# IFIP Advances in Information and Communication Technology 597

## Editor-in-Chief

*Kai Rannenberg, Goethe University Frankfurt, Germany*

## Editorial Board Members

## IFIP – The International Federation for Information Processing

IFIP was founded in 1960 under the auspices of UNESCO, following the first World Computer Congress held in Paris the previous year. A federation for societies working in information processing, IFIP's aim is two-fold: to support information processing in the countries of its members and to encourage technology transfer to developing nations. As its mission statement clearly states:

*IFIP is the global non-profit federation of societies of ICT professionals that aims at achieving a worldwide professional and socially responsible development and application of information and communication technologies.*

IFIP is a non-profit-making organization, run almost solely by 2500 volunteers. It operates through a number of technical committees and working groups, which organize events and publications. IFIP's events range from large international open conferences to working conferences and local seminars.

The flagship event is the IFIP World Computer Congress, at which both invited and contributed papers are presented. Contributed papers are rigorously refereed and the rejection rate is high.

As with the Congress, participation in the open conferences is open to all and papers may be invited or submitted. Again, submitted papers are stringently refereed.

The working conferences are structured differently. They are usually run by a working group and attendance is generally smaller and occasionally by invitation only. Their purpose is to create an atmosphere conducive to innovation and development. Refereeing is also rigorous and papers are subjected to extensive group discussion.

Publications arising from IFIP events vary. The papers presented at the IFIP World Computer Congress and at open conferences are published as conference proceedings, while the results of the working conferences are often published as collections of selected and edited papers.

IFIP distinguishes three types of institutional membership: Country Representative Members, Members at Large, and Associate Members. The type of organization that can apply for membership is a wide variety and includes national or international societies of individual computer scientists/ICT professionals, associations or federations of such societies, government institutions/government related organizations, national or international research institutes or consortia, universities, academies of sciences, companies, national or international associations or federations of companies.

More information about this series at http://www.springer.com/series/6102

Denis Cavallucci · Stelian Brad ·
Pavel Livotov (Eds.)

# Systematic Complex Problem Solving in the Age of Digitalization and Open Innovation

20th International TRIZ Future Conference, TFC 2020
Cluj-Napoca, Romania, October 14–16, 2020
Proceedings

 Springer

*Editors*
Denis Cavallucci (iD)
INSA Graduate School of Science
and Technology of Strasbourg
Strasbourg, France

Stelian Brad
Technical University of Cluj-Napoca
Cluj-Napoca, Romania

Pavel Livotov
Offenburg University of Applied Sciences
Offenburg, Germany

ISSN 1868-4238          ISSN 1868-422X  (electronic)
IFIP Advances in Information and Communication Technology
ISBN 978-3-030-61297-9          ISBN 978-3-030-61295-5  (eBook)
https://doi.org/10.1007/978-3-030-61295-5

This Springer imprint is published by the registered company Springer Nature Switzerland AG
The registered company address is: Gewerbestrasse 11, 6330 Cham, Switzerland

# Preface

The 20th anniversary edition of ETRIA TRIZ Future conference will be like no other. The international health situation is forcing us to change the way articles are presented and exchanges are performed. As in most activities at the moment, the use of video conferencing tools has allowed authors to present their work, keynotes to present their points of view, and the master classes to experiment with a new form of teaching that may become the norm if such situations persist or come back to us on a recurring basis.

This 2020 edition is resolutely placed under the sign of the digital age. Even if the first publication on the Theory of Inventive Problem Solving (TRIZ) dates back to the year 1956, the world had widely discovered TRIZ about 30 years ago. As the first years were dedicated to understanding what TRIZ was all about, we had to get around it. Now activities of a different nature need to further develop to reinvent TRIZ and to get it through the next decades. Of course, this challenge cannot be solved by simply replicating, modifying, or extending what the early experts taught us. Today, it is also necessary to critically evaluate TRIZ, to understand its limitations, inaccuracies, and internal inconsistencies, and to confront them through a combination of research and professional use. It was the specific role of the European TRIZ Association ETRIA to address these issues. Moreover, ETRIA has pioneered and supported the application of scientific standards in international TRIZ research and development. Since its foundation in 2000 and the first TRIZ Future Conference, held at the University of Bath, UK in 2001, ETRIA annual conferences far exceed the geographical boundaries of Europe as about half of the submitted papers came from all over the world.

Already 20 years old, ETRIA is bringing together the contributions from academic research and industrial practice. Each annual TRIZ Future conference presents a collection of the achievements of not only research teams, companies, and TRIZ professionals, but also beginners who have just discovered the TRIZ methodology and its corpus of knowledge. Of course, we do not claim to offer an exhaustive vision of what is happening around TRIZ in the world, but we believe that ETRIA is a representative sample of it, and that it remains useful for the world of TRIZ to have this regularity in productive exchanges that can take place between scientists, experts, practitioners, and newcomers from academia and industry.

But the TRIZ Future conference is not only that. We all operate in a changing world and from year to year, from decade to decade, the paradigms, that our society goes through, influence the trajectory of TRIZ and the activities of ETRIA members. The 20th edition shows a strong influence of digital technology in the work of the teams. In addition, there has been an ongoing desire in recent years to formalize the approaches resulting from TRIZ. This will probably arise from the observation that the use of TRIZ was somewhat lacking in rigor and that TRIZ practices were mainly based on extensive expertise and skills. Learning TRIZ "with pain" seemed to be the keyword at the time. The analogy was often made to learning a foreign language: one only progresses by practicing a new language intensely, with time and the help of a mentor. While this remains true in many learning situations, the fact is that our world has become versatile and complex, requiring everyone to be able to quickly absorb new knowledge and just as quickly change direction in the professional trajectories.

Therefore, the general trend towards automation of the intellectual tasks of reading and compiling information, expertise prior to a study, and patent databases is becoming more noticeable in some contributions of the TFC 2020. Some papers discuss the use of knowledge management techniques and techniques derived from artificial intelligence. We are approaching the age of using collective intelligence in a much better way by transforming big data into information and further into knowledge by means of artificial intelligence algorithms. Nevertheless, it will probably take some time until automated systems and artificial intelligence will be capable of generating understanding and wisdom from knowledge. Thus, the involvement of experts in interpreting results generated by such systems and to continuously feed them with new ideas, algorithms, and data will still be crucial for the success of AI-driven innovations. These techniques are also applied to build around TRIZ, or to revisit the historical tools of TRIZ, either through enhancing them through hybridization with other tools of the design sciences or by updating them with the use of techniques either empirically or inspired by artificial intelligence.

Finally, as in the preceding TFC editions, some contributions are more related to humanities, social sciences, or education and clearly raise the stakes of TRIZ impact in their discipline. Work in distributed environments for problem solving using open innovation platforms and secured frames for IP tracking is also highlighted in some works at this TFC edition. This kind of context might influence the future of TRIZ frameworks, because more complexity seems to be brought into problem resolution and multidisciplinary expertise is necessary to tackle cutting-edge technological projects, etc.

All papers published in this book were triple peer-reviewed by several members of the Scientific Committee and the authors were given the opportunity to amend their paper in light of these reviews before the decision to accept and publish their papers. The book is composed of the 34 selected articles divided into 7 chapters as follows:

- A section dedicated to "Computing TRIZ" composed of 8 papers.
- A session dedicated to "Education and Pedagogy" composed of 4 papers.
- A session dedicated to "Sustainable Development" composed of 4 papers.
- A session dedicated to "Tools and techniques of TRIZ for enhancing Design" composed of 4 papers.
- A session dedicated to "TRIZ and system engineering" composed of 4 papers.
- A session dedicated to "TRIZ and Complexity" composed of 4 papers.
- A session dedicated to "Cross-fertilization of TRIZ for Innovation management" composed of 6 papers.

All papers were presented at the 20th edition of the TRIZ Future conference remotely with a pre-recorded video. Then a live question and answers session followed.

October 2020                                                        Denis Cavallucci
                                                                         Stelian Brad
                                                                         Pavel Livotov

# Organization

## General Chair

Stelian Brad — Technical University of Cluj-Napoca, Romania

## Scientific Chair

Denis Cavallucci — INSA Strasbourg, France

## Steering Committee

Stelian Brad — Technical University of Cluj-Napoca, Romania
Denis Cavallucci — INSA Strasbourg, France
Pavel Livotov — Offenburg University of Applied Sciences, Germany

## Scientific Committee

Roland DeGuio — INSA Strasbourg, France
Sébastien Dubois — INSA Strasbourg, France
Hicham Chibane — INSA Strasbourg, France
Iouri Belski — Royal Melbourne Institute of Technology, Australia
Barbara Gronauer — Strategie Innovation, Germany
Christian M. Thurnes — Hochschule Kaiserslautern, Germany
Karl Koltze — Krefeld University of Applied Sciences, Germany
Stelian Brad — Technical University of Cluj-Napoca, Romania
Denis Cavallucci — INSA Strasbourg, France
Amadou Coulibaly — INSA Strasbourg, France
Amir Nafi — National School for Water and Environmental Engineering, France

Yuri Borgianni — Free University of Bozen-Bolzano, Italy
Stéphanie Buisine — Training Center CESI Paris-Nanterre, France
Cecilia Zanni-Merk — INSA Rouen, France
Christian Spreafico — University of Bergamo, Italy
Davide Russo — University of Bergamo, Italy
Donald Coates — Kent State University, USA
Amira Essaid-Farhat — Training Center CESI Paris-Nanterre, France
Fatima Z. Ben Moussa — Marrakech Prefecture, Morocco
Federico Rotini — University of Florence, Italy
Hans-Gert Gräbe — Leipzig University, Germany
Camille Jean — Arts et Métiers ParisTech, France
Jean Renaud — INSA Strasbourg, France
Jerzy Chrząszcz — Warsaw University of Technology, Poland

| | |
|---|---|
| Justus Schollmeyer | Leibniz Institute for Interdisciplinary Studies, Germany |
| Kalle Elfvengren | LUT School of Engineering Science, Finland |
| Fabrice Mantelet | Arts et Métiers ParisTech, France |
| Nicolas Maranzana | Arts et Métiers ParisTech, France |
| Marco De Carvalho | Universidade Tecnológica Federal do Paraná, Brazil |
| Kai Hiltmann | Coburg University of Applied Sciences and Arts, Germany |
| Claudia Hentschel | Hochschule für Technik und Wirtschaft Berlin, Germany |
| Pei Zhang | INSA Strasbourg, France |
| Rachid Benmoussa | Cadi Ayyad University, Morocco |
| Remy Houssin | University of Strasbourg, France |
| Sebastian Koziolek | Wroclaw University of Technology, Poland |
| Pavel Livotov | PPI, Offenburg University, Germany |
| Leonid Chechurin | LUT School of Engineering Science, Finland |
| Stephane Negny | Toulouse Graduate School, France |
| Toru Nakagawa | Osaka Gakuin University, Japan |
| Mikael Collan | Lappeenranta University of Technology, Finland |
| Yongwon Song | Korea Polytechnic University, South Korea |
| Sungjoo Lee | Ajou University, South Korea |
| Ahmed Samet | INSA Strasbourg, France |
| Claude Gazo | Arts et Métiers ParisTech, France |

# Contents

## Sustainable Development

## Tools and Techniques of TRIZ for Enhancing Design

# Computing TRIZ

# Managing AI Technologies in Earthwork Construction: A TRIZ-Based Innovation Approach

Nino Hoch[(✉)] and Stelian Brad

Research Centre for Engineering and Management of Innovation, Technical University of Cluj-Napoca, Cluj-Napoca, Romania
nino.hoch@hoch-baumaschinen.de

**Abstract.** Artificial Intelligence (AI) is becoming more prevalent across various industries. However, the construction industry and its suppliers have not yet recognized its full potential as it relates to efficiency and competitiveness. This study aims to increase the understanding of AI in the environment of construction by presenting a case applying tools referring to the Theory of Inventive Problem Solving (TRIZ) and Six Sigma to show how to implement selected AI technologies in a systematic way in order to improve processes. Thus, this paper presents a novel approach for solving business process and management problems combining TRIZ and Six Sigma tools. We specifically focus on extending TRIZ with Six Sigma. To demonstrate the successful application of the developed TRIZ-Six Sigma framework a case study is included. Overall, this paper provides an illustrative example of successful systematic innovation and demonstrates how AI technology can be implemented within a real company by identifying the use of cases with the support of TRIZ. This case report can help practitioners in planning and executing similar projects towards business process optimization since fast and efficient processes have been obtained in a real world scenario.

**Keywords:** Business process innovation · Earthwork construction · Artificial intelligence · TRIZ · Six Sigma · Systematic innovation · Business process optimization

## 1 Introduction

In planning for the future improvement of processes and operations, many sectors including construction are increasingly looking for possibilities to implement advanced technologies related to artificial intelligence (AI). Applications of AI have become a topic of central importance to the ways in which construction will change in the upcoming future, with recent use cases addressing potential transformations in earthmoving machines and earthwork construction [1]. It represents a core set of capabilities that can be combined to perform a variety of tasks in different contexts of application, together having the potential to substantially reconfigure the whole industry. Although AI presents valuable opportunities in terms of increased competitiveness and enhancing efficiency, companies struggle in how to implement and how to apply

© IFIP International Federation for Information Processing 2020
Published by Springer Nature Switzerland AG 2020
D. Cavallucci et al. (Eds.): TFC 2020, IFIP AICT 597, pp. 3–14, 2020.
https://doi.org/10.1007/978-3-030-61295-5_1

selected technologies to the right business process or even business model in a meaningful way [2]. Due to this fact, we suggest that both researchers and practitioners make a commitment to more fully analyze and consider the full range of issues that relate to the implementation phase of AI. Therefore, a set of sophisticated tools is needed to develop a systematic approach, considering all phases of the associated management problem solving process. In this context, we specifically focus on a combination of tools referring to the Theory of Inventive Problem Solving (TRIZ) and Six Sigma to develop a process-based method of generating new ideas and solution strategies. By extending TRIZ with Six Sigma we assume to more systematically reach target-oriented and robust results regarding the implementation of AI technologies. Despite the known advantages of both approaches, we anticipate that their combination has the potential for far-reaching improvements in terms of systematic process innovation. While Six Sigma helps us in identifying the root causes of low performance in the process, TRIZ is considered to be the appropriate tool, for associated systematic problem solving [3].

Thus, the objective of this paper is to introduce a novel framework, incorporating TRIZ and Six Sigma, which supports the process of implementing AI technology systematically. To test its efficacy a case study is conducted additionally. The research paper is organized as follows. Section 2 provides an overview on the research background, indicating the research gap. Section 3 illustrates the methodology, the tools applied and the roadmap of the proposed Six-Sigma framework. The application of the theory is demonstrated within a real case study of process improvement together with results in Sect. 4. The paper ends with a conclusion and future research direction.

## 2   Background

This section explores fundamental aspects of AI in context to business process optimization and more specifically its application in the area of earthwork construction. Moreover, it identifies the research gap and scientific challenge of systematically managing AI technologies in earthwork construction.

### 2.1   AI in Earthwork Construction

At present, AI is assumed to be one of the most disruptive technologies, impacting whole industries and businesses, and thus is said to be a catalyst of business process innovation [4]. AI comprises a set of several technologies, enabling automation and including several approaches such as machine learning, machine reasoning and robotics [5]. According to [6] "artificial intelligence is the study of how to make computers do things at which, at the moment, people are better". Hence, AI refers to a technology which develops sophisticated methods, techniques and applications in order to make machines capable of doing complex work tasks which required human intelligence in the past [7]. AI is based on the ability of a machine or computer to analyze a complex situation, draw conclusions from it and act accordingly [8]. Regarding earthwork construction, AI encompasses a wide range of applications such as platforms (e.g. Fleet Management, Building Information Modeling- BIM),

Augmented Reality (AR), Robotics, Autonomous Vehicles (AV), Unmanned Aerial Vehicles (UAVs). In this context, they offer advantages in terms of schedule optimization, predictive maintenance, waste reduction, increased environmental sustainability, increased on-site safety and increased jobsite productivity. In practice, the functions of AI are achieved by accessing, processing and analyzing big data via certain algorithms [9]. This data can be either structured or unstructured and gathered from multiple data sources such as advanced Internet of Things (IoT) sensors [10].

## 2.2 Gap Formulation and the Scientific Challenge

The implementation of AI not only implicates technological challenges, but also behavioral and environmental influence factors as well. In this context, the biggest issues in implementing new technologies are the identification of a specific need, the identification of appropriate and available technology as well as the formulation of effective implementation strategies and goals. Hence, several studies analyze the challenges of implementing new technologies in construction companies, albeit not providing any structured guidance on how to overcome these [11, 12]. Particularly, no structured approach can be found in academic literature, providing systematic guidance on how to implement and how to apply selected technologies to the right business process or even business model in a collaborative and meaningful way. Thus, from a scientific point of view, there is a need for a structured approach to tackle these issues. In this respect, we propose a combination of tools using TRIZ and Six Sigma to guide the problem-finding process and to develop systematic solutions referring to the AI implementation challenges identified.

## 3 Methodology

### 3.1 TRIZ and Six Sigma

Initially, the Theory of Inventive Problem Solving (TRIZ) was proposed 1984 by the Russian researcher Altshuller as a helpful tool for systematically generating breakthrough ideas and delivering solutions [13]. In the course of time, TRIZ has been applied to various fields and research topics as a knowledge-based systematic methodology of inventive problem solving [10]. In the past, TRIZ particularly has been proved effective at modeling problems in context to engineering. But TRIZ is also valuable for modeling problems within business processes and business models, opening new directions for major improvements and innovations [15, 16]. In this regard, this study applies TRIZ as a framework for innovating business processes, avoiding the "blank sheet paper" problem by systematically opening dialogues between stakeholders and team members, and stimulating the flow of ideas [17, 18]. Although TRIZ has been applied to innovation theory in the past, this study offers a novel and structured methodology, proposing a systematic framework for business process innovation.

Six Sigma was established by Motorola in 1987 as a strategic initiative to identify problematic areas within the business, to define improvements and to develop breakthrough solutions in a predictable and repeatable manner [19]. Following a common Six Sigma methodology a process can be aligned to critical customer requirements and constantly analysed in order to continuously improve the process. Thus, Six Sigma is a process improvement approach that uses conventional and advanced tools of quality management to optimize processes [20, 21]. In this context Table 1 presents the Six Sigma DMAIC (define, measure, analyze, improve and control) approach which offers a structured framework in following steps to establish systematic continuous process improvement.

**Table 1.** Six Sigma DMAIC Model.

| DMAIC | Course of Action |
|---|---|
| D | **Define** the goals of the improvement activity |
| M | **Measure** the existing system |
| A | **Analyse** the system to identify ways to eliminate the gap between the current performance of the process and the desired goal |
| I | **Improve** the system by finding new ways to do things better, cheaper or faster |
| C | **Control** the new system by modifying procedures, operating instructions and other management systems |

Thus far, the Six Sigma DMAIC approach has been successfully applied for process improvement in the service and manufacturing industry and now is gaining increasing awareness regarding its application in the construction environment [22]. In this context, DMAIC can be assessed to be a team-based approach to problem solving and process improvement [23].

By extending TRIZ with Six Sigma we assume to more systematically reach target-oriented and robust results regarding the implementation of AI technologies [24]. Despite the known advantages of both approaches, we anticipate that their combination has the potential for far-reaching improvements in terms of systematic process innovation. While Six Sigma supports the identification of root causes referring to low performance in the process, TRIZ is chosen because of its strengths regarding systematic problem solving. Consequently, the proposed roadmap for systematic business process innovation is elaborated through the combination of TRIZ and Six Sigma and presented in the next section. Moreover, its application is tested in a real-world application within a case study.

### 3.2    Roadmap of TRIZ-Six Sigma Framework

To contribute to the existing literature, we designed a framework, fostering systematic innovation by combining TRIZ (Russian acronym for Teoriya Resheniya Izobretatelskikh Zadatch) and Six Sigma in a sophisticated way. Accordingly, Fig. 1 presents the roadmap for systematic business process innovation under a grid of nine windows, where the number in each box shows the order for tackling issues within the proposed innovation process. The framework comprises a combination of methods, such as

System Operator Technique (SOT) which is a proven TRIZ technique for inventive problem solving, developed by Genrich Altshuller [25]. It is estimated to be a suitable tool to look at a problem from different viewpoints, considering time (past, present, future) and abstraction level (system, super-system, sub-system) [26]. The reason for choosing it, is its flexibility and feasibility to investigate a problem, to discover resources, and to generate solutions systematically [17, 27]. In addition, we applied the Six Sigma DMAIC model previously presented in Table 1 and integrated it into the grid of nine windows (SOT). This Six Sigma methodology was adopted in addition to TRIZ because of the following three reasons. First, it facilitates a data and fact driven approach, second it is capable to streamline the information flow within the organization, third it has the capability to integrate the human and process aspects of process improvement and thus helps to better identify the root causes of the problem [28].

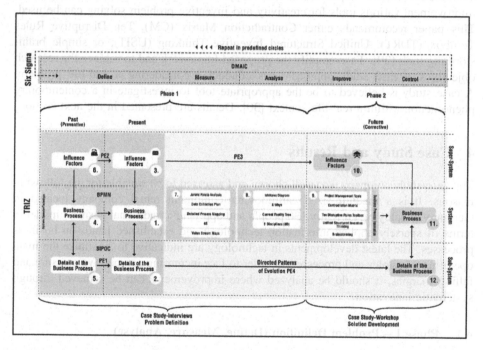

**Fig. 1.** Proposed Architectural TRIZ-Six Sigma Framework. Source: Own presentation

Before demonstrating the model in practice, we explain the terminology, the course of action, the single process steps, and the best practices on how to apply the model. 'Past' refers to 5 to 10 years ago. 'Future' is 1 to 3 years in the future. 'Present' represents the current situation and/or expected situation in the very near future. 'System' explains the business process whereas 'Sub-System' describes the details of each block of the business process. 'Super-System' is the external environment and, thus, the context where the business process exists, mainly by means of key influence factors. 'Patterns of evolution' are the routes through which influence factors and business processes have evolved from past to present, but also estimates of the future evolution of the influence factors. They are determined by collecting historical data and mapping out the lines of evolution. 'Conflicts' occur at the intersection between the forecasted future factors of influence and the current business process, along the following Predefined Areas of Investigation (PAI): a) determinants leading to the development of the current business process that embed it in traditions; b) natural interdependencies that block the current process, due to the concern of provoking instabilities; c) limitations that favour current consolidated mechanisms; and d) strengths that intend to keep the status-quo.

Most importantly, DMAIC analyses the "System" from a superordinate level, also considering the 'Super-System' and "Sub-System", providing a structured framework in following steps (define, measure, analyse, improve, control) to establish systematic continuous process improvement. To support the process of business process improvement various tools for creativity and inventive problem solving can be used. This paper recommends either Contradiction Matrix (CM), Ten Disruptive Rules Toolbox (TDRT), Unified Structured Inventive Thinking (USIT), or simple brainstorming tools [29]. To exemplify the proposed framework and to achieve the research objectives, a case study approach was conducted considering a real-life problem. A case study is believed to be the appropriate tool to investigate in a contemporary phenomenon within a real-life context [30]. Details are presented in the next section.

## 4   Case Study and Results

The case-study company was well-chosen and assessed to be suitable for the following reasons. It is a medium-sized earthmoving equipment rental company located in Germany, employing currently 130 people and applying a traditional business model in terms of sparsely applied information technology and established hands-on business processes. The latest developments in technology are indicative to scrutinize the main operating principles and processes. In order to face increasing competitive pressure and falling margins, it should be analyzed where improvements can be achieved through systematic innovation.

### 4.1   Phase 1 – Problem Definition (Define, Measure, Analyse)

Phase 1 (problem definition) of the proposed TRIZ-Six Sigma Framework on systematic innovation took place during January 2020, intending to gain insights on the company's past and present rental process, referring to the first 3 phases of DMAIC, which are namely "define", "measure" and "analyse". In this respect, three semi-structured interviews were conducted with 3 managers (M1-Rental Division, M2-Rental Division and S3-Service Division) at the case company. The main interview used open-ended questions designed to allow the subject to discuss topics such as the recently applied rental business process, its details, influence factors, the value chain, customer-value, and key stakeholders. The second interview was a follow-up interview to address topics not sufficiently covered by the first interview. This follow-up interview was conducted to gain deeper information on the companies' rental process and its linkages to the service department as well as on the participants considerations on possible business process improvements applying AI technology.

During the *define phase* the information used to inform the framework was categorized by each components' name and corresponding number within the framework. During the define phase, various tools were applied to determine the focus points of the project, the scope of the problem and the in- and outputs of the process. For Instance, BPMN (Business Process Model and Notation) was used to model the businesses processes at "System" level for the past and present (points 1, 2). Moreover, SIPOC (Supplier, Input, Process, Output, Customer) was applied to define the details of the business process, identifying and mapping all basic relationships between suppliers, inputs, process steps, outputs and customers at "Sub-System" level (points 2, 5) [28]. Additionally, the impact of AI technology as a positive or negative influence factor on the business process was discussed on "Super System" level by means of a planned discussion and interview with the small group of people (M1, M2; S3), conducted by one of the researchers as moderator. (points 3,6). The patterns of evolution (PE1 + PE2) revealed how the advancements in technology "Super System" had impact on the details of the business process on "Sub-System" level in terms of efficiency and productivity (in our case moving from typewriter and paper planning to personal computer and excel planning) Finally, we explored the estimated patterns of evolution (PE3) for 1 to 3 years from the present patterns. Considering the estimated patterns of evolution, the future factors of influence at the future-super-system [10] were examined based on, but not limited to AI, smart sensors, IoT enabled machines, platform technology, big data, machine learning, deep learning. Thus, this evolution will impose a directed pattern of evolution (PE4) at the sub-system level between the present and future, such as increased efficiency and productivity and increased integration of AI into machines, rental solutions, and work processes. The following issues were revealed during the define phase: (a) The current rental process is old-fashioned and too slow in view of the current and expected technological possibilities, because many work steps could potentially be automated, (b) the information flow among process stakeholders is considered to be ineffective due to manual work steps, (c) identified stakeholders of the process are rental department, maintenance department, customer, software supplier, machine supplier, customers. This assessment indicates that the currently applied (in this case, not digitized or automated) business process should transition to a more automated and intelligent business process.

The first step during the *measure phase* is to identify the defects (anything not complying with the requirement of the process) within the process. For that reason, we applied a detailed process mapping. As a result, we identified the weaknesses to be in our case (a) working days not billed due to reported machine downtimes, (b) to long process duration due to untapped automation potential, (c) insufficient rental prices. As a result, the measure phase involves the constitution of valid and reliable metrics helping to monitor the progress towards a more effective rental process. But, in our case study it is almost impossible to set reliable KPIs because every rental process differs in detail. Although the process duration might be an obvious indicator, it cannot be used because each rental agreement differs regarding the availability of machines and associated components. Because of this, we have decided to focus on (a) the long-term capability, which in our case study is assumed to be an increasing billed rental turnover, assuming a constant rental fleet, (b) a decreasing number of credit notes issued due to reported machine downtimes, (c) a reduced total working time per day of the rental department.

The purpose during the *analyse phase* was to find an innovative way to eliminate the gap between the performance of the initial business process and the aspired goal. Therefore, we applied a root cause analysis which revealed several weaknesses that must be addressed. Regarding the machine fleet, we figured out that the rental fleet includes different OEMs, each of them having their own data standard with inconsistent API and own IoT platform. This means that necessary information about the machines must be queried through countless portals, which makes the process of information retrieval very slow. In addition, there is a non-integrated ERP system for, without an API to the individual portals. This implies that the different departments have no central source of information and therefore work independently. This in turn means that despite the existing technological possibilities, the rental process can be assessed to be very old-fashioned due to the lack of networking. Finally, these work procedures lead to potentially higher sources of error, which in turn has a negative impact on productivity and thus also on customer satisfaction, revenue and costs.

By incorporating AI, the turnover might increase and the rental process can be accelerated, although delivering customer-added value at the same time.

### 4.2  Phase 2 – Solution Development (Improve, Control)

Phase 2 (solution development) of the proposed framework was initiated on March 7, 2020, as an interactive workshop, referring to the last two phases of the DMAIC, which are namely "improve" and "control". Considering the results from phase 1 (problem definition phase) and in order to encourage engagement and collaboration [31] we invited two stakeholders (software supplier & developer and one CEO of a top 10 customer). The workshop was moderated under the proposed framework by one of the researchers, who also actively participated in the discussion. The aim of this workshop was to innovate and improve the company's rental process systematically as a solution to the problems identified within phase 1. This was realized by collaborating with several stakeholders that might have similar interests [32].

The *improve phase* encompasses the development of a suitable solution relevant to the problems and weaknesses identified within the previous phases. In our study this was achieved through collaborative brainstorming with two major stakeholders (software supplier & developer and one CEO of a top 10 customer). By means of interactive discussion and brainstorming a solution referring to the problems identified within phase 1 was collaboratively developed. As a result, we propose a solution on how to transform the traditional rental process into a sophisticated digital process incorporating AI technology. The following Fig. 2 provides deeper information on the applied components and their interaction.

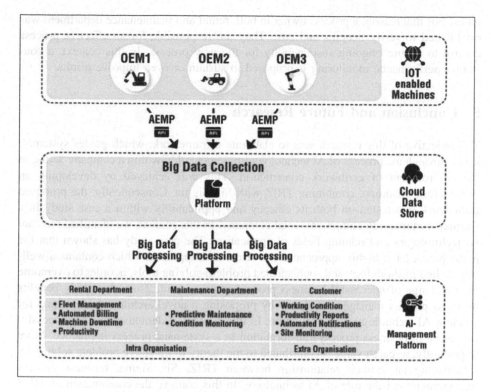

**Fig. 2.** Case Study Result - Innovated business process

For this purpose, a platform was developed together with a software engineer receiving data of various IoT enabled machines via a standardized application programming interface (API), which are collected and bundled within a cloud storage. To also integrate older machines, they were retrofitted with an IoT device. The data collected is now processed accordingly and distributed subsequently to predefined recipients, which are the rental department, the maintenance department and selected customers. Regarding rental department, this enabled unified fleet management, automated billing of rental orders (performance based or power by the hour), automated information on machine downtimes and thus higher productivity due to less of manual work steps. In addition, the service department transforms their work procedures from incident-based to predictive maintenance processes including real-time machine monitoring. Finally, the customer can be supplied with automated reports, providing him real time information of his construction site including machine productivity, machine working condition and building progress. With the help of AI, the customer can be periodically supplied with purchase offers including the current takeover price of the rental machine. Moreover, AI and machine learning enable the implementation of intelligent rental fees, automatically considering several influence factors such as weather, customer group, fleet utilization and purpose of machine application. The future control phase should be documented within the company to ensure long-term gains. For that reason, a process owner in both rental and maintenance department was established to verify benefits and cost. They are responsible for an effective process control to ensure ongoing sustainability for the new process. In this context, a constantly performance monitoring is proposed to sustain or even improve results.

## 5  Conclusion and Future Research

The objective of this research was to elaborate a framework, which guides systematically through the process of AI technology implementation within a company acting in the environment of earthwork construction. This was achieved by developing an architectural roadmap, combining TRIZ with Six Sigma. Consequently, the proposed framework was tested on both its efficacy and applicability within a case study in a German earthmoving equipment rental company. In this context, we identified relevant AI technologies and relating fields of application. The case study has shown that the participants, have highly appreciated the structured approach, which contains a well-established methodology and sophisticated problem-solving tools, in order to overcome the challenge of successful business process improvement. Thus, this study benefits business process management theory by proposing a novel architectural roadmap for efficient AI technology implementation. In this context, it demonstrates the successful execution of business process transformation as a systematic process in practice. More importantly, research value is contributed to the theory of inventive problem solving by establishing an explicit relationship between TRIZ, Six Sigma, business process management and the role of AI technology. In this context, the combination of TRIZ and Six Sigma for business processes innovation is a novelty, revealing new perspectives in the process of creative problem solving. Moreover, the case study company involved is gaining new ideas for AI technology-based business process innovation in a systematic way, thereby also identifying weaknesses and gaps in the business processes currently applied. Further Future research should collect more empirical data und investigate in experiences done by other industries, applying the proposed framework.

## References

1. Klashanov, F.: Artificial intelligence and organizing decision in construction. In: 15th International Scientific Conference "Underground Urbanisation as a Prerequisite for Sustainable Development", Procedia Engineering vol. 165, pp. 1016–1020 (2016)
2. Schia, M.H., Trollsås, B.C., Fyhn, H., Lædre, O.: The introduction of AI in the construction industry and its impact on human behavior". In: Pasquire, C., Hamzeh, F.R. (ed.) Proceedings 27 th Annual Conference of the International. Group for Lean Construction (IGLC), Dublin, Ireland, pp. 903–914 (2019)
3. Brad, S.: Sigma-TRIZ: algorithm for systematic integration of innovation within six sigma process improvement methodologies. In: Coskun, A. (ed.) Quality Management and Six Sigma, pp. 89–108 (2010)
4. Lee, J., et al.: Emerging technology and business model innovation: the case of artificial intelligence. J. Open Innov. Technol. Market Compexity 5(44), 1–13 (2019)

5. Mucha, T., Seppälä, T.: Artificial intelligence platforms - a new research agenda for digital platform economy. In: ETLA Working papers No. 76 (2020)
6. Rich, E.: Artificial Intelligence McGraw-Hill (1983)
7. Deloitte: Artificial Intelligence, pp. 1–33 (2018)
8. Vinci Construction: Artificial intelligence and its contribution to construction. 09 September 2019. https://vinci-construction.com/en/news/artificial-intelligence-construction/832/ (2019)
9. Parveen, R.: Arificial intelligence in construction industry: legal issues and regulatory challenges. Int. J. Civil Eng. Technol. 9(13), 957–962 (2018)
10. Pramanik P.K.D., Pal, S., Choudhury, P.: Beyond automation: the cognitive IoT. artificial intelligence brings sense to the internet of things. In: Sangaiah, A., Thangavelu, A., Meenakshi Sundaram, V. (eds.) Cognitive Computing for Big Data Systems Over IoT. Lecture Notes on Data Engineering and Communications Technologies, vol 14. Springer, Cham (2018)
11. Henderson, J.R., Ruikar, K.: Technology implementation strategies for construction organisations. Eng. Construct. Archi. Manage. 17(3), 309–327 (2010)
12. Tulenheimo, R.: Challenges of implementing new technologies in the world of BIM – case study from construction engineering industry in Finland. Procedia Econ. Finance 21, 469–477 (2015)
13. Altshuller, G.: The innovation algorithm: TRIZ, systematic innovation and technical creativity. In: Shulyak, L., Rodman, S. (eds.) Worcester, Technical Innovation Center, Inc. (1999)
14. Boavida, R., Navas, H., Godina, R., Carvalho, H., Hasegawa, H.A.: Combined use of TRIZ methodology and eco-compass tool as a sustainable innovation model. Appl. Sci., 10, 10 (2020)
15. Sheu, D., Chiu, M.-C., Cayard, D.: The 7 Pillars of TRIZ Philosophies. Comput. Ind. Eng. 146 (2020)
16. Lassnig, M., Klieber, K.: IoT-based business model innovation with an adapted TRIZ multi-screen approach. In: ISPIM Conference Proceedings, Manchester (2020)
17. Livotov, P., et al.: Systematic Innovation in process engineering: linking TRIZ and process intensification. In: Chechurin, L., Collan, M.: Advances in systematic Creativity. Palgrave Macmillan, Cham, pp. 27–44 (2019)
18. Souchkov, V.: Systematic business innovation: a roadmap. TRIZ Rev. J. Int. TRIZ Assoc. 1 (1), 122–132 (2019)
19. Toivonen, T.: Continuous innovation - combining Toyota Kata and TRIZ for sustained innovation. In: Proceedia Engineering, World Conference TRIZ FUTURE, TF 2011–2014, vol. 131, pp. 963–974 (2015)
20. Yadav, N., Shankar, R., Singh, S.P.: Impact of Industry4.0/ICTs, Lean Six Sigma and quality management systems on organisational performance. TQM J. 32(4), 815–835 (2020)
21. Indrawati, S., Azzam, A., Adrianto, E., Miranda, S., Prabaswari, A.: Lean concept development in fast food industry using integration of six sigma and TRIZ Method. IOP Conference Series: Materials Science and Engineering, 722 (2020)
22. Alaloul, W., Liew, M.S., Wan, A.Z., Noor, A., Kennedy, I.: Industrial Revolution 4.0 in the construction industry: challenges and opportunities for stakeholders. AIN Shams Eng. J. 11 (1), 225–230 (2019)
23. Karout, R., Awasthi, A.: Improving software quality using Six Sigma DMAIC-based approach: a case study. Bus. Process Manage. J. 23(4), 842–856 (2017)
24. Soti, A., Shankar, R., Kaushal, O.P.: Six Sigma with innovation tool kit of TRIZ. Int. J. Bus. Innov. Res. 6(2), 220–237 (2012)
25. Seed, I.E.: Successful Problem Solving, 1st edn. Cogentus Consulting Limited, Reading (2016)

26. Teplov, R., Chechurin, L., Podmetina, D.: TRIZ as innovation management tool: insights from academic literature. Int. J. Technol. Market. **12**(3), 207–229 (2018)
27. Ding, Z., et al.: A new TRIZ-based patent knowledge management system for construction technology innovation. J. Eng. Des. Technol. **15**(4), 456–470 (2017)
28. Antony, J., et al.: Application of Six Sigma DMAIC methodology in a transactional environment. Int. J. Qual. Reliab. Manage. **29**(21), 31–53 (2012)
29. Brad, S., Brad, E.: Directed innovation of business models. Int. J. Manage. Knowl. Learn. **5** (1), 97–119 (2016)
30. Yin, R.: Case Study Research: Design and Methods. London: Sage, 3rd edition (2003)
31. Numa, K., Toriumi, K., Tanaka, K., Akaishi, M., Hori, K.: Participatory workshop as a creativity support system. In: Lovrek, I., Howlett, R.J., Jain, L.C. (eds.) KES 2008. LNCS (LNAI), vol. 5178, pp. 823–830. Springer, Heidelberg (2008). https://doi.org/10.1007/978-3-540-85565-1_102
32. Dalsgaard, P., Halskov, K.: Innovation in participatory design. In: Proceedings of the 11th Conference on Participatory Design, PDC 2010, Sydney, Australia, November 29–December 03, 2010 (2010)

# TRIZ Driven Identification of AI Application to Improve Navigation of Mobile Autonomous Robots

Andrei Vlad Florian[1][✉] and Stelian Brad[2]

[1] Braintronix, Taietura Turcului, 47C1, 400285 Cluj-Napoca, Romania
vlad.florian@muri.utcluj.ro
[2] Technical University of Cluj-Napoca, Memorandumului 28,
400441 Cluj-Napoca, Romania
stelian.brad@staff.utcluj.ro

**Abstract.** Increase of effectiveness of navigation in the case of autonomous mobile robots with limited sensory systems integrated that operate in different types of production facilities is considered in this research work. The challenge is to define a reliable solution in a cost-effective design. The research methodology integrates TRIZ within the framework of voice-of-use-table-performance function deployment (VOUT-PFD) design planning framework. The key user requirements and engineering specifications defined with VOUT-PFD have been analyzed in terms of correlations. For the identified sets of negative correlations, TRIZ Contradiction Matrix has been considered to formulate the generic areas for inventive problem-solving. Using the method of weighted analysis of interdependencies (AIDA), the compatible TRIZ vectors have been selected for guiding the design of the artificial intelligence (AI) algorithm. These vectors have been introduced in the framework of Complex System Design Technique (CSDT) in relation with generic modules of the AI system (algorithm, related inputs from the sensors and mechanical limitations of the robotic system) in order to design the navigation solution. In this article eight areas of possible improvements using AI algorithms have been found and the first area of research, which represents the robot construction is further detailed. The major result of this paper is that it shows a structured way in which inventive problem-solving thinking can lead to possible improvement areas regarding navigation of autonomous mobile robots (AMRs) in industrial environment.

**Keywords:** AMR · Structured environment · Navigation · ROS · TRIZ · Decision making algorithm

## 1 Introduction

Nowadays, the industry standards and requirements regarding autonomous robots in terms of safety, reliability, precision of positioning and orientation, robustness to a changing environment are high. Highly dynamic spaces need to be mapped correctly and the robots need to be aware of the spaces around them. They need to adapt their behavior based on their location inside a factory and by the dynamicity of the environment.

© IFIP International Federation for Information Processing 2020
Published by Springer Nature Switzerland AG 2020
D. Cavallucci et al. (Eds.): TFC 2020, IFIP AICT 597, pp. 15–29, 2020.
https://doi.org/10.1007/978-3-030-61295-5_2

From an economic point of view there are numerous studies, papers and articles [2–4] that sustain the logic that the manufacturing, retail, warehouse logistics industries have and will have an increased need for autonomous mobile robots (AMR). This is due to the fact AMRs will have reduced costs, products can be stored efficiently using less storage space, delivery routes can be optimized for faster traffic and less damaged goods during the transport. The companies that take advantage of these products can disrupt the market in this way and gain numerous competitive advantages [1].

However, using complex AMRs in a dynamic and flexible manufacturing environment still pose unsolved challenges in terms of navigation as seen in [5]. The influencing factors can be people, other AMRs or other moving obstacles such as fork-lifts. This can lead to different types of failures that require human intervention and increased risks related to safety. A detailed analysis in terms of safety regarding AMRs is presented in [6].

Using the above information, we can say that the AMRs are still an increased area of research both from a mechanical point of view and as well from the technical demands of the global market. Making the processes more robust and easier to handle, this type of equipment will be able to penetrate the market of even smaller industrial facilities because of the reduces prices and because of the continuous improvements that are done on the software side. By following the presented methodology based on TRIZ [13] principles of innovation and problem-solving, AMR navigation areas that still need to be addressed are discusses and the paper ends with future research directions.

## 2   Background

As already presented, AMRs navigation is a vast domain that considers locomotion types, path planning, environment perception, dynamic control, data transfer and decision making. The state-of-the-art research on autonomous robot navigation and TRIZ for inventive solving problems was conducted using several databases: Scopus, Springer Link, Elsevier, IEEE Explorer, Research Gate. The searching criteria included different combinations, such as "autonomous navigation" AND "innovation", "autonomous robots" AND "navigation" AND "TRIZ", "navigation" AND "indoor" AND "industry" AND "autonomous robot" AND "requirement", "TRIZ" and "industry", "autonomous robot" AND "navigation" AND "corridor", "autonomous mobile robot" AND "future trends" AND "industry", "TRIZ" AND "methodology". One of the search results conclusions is that autonomous navigation is a highly debated subject of interest and new advances and improvements are still in focus. Most of the papers dive into the subject of path planning in different environments and improvements on niche subjects, the papers related to autonomous robots in industry focus on safety and human robot interaction and with the development of the different cloud infrastructures, in recent years, papers related to deploying the robot processing in Cloud continue to rise. The steady rise in the publications demonstrates that the possible developments or a new way of thinking related to autonomous robot navigation remains a subject of interest to this day.

AMRs navigation is based on interactions between sensors, actuators and control units. Navigation can be divided into four categories: map-based navigation, behavior-based navigation, learning-based navigation and communication-based navigation. In [7] there are presented all the four types of navigation methods and their lacks. Although improvements toward all the above presented navigation methods appeared, as presented in [8–10], there are still issues that need to be addressed, as seen from [6, 11].

There are few research articles that incorporate the TRIZ methodology directly related to robotic systems, a total of 122 papers, and most of them are not related to the navigation of autonomous mobile robots. One of the best papers in which TRIZ methodology and tools for inventive problem-solving regarding AMRs is presented in [12], in which scheduling and autonomous navigation is discussed for multiple agents.

In this paper an out of the box way of thinking is presented that analyses the different steps into dealing with the AMRs navigation subdomains. Approaching the autonomous navigation domain in a structured manner, can provide more insight and generic directions for further research of AMRs in industrial environments can be drawn.

## 3 Research Methodology

In order to have a structured approach over the complex system that navigation represents for AMRs and involve a creative and innovative way of thinking, the next steps were taken into account regarding the methodology: planning framework of voice-of-use-table-performance function deployment (VOUT-PFD), correlation between defined functions and KPI list, TRIZ contradiction matrix [14], method of weighted analysis of interdependencies (AIDA) [15], framework of Complex System Design Technique (CSDT) [16, 17] in relation with generic modules of the AI system. The above methods and techniques will be further described in this chapter, considering the complex system of autonomous robot navigation in an industrial environment setup.

### 3.1 VOUT-PFD Design Planning Framework

As a first step in order to construct this method, the engineering specifications must be defined as functions. The method through which the functions are chosen is based on the "Why" and the "Criticality" of the function regarding the overall needed solution. Then, for the defined functions different options for solving every function are presented. The result of this framework constitutes a morphological map that can produce generic clusters for the addressed navigation requirement.

In Fig. 1, just the identified functions and examples of the solving options are presented from the VOUT-PFD, because the whole table and the representation by lines of the considered clusters would not have been possible to fit in the paper limits and also the readability of the table would have lacked.

| No. | Function | Criticality | Means through which we can achive them | | | | |
| --- | --- | --- | --- | --- | --- | --- | --- |
| | | | option 1 | option 2 | option 3 | option 4 | option 5 |
| 1 | adapt optimal velocities and accelerations | critical | Use AI and analitics from both control algorithm and environment perception | risk assessment of perturbatory factors inside path boundary | utilising mixture of ROS local planners without further interrogations | | |
| 2 | smart obstacle avoidance | critical | using the information from 2D and / or 3D grid maps | behaviour based | combining grid maps with continuous learning solutions | communication based | learning based |
| 3 | compute trajectories only inside boundaries of predefined path | critical | contain the path with virtual walls | contain the path using physical path delimiters | use goal sequencing in order to reach the targeted position | | |
| 4 | optimize trafic on route | critical | create system scheduler | use IoT technologies and smart devices combined with custom path planners | using clasical path planners | | |
| 5 | obstacle detection on route and near route | high | utilising Lidar sensors | utilising sensor mixture for environment perception | utilising sonar sensors | utilising 3D cameras | |
| 6 | predict dynamic obstacle trajectories on and around given route | critical | by using active navigation: object classification classes, predict different object clases behaviour, while taking into account all involved AMR informations [cu ex: 49 din votre formulaire] | reactive method: by using obstacle detection methods and compute in real time the object velocities and accelerations | | | |
| 7 | obstacle tracking | high | using 2D lidar sensors with respect to generated Map | combining visual processing, pointcloud information, and data from other AMR systems in the vicinity with respect to the map | using visual processing and classification | using 3D pointcloud information with respect to generated map | |
| 8 | map and costmap clearing | critical | fast update time based on sensor information | utilise prediction | utilise prediction, sensor information and centralized map between AMR agents | by using costmap clearing maneuvers [ROS] | |
| 9 | automatically adapt robot behaviour based on factory location or by situation | critical | using classical path planning algorithm and DWA | using safe global path planning and DWA methods | using continuous learning and predictions while taking into account the sensors information inside map zones | by creating custom paths at safe distances from environment stationary obstacles and utilising sensor infrmation for sensing the unnacounted situations | split map into zones with different characteristics and use custom robot behaviours in the zones |
| 10 | environment perception | critical | data fusion and classification | using 2D sensors | using computer vision | using IoT technologies | |
| 11 | increase precision positioning of the robot near goal | high | using SLAM | using innertial navigation system | using visual odometry | using immage processing and 2D/3D sensor information | using markers |
| 12 | smart robot selection for ongoing and new tasks | critical | prioritise jobs based on battery usage | prioritise jobs based on closest available robot near the starting point of the job | create complex scheduler that takes into account KPI's of each unit and robots current job status | | |
| 13 | fast decision making in intersections | critical | zipper way | prioritize entering the intersection based on job weight | using clasical path planners algorithms | first come first served | |
| 14 | easy user creation, modification, deletion and visualization of a routes | high | by means of custom GUI where the user can interaction with the map | by saving the path in real time while the robot is autopiloted | using ROS tools and clasical navigation in order to reach goal | | |
| 15 | optimize mechanical structure of the robot | critical | using AI for mechanical design and simulation | using complex mechanical design programs that have static and dynamic finite element analisys | optimize mechanical structure by trail and error | | |

**Fig. 1.** Condensed representation of the morphological map from the VOUT-PFD planning framework.

The considered functions seen in the above figure were considered after conducting several physical tests and experiments with two AMRs platforms with non-holonomic drive [8], one with tracks and the other with four wheels in different indoor environments, while using robot operating system (ROS) as middleware infrastructure for distributed systems. Nonetheless, from the literature it is observed that the same areas of research are in continuous investigation, as indicated by older papers like [19, 20] to more recent ones [6, 11]. The drive type for robotic platforms can be either holonomic or nonholonomic. For a mobile terrestrial robot moving in a plane, a nonholonomic drive states that the robot has less than three degrees of freedom.

In Fig. 1, it can be seen that all the considered functions have a high importance and eleven of the fifteen functions are of greater criticality regarding AMRs navigation. The functions presented as critical are function that have stronger correlation with the other ones and treating them with lower importance has a big impact over the behavior, robot functionalities and can add impediments to robot programming. One important function that is usually left out when addressing robot navigation is presented in function fifteen. Even if the navigation type is chosen, the designer of the robotic system will create the product based on specific criteria and then once the robot is finished, intelligence is going to be placed on it. Having an already existing robot, the programmers will encounter different restrictions while dealing with robot navigation for specific tasks. If these restrictions can be encountered from the designing phase and solved from a mechanical point of view, then the results will have a big impact in the next programming steps. When a proposed mechanical or software component has to reach a Technology Readiness Level (TRL) of 8, that stands for system complete and qualified then all the components must reach a mature and already proven to work in the relevant industrial environment, in order to present a viable solution for the targeted market. The "Why" column, that is not represented in the above figure, is mainly concentrated towards reaching a viable product that can be used in industrial setups for handling goods, automate certain tasks that require multiple robots and also making the human robot interaction more pleasant.

In this example there are five different clusters that were considered. In order to present each cluster, based on Fig. 1, each function was noted with F1 to F15 and each option with O1 to O5. Based on the proposed options, the considered combinations are further presented. Cluster 1: F1-O1; F2-O3; F3-O1; F4-O2; F5-O2; F6-O1; F7-O2; F8-O3; F9-O3; F10-O1; F11-O4; F12-O3; F13-O2; F14-O1; F15-O1. Cluster 2: F1-O2; F2-O2; F3-O1; F4-O1; F5-O2; F6-O1; F7-O3; F8-O1; F9-O2; F10-O3; F11-O3; F12-O1; F13-O4; F14-O1; F15-O1. Cluster 3: F1-O1; F2-O3; F3-O1; F4-O2; F5-O2; F6-O1; F7-O2; F8-O3; F9-O3; F10-O1; F11-O4; F12-O3; F13-O2; F14-O1; F15-O1. Cluster 4: F1-O1; F2-O3; F3-O1; F4-O2; F5-O2; F6-O1; F7-O2; F8-O3; F9-O4; F10-O1; F11-O5; F12-O3; F13-O2; F14-O1; F15-O1. Cluster 5: F1-O3; F2-O1; F3-O3; F4-O3; F5-O1; F6-O2; F7-O1; F8-O2; F9-O1; F10-O2; F11-O1; F12-O2; F13-O3; F14-O3; F15-O3. Cluster 1 is the most complex and could present the highest results from the considered options. Clusters from two to four are combinations extracted from Cluster 1 that reduce some of the complexity. Cluster 2 represents the second complex solution. Cluster 3 presents a more reactive navigation approach and Cluster 4 comes with more human robot interaction. Cluster 5 can be the easiest to program among the five clusters but can only address specific needs.

### 3.2 Correlation Between Defined Functions and KPIs List

In order to be able to improve and innovate a system the requirements for that specific system must be well understood and analyzed. One way of doing this is by properly defining the Key Performance Indicators (KPIs) for the task at hand. Examples of addressing the correct KPIs, related to the discussed subject in this paper, can be found on the following works [21, 22].

Considering the scope of the project and the literature, the following KPIs list was constructed, presented in Fig. 2. Each KPI was given an importance factor followed by the measuring system and the specific values targeted for this specific scope of work. The most critical KPIs, when considering the navigation for an AMR in an industrial environment, are: the cycle time, the safety factor, the average moving speed and the cost per robot unit.

| No. | KPI list | KPI importance | Measuring system | Project target |
|-----|----------|----------------|------------------|----------------|
| 1 | Deviation from planned route | high | % | <0.5% |
| 2 | Path repetability | high | % | >95% |
| 3 | Nr. of times robot leaves planned route | high | number | 0 |
| 4 | Cycle time | critical | time | > 1 min than mean time on that path with load (worst case scenario) |
| 5 | Completed jobs per hour | high | number | >=20 |
| 6 | Failed jobs per hour | critical | number | 0 |
| 7 | Distance traveled per hour | medium | distance | > 2700 m |
| 8 | Mean time between jobs per hour | high | time | < 30 sec |
| 9 | Wait time between jobs per hour | high | time | < 30 sec |
| 10 | Utilisation factor per hour | high | % | >70 |
| 11 | Efficiency factor per hour | high | % | >95 |
| 12 | Safety | critical | % | 100% (ideally) |
| 13 | Obstacles detected on path and avoided per hour | high | number | < 50 |
| 14 | Nr of halted navigation state because of obstacle blocking path per hour | high | number | < 5 |
| 15 | Mean halted time due to obstacles per hour | high | time | < 2 min |
| 16 | Ratio of human intervention time - to robot time | high | time | <1:12 ratio per hour |
| 17 | Average moving speed | critical | speed | >1.5 m/s (depending on environmental conditions, and on type of job) |
| 18 | Mean time between failure | high | time | > 10000 hours |
| 19 | Idle state after robot started job per hour | high | time | <2 min |
| 20 | Cost per robot unit | critical | eur | <15000 |

**Fig. 2.** KPIs list considered for autonomous navigation.

The first KPI from Fig. 2 represents by how much the robot is allowed to exit the path boundaries in order to avoid obstacles and then re-enter the path to reach the designated target. The AMR has multiple types of tasks that can be received and a task is not considered finished before loading and unloading of the robot is done. The safety factor is influenced by KPI one and three which tend to zero, also no collisions, respecting the safety distances and adaptive control of speed and accelerations for the robot in regards to the environment. The distance traveled per hour has to be set in regards to the type of tasks the robot is subjected to.

Following the construction of the relevant KPIs list, a correlation matrix was used, between the already defined functions and the newly defined KPIs. The results can be seen in Fig. 3. In the figure the functions index coincides with the indexing in the VOUT-PFD method and the KPIs are put in the same order as in Fig. 2.

In Fig. 3, both positive and the negative correlations are indicated between the functions and the KPIs. The negative correlations are also highlighted in order to be faster identified. In the below table obvious high impact negative correlations like the ones between the KPI 15 related to cost and F15 mechanical structure of the robot and also towards F10 that deals with the environment perception. But there are also other high impact negative correlations that are not so easy to discover, like the one between KPI1 that deals with the deviation from planned path and F9 – automatically adapt robot behavior based on factory location and situation. Also, these two functions have one of the highest positive correlation factors with the other KPIs that indicate issues that need increased attention. The values for positive and negative correlations were drawn from practical experiments over four years of work and by drawing conclusions from the literature [7–9, 11].

| | Neg. | Pos. | KPI1 | KPI2 | KPI3 | KPI4 | KPI5 | KPI6 | KPI7 | KPI8 | KPI9 | KPI10 | KPI11 | KPI12 | KPI13 | KPI14 | KPI15 | KPI16 | KPI17 | KPI18 | KPI19 | KPI20 |
|---|---|---|---|---|---|---|---|---|---|---|---|---|---|---|---|---|---|---|---|---|---|---|
| Negative Correlation | | | -15 | -15 | -15 | -3 | -3 | | -3 | | | | | -9 | | -12 | -1 | | -30 | -1 | -3 | -18 |
| Positive Correlation | | | 31 | 32 | 19 | 66 | 59 | 80 | 50 | 25 | 25 | 75 | 75 | 82 | 87 | 30 | 46 | 74 | 38 | 37 | 36 | 25 |
| F1 | -21 | 62 | 9/ | 9/ | 1 | /-3 | /-3 | 9/ | /-3 | / | / | 9/ | 9/ | 3/ | 9/ | /-3 | 3/ | 3/ | /-9 | 3/ | 1/ | 3/ |
| F2 | -22 | 90 | /-3 | /-3 | /-3 | 3/ | 3/ | 9/ | 3/ | / | / | 9/ | 9/ | 9/ | /-9 | 9/ | 9/ | 9/ | /-3 | /-1 | 9/ | 3/ |
| F3 | -10 | 67 | 9/ | 9/ | 9/ | 3/ | 3/ | 9/ | 9/ | / | / | 3/ | 3/ | 9/ | /3 | /-9 | /-1 | 1/ | 9/ | 3/ | 1/ | 3/ |
| F4 | -18 | 105 | /-3 | /-3 | /-3 | 9/ | 9/ | 9/ | 9/ | 9/ | 9/ | 9/ | 9/ | 9/ | 9/ | 9/ | 9/ | 9/ | 3/ | 3/ | /-9 | 1 |
| F5 | | 39 | / | / | / | 1/ | 1/ | / | 1/ | 1/ | 1/ | / | / | 9/ | 9/ | 1/ | 1/ | 3/ | / | / | 1/ | / |
| F6 | -9 | 58 | 1/ | 1/ | 1/ | 3/ | 3/ | 3/ | 3/ | 3/ | 3/ | 3/ | 3/ | 9/ | 9/ | 1/ | 1/ | 3/ | /-9 | 3/ | 1/ | 1/ |
| F7 | | 26 | / | / | / | 1/ | / | 1/ | / | / | / | 1/ | 1/ | 9/ | 3/ | 1/ | / | 1/ | / | / | / | / |
| F8 | | 80 | 3/ | 3/ | 1/ | 9/ | 9/ | 1/ | 3/ | 1/ | 1/ | 3/ | 3/ | 1/ | / | / | 9/ | 9/ | / | / | 9/ | 1/ |
| F9 | -15 | 115 | /-9 | /-3 | /-3 | 9/ | 3/ | 9/ | 3/ | 1/ | 1/ | 9/ | 9/ | 9/ | 9/ | 1/ | 1/ | 9/ | 3/ | 3/ | 3/ | 3/ |
| F10 | -9 | 105 | 3/ | | 3/ | 3/ | 3/ | 9/ | 3/ | 1/ | 1/ | 9/ | 9/ | 9/ | 9/ | 3/ | 9/ | 9/ | 3/ | 3/ | 1/ | /-9 |
| F11 | -9 | 15 | / | / | / | 9/ | 3/ | / | / | / | / | 1/ | 1/ | 3/ | / | / | / | 1/ | /-9 | / | / | / |
| F12 | | 88 | / | / | / | 1/ | 9/ | 9/ | 9/ | 9/ | 9/ | 9/ | 9/ | 3/ | 1/ | / | / | 9/ | 1/ | 9/ | 1/ | 9/ |
| F13 | | 58 | 3/ | 1/ | 1/ | 3/ | 3/ | 9/ | 3/ | / | / | 3/ | 3/ | 3/ | 9/ | / | / | 3/ | 9/ | 1/ | 9/ | / |
| F14 | | 18 | / | / | / | 3/ | 1/ | 1/ | 1/ | / | / | 1/ | 1/ | 3/ | / | 3/ | 3/ | 3/ | / | / | / | 1/ |
| F15 | -9 | 103 | 3/ | 9/ | 3/ | 9/ | 9/ | 3/ | 3/ | / | / | 9/ | 9/ | 9/ | 3/ | / | / | 3/ | 9/ | 9/ | / | /-9 |

**Fig. 3.** Correlation matrix between the defined functions and the KPIs list.

## 3.3 Applying TRIZ Contradiction Matrix

| No. | Functions to improve | Highest Conflicting KPI | Selected TRIZ principles translated in application dommain - Generic guiding lines | Vector Index |
|---|---|---|---|---|
| A | Adapt optimal velocities and accelerations | Average moving speed | Beside the adopted navigation method used, suggest through Ai algorithms specific routes from A to B that are with less corners, less trafic from other systems (TRIZ 5) | A1 |
| | | | Train an active navigation method that takes into account the behaviour of the specific classified dynamic objects in order to obtain paths where higher velocityes are possible and safe (TRIZ 20) | A2 |
| | | | Use IoT devices that communicate among them in order to create a new robot behaviour that facilitate the robot to operate at higher speeds with reduced risks (TRIZ 1) | A3 |
| I | Optimize mechanical structure of the robot | Cost per robot unit | Add, prior to final robot concept, AI that can suggest improvements in the mechanical design of the robot (TRIZ 10) | I1 |
| | | | Use passive elements in the mechanical structure in order to eliminate need for more actuators and in order to improve the dinamics of the system (TRIZ 28) | I2 |
| | | | Use unconventional materials and production techniques (TRIZ 35) | I3 |

**Fig. 4.** Part of the TRIZ contradiction matrix between the AMR functions that need improvement and the conflicting

In order to maintain the inventive problem-solving way of thinking over the negative correlations indicated by Fig. 2, the TRIZ contradiction matrix was used. This was done in order to obtain the innovation vectors that can solve the functions that need improvement by addressing the conflicting KPIs. In this way all the functions that need improvement and the adjacent conflicting KPIs were given between three and four TRIZ inventive principles as indicated in [14, 18]. Then for each function that had multiple conflicting KPIs, the TRIZ principles were selected that could solve the highest degree of negative correlation and could also solve the lesser conflicts. After applying this reduction, for each function were selected between three and four principles resulting into a total of 28 possible innovation vectors. Then each selected innovation vector was translated in application domain by suggesting generic guiding lines to follow. This was done by investigating the analogies between the TRIZ 40 Inventive principles [18] and possible examples in software domain presented in [23]. Because the whole table could not fit in this paper, in Fig. 4 were selected two results, considering two different conflicting situations and the proposed generic guiding lines and an index associated with each vector in order to keep track on them.

### 3.4   Method of Weighted Analysis of Interdependencies (AIDA)

For reducing the number on innovation vectors while keeping the TRIZ methodology in mind and in order to achieve the highest result from the proposed vectors the improved AIDA method was used. This method was first proposed in [15] and an exemplification of the method in the software domain is presented in [24]. As stated in [15] this improved version has better results when dealing with complex projects as it is the case in this work.

The constraints for reducing the 28 innovation vectors were selected based on the possibility to improve and innovate the algorithms that need work. The chosen constraints are: o1 – detection time, o2 – accuracy of identification of hazardous factors, o3 – accuracy of maintaining the robot footprint on the given trajectory, o4 – robust system, o5 – adaptability time to new environment, situations, o6 – increased safety. For every set of innovative vectors resulted from the previous used method, nine tables were created. In the below figure it is presented the case for the two-ways causality between the above selected constraints and the identified vectors I1 – I3 from Fig. 4.

Figure 5 clearly indicates that the best innovative vector in the decision area I is I1, (add, prior to final robot concept, AI that can suggest improvements in the mechanical design of the robot – based on TRIZ 10, Prior Action). Also, one constraint is less critical in the decision area I is o3 – accuracy of maintaining the robot footprint on the given trajectory. This means that accomplishing this condition will not influence the decisions needed for the decision area I.

|    | I1 | I2 | I3 |
|----|----|----|----|
| o1 | 3 | 2 | 1 |
| o2 | 3 | 1 | 1 |
| o3 | 3 | 3 | 1 |
| o4 | 3 | 2 | 2 |
| o5 | 3 | 1 | 1 |
| o6 | 3 | 2 | 1 |

Step 1: influence of constraints over options by atributing a score [1 - low; 2 - medium; 3 - high]

Step 2: influence of options over constraints

|    | o1 | o2 | o3 | o4 | o5 | o6 |
|----|----|----|----|----|----|----|
| I1 | 3 | 3 | 3 | 3 | 3 | 3 |
| I2 | 2 | 1 | 2 | 2 | 1 | 2 |
| I3 | 1 | 1 | 1 | 2 | 1 | 2 |

|     | I1 | I2 | I3 | ΣC/3 |
|-----|----|----|----|------|
| o1  | 9 | 4 | 1 | 4.67 |
| o2  | 9 | 1 | 1 | 3.67 |
| o3  | 9 | 6 | 1 | 5.33 |
| o4  | 9 | 4 | 2 | 5.00 |
| o5  | 9 | 1 | 1 | 3.67 |
| o6  | 9 | 4 | 2 | 5.00 |
| O/6 | 9.00 | 3.33 | 1.33 | |

Step3: products of the coefficients from previous steps. The results are the averages from the lines and columns

**Fig. 5.** Table for analyzing the two-way causality between the innovation vectors and the proposed constraints for the decision area I.

Similar tables were constructed for all the decision areas and the result is presented through the simplified option graph shown in Fig. 6.

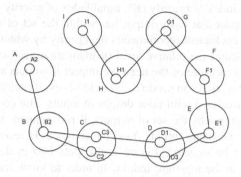

**Fig. 6.** Simplified option graph for all the six decision areas.

Figure 6 presents two compatible combinations of the vectors: A2-B2-C3-D1-E1-F1-G1-H1-I1 and A2-B2-C2-D3-E1-F1-G1-H1-I1. Based on the accumulated experience in the navigation domain, the first combination was chosen. The innovation vector representing the generic guiding lines are: V1(A2) - Train an active navigation method that takes into account the behavior of the specific classified dynamic objects in order to obtain paths where higher velocities are possible and safe; V2(B2) - Beside the path planner adopt a learning based navigation that is trained to deal with a variety of situations; V3(C3) - Inform that obstacle is blocking and based on obstacle properties automatically determine to either try different route towards the goal or wait for further instructions; V4(D1) - Use AI in a system scheduler that monitors and plans all traffic inside the facility; V5(E1) - Use AI to predict specific human or machine behavior; V6 (F1) - Use AI to extract patterns and make predictions over the already classified objects in the environment and use them in simulation scenarios regarding the system parameters; V7(G1) - Use AI for classification and training and data storage for computer vision, point-cloud processing, sound processing, thermal images processing; V8(H1) - Use AI to increase dynamic and position control of the system; V9(I1) - Add prior to final robot concept, AI in the mechanical design of the robot.

### 3.5 CSDT Framework

In order to further investigate the identified combination of vectors and provide a roadmap for reaching end results CSDT framework was used. Figure 7 shows the CSDT planning matrices. Each input has a relative importance rank (R), given by engineers to meet the short list of inventive directions (outputs). Each output has a relative difficulty rank (D) from the perspective of achievement. Both R and D coefficients were introduced by applying Analytic Hierarchy Process (AHP) between the inputs and then between the outputs. The AHP method is first described in [25]. To quantify the relationship coefficients between inputs and outputs a specific algorithm is considered, called CSDT [16]. The CSDT planning framework also considers several other coefficients. In this example the following CSDT coefficients are introduced (see Fig. 7): value weight (W), technical index of priority (I), relative technical effort (Z), impact depreciation (Q), technical depreciation (O), input risk (J), difficulty to satisfy inputs (d), correlation index of priority (K), input index of priority (H). W indicates the maximum relative impact that each output has within the set of outputs to define an innovative solution. I coefficient recommends the priority by which each output should be approached. Z indicates the relative level of innovation necessary to be induced in each output. Q gives a measure of the negative impact if outputs are not well satisfied. O is related to the implications on product competitiveness if inputs are not well solved. J is about the risks associated with poor design of inputs. The coefficient d shows the difficulty to satisfy an input by the set of outputs. K recommends the priority by which the interdependencies between outputs must be analyzed. H recommends the priority by which inputs must be satisfied. Figure 7 also puts into evidence the correlations (C) between outputs, in the top-right matrix. In order to know more details about the calculation of the above-mentioned coefficients, reference [16] must be consulted.

Information from Fig. 7 show that "Train an active navigation method that takes into account the behavior of the specific classified dynamic objects in order to obtain paths where higher velocities are possible and safe" and "Beside the path planner adopt a learning based navigation that is trained to deal with a variety of situations" have the highest impact on the AI system (W = 7.03), followed by "Inform that obstacle is blocking and based on obstacle properties automatically determine to either try different route towards the goal or wait for further instructions" (W = 6.56) and close by "Use AI to increase dynamic and position control of the system" (W = 6.37).

Figure 7 highlights that priority for AI system is on "Use AI to increase dynamic and position control of the system" (I = 70.02), followed by "Add prior to final robot concept, AI in the mechanical design of the robot" (I = 58.19), and close by "Use AI for classification and training and data storage for computer vision, point-cloud processing, sound processing, thermal image processing" (I = 56.49). The highest level of innovation is required in "Train an active navigation method that takes into account the behavior of the specific classified dynamic objects in order to obtain paths where higher velocities are possible and safe" (Z = 115.98), followed by "Beside the path planner, adopt a learning based navigation that is trained to deal with a variety of situations" (Z = 104.73). Usually in a production facility there are many workflows to be considered, the personnel vary from well to underqualified and in most case emotional or physical stress and tiredness can affect their process of work. In this way certain procedures can be handled in multiple ways. In most of these cases it is meaningful to understand what the specific human or other device is doing in order to adopt a proper navigation inside a facility.

"Inform that obstacle is blocking and based on obstacle properties automatically determine to either try different route towards the goal or wait for further instructions" is on the third place in terms of innovation challenges (Z = 97.82), followed at some distance by "Use AI in a system scheduler that monitors and plans all traffic inside the facility" (Z = 73.14). The goods and other vehicles inside a production facility are usually just identified as obstacles. It is important to understand more about the vehicles and how do they move. For example, a forklift can be with a human inside or not, if there is a human inside then is the forklift already loaded or not, is the forklift near the start or the end of operation of displacing the goods on shelves. In the same cases we can have a look over the merchandise that is blocking the path. Is this due to poor handling and it fell, is the merchandise displaced on top of a euro pallet or not. All this information can provide insight over how to address the navigation of the AMRs in the vicinity of these obstacles. Also, information exchanged between robots must be selected and be meaningful in order to reduce the data traffic on the network.

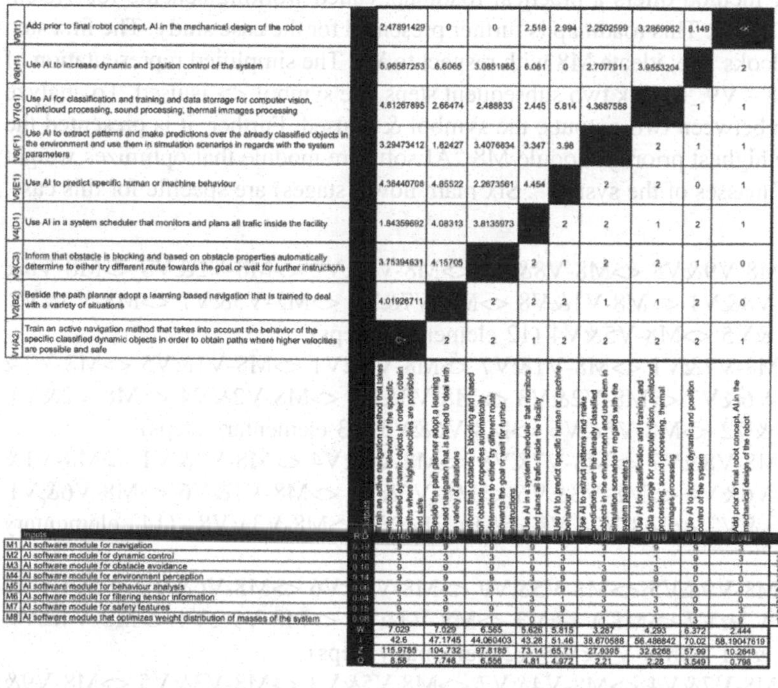

| | | | | | | | | | |
|---|---|---|---|---|---|---|---|---|---|
| Add prior to final robot concept, AI in the mechanical design of the robot | 2.47891429 | 0 | 0 | 2.518 | 2.994 | 2.2502599 | 3.2869962 | 8.149 | ∞ |
| Use AI to increase dynamic and position control of the system | 5.96587253 | 6.6065 | 3.0851965 | 6.061 | 0 | 2.7077911 | 3.9553204 | | 2 |
| Use AI for classification and training and data storrage for computer vision, pointcloud processing, sound processing, thermal immages processing | 4.81267895 | 2.66474 | 2.488833 | 2.445 | 5.814 | 4.3687588 | | 1 | 1 |
| Use AI to extract patterns and make predictions over the already classified objects in the environment and use them in simulation scenarios in regards with the system parameters | 3.29473412 | 1.82427 | 3.4076834 | 3.347 | 3.98 | | 2 | 1 | 1 |
| Use AI to predict specific human or machine behaviour | 4.38440708 | 4.85522 | 2.2673561 | 4.454 | | 2 | 2 | 0 | 1 |
| Use AI in a system scheduler that monitors and plans all traffic inside the facility | 1.84359692 | 4.08313 | 3.8135973 | | 2 | 2 | 1 | 2 | 1 |
| Inform that obstacle is blocking and based on obstacle properties automatically determine to either try different route towards the goal or wait for further instructions | 3.75394531 | 4.15705 | | 2 | 1 | 2 | 2 | 1 | 0 |
| Beside the path planner adopt a learning based navigation that is trained to deal with a variety of situations | 4.01926711 | | 2 | 2 | 2 | 1 | 1 | 2 | 0 |
| Train an active navigation method that takes into account the behavior of the specific classified dynamic objects in order to obtain paths where higher velocities are possible and safe | ∞ | 2 | 2 | 1 | 2 | 2 | 2 | 2 | 1 |

| inputs | | | | | | | | | | | | |
|---|---|---|---|---|---|---|---|---|---|---|---|---|
| M1 AI software module for navigation | | 9 | 9 | 9 | 9 | 3 | 3 | 9 | 9 | | 7.56 | 40 | 1428.8 | 11.907 |
| M2 AI software module for dynamic control | | 3 | 3 | 3 | 3 | 3 | 1 | 1 | 9 | | 3.224 | 17.714 | 586.77 | 5.278 |
| M3 AI software module for obstacle avoidance | | 9 | 9 | 9 | 9 | 9 | 1 | 9 | 9 | | 7.696 | 46.939 | 1262.5 | 10.004 |
| M4 AI software module for environment perception | | 9 | 9 | 9 | 9 | 9 | 9 | 9 | 0 | | 7.023 | 52.022 | 948.11 | 7.895 |
| M5 AI software module for behaviour analysis | | 9 | 9 | 3 | 3 | 9 | 1 | 0 | 0 | | 4.761 | 74.234 | 304.06 | 2.24 |
| M6 AI software module for filtering sensor information | | 9 | 9 | 3 | 1 | 3 | 9 | 0 | 0 | | 2.077 | 51.925 | 83.08 | 0.66 |
| M7 AI software module for safety features | | 9 | 9 | 9 | 3 | 9 | 9 | 3 | 3 | | 7.782 | 53.301 | 1136.2 | 9.198 |
| M8 AI software module that optimizes weight distribution of masses of the system | | 1 | 1 | 1 | 0 | 1 | 9 | 0 | 9 | | 1.388 | 17.136 | 112.43 | 1.458 |
| W | 7.029 | 7.029 | 6.565 | 5.626 | 5.815 | 3.287 | 4.293 | 6.372 | 2.444 | | | | |
| I | 115.9785 | 104.732 | 97.8185 | 73.14 | 65.71 | 27.9395 | 32.6268 | 57.99 | 10.2848 | | | | |
| O | 8.56 | 7.746 | 6.556 | 4.81 | 4.972 | 2.21 | 2.28 | 3.549 | 0.796 | | | | |

**Fig. 7.** CSDT matrix for the case study.

According to the information in Fig. 7, the highest drawback of the system (if it is not properly solved) stands on "Train an active navigation method that takes into account the behavior of the specific classified dynamic objects in order to obtain paths where higher velocities are possible and safe" (Q = 8.58). An active navigation means that reasoning is performed in a predictive manner in order to enable smooth evasive maneuvers instead of abrupt collision avoidance maneuvers. The work in [26] provides insight and better results than traditional path planners, but also in this work the mean velocities for handling obstacle avoidance maneuvers were underneath the desired KPI of this project by a third. In this case, in order to reach an average of 1.5 m/s, unsafe accelerations and velocities must be adopted after passing an obstacle. In this way specific individual behavior in open spaces, like the inside of production facilities may have to be captured for better results in terms of speed and safety of the AMR system.

"AI software module for safety features" and "AI software module for obstacle avoidance" are the top two modules of the AI system that are equally most difficult to satisfy, closely followed by "AI software module for navigation" and "AI software module for environment perception" (see the coefficient d in Fig. 7). However, in terms of priority to satisfy, on the first place is the "AI software module that optimizes weight distribution of masses of the system" (H = 17.14), and on the last place is "AI software module for behavior analysis" (H = 74.23). Both AI system competitiveness and risks are related to "AI software module for navigation" (see coefficients O and J in Fig. 7).

In order to manage complexity during the conceptualization process of the AI system, CSDT method offers a practical roadmap, called working scheme for system design (WSSD) [16]. This roadmap is further presented for the case study. The first step of the WSSD looks like: ideate M8 with respect to V9. The simplified representation of this step is: M8 – V9. To link two subsequent steps, the symbol <> is used. To analyze the correlation between two outputs, the symbol & is used. Further, it is presented the WSSD for the highest priority module M8 "AI software module that optimizes weight distribution of masses of the system". Six main flows (stages) are specific for this case, as follows:

- Flow 1: M8-V9&V8 <>M8-V8&V9 <>M8-V8&V2 <>M8-V2&V8 <>M8-V8& V4 <>M8-V8&V1 <>M8-V1&V8 <>M8-V7&V5 <>M8-V5&V7 <>M8-V5&V2 <>M8-V2 &V5 <>M8-V5&V4 (12 elementary steps)
- Flow 2: M8-V7&V1 <>M8-V1&V7 <>M8-V5&V1 <>M8-V1&V5 <>M8-V7& V6 <>M8-V6&V7 <>M8-V2&V3 <>M8-V3&V2 <>M8-V2&V4 <>M8-V2&V1 <>M8-V1 &V2 <>M8-V5&V6 <>M8-V6&V5 (13 elementary steps)
- Flow 3: M8-V8&V7 <>M8-V7&V8 <>M8-V3&V4 <>M8-V3&V1 <>M8-V1& V3 <>M8-V6&V4 <>M8-V3&V6 <>M8-V6&V3 <>M8-V1&V6 <>M8-V6&V1 <>M8-V9 &V7 <>M8-V7&V9 <>M8-V8&V3 <>M8-V3&V8 (14 elementary steps)
- Flow 4: M8-V9&V5 <>M8-V5&V9 <>M8-V8&V6 <>M8-V6&V8 <>M8-V7& V2 <>M8-V2&V7 <>M8-V7&V3 <>M8-V3&V7 <>M8-V9&V4 <>M8-V4&V9 <>M8-V9 &V1 <>M8-V1&V9 (12 elementary steps)
- Flow 5: M8-V7&V4 <>M8-V4&V7 <>M8-V5&V3 <>M8-V3&V5 <>M8-V9& V6 <>M8-V6&V9 <>M8-V1&V4 <> M8-V6&V2 <>M8-V2&V6 (9 elementary steps)
- Flow 6: M8-V2 <>M8-V3 <>M8-V5 (3 elementary steps)

The six flows above presented can be approached in several cycles (usually 2–3) if the results are not enough mature after the first cycle. As the flows show, the conceptualization (design) process of M8 is divided into 63 elementary steps. At each increment, an elementary problem is approached. Thus, complexity is better administrated. As it can be seen, the design process is an evolutionary one. The WSSD provides a structured space for search and ideation. It follows the laws of ideality and convergence, too.

## 4 Case Study

As seen from the CSDT method, the order in which the AI software modules are to be addressed is based on the H coefficient from low to high. In this way the iterations follow a logical order M8-M2-M1-M3-M6-M4-M7-M5 (see Fig. 7). In order to improve and innovate in a complex subject such as navigation, the order for addressing the requirements must start from the bottom up, which in this case is to optimize the mechanical structure of the robot, AI Module 8. In this case a really strong influence in terms of navigation holds the weight distribution of masses because they introduce inertial moments in respect to the robot motors axes, it will affect the stability of the robot, has effects upon both kinematics and dynamics of the robot. The first flow proposed by the WSSD method to manage the complexity of the AI Module 8 is briefly presented in this case study.

The first flow in the WSSD process is to follow M8 with respect to V9 but the results should not affect V8. For this case it means that the "AI software module that optimizes the weight distribution of masses in the system" should be solved in respect to "add prior to final robot concept, AI in the mechanical design of the robot" without influencing the "Use AI to increase dynamic and position control of the system". The first problem basically solves itself because if weight distribution is done before the concept is finalized then the dynamics and position control can also be foreseen beforehand. In order to address the weight distribution, the mechanical system must be first brought down to individual components. The main components of the robot to be defined are: the drive train – non-holonomic, holonomic, Ackermann; the chassis – shape and execution; the type of servo-motors; the control unit, batteries, power source, motor drivers, sensors and sensor drivers. Because there are many possible lits already on the market, this work will also address integrating the needed components in the system. In order to have a general view over each component, they will be represented as primitives in the system allowing different dimensions and masses. The challenge is to obtain the ideal placement for all the equipment in order to respect all the steps in the workflows presented by the WSSD process. This leads to complex tables in which mathematical and mechanical constraints intervene between the elements. The objective functions that were considered when constructing the tables were to optimize the system masses in order to increase stability, the moment of inertia at the motor axes should be minimal. After choosing the components of the system and all the mathematical restrictions between them, in order to optimize the weight distribution of masses in the system, particle swarm optimization is considered (PSO) and in order to optimize the mechanical structure of the robot generative design techniques are to be addressed. The case study would not have been reached without utilizing TRIZ principles and the suggested problem-solving methodology.

## 5 Conclusions and Future Work

The main contribution of this paper is that it shows a structured way in which inventive problem-solving thinking can lead to possible innovations regarding integration of AI algorithms in the complex system of navigation for autonomous mobile robots. Using the proposed steps in the methodology, eight research direction were identified and with the help of CSDT method, an order for addressing them was established. Using WSSD, each of the eight modules is broken into elementary steps, thus providing a path for addressing each topic. Keeping into account the complexity of each module with respect to the established innovation vectors justifies the need for a large team with strong competences in mechanical engineering, AI, mechatronics, computer vision, to be part of the project. In this way the CSDT inputs can be addressed in a concurrent way and each decision taken at any of the modules if it has implications over the rest, then the issues can be solved quicker and in an Agile way.

The case study briefly presents the approach over how the first module related to autonomous navigation must be addressed regarding optimization of weight distribution of masses in the robot system. The main objective functions are identified and AI algorithms in order to implement the first module are proposed.

The first research direction is to finalize the implementation of the first AI module extracted from CSDT framework and then to follow the proposed order into addressing and implementing all the remaining AI software modules. TRIZ tools and techniques will also be incorporated in the future work in order to increase the degree of possible innovations along the way. Testing the software modules will need to be done periodically, as the modules evolve and the final acceptance testing, combining all modules will be presented last.

## References

1. Rajana, S.: Robotics for the supply chain. Techn. Rep. (2018). https://doi.org/10.13140/RG.2.2.28081.43361
2. Sander, A., Wolfgang, M.: The Rise of Robotics. Boston Consulting Group. https://www.bcg.com/publications/2014/business-unit-strategy-innovation-rise-of-robotic.aspxs. Accessed 27 Aug 2014
3. Sun, A., Faulkner, D., Jeong, H.: Glimpsing the road ahead: reshaping the logistics market. Colliers International. https://www2.colliers.com/en-IN/Research/Glimpsing-the-Road-Ahead-Reshaping-the-Logistics-Market. Accessed 17 June 2019
4. Kumar, R.: Mobile Robotics Market: Opportunities and forecasts. 2019–2026 (2019). https://www.alliedmarketresearch.com/mobile-robotics-market. Accessed 17 June 2019
5. Liaqat, A., et al.: Autonomous mobile robots in manufacturing: highway Code development, simulation, and testing. Int. J. Adv. Manuf. Technol. **2019**, 4617–4628 (2019). https://doi.org/10.1007/s00170-019-04257-1
6. Bozhinoski, D., Di Ruscio, D., Malavolta, I., Pelliccione, P., Crnkovic, I.: Safety for mobile robotic systems: a systematic mapping study from a software engineering perspective. J. Syst. Software **151**, 150–179 (2019). https://doi.org/10.1016/j.jss.2019.02.021
7. Nurmaini, S., Tutuko, B.: intelligent robotics navigation system: problems, methods, and algorithm. Int. J. Electric. Comput. Eng. **7**(6), 3711–3726 (2017). https://doi.org/10.11591/ijece.v7i6
8. Tzafestas, S.G.: Introduction to mobile robot control. 1$^{st}$ edition, Elsevier Insights, London, Waltham (2014). https://doi.org/10.1016/c2013-0-01365-5

9. Patle, B.K., Ganesh Babu, L., Pandey, A., Parhi, D.R.K., Jagadeeshm, A.: A review: on path planning strategies for navigation of mobile robot. Defence Technol. **15**(4), 582–606 (2019). https://doi.org/10.1016/j.dt.2019.04.011

10. Liu, Y., Li, Z., Liu, H., Kan, Z.: Skill transfer learning for autonomous robots and human–robot cooperation: a survey. Robot. Autonom. Syst. **128** (2020). https://doi.org/10.1016/j.robot.2020.103515

11. Engemann, H., Badri, S., Wenning, M., Kallweit, S.: Implementation of an autonomous tool trolley in a production line. Adv. Intell. Syst. Comput. **980**(28), 117–125 (2019)

12. Petrović, M., Miljković, Z., Babić, B.: Integration of process planning, scheduling, and mobile robot navigation based on TRIZ and multi agent methodology, FME. Transactions **41**, 120–129 (2013)

13. Altshuller, G.: TRIZ the Theory of Inventive Problem Solving. Technical Innovation Center, Worcester (1996)

14. Kaplan, S.: An Introduction to TRIZ The Russian Theory of Inventive Problem Solving. Ideation International Inc., Farmington Hills, Northwestern Hwy, Suite 145, Michigan (1996)

15. Brad, S.: Improving the use of AIDA method. ACTA TECHNICA NAPOCENSIS, Series: Appl. Math. Mech. **50**(2), 56 (2007)

16. Brad, S.: Complex system design technique. Int. J. Prod. Res. **46**(21), 5979–6008 (2008)

17. Brad, S., et al.: TRIZ to Support Blue-design of Products. Procedia CIRP **39**, 125–131 (2016). https://doi.org/10.1016/j.procir.2016.01.177

18. Altshuller, G.S., Shulyak, L., Rodman, S.: 40 Principles: TRIZ Keys to Technical Innovation. 1st. ed. Technical Innovation Center, Inc. (1997)

19. Park, J.H., Huh, U.Y.: Path Plan. Autonomous Mob. Robot Based Safe Space. J. Electric. Eng. Technol. **11**(5), 1441–1448 (2016). https://doi.org/10.5370/JEET.2016.11.5.1441

20. Marin, P., Hussein, A., Gomez, D.M., Escarla, A.: Global and local path planning study in a ROS-based research platform for autonomous vehicles. J. Adv. Transport 2018, Article ID 6392697, p. 10 (2018). https://doi.org/10.1155/2018/6392697

21. Vermesan, A., et al.: AUTOmated driving Progressed by Internet Of Things D. 5.3 Performance and KPIs for autonomous vehicles and IoT pilot impact measurement. Project co-funded by the European Commission within Horizon 2020 and managed by the European GNSS Agency (GSA) (2017)

22. Voronova, D., Berezhnaya, L.: Logistic approach to a company's performance assessment based on a KPI system. OP Conference Series: Materials Science and Engineering, volume 817, All-russian scientific-practical conference with international participation "Actual issues of transport in the forest sector, 28–29 November 2019, St. Petersburg, Russia (2019)

23. TRIZ Journal Homepage. https://triz-journal.com/triz-software-40-principle-analogies-sequel/. Accessed 12 Jan 2006

24. Brad, S., Brad, E., Homorodean, D.: CALDET: a TRIZ-driven integrated software development methodology. In: Benmoussa, R., De Guio, R., Dubois, S., Koziołek, S. (eds.) TFC 2019. IAICT, vol. 572, pp. 400–416. Springer, Cham (2019). https://doi.org/10.1007/978-3-030-32497-1_32

25. Whitaker, R.: The analytic hierarchy process – what it is and how it is used. Math. Model. **9** (3–5), 161–176 (1987). https://doi.org/10.1016/0270-0255(87)90473-8

26. Kretzchmar, H., Spies, M., Sprunk, C.: Socially compliant mobile robot navigation via inverse reinforcement learning. Int. J. Robot. Res. **35**(11), 1289–1307 (2016)

# Setting Up Context-Sensitive Real-Time Contradiction Matrix of a Given Field Using Unstructured Texts of Patent Contents and Natural Language Processing

Daria Berdyugina[✉] and Denis Cavallucci[✉]

INSA, Strasbourg, France
dberdyugina@etu.unistra.fr,
denis.cavallucci@insa-strasbourg.fr

**Abstract.** It is well known that Altshuller matrix is the most frequently used tool by TRIZ practitioners. While experts often turn away from it in favor of more recent (and reputedly more effective) tools such as Vepoles and ARIZ85C, it is clear that beginners prefer the matrix because of its simplicity. Nevertheless, two sensitive phases in its use call it into question. The association of the user's specific problem with one of the 39 generic parameters that listed in matrix and the interpretation that can be made of the inventive principles proposed to users. We have developed an approach based on Natural Language Processing to process a specific corpus of patents corresponding to a given technical field in real time. This leads to a new approach developed in this article to propose to users a new matrix for each study but which considers the vocabulary of a given domain to describe the oppositions between parameters. Such a matrix could constitute a state of the art in form of contradictions of the field being explored, which we believe will ease its use upstream of inventive studies processes in order to target the resolution of key and up-to-date contradictions of the same field.

**Keywords:** Altshuller matrix · Automatic extraction · NLP

## 1 Introduction

Nowadays, many tools for TRIZ applications have been developed by experts, for example, Vepoles and ARIZ85C [1]. However, the contradiction matrix (CM), created in 1969, is still popular among TRIZ users because of its simplicity despite several attempts to replace it by a newer one.

Nevertheless, the effectiveness of this tool becomes questionable due to today's ever increasing scientific progresses. Many new technologies, new methods and even new fields of science have emerged since the creation of Altshuller's matrix. The terminology is becoming obsolete, making the CM out of date.

Its generic nature is another problem. For beginners that just started to use TRIZ it can be difficult to formulate a relevant contradiction and to link up the terms of their own field of expertise with technical parameters used in the CM, resulting is a misuse of this latter.

© IFIP International Federation for Information Processing 2020
Published by Springer Nature Switzerland AG 2020
D. Cavallucci et al. (Eds.): TFC 2020, IFIP AICT 597, pp. 30–39, 2020.
https://doi.org/10.1007/978-3-030-61295-5_3

As we know, the creator of the CM analyzed manually about 40 000 the most inventive patent texts [2]. Nowadays, the capacity of automatic text-mining techniques became more important. Patents represent an abundant and numerically available source of inventive information. Thus, we aim to exploit the corpus of patent texts issued from the newest field of science in order to manage to create a CM issued by the user's selection of patents. Nowadays, the patent analyzing applications gain the popularity among industry and engineers, thus it is important to find adequate methods and processing tools. The better processing tool is used, the better are the results in any patent-related activity.

Patent texts are often very difficult to understand because of their long and complex sentence structures with peculiar style. This feature is due to the double nature of patent text which is at the same time a legal and technical document aiming to protect the inventor and identify the boundaries of the invention. That is why, due to a number of patents published every day, it is more convenient for industry and scientists to have a more compact TRIZ-based representation form of concerned patents.

The IDM (Inventive Design Method) was created in order to extend the limitations of TRIZ: one of them was the absence of a formalized ontology. Another drawback of the grounding theory resolved by IDM is the difficulty to perform any computation on the abstract concepts [3]. The main core concepts of IDM are problems, partial solutions and parameters. There are mandatory for a complete problem-solving process [4]. However, for CM reconstruction on the user's patent corpus, it is mandatory to focus on the parameters because they give the summarized information about the inventions mentioned in the patents. Moreover, the parameters construct the "borders" of CM.

The requirements for doing an automatic analysis of patents are extremely high. It demands a certain level of expertise in domain-specific technologies and information retrieval techniques. Such analysis is costly and hard to train. Such typical analyzing scenario is hard to perform manually.

Our laboratory's automatic extraction tool [5] is providing good results for parameters extraction. However, this tool does not take into account the context information and the semantic distribution of terms. Topic mapping is one of the most popular techniques in text mining field. This technique allows to classify and to cluster the terms extracted manually into the topics. Each topic contains terms unified by common semantic characteristic. Such representation is useful to observe the current state of art in chosen domain. Moreover, the link between IDM parameters and machine-identified topics extend the capability of finding the contradiction thanks to the distributional hypothesis: *linguistic items with similar distributions have similar meanings* [6]. i.e., the more semantically similar two words are the more that they will tend to occur in similar linguistic contexts. Originated as a linguistic hypothesis [7], it gains the popularity among the cognitive scientists and becomes the base for some of NLP researches. Representation the patent text as a distributional model helps not only efficiently reduce the noise of parameters extraction but also provide the information about the context and synonyms of each parameters.

The goal of our research is to find the most suitable way of automatic extraction of parameters in order to populate the CM's rows and columns.

In this article, we propose to look through an overview of IDM-methods and its tool for automatic knowledge extraction from patent documents and literature review about Topic Modeling techniques (2). Thereafter, we present the tool of automatic extraction of IDM-related information from patents, notably the parameters, which is recently created by our laboratory (3). Then, we describe the methodology concerning the improvement and the enhancing the parameters extraction process using the topic modeling techniques (4). Thereafter, we present the results of our experimental work (5).

## 2   State of Art

### 2.1   Inventive Design Method

For the goal of extract the IDM-related information (notably the parameters), we have to define the main notions of these terms.

TRIZ developed by Genrich Altshuller is the basis for a significant part of the work carried out by our laboratory. The Inventive Design Method (IDM) based on TRIZ extend the limitations of the grounding theory.

According to IDM, the problem-solving process consists of four steps [4]:

1. Information extraction, comprising "problems" and "partial solutions"
2. Contradiction formulation
3. Solving of each key contradiction
4. Selection of the most suitable solution concept

The IDM proposes a practical definition of the contradiction notion for making TRIZ useful for industrial innovation. According to this definition, the contradiction is "[…] characterized by a set of three parameters and where one of the parameters can take two possible opposite values $Va$ and $V\overline{a}$" [8]. Thus, it is necessary to give the definition of two types of parameters.

The first one, the action parameter (AP), "[…] is characterized by the fact that it has a positive effect on another parameter when its value tends to $Va$ and that it has a negative effect on another parameter when its value tends to $V\overline{a}$. (That is, in the opposite direction)" [8].

The two other parameters in a contradiction definition are called an evaluation parameter (EP) which "[…] can evolve under the influence of one or more action parameters" and which make possible to "evaluate the positive aspect of a choice made by the designer" [8].

In order to make the definition clearer, we add the graphical representation of the model of contradiction according to IDM postulates [8]:

$$AP \frac{Va}{Va} \begin{pmatrix} EP_1 & EP_2 \\ -1 & 1 \\ 1 & -1 \end{pmatrix}$$

The understanding the way of contradiction formulation helps in the process of information retrieval and information extraction. The information that we aim to extract from patent text comprises APs and EPs, moreover, if it is possible, their $Va$ and $\overline{Va}$ Values.

## 2.2    Topic Modeling Techniques for Patent Analysis

Patent map is the way to represent the patent text graphically. The large amount of research was focused on this task, for example, [9, 10] and [11]. The most important approaches in patent analysis and patent mapping are based on structured information: dates, assignees, or citations. These data can be analyzed by traditional bibliometric techniques [12].

Nowadays, the most used techniques for patent mapping are data mining, especially text mining [13]. Other researches concentrate on creating automatic summarization of patent texts [14]. The data mining technic is used for the same purposes [15].

Machine-learning field becomes more stable that is the reason why the research start to focus on computational methods. For example, unsupervising learning methods such as Latent Dirichlet Allocation (LDA) [16] is a useful tool for statistical corpus analysis. This method can be described as follows: *"The LDA model assumes that the words of each document arise from a mixture of topics, each of which is a distribution over the vocabulary"* [17].

Unsupervised learning generates results based on input data without any feedback from the environment. This technique is distinguished from supervised or reinforced learning in that it employs a formal structure that allows the algorithm to find patterns.

Most unsupervised methods are built on a probabilistic input model. An unsupervised learning method evaluates a model that represents a probabilistic distribution for the input data, based either on the preliminary input or independently of each other. Topic modeling belongs to unsupervised learning methods and LDA draws out latent patterns from text.

In the LDA, each document can be considered as a set of different topics. This approach is similar to Probabilistic Latent Semantic Analysis (pLSA) [18] with the difference that the LDA assumes that the distribution of topics has as a priori Dirichlet distributions. In practice, the result is a more correct set of topics. According to existing methodology, topic models *"... can extract surprisingly interpretable and useful structure without any explicit 'understanding' of the language by computers"* [17].

For a detailed explanation on the algorithm refer to [19, Ch. 4] and for an evaluation analyzing scientific publications refers to Yau et al. [20].

## 3    Extraction Tool

In this chapter, we shortly present the tool that allows to extract the IDM-related concepts. In this article, we do not focus on the problems or partial solution extraction. We interest only on parameters extraction and our tool is performing the good result in this task.

The patent text represents the unstructured data that is the reason why this tool was constructed using the knowledge-oriented approach (comparing the data-oriented approach which used more frequently on structured data). This tool is based on linguistic and statistical approaches [3].

This approach consists of an automatic extraction of the relevant linguistic patterns for each concept (problem, partial solution and parameters). Firstly, two corpora of patent texts were built (the first corpus was used to complete the list of linguistic markers and the second one for the result evaluation). The classical NLP approaches such as corpus reprocessing, stop word elimination, linguistic marker weighting, part of speech tagging and lemmatization were applied for the training corpus [21].

The linguistic markers are extracted from the patent corpus with help of the TF-IDF methods (term frequency—inverse documents frequency) [22] and the identification of a contiguous sequence of n items methods, also called n-gram identification. The last one is based on the extraction of all the word sequences from 1 to 10 tokens and on the calculation of the most frequents.

This approach conducted to analyze all the n-grams to choose the most relevant linguistic markers and to study it in the context. For example, the problems are preceded by markers such as "it is known that..." or "resulting in...". And the partial solution is preceded by the phrases like "the present invention relates to..." or "... an object of this invention is to..." [13].

After construction of the list of linguistic markers for each IDM concept and its classification, the API was built to operate this extracted data using the Python language. At the input, a user gives a patent text, and then the algorithm perform the extraction based on the lists of linguistic markers.

## 4   Methodology

As mentioned above, our goal consists of real-time reconstruction of contradiction matrix using machine learning techniques. We use unsupervised learning technique because we aim to construct a universal tool, which can be a process any patent corpus regardless its domain. That is the reason why the training can have an influence on the result.

### 4.1   Corpus Reprocessing

Before presenting the methodology, we describe the data on which we apply the topic modeling techniques.

The corpus data that we use belongs to the biotech field, more precisely, to the cryoprotectant theme. In our research, we use only English-language data. However, the part of collected patent contain the sections edited in other languages. Thus, before start the corpus preparation, we manually clean the data from these sections. Table 1 shows the corpus statistics after cleaning.

**Table 1.** Corpus statistics

| Number of documents | 94 patents |
|---|---|
| Number of words | 2 068 732 words |
| Number of tokens | 12 980 481 tokens |
| Language | English |

Preprocessing pipeline consists on applying classical steps on any NLP task. As an input for LDA-building tools, we need to obtain a vector (i.e. Word Embeddings model) [23] representation of our corpus.

First, we need to prepare the list of stop words (the most frequently used words in language such as function words, for example, the articles, prepositions). Thus, we apply the special tool for statistical corpus analysis—Antconc [24]. This software allows extracting automatically the most used words from custom corpus. We can not apply the standard list of stop words for English language because of the number words and collocation rarely used in common corpus are frequently used in patent texts. Our list contains approximately 100 words including specific legal-related constructions, name of sections of documents and, obviously, function words.

Second step consists of tokenization of the data and of removing the punctuation. In order to take into account the polylexical construction and terms (i.e. the collocation containing two and more words), we apply the function that searches for the words having tendency to collocate. The threshold measure allows reducing the number of phrases, where random words placed together, to be considered as polylexical terms. The units of collocation are linked together using "_" character (for example, "nitric oxide inhibitors" becomes "nitric_oxide_inhibitor"). This step is necessary for further processing because we need that the algorithm recognize the polylexical terms as a same token.

For this experiment, we identify only bi- and tri-grams and we take into account the noun phrases (the collocation with the noun as a headword) because of time limitations. The next step in the reprocessing pipeline is the identification of allowed part of speech. As we aim to extract noun phrase, we take nouns, adjectives, prepositions and determinants.

The final step in the pipeline is the transformation the text data into the word embeddings. We use the list to stop words generated at the first step for cleaning the corpus and apply the lemmatization on each token.

## 4.2    Topic Modeling Workflow

Nowadays, there are a lot of open-source software framework for topic modeling such as BigARTM[1], Mallet[2], Stanford Topic Modeling Toolkit[3], topicmodels R package[4] and others. However, in our project we use Gensim Framework [25], a Python open-source library permits to accomplish an important number of NLP tasks such as topic modeling and similarity queries.

The first step after creation of word embeddings dictionary from preprocessed corpus, we need to filter it applying tf-idf measure. It is necessary in order to rank the input according to the frequency of each entry.

---

[1] Availible at https://github.com/bigartm/bigartm.

[2] Availible at http://mallet.cs.umass.edu.

[3] Availible at http://nlp.stanford.edu/software/tmt/tmt-0.4/.

[4] Availible at https://cran.r-project.org/package=topicmodels.

For this step, we assign the random number of topics to extract because at this stage, we can not predict the exact amount of topics which gives the better coherence score for the model. Apart from that, we need to provide the number of chunk size (controls how many documents are processed at a time in the training algorithm; increasing chunk size will speed up training) and passes (controls how often we train the model on the entire corpus). We use default options.

The second step consists of training the model. As a result, we obtain the 10 topics containing 10 terms each. We measure the coherence score (based on one-set segmentation of the top words and an indirect confirmation measure that uses normalized pointwise mutual information [NPMI] and the cosine similarity) in order to estimate the quality of the model.

Mallet version [26], mentioned above, however, is known by a better quality of topics compared with Gensim. It is an implementation for standard Gensim version that allows computing the number of topics, which gives the best result of coherence score.

### 4.3  Parameters Extraction Validation

We extract the topics for the purpose to validate the parameters extracted by the tool mentioned in 3. However, the tool is capable of extracting not only the parameters but also the problems and partial solutions. That is the reason why we adjust the tool for our purposes: we limit the extraction on the parameters.

After extracting the list of parameters, it is necessary to associate each extracted entry with topics. In order to achieve this, we compute the similarity between vector representation of extracted parameters and vector representation each member of topics using cosine similarity metrics.

The result of each computation is stocked in order to allow the algorithm to choose the best match.

## 5  Result and Evaluation

In this chapter, we report the result of each step described in methodology. It is important to specify that we employ only default options for topic modeling training because of lack of time. Moreover, due to the same reason, we do not compare the performance of LDA models with other topics modeling techniques such as, for example, HDP (Hierarchical Dirichlet Process) or pLSA (Probabilistic latent semantic analysis).

The first trained LDA model contains 10 topics with 10 terms. The coherence score for this model is 0.41. The next step is the use of Mallet implementation. We compute the coherence score for the same number of topics as a raw model. We obtain the coherence score equal to 0.42. Obviously, we obtain a small improvement of the result. However, with adjusting the number of topics to extract, we can improve the coherence score and, by consequence, the quality of extraction. In order to estimate the suitable number of topics, we calculate the result of coherence score for each iteration of topics number from 2 to 40. The best model, according to calculation, is the model containing 14 topics. The coherence score for this model is 0.45.

As a result of parameters extraction, we obtain the 40 candidates. The 29 of these candidates are related with LDA topics. The experts from biotech domain validated 23 of candidates linked with LDA topics and 2 candidates not linked with topics.

We calculate the statistical measures for extraction quality estimation and we provide the result in the Table 2. However, for calculating the recall, it is necessary to calculate the number of parameters containing in the corpus. Because of the lack of time, we suppose hypothetically that extraction tool does not miss any parameters and we assign the recall by 1.

**Table 2.** Statistical measures of quality of extraction

|           | Raw extraction | Extraction with LDA validation |
|-----------|----------------|--------------------------------|
| Precision | 0.525          | 0.90                           |
| Recall    | 1              | 1                              |
| F-measure | 0.68           | 0.94                           |

## 6  Conclusion

In this article, we descried the methodology of validation of extracted parameters by topic modeling technique. This technique allows enhancing the semantic information about each extracted candidate. The additional information helps to clean the output and achieve the purest extraction as possible.

However, the goal of our research is the finding the way to automate contradiction retrieval in text data. That is the reason why we aim to obtain the most semantic links among the elements of the corpus as possible. Using this information, we can compute, for example, the predominant topic in each document of collection. Moreover, we also obtain the information about synonym constructions, which is the key of identification of hidden contradictions.

The validation of extracted parameters with extracted topics contributes to the reconstruction of the "borders" of contradiction matrix. Using the methodology described in this article, we arrived to improve the extraction by 26%, which is an important contribution.

As a further work, it is necessary to apply other techniques of topic modeling in order to compare and chose the best training model. Moreover, for improving the quality of training model it is necessary to identify the key type of collocation for better model representation and to process more voluminous polylexical terms and collocation and adjust the algorithm of its identification.

In view of the continuation of the matrix reconstruction project, the important step is to verify if the proposed methodology works for another domain. For the same purpose, it is important to implement described methodology on other sources of inventive information such as scientific articles.

In order to identify the contradictory parameters, we have to exploit the enhanced semantic information to mine the hidden pragmatic structure of texts.

# References

1. Петров, В.: Основы ТРИЗ. Теория решения изобретательских задач. Издание 2-е, исправленное и дополненное. Litres (2019)
2. Altshuller, G.: 40 Principles: TRIZ Keys to Innovation. Technical Innovation Center, Inc. (2002)
3. Souili, A., Cavallucci, D.: Automated extraction of knowledge useful to populate inventive design ontology from patents. In: Cavallucci, D. (ed.) TRIZ – The Theory of Inventive Problem Solving, pp. 43–62. Springer, Cham (2017). https://doi.org/10.1007/978-3-319-56593-4_2
4. Cavallucci, D.: From TRIZ to Inventive Design Method (IDM): towards a formalization of Inventive Practices in R&D Departments (2012)
5. Souili, A.W.M.: Contribution à la méthode de conception inventive par l'extraction automatique de connaissances des textes de brevets d'invention, Université de Strasbourg, École Doctorale Mathématiques, Sciences de l'Information et de l'Ingénieur Laboratoire de Génie de la Conception (LGéCo), INSA de Strasbourg (2015)
6. Harris, Z.S.: Distributional Structure, WORD, vol. 10, no. 2–3, pp. 146–162, August 1954. https://doi.org/10.1080/00437956.1954.11659520
7. Sahlgren, M.: The Distributional Hypothesis, pp. 33–53 (2008)
8. Rousselot, F., Zanni-Merk, C., Cavallucci, D.: Towards a formal definition of contradiction in inventive design. Comput. Ind. **63**, 231–242 (2012). https://doi.org/10.1016/j.compind.2012.01.001
9. Yoon, B., Yoon, B., Park, Y.: On the development and application of a self–organizing feature map–based patent map. R&D Manage. **32**, 291–300 (2002). https://doi.org/10.1111/1467-9310.00261
10. Lee, S., Yoon, B., Park, Y.: An approach to discovering new technology opportunities: keyword-based patent map approach, Technovation, **29**(6), 481–497 (2009). https://doi.org/10.1016/j.technovation.2008.10.006
11. Kim, Y.G., Suh, J. H., Park, S.C.: Visualization of patent analysis for emerging technology. Expert Syst. Appl. **34**(3), 1804–1812 (2008). https://doi.org/10.1016/j.eswa.2007.01.033
12. Archibugi, D., Planta, M., Measuring technological change through patents and innovation surveys, Technovation, vol. 16, no. 9, pp. 451–519 (1996). https://doi.org/10.1016/0166-4972(96)00031-4
13. Tseng, Y.-H., Wang, Y.-M., Lin, Y.-I., Lin, C.-J., Juang, D.-W.: Patent surrogate extraction and evaluation in the context of patent mapping. J. Inf. Sci. **33**, 718–736 (2007). https://doi.org/10.1177/0165551507077406
14. Tseng, Y.-H., Lin, C.-J., Lin, Y.-I.: Text mining techniques for patent analysis. Inf. Process. Manage. **43**(5), 1216–1247 (2007). https://doi.org/10.1016/j.ipm.2006.11.011
15. Yoon, B., Phaal, R.: Structuring technological information for technology roadmapping: data mining approach. Technol. Anal. Strategic Manage. **25**(9), 1119–1137 (2013). https://doi.org/10.1080/09537325.2013.832744
16. Blei, D.M., Ng, A.Y., Jordan, M.I.: Latent dirichlet allocation. J. Mach. Learn. Res. **3**, 993–1022 (2003)
17. Blei, D.M., Lafferty, J.D.: A correlated topic model of Science. Ann. Appl. Stat. **1**(1), 17–35 (2007). https://doi.org/10.1214/07-aoas114
18. Hofmann, T.: Probabilistic latent semantic indexing. In: Proceedings of the 22nd Annual International ACM SIGIR Conference on Research and Development in Information Retrieval, Berkeley, California, USA, August 1999, pp. 50–57. https://doi.org/10.1145/312624.312649

19. Srivastava, A.N., Sahami, M.: Text Mining: Classification, Clustering, and Applications. CRC Press (2009)
20. Yau, C.-K., Porter, A., Newman, N., Suominen, A.: Clustering scientific documents with topic modeling. Scientometrics **100**(3), 767–786 (2014). https://doi.org/10.1007/s11192-014-1321-8
21. Souili, A., Cavallucci, D., Rousselot, F.: A lexico-syntactic pattern matching method to extract IDM- TRIZ knowledge from on-line patent databases. Procedia Eng. **131**, 418–425 (2015). https://doi.org/10.1016/j.proeng.2015.12.437
22. Salton, G., Yang, C.S.: On the specification of term values in automatic indexing, June 1973. https://ecommons.cornell.edu/handle/1813/6016. Accessed 31 May 2020
23. Mikolov, T., Sutskever, I., Chen, K., Corrado, G., Dean, J.: Distributed Representations of Words and Phrases and their Compositionality. arXiv:1310.4546 [cs, stat], October 2013 (2020). http://arxiv.org/abs/1310.4546. Accessed 31 May 2013
24. Anthony, L.: AntConc. Tokyo, Japan: Waseda University (2019)
25. Řehůřek, R., Sojka, P.: Software framework for topic modelling with large corpora. In: Proceedings of the LREC 2010 Workshop on New Challenges for NLP Frameworks, Valletta, Malta, pp. 45–50 (2010)
26. McCallum, A.K.: MALLET: A Machine Learning for Language Toolkit (2002)

# Algorithm for Idea Landscaping
# and Prioritization

Nikhil Phadnis[(✉)] [iD]

Department of Industrial Engineering and Management, Lappeenranta University
of Technology, Lappeenranta, Finland
nikhilphadnis29@gmail.com

**Abstract.** In a competitive world as ours, knowledge management has become
a crucial part of innovation in organizations. Further, with the trend of open
innovation being practiced throughout the different hierarchies of an organization, the inflow of knowledge has been higher than ever. The inbound open
innovation principles by Chesbrough have been replicated across many large
companies in practice where ideas for new products, processes or businesses
come from external sources such as customers, suppliers, different departments,
and competitors. However, prioritizing these ideas or concepts are based on
subjective experience and intuition of decision makers. This research aims to
eliminate subjectivity for prioritization and selection of ideas and concepts. It
proposes a systematic method of idea landscaping, prioritization, and screening
to aid in decision making thereby reducing time, bias in decision-making and
risk in innovation failures.

**Keywords:** TRIZ · Idea prioritization · Innovation management · Knowledge
management · Inventive problem solving · Idea-landscaping

## 1 Introduction

In recent years, the word "Innovation" has transitioned into "Systematic innovation"
throughout organizations where industries are prioritizing "Innovation methods". One
reason for this shift is that professionals believe in a structured approach that can be
reliable, repeatable, and most importantly teachable to upcoming innovation professionals. Systematic innovation is a buzzword and a new norm that companies adopt to
showcase their strengths of their research and development within innovation teams.
Different methods have been applied and adopted in organizations to make the "innovation spaghetti" structured, organized, and methodical in nature. Agile, design
thinking, theory of inventive problem-solving, theory of constraints and many other
such innovation methods have received considerable attention in recent years that
focused on systematic innovation and have been successful in different areas of the
problem-solving domain.

The application of the above-mentioned methods results in a set of ideas, concepts
or solutions that must be evaluated against the set of given constraints and requirements. This process most commonly is known as idea screening and evaluation where
ideas are essentially screened across a set of criteria defined by individuals (Rochford

© IFIP International Federation for Information Processing 2020
Published by Springer Nature Switzerland AG 2020
D. Cavallucci et al. (Eds.): TFC 2020, IFIP AICT 597, pp. 40–53, 2020.
https://doi.org/10.1007/978-3-030-61295-5_4

1991). Therefore, one might say that the process is structured. However, the evaluation scores allocated by the individual or the team for a proposed criterion is based on personal experience, subject matter expertise and intuition. Moreover, such situations are significantly biased when raw ideas at the "fuzzy front end of innovation" must be selected to flow through the funnel of innovation (Herstatt and Verworn 2003).

Furthermore, organizations practicing "open innovation", collects ideas and concepts from customers, suppliers, internal teams, universities as a part of co-creation falling within the inbound open innovation umbrella that results in thousands of raw ideas that must be evaluated and screened (Chesbrough, et al. 2006). Moreover, idea screening process does not give clear roadmap on prioritization of the most promising ideas i.e some of the most promising ideas may be short term or long term. An algorithmic method that can create such an idea landscape would be practically relevant in terms of business potentials and new product development.

In such situations, a systematic method that can objectively screen the best ideas to create an idea landscape is needed. This research creates an objective tool to aid in decision making thereby reducing time, bias in and risk in innovation. The research question that we attempt to address is "how to make the idea screening process as objective as possible?"

## 2  Background

The problem of having numerous ideas for a product and having to choose only a few of them to implement is very common amongst the innovation industry. Extensive research has already been conducted on how to prioritize a list of requirements from customers. Some empirical research has also been conducted to verify which of the multitude of methods is the best in terms of ease of use, accuracy and scalability (Vestola 2010). Some of the most popular ones are analytical hierarchical process, numerical assignment, the MoSCoW technique, the hundred-dollar method and many others. Some of these methods are described below in brief:

### 2.1  Numerical Assignment Technique

It is the simplest form of methods where we assign priority in a numerical form, usually done in groups of three. Such as "low", "medium" and "high". This results in a group of entities into different priority groups (Vestola 2010).

### 2.2  MoSCoW Technique

This method can be a modification of the Numerical assignment technique where four priority groups namely "Must have", "Should have", "could have" and "won't have" are created. Entities are prioritized accordingly. This method on mostly used for prioritizing requirements as well as idea evaluation.

The Numerical assignment techniques also have studies related to its ineffectiveness and low accuracy when number of entities to be compared is low (Danesh and Ahmed 2009).

## 2.3    Hundred-Dollar Test

The idea is that the stakeholders participating at prioritization are given a number of imaginary units (100 dollars, 1000 points, etc.) which are allocated to the entities that need to be prioritized. The number of units assigned to a requirement represents its priority. The results are presented on a ratio scale which provides the information on how much one requirement is more/less important than another (Vestola 2010).

All of the mentioned methods have their pros and cons and they are suited for various applications; however, the methods do not provide an innovation landscape of all ideas that allow decision makers to see the bigger picture. They are somehow constrained in terms of their applicability with respect to providing a relatively clear vison upfront to innovation drivers of the organization. The main concept behind this paper is to allow a decision maker to see a guided roadmap of what do with all the ideas that they collect and which ones to focus on for further feasibility, investigations, and implementations upfront to strategically make informed decisions.

# 3    Methodology

The method proposed was a result of a university project in collaboration with a swiss-company based on a specific problem statement provided to students. The goal of the project was to provide an objective criterion for a portfolio of products that the company manufactures. These criteria would allow them to sort, prioritize and investigate those ideas that are worth the effort during the fuzzy front end of innovation products have not entered their stage gate innovation process.

The proposed method was exploratory in nature and was experimental. During the research, two hypothesis were put forward asking "is it possible to have a structured method that could potentially reduce subjective bias during the idea selection phases?" and "is it possible create a method to provide an innovation landscape in the fuzzy front end to innovation managers?". The proposed method was tested out with the swiss company for validity and reliability. The company provided the author a list of ideas that were collected years ago and asked him to prove the method. The author had no knowledge of the results of the ideas or which ones were practically implemented. Post the "testing phase" results of the method proposed were qualitatively confirmed with the swiss company with good accuracy and reliability wherein all outcomes of the method matched the outcomes in real life.

The method is born out of an existing set of well-known methods and problem-solving approaches such as AHP, TRIZ, risk versus reward plot and applied in a new context to be combined and adapted to the problem to provide different insights.

# 4    Results

The method proposed includes some aspects of Theory of Inventive Problem Solving (TRIZ), an innovation methodology, created by Genrikh Altshuller. His findings categorized various inventive problems into five distinct classes. They were known as "5 levels of inventions". The criteria created within this framework considers the number of attempts required to solve the inventive problem at a specific level and the degree of change imposed on the original system (Altshuller 1999).

This discovery was further improved and developed upon by Zlotin and his colleagues in 2003 by adding definitions to the criteria that were created. This research was an extension of Altshuller's above-mentioned criteria and utilized in to "Ideation software", a proprietary software created by Zlotin's consulting company, Ideation Inc (Zlotin and Zusman 2003). The criteria for identifying levels of inventions were increased multifold and had five levels of definitions allocated to it. The identified criteria was as follows:

- Problem type
- Direction type
- Information utilized
- Solution type
- Changes to the system
- Changes to system functions
- Transforming an idea into a design
- Counteraction against psychological inertia
- Application/market value
- Application of resources
- Generation of evolutionary resources

These criteria had well defined statements that an individual to classify his inventions The practical application of the tool was aimed towards "classifying inventions". The general idea behind this tool has been chosen as a part of the proposed method.

As mentioned earlier criteria had a set of guidelines that was well-defined to categorize inventions into five levels. A similar approach has been created as a part of this exploratory research where, criteria have been defined along with their respective guidelines. Based on these guidelines, the ideas are allocated a predetermined score. The range of the score can be changed in proportion if needed or can follow the Likert scale. The criteria were created based upon a powerful TRIZ based method known as Anticipatory Failure Determination (AFD) (Kaplan, et al. 1999). The method proposed is a modification of the existing method of weighted averages used for traditional idea screening where Analytical hierarchical process is used to rule out inconsistencies for the weightage given for each criterion (Saaty 2002).

## 4.1 Algorithm for Idea Landscaping and Prioritization

The systematic algorithm for idea landscaping and prioritization proposed comprises of the following steps that have been elaborated upon:

1. Creation of a Criteria: Use analytical tools, subject matter expertise, innovation methods like TRIZ based AFD to create a set of criteria for evaluating ideas.
2. Creation of guidelines with levels - Use analytical tools, subject matter expertise, innovation methods to create guidelines for the identified with a range of levels.

3. Grouping criteria: group the criteria created into two major classes in such a way that scores that are "higher the better" and "lower the better" are separated. They will be treated as X axis and Y axis during a scatter plot.
4. Add a weightage coefficient- using Analytical Hierarchical process or pairwise comparison to assign weightage coefficient(K) to the identified criteria. This process eliminates bias in decision making.
5. Compute the scores- calculate scores weighted averages method separately for the two classes created in step 3. Therefore, each idea will have two scores, one for the X axis and another for the Y axis.
6. Perform a scatter plot: plot the final scores of the ideas on the scatter plot to create a 2 × 2 matrix.
7. Recording results: interpret the results of the plot.

### Anticipatory Failure Determination to Identify Criteria for Failures

Subversion analysis later known as AFD is a TRIZ tool aimed to reveal failure mechanisms technical systems using existing resources to prevent them from happening at later stages (Chybowski et al. 2018). This approach is mainly utilized for engineering systems but was adapted and applied for a business scenario. An AFD was created for making an innovation "Fail" to recognize all possible factors for the success of the innovation. The factors were identified based on existing literature that analyzed causes of failures and successes for innovations (Van der Panne 2003). Application of AFD resulted in some major potential causes for failure of ideas. Therefore, these key failures were chosen as criteria from Zlotin's database. As a part of an exploratory research, some criteria were created with similar logic to that of the "levels of inventions".

### Creation of Guidelines with Levels

The criteria are placed in a systematic format wherein each identified criterion consists of guidelines or definitions that are in the form of "Levels". The guidelines proposed below are created by Zlotin from his experience in hundreds of innovation projects performed for clients however, an individual or an organization may create their own criteria to evaluate ideas (Zlotin and Zusman 2003).

Scoring of the idea can follow a different scale from the one proposed below. The scale proposed consists of even numbers ranging from 0 to 10 as there are five levels defined

*Criteria Selected - Market Potential*

The predetermined score for this criterion ranges from 0 to 10 points,10 being the best.

- Level 5(10 points)- Idea has potential to create a new product or service or a very large/mass expansion of existing market for large groups of people with possible volumes up to dozens of billions.
- Level 4(8 Points)- Idea has potential to create a new product or service or a substantial expansion of existing market for large groups of people with possible volumes up to billions.

- Level 3(6 points)- Idea has potential to create a new product or service or a moderate expansion of existing market for small groups of people with possible volumes in dozens of millions.
- Level 2(4 points)- Idea has potential to create a new product or service or a moderate expansion of existing market for small groups of people with possible volumes up to 12 million.
- Level 1(2 points)- Idea has very limited potential with returns less than 1 million$.

*Areas of Application*
The predetermined score for this criterion ranges from 0 to 10 points,10 being the best.

- Level 5(10 points)- Idea can be utilized for different markets that you serve or different businesses and new markets that you do not currently serve.
- Level 4(8 points)-Idea can be used in different markets that you currently serve for different products and categories.
- Level 3(6 points)- Idea can be used and replicated for different product categories of the same market.
- Level 2(4 points)-Idea can be used for different Products of the same product categories of the same market.
- Level 1(2 points)-Idea is focused on the existing market and to make the product slightly more efficient.

*IP Potential of the Idea*
The predetermined score for this criterion ranges from 0 to 10 points,10 being the best.

- Level 5(10 points)-Idea has strong IP and multiple industries and domains very far from yours are interested in licensing the IP, Cross licensing possibilities exist.
- Level 4(8 points)- Idea has very strong IP and you are very well protected, however lots of Buyers are interested in the IP in your domain.
- Level 3(6 points)- idea has strong IP and you will be well protected in your market and some players are interested in licensing the IP in your domain.
- Level 2(4 points)-Idea has may or may not have IP, even if it has IP value is very low, no would be interested.
- Level 1(2 points)-Idea has no IP.

*Solution Type*
The predetermined score for this criterion ranges from 0 to 10 points,10 being the best.

- Level 5(8 points) Solution is from a different field or domain, it is a major invention, a change of action principle or a discover.
- Level 4(8 points)- Solution has been adapted and borrowed from a different domain and different field, this sort of solution gives a considerable competitive advantage, is a Patent or cannot be predicted by the competition, it's also difficult to replicate.
- Level 3(6 points)- Solution that was applied to different product category or businesses has now been adapted and modified. It is either a Hybrid of conventional solution and the adapted solution or its completely the adapted solution.
- Level 2(4 points)- Conventional solution has changed and has been modified, refined, perfected, optimized or matured but it is still is from the same domain (within one's professional field.

- Level 1(2 points)- Conventional solution (probably not completely optimized) from the same domain is applied, existing solution has not substantially changed (within one's professional field).

*Implementation Time Based on Infrastructure Required*
The predetermined score for this criterion ranges from 0 to 10 points,10 being the worst.

- Level 5(2 points)- Time of implementation is easy with little modification of processes to existing infrastructure. Expected time is less than 1 year for a fast market and less than 3 years for slow, markets.
- level 4(4 points)- Time of implementation is less than 3 years for a fast market and less than 6 years for a slow market but the idea can be implemented using existing manufacturing equipment with, moderate modifications. It still requires some testing.
- Level 3 (6 points)- Time for implementation is more than 3 years for a fast-growing industry and more than 6 yrs for a slow growing industry with substantial new equipment with additional significant R and D requirements.
- Level 2 (8 points)- time for implementation is long and expensive to make proof of concepts, various legislative approvals needed heavy investments in technology, new factories, almost like building a whole new business.
- Level 1 (10 points)- Time for implementation cannot be predicted, Long R and D process, many additional inventions or technologies are required for the idea to be practical.

*Reliability of the Concept/Idea Proposed*
The predetermined score for this criterion ranges from 0 to 10 points,10 being the worst.

- Level 5 (2 points)- idea/concept is perfected and proven in practice and can be implemented quickly.
- level 4 (4 points)- Idea/concept is proven by at least calculations, simulations, or research papers.
- Level 3 (6 points)- idea/concept was confirmed by verbal expert opinions.
- Level 2 (8 points)- idea/concept is confirmed by general considerations and comparisons (if it works for them, it should work for us philosophy).
- Level 1 (10 points)- idea/concept is very raw and needs to be tested/researched worked upon to be tested.

*Based on Internal Structures Required*
The predetermined score for this criterion ranges from 0 to 10 points,10 being the worst.

- Level 5 (2 points)- Project can be performed within internal structures, no new project teams need to be created and project can kick-off almost immediately.
- Level 4 (4points)- Project can be performed within internal structures but requires some modification of structures. Eg: teams need to be "reshuffled" new people (experts) need to be added to the existing team, Project can still kick-off almost immediately.

- Level 3(6 points)- Project can be performed within internal structures but requires some modification of structures. Eg: teams need to be significantly "reshuffled" new people(experts) need to be added to the existing team, Project will take some amount time to kick-off.
- Level 2(8points)- Project needs new internal structures to be made such as new teams, departments, people, team leaders as the project. However, the expertise that is required for the project is available with the company, in different areas/departments or businesses of the same company.
- Level 1(10 points)- Project needs new internal structures to be made such as new teams, departments, people, team leaders as the project. However, the expertise that is required for the project is NOT available with the company. There must be recruitment of new third party experts, or professional consultants, or university collaborations and experts, new Joint ventures, buying IP/in licensing IP.

**Grouping of Criteria**
We create two major classes to group the criteria mentioned above. Firstly, those related to "Potential of an idea" and secondly those related to "Effort required for implementation of the idea". This step is very similar to creation of the risk vs reward plot where we identify our groups as "potential" against "effort". Table 1 shows the grouping of identified criteria into two classes.

**Table 1.** Grouping of identified criteria

| Group 1: Potential of the Idea (scoring higher the better logic) | Group 2: Effort of Implementation (scoring lower the better logic) |
|---|---|
| Market Potential | Implementation time based on infrastructure required |
| Areas of Application | Reliability of the concept/idea proposed |
| IP potential of the Idea | Based on internal structures required |
| Solution Type | |

**Adding a Weightage Coefficient Using Analytical Hierarchical Process**
The next step is to assign weightage coefficients to the criteria. Analytical Hierarchy Process (AHP) is a method of "measurement through pairwise comparisons and relies on the judgments of experts to derive priority scales" (Saaty 2002). AHP is a systematic method to support decision-making by ironing out inconsistencies in judgements that attempts to eliminate subjective bias. It allows for qualitative as well as quantitative criteria in evaluation (Russo and Camanho 2015). The method is well established and is used by the research community however, the application of AHP in the industry is questionable. The objective of an AHP is to provide appropriate weightage coefficients

to the criteria identified instead of the traditional ad hoc unstructured and brainstormed weightage coefficients. The method utilizes mathematics, matrices and eigen vectors to calculate "consistency" in judgements (Saaty 2002).

AHP algorithm in brief is basically composed of two steps and must be performed for the two identified subclasses separately. In this case, they will be "potential of an idea" and "effort for implementation".

1. Determine the relative weights of the decision criteria
2. Determine the relative rankings (priorities) of alternatives

Pairwise comparisons are made with the grades ranging from 1–9. A basic, but very reasonable assumption for comparing alternatives: "If attribute A is absolutely more important than attribute B and is rated at 9, then B must be absolutely less important than A and is graded as 1/9." This logic is followed throughout the entire process and the matrix is completed (Saaty 2002). AHP tools are available as online open source software's.

For convenience purposes, we propose using such online tools developed by well-recognized and reliable sources such as Business Performance Management Singapore (BPMSG). The advantage of using an online tool is that all the mathematical calculations are performed by the tool instantaneously.

An individual must perform the AHP by rating criteria from the integer range of 1–9 with respect to another criteria. All such combinations must follow similar logic. The next step is to calculate a Consistency Ratio (CR) to measure how consistent the judgments have been relative to large samples of purely random judgments. If the CR is greater than 0.1(10%) the judgments are untrustworthy because they are too close for comfort to randomness and the exercise is valueless or must be repeated (Saaty 2002). In this step the overall subjective bias can be minimized. Very often when there are multiple screening criteria, managers simply allocate a number "they think" would be appropriate and end up creating an overall bias in the process. This step ensures that managers do not put more than required or less than required weightage coefficients to all criteria to "balance" the AHP.

Once the consistency ratio is calculated and is less than 0.1, a relative ranking is developed based upon priorities. This relative ranking is selected as the weightage coefficient for the weighted average method and is added to Table 2 as weightage coefficients K.

**Computing of Scores**
Post the addition of weightage coefficients(k), we list all the ideas to be evaluated in a separate column. Each idea is evaluated by allocating a score based on the guidelines that were defined for the identified criteria. Two final scores will be calculated at the end of this step i.e one for each subclass created. Table 2 shows a template of ideas to be evaluated and computed as an illustration.

**Table 2.** Template of Evaluation for ideas/concepts

| Ideas/Concept names | Subclass X Criteria 1,2,3... | Subclass Y Criteria 1,2,3... | Weighted score for Subclass X | Weighted score for Subclass Y |
|---|---|---|---|---|
| Weightage coefficients (K) from AHP | Score a | Score b | | |
| Idea 1,2,3... | n,n1,...scores for number of criteria in subclass X | m,m2... scores for number of criteria in subclass Y | =(n*a) +(n1*a)+ ... | =(m*b) +(m1*b)+ ... |

## 4.2    Interpretation of Results

The weighted scores obtained for subclasses X and Y can now be plotted onto a scatter diagram that results in a 2 × 2 matrix. In this case, the use statistical software Minitab 19 to interpret results and draw conclusions.

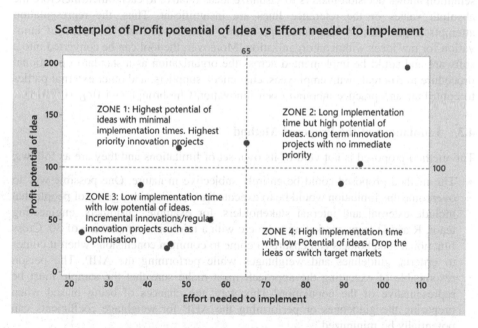

**Fig. 1.** Scatterplot representing innovation landscapes

The goal of this plot is to provide approximate insights into different clusters of ideas and figure out strategies for them. Figure 1 shows a representation for decision makers to prioritize ideas and create innovation roadmaps. Firstly, the scatter plot is relative in nature, therefore we would always end up in a good spread. Four distinct zones are created once we plot approximately reference line through the medians.

- Zone one represents the highest potential of ideas with minimal effort required to implement the ideas. They make the highest priority projects and are an ideal zone as the returns are substantially higher than the effort.
- Zone two can be termed as a long-term project where implementation efforts are large however, the potential of the ideas is also high. These projects are not an immediate priority however, some preliminary research for these innovation projects must begin in a short time.
- Zone three represents ideas that require low amount of effort but offer a low potential of the idea as well. They can be termed as incremental innovations or regular research and development projects within a professional field. The type of projects generally consists of optimizations, minor improvements to products or frequent revision of innovations.
- Zone four represents significant implementation times with low potential of ideas. These are set of ideas can either be dropped or it is necessary to look for new markets or adjacent markets to increase their potential.

The representation of results depends upon the variables on the X and Y axis and must be interpreted in correspondence to the change. Moreover, this graphical representation allows decision-makers to visualize ideas relative to each other, therefore the absolute values or the reference lines are insignificant. Thus, the representation attempts to provides an idea landscape mainly towards the fuzzy front end of innovation for raw ideas within an organization. Moreover, the tool can be converted into a software and could be implemented across the organization as a standard operational procedure to co-create with employees, customers, suppliers, and other external parties to contribute and practice inbound open innovation(Chesbrough and Bogers, 2014).

### 4.3   Limitations of the Proposed Method

The method proposed is not void of its own set of limitations and they are as follows:

- The method proposed could be entirely subjective in nature. One possible way to overcome this limitation would be to execute the process with a group of people that include external and internal stakeholders. for example: customers, engineering team, R and D team, marketing team etc with a minimum sample size of 30. Cross functional stakeholders can ensure to come to common conclusions when it comes to criteria, guidelines and weightages while performing the AHP. The person responsible of executing the approach must make sure that the sample must be representative of the population. This way, the chances of being biased when preparing the guidelines or performing the AHP for weightage coefficients can potentially be minimized.
- The linearity of the proposed method was identified as a limitation of the research. In the innovation context, its possible that an idea that appears within the "incremental innovation zone" (zone 3) may create more value for the customer than the idea in other zones. This is a function of the customer need that he is willing to pay for. Improving something in a product and happiness of a customer is nonlinear. Companies improve a small feature and the customer is willing to pay much more than the company expected, whereas sometimes companies improve a parameter

twice or thrice, however the customer is not satisfied with it and the product fails. Therefore, its assumed that all ideas are generated for the "true customer needs".

- Every idea could have a high potential in a certain market but could have a low potential in another. Such a situation creates a contradiction in the idea landscaping representation. Therefore, it is recommended to fixate a target market throughout the method.
- Some mathematical limitations also exist within AHP. Firstly, when we add new criteria to be compared in the AHP the priorities are altered for the existing ones as a result the reliability of the result may be lowered.
- It is assumed that the elements in the sublevels are dependent on those in the upper level in AHP, and if the hierarchy structure does not satisfy this assumption, then errors will be generated in the result.
- A CR value is suggested to maintain the consistency of responses, but the result is reliable only when the value is 0.1 or less. However, if the number of entities to compare is increasing, it is challenging to keep the CR below 0.1. (Song and Kang 2016)

Despite the limitations, the method is easy to implement, adaptable, usable and much more structured as compared to the traditional method of using intuition for input of values. We cannot directly say that its objective in nature, but we could say that it attempts to reduce subjectivity as its better structured rather than being completely ad-hoc. Moreover, the research creates additional value for any decision makers in the industry or academia.

## 5 Discussions

Lyubomirskiy's TRIZ based benchmarking using integral S-curve analysis and his nonlinear equation for value, is a superior method to the one proposed as it takes into account multiple factors such as market saturation coefficient, satisfaction and value in the same equation. Moreover, his research also takes into account every main parameter of value on the S-curve that provides insights into developmental limits of the main parameter of value that allows for better prioritization of ideas and concepts. (Lyubomirskiy 2017). However, Lyubomirskiy's method is quite complex and difficult to implement without expertise or facilitation. The "TRIZ-assisted stage gate process" as an alternative to idea landscaping would significantly improve the success rates of innovation, as "voice of the product" is considered from the beginning of the inno-vation journey (Abramov 2015, 2018). This results in a smaller number of ideas but better ideas that can potentially eliminate the process of idea evaluation itself. How-ever, companies often refrain to make such radical changes to their innovation pro-cesses because implementing the "TRIZ assisted stage gate approach" requires extensive knowledge and application of the methodology of TRIZ. Further, the amount of time required to train employees would be expensive. Therefore, this proposed idea prioritization tool would be faster to implement and does not require extensive training for the employees, serving as a doorway to accept TRIZ completely in an organiza-tion's innovation processes. Every tool has its disadvantages; however, they can be overcome by combination of different methods. The proposed approach can be coupled with Abramov's quantum economic analysis (QEA) screening tool, that presents a combination of only thirteen combinations of product, size of the company and stage in the S-curve that are successful (Abramov, Markosov and Medvedev 2018). The researcher recommends using the guidelines and criteria provided in the paper to ensure appropriate outcomes as testing was carried out using the mentioned literature.

# 6 Conclusions

The discussion on subjectivity and objectivity could be a long debate in the world of innovation. However, the truth is we deal with a contradiction between subjectivity and objectivity. On one hand subjectivity will be required in order to create the criteria and its guidelines suited to one's business and on the other, allocating weightage coefficients must be more objective rather than an ad hoc unstructured method that is traditionally followed. This method targets a specific segment in the innovation domain wherein a large number of ideas need to be screened and taken forward at the early stages of development. The proposed method attempts to provide an innovation landscape to aid in decision making for innovation managers to prioritize a few ideas relative to others amidst the chaos of idea screening. To answer the question, "is this the best method available?", The answer is no. There are better methods and approaches that exist. However, most methods require extensive knowledge, experience and expertise to execute, as a result it makes it harder to implement in large organizations. We could say that there is a systematic and a structured approach towards idea screening in the fuzzy front end of innovation and it is more objective than the traditional ad hoc methods. This is because creation of guidelines under every criterion allows people to allocate the similar scores during the idea evaluation process and AHP allows decision-makers to minimize overall subjective bias when providing weightage coefficients to their criteria. Future scope of work includes extensive quantitative data being gathered to assess the reliability, accuracy and repeatability of the criteria as well as the method proposed. The proposed method is currently being tested for different industries such as services, products and B2B process industries to expand its applicability and to empirically prove it.

# References

Abramov, O., Markosov, S., Medvedev, A.: Experimental validation of quantum-economic analysis (QEA) as a screening tool for new product development. In: Koziołek, S., Chechurin, L., Collan, M. (eds.) Advances and Impacts of the Theory of Inventive Problem Solving, pp. 17–25. Springer, Cham (2018). https://doi.org/10.1007/978-3-319-96532-1_2

Abramov, O.Y.: Voice Of the Product To Supplement "Voice Of the Customer", TRIZfest (2015)

Altshuller, G.S.: The innovation algorithm: TRIZ, systematic innovation and technical creativity, Technical Innovation Center, Inc., p. 312 (1999). http://www.amazon.com/dp/0964074044

Chesbrough, H., Vanhaverbeke, W., West, J.: Open Innovation: Researching a New Paradigm - Chapter 1: Open Innovation: A New Paradigm for Understanding Industrial Innovation, pp. 1–25 (2006)

Chybowski, L., Gawdzińska, K., Souchkov, V.: applying the anticipatory failure determination at a very early stage of a system's development: overview and case study. Multidisciplinary Aspects Prod. Eng. 1(1), 205–215 (2018). https://doi.org/10.2478/mape-2018-0027

Herstatt, C., Verworn, B.: The, "fuzzy front end" of innovation bringing technology and innovation into the boardroom. Strategy, Innov. Competences Bus. Value 4, 347–372 (2003). https://doi.org/10.1057/9780230512771

Kaplan, S., et al.: New Tools for Failure & Risk Analysis, Ideation International, Inc. Dearborn (1999). http://scholar.google.com/scholar?hl=en&btnG=Search&q=intitle:New+Tools+for +Failure+and+Risk+Analysis#5

Van der Panne, G.: Dept. Economics of Innovation, Delft University of Technology The Netherlands, Int. J. Innov. Manage., 7(3), 1–29 (2003). https://doi.org/10.1142/s136391960300 0830

Rochford, L.: Generating and screening new products ideas. Ind. Market. Manage. 20(4), 287–296 (1991). https://doi.org/10.1016/0019-8501(91)90003-X

Russo, R.D.F.S.M., Camanho, R.: Criteria in AHP: a systematic review of literature, Procedia Computer Science. Elsevier Masson SAS, 55(Itqm), pp. 1123–1132 (2015). https://doi.org/ 10.1016/j.procs.2015.07.081

Saaty, T.L.: Decision making with the analytic hierarchy process. Scientia Iranica 9(3), 215–229 (2002). https://doi.org/10.1504/ijssci.2008.017590

Zlotin, B., Zlotin, A.: Levels of Invention and Intellectual Property Strategies, Innovation, pp. 1–17. GIPO, Geneva (2003)

Chesbrough, H., Bogers, M.: Explicating Open Innovation, in New Frontiers in Open Innovation (2014). https://doi.org/10.1093/acprof:oso/9780199682461.003.0001

Kavitha, K., Vijayan, R, Sathishkumar, T.: Fibre-metal laminates: a review of reinforcement and formability characteristics. Materials Today: Proc. Elsevier Ltd. 22, 601–605 (2019). https:// doi.org/10.1016/j.matpr.2019.08.232

Song, B., Kang, S.A.: Method of assigning weights using a ranking and nonhierarchy comparison. In: Pardalos, P. (ed. ) Advances in Decision Sciences. Hindawi Publishing Corporation, p. 8963214 (2016). https://doi.org/10.1155/2016/8963214

Alex Lyubirmirskiy - Intergral S-Curve Analysis. The 13th international conference TRIZ fest - 2017, p 222 (2017)

Vestola, M.: (2010) A Comparison of Nine Basic Techniques for Requirements Prioritization

Danesh, A.S., Ahmad, R.: Study of prioritization techniques using students as subjects. In: ICIME 2009: Proceedings of the 2009 International Conference on Information Management and Engineering. Washington, DC, USA: IEEE Computer Society, pp. 390–394 (2009)

# Conceptual Semantic Analysis of Patents and Scientific Publications Based on TRIZ Tools

Vasilii Kaliteevskii[1]([⊠]), Arthur Deder[3], Nemanja Peric[2], and Leonid Chechurin[1]

[1] Lappeenranta-Lahti University of Technology, 53850 Lappeenranta, Finland
vkalit@gmail.com
[2] Univ. Lille, CNRS, Centrale Lille, ISEN, Univ. Valenciennes,
UMR 8520 - IEMN, 59000 Lille, France
[3] Baltic State Technical University "Voenmeh" D.F. Ustinov,
190005 Saint Petersburg, Russia
arthurdeder@gmail.com

**Abstract.** Being committed to the idea that problems from completely different fields could have conceptually similar solutions, Altshuller has analyzed more than 40,000 patents to identify and interplay those common inventive principles. However, reliable extraction and identification of different solutions among millions of patents and scientific publications is still a challenge. Inspired by the core notion behind the TRIZ, we have decided to build upon it by exploiting modern-day advances in both processing power and software engineering. In particular, the idea behind our methodology is to extract semantic features from large amount of source documents and subsequently subject them to analysis which is based on building the semantic boxes of their underlying concepts. Being created and identified, the semantic box allows extracting out-of-the-box ideas from different fields. To this day, our analysis has proved successful in processing 8 million patents and scientific publications with the use of machine learning and natural language-based processing techniques.

**Keywords:** TRIZ · Data analysis · Patent analysis · Conceptual design · Semantic design

## 1 Introduction

To effectively solve engineering and scientific challenges on demand, some conceptual design tools as TRIZ [1] have been introduced. The Theory of Inventive Problem Solving (TRIZ) was invented by Genrich Altshuller in 1956, and was based on a manual analysis of the author with a group of engineers of more than 40,000 patents in order to extract some general principles that are behind similar problems solutions in different fields [2]. Altshuller believed that patents from different fields could have the same idea or solution behind and thus will allow systematic problem solving approaches generalization and development. Hence, all the identified generally applicable heuristics approaches such as the Ideal Final Result, the Altshuller Matrix, Trends of

D. Cavallucci et al. (Eds.): TFC 2020, IFIP AICT 597, pp. 54–63, 2020.
https://doi.org/10.1007/978-3-030-61295-5_5

Engineering System Evolution found by Altshuller formed the basis of the TRIZ theory, that have been further developed by inventor's followers and strengthened with Functional Analysis and other more formal modelling tools [3].

Although TRIZ has proven itself as a powerful tool for solving inventive engineering problems, the main limitation was the requirement of a mastering of TRIZ skill in order to successfully apply it in practice. Thus, in order to make the tool more accessible and applicable for engineers, the next generation of TRIZ tools has been introduced as attempts to digitalization of main TRIZ concepts and supplementary knowledgebases in form of the software products (TechOptimizer, GoldFire [4, 5] and others), integration of TRIZ tools to CAD/CAM software and automatic patent analysis with relation extractions based on TRIZ philosophy [6–8].

Thus, the main trend for TRIZ development in XXI century was the digitalisation of TRIZ tools and systematization of information and data that might be of help for engineers during the conceptual design stage and product related decision making. Being quite useful for TRIZ engineers, those digital TRIZ-based tools still stayed inaccessible for a bigger audience and required certain TRIZ skills from users.

The present article brings together the core TRIZ principle, TRIZ tools digitalisation trend and modern approaches to Big Data analysis, Machine Learning and Natural Language Processing. The main idea behind is automatic semantic extraction of patents and scientific publications general concepts with an aim to build a navigable environment of those concepts as an alternative ideation tool for engineers, scientists and decision-makers. In specific, 3,514,730 of patents and 4,875,744 of scientific publications have been downloaded/extracted from USPTO and UK CORE collection to the database; semantic (Doc2Vec, LDA) and clustering (K-means) algorithms have been used in order to build a navigable data environment and the resulting semantic concepts (or semantic boxes) have been put to the database with additional user interface.

The structure of the paper is as follows: first, it comes the Dataset (patents and scientific publications sources) description, then the notion of a semantic concept described and the algorithm of extraction is presented. Second, the search engine algorithm over a dataset is suggested, and, finally, there is presented a case study with "nanowires", followed by Discussion and Conclusion parts of the paper.

## 2 Semantic Exploration

### 2.1 Dataset

Semantic data analysis part includes several steps depicted on Fig. 1. First, it's necessary to extract data, i.e. to get text documents from the scientific publications and patents sources, then to complete data preprocessing in order to remove unwanted or semantically valueless parts of text. In this way the data is prepared for further analysis by performing concept extraction powered by a search engine over the preprocessed data.

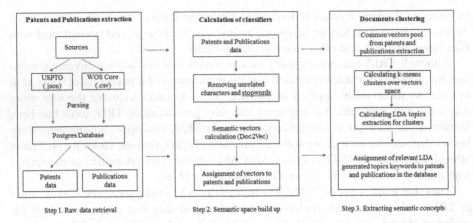

Step 1. Raw data retrieval         Step 2. Semantic space build up         Step 3. Extracting semantic concepts

**Fig. 1.** The semantic concepts extraction built within several steps: 1. Raw patents and publications data extraction 2. Semantic space (Doc2vec) of documents vectors buildup, and 3. Clustering of semantic space with k-means and LDA concepts calculation.

There are different well-known sources for scientific publication and patent data materials, such as Google Scholar, Web of Science, Scopus, ScienceDirect for publications and Google Patents, Patenscope, Espacenet, Lens and others for patents [9–15]. But automatic text analysis usually requires text materials to have a suitable format, since pdf-documents may require efforts to parse them in order to analyse the structure of document and extract the content. The Web of Science Core Collection and Web of Science Derwent Innovation Index are suitable sources for patents and publications analysis but it requires special access to the data since WoS is a commercial product. It's also a benefit that the WOS sources provide the possibility to extract the data in similar csv format, suitable for automatic extraction and analysis [16]. One of the biggest open-access sources for patent data kept in machine-suitable format is United States Patent and Trademark Office (USPTO) [17] bulk data source, as it allows to retrieve all the Unites States patents in xml format. The large open-access source of data for publications in machine-suitable format is the CORE UK Articles Collection [18]. Though both sources require additional efforts and programming skills to retrieve the data, USPTO and CORE UK data sources have been chosen for a final solution and thus 3,514,730 patents and 4,875,744 scientific publications have been extracted and used in the analysis. Another feature of USPTO database is its diversity — as a large portion of patent applications are published in the US, besides other countries, so all together they should provide a more complete picture and a solid collection for deciphering the inventive backgrounds behind them. Patent documents have been limited to 2005 and only newer ones took part in the analysis. The distribution of number of patent applications and scientific publications is depicted over a set timescale in the Fig. 2 below.

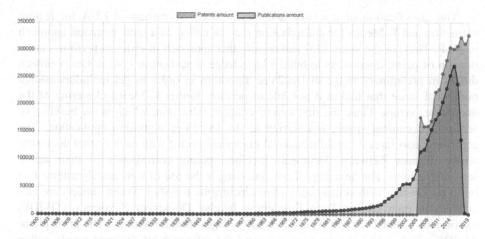

**Fig. 2.** The distribution of patents and scientific publications documents that have been retrieved from USPTO and CORE UK data sources over years. The leap of patent documents near 2005 related to the fact that patents only after 2005 have been extracted. The decrease in publication documents regarding patents in last years is due to the fact that CORE UK is an aggregating database of open-access journals, and therefore there may be delays in filling it with relevant publications

## 2.2 Preliminary Data Preprocessing

The main idea of the developing product is to build a navigable space of concepts with a relevant patents and scientific publications. To be able to effectively navigate within hundreds of thousands of textual documents, the extensive preprocessing steps should be performed.

Thus, the concept extraction starts with row textual documents preprocessing, including stopwords removal (removing the redundant symbols such as commas, quotation marks, and digits and removing the common words such as "the", "are", "being" and others that are hard to extract semantic meaning), stemming and lemmatization (which reduces inflected forms of a word to their lexical root, e.g., "wires", "wiring" to "wire" or "better" to "good") as more or less standard Natural Language Processing steps with a help of NLTK toolkit [19]. Another step is a filtering out only documents published in English, since it is reasonable to build a semantic space of a single language, but those spaces in different languages could be built separately.

## 2.3 Concept Extraction

Concept extraction is a continuation (or a part) of preprocessing as well, since it is a discrete process that is made only once and does not happen in real time when a user interacts with concepts. This part includes bag of words models building, textual features extraction, building a semantic space of documents (Doc2Vec algorithm [20]), words contextual frequency and relevancy calculation (TF-IDF metrics [21]), further clusterization (K-means [22]), and finally concepts' relevant keywords extraction part (LDA algorithm [23, 24]).

The classification of a textual documents based on pairing of LDA for feature extraction and K-Means for clusterization may be called as a quite common approach in NLP. Thus, in the study [25] authors use this approach in order to perform classification of patent documents to build a knowledge organization system. Our approach differs in preliminary usage of Doc2Vec algorithm in order to get multidimensional numerical space that makes it possible to perform further K-Means clustering of the document vectors. Thus, the first step of concept extraction, which is the building of semantic document space, is referring to the Doc2Vec algorithm application. The algorithm associates a multidimensional numerical vector with each textual document where distance between documents (vectors) points corresponds to their actual semantic affinity. The next step of preprocessing is the use of k-means algorithms that build up clusters with semantically close documents together. When clusters are calculated, in each cluster Term Frequency- Inverse Document Frequency (TF-IDF) metric and Latent Dirichlet Allocation (LDA) algorithm are applied. The principle of TF-IDF which calculates the frequency and the relevancy of different words within different documents is depicted on the Formulae:

$$idf(t, D) = log \frac{N}{|\{d \in D : t \in d\}|}, \tag{1}$$

where N is the total number of documents in the corpus and D is a number of documents where the term t appears. Thus, the term frequency which is proportional to frequency of the word within a document and inverse document frequency which is inversely proportional to frequency of the word in other documents shows the relevant frequency of the word. Based on that model LDA algorithm may be applied which builds the map of cloud of words that forms topics, i.e. the sets of words which are, in a sense, the centers of mass of documents distributed between different groups, thus mapping documents between topics, where each topic also consisting of words and their frequency. The scheme of this algorithm is shown in Fig. 3.

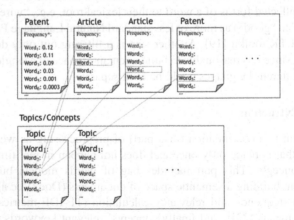

**Fig. 3.** The LDA algorithm scheme for topic (expressed as a set of relevant keywords) extraction from the corpus of text documents.

The number of clusters and topics within them are the input parameters to the whole algorithm and may be a subject for a separate research and further optimization. In our study we have separated the 8,390,474 documents between 500 clusters and extracted 1000 semantic concepts in each cluster. Both numbers 500 and 1000 have been got empirically and the optimal numbers (which may be dynamic) are for further research. Thus, the sorted distribution of documents per concept amounts is depicted on Fig. 4. It can be seen from the distribution that without counting a number of concepts at the beginning and at the end, mainly, documents are distributed between concepts without strong outliers.

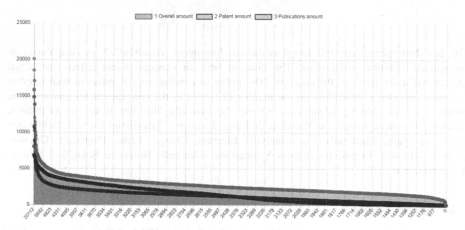

**Fig. 4.** The distribution between concepts and the number of documents in each concept. (Each point on the graph contains 200 concepts)

As a result of algorithm work, which is implemented in Python with the help of *nltk*, *sci-learn* libraries the result is a set of topics where each topic is represented as a set of keywords with the coefficient of relevancy of the keyword to the topic. Keywords of topics include all the unique words of the original documents' pool.

Thus, the result of the algorithm in the form of presented found concepts is depicted in the Fig. 5. Each circle represents a topic, i.e. the set of relevant keywords. These circles are generated as a result of "nanowire" searching query. It may be seen that meaningful concepts have been generated and maybe easily interpreted. Thus, the top 5 generated topics have been identified as "Optics", "Transistor", "Photonics", "Growth" and "Solar cells". Each topic represents a field, either a device or an application/method that are highly relevant to the modern technology related to nanowires field.

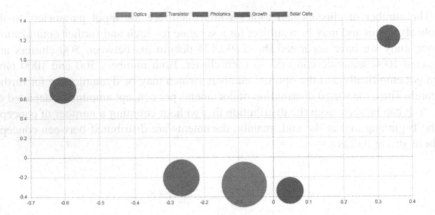

**Fig. 5.** Identified concepts resulting from the searching query "nanowire". X-axis and Y-axis are normalized closeness coefficients. The distance between concept points reflects the actual semantic distance between the concepts. The radius of concept' circles refers to their relevant semantic importance depending on the number of related to the concept patents and scientific publications. The top-5 relevant keywords for the manually identified topics are as follows. **Optics**: Absorption, Plasmonic, Wavelength, Laser, Nanowire; **Transistor**: Current, Field, Gate, Drain, Insulator; **Photonics**: Photocatalytic, Electron, Charge, Light, Photonics; **Growth**: Growth, Nanowire, Deposition, Process, Synthesized; **Solar cells**: Nanowire, Solar, Cell, Silicon, Semiconductor.

## 2.4   Search Engine

The idea of a developed solution is an adaptation of TRIZ philosophy to modern reality, that is, to automatically extract semantic concepts from patents extended with scientific papers and build an up-to-date navigable space from them. Thus, to make the extracted concepts navigable the server on Django [26] has been set up, and Post-greSQL [27] database has been filled with extracted concepts. Ideally, the searching algorithm should work in real time, which is possible due to the extensive data pre-processing. The search algorithm works as follows. Each individual word of the search query sentence is separately compared with keywords representing concepts, so that, if the keyword of some concept fell into the search string, then such a topic is displayed in the search results.

Since each topic is represented by a certain number of documents, each of which has a publication or grant date, and each search query corresponds to a certain number of concepts, we can build trends in scientific publications and patents corresponding to this search query. Such an example for searching query "nanowire" is shown in Fig. 6.

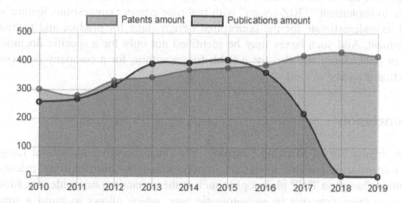

**Fig. 6.** Trending of patents and scientific publications over years by "nanowire" searching query. The parallel with TRIZs S-Curve concept may be built.

Based on the extracted concepts the evolution of them can be build, that show the trending of the concept, expressed as the amount of patents/publications per year. Notably, each keyword has a relevancy coefficient for the document, and reciprocally, each document has a relevancy coefficient for the topic. This means that each document relates to different topics, what is reasonable, since the patent may refer to the "Optics" and "Photonics" topics at the same time. So, when we want to build the trending graph for topic per year, we count the relevancy coefficient of each document of that topic for that year.

## 3 Discussion

Since in the presented implementation the algorithm still depends on expert assessment and interpretation, there is still a gap remaining for future work. But a few important thoughts need to be formulated. First of all, the idea that currently the model allows to automatically identify concepts over a certain selection of documents. Moreover, the concepts are meaningful and interpretable. Moving toward the smart data, from the sample of documents, the approach has important consequences and future possibilities. First of all, with such an approach publications and patents from many different fields may be analysed, what will allow to see the specific semantic correlations not only within a field, but within fields distant from each other. And TRIZ ideology may be applied for such a general model, where it's believed that patents even from different fields may and do have some common principles in their solutions. With such an approach the semantic distance between documents and even fields may be measured, providing the future user with the insights from many different perspectives.

Another idea is that each concept represents some semantic "box". It means that, if a box has been formulated than out-of-the-box may be clearer and may be find with the help of a machine. To find out-of-the-box idea is a main goal of such tools as TRIZ and other ideation tools. So if consider each concept as the semantically expressed idea of the box, then out-of-the-box ideas can be suggested by a machine. This will make it possible to implement "TRIZ-on-go" with real-time concept suggestions feature which is hard to underestimate for the conceptual design stage for product and technology development. And such boxes may be identified not only for a specific document as patent or publication, but also for a field, for an author, for a company or a country intellectual property as well.

## 4  Conclusion

Modern approaches of Machine Learning, Big Data analysis and Natural Language Processing make it possible to extract important insights from existing patents and publications based on TRIZ philosophy, such as the semantic concept identification and trending of these concepts in an automatic way, which allows to build a space of concepts and related scientific publications and patents within a different fields.

In the framework of this article, a pool of documents was collected consisting of 3 514 730 patents and 4 875 744 scientific publications from USPTO and CORE UK has been built. Natural Language Processing techniques and Machine Learning methods were applied to these documents in order to extract information about this pool and prepare it for further semantic analysis. A comparison of similar concepts in publications and patents was provided on the example of nanowires. The concepts constructed by automatic methods are meaningful and easily interpreted, which makes them ready for future analysis, including automatic classification of related keywords based on the Word2Vec neural network algorithm, concept suggestion, automatic concept name identification, and TRIZ tools integration.

**Acknowledgement.** This project has received funding from the European Union's Horizon 2020 research and innovation programme under the Marie Skłodowska Curie grant agreement № 722176.

## References

1. Salamatov, Y., Souchkov, V.: TRIZ: the right solution at the right time: a guide to innovative problem solving, p. 256. Hattem: Insytec (1999)
2. Altshuller, G., Altov, H.: And suddenly the inventor appeared: TRIZ, the theory of inventive problem solving. Technical Innovation Center, Inc. (1996)
3. Savransky, S.D.: Engineering of Creativity: Introduction to TRIZ Methodology of Inventive Problem Solving. CRC Press (2000)
4. http://invention-machine.com/custsupport/to_install.cfm. Accessed May 2020
5. https://ihsmarkit.com/products/enterprise-knowledge.html. Accessed May 2020
6. Cascini, G.: State-of-the-art and trends of computer-aided innovation tools. In: Building the Information Society, pp. 461–470. Springer, Boston (2004). https://doi.org/10.1007/978-1-4020-8157-6_40
7. Efimov-Soini, N.K., Chechurin, L.S.: Method of ranking in the function model. Procedia CIRP **39**, 22–26 (2016)

8. Renev, I., Chechurin, L., Perlova, E.: Early design stage automation in architecture-engineering-construction (AEC) projects. In: Proceedings of the 35th eCAADe Conference, pp. 373–382 (2017)
9. EPO World Patent Statistical Database. https://www.epo.org/searching-for-patents/business/patstat.html#tab-1
10. European Patent Office Database. https://worldwide.espacenet.com/?locale=en_EP. Accessed May 2020
11. WIPO Patentscope. https://patentscope.wipo.int/search/en/search.jsf
12. Lens Patent analysis tool. https://www.lens.org/lens/. Accessed May 2020
13. TEQMINE Patent analysis tool. https://teqmine.com. Accessed May 2020
14. CIPHER Patent analysis tool. http://cipher.ai/. Accessed May 2020
15. Web Of Science publisher-independent global citation database https://www.webofknowledge.com. Accessed May 2020
16. Ranaei, S., Knutas, A., Salminen, J., Hajikhani, A.: Cloud-based patent and paper analysis tool for comparative analysis of research. In: CompSysTech, pp. 315–322 (2016)
17. https://www.uspto.gov/. Accessed May 2020
18. https://core.ac.uk/.. Accessed May 2020
19. Loper, E., Bird, S.: NLTK: the natural language toolkit. arXiv preprint cs/0205028 (2002)
20. Mikolov, T., Sutskever, I., Chen, K., Corrado, G. S., Dean, J.: Distributed representations of words and phrases and their compositionality. In: Advances in Neural Information Processing Systems, pp. 3111–3119 (2013)
21. Huang, C.H., Yin, J., Hou, F.: A text similarity measurement combining word semantic information with TF-IDF method. Jisuanji Xuebao (Chinese J. Comput.) **34**(5), 856–864 (2011)
22. Likas, A., Vlassis, N., Verbeek, J.J.: The global k-means clustering algorithm. Pattern Recogn. **36**(2), 451–461 (2003)
23. Blei, D.M., Ng, A.Y., Jordan, M.I.: Latent dirichlet allocation. J. Mach. Learn. Res., **3**, 993–1022 (2003)
24. Řehůřek, R., Sojka, P.: Gensim - statistical semantics in python. statistical semantics; gensim; Python; LDA; SVD (2011)
25. Hu, Z., Fang, S., Liang, T.: Empirical study of constructing a knowledge organization system of patent documents using topic modeling. Scientometrics **100**(3), 787–799 (2014). https://doi.org/10.1007/s11192-014-1328-1
26. https://www.djangoproject.com/. Accessed May 2020
27. https://www.postgresql.org/. Accessed May 2020

# Build Links Between Problems
# and Solutions in the Patent

Xin Ni[1(✉)], Ahmed Samet[2], and Denis Cavallucci[1]

[1] ICUBE/CSIP, INSA de Strasbourg, 24 Boulevard de la Victoire,
67084 Strasbourg, France
{xin.ni,denis.cavallucci}@insa-strasbourg.fr
[2] ICUBE/SDC, INSA de Strasbourg,
300 Bd Sebastien Brant, 67412 Strasbourg, Illkirch, France
ahmed.samet@insa-strasbourg.fr

**Abstract.** Inventive Design Method mostly relies on the presence of
exploitable knowledge. It has been elaborated to formalize some aspects
of TRIZ being expert-dependent. Patents are appropriate candidates
since they contain problems and their corresponding partial solutions.
When associated with patents of different fields, problems and partial
solutions constitute a potential inventive solution scheme for a target problem. Nevertheless, our study found that links between these
two major components are worth studying further. We postulate that
problem-solution effectively matching contains a hidden value to automate the solution retrieval and uncover inventive details in patents in
order to facilitate R&D activities. In this paper, we assimilate this challenge to the field of the Question Answering system instead of the traditional syntactic analysis approaches and proposed a model called IDM-
Matching. Technically, a state-of-the-art neural network model named
XLNet in the Natural Language Processing field is combined into our
IDM-Matching to capture the corresponding partial solution for the given
query that we masked using the related problem. Then we construct links
between these problems and solutions. The final experimental results on
the real-world U.S. patent dataset illustrates our model's ability to effectively match IDM-related knowledge with each other. A detailed case
study is demonstrated to prove the usage and latent perspective of our
proposal in the TRIZ field.

**Keywords:** TRIZ · Patent analysis · Question answering system ·
Neural networks · XLNet

## 1 Introduction

The foundations of TRIZ [1] taught us that associating a problem with a piece of
information from a domain distant from the domain where the problem occurs
was an appropriate inventive scheme. In this scenario, the two fundamental elements "problem" and "solution" appear to be indispensable for the implementation of an approach that would aim at automating their association on the

© IFIP International Federation for Information Processing 2020
Published by Springer Nature Switzerland AG 2020
D. Cavallucci et al. (Eds.): TFC 2020, IFIP AICT 597, pp. 64–76, 2020.
https://doi.org/10.1007/978-3-030-61295-5_6

assumption that they must respectively come from different domains. These three elements are all three present in the corpus of patents. The problems are explained under the heading "description" and the solutions under the heading "claim" [6]. Each patent is also classified in a category called IPC. With this database of more than 130 million texts, we are therefore in the presence of the elements essential to the automation of a TRIZ-based process. In our previous research, we have developed a Patextractor API [18], capable of isolating from unstructured texts in the patent corpus, Problems, and Partial Solutions when they respect the formalism of IDM-TRIZ and its problem graph. Although offering precision scores that needed to be improved, these sentences were isolated from the perspective of constructing a problem graph, a state of the art of an initial situation of an inventive problem. Our objective in this new research is to provide a base for the hypothesis that two semantically close problems from two distant domains, logically associated with partial solutions, may present inventive opportunities when the problem of one domain is associated with the solution of the other [10].

In order to ensure the quality of problem-solution associations from different domains, we proposed our IDM-Matching model in this paper. It combines a state-of-the-art natural language processing model called XLNet to capture the partial solutions. The problem-solution links are then proposed to the user through an online software interface. Specially, we treat this task as a question answering system [15] and convert each problem into a query to make full use of XLNet neural networks and avoid the drawbacks of lexico-syntactic pattern matching methods. To summarize, the main contribution of this paper is proposing a novel method for automatic matching problems and corresponding solutions in patent documents. The final experiments on the open-source SQuAD dataset [14] and real-world patent dataset illustrate our model's performance. Though, the patent base with which we perform our initial tests is for the moment limited to USPTO patents (thus only American) but its scope nevertheless allows us to verify the validity of our hypotheses. Especially, a detailed case study eventually proves our model's usage and latent perspective on reality.

This article is composed of 5 parts after the introduction, the second part is dedicated to the state of the art on the subject and cites the main contributions that have been useful to our research. It is in the third part that our methodology is presented, as well as the framework of our experiments. The forth part is dedicated to the case study; it constitutes a part both of verification of our hypotheses but also with the didactic aim of presenting the logic of our approach by example. It is followed by discussions, conclusions, acknowledgments, and references.

## 2 Related Work

Inventive Design Method (IDM) is based on the Theory of Inventive Problem Solving - TRIZ [21]. It represents an extension of TRIZ and is perceived as more guided. Different from other ontologies, IDM ontology is generic and applicable in all fields [3]. In addition, Cavallucci et al. [6] proposed the main concepts of IDM that are problems, partial solutions, and contradictions including element parameters and values. In patents, problems normally describe unsatisfactory features of existing methods or situations. Partial solutions provide improvements or changes to the defined problems. Each problem may cause one or more contradictions the patent solves. Besides, partial solutions must be the simplest possible. The correct pairwise between problems and corresponding solutions has great value for engineers to capture the hidden inventive details in patents.

Recent years, most of researchers focus on making use of images [9,13], tabulations [13] or novel proposals [19] in patent documents to facilitate TRIZ or R&D activities. Nevertheless, only a few of research works notice the hidden value of relation between problems and corresponding solutions in IDM-related knowledge. Among them, syntactic analysis is used as the main research method. The syntactical structure of subject (noun phrase), action (verb phrase), and object (noun phrase) is leveraged to explicitly represent relationships between the components of a patent by several researchers [4,5,16,18].

Especially, Souili et al. [17] leverage generic linguistic markers to build patent lexicon database for extracting IDM-related knowledge and building links between problems and partial solutions. Our study also leverages this work to extract problems in patents but the links it provides always are weak and not precise. Besides, our study found that, in patent documents, inventors always provide several inventive details for solving different problems in order to construct an entire inventive plan or object. Furthermore, these inventive details are contained in different corresponding solutions of IDM-related knowledge. It makes us cannot ignore the latent value of building precise links between problems and corresponding solutions in patent documents. Therefore, in this work, we proposed a model called IDM-Matching that combined state-of-the-art natural language processing model called XLNet [20] in order to match problems to corresponding solutions in patents. XLNet integrates the segment recurrence mechanism and relative encoding scheme of Transformer-XL [7] into pretraining, which empirically improves the performance especially for tasks involving a longer text sequence like patent text. In order to leverage its specialty, we especially convert our task as a question answering system task [2]. The answers to the queries that are packed by problems become the corresponding solutions. The links between these IDM-knowledge are eventually built by IDM-Matching.

## 3   Methodology and Experiments

In this section, we introduce our IDM-Matching model for building links between problems and partial solutions. Our work aims to match the corresponding solution with the target problem in each patent document in order to help engineers conveniently find out as many inventive sub-solutions as the inventor provided in the patent. As shown in Fig. 1, IDM-Matching first extracts problems from patent documents by Patentextractor [18] to prepare a list of related problems. Then, we assume these problems as several queries and convert them into related

questions. These packed queries are sent to the Question Answering system–
pretrained with XLNet neural networks [20] to compute an answer list. After a
filtering mechanism, the corresponding solutions are extracted so that we can
build links between the corresponding solution and the target problem.

Formally, the extracted IDM-related knowledge set $k_i = \{P_i, PS_i\}$ is from
$i$-th patent document where $P_i$ and $PS_i$ are problems and partial solutions
respectively in the $i$-th patent document. Given the $j$-th problem $P_i^j =
\{(X_i^{j1}, z_1); (X_i^{j2}, z_2); \dots (X_i^{j|x_i|}, |z_t|)\}$ in the $i$-th patent document where $X_i^{j|x_i|}$
is the $|x_i|$-th word that is located in the $|z_t|$-th position.

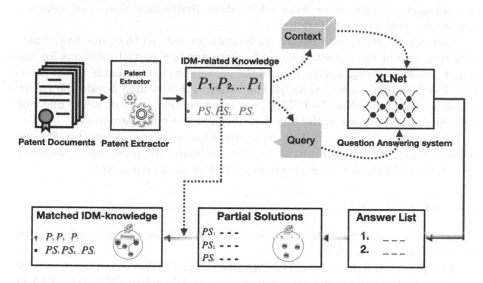

**Fig. 1.** An overview of IDM-Matching

### 3.1 Pack Problem

We aim to build links between problems $P$ and partial solutions $PS$ via Question
Answering system.

Indeed, we first leverage Patentextractor to capture IDM-related knowledge
including problems and partial solutions from patent documents. For $i$-th patent
document, we build a problem database without partial solutions since it fails
extract precise corresponding solutions for the given problems. For each single
problem $P_i^j$ in $i$-th patent document, we then pack it into a query sentence
with a fixed format, for instance "*What is the solution for the problem that___?*".
With this type of converting, each problem can be seen as a query sentence
in the question answering system. Besides, we do not need to make a custom
design for several different types of problems in the IDM-related knowledge in
patent documents. More importantly, the head of "*What is the solution for the
problem that*" is apparent to let model learn that finding solutions are the target

and given problem is the sentence after *"problem that"*. This type of packing is helpful, especially when the problem sentences are not obvious to be seen as problems or lacking some unique negative words. Besides, *"solution"* in the design is useful for the model to locate the corresponding solution sentence when the related context information is containing the key word *"solution"*.

## 3.2  Define Context Information

Context information plays a significant role in the question answering system. The model captures related answers for the given query. Longer context information normally contains more noisy information. Redundant context information also leads to bigger computational cost.

Through the study over patent documents, we noticed that, due to the natural structure of the patent document, corresponding partial solutions for the target problems always appear near to the paragraph containing the target problem. Furthermore, some obvious partial solutions are located beside the target problem the patent described. Thus, for this situation, we can easily find out corresponding solutions to the target problem in the same paragraph.

Due to these reasons, in this task, we define context information for our IDM-Matching as 3 paragraphs of context, including the paragraph containing the target problem as well as an upper and lower single paragraph.

## 3.3  XLNet Model

A state-of-the-art natural language model called XLNet [20] is combined into our IDM-Matching model.

As a pre-trained permutation language modeling, XLNet solves the drawback that the traditional autoregressive language modeling like GPT [12], ELMO [11] etc. cannot learn the forward context and backward context information at the same time to predict the target word. Moreover, XLNet is able to solve the drawback that the artificial symbols like [MASK] used by BERT [8] during pretraining are absent from real data at netuning time, resulting in a pretrain-netune discrepancy.

According to XLNet, it captures bidirectional context via the permutation based dependency rule. Indeed, take a problem sentence in patent as an example. For the given length $(T = 3)$ problem $P_i^j = \{(X_i^{j_1}, z_1); (X_i^{j_2}, z_2); (X_i^{j_3}, z_3)$ in the $i$-th patent document, there are $T!$ different orders to perform a valid autoregressive factorization for the tokens that the problem sentence $P_i^j$ contained:

$$p(\mathbf{X}) = p(x_i^{j_1})p(x_i^{j_2}|x_i^{j_1})p(x_i^{j_3}|x_i^{j_1}x_i^{j_2}) \Rightarrow 1 \to 2 \to 3 \tag{1}$$

$$p(\mathbf{X}) = p(x_i^{j_1})p(x_i^{j_2}|x_i^{j_1}x_i^{j_3})p(x_i^{j_3}|x_i^{j_1}) \Rightarrow 1 \to 3 \to 2 \tag{2}$$

$$p(\mathbf{X}) = p(x_i^{j_1}|x_i^{j_2})p(x_i^{j_2})p(x_i^{j_3}|x_i^{j_1}x_i^{j_2}) \Rightarrow 2 \to 1 \to 3 \tag{3}$$

$$p(\mathbf{X}) = p(x_i^{j_1}|x_i^{j_2}x_i^{j_3})p(x_i^{j_2})p(x_i^{j_3}|x_i^{j_2}) \Rightarrow 2 \to 3 \to 1 \tag{4}$$

$$p(\mathbf{X}) = p(x_i^{j_1}|x_i^{j_3})p(x_i^{j_2}|x_i^{j_1}x_i^{j_3})p(x_i^{j_3}) \Rightarrow 3 \to 1 \to 2 \tag{5}$$

where $p(x_i^{j_2}|x_i^{j_1}x_i^{j_3})$ denotes the possibility $p$ of second word $x_i^{j_2}$ with the constraint condition that first word is $x_i^{j_1}$ and third word is $x_i^{j_3}$. This mechanism makes XLNet could capture bidirectional context information at the same time.

For predicting target word $x_i^{j|x_i|}$ with its position $z_t$, the function is as follows:

$$p_\theta\left(X_{z_t} = x_i^{j|x_i|}|\mathbf{x}_{z<t}\right) = \frac{\exp\left(e(x_i^{j|x_i|})^T g_\theta\left(\mathbf{x}_{z<t}, z_t\right)\right)}{\sum_{x'}\exp\left(e\left(x_i^{j|x_i|'}\right)^T g_\theta\left(\mathbf{x}_{z<t}, z_t\right)\right)} \tag{6}$$

where $\mathbf{x}_{z<t}$ denotes previous words for the target word $x_i^{j|x_i|}$.

Additionally, as an unsupervised language representation learning method, XLNet also profits the pros of Transformer-XL so that it exhibits better performance on language tasks involving long context. We thus combine it into our IDM-matching model to be as a question answering system to capture corresponding solutions.

### 3.4 Experimental Settings

We detail the experimental settings in this section.

**Datasets and Evaluation Metrics:** In this work, as a notable benchmark in question answering, we leverage open-source Stanford Question Answering Dataset (SQuAD 2.0)[1] to train and evaluate our model. SQuAD is a reading comprehension dataset, consisting of questions posed by crowdworkers on a set of Wikipedia articles, where the answer to every question is a segment of text, or span, from the corresponding reading passage. It contains 100,000 questions with corresponding labelled answers. Furthermore, due to lacking labelled patent datasets, we choose 50 U.S. patent documents that are issued on 03, January 2017 by the United States Patent and Trademark Office (USPTO)[2] to evaluate IDM-Matching's performance on our task by manual work. The final EM (Exact Match) and F1 score are used as evaluation metrics.

**Parameter and Computer Settings:** In this work, we tune our IDM-Matching on SQuAD dataset and use the grid search to determine the optimal parameters. We use Huggingface's pretrained XLNet-base-cased model[3] as our question answering system. It contains 12-layer, 768-hidden, 12-heads, 110M parameters. For training the model, we select the epochs among {3, 4, **5**, 6}, batch size among {**5**, 10, 15}, learning rate among {$2e^{-5}, 3e^{-5}, 4e^{-5}$}, and others are as default.

---

[1] https://rajpurkar.github.io/SQuAD-explorer/.
[2] https://bulkdata.uspto.gov/data/patent/grant/redbook/fulltext/2017/.
[3] https://huggingface.co/transformers.

The optimal parameters are highlighted with bold faces. Besides, the model is trained on 1 T P100 GPU for around 15 h.

**Overall Results:** We first evaluate our model on the evaluation dataset and achieves 70.99% EM and 72% F1. On the 50 real-world U.S. patent datasets, IDM-Matching achieves average 72.43% accuracy.

## 4   Case Study

In this section, we demonstrate a real-world case study on an U.S. patent document in order to show our model's practical performance.

**US8847930B2:** *"Electrically conductive touch pen"* is an U.S. patent from physics field. As shown in Fig. 2, it presents a multi-function writing devices that can physically mark on traditional writing surfaces and can also digitally mark on, or be used as other input means in association with, computerized digital displays. This invention has an internal ink cartridge deployable through a hole in the stylus tip. The stylus tip extends from a sleeve that is formed of a conductive elastomeric material. The sleeve extends up a rigid shaft of the device such that it contacts a sufficient ground. The stylus tip is coated with a protective material that adjusts the coefficient of friction and prevents carbon deposits on the touch screen. A sufficient contact patch is achieved to simulate a human finger so as to overcome false positives from common touch screen logic.

Patentextractor extracted, as shown in Fig. 3, several problems (red circles)

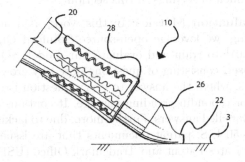

**Fig. 2.** An overview of the invention

from the patent. We picked up 7 correct problems (red circles with yellow edges) as inputs for the IDM-Matching and convert them into 7 queries. The questions, answers that our model extracted, correct answers, and the related context information are as follows:

1. [Question]: What is the solution for the problem that this would hamper a user's ability to operate the touch pen 10 with gloves?

PatentSolver : ELECTRICALLY CONDUCTIVE TOUCH PEN

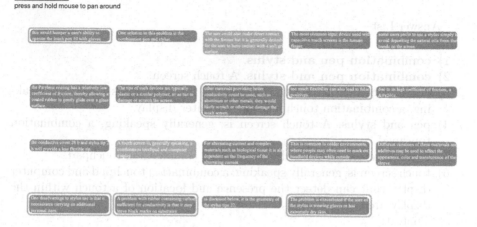

**Fig. 3.** The extracted problems (Color figure online)

—Answer List—

1) **The inner molding 29 is replaced by a former 39 that is ideally metallic. This alternative embodiment is designed to address the aforementioned problems attendant to a user wearing gloves,** having very dry skin, or situations in which the user does not make good conductive contact with the touch pen 10. In such cases the conductive cover 28 needs to be in good electrical contact with a volume of metal V (m3) of conductivity.

2) conductive cover 28 needs to be in good electrical contact with a volume of metal V (m3) of conductivity a (Siemens per meter S/m).

2. [Question]: What is the solution for the problem that too much flexibility can also lead to false positives?

—Answer List—

1) The larger the air cavity 32, the more flexible the stylus tip 22 will become. However, too much flexibility can also lead to false positives. As shown, the former 39 comprises an extension 41 of various sizes.

2) The larger the air cavity 32, the more flexible the stylus tip 22 will become. However, too much flexibility can also lead to false positives. As shown, the former 39 comprises an extension 41 of various sizes. **The size of this extension directly controls the size of the air cavity 32. In some embodiments, this extension may be a controllable feature of the touch pen 10.**

3. [Question]: What is the solution for the problem that one disadvantage to stylus use is that it necessitates carrying an additional personal item?

—Answer List—

1) **combination pen and stylus**.
2) **combination pen and stylus**. A touch screen.
3) **the combination pen and stylus**. A touch screen is, generally speaking, a combination touchpad and computer display.
4) pen and stylus. A touch screen is, generally speaking, a combination touchpad.
5) A touch screen is, generally speaking, a combination touchpad.
6) touch screen is, generally speaking, a combination touchpad and computer display that can detect the presence and location of a touch within the display area.
   Context:
   One solution to this problem is the combination pen and stylus.

4. [Question]: What is the solution for the problem that a problem with rubber containing carbon sufficient for conductivity is that it may leave black marks on substrates to which it comes into contact?

—Answer List—

1) **coating the rubber, or selectively the rubber tip, with a very thin layer of Parylene**.
2) **selectively the rubber tip, with a very thin layer of Parylene**. This conformal coating.
3) very thin layer.
   Context:
   These problems can be solved by coating the rubber, or selectively the rubber tip, with a very thin layer of Parylene.

5. [Question]: What is the solution for the problem that the problem is exacerbated if the user of the stylus is wearing gloves or has extremely dry skin?
   —Answer List—

1) **films made from graphene (carbon nanotubes), or other suitable material**. Conductive materials that touch or are in very close proximity to this type of touch screen alter the electrostatic field of the screen, thereby creating a registerable change in capacitance.
   Context:
   Traditional plastic or polymer-based styli are not effective in marking on capacitive touch screens because they are not sufficiently conductive. The problem is exacerbated if the user of the stylus is wearing gloves or has extremely dry skin.
   Correct Answer:

Capacitive touch screens generally comprise a flat insulative transparent sheet such as glass having an inside portion coated with a transparent conductor such as **indium tin oxide (ITO), films made from graphene (carbon nanotubes), or other suitable material.**

6. [Question]: What is the solution for the problem that this is common in colder environments, where people may often need to mark on handheld devices while outside?

—Answer List—

1) Capacitive touch screens are quickly replacing resistive touch screens.
2) sink or source of electrons.
3) films made from graphene (**carbon nanotubes**), or other suitable material. Conductive materials that touch or are in very close proximity to this type of touch screen alter the electrostatic field of the screen, thereby creating a registerable change in capacitance.
4) sink or source of electrons, sometimes called a "ground.
   Correct Answer:
   One solution that enables a stylus to be used with a capacitive touch screen is the use of conductive rubber or a similar conductive elastomeric material.
   Context:
   One solution that enables a stylus to be used with a capacitive touch screen is the use of **conductive rubber** or a similar conductive elastomeric material. **Conductive rubber** is a rarer and more expensive form of rubber that **contains** suspended graphite carbon, **carbon nanotubes**, nickel or silver particles.

7. [Question]: What is the solution for the problem that other materials providing better conductivity could be used, such as aluminum or other metals, they would likely scratch or otherwise damage the touch screen?

—Answer List—

1) **Conductive materials** that touch or are in very close proximity to this type of touch screen.
2) films made from graphene (carbon nanotubes), or other suitable material. textbfConductive materials that touch or are in very close proximity.
3) films made from graphene.
4) ions–cations.
5) conductive materials such as biological tissue, these charged carriers could be predominantly ions–cations and/or anions.
   Correct Answer:
   One solution that enables a stylus to be used with a capacitive touch screen is the use of **conductive rubber or a similar conductive elastomeric material.**

The correct predictive answers have been labelled with bold faces. Instead of some obvious correct answers, we especially mention 2 answers that represent the latent perspective that IDM-Matching in the automatic of IDM-related knowledge. For instance, Question 5 presents the problem that the finger with gloves or dry skin cannot use the stylus well. Actually, the plastic or polymer-based stlyli contributes to this problem but this important information does not appear in the question. IDM-Matching still successfully learned the related information and achieve the correct answer of films made from graphene (carbon nanotubes), or other suitable material. Besides, Question 6 provides a problem that people need to mark on handheld devices while outside in colder environments. This situation leads to insulation from the stylus with the human body. The answer list that our model proposed does not illustrate a precise answer. The correct answer is the use of a conductive rubber or a similar conductive elastomeric material. However, we see the carbon nanotubes appeared in our answer list and conductive rubber exactly contains carbon nanotubes. It means our model still learned some significant information in order to build the link between the problem and the corresponding solution.

In the conclusion of this detailed case study, we note that the final corresponding solutions that IDM-Matching extracted are precise and have significant practical value for automatic matching the target problems. It illustrates that the built links between problems and partial solutions can facilitate engineers to face a large number of patent documents to extract problems the target patent faced and corresponding inventive solutions it provides.

## 5    Conclusion and Future Work

In this paper, we proposed an IDM-related knowledge association model called IDM-Matching for matching problems and corresponding solutions in patent documents. Our approach can automate the solution retrieval and match with corresponding problems in patents. This work will facilitate engineers to find out inventive details hidden in patent documents in order to speed the R&D activities. More importantly, this work can further improve inventive solutions retrieval for the target problem by associating with different domains' similar problems [10] in patent documents. By that time, engineers without a broad understanding of the different domains' knowledge to make full use of inventive knowledge from a wide range of patent documents to facilitate their inventive manufacturing inspirations. Final experimental results on the real-world patent dataset illustrate the performance of our model. In particular, a detailed case study demonstrates the usage of our model in reality and shows its latent perspective on TRIZ field.

In the future, we will explore the following directions:

(1) Fine-tune our IDM-Matching model in order to further improve its final accuracy in patent datasets.
(2) Combine it with similarity computation approaches of different domains' IDM-related knowledge in order to leverage different domains' inventive solutions to facilitate R&D activities.

**Acknowledgement.** This work is supported by China Scholarship Council (CSC). The statements made herein are solely the responsibility of the authors.

# References

1. Altshuller, G.: 40 Principles: TRIZ Keys to Innovation, vol. 1. Technical Innovation Center Inc., Worcester (2002)
2. Brill, E., Dumais, S., Banko, M.: An analysis of the AskMSR question-answering system. In: Proceedings of the ACL-02 Conference on Empirical Methods in Natural Language Processing, vol. 10, pp. 257–264. Association for Computational Linguistics (2002)
3. Bultey, A., De Bertrand De Beuvron, F., Rousselot, F.: A substance-field ontology to support the TRIZ thinking approach. Int. J. Comput. Appl. Technol. **30**(1–2), 113–124 (2007)
4. Cascini, G., Fantechi, A., Spinicci, E.: Natural language processing of patents and technical documentation. In: Marinai, S., Dengel, A.R. (eds.) DAS 2004. LNCS, vol. 3163, pp. 508–520. Springer, Heidelberg (2004). https://doi.org/10.1007/978-3-540-28640-0_48
5. Cascini, G., Russo, D., et al.: Computer-aided analysis of patents and search for TRIZ contradictions. Int. J. Prod. Dev. **4**(1), 52–67 (2007)
6. Cavallucci, D., Rousselot, F., Zanni, C.: Initial situation analysis through problem graph. CIRP J. Manuf. Sci. Technol. **2**(4), 310–317 (2010)
7. Dai, Z., Yang, Z., Yang, Y., Carbonell, J., Le, Q.V., Salakhutdinov, R.: Transformer-xl: attentive language models beyond a fixed-length context. arXiv preprint arXiv:1901.02860 (2019)
8. Devlin, J., Chang, M.W., Lee, K., Toutanova, K.: Bert: pre-training of deep bidirectional transformers for language understanding. arXiv preprint arXiv:1810.04805 (2018)
9. Jiang, S., Luo, J., Pava, G.R., Hu, J., Magee, C.L.: A CNN-based patent image retrieval method for design ideation. arXiv preprint arXiv:2003.08741 (2020)
10. Ni, X., Samet, A., Cavallucci, D.: An approach merging the IDM-related knowledge. In: Benmoussa, R., De Guio, R., Dubois, S., Koziołek, S. (eds.) TFC 2019. IAICT, vol. 572, pp. 147–158. Springer, Cham (2019). https://doi.org/10.1007/978-3-030-32497-1_13
11. Peters, M.E., et al.: Deep contextualized word representations. arXiv preprint arXiv:1802.05365 (2018)
12. Radford, A., Wu, J., Child, R., Luan, D., Amodei, D., Sutskever, I.: Language models are unsupervised multitask learners. OpenAI Blog **1**(8), 9 (2019)
13. Rahim, Z.A., Yusof, S.M., Bakar, N.A., Mohamad, W.M.S.W.: The application of computational thinking and TRIZ methodology in patent innovation analytics. In: International Conference of Reliable Information and Communication Technology, pp. 793–802. Springer (2018). https://doi.org/10.1007/978-3-319-99007-1_73
14. Rajpurkar, P., Zhang, J., Lopyrev, K., Liang, P.: Squad: 100,000+ questions for machine comprehension of text. arXiv preprint arXiv:1606.05250 (2016)
15. Ravichandran, D., Hovy, E.: Learning surface text patterns for a question answering system. In: Proceedings of the 40th Annual Meeting on Association for Computational Linguistics, pp. 41–47. Association for Computational Linguistics (2002)
16. Savransky, S.D.: Engineering of Creativity: Introduction to TRIZ Methodology of Inventive Problem Solving. CRC Press, Boca Raton (2000)

17. Souili, A., Cavallucci, D.: Toward an automatic extraction of IDM concepts from patents. In: Chakrabarti, A. (ed.) CIRP Design 2012, pp. 115–124. Springer (2013). https://doi.org/10.1007/978-1-4471-4507-3_12

18. Souili, A., Cavallucci, D., Rousselot, F.: A lexico-syntactic pattern matching method to extract IDM-TRIZ knowledge from on-line patent databases. Procedia Eng. **131**, 418–425 (2015)

19. Strumsky, D., Lobo, J.: Identifying the sources of technological novelty in the process of invention. Res. Policy **44**(8), 1445–1461 (2015)

20. Yang, Z., Dai, Z., Yang, Y., Carbonell, J., Salakhutdinov, R.R., Le, Q.V.: XLNet: generalized autoregressive pretraining for language understanding. In: Advances in Neural Information Processing Systems, pp. 5754–5764 (2019)

21. Yeap, T., Loo, G.H., Pang, S.: Computational patent mapping: intelligent agents for nanotechnology. In: Proceedings International Conference on MEMS, NANO and Smart Systems, pp. 274–278. IEEE (2003)

# Summarization as a Denoising Extraction Tool

Guillaume Guarino[1]([⊠]), Ahmed Samet[2], and Denis Cavallucci[1]

[1] ICUBE/CSIP Team (UMR CNRS 7357), INSA Strasbourg, Strasbourg, France
guillaume.guarino@insa-strasbourg.fr
[2] ICUBE/SDC Team (UMR CNRS 7357), INSA Strasbourg, Strasbourg, France

**Abstract.** Altshuller's matrix, over various conducted surveys on the frequency of use by practitioners, remains systematically in the lead despite criticism of its obsolescence. Consequently, attempts have emerged to update it, both in terms of principle's quantity and their statistical distribution in generic technical conflicts. Nevertheless, up to now, none of them has supplanted the effectiveness of the Altshuller matrix. These attempts as well as other approaches introducing new tools for patent classification and information retrieval often suffer from poor accuracy in data extraction. In this paper, we introduce a new TRIZ-dedicated extraction tool based on a deep neural network summarization called SummaTRIZ. We also introduce a method including SummaTRIZ to update TRIZ matrix and create a whole new matrix based on patents and independent from potentially obsolete inventive principles.

**Keywords:** Summary · Extraction · Deep learning

## 1 Introduction

Patents are underused source of knowledge for two main reasons. A human being has the ability to produce a fine-grained analysis of the patent content in order to extract usable information. However, an engineer cannot analyze millions of patents. On the contrary, NLP algorithms can analyze large amounts of data but the extracted information is often very noisy. The inventiveness of TRIZ problem solving method can be taken one step further by the targeted extraction of knowledge from patents. The extraction of TRIZ parameters and contradictions is, in particular, one of the most necessary tasks in this field. However, this targeted extraction faces the problem of the low precision and recall (see Eqs. 1 and 2 with $TP$ the True Positives, $FP$ the False Positives and $FN$ the False Negatives) of information retrieval algorithms. Therefore, there is a significant need to develop an algorithm to reduce noise in information retrieval.

$$Precision = \frac{TP}{TP + FP} \tag{1}$$

ⓒ IFIP International Federation for Information Processing 2020
Published by Springer Nature Switzerland AG 2020
D. Cavallucci et al. (Eds.): TFC 2020, IFIP AICT 597, pp. 77–87, 2020.
https://doi.org/10.1007/978-3-030-61295-5_7

$$Recall = \frac{TP}{TP + FN} \tag{2}$$

In this paper we propose a new extraction algorithm to reduce noise in information extraction. This method allows TRIZ parameters extraction with an improved accuracy and would pave the way for a complete detection of patent contradictions. In addition to this new extraction algorithm, we will also propose a novel method to update a TRIZ matrix from patents extracted knowledge.

The main contributions of this paper are:

- the adaptation of a deep neural summarization network called SummaTRIZ to retrieve sentences containing parameters from a patent and reconstruct the solved contradictions
- a method to build a whole new TRIZ matrix based on patents independent from inventive principles
- a pre-study to evaluate the quality of the sentences extraction

The paper consists of the following sections. Section 2 presents a brief state of art about information retrieval, contradictions and parameters extraction from patent documents. In Sect. 3 we introduce our model SummaTRIZ and we show some qualitative results of our method in Sect. 4. We finally conclude our work and show perspectives for future works.

## 2 Related Work

Several approaches attempted to address the problem of patents classification, information and parameters retrieval in the context of TRIZ. They rely on simple classification tools and the analysis of the proposed methods are often restrictive.

Information may be extracted from patents with linguistic tools [14]. These information are related to Inventive Design Method concept which is a particular framework made to apply TRIZ theory easily, in particular through the use of patents. The data extracted may then be represented in graphs.

Keywords linked to a patent database simplifies the problems extraction [15]. The user must analyse the patents to select the best information sources. Results are then organized into a discovery matrix to associate, for instance the keywords linked to the technological systems to the keywords linked to the physical parameters. Finally the matrix is exploited through the technology used or physical phenomena. The purpose of such a method is assisting ideas generation for engineers but it is not automatized.

TF-IDF (Term Frequency-Inverse Document Frequency) and LDA clustering may also be utilized for physical effects retrieval [7].

Some attempts were made to classify patents in accordance with the inventive principle they use to solve a problem [5,12]. Nevertheless, Loh et al. use a small database of 200 patents and the patents are only classified using 6 inventive principles due to a lack of precision. He et al. use all the inventive principles but, to deal with the lack of data and to make the training possible, groups of inventive principles are created. The purpose of the method is therefore to recognize which groups of inventive principles are linked to the patents. Despite this simplification, the results are noisy with a very low recall value.

Methods for TRIZ parameters extraction already exist [2]. Chang et al. assume that a patent solves one contradiction and two TRIZ parameters are therefore improved (or at least not degraded). The method consists in keyphrases detection. One of the parameters is supposed to be in a sentence similar as "to be prevented from worsening" and the second one in a sentence with "to be improved". The detection method is therefore very limited and it works only for Chinese patents as the syntax does not vary much.

Patents may be retrieved according to the targeted contradictions [18]. Nevertheless, this approach uses Wordnet dictionary but no attempt to test the approach has been made. Therefore, it cannot be really considered as a prior art method. Liang et al. published another paper [9] dealing with patent classification. This time it was not a classification in accordance to the solved contradictions but in accordance to the used inventive principle. First the initial contradiction is found. The most suitable inventive principles are then chosen and patents potentially related to the inventive principle are suggested to the user. To measure relevancy of patents, a traditional TF-IDF algorithm with Chi-square method is used.

A methodology based on clustering methods was also proposed [10]. The idea is to recognize patterns associated with the problems or the way of solving these problems.

A position criteria on the parameters forming contradictions in the patent make the extraction easier [1]. It is assumed that the worsening factor is located in the background of the invention/state of the art and the improving factor in the claims. Nevertheless, because of this strong hypothesis, the method is not workable with all patents and it is limiting the scope of the approach.

Content may be extracted automatically [17]. In this case, process patents parameters are recognized using semantic databases. These parameters are then associated with the general parameters from TRIZ matrix. Process contradiction solving principles are also clustered to build a new TRIZ matrix for process patents.

These approaches do not use the potential of deep learning and summarization method to retrieve information from patents. In this paper, we focus on filling this gap and show that these new tools help to reach new achievements in patents information retrieval.

## 3  SummaTRIZ, A Summarization-Based Approach

SummaTRIZ aims at retrieving information (i.e. sentences containing contradictions and TRIZ parameters) with neural based summarization methods. A summary may be inferred in an extractive or abstractive way. Extractive summarization aims at selecting sentences that contains main information. The syntax of the summary is therefore correct. Nevertheless, an extractive summary may lose coherence as it is the result of pasting different sentences from different paragraphs. On the contrary, abstractive summarization aims at writing a summary from scratch using text generation models. The abstractive summaries are coherent but they often show syntax errors, misinterpretation and they sometimes tend to copy the original text. Based on this, we chose to focus on extractive summarization to keep the information unbiased.

We are also focusing on transfer learning and pretrained models to avoid having to create a huge database to learn the networks. Some encoding models are designed to be trainable in a non-supervised way. They can be trained on all sort of documents like Wikipedia pages, articles, journals. These models learn therefore words representations on various dataset before being applied to a specific domain. Due to the lack of summarization dataset, these models are largely used. If the encoder is already pre-trained on an other dataset, then a small dataset may be enough to learn how to summarize without overfitting. Sometimes, even finetuning the model is not necessary.

BERT [4] is a Transformer Network [16]. Transformer Networks are interesting for language understanding and language generation because of their bidirectionality. It means that these networks were developed to take into account the words and sentences placed before a certain sentence but also after this sentence. Until the appearance of this type of networks, the models could only take into account either only the sentences placed before or only the sentences placed after. That is why the Transformer networks are now largely used in NLP tasks. They are composed of several stacked Attention Mechanisms. An Attention Mechanism is designed to select the best information from a flow of data.

BERT encoder shows incredible results and helped establishing the state of the art in a great number of nlp tasks. BERT [4] adapted for summarization task [11] (see Fig. 1) is used to summarize patents and extract useful information. A binary classifier on top of the encoder takes as input the sentences representation and decides whether it will be part of the summary or not. The model uses a sentence level extractor which is particularly interesting for patents summaries in which the length of the summaries are varying. It means that no matter the number of useful sentences, they can all potentially be part of the summary.

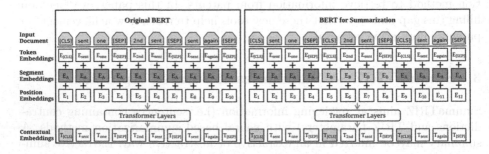

**Fig. 1.** Summarization network

## 4   TRIZ Matrix Update and Other Applications

The summarization model is meant to extract meaningful data from patents. In TRIZ applications, meaningful data is often a synonym of the potential presence of a contradiction. The definition of a contradiction solved by the patent is an important step for being able to utilize the content of the patent. If patents are classified in accordance to the contradiction they solve it would be straightforward to link some patents to engineers contradiction in real life problems. Given a problem, if the user gets patents which are able to solve his contradiction, then the chances of solving this problem in an inventive way increase. With lexical distance measure the user would even be able to scan patents relative to his contradiction among different domains, from his domain to completely different domains (Fig. 2).

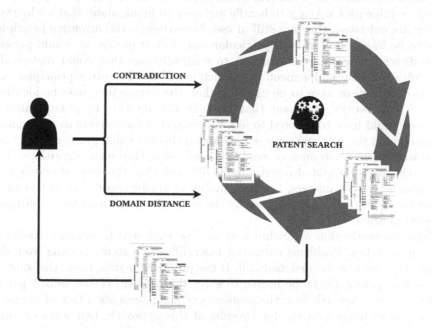

CONTRADICTION

PATENT SEARCH

DOMAIN DISTANCE

**Fig. 2.** Relevant patents scanning

The definition of a contradiction consists basically in finding at least two TRIZ parameters that are contradictory i.e. when one parameter is improved another one is degraded. Usually finding the parameters which are part of the contradiction is not an easy task and require a full analysis of the patent by an expert. Nevertheless, an approach using the state of the art is possible. If a patent solves a contradiction, it means that prior art patents presented in the state of the art do not solve this contradiction. Then, the task of finding the solved contradiction in the patent would be slightly modified into finding the unsolved contradiction of the prior art patents. Generally, the unsolved contradiction of prior art patents is expressed or explained in the state of the art of the patent. Consequently, the analysis of the state of the art part of the patent would be sufficient to extract the solved contradiction.

The relevancy of the analysed patents is an important question. Since there is no clear written indication that a patent is inventive, the measure of the inventiveness for which some approaches were developed [3,6,8] remains a field of interest and we will more likely introduce some inventiveness evaluation tools in SummaTRIZ.

The summarization model could also be used to recreate a brand new TRIZ matrix (see Fig. 3). If TRIZ parameters can be extracted with the right order in the parameters i.e., which parameter degrades when the other parameter is improved, there is no obstacle, besides the measure of inventiveness, to the construction of a new matrix. This matrix would be different from the original matrix as the content of the matrix would be patents and not inventive principles. Inventive principles are easy to handle and easy to manipulate, that's why even if they are outdated, they are still in use. Nevertheless, the inventive principles have to be interpreted in each particular case. In our matrix we would present some direct applications of solutions to contradictions that could replace the principles but also supplement the principles. If the inventive principles and the patents content have to be used together, the parameters must be identical in both frameworks. It means that keyword classification or some similarity measure would have to be used to link the extracted parameters to the original parameters. If the new matrix is self-sufficient, this matching problem would not exist and different parameters would be used using clustering algorithms. The size of the matrix would also certainly be different than the original matrix size. The number of parameters, i.e. the number of clusters would be determined, either by an arbitrary choice either by the value of the minimal lexical distance between clusters.

The summarization algorithm may also be exploited to enhance results of other approaches. Problems extracted from different patents coming from different domains may be matched [13]. If the problems match, then, the solution of the first patent might be usable to solve the problem of the second patent and vice versa. Nevertheless, the problem extractor presents a lack of precision which has an impact on the final results of this approach. Our work on summarization could provide a robust extractor which would improve the results of this approach.

## 5    Experiments

In this part, we show qualitative results of the summarization model with several patent's state of the art as input. The summarization model is trained on newspapers as a dataset is already available and may help to distinguish the sentences to keep in the summary even if the structure of a patent is very different from a newspaper article. The results showed that this training on newspaper improved the results compared to a model without training, using original BERT weights.

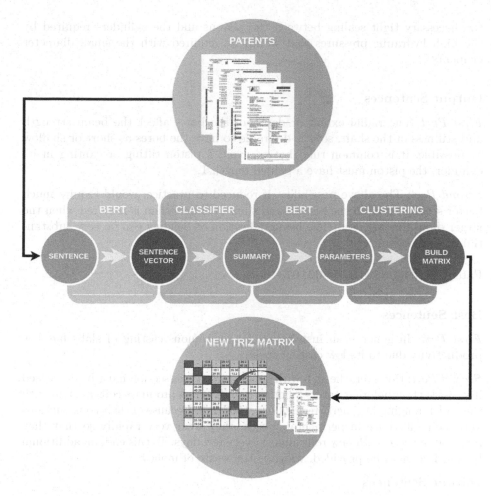

**Fig. 3.** Building a new TRIZ matrix

Patent **US043086519-19791003**

**Best Sentences**

*First Part*: The radial extent or depth of the bores affect the beam strength and stiffness of the shaft, so it is desirable to have the bores as short or shallow as possible. It follows that in the case of the described roll the bores forming the cylinders must extend undesirably far into the fixed shaft in its radial direction with a consequent undesirable reduction in the shaft's beam strength and stiffness.

*Second Part*: With such deflections, which would be exaggerated if the shaft were to be bored to form even very small diameter cylinders, the small cylindrical shapes would distort from true cylinders to slightly elliptical shapes preventing the necessary tight sealing between the pistons and the cylinders required by the high hydraulic pressures that would be required with the small diameter elements.

## Output Sentences

*First Part*: The radial extent or depth of the bores affect the beam strength and stiffness of the shaft, so it is desirable to have the bores as short or shallow as possible. It is common rule that to avoid a piston tilting or canting in its cylinder, the piston must have a guided length 1.

*Second Part*: The above possibility, if reduced to practice, would require much better sealing between the pistons and their cylinders than is required when the larger diameters are used. The beam deflection or bending can be very substantial in some instances.

Patent **US043087418-19800107**

## Best Sentences

*First Part*: In general, an installation for continuous casting of slabs has low productivity due to its low casting speed.

*Second Part*: However, the slab with such a large cross section must be decreased in cross section before it enters a hot strip mill which produces coils of strip with the width ranging in general from 800 to 1500 mm. Because of their constructions and their difference in peripheral speeds, they wear very rapidly so that they must be replaced with new rolls almost every few days. To this end, an additional bypass line must be provided, which is the waste of money.

## Output Sentences

*First Part*: Because of their constructions and their difference in peripheral speeds, they wear very rapidly so that they must be replaced with new rolls almost every few days. When the continuous casting of slabs is interrupted whenever the caliber rolls are changed, it is impossible to improve productivity. However, the slab with such a large cross section must be decreased in cross section before it enters a hot strip mill which produces coils of strip with the width ranging in general from 800 to 1500 mm.

*Second Part*: To this end, an additional bypass line must be provided, which is the waste of money. When the continuous casting of slabs is interrupted whenever the caliber rolls are changed, it is impossible to improve productivity. Because of their constructions and their difference in peripheral speeds, they wear very rapidly so that they must be replaced with new rolls almost every few days.

Patent **US043087787-19800528**

## Best Sentences

*First Part*: Another difficulty is that the hook members on the blade holder must pass between the hook members on the other blade holder during reciprocal moving, so the minimum space between said adjoining knife blades is limited to a space larger than the thickness of said hook members. This results in the minimum spacing between said adjoining knife blades being limited to a size larger than half of the diameter of said coil springs, so that an extremely small space, for example, 2.5 mm, is not possible. For these reasons, in slicing foodstuff into very thin slices with a conventional slicer, the knife blades can't be pulled with enough tension to slice the foodstuff into even thickness slices due to weak resilient means and thin hook means and weak supporting parts.

*Second Part*: This causes difficulty in slicing in even thicknesses. Such a blade assembly requires a complex adjustment to achieve even blade tension. In the slicers described in my 3,628,501, however, a great deal of complexity is involved in construction and assembly when the hook member is mounted on the blade holder since the vertical and diagonal hook members are alternately interconnected with each other. Otherwise it is difficult to slice the foodstuff into even thickness slices due to the uneven blade tension.

## Output Sentences

*First Part*: This results in the minimum spacing between said adjoining knife blades being limited to a size larger than half of the diameter of said coil springs, so that an extremely small space, for example, 2. For these reasons, in slicing foodstuff into very thin slices with a conventional slicer, the knife blades can't be pulled with enough tension to slice the foodstuff into even thickness slices due to weak resilient means and thin hook means and weak supporting parts.

*Second Part*: This causes difficulty in slicing in even thicknesses. Otherwise it is difficult to slice the foodstuff into even thickness slices due to the uneven blade tension. Further, when the length of each blade from holding pin to holding pin is slightly different, the edge of each knife blade is not arranged in a straight line.

The "Best sentences" are the sentences where the parameters are the most obvious. Some of these sentences where extracted by the model. Even if the sentences extracted are not the same, these qualitative (and random) results show that some parameters are still present in the sentences. It means that the model is already performative without proper training on patents. Sometimes the model is completely wrong and extract sentences which do not contain parameters but there are often at least one extracted parameter. Nevertheless, even if some of the parameters are extracted, it is not sufficient to reconstruct a contradiction. The difference between extracting meaningful sentences in the context of a press article and extracting meaningful sentences in a context of TRIZ and patents is the main cause of this loss of precision in the extraction. That's why a training on patent database to learn in particular the extraction of sentences containing the parameters forming a contradiction will be necessary.

# 6    Conclusion

In this paper we presented a new information retrieval method through summarization that could make possible a clean extraction of contradiction and parameters from patents. The model is based on a deep learning summarization method using BERT encoder. A pre-study shows encouraging qualitative results for the extraction of sentences containing parameters even if the accuracy is not high enough yet to reconstruct the full contradictions.

Future works include the creation of a patents database to fine-tune the model on contradiction extraction and the development of an approach to estimate which patents are the most inventive.

With an ultimate goal in mind, an ideal matrix would be a real-time matrix, which would be reconstructed as new patents arrive. Finally, wouldn't the ideal matrix be the absence of a matrix at all? We could then imagine instead of this matrix an online algorithm that would process all the patents at the moment a user requests it and finally provide a real-time answer. A nice immaterial answer to the contradiction of having one matrix and an infinity of matrices at the same time.

# References

1. Cascini, G., Russo, D.: Computer-aided analysis of patents and search for TRIZ contradictions. Int. J. Prod. Dev. **4**, 52–67 (2007). https://doi.org/10.1504/IJPD. 2007.011533
2. Chang, H.T., Chang, C.Y., Wu, W.K.: Computerized innovation inspired by existing patents, pp. 1134–1137 (May 2017). https://doi.org/10.1109/ICASI.2017. 7988268
3. Cremers, K., Harhoff, D., Narin, F., Scherer, F., Vopel, K.: Citation frequency and the value of patented inventions. Rev. Econ. Stat. **81**, 511–515 (1999). https://doi. org/10.1162/003465399558265
4. Devlin, J., Chang, M.W., Lee, K., Toutanova, K.: Bert: pre-training of deep bidirectional transformers for language understanding. In: NAACL-HLT (2019)
5. He, C., Loh, H.T.: Grouping of TRIZ inventive principles to facilitate automatic patent classification. Expert Syst. Appl. **34**, 788–795 (2008)
6. Jugulum, R., Frey, D.D.: Toward a taxonomy of concept designs for improved robustness. J. Eng. Des. **18**(2), 139–156 (2007). https://doi.org/10.1080/ 09544820600731496
7. Korobkin, D.M., Fomenkov, S.A., Kravets, A.G.: Extraction of physical effects practical applications from patent database. In: 2017 8th International Conference on Information, Intelligence, Systems Applications (IISA), pp. 1–5 (August 2017). https://doi.org/10.1109/IISA.2017.8316402
8. Lanjouw, J., Schankerman, M.: Patent quality and research productivity: measuring innovation with multiple indicators. Econ. J. **114**, 441–465 (2004). https://doi. org/10.1111/j.1468-0297.2004.00216.x
9. Liang, Y., Tan, R., Wang, C., Li, Z.: Computer-aided classification of patents oriented to TRIZ. In: 2009 IEEE International Conference on Industrial Engineering and Engineering Management, pp. 2389–2393 (2009)

10. Liang, Y., Tan, R.: A text-mining-based patent analysis in product innovative process. In: León-Rovira, N. (ed.) CAI 2007. ITIFIP, vol. 250, pp. 89–96. Springer, Boston, MA (2007). https://doi.org/10.1007/978-0-387-75456-7_9
11. Liu, Y., Lapata, M.: Text summarization with pretrained encoders. In: EMNLP/IJCNLP (2019)
12. Loh, H., He, C., Shen, L.: Automatic classification of patent documents for TRIZ users. World Pat. Inf. **28**, 6–13 (2006). https://doi.org/10.1016/j.wpi.2005.07.007
13. Ni, X., Samet, A., Cavallucci, D.: An approach merging the IDM-related knowledge. In: Benmoussa, R., De Guio, R., Dubois, S., Koziołek, S. (eds.) TFC 2019. IAICT, vol. 572, pp. 147–158. Springer, Cham (2019). https://doi.org/10.1007/978-3-030-32497-1_13
14. Souili, A., Cavallucci, D.: Automated extraction of knowledge useful to populate inventive design ontology from patents. TRIZ – The Theory of Inventive Problem Solving, pp. 43–62. Springer, Cham (2017). https://doi.org/10.1007/978-3-319-56593-4_2
15. Valverde, U.Y., Nadeau, J.P., Scaravetti, D.: A new method for extracting knowledge from patents to inspire designers during the problem-solving phase. J. Eng. Des. **28**(6), 369–407 (2017)
16. Vaswani, A., et al.: Attention is all you need. In: Guyon, I., et al. (eds.) Advances in Neural Information Processing Systems, vol. 30, pp. 5998–6008. Curran Associates, Inc. (2017). http://papers.nips.cc/paper/7181-attention-is-all-you-need.pdf
17. Wang, G., Tian, X., Geng, J., Evans, R., Che, S.: Extraction of principle knowledge from process patents for manufacturing process innovation. Procedia CIRP **56**, 193–198 (2016). https://doi.org/10.1016/j.procir.2016.10.053
18. Liang, Y., Tan, R., Ma, J.: Patent analysis with text mining for TRIZ. In: 2008 4th IEEE International Conference on Management of Innovation and Technology, pp. 1147–1151 (2008)

# Problem-Solving Tools as Methods for Managing the Information Content of Systems

Igor Zadesenets[✉]

Ramat Gan, Israel

**Abstract.** The time limitation sets one of the major obstacles for finding creative solutions. Reserves for expediting the productivity of unrestricted search are exhausted. Thus, knowledge should be engaged. Engaging specific knowledge is simple but does not provide creative solutions. Engaging general knowledge, despite difficult interpretation, helps to uncover blind spots. In general, the problem-solving process is considered as exploring the space of possibilities for defining one result. So, this is the process of compensation of Uncertainty. The Requisite Variety Law defines Information as of the only means for compensation of Uncertainty (Entropy). Most of the problems are solved by humans or nature engaging some entities (tools). Therefore, such entities contain information, helps to resolve problems. The development of tools can be described as improving the ability to store and transmit information. Thus, the simplification of tools is skipping excessive (unnecessary) information. For finding the ways for the improvement of tools, the equations of Shannon's Information Theory can be analyzed. The ways defined, for the most part, match the TRIZ trends and principles and some techniques of other experience-based methods, such as SIT, Lean, Axiomatic Design. This gives hope for the creation of the formal theory for the area, which can be defined as 'Solving Problems by improving tools.' The theoretical explanation is one of the crucial parts of the scientific justification of methods. Without scientific validation, creative problem-solving tools are doomed to stagnation.

**Keywords:** Problem solving · Information theory · Free idea generation · Thinking tools · Heuristics · Evolution trends · TRIZ · SIT · Lean thinking

## 1 About Terminology: Tools and Systems

In the Engineering Design literature, the terms 'system' and 'technical system' are commonly used, despite the lack of the universally accepted definition of the System concept. The last usually implies the concept of unity [1], which is only slightly related to our considerations. So, in the present work, author tries to use words 'tool' and 'entity' instead. Under the "tool" refers to an entity or a set of entities that can be used for some purposes. Thus, the consideration is refocused from the composition and structure of

I. Zadesenets—Independent Researcher.

D. Cavallucci et al. (Eds.): TFC 2020, IFIP AICT 597, pp. 88–100, 2020.
https://doi.org/10.1007/978-3-030-61295-5_8

studied entities to their purposes. This definition is surprisingly wide. It covers not only ordinary tools as simple as an ax or as complicated as a super-computer, but also organizations, methods, and even theories. Taking the assumption that living things try to fulfill some purposes, at least - surviving, their organisms can also be considered tools.

The author does not underestimate the importance of the System Approach and such useful tools as Nine Screen Vision, Flow Analysis, 5 Whys or Value Stream Mapping. The approach, proposed in this article, probably can be used for or improving these tools, but this is out of scope of the present work.

## 2 On the Importance of the Theoretical Approach for the Idea Generation Methods

One of the brilliant solutions, found during the latest epidemic was organizing the drive-through test points. It was applied first in South Korea, the country, where different idea generation techniques are most widely used. A TRIZ specialist will say, that this solution was found with the help of the 'Preliminary Action' principle or 9-screen vision concept [2, 3]. A Lean Production specialist will argue that this is the classic case of implementation of one of the '8 Wastes Elimination' principles - excluding the waiting. The Design Thinker will recall Tim Brown's example of 'customer journey' taken as part of improving the service of Amtrak company project [4]. During this travel, it was realized that the customers' experience starts from the parking; and taking the seat on the train is only the 8-th step from 10.

There could be many more such examples if the Systematic Innovation Methods were used wider. Meanwhile, the current situation is far from the desirable. The most suitable definition for a niche occupied by the TRIZ is 'marginal'. The presence on the market of individual consultants and companies capable of finding brilliant solutions cannot radically improve the situation. Moreover, the fact, that some specialists can produce incredible ideas while others, using the same tools, produce only trivial solutions, rather testify different innate abilities. Actually, this can even awake distrust. Beside this, in most cases, a solution must be found not by consultant, but by problem owner, just in time. The usage of Lean Production Method is wider but far from the overall. There are some discussions about why such the state of affairs is so dull [5]. One of the explanations may be the lack of scientific validity of these methods.

Scientific justification relies on strict facts checking and consistency with known theories [5, 6]. No set of facts without relying on theory cannot be admitted enough for scientific justification. It concerns also success stories and studies confirming the positive effect of the technique implementation, even with sophisticated statistics [7–9]. As Valeri Souchkov wrote: 'However, if we look at TRIZ from the point of view of modern understanding of science and a broad range of demands and requirements which are used to confirm scientific validity of research, method or theory, we can say that at the moment, TRIZ is a well-developed science only by a stretch of imagination'. The same can be said of other sophisticated Idea Generation Methods.

The method which describes the technologies development laws, teaches 'strong thinking', boosting creativity should be one of the cornerstones of engineering and management education. In fact, TRIZ is taught in a few dozen universities and colleges in the world. The lack of scientific validity is one of the main reasons for this.

In the absence of scientific support, management of companies relies on vague criteria, mostly on 'popularity'. Thus, methods spread according to an epidemic-like scenario. The more popular is the tool, the more chances it has. We are now at the peak of the Design Thinking epidemic, which is largely spread by former Industrial Design students. Just imagine what popularity can acquire a method, studied in most universities and colleges. The situation is intricated by a lot of existing techniques. For example, in [10] 87 different 'Idea Generation Techniques' are listed.

The theoretical approach should also help to put this bunch of tools in order. Relying on experience provides an incredible variety of tools but can never guarantee the absence of 'gaps'. The existence of such gray zones explains the extreme differences in the productivity of users.

The theory allows for chaining different facts and other theories. In such a way the medical diagnosis can rely on a physiological theory, which in turn can base on a biological observation, which is consistent with Darwin's theory and Genetics, the last is closely related with the Chemistry, Physics, and so on up to the Big Bang theory.

## 3   Directed and Undirected Search for Solutions

There is a widely accepted view on the problem-solving process as on exploring a field of possibilities [11, 12]. As a result, only one, maybe a few of the possibilities should be selected. Therefore, problem-solving can be defined as compensation of Uncertainty. The search can be based on the divergent and the convergent strategy. The divergent strategy implies covering as much area as possible. Theoretically, this allows for resolving any problem. On the other hand, even for simple problems, like the simplest puzzles solving, the number of choices often is appeared too large. For finding the solution in a reasonable time, the search must be directed, convergent. This is realized by using special 'rules of thumb' (heuristics). The correctness of all known heuristics has not formally proved. So, their usage can lead to losing useful solutions. A brain constantly uses heuristics for solving routine problems. Unconsciousness attempts to apply these rules to creative problems often leads to impasses.

In short: directed search allows drastic improving productivity but increases the risk of omitting some solutions. Psychologists favor undirected search, as a panacea for impasses and lost solutions [13, 14]. Using ready-made lists of clues or principles, such as TRIZ 40 Inventive principles, Osborn's checklist [15], Lean 8 wastes, or various Design Heuristics [16] also are not welcomed for the same reasons. Proponents of the directed search emphasize its productivity.

In fact, the question has never been so categorical. Solving a problem using heuristics implies backtracking just like the free search. Prioritization based on heuristics does not eliminate the possibility of finding the best and most original solution, increasing only expected productivity. The same is true of using lists of clues, inventive principles, or checklists for overcoming impasses. To prevent the loss of solutions, such lists should be treated as notoriously incomplete. Strict success criteria also can be applied. Other techniques, such as collective work or morphological analysis can be used auxiliary.

The preceding does not abolish the need to seek proven rules and compile as complete a list of inventive principles as possible. These requirements do not imply dumping a bunch of randomly selected heterogeneous clues or drawing up specific instructions for all cases. The contradiction between the universality of general and ease of use of specific recommendations can be solved by the creation of a system, organically combined universal recommendations, and specific examples [17]. Thus, the theoretical approach is no less important than the experience-based.

## 4  The Information Hypothesis and Its Application for Problem Solving

The proposed view is based on the author's Information Hypothesis [18].

Tools, intended for compensating entropy under restrictions, are developed in specific ways. Mainly the progress is realized by collecting adequate information about potential challenges. Increasing the information content inevitably leads to increasing the complexity. At some stages, development is carried out by skipping unnecessary information, simplifying the tool.

Solving a problem anyway goes along existing possibilities and cannot avoid restrictions set by nature. Objective structures, objective laws define the search [3, 4, 11, 12]. This allows us to equate problem-solving processes and evolution.

Let us assume, that there is a class of problems consisting of transferring some entity from one state to another or maintaining its current state despite the environment changes. In short: the problem is to control the entity. Intuitively we can argue that this class contains most of the problems, solved by humans, societies, or nature. Some 'controlling' entities or regulators can be used for providing the job. In some cases, the role of the regulator can be performed by the controlled entity itself. This is the starting point of our consideration, and at the same time, the determination of our domain.

One of the fundamental conditions for providing good control is enough variety (entropy) of the regulator. This requirement is established by the Requisite Variety Law. In the form of the Ashby Theorem [19, 20], this is one of the most fundamental science findings. The law was further elaborated by Conant and Ashby with the requirement for the good regulator to contain the internal model of the regulated entity [21]. The internal model concept can be interpreted as the adequate information about the object and its possible behavior. Therefore, to resolve a problem, adequate information about a controlled entity must be implemented into a regulator. We will try to show, how the analysis of the concept of information and equations of Shannon's Information Theory [22] allows defining some general ways for improving tools and thus, resolving problems.

## 4.1    Problem Solvers - Brains and Techniques

A human brain is amazingly complicated, it is the most complicated thing we ever met. This has a sense only because the brain contains models of all human environments and used for resolving an incredible variety of problems. The difference between problem-solving and classical 'cybernetic' regulation upon closer examination becomes blurred. Some problems can be solved on the locomotion level. For example, a baby tries to reach a favorite toy by performing stochastic moving showing a definite focus on it [23]. A grown person usually uses a more effective method - choosing and testing in the imagination models of the environment, goals and possible means. The control in the 'cybernetic' sense can imply the selection of proper regulators, for example, an injection of different substances, which is the common case in biology. Some of the biological substances can be fairly called 'sophisticated' due to complex structures and accurate action. The last example illustrates the idea of a tool as a means for solving problems. The difference between problem-solving and sophisticated regulation lies in the number of achievable tools.

Without proper tools, the problem is more difficult. Thus, the information contained in a tool saves the efforts to find a solution. Increasing the content of adequate information in the tool allows saving more effort, to resolve more difficult problems. So, the main trend of tools development is increasing information content.

## 4.2    The Information Formula and the Trends of Development

Both Information and Entropy are fundamental, many-sided, and therefore vague concepts. Fortunately, the formulas for measuring their quantity are simple. Claude Shannon proved, that the Entropy formula, is the only equation that fits the criteria of measuring uncertainty [22]. The same equation is used for measuring the amount of information, as a means of compensation of uncertainty:

$$I = -\Sigma_{i=1}^{N} * p_i * log_2(p_i) \tag{1}$$

Where:

N - number of events
$p_i$ - the probability of the i-th event.

Usually, peculiarities of the formula are illustrated by transmitting a text message.

### The Development Trends in the Discrete Determined World

Suppose, that a text is transmitted to some device which can take N states, corresponding to the characters used. If the probability of the occurrence of any character is equal, the formula will be as follows:

$$I = -N * \frac{1}{N} * log_2\left(\frac{1}{N}\right) = log_2(N) \tag{2}$$

From this, the first simple conclusion can be derived. The more states the entity can take (the more characters there are in the alphabet), the more information it can contain. An entity can consist of elements or features, similarly as a text consists of signs. So, increasing the number of entity elements leads to increasing its content of information. Signs in the message should differ one from another. Similarly, the information content of the entity grows when elements differ.

These two trends - increasing the number of elements and increasing the differences are well known in TRIZ. The number of elements can be increased by adding elements or by dividing one entity into elements. The first way corresponds with classical TRIZ Transition to Supersystem Trend (line mono-by-poly), the second - with Transition to Micro Level Trend as described in [24–26]. Increasing the number of states can be achieved also by increasing the number of variable parameters. This way of improving tools is also one of the basic in the TRIZ. It is recommended by some lines of the Dynamicity Trend, Parameters Changes Principle, etc.

Formula (2) gives one more argument for the support of our considerations. Using a tool can increase the number of states, which combined system (a person or machine equipped with a tool) can take. For example, we cannot change the body temperature. Thus, for example, for preparing and preserving food, special devices are used.

### The Development Trends in the Discrete Probabilistic World

The edge case, described by the formula (2), when all the entity states have equal probability, coincident also with the maximum Information/Entropy value. Claude Shannon illustrated this peculiarity by the graph for two alternative states ($p_1 + p_2 = 1$). Maximum Entropy/Information value is reached when $p_1 = p_2 = 0.5$ (see Fig. 1). Thus, for maximizing the information content, all entity states must be equally achievable.

Equality of entity states can be achieved only in case of absence of any restrictions for transitions between states, that is by creating a flexible organization. For example, the flexible production means the absence of restrictions imposed by the batch size, readjustment time, achievable materials, subcontractors, etc.

The notion about independency leads to interesting observation. The independency/autonomy/encapsulation should be one of the most effective principles just like the flexibility. This assumption is confirmed by numerous examples, such as mobile phone, wireless vacuum cleaner or independent military squads.

Symmetry is another antagonist for Information. This is also one of the fundamental concepts. In modern science, Symmetry is understood as any value that remains constant (invariant) under some transformations. The examples can be taken from Geometry, where a figure features can be preserved under reflection, rotation, translation, or scaling. In Physics, the conservation laws are regarded as a manifestation of Symmetry. The Asymmetry principle is one of the most powerful (however, underestimated) in the TRIZ. Any deviation from the constant order in space, in time, an uneven distribution of features can be considered as a violation of Symmetry. So, for example, the Local Quality principle is a manifestation of the Asymmetry.

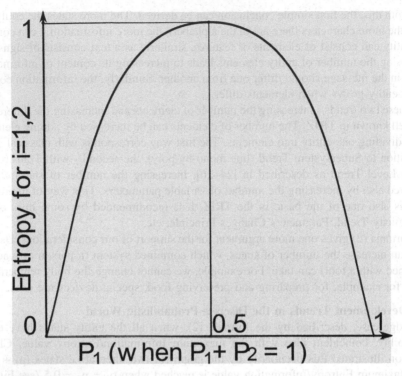

**Fig. 1.** Entropy/Information value for two alternative events. The maximum value is reached when $p_1 = p_2 = 0, 5$, i.e. both events are totally independent from previous state.

## The Development Trends in the Analogical World

Suppose, that letters in a text differ one from another not only by shape but also by color, thickness, incline, dimensions, etc. It can allow drastically increase the information, transmitted by the message. We can imagine differences that cannot be caught by eyes, for example, a chemical compound of the ink, which can be used, for example, for classified messages. Let us take for example colors. How many colors can be used? Seven colors of the rainbow? OK, and how about olive or magenta? It sounds reasonable to use as many colors as possible. The number of colors can be limited only by the ability of eyes or another detector to distinguish similar colors.

The last case illustrates the information transfer by an analog signal. The amount of information transferred by an analog channel is defined by the Shannon - Hartley formula [20]:

$$C = B * log_2\left(1 + \frac{S}{N}\right) \tag{3}$$

Where:

- **C** is the channel capacity.
- **B** is the bandwidth of the channel. For our purposes, it is enough to consider the bandwidth as the working frequency.
- **S** is the average received signal power over the bandwidth.
- **N** is the average power of the noise and interference over the bandwidth.

The last two parameters define the maximum theoretical accuracy of signal change detection. Formula shows, that the information content, measured in time, grows with an increased time interval, frequency, and power. The same formula can be applied to the Information distribution in space. The information content grows with an increasing space interval (length, area, volume), 'symbols' compaction, and differences. Many Inventive Principles can correspond to the formula parameters (see also Fig. 2).

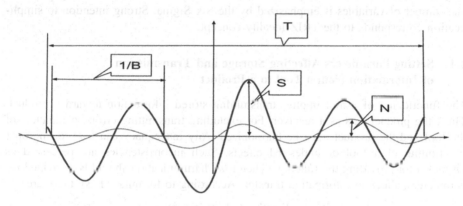

**Fig. 2.** Analogical signal parameters influence to information transfer

Increasing the information content can be achieved by increasing the communication duration (parameter T on the graph). Thus, involving the time before and after session can be useful. The TRIZ Preliminary Action principle is related to the preceding time, Repairing, regeneration or rejecting parts – to after-going time. Performing operations before and after 'Zero Hour' is widely used in the Lean SMED tool. Similarly, engaging inner and outer space of objects are suggested by TRIZ Nested Doll, and Other Way Round principles.

The Partial and Excessive Action, Strong Oxidants principles, and some others deal with amplitude. The Periodic Action, Mechanical Vibration principles, and all lines of transition to Micro-Level Law deal with frequency and 'compaction'. The Anti-Weight, Anti-Action principles deal with the negative values on amplitude axis. The Preliminary Anti-Action is related to preceding time and negative amplitude axis.

## 4.3 Simplification as Getting Rid of Excessive Information

The evolution of tools by increasing information content has a downside – increasing complexity. This can lead to reduced reliability and uncontrolled behavior. Storing and transmitting information also requires carrier (resources). Due to various reasons, for example, suboptimal design, the complexity of a tool can be excessive.

For the reduction of the complexity (decreasing the information content), the means, opposite to described above, may be used. The list of such means includes decreasing the number of system elements by 'trimming', aggregation or encapsulation, unification between elements and within elements, decreasing the number of variable parameters, narrowing the application areas, reducing the amplitudes, the transition to symmetrical shapes. Probably, in some cases, even amplifying the noise may be useful. Some of these ways are proposed by such TRIZ principles as merging, continuity of useful action, equipotentiality, homogeneity. The tendency to standardization and unification clearly prevails in the Lean Production, the tendency to reduce the number of variables is emphasized by the Six Sigma. Strong intention to simplification corresponds to the TRIZ Ideality concept.

## 4.4 Setting Parameters Affecting Storage and Transmission of Information from a Tool to a Product

The functioning of a tool implies transmitting stored information toward a product. Thus, the product acts as a receiver. For excluding transmitting errors, parameters of the tool and the product must be harmonized. Any inadequacy can lead to improper functioning of a tool or undesired effects. Such inconsistencies are perceived as obstacles for providing the function. Therefore, harmonization should be provided for parameters, affecting information transfer. According to formulas (1–3), these are:

- space parameters (positions, directions, dimensions);
- time parameters (start, end, duration);
- number of objects (tools and products);
- number, kind, range (amplitude) and period of changes (variables).

Setting parameters can be illustrated by the metaphor of finding the bypass for an obstacle in the n-dimensional space. A function or attribute must be assigned only at a certain time (time axis), in a certain location (space axes), with a certain amplitude (amplitude axis), etc., in order to avoid obstacles. This can be achieved by applying the OTSM-TRIZ Tongues Model [27], by resolving physical contradictions, or even by asking corresponding questions (where to assign, when to stop, etc.). Such Inventive Principles, as Taking Out, Local Quality, Skipping, Partial or Excessive Action correspond with adjustment in space, time, and amplitude. Just in Time principle of Lean Production can also be attributed to this class.

Along with previously described principles, the listed tools cover most of the Inventive Principles and a lot of other TRIZ tools, expanding on the Lean Production, Axiomatic Design, Six Sigma, etc. [16].

# 5 About the Optimal Search Strategy

In the present work, the promising generalization based on Information Theory for Idea Generation Methods is proposed. This approach can pretty well describe a significant part of TRIZ tools. The generalization extends also to some tools of other methods. To be accepted, this approach should show some predictive value. The variety of different tools and algorithms in modern techniques is excessive. There is no need in increasing this variety. The predictive power of the proposed approach should be aimed at simplifying these methods.

One of the non-trivial conclusions from the Information Approach is the existence of distinct groups of Inventive Principles. From an Information point of view, a tool can be changed in two ways. Its information content can be increased for better functioning or reduced for simplification. Besides this, parameters, influence on information transfer, can be adjusted for excluding functioning errors (undesired effects). Thus, three kinds of improvement goals can be set, and three different (although, partially intersected) sets of Inventive Principles applied. The first nice consequence of this is the relatively small amount of principles in each category. By defining a goal of improvement of a tool, a set of principles, which should be considered for resolving a specific problem can be significantly reduced. All principles in the specific set are logically related. Thus, the solving process can be even simpler. The tool is not functioning well? Its information content should be increased by increasing the number of elements, differences between elements, flexibility, asymmetry, incorporating adjacent time, and space areas. The tool is too complicated? The opposite measures should be taken, including increasing the degree of symmetry, stiffness, narrowing occupied time, and space. Undesired effects are observed? Try to adjust time, space, amplitude, qualitative parameters.

As an example of increasing information content, the solution described in [28] can be taken. For destroying cancer tumors, proton beam treatment can be applied. For minimizing the harm, caused by proton beams, the bolus (compensator) can be used. The thickness of the bolus is varied depending on the location and therefore: - "...it will modify the energy of different parts of the proton beam, and correspondingly modify the penetration depth of the protons, matching the shape of the cancer site" [26]. The bolus appears as the source of information, reframing the proton beam.

Applying Information Theory to TRIZ leads to one more surprising find. The number of principles aimed at increasing the information content significantly exceeds the number of simplification principles. For example, the Asymmetry Principle has no antagonists (the Symmetry Principle). The Law of Transition to Super systems contains a line of increasing differences between elements and does not contain a line of standardization. Meanwhile, the simplification principles can be illustrated by numerous examples.

For example, at the very start of the railway age, numerous locomotion principles were tested. For propelling trains, gear wheels moving on gear racks, artificial legs, cable traction, etc. were offered. Eventually, the most symmetrical round wheel moving on the most symmetrical smooth rail won the competition.

Another example. Two complementary methods of initial problem state description are widely used. The Object-Relation description can be easily represented in the tabular forms. Descriptions of causal relationships are usually presented in graphical form, such as the Ishikawa diagram. Both representations can be useful for creating TRIZ-based software. The software interface can be simplified by combining both representations in one window (the Merging Principle), for example, by connecting the Object-Relation table rows with arrows [29]. This solution is only suitable for very simple descriptions. A chart with more than 6–7 interconnected rows will look like a plate of spaghetti. The solution can be further simplified by the transition to the ordered structure. In the TRIZ-based experimental program created by the author, the table was additionally divided into columns. The first column corresponds to the first raw, second – with the second raw, and so on. Consequences of any Relation of Objects described in raw can be represented in the corresponding column by arrows. The solution proved so simple that it was implemented in form of the Internet-site (Fig. 3)

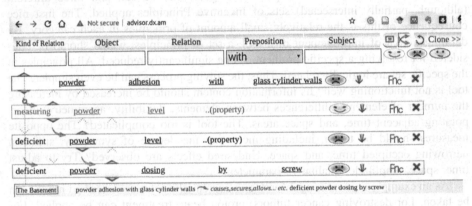

**Fig. 3.** The problem description in the experimental TRIZ-based software (screenshot). Relations between objects are presented in table rows. Blue arrows show causal relations. (Color figure online)

## 6 Conclusion

The Information Theory outcomes show good consistency with practical findings. Our tools help us solve our problems thanks to adequate information content. Acquiring the proper and excluding unnecessary information are the main development trends of human tools, living creature's organs and human's organizations.

Information is just another name for means for compensating Uncertainty, or, which is the same, for resolving problems. This makes the main statement of the present article almost tautology. Increasing the ability of tools for resolving problems is reached by increasing the content of means for resolving problems. The case resembles Darwin's theory which explains the adaptability of living creatures by adaptation. TRIZ and other Systematic Innovation Methods describe, but not explain the ways in which adaptability can be acquired by human tools. Qualitative analysis of the Information

Theory equations can help to explain and systematize these ways and, in perspective, propagate the knowledge to organizations and living creatures.

Many classical TRIZ trends, such as Dynamisation, Transition to Micro-Level, Transition to Super-System are directly followed from the very basic Information Formula. Most of the Inventive Principles can be easily represented on the Information Transfer Graph (Fig. 2). Many principles suggested by other methods are consistent with the Information Theory findings. With enough consideration, most of the examples can be explained by the Information Theory outcomes. Reinventing solutions by applying Information Theory, just like the TRIZ adepts [24] used to reinvent things with numerous TRIZ tools, is an exciting activity.

Without huge data, collected in Systematic Innovation Methods, primarily, in TRIZ, the theoretical considerations would be lifeless. On the other hand, without the theoretical approach, we can improve our skills, but cannot acquire knowledge.

# References

1. Von Bertalanffy, L.: General System Theory: Foundations, Development, Applications. George Braziller, New York (1968)
2. Altshuller, G.S.: Creativity as an Exact Science: The Theory of the Solution of Inventive Problems. Gordon and Breach, UK (1984)
3. Altshuller, G.S.: The Innovation Algorithm: TRIZ, Systematic Innovation and Technical Creativity. Technical Innovation Center, Inc., Worcester (1999)
4. Brown, T.: Change by Design: How Design Thinking Transforms Organizations and Inspires Innovation. Harper Collins, New York (2009)
5. Souchkov, V.: TRIZ in the world: history, current status, and issues of concern. In: 8th MATRIZ International Conference, Moscow, Russia, p. 23 (2016)
6. Popper, K.R.: Objective Knowledge. Oxford University Press, Oxford (1972)
7. Chang, Y.-S., Chien, Y.-H., Yu, K.-C., et al.: Effect of TRIZ on the creativity of engineering students. Think. Skills Creat. 19, 112–122 (2016). https://doi.org/10.1016/j.tsc.2015.10.003
8. Ogot, M., Okudan, G.E.: Integrating systematic creativity into first-year engineering design curriculum. Int. J. Eng. Educ. 22, 109 (2006)
9. Jafari, M., Akhavan, P., Reza Zarghami, H., Asgari, N.: Exploring the effectiveness of inventive principles of TRIZ on developing researchers' innovative capabilities: a case study in an innovative research center. J. Manuf. Technol. Manag. 24, 747–767 (2013)
10. Wang, K.: Towards a taxonomy of idea generation techniques. Found. Manag. 11, 65–80 (2019)
11. Newel, A., Shaw, J.C., Simon, H.A.: Report on a general problem-solving program for a computer, information processing. In: Proceedings of the International Conference of Information Processing, pp. 256–264 (1960)
12. Simon, H.A.: The Sciences of the Artificial, 3rd edn. MIT Press, Cambridge (1996)
13. Simonton, D.K.: Creative thought as blind-variation and selective-retention: combinatorial models of exceptional creativity. Phys. Life Rev. 7, 156–179 (2010). https://doi.org/10.1016/j.plrev.2010.02.002
14. Simonton, D.K.: Creativity and discovery as blind variation: Campbell's (1960) BVSR model after the half-century mark. Rev. Gen. Psychol. 15, 158–174 (2011). https://doi.org/10.1037/a0022912

15. Osborn, A.: Your Creative Power: How to Use Your Imagination to Brighten Life, to Get Ahead. University Press of America, Lanham (2008)
16. Yilmaz, S., Daly, S.R., Seifert, C.M., Gonzalez, R.: Evidence-Based Design Heuristics for Idea Generation. Des. Stud. **46**, 95–124 (2016)
17. Khomenko, N., Ashtiani, M.: Classical TRIZ and OTSM as a scientific theoretical background for non-typical problem-solving instruments. In: Conference Proceedings of TRIZ Future 2007, Frankfurt am Main, Germany (2007)
18. Zadesenets, I.: The key to idea generations: improvement of the system is the management of its information content. https://www.researchgate.net/publication/336838485_The_key_to_idea_generations_Improvement_of_the_system_is_the_management_of_its_information_content (2019)
19. Ashby, W.R.: An Introduction to Cybernetics. Chapman & Hall, London (1956)
20. Ashby, W.R.: Requisite variety and its implications for the control of complex systems. Cybernetica **1**(2), 83–99 (1958)
21. Conant, R.C., Ross Ashby, W.: Every good regulator of a system must be a model of that system. Int. J. Syst. Sci. **1**, 89–97 (1970)
22. Shannon, C.E.: Communication in the presence of noise. Proc. IRE **37**, 10–21 (1949)
23. Duncker, K.: On Problem-Solving. Psychol. Monogr. **58**(5), i (1945)
24. Orloff, M.A.: Inventive Thinking Through TRIZ: A Practical Guide. Springer, Heidelberg (2003). https://doi.org/10.1007/978-3-540-33223-7
25. Petrov, V.: The laws of system evolution. TRIZ J. **3**, 9–17 (2002)
26. Souchkov, V.: Glossary of TRIZ and TRIZ-related terms (2014)
27. Khomenko, N., Cooke, J.: Inventive problem solving using the OTSM-TRIZ "TONGS" model (2011)
28. Seraia, E., Seryi, A.: Accelerating science TRIZ inventive methodology in illustrations. arXiv:1608.00536 (2016)
29. Govindarajan, U.H., Sheu, D.D., Mann, D.: Review of systematic software innovation using TRIZ. Int. J. Syst. Innov. **5**, 72–90 (2019)
30. Zadesenets, I., Advisor: Experimental TRIZ-based software. http://advisor.dx.am/. Accessed 14 Aug 2020

# Education and Pedagogy

# Easy-to-Use Ideation Technique Based on Five Cross-Industry Analogies Enhances Engineering Creativity of Students and Specialists

Pavel Livotov[✉]

Offenburg University of Applied Sciences, Badstr. 24, 77652 Offenburg,
Germany
pavel.livotov@hs-offenburg.de

**Abstract.** Cross-Industry Innovation is commonly understood as identification
of analogies and interdisciplinary transfer or copying of technologies, processes,
technical solutions, working principles or models between industrial sectors. In
general, creative thinking in analogies belongs to the efficient ideation techniques. However, engineering graduates and specialists frequently lack the skills
to think across the industry boundaries systematically. To overcome this
drawback an easy-to-use method based on five analogies has been evaluated
through its applications by students and engineers in numerous experiments and
industrial case studies. The proposed analogies help to identify and resolve
engineering contradictions and apply approaches of the Theory of Inventive
Problem Solving TRIZ and biomimetics. The paper analyses the outcomes of
the systematized analogies-based ideation and outlines that its performance
continuously grows with the engineering experience. It defines metrics for
ideation efficiency and ideation performance function. Finally, a comparison
with other TRIZ inventive techniques, such as nine fields of the Substance-Field
Analysis and 40 Inventive Principles is presented.

**Keywords:** Engineering creativity · Ideation performance function · Ideation
efficiency · Cross-industry innovation · TRIZ

## 1 Initial Situation

### 1.1 Introduction

The paper is addressing the needs of the universities, enterprises, and society regarding
qualification of students and specialists in engineering creativity and inventiveness.
Analysis of the relationship between creativity and engineering education outlines the
necessity of special activities and courses that would enhance innovative skills of
graduate engineers [1]. The engineering educators have proposed in the last two
decades different education approaches in the systematic innovation. The analysis of
the top cited scientific publications on innovative design [2] confirms that the theory of
inventive problem solving TRIZ developed by Altshuller and his co-workers [3]
belongs today to one of the most organized and comprehensive methodologies for

© IFIP International Federation for Information Processing 2020
Published by Springer Nature Switzerland AG 2020
D. Cavallucci et al. (Eds.): TFC 2020, IFIP AICT 597, pp. 103–121, 2020.
https://doi.org/10.1007/978-3-030-61295-5_9

invention knowledge and creative thinking. Cascini et al. [4] report about the enhancement of problem-solving skills of engineering students with TRIZ. In a series of experiments Belski and co-authors demonstrate that TRIZ inventive heuristics such as fields and interactions of the Substance-Field Analysis can statistically significantly improve the ideation productivity of engineering students [5]. Among other TRIZ tools, the 40 Inventive Principles remain the most frequently used tool in practice. A recent study evaluates 194 experiments and outlines that the less abstract and problem specific formulation of TRIZ Inventive Principles improves idea generation outcomes both in the quantity and variety of proposed ideas [6].

Another approach for faster and easier ideation and inventive problem solving is based on the interdisciplinary analogies. Gordon, the co-creator of the Synectics method, outlined that creative thinking in analogies belongs to efficient creativity techniques [7]. The identification of analogies and transfer of technologies, technical solutions, working principles between industrial sectors is commonly defined as cross-industry innovation [8]. It promises advantages for enterprises in reduction of their R&D expenditures and has in accordance with [9] a high potential to create radical ideas. The VDI Standard [10] includes modern TRIZ tools supporting cross-industry innovation such as Function-Oriented Search and Feature Transfer. However, engineering graduates and specialists often lack the skills to think across the industry boundaries systematically. To overcome this drawback this paper presents an easy-to-use method based on interdisciplinary analogies. It analyses the gain in quantity, variety and efficiency of ideation based on the systematized thinking in analogies for individual and collective use in a group. Finally, it discusses merging opportunities with TRIZ 40 Inventive Principles and a heuristic based on the fields of the Substance-Field Analysis.

## 1.2    Creative Thinking in Interdisciplinary Analogies

To help increase the ideation capability of engineering students and specialists, a fast and easy-to-use technique applying five interdisciplinary analogies has been initially proposed by the author in [11]. Table 1 shows 5 ideation steps of this cross-industry heuristic and outlines corresponding innovative design tools and approaches.

**Table 1.** Five interdisciplinary analogies for rapid cross-industry idea generation.

| N° | Analogy | Corresponding innovative design tool or approach |
|---|---|---|
| Step 1 | How is a similar problem solved in technical domains or fields like yours? | Morphological analysis, feature transfer (TRIZ) |
| Step 2 | Extract the primary useful function UF. How is a similar UF realized in other technical domains? | Function-oriented search FOS (TRIZ) |
| Step 3 | Extract the primary negative effect NE. How is a similar NE counteracted in other technical domains? | Function-oriented search FOS (TRIZ) |
| Step 4 | How similar problem is solved in very small systems up to the micro or nano-level (downscale) and in the huge macro- and giga-systems (upscale)? | TRIZ operators: size-time-costs; transfer to micro-level |
| Step 5 | How is a similar problem solved in the nature (living organisms, cells, plants, insects, animals, humans)? | Bionic/biomimetics |

The application of the analogies starts with the problem definition. Let us illustrate it with a problem of roadway condition monitoring in autonomous cars: "A sensor, for example a camera, for detection of road condition (dry, wet, dirty, icy) is placed in a vehicle close to the road surface to detect its properties. This working principle requires a protection of the sensor from getting dirty or damages". The primary useful function can be formulated as "Control or analysis of surface properties" and the task for elimination of primary harmful effect can be defined as "Protection of sensitive surfaces from getting dirty or damages".

After a problem has been defined, the user(s) can start idea generation phase working individually with the help of the idea-generation form (see Table 1) and trying to record as many ideas as possible within 20...25 min with a recommendation to spend about 4...5 min for each analogy. If several persons are participating in the problem solving, their individual contributions must be merged to the common idea pool, where the duplicate or similar entries must be deleted during the idea evaluation step.

## 2 Experimental Verification of the Ideation Technique

### 2.1 Experimental Method

In the initial experiment performed by the author in 2018 [11], the Roadway condition monitoring problem has been offered to three groups of mechanical and process engineering students and one interdisciplinary group of engineers, as presented in the Table 2. The Control group did not use the analogies or any other creativity tools for idea generation. All other groups used five analogies for idea generation and were supervised by the same tutor. The experiment participation was voluntary and anonymous. The form to record ideas was distributed to the participants just before the problem definition was presented. The number of different ideas proposed by each individual participant, the distribution of these ideas over analogies, number of different ideas within each group were estimated by two independent assessors. Similar to the approach proposed by Belski [5], the ideas were also assigned to the nine fields of MATCEMIBD knowledge domains (known from Substance-Field Analysis in TRIZ): Mechanical, Acoustic, Thermal, Chemical, Electric, Magnetic, Intermolecular, Biological and Data processing (Digitization).

**Table 2.** Participant groups in the first experiment [11].

| Group 1 | 40 bachelor students: 15 persons in 4th semester of mechanical engineering degree and 25 persons in 4th semester of process engineering degree |
|---|---|
| Group 2 | 25 master's students enrolled into the master's degree in mechanical engineering in 8th or 9th semesters |
| Group 3 | Industrial group of 13 engineers from 8 companies: mechanical, electrical, energy, constriction engineers and physicists involved in R&D activities |
| Group 4 | Control group: 40 bachelor students in 4th semester of the bachelor of mechanical engineering degree |

Among typical objective metrics of ideation effectiveness such as quantity, variety, novelty, feasibility, and quality of proposed ideas [12], only the quantity and variety of ideas have been evaluated in the experiment. Table 3 presents the set of metrics which were selected for the ideation performance assessment.

**Table 3.** Metrics for ideation performance assessment used in experiments.

| S. | Description | Category |
|---|---|---|
| $N_t$ | Total number of ideas generated in a group with $n$ members | Group metric |
| $N_d$ | Total number of different (unique) ideas generated in a group | Group metric |
| $P_m$ | Mean number of ideas proposed by individual participant within one ideation session (average ideation productivity): $P_m = N_t/n$ | Individual metric |
| $P_{md}$ | Mean number of different (unique) ideas per person within a group with $n$ members within one session: $P_{md} = N_d/n$ | Group metric |
| $E_r$ | Relative efficiency of ideation, defined as quotient of number of different ideas in a group to the total ideas number: $E_r = N_d/N_t$ | Group metric |
| $V_1$– $V_9$ | Variety of ideas proposed by individual participants as distribution of different ideas over the nine MATCEMIBD domains as percentage of mechanical ideas $V_1$, acoustic ideas $V_2$ etc. | Individual and group metric |
| $t_m$ | Average time expenditures for generation of one unique idea within a group during one ideation session | Group metric |

## 2.2  Discussion of Results

The quantitative analysis of the results in different groups, presented in Table 4, shows that the cross-industry analogies effectively support the ideation process. A participant from each experimental group 1, 2 or 3 generated on average significantly more ideas than a student from the Control group 4. The following are some outcomes of the Mann-Whitney Test that was used for the statistical comparison of responses in the experiments: Control group 4 versus Bachelor group 1 with $Z = -6{,}22$, $p < 0{,}001$; Bachelor group 1 vs. Master group 2 with $Z = -2{,}97$, $p < 0{,}01$; Master group 2 vs. Industrial group 3 with $Z = -1{,}40$, $p < 0{,}1$.

It is also interesting to compare the ideas productivity over cross-industry analogies. As presented in Fig. 1, the Industrial group 3 has rather uniform distribution of ideas over all five analogies. On the contrary, the students in the groups 1 and 2 demonstrate their weakness in abstract thinking with the scaling-analogy N.4: Bachelor group 1 vs. Industrial group 3 with $Z = -2{,}61$, $p < 0{,}01$; Master group 2 vs. Industrial group 3 with $Z = -1{,}46$, $p < 0{,}1$. In general, the evaluation of the experiment confirms the advantages of applying all five analogies. The study also reveals that the ideation performance, based on the systematized analogical thinking, continuously grows with the engineering experience.

The results also demonstrate a higher degree of analogies-based creativity of the graduate students (Group 2) versus the undergraduate students (Group 1). There is no statistically significant difference in ideation productivity within the Bachelor group 1 between 15 mechanical engineering students with 6,80 ideas per person (SD = 3.17) and 25 process engineering students with 6,76 ideas per person (SD = 2.69).

The variety of different ideas, defined as their distribution over the nine MAT-CEMIBD fields, was significantly broader in the Groups 1 and 2 in comparison with the Control group 4. Substantial differences were found in a high percentage of purely mechanical ideas (67%) and no biological ideas at all in the Control group.

## 2.3   Evaluation and Modeling of Ideation Efficiency

Idea generation can be carried out in a group or individually. The number of high-quality ideas positively correlates with the total number of proposed ideas. The ratio of high-quality ideas number to a total ideas number is usually specified as ideation quality function [13]. Thus, a major outcome of any ideation technique is the number of different or independent ideas which can be proposed by the group of $n$ users ($n \geq 1$) within a given time. The number of different ideas $N_d$ proposed in each group in one ideation session divided by the total number of the ideas in the session $N_t$ can be defined as a relative ideation efficiency of a group $E_r$ (see Table 4).

**Table 4.** Ideation performance assessment for different participant groups.

| Group | Number of participants | Total number of ideas | Total number of unique ideas | Number of ideas per person: mean (SD) | Percentage of mechanical ideas | Mean number. of unique ideas per person | Relative. Efficiency of a group | Average time for one unique idea in a group, min |
|---|---|---|---|---|---|---|---|---|
| | $n$ | $N_t$ | $N_d$ | $P_m$ | | $V_1$ | $P_{md}$ | $E_r$ | $t_m$ |
| 1. Bachelor students | 40 | 271 | 59 | 6,78 (SD = 2,88) | 42% | 1,48 | 0,22 | 13,6 |
| 2. Master students | 25 | 240 | 73 | 9,60 (SD = 3,75) | 41% | 2,92 | 0,30 | 6,9 |
| 3. Engineers (industrial) | 13 | 152 | 70 | 11,69 (SD = 4,10) | 47% | 5,38 | 0,46 | 3,7 |
| 4. Control (students) | 40 | 114 | 39 | 2,85 (SD = 1,42) | 67% | 0,98 | 0,34 | 20,5 |

The relative ideation efficiency value $E_r = N_d/N_t$ can be influenced by many factors and variables, such as qualification, experience, creativity, or educational diversity of individual participants, but also by the number of group members $n$ and the total number of generated ideas $N_t$. Noteworthy that in the experiment the relative ideation efficiency $E_r$ does not exceed the value of 35% for the number of group members higher than 20. Moreover, by the same number of participants $n = 40$ in the Students' groups 1 and Control group 4, the relative ideation efficiency $E_r$ of the Control group 4 is higher. It is possible that due to the creative impact of the cross-industry analogies the students of the Group 1 could generate significantly more ideas but the growth of the total number of different ideas $N_d$ has slowed. This aspect is further analyzed below.

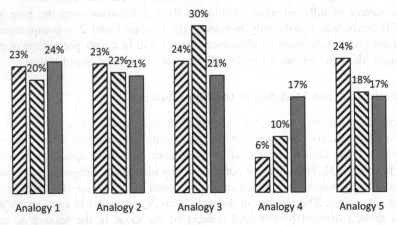

**Fig. 1.** Distribution of total amount of ideas created with different analogies [11].

Obviously that in a group consisting of one person ($n = 1$) the number of different ideas $N_d$ equals the total number of ideas $N_t$: $N_d = N_t$. In a group with an infinite number of members ($n \rightarrow \infty$) the relative ideation efficiency value $E_r = N_d/N_t$ tends towards zero ($E_r \rightarrow \infty$) if a finite total number of solution ideas is presumed. Such assumption is reasonable for the so called closed-ended problems with a finite number of feasible solution alternatives or with a limited search field [13]. Under these constrains the following exponential model can be applied for assessment of the relative ideation efficiency:

$$E_r = N_d/N_t = exp\left[-\alpha \cdot (n-1)^\beta\right] \tag{1}$$

The coefficients $\alpha$ and $\beta$ can be determined using existing experimental data for known values of $N_d$, $N_t$ and $n$. Assuming the average individual ideation productivity $P_m$ in a group ($P_m = N_t/n$ - mean number of ideas per person) as a constant, it is possible to determine the *ideation performance function* as a number of different ideas $N_d$ in a group with the Eq. (2):

$$N_d(n) = n \cdot P_m \cdot exp\left[-\alpha \cdot (n-1)^\beta\right] \tag{2}$$

The shape coefficient $\beta$ varies between 0 and 1. For the practical use, it appears to be helpful to postulate a maximum number of group members (e.g. $n_{max} = 150$) which will reach the ideation limit and corresponds to the maximum quantity of different ideas

$N_{dmax}$ generated by a group in a given time. In other words, a group with the number of participants $n > n_{max}$ will not be able to propose more different ideas than $N_{dmax}$ value. In this case the formula (2) can be applied in the range between $n = 1$ and $n = n_{max}$ values.

Figure 2 illustrates a calculation example for the Group 1 (see Table 4) with $n = 40$, $N_t = 271$, $N_d = 59$, $P_m = 6{,}78$, $n_{max} = 150$, $\alpha = 0{,}368$ and $\beta = 0{,}388$. The ideation performance curve $N_d(n)$ hits properly two independent experimental points ($n = 16$; $N_d = 33$) and ($n = 24$; $N_d = 53$) with the relative error between the simulated and experimental values less than 12,9%. Interestingly, the simulation reveals that the assumed maximum number of group members ($n_{max} = 150$) leads to the ideation limit of $N_{dmax} = 78$. That means that the undergraduate students using the same ideation technique and with the same qualification as in the Group 1 most likely will not generate more the 78 different ideas in total, independently of the number of persons participating in the ideation session.

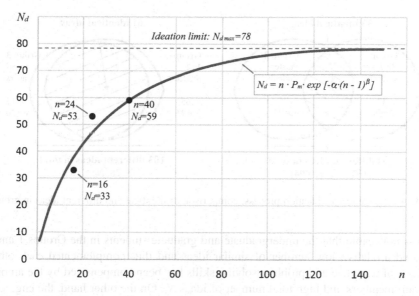

**Fig. 2.** Ideation performance function: estimation of total quantity of different ideas $N_d$ in one ideation session as a function of the group members number $n$ (Group 1: $n = 40$, $N_d = 59$, $P_m = 6{,}78$) and comparison with experimental data ($n = 16$; $N_d = 33$) and ($n = 24$; $N_d = 53$).

Additional parameter, which can be applied as a group metric of ideation effectiveness, is the average time required to generate one unique idea. This parameter has been estimated for the Bachelor group 1 with 13,6 min, for the Master group 2 with 6,9 min, for the Industrial group 3 with 3,7 min, and for the Control group 4 with 20,5 min. These results speak for themselves: the examined analogies-based ideation method enhances the engineering creativity of students and specialists.

## 2.4    Completeness of the Ideation Process

An important question to be discussed in the context of the effectiveness of any ideation method is how to evaluate the completeness of the ideation process. In other words, it is necessary to estimate the ideation limit of the method and to clarify how comprehensive the ideation technique helps to approaching the closed-ended problems with a finite number of feasible solutions. In this respect, it was found that the students of the Control group did not propose any different ideas that were not generated by the Students in the groups 1 and 2 with the cross-industry analogies. At the same time, a direct comparison of 132 different ideas from the Students' groups 1 and 2 identifies 38 identical ideas only. Thus, the total number of different ideas proposed by the students from the Groups 1 and 2 is $N_d = 94$. Comparing these 94 different ideas with 70 different ideas of the Industrial group 3, one can identify 61 identical ideas. Therefore, the total number of different ideas generated in the experiment in the Groups 1, 2 and 3 with a total of 78 participants reaches $N_d = 103$, as illustrated in Fig. 3.

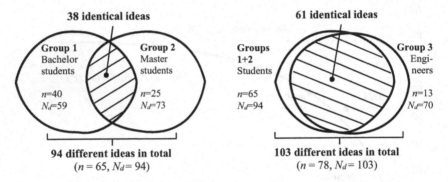

**Fig. 3.** Completeness of ideation process: comparison of identical and different ideas in groups.

It is noticeable that the undergraduate and graduate students in the Groups 1 and 2 proposed a relative low number of similar ideas and thus complemented each other. The lack of expertise and problem-solving skills has been compensated by the amount of group members and high total number of ideas $N_t$. On the other hand, the engineers in the smaller Group 3 generated about 70% of all different ideas in experiment and proposed among them 9 unique solution ideas overseen by the students. This fact underlines the advantages of the interdisciplinary analogies for rapid cross-industry idea generation for all groups of users. The proposed ideation technique is suitable both for use in a group and for individual work. But it is important to emphasize the benefits of the application in a group because of a significant gap between the average individual ideation productivity with $P_m = 7,8...11,7$ ideas per session and the ideation performance of a group with $N_d = 59...103$ different ideas per session.

The data collected in this study allows to evaluate the ideation limit of the suggested creativity technique for the experimental problem of Roadway condition monitoring. Figure 4 presents the ideation outcomes of all Groups and shows the course of the ideation performance function (2) for the merged group combined from the Groups 1, 2 and 3. The simulation is based on the following data: total number of participants $n = 78$, total number of ideas $N_t = 663$, total number of different ideas $N_d = 103$, average individual productivity $P_m = 8,50$, maximum number of group members $n_{max} = 150$, calculated coefficients $\alpha = 0,316$ and $\beta = 0,408$. The estimated ideation limit of the combined group has a value of $N_{dmax} = 112$ ideas. A comparison of the *ideation performance* curves presented in Fig. 2 and Fig. 4 reveals that the ideation limit $N_{dmax}$ depends on the relative ideation efficiency $E_r$ of a group and on the average individual productivity $P_m$ of the group members. Consequently, the Industrial group 3 has the highest anticipated ideation limit of $N_{dmax} = 175$ ideas, the students' groups show correspondingly the ideation limit values $N_{dmax}$ of 121 for the Master group 2 and 78 for the Bachelor group 1. The lowest ideation limit of $N_{dmax} = 52$ can be expected in the Control group of the Bachelor students who did not use any ideation method in the experiments.

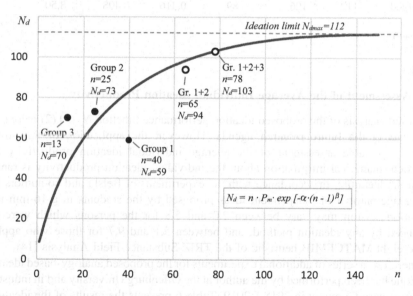

**Fig. 4.** Estimation of the average ideation limit for the proposed creativity technique ($N_d$ - total number of different ideas in ideation session, $n$ – number of the group members).

The simulated ideation limit values will be reached in the merged group with a max. number of $n_{max} = 150$ participants. In the practice it is important to estimate the number ideation session participants $n_{95}$ which is required to achieve 95% of the ideation limit $N_{dmax}$. The results of the calculations performed with the formula (2) are summarized in Table 5.

**Table 5.** Estimation of practical ideation limit and corresponding practical group size.

| Group | Ideation limit | Practical ideation limit | Pract. group size | Form coefficient | Shape coefficient | Average ideation productivity |
|---|---|---|---|---|---|---|
| | $N_{dmax}$ | $0{,}95{\cdot}N_{dmax}$ | $n_{95}$ | $\alpha$ | $\beta$ | $P_m$ |
| 1. Bachelor students | 78 | 74 | 86 | 0,368 | 0,388 | 6,78 |
| 2. Master students | 121 | 115 | 89 | 0,333 | 0,401 | 9,60 |
| 3. Engineers | 175 | 166 | 89 | 0,265 | 0,432 | 11,69 |
| 4. Control (bach. students) | 52 | 49 | 78 | 0,181 | 0,484 | 2,85 |
| 5. Students' groups 1 + 2 | 107 | 101 | 86 | 0,302 | 0,414 | 7,86 |
| 6. Merged group 1 + 2 + 3 | 112 | 106 | 89 | 0,316 | 0,408 | 8,50 |

## 2.5   Assessment of the Average Individual Ideation Productivity

A detailed analysis of the proposed ideation performance function $N_d(n)$ (2) belongs to the issues of the future research agenda. However, the application of this model requires a reliable assessment of the average individual ideation productivity $P_m$. Consistent numerical information about the individual ideation productivity is rare to find in the literature. In accordance with the experiments of Belski and co-authors [5], the average number of independent ideas proposed by the students in a 16-min idea generation session may vary between 2,0 and 5,8 for the persons which were not influenced by any ideation method, and between 5,1 and 9,7 for those who applied simple eight MATCEMIB heuristic of the TRIZ Substance-Field Analysis [14].

   Therefore, a series of additional experiments for the proposed analogy-based ideation technique has been performed by the author at the Offenburg University and in industrial environment in Germany in 2018…2019. Table 6 presents the results of the idea generation sessions in the course "Innovative Product Development" for the graduate students enrolled into the Master's degree in mechanical engineering. The students worked under supervision of the tutor in a classroom in small teams on their semester projects using the idea-generation form (see Table 1). The students tried to generate personally as many ideas as possible within 20…25 min with a recommendation to spend about 4… 5 min for each analogy. After the individual idea generation session, the students' contributions have been merged to the team idea pool, where the duplicate or similar entries were identified and deleted. As shown in Table 6, the average individual ideation productivity $P_m$ in the projects varies between 6,50 and 12,25 with a mean value of 9,35 that corresponds to the results of other studies. For example, in the experiment discussed in the Sect. 2 the average $P_m$ value of the Master students' group 2 was 9,60.

**Table 6.** Ideation performance assessment in students' product development projects.

| Team number and project domain | Number of team members | Total number of ideas | Total number of unique ideas | Average ideation productivity (ideas per pers.) | Mean number. of unique ideas per person | Rel. efficiency of a group | Average time for one unique idea in group |
|---|---|---|---|---|---|---|---|
| | $n$ | $N_t$ | $N_d$ | $P_m$ | $P_{md}$ | $E_r$ | $t_m$, min |
| 1. Automotive sector | 4 | 41 | 24 | **10,25** | 6,00 | 0,59 | 3,3 |
| 2. Payment service | 2 | 13 | 11 | **6,50** | 5,50 | 0,85 | 3,6 |
| 3. Bakery service | 5 | 50 | 25 | **10,00** | 5,00 | 0,50 | 4,0 |
| 4. Petrol station | 4 | 27 | 17 | **6,75** | 4,25 | 0,63 | 4,7 |
| 5. Charging of e-cars | 3 | 26 | 18 | **8,67** | 6,00 | 0,69 | 3,3 |
| 6. Water treatment | 3 | 33 | 26 | **11,00** | 8,67 | 0,79 | 2,3 |
| 7. Fuel cell system | 4 | 49 | 31 | **12,25** | 7,75 | 0,63 | 2,6 |
| *Mean values* | *3,6* | *34,1* | *21,7* | ***9,35*** | *6,17* | *0,67* | *3,4* |

Results of practical application of the proposed analogies-based ideation technique in German industrial companies are presented in Table 7. These data stem from a series of problem-solving workshops moderated by author in 2018–2019. The ideation tool was applied in the initial phase of the workshops just after the problem definition. The workshop participants were R&D engineers, production and process engineers and product managers. They worked individually within 20…25 min using the idea-generation form (see Table 1). The proposed ideas have been processed by the workshop moderator.

**Table 7.** Ideation performance assessment in industrial problem-solving workshops.

| Workshop number and project domain | Number of team members | Total number of ideas | Total number of unique ideas | Average ideation productivity (ideas per person) | Mean number. of unique ideas per person | Relative. Efficiency of a group | Average time for one unique idea in a group |
|---|---|---|---|---|---|---|---|
| $n$ | $N_t$ | $N_d$ | $P_m$ | $P_{md}$ | $E_r$ | $t_m$, min |
| 1. Sensor technology | 17 | 220 | 84 | 13,75 | 4,94 | 0,38 | 4,0 |
| 2. Civil engineering | 16 | 245 | 78 | 15,31 | 4,88 | 0,32 | 4,1 |
| 3. Bonding technology | 15 | 236 | 93 | 15,73 | 6,20 | 0,39 | 3,2 |
| 4. Sealing technology | 14 | 188 | 52 | 13,43 | 3,71 | 0,28 | 5,4 |
| 5. Measuring technique | 15 | 213 | 92 | 14,12 | 6,13 | 0,43 | 3,3 |
| 6. Medical equipment | 14 | 164 | 51 | 11,71 | 3,64 | 0,31 | 5,5 |
| *Mean values* | *15,2* | *211* | *75* | *14,01* | *4,92* | *0,35* | *4,25* |

The average individual ideation productivity $P_m$ in the industrial problem-solving workshops varies between 11,75 and 15,73 with a mean value of 14,01 that is higher than the value of $P_m = 11,69$ shown by the engineers from the Group 3 in the experiment evaluated in the Sect. 2.

The estimated mean values in Table 7 allow to determine coefficients of the Eq. (2) for prediction of the ideation performance of the analogies-based techniques in the practice: $\alpha = 0,374$, $\beta = 0,386$. The resulting ideation limit for the individual ideation productivity $P_m = 14,0$ ideas, max. group size $n_{max} = 150$ and ideation time of 20…25 min is $N_{dmax} = 160$. The group size corresponding to the practical ideation limit of $(0,95 \cdot N_{dmax}) = 152$ is $n_{95} = 88$. Thus, the number of different ideas $N_d$ in an ideation session with 25 engineers ($n = 25$) can be anticipated with the following formula:

$$N_d(25) = 25 \cdot 14,0 \cdot exp\left[-0,374 \cdot (25-1)^{0,386}\right] \approx 98 \qquad (3)$$

It should be underlined that the estimated results are based on the individual contributions of the participants of the ideation sessions. Consequently, the idea generation can be performed by individual contributors asynchronously at different times. The ideation session manager is responsible for merging of proposed ideas to the idea pool.

# 3   Enhancement Potential Through TRIZ Inventive Methods

## 3.1   Limitations of the Analogies-Based Ideation Technique

The proposed ideation technique can be characterized by its simplicity and a relatively high quantity of ideas generated in a short time. As a matter of fact, the time expenditures of each idea contributor can be considered with 20...25 min as low. With the number of contributors larger than 10 the ideation technique allows to record a considerable quantity of ideas. In accordance with Alex Osborn, the creator of Brainstorming, increasing of ideas quantity helps to generate more ideas of higher quality [15]. Altshuller, the creator of the Theory of Inventive Problem Solving TRIZ [3], and contemporary researchers [13] underline that the idea quantity does not significantly increase the number of high-quality ideas. Moreover, the application of the analogies-based technique by a single person or in smaller groups with less than 10 participants remains clearly behind the ideation limit values. Therefore, a series of additional ideation experiments using simple TRIZ tools such as MATCEMIBD heuristic and selected 40 Inventive Principles has been conducted with an objective of enhancing the analogies-based creativity method.

## 3.2   Applied TRIZ Ideation Tools and Experimental Method

The nine MATCEMIBD fields of the TRIZ Substance-Field Analysis is a simple and easy-to-use heuristic that improves the ideation productivity [6, 14]. Its usefulness stems from the ability to effectively act as prompts to search for solutions that are relevant to a particular field of MATCEMIBD [14]. The ninth Informational field (D) has been proposed in [6] in order to underline the role of the Data processing, Artificial Intelligence and Digitalization in modern technical systems. Table 8 presents the nine fields of MATCEMIBD together with some examples of interactions related to each individual field.

Among other TRIZ tools, the 40 Inventive Principles [3, 10] can be easily used for structured idea generation and directed brainstorming. They act as inventive operators proposing directions for transformation of a technical system and its components to enhance useful functions, eliminate harm and consequently to overcome engineering contradictions. One of the latest updates of this tool for process engineering [6] contains 160 sub-principles with nearly 70 additional sub-principles. These 160 sub-principles can be assigned to three categories: field-independent, field-universal, and field-oriented. The field-independent category includes sub-principles, which do not relate directly to any field or engineering domain, like for example *1e) Segment process* or *2d) Trim process steps*. The category "field-universal" includes the sub-principles which can be assigned to any of MATCEMIBD-fields, like *4b) Enhance asymmetry*. To these two categories belong respectively 36 and 29 sub-principles. The idea generation with the field-independent or field universal sub-principles does not necessarily cause a change of the "field" in the working principle of a technical system. Other 95 field-oriented principles can be assigned directly to one of the MATCEMIBD-fields [16]. Table 9 presents a balanced combination of 10 TRIZ Inventive Principles with 15 field-independent, field-universal, field-oriented inventive sub-principles selected for the ideation experiment. These sub-principles are suitable for solving engineering design problems and do not duplicate the MATCEMIBD heuristic. The outcomes of ideation work with the TRIZ Inventive Principles may depend on a certain interpretation of the abstract terms like "object", "action" or "function. To reduce the level of abstractness in the experiment, the term "object" was additionally illustrated in the idea generation form with a context-specific name of a real system component.

**Table 8.** Nine fields of MATCEMIBD with examples of interactions for fast idea generation.

| Field | Examples of interactions |
|---|---|
| 1. Mechanical | Gravitation, centrifugal force, collisions, friction, mechanical treatment, vibration, resonance, gas/fluid dynamics, vacuum, …, etc. |
| 2. Acoustic | Sound, ultrasound, infrasound, cavitation |
| 3. Thermal | Heating, cooling, insulation, thermal expansion, phase/state change, endo- or exothermic reactions, fire, burning, heat radiation, …, etc. |
| 4. Chemical | Chemical reactions, explosion, compounds, catalysts, inhibitors, indicators (pH), dissolving, crystallization, polymerization, odour, taste, …, etc. |
| 5. Electrical | Electrostatic charges, conductors, insulators, semiconductors, electric field, current, electrolysis, piezo-electrics, ionisation, discharge, …, etc. |
| 6. Magnetic | Magnetic field, forces and particles, induction, electromagnetic waves (X-rays, microwaves.), optics, optical effects, translucence change, …, etc. |
| 7. Intermolecular | Subatomic (nano) particles, capillary, pores, radiation, fusion, laser, surface tension, adhesion, cohesion, Lotus effect, …, etc. |
| 8. Biological | Microbes, bacteria, living organisms, plants, fungi, cells, enzymes Bionic/biomimetics. Human resources |
| 9. Data processing | Information and data processing, automatic control, sensors, cloud computing, big data, digitalization, virtual reality, artificial intelligence, …, etc. |

The problem of vacuum cleaning of carpets was proposed for the experiments in form of engineering contradiction: the powerful suction floor and carpet nozzle efficiently removes dust, dirt and pet hair from the carpet (*positive function*) but can damage carpet fibers (*negative property*).

Two groups of undergraduate and graduate students from different years of study in Offenburg University of Applied Sciences, Germany participated in the experiment. 18 undergraduate students belonged to the 5–6th semester of Mechanical and Process Engineering program, whilst 15 graduate students were in their 8th and 9th study semesters of the Master Degree in Mechanical Engineering. All experiment participants were comprehensively advised in application of ideation tools by the same tutor. The experiment included three ideation sessions with one session per week. In the first session with a duration of 20…25 min the analogies-based ideation technique has been applied in initial phase of problem-solving. In the second session with the duration of 25...30 min students extended their idea collections with the help of the MATCEMIBD fields (Table 8) with about 3 min for each field. And finally, in the third session with the duration of 40...50 min the selection of inventive sub-principles in Table 9 has been applied with about 4...5 min per inventive principle. In each session the students worked individually using idea generation forms. In each ideation session the duplicates or similar ideas were deleted, and only different ideas were documented by the students.

**Table 9.** Inventive TRIZ sub-principles selected for the ideation experiment.

| Name of TRIZ inventive principle | Inventive sub-principles selected for idea generation |
| --- | --- |
| 1. Segmentation: | 1(a) Divide the object into independent objects or parts. |
| 2. Leaving out | 2(b) Remove disturbing components, parts or substances |
| 3. Local quality | 3(a) Change the uniform structure of an object to a non-uniform. 3(c) Various parts of the object should fulfil different functions. |
| 4. Asymmetry | 4(a) Replace the symmetrical object shape or property by asymmetrical. |
| 5. Combining | 5(a) Combine identical objects in space to perform parallel operations, use simultaneously two or more objects instead of one. |
| 6. Universality: | 6(a) Make an object universal, performing multiple functions. |
| 7. Nesting and integration | 7(a) Place an object inside another one, which, in turn, is placed inside a third object and so on. 7(c) Use telescoping objects. |
| 13. Inversion: | 13(b) Make moving parts of the object fixed, and the fixed parts movable. 13(c) Turn the object or process upside down. |
| 14. Sphericity | 14(a) Replace rectilinear form of the object with curved or ball shaped. 14(c) Provide rotary motion of parts, substances or force fields. |
| 15. Dynamism and adaptability | 15(a) Make an object adjustable to enable optimal performance at each stage of operation. 15(b) Make the object parts movable to each other. |

## 3.3   Discussion of Results

Table 10 presents the average number of different ideas proposed by each individual student in each ideation session as well as the total number of different ideas in the experiment. The individual ideation performance $P_m$ of the graduate students was slightly higher than the performance of the undergraduate students. The application of the cross-industry analogies in the first session results in $P_m = 8...23$ ideas per person with the mean values of 15,2 and standard deviation of SD = 3,9 for undergraduate students and with mean values of 15,9 (SD = 3,7) for graduate students. Interestingly that the outcomes of the second MATCEMIBD session ($P_m = 8...33$) and of the third session with the selected TRIZ inventive sub-principles ($P_m = 6...28$) show significantly higher variance in individual ideation performance. However, the average values of $P_m$ remain almost the same in all phases of experiment.

This fact can be explained by the observed five segments of the participants with the increasing, constant and decreasing individual ideation performance during the experimental sessions, as illustrated in Fig. 5. The first segment (I) includes 4 persons (12,1% of all participants) with a high ideation performance in the first ideation session $P_m \geq 15$ and a continuous growth in number of different ideas proposed in each following ideation session. The second segment (II) includes 4 persons who also demonstrate a continuous growth in number of different ideas proposed in each following session but has a lower ideation performance in the first ideation session $P_m$ 10. Apparently, in the second segment a lower ideation outcome of the first session is compensated by the application of inventive tools in the sessions 2 and 3. The third segment (III) of 7 students (21,2% of participants) shows a stable number of on average 15 new ideas in each ideation session. Finally, the students in the segments IV and V, with 13 persons (39,4%) and 5 persons (15,2%) respectively, generate in each new ideation session less ideas compared to the previous one. In other words, their individual ideation performance is continuously decreasing over the entire experiment. The students from the fourth segment (IV) demonstrate a high ideation performance in the first ideation session with $P_m \geq 15$, whereas the students from the fifth segment (V) show a lower ideation performance in the first ideation session $P_m \leq 14$.

**Table 10.** Different ideas generated by students in three successive ideation sessions.

| Group information | Group size | Individual ideation productivity $P_m$ in different ideas per person (mean value and standard deviation) | | | |
|---|---|---|---|---|---|
| | $n$ | Session 1: interdisplin. analogies | Session 2: MATCEM-IBD fields | Session 3: inventive principles | Total value for all 3 sessions |
| 1. Undergraduate students | 18 | 15,2 (SD = 3,9) | 14,1 (SD = 3,7) | 14,4 (SD = 5,3) | 43,8 (SD = 8,6) |
| 2. Graduate students | 15 | 15,9 (SD = 3,7) | 15,5 (SD = 6,2) | 16,2 (SD = 6,3) | 47,7 (SD = 14,0) |
| 3. Students' group 1 + 2 | 33 | 15,5 (SD = 4,0) | 14,8 (SD = 5,2) | 15,2 (SD = 6,0) | 45,5 (SD = 12,0) |

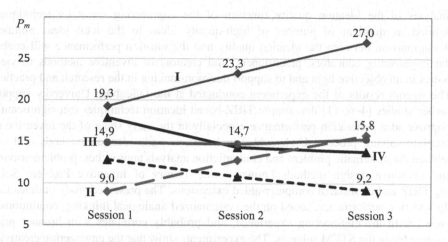

**Fig. 5.** Average growth of individual ideation productivity $P_m$ in each ideation session: segments I and II – increasing, segment III – constant, and segments IV and V – decreasing values.

According with [14], there are four main variables that could contribute to dissimilar ideation performance: knowledge level, creativity skills, motivation during idea generation and the influence of the experimental setting. Furthermore, the long-term observation and experience of the author allows to assume that the successful application of TRIZ Inventive Principles requires an ability to think abstractly and to transform technical systems by exactly following the instructions given in the subprinciples. Due to the similar experimental conditions and student motivation, the students obviously differed in their knowledge levels using MATCEMIBD-fields and, possibly, had dissimilar levels of engineering creativity and different skills applying TRIZ Inventive Principles.

Remarkably, the application of three simple engineering creativity tools (5 Analogies, 9 MATCEMIBD fields and 15 TRIZ inventive sub-principles) demonstrates a potential to triple the average individual ideation performance up to 45 different ideas within 1,5…2 h. A thorough analysis of the variety, quality, and feasibility of the 1503 ideas documented in the experiment is a subject of future research activities. It should also help to evaluate the validity and application range of the ideation efficiency model (1) and ideation performance function (2) and to estimate the ideation limit of combined approaches successively using different ideation techniques.

## 4 Concluding Remarks and Outlook

Through a series of experiments the paper wish to objectify the individual and collective ideation performance of easy-to-use engineering creativity techniques. It is essential that quantitative criteria and mathematical models should be established, regarding quantity, variety, quality, and novelty of ideas to compare different ideation tools and their combinations. The future research should focus on determination and analysis of the ideation quality function of the engineering creativity techniques, defined as quotient of number of high-quality ideas to the total ideas number. A comparison between the ideation quality and the ideation performance will enable the engineering educators, practitioners, and creators of inventive methods to view issues in an objective light and to support decision-making in the research and practice. The overall results of the experiment conducted at the Offenburg University support earlier studies [4–6, 11] that simple TRIZ-based ideation techniques can significantly improve idea generation performance especially in the early stage of the inventive or problem-solving process. Undeniably, such fast or agile ideation methods will not replace the systematic problem and contradiction analysis approaches, problem-solving and inventive design methods known in the Theory of Inventive Problem Solving TRIZ and its modern computer-aided extensions. The presented study outlines that the ideation performance, based on the systematized analogical thinking, continuously grows with the engineering experience, and probably correlates with broader prior knowledge in the STEM subjects. The experiments show that the engineering creativity of the undergraduate and graduate students is in general lower than the benchmark performance of the interdisciplinary group of engineers. However, the students trained in the ideation techniques demonstrate significantly better creativity skills that results in the ideation performance similar to the creativity level of the engineers. Even though the reasons for this finding are not sufficiently explored, the outcomes of the study should be taken into consideration by the educators in creativity and innovation.

# References

1. Badran, I.: Enhancing creativity and innovation in engineering education. Eur. J. Eng. Educ. **32**(5), 573–585 (2007). https://doi.org/10.1080/03043790701433061
2. Chechurin, L., Borgianni, Y.: Understanding TRIZ through the review of top cited publications. Comput. Ind. **82**, 119–134 (2016). https://doi.org/10.1016/j.compind.2016.06.002
3. Altshuller, G.S.: Creativity as an Exact Science. The Theory of the Solution of Inventive Problems. Gordon & Breach Science Publishers, New-York (1984). ISSN 0275-5807
4. Cascini, G., Regazzoni, D., Rizzi, C., Russo, C.: Enhancing the innovation capabilities of engineering students. In: Horváth, I., Rusák, Z. (eds.) Proceedings of the TMCE Conference, Izmir, Turkey, pp. 733–742, April 21–25 2008. ISBN 978-90-5155-045-0
5. Belski, I., et al.: Can simple ideation techniques influence idea generation: comparing results from Australia, Czech Republic, Finland and Russian Federation. In: Proceedings of the Annual Conference of the Australasian Association for Engineering Education AAEE 2015, pp. 474–483. Deakin University, School of Engineering, Geelong (2015)
6. Livotov, P., Chandra Sekaran, A.P., Mas'udah: Lower abstraction level of TRIZ inventive principles improves ideation productivity of engineering students. In: Benmoussa, R., De Guio, R., Dubois, S., Koziołek, S. (eds.) New Opportunities for Innovation Breakthroughs for Developing Countries and Emerging Economies, TFC 2019. IFIP Advances in Information and Communication Technology, vol. 572, pp. 526–538, Springer, Cham (2019). https://doi.org/10.1007/978-3-030-32497-1_41
7. Gordon, W.: Synectics: The Development of Creative Capacity. Harper, New York (1961)

8. Enkel, E., Gassmann, O.: Creative imitation: exploring the case of cross-industry innovation. R&D Manag. **40**(3), 256–270 (2010). https://doi.org/10.1111/j.1467-9310.2010.00591.x
9. Echterhoff, N., Amshoff, B., Gausemeier, J.: Cross-industry innovations – systematic identification of ideas for radical problem solving. In: International Conference on Innovation and Management (ICIM), February 27–28, 2013, Barcelona, vol. 74, pp. 935–944 (2013)
10. VDI Standard 4521: Inventive problem solving with TRIZ. Fundamentals, Terms and Definitions. The Association of German Engineers (VDI), Beuth publishers, Duesseldorf, Germany (2016)
11. Livotov, P.: Enhancing innovation and entrepreneurial competences of engineering students through a systematic cross-industry innovation learning course. Paper Presented at the 29th Annual Conference of the Australasian Association for Engineering Education, Hamilton, New Zealand (2018)
12. Shah, J.J., Vargas-Hernandez, N., Smith, S.M.: Metrics for measuring ideation effectiveness. Des. Stud. **24**(2), 111–134 (2003)
13. Briggs, R., Reinig, B.: Bounded ideation theory. J. Manag. Inf. Syst. **27**, 123–144 (2010). https://doi.org/10.2753/mis0742-1222270106
14. Belski, I., Livotov, P., Mayer, O.: Eight fields of MATCEMIB help students to generate more ideas. Procedia CIRP **39**, 85–90 (2016)
15. Osborn, A.F.: Applied Imagination. Scribner, New York (1963)
16. Chandra Sekaran, A.P., Livotov, P., Mas'udah: Classification of TRIZ inventive principles and sub-principles for process engineering problems. In: Benmoussa, R., De Guio, R., Dubois, S., Koziolek, S. (eds.) New Opportunities for Innovation Breakthroughs for Developing Countries and Emerging Economies. TFC 2019. IFIP Advances in Information and Communication Technology, vol. 572, pp. 314–327. Springer, Cham (2019). https://doi.org/10.1007/978-3-030-32497-1_26

# MOOC vs Face to Face (F2F) Model: What Relevance for Creativity Development?

Rachid Benmoussa[✉]

ENSA Marrakech, Cadi Ayyad University, Marrakesh, Morocco
benmoussa.ensa@gmail.com

**Abstract.** Teaching invention problem solving methods is complex because it aims to improve the learner's creativity, which is not a knowledge but an intrinsic competence. This paper presents an empirical study to compare the effectiveness of the MOOC's model and the Face to Face (F2F) model for teaching methods of solving invention problems. It answers the following research question: Is MOOC's model more relevant than F2F model for learners' creativity development?

Our methodology consists in observing a population of 28 students who have followed a solving invention problems course simultaneously in two forms: a part delivered through a MOOC and a part delivered in F2F classroom. Correlations analysis between the evaluations carried out on the MOOC and F2F of the two parts of the course led to several conclusions:

- The overall assessment through the MOOC and F2F of all the parts delivered in the course are not correlated. There is therefore no correlation between the level of competence acquired through the MOOC and the level of competence acquired in the classroom.
- The Multiple Choice Question (MCQ) evaluation of the part delivered on the MOOC is weakly but positively correlated with the F2F MCQ evaluation of the same content. This proves the low reliability of the MOOC assessment. The same analysis dealing with exercise activities showed, on the other hand, that there is no correlation between the MOOC and F2F evaluation. Thus, MOOC's assessment of exercise activities is not at all reliable.
- Finally, evaluation on table of the part delivered by the MOOC and the part delivered in F2F classroom does not show any correlation. This proves that learners who appreciate the F2F model do not necessarily appreciate the MOOC's model and vice versa. But the analysis of these assessments shows that the MOOC's model gives slightly better results than F2F one.
- The experiment conducted on a limited sample does not allow to draw definitive conclusions. It will be reproduced next year with a larger student sample, some teaching material improvements and learners' motivation support.

**Keywords:** TRIZ learning · Creativity development · MOOC · F2F learning

© IFIP International Federation for Information Processing 2020
Published by Springer Nature Switzerland AG 2020
D. Cavallucci et al. (Eds.): TFC 2020, IFIP AICT 597, pp. 122–132, 2020.
https://doi.org/10.1007/978-3-030-61295-5_10

# 1 Introduction

Considered a useful resource for personal, professional development and societal transformations, creativity consists in producing new and useful ideas to solve a problem or reach a goal. In recent years, the socio-economic world (re)discovers the virtues of creativity to face new needs for transversal and collaborative skills useful for innovation development in companies and more broadly in society. The World Economic Forum, in its report on human capital entitled "Preparing for the future of work", ranks creativity as one of the three skills that businesses will need the most [7]. But how to develop student's creativity? One of the solutions widely adopted in universities is "TRIZ invention problem solving methods" teaching. But this teaching is complex due to its nature, because it aims to improve a learner intrinsic skill (creativity) as opposed to a knowledge. A fundamental question then arises in relation to the relevance of classical transmissive models compared to collaborative and distance models (such as MOOCs) for this teaching.

The concept of MOOC (Massive Open Online Course), based on the exchange between learners and the teacher, supposedly interactive, is a form of online education [3]. Several authors have studied the interest and the challenges of using MOOCs [1, 4, 6]. MOOCs offer online resources, multiple choice questions and forums, video presentations and PowerPoint slides. The MOOCs stress the need to refocus the teaching process on the learner, on the skills to be acquired by the latter and on the primacy of the progressive integration of ICT in teaching [6].

The research question addressed in this paper is the following: "Is the MOOC more relevant than the transmissive model for creativity development of a learner who takes a course in solving invention problem?" To answer this question, we have adopted an experimental approach which consists in observing a population of 28 students who followed a MOOC on "solving invention problems" made available by the Moroccan Ministry of Higher Education on the "Morocco Digital University" platform [5]. This MOOC was developed, within the framework of a call for projects, by our team at ENSA of Marrakech in collaboration with a TRIZ specialized team at INSA of Strasbourg. The MOOC covers the majority of Triz tools. The same population followed in parallel a face-to-face course on two chapters that the MOOC does not cover. The first chapter concerns the ASIT method (Advanced Systematic Inventive Thinking) for which we did not have the copyright required to its integration into the MOOC. The second chapter concerns the ARIZ algorithm, too complex to be integrated into the MOOC as well. The objective of this experiment is to analyze the correlation between the results of this population for the two models of education. It was conducted for about 3 months between November 2019 and January 2020.

This paper is structured as follows. After an introduction, Sect. 2 presents the experience modalities in detail according to the two considered pedagogical models. Section 3 presents the results of the correlation analysis between the different students grades. The conclusion presents the limits of the study and leads to the perspectives which will be taken into account in a future experiment.

## 2  Modalities of Running the Experience

### 2.1  Training Objective

**MOOC Training.** The general objective of the MOOC is to provide registrants with the knowledge necessary to understand the concepts of innovation, creativity and invention as well as to gain insight into various tools known in this field for their ability to help solving invention problems. The learners, according to their levels of engagement, will be able to improve their creativity and to grasp specific problem situations to solve them. This content is divided in six weeks. Week 0 "Course discovery" does not cover any course. During this week, learners are called upon to discover the work environment and to introduce themselves to each other through the discussion forum. Week 1, entitled "Innovation: Concepts and Approaches" covers 3 introductory sections: "What is innovation, creativity, invention?", "Problem solving: finding a solution" and "Characterization of problem solving methods". Week 2, entitled "Recognizing the problem" covers the three most used TRIZ tools to identify a problem: "The Multiscreen tool", "The Intensification tool (DTC)" and "The Golden Fish tool". Week 3, "Analyzing the problem" covers different facets of the contradiction concept: "Technical contradiction", "Physical contradiction" and "The system of contradictions". Week 4, "Synthesizing solution concepts" presents: "Inventive principles", "Separation principles" and "Standards". Week 5, "Realizing and Evaluating Solutions" covers three areas: "Resource Mobilization", "Effect Pointer" and "Evaluation and Ranking". Week 6, entitled "Inventive resolution scenarios", presents two resolution scenarios (by principles and by ARIZ) as well as a final synthesis.

**Face to Face Training.** F2F training covers two chapters: ASIT and ARIZ. The ASIT course covers "the rule of the closed world and of qualitative change" as well as the tools "Unification, Multiplication, Division, Subtraction". The ARIZ course covers essentially the first three steps of the algorithm "Analyze the System", "Analyze the Resources" and "Define the Ideal Final Result and Formulate the Physical Contradiction".

### 2.2  Learning Environment

The face-to-face course took place in a classic passive learning environment. The learning model was predominantly transmissive. The trainer, through PowerPoint presentation, delivered the content to the students. A series of tutorials is used to involve students in the training and to illustrate the content. The environment is physical. Both the learner and the trainer have the ability to see, hear and pick up physical signals and body language.

However, the MOOC uses a more active learning environment. Students must watch three videos per week and carry out activities in the form of exercises (drag and drop) and multiple choice questions (MCQ) to assimilate the content. Through interaction and participation via forums dedicated to the theme of each week, students play an active role in the material and the courses delivery.

## 2.3   Course Pace

The face-to-face course, lasting 4 h/week, takes place in a classroom for four weeks. In class, the trainer sets the pace according to learner's audience and responsiveness.

For the MOOC, the content of the week is launched every Wednesday. Exercises and multiple choice questions are open all the week until the following Wednesday. It is up to the student to define his own rhythm for the work that must be accomplished during the week using the MOOC. Students therefore have flexibility in determining where and at what time of the day they participate in the MOOC.

## 2.4   Discussions

For face-to-face course, the discussion takes place in the restrictive environment of a physical classroom. The trainer often leads and controls the purpose of the discussion to reach a conclusion in a limited amount of time. As time is limited, responses generally need to be made quickly. For some students, there may also be some intimidation of speaking live in a classroom, but there is also the benefit of visual cues from other students and the trainer.

With MOOC, students have more opportunity to develop well thought-out and researched responses to the discussion. Students often carry most of the discussion interaction with the trainer acting as a facilitator and only intervene when necessary. The online discussion progresses over a longer period of time than that of the face-to-face class (often more than a week), which allows all the students of the course to contribute and draw conclusions together.

## 2.5   Exams and Quizzes (Assessments)

For the face-to-face course, the examination on table is individual. It took place in the classroom according to the schedule established by the administration. Students were monitored during the exam period which was limited to 3 h.

For the MOOC, self-assessment activities based on multiple choice questions and drag and drop exercises, are submitted each week to students through the software components provided by the OpenEdx platform. The parameters chosen by the teaching team, gave students the opportunity to choose the correct answers from a list of proposals and to check their answers twice before submitting their assignment. The activity most often focused on questions directly related to the content of the videos to verify that the student had correctly viewed them. It also covered other types of questions to verify that the learner understood the concepts studied. Both drag and drop exercises and multiple choice questions have specific opening and closing dates for students to respect. The review of rated work took place online automatically, since it had already been scheduled by the trainers. After submission, students can view correction and comment for each exercise and each question. They could also constantly view their progress. The final exam took up the content of all weeks. Compared to the self-assessment, the exam required consulting a set of online resources before answering the questions. This made it possible to involve the learner even more in the content appropriation. The final score was automatically calculated by the platform using the following scales: 30% for MCQs of each week (6 MCQs), 30% for drag and drop exercises (2 exercises) and 40% for final exam.

## 2.6 Group Work

Since the students are physically located in the same place at the same time, a face-to-face course is more convenient to group work. Class time can be used for this collaboration and work can be continued between students after the end of the class through scheduled meetings. The tutorials were mainly conducted in class and in groups.

Online courses also often include group work. Trainers have the ability to divide their online students into teams to work collaboratively on projects and interact using the discussion tools. However, since most online courses are asynchronous, the advantage of being in the same place at the same time does not exist in the online class. It is therefore up to each learner in the group to follow the work and do its part. Group work has not been used explicitly in this MOOC.

## 2.7 Learning Material Assessment

The evaluation of the face-to-face teaching material was not carried out because its manual completion was tedious. It required the distribution of a paper questionnaire to be completed by the students anonymously and then its counting to draw conclusions.

Unlike F2F course, the evaluation of teaching materials is easy in a MOOC. The assessment of course materials, self-assessment activities and additional resources deposited online was carried out by the learners through an online questionnaire developed by the "Survey" software component of the OpenEdx platform. The questions asked to learners were as follows:

Q01: Is the quality of video 1 suitable: sound, graphics, text?
Q02: Is the quality of video 2 suitable: sound, graphics, text?
Q03: Is the quality of video 3 suitable: sound, graphics, text?
Q04: Are the instructions given in the self-assessment and the exercises clear?
Q05: Was the content of video 1 clear and understandable?
Q06: Was the content of video 2 clear and understandable?
Q07: Was the content of video 3 clear and understandable?
Q08: Do the 3 videos have synchronized content?
Q09: Did the self-assessment and exercises help you better understand the content provided in the videos?
Q10: Did the references presented at the end of the course help you to better complete the content delivered in the videos?
Q11: Did you actively participate in discussions between learners through the forum?
Q12: Have the discussions between learners been beneficial for the assimilation of the course presented in the videos?

The scale used to score the questions varied from 5 (Very Good) to 1 (Very Bad). Between these two extremes, the intermediate levels 2, 3 and 4 was considered.

# 3  Analyzes and Results

As a reminder, the experience described in this paper consists in observing a population of 28 students who followed both the MOOC and the face-to-face course. The results of this experiment relate to two points: the evaluation of students and the evaluation of the quality of content and teaching materials.

## 3.1  Learners' Evaluation

Learners' evaluation gave rise to 8 types of grades whose relation was analyzed by linear correlation. To do so, we used the two factors Bravais-Pearson coefficient [2]:

$$r = \frac{Cov(X, Y)}{\sigma_x \sigma_y} \tag{1}$$

$$Cov(X, Y) = \frac{E[(X - E(X))(Y - E(Y))]}{\sigma_x \sigma_y} = \frac{E(XY) - E(X)E(Y)}{\sigma_x \sigma_y} \tag{2}$$

This coefficient is equal to 1 in the case where one of the variables is an increasing affine function of the other variable, to −1 in the case where a variable is an affine and decreasing function. The intermediate values provide information on the degree of linear dependence between the two variables. The closer the coefficient is to the extreme values −1 and 1, the stronger the linear correlation between the variables; the term "highly correlated" is simply used to qualify the two variables. A correlation equal to 0 means that the variables are not linearly correlated, they can nevertheless be correlated non-linearly [9].

The fundamental principle of the analyzes is based on the fact that the evaluation on table, since it is individual and supervised, reflects well the real competence acquired by the learner in terms of creativity.

Analysis 1 seeks to calculate the correlation between "The final grade of the MOOC which includes the self-assessment (MCQ and Drag and Drop exercises) and the final exam" and "The evaluation on table grade covering the content of the face-to-face course and the content of week 1, 2, 3 and 4 from the MOOC". The interest of this analysis is to answer the question: does the MOOC generally reflect "the level of competence acquired by the learner?"

Analysis 2 seeks to calculate the correlation between "The grade concerning the multiple choice questions of the MOOC" and "The grade concerning the MCQ of the evaluation on table, which deals with the same content of MOOC MCQ". It also seeks to calculate the correlation between "The grade concerning the MOOC Drag and Drop exercises" and "The grade concerning the exercises of the evaluation on table which relates to the same content of the MOOC exercises". The interest of this double analysis is to answer respectively the questions: does the MOOC reflect "the seriousness and the implication of the learner when replying to MCQ" and "the seriousness and the implication of the learner when replying to the Drag and Drop exercises".

Analysis 3 finally seeks to calculate the correlation between "The grade of the evaluation on table which covers parts studied only on the MOOC" and "The grade of the evaluation on table which covers only the chapters studied face-to-face". The interest of this analysis is to answer respectively the questions: "do the learners have a preference for training by MOOC compared to face-to-face training" and "does training by MOOC give better results than training face-to-face".

The analyzes and the results are summarized in Table 1 and show that:

- The MOOC does not reflect "the learner's level of acquired competence"
- The MOOC weakly reflects the "seriousness and involvement" of the learner when replying to MCQ.
- The MOOC does not reflect the "seriousness and involvement" of the learner when replying to exercises.
- Those who appreciate face-to-face model do not necessarily appreciate the MOOC model and vice versa. But the MOOC model gives slightly better results.

## 3.2    Learning Content Evaluation

Table 2 summarizes the results of the six questionnaires intended to assess the quality of the teaching material used during the six weeks of learning. This material includes videos, self-assessment (multiple choice questions and drag and drop exercises), additional resources and discussion forums.

If we assume that the students' answers are reliable, the analysis of Table 2 allows us to draw several conclusions:

1. The respondent rate is low. It does not indeed exceed in average 6.5 respondents by week, namely 23.2%
2. The audio visual quality of the videos is satisfactory: 65.6% of the respondents gave a mark 5 (very good) to questions dealing with this criterion.
3. The clarity of the self-assessment instructions is insufficient: only 40% of respondents gave a mark 5 (very good) to this question.
4. The clarity of the content of the videos is also insufficient: only 37.8% of the respondents gave a mark 5 (very good) to questions dealing with this criterion.
5. The synchronization of the videos in terms of content is insufficient: only 25.5% of the respondents gave a mark 5 (very good) to this question.
6. The usefulness of the self-assessment to understand the course is satisfactory: 57.8% of the respondents gave a mark 5 (very good) to this question.
7. The usefulness of the additional resources to understand the course is insufficient: only 30% of the respondents gave a mark 5 (very good) to this question.
8. Participation in the forums is very low: no respondent assumed to have used the forums heavily (0% gave a mark 5) to this question.
9. The usefulness of the exchanges via the Forums to understand the course was also too weak: only 3.3% of the respondents gave a mark 5 (very good) to this question.

**Table 1.** Analyzes and results synthesis of the experiment

| Learners | Analyze 1 | | Analyze 2 (a) MCQ | | Analyze 2 (b) Exercise | | Analyze 3 MOOC/F2F | |
|---|---|---|---|---|---|---|---|---|
| | Final Grade MOOC | Grade Evaluation on Table | MOOC Grade | Grade on Table | MOOC Grade | Grade on Table | Grade MOOC Content on Table (MCQ/Exercise) | Grade F2F Content on Table : ASIT/ARIZ |
| Correlation | -0,004977317 | | 0,44919702 | | -0,0979021 | | -0,027104331 | |
| Learners Average Grade | 17,48 | 12,58 | 18,31 | 15,43 | 16,05 | 12,29 | 13,86 | 11,30 |
| Results | No Correlation The MOOC does not reflect the "learner's level of acquired competence" | | Weak Positive Correlation The MOOC weakly reflects the "seriousness and involvement" of the learner when replying to MCQ | | No Correlation The MOOC does not reflect the "seriousness and involvement" of the learner when replying to exercises | | No Correlation Those who appreciate face-to-face model do not necessarily appreciate the MOOC model and vice versa. But the MOOC model gives slightly better results | |

**Table 2.** Questionnaire results (in %)

| MARK | Week 1 | | | | | Week 2 | | | | | Week 3 | | | | | Week 4 | | | | | Week 5 | | | | | Week 6 | | | | | Average Mark 5 |
|---|---|---|---|---|---|---|---|---|---|---|---|---|---|---|---|---|---|---|---|---|---|---|---|---|---|---|---|---|---|---|---|
| | 5 | 4 | 3 | 2 | 1 | 5 | 4 | 3 | 2 | 1 | 5 | 4 | 3 | 2 | 1 | 5 | 4 | 3 | 2 | 1 | 5 | 4 | 3 | 2 | 1 | 5 | 4 | 3 | 2 | 1 | |
| Q1 | 53 | 20 | 20 | 7 | 0 | 80 | 0 | 0 | 20 | 0 | 60 | 40 | 0 | 0 | 0 | 60 | 40 | 0 | 0 | 0 | 80 | 20 | 0 | 0 | 0 | 80 | 20 | 0 | 0 | 0 | 68,8 |
| Q2 | 60 | 33 | 0 | 7 | 0 | 80 | 20 | 0 | 0 | 0 | 60 | 40 | 0 | 0 | 0 | 60 | 40 | 0 | 0 | 0 | 60 | 40 | 0 | 0 | 0 | 60 | 40 | ◊ | 0 | 0 | 63,3 |
| Q3 | 67 | 20 | 13 | 0 | 0 | 80 | 20 | 0 | 0 | 0 | 60 | 40 | 0 | 0 | 0 | 60 | 40 | 0 | 0 | 0 | 60 | 20 | 20 | 0 | 0 | 60 | 20 | 20 | ◊ | 0 | 64,5 |
| Average Q1, Q2, Q3 | 60,0 | 24,3 | 11,0 | 4,7 | 0,0 | 80,0 | 13,3 | 0,0 | 6,7 | 0,0 | 60,0 | 40,0 | 0,0 | 0,0 | 0,0 | 60,0 | 40,0 | 0,0 | 0,0 | 0,0 | 66,7 | 26,7 | 6,7 | 0,0 | 0,0 | 66,7 | 26,7 | 10,0 | 0,0 | 0,0 | 65,6 |
| Q4 | 40 | 27 | 20 | 13 | 0 | 40 | 60 | 0 | 0 | 0 | 20 | 60 | 20 | 0 | 0 | 40 | 20 | 40 | 0 | 0 | 40 | 60 | 0 | 0 | 0 | 40 | 60 | 0 | 0 | 0 | 40,0 |
| Q5 | 47 | 33 | 20 | 0 | 0 | 80 | 0 | 20 | 0 | 0 | 20 | 60 | 20 | 0 | 0 | 20 | 60 | 20 | 0 | 0 | 40 | 60 | 0 | 0 | 0 | 40 | 60 | 0 | 0 | 0 | 41,2 |
| Q6 | 53 | 33 | 13 | 0 | 0 | 80 | 20 | 0 | 0 | 0 | 20 | 60 | 20 | 0 | 0 | 20 | 60 | 20 | 0 | 0 | 20 | 40 | 0 | 20 | 20 | 20 | 40 | 0 | 20 | 20 | 35,5 |
| Q7 | 60 | 27 | 13 | 0 | 0 | 80 | 20 | 0 | 0 | 0 | 20 | 40 | 40 | 0 | 0 | 20 | 60 | 40 | 0 | 0 | 20 | 60 | 0 | 20 | 0 | 20 | 60 | 0 | 20 | 0 | 36,7 |
| Average Q5, Q6, Q7 | 46,7 | 31,0 | 17,7 | 4,3 | 0,0 | 66,7 | 26,7 | 6,7 | 0,0 | 0,0 | 26,7 | 46,7 | 26,7 | 0,0 | 0,0 | 26,7 | 46,7 | 26,7 | 0,0 | 0,0 | 33,3 | 53,3 | 0,0 | 6,7 | 6,7 | 33,3 | 53,3 | 0,0 | 6,7 | 6,7 | 37,8 |
| Q8 | 33 | 47 | 13 | 7 | 0 | 40 | 40 | 0 | 20 | 0 | 20 | 40 | 40 | 0 | 0 | 40 | 40 | 20 | 0 | 0 | 20 | 60 | 20 | 0 | 0 | 20 | 60 | 20 | 0 | 0 | 25,5 |
| Q9 | 47 | 27 | 27 | 0 | 0 | 60 | 40 | 0 | 0 | 0 | 60 | 20 | 20 | 0 | 0 | 60 | 20 | 20 | 0 | 0 | 60 | 0 | 40 | 0 | 0 | 60 | 0 | 40 | 0 | 0 | 57,8 |
| Q10 | 40 | 47 | 13 | 0 | 0 | 20 | 60 | 0 | 20 | 0 | 40 | 40 | 20 | 0 | 0 | 40 | 20 | 20 | 0 | 20 | 20 | 0 | 40 | 20 | 20 | 20 | 0 | 40 | 20 | 20 | 30,0 |
| Q11 | 0 | 7 | 27 | 20 | 47 | 0 | 0 | 20 | 20 | 60 | 0 | 0 | 20 | 20 | 60 | 0 | 0 | 20 | 0 | 60 | 0 | 0 | 0 | 20 | 40 | 0 | 0 | 0 | 20 | 40 | 0,0 |
| Q12 | 0 | 7 | 47 | 13 | 33 | 20 | 0 | 40 | 0 | 40 | 0 | 20 | 40 | 0 | 40 | 0 | 20 | 40 | 0 | 40 | 0 | 20 | 60 | 0 | 20 | 0 | 20 | 60 | 0 | 20 | 3,3 |
| Respondents Number | 15 | | | | | 5 | | | | | 5 | | | | | 3 | | | | | 5 | | | | | 6 | | | | | 6,5 |

# 4  Conclusion and Perspective

This paper raises a general research question regarding the relevance of the distance education model via MOOC in comparison with the conventional face-to-face model. It more specifically addresses the relevance of this model learners' creativity development through solving invention problems methods teaching.

The experiment, which was conducted at the national school of applied sciences in Marrakesh, concerned 28 engineering students from the industrial engineering department. Although it leaned slightly towards the MOOC model, this study did not provide a conclusive and definitive answer to our research question. Several reasons for this can be cited:

- The limited number of participants: indeed, 28 students are not a significant population for MOOCs.
- The motivation of the learners regarding the use of MOOCs: almost all learners have never experienced distance learning through a MOOC. The rate of participation in discussion forums, consultation of additional resources and response to content assessment questionnaires clearly demonstrate this non-motivation. The students therefore had a kind of psychological inertia with regard to this new model, accentuated by their dependence on the classical face-to-face model.
- The quality of the content itself as well as its synchronization also seem contribute to this limit (if we believe the respondents).
- The full power of distance education has not really been harnessed. More specifically, group work tools in synchronous and asynchronous mode were not used to support learning.

Beyond its success, this experiment allowed us to test the relevance of the methodology applied to compare F2F and MOOC teaching. As a perspective, several actions will be considered for the next experiment in order to counteract the limits mentioned above:

- Given the increase in enrollment in the industrial engineering department, at least 50 students will be able to participate in the experiment next year.
- The motivation of the learners will also be supported by several actions:
  - Give open questions to discuss via forums
  - Make explicit references, to consult in learning activities, to additional resources
  - Require the filling of questionnaires through personalized monitoring of learners
  - ...
- Improve the quality of the videos and their synchronization as well as the self-assessment instructions.
- Give mini projects to be realized by groups of 4 to 6 learners using the synchronous and asynchronous collaboration tools.
- ...

# References

1. Daniel, J.: Making Sense of MOOCs: Musings in a Maze of Myth, Paradox and Possibility. Korean National Open University, Seoul (2012)
2. Dodge, Y., Rousson, V.: Analyse de régression appliquée - 2ème édition, Collection: Éco Sup, Dunod, Parution, Octobre 2004
3. Karsenti, T.: MOOC, révolution ou simple effet de mode? RITPU **10**(2), 6–37 (2013)
4. Siemens, G., Downes, S.: The connectivism and connective knowledge course (CCK08), référencé sur (2008) https://sites.google.com/site/themoocguide/3-cck08—the-distributed-course. Accessed 07 Apr 2020
5. Maroc Université Numérique. www.mun.ma. Accessed 07 Apr 2020
6. Nouib, A., Oulhadj, B.: L'enseignement à distance: l'émergence des MOOCs au Maroc, la revue internationale francophone des innovatrices et des innovateurs, V4 – N° 1, 15 Octobre 2017 (2017)
7. The Innovation Management de l'innovation et de la créativité. https://www.theinnovation.eu/category/creativite. Accessed 07 Apr 2020

# Effective Improvement Solutions in Organizations Using Data Envelopment Analysis (DEA) and TRIZ: A Case Study in Higher Education

Gabriela Vica Olariu[✉] and Stelian Brad

Research Centre for Engineering and Management of Innovation, Technical University of Cluj-Napoca, Cluj-Napoca, Romania
{gabriela.olariu,stelian.brad}@staff.utcluj.ro

**Abstract.** The aim of this study is to investigate how systematic innovation can be applied to define effective action plans for improvement in lagging behind operational units of an organization. The value of this research stands in the combination of DEA and TRIZ for systematic analysis and innovation of decision-making units in organizations. The constant returns to scale (CRS) model and the variable returns to scale (VRS) model (output oriented) is used to determine the output maximization of eleven faculties (DMUs) within the analyzed university. Analysis has been done for five academic years (between 2013 and 2018). Research ends with the identification of variables that affect the results in the less efficient DMUs. In the attempt of improving these variables, some other variables might be affected. Here, TRIZ is introduced to tackle conflicts in an inventive manner. The results of this study show the relative most efficient faculty (DMU) during the period 2013–2018 (taken as Ideal Final Result). In comparison to this, some directions of intervention have been identified and a set of innovative solutions have been generated for the most inefficient DMU. The methodology has a general applicability in practice, for all cases where benchmarking analyses are required, and innovative plans are necessary as a course of action.

**Keywords:** DEA · Higher education · Efficiency · Performance · Innovative solutions · TRIZ · DMU

## 1 Introduction

There are many situations in organizations when managers and employees must solve conflicting problems and make good decisions. The variety in dimensions and nature of the problems and obstacles to which organization encounter, requires manager to use different tools for solving its problems. Consequently, it is essential for any organization to understand its problems and know how the problem-solving tools work [1].

The purpose of this study is to investigate how systematic innovation can be applied to define effective action plans for improvement in lagging behind operational units of an organization, in this case, in higher education institutions.

© IFIP International Federation for Information Processing 2020
Published by Springer Nature Switzerland AG 2020
D. Cavallucci et al. (Eds.): TFC 2020, IFIP AICT 597, pp. 133–144, 2020.
https://doi.org/10.1007/978-3-030-61295-5_11

The mission of a higher education institution is to generate and transfer knowledge to the society through initial and continuing education and training at university level. In their complexity, these organizations need the ability to solve difficult problems through identification of the best innovative solutions. Most of the solutions could be derived from knowledge and information that already exist. For solving the complex problems, a systematic approach is required in order to ensure that the solution solves the current problem satisfactory. TRIZ method is a systematic approach for finding advanced and creative solutions to difficult problems in a more efficient and effective manner to ensure the solutions are up-to-date and still relevant during launching [2].

In order to generate effective solutions, a highly pragmatic approach to examine the efficiency of a complex system is Data Envelopment Analysis (DEA). It has been designed to assess the relative efficiencies of units within a set where inputs and outputs are incommensurate so that simple efficiency measures are difficult to obtain [3]. This is also the case of higher education institutions.

The value of this research stands in the combination of DEA and TRIZ for systematic analysis and innovation of decision-making units in organizations. The article is organized as follows. In section two, basic aspects of DEA method and TRIZ problem-solving methodology are introduced. Section three is dedicated for the theoretical descriptions of the methodology. Even though TRIZ was developed to solve inventive problems in engineering, nowadays it has gained in other domains such as education, business, services. On the other hand, the DEA was developed as a method for assessing the comparative efficiency of organizational units. Application of the theory on a real case study in the higher education institution is illustrated in section four. The paper ends with conclusions and underlining of research limitations.

## 2  DEA and TRIZ Methodology

In this section basic rules and some references of DEA and TRIZ use in higher education are introduced.

### 2.1  DEA Methodology

Data Envelopment Analysis was developed by Charnes, Cooper and Rhodes (1978) [4] will be endorsed by the Banker, Charnes and Cooper (1984) [5]. The purpose of this review is to evaluate the efficiency of some decision-making units (DMU) through the use of input elements (inputs) that produce one or more output elements (outputs). The efficiency of a unit formula with a single input and output is defined by the relationship:

$$\text{Efficiency} = \frac{\text{output}}{\text{input}} \tag{1}$$

and for more outputs and inputs is defined by the relationship:

$$\text{Efficiency} = \frac{\text{weighted sum of outputs}}{\text{weighted sum of inputs}}. \tag{2}$$

The DEA analyze relative efficiency by a ratio between inputs and outputs for evaluation of each DMU and measuring its effectiveness compared to other units. Models used for the measure efficiency can be with constant returns to scale (CRS) or variable returns to scale (VRS), oriented toward minimizing the inputs or maximizing the outputs. The efficiency scales are associated with each type of surface envelope caused by each DMU and this surface refers to the efficiency frontier [4]. Those elements which belong to this surface (or determine it) are considered efficient and those that do not belong to are considered inefficient. To make inefficient decision-making units becoming efficient, one can choose from the following variants: reducing input while output remains constant (input-oriented analysis); output increasing while inputs remain constant (output-oriented analysis); output increasing in the same time as reducing input (dual version). Input-oriented measurement equals output-oriented measurement of technical efficiency (TE) only in the case of constant returns to scale (CRS) [6].

A model oriented to CRS input with constant returns to scale (CRS DEA) is obtained by the considering the following optimisation framework:

$$\begin{aligned} &\min_{\theta\lambda}\theta \\ \text{st } &-y_i + Y\lambda \geq 0 \\ &\theta x_i + X\lambda \geq 0 \\ &\lambda \geq 0, \end{aligned} \tag{3}$$

where: $x_i$ describes all inputs related to the $i$-th DMU, $y_i$ describes all outputs related to the $i$-th DMU, $X$ is the input matrix of size $K \times N$ for all DMU units decision ($N$ is the number of DMU decision units, $K$ is the number of inputs for each DMU, $M$ is the number of outputs for each DMU), $Y$ is the output matrix of size $M \times N$ for all DMUs, $\theta$ is a scalar and $\lambda$ represents a vector of constants by size $N \times 1$. The value obtained for $\theta$ will be the efficiency score for the $i$-th DMU. It will satisfy $\theta \leq 1$, where a value of 1 represents a point on the frontier and indicates a technically efficient DMU, according to the Farell's (1957) definition. The linear programming problem must be solved $N$ times, for each DMU. A value of $\theta$ is then obtained for DMU [7].

Branker, Charnes and Cooper (1984) [5] suggested an extension of the constant return to scale (DEA CRS) to account for variable return to scale (DEA VRS). The problem of linear programming to explain CRS to VRS, adding the condition of convexity, $N_1'\lambda = 1$ to (3) is the following:

$$\begin{aligned} &\min_{\theta\lambda}\theta \\ \text{st } &-y_i + Y\lambda \geq 0 \\ &\theta x_i + X\lambda \geq 0 \\ &N_1'\lambda = 1 \\ &\lambda \geq 0, \end{aligned} \tag{4}$$

where $N_1$ is an $N \times 1$ vector of 1. If there are differences between technical efficiency determined with CRS ($TE_{CRS}$) and technical efficiency determined with VRS ($TE_{VRS}$), then DMU has *a lack of scale* obtained by the difference between $TE_{VRS}$ and $TE_{CRS}$. It results that CRS technical efficiency measure is discomposed into "pure" efficient technique VRS and scale efficiency (SE), that means: $TE_{CRS} = TE_{VRS} \times SE$.

A model oriented to VRS output with variable returns to scale (VRS DEA) is obtained by the linear programming model:

$$\min_{\theta\lambda}\phi$$
$$\text{st} -\phi y_i + Y\lambda \geq 0$$
$$x_i + X\lambda \geq 0 \tag{5}$$
$$N_1'\lambda = 1$$
$$\lambda \geq 0,$$

where $\phi$ is a scalar and the other symbols have the same meaning as in (3) and (4). The obtained value of $\phi$ will be the efficiency score for the $i$-th DMU. It will satisfy $\phi \leq 1$, where a value of 1 represents a point on the frontier and indicates a technically efficient DMU, according to the Farell (1957) definition. $1 \leq \phi \leq \infty$ and $\phi - 1$ represents proportional increase in outputs with input quantities held constant for each $i$-th DMU. The linear programming problem must be solved $N$ times, for each DMU. A value of $\phi$ is then obtained for DMU [7].

There are a variety of references of this analysis in the specialized literature abroad such as: Application of the Data Envelopment Analysis and Panel Tobit Model to determine factors on the efficiency of 51 universities in Turkey in 2006–2010. The analysis used five inputs (central government budget appropriations, own revenue, project allocations-The Scientific and Technological Research Council of Turkey - TÜBİTAK, project allocations - Scientific Research Projects and the total academic staff) and five outputs (number of graduate students, post-graduate students and number of doctorate students per academic, number of publications and number of employment. The selected DEA method was BCC Model (VRS surface) oriented towards maximizing the outputs and panel tobit model [8]; Comparative Departmental Efficiency Analysis within a University with DEA was illustrated by Nur Azlina Abd Aziz [9]. The inputs (numbers of academic staff, number of non-academic staff and yearly operating expenses) and outputs (number of graduates for the year 2011, total amount of research grants and number of academic publications by faculty member) contribute to investigate the performance of departments with different dimensions (science and social science). Four models with different input-output combinations were defined and this analysis suggests that almost all departments utilize their resources efficiently in producing graduates.

Avkiran [10] examined the relative efficiency of Australian universities by using DEA in three models, namely, overall performance, performance on delivery of educational services and performance on fee-paying enrolments. In all models he used the same inputs (academic staff and non-academic staff) and outputs were different depending on the model (undergraduate enrolments, postgraduate enrolments and research quantum for the first model; student retention rate, student progress rate and graduate full-time employment rate for the second model; overseas fee-paying enrolments, non-overseas fee-paying postgraduate enrolments for the third model).

## 2.2  TRIZ Methodology

Theory of Inventive Problem Solving (TRIZ) has been developed by Genrich Altshuller, a Russian Inventor and it is based upon an exhaustive patent search that was conducted by him. His curiosity about problem solving led him to search for standard methods. Thus, Altshuller felt a theory of invention should satisfy the following conditions: to be a systematic, step-by-step procedure; be a guide through a broad solution space to direct to the ideal solution; be repeatable and reliable and not dependent on psychological tools; be able to access the body of inventive knowledge; be able to add to the body of inventive knowledge; be familiar enough to inventors by following the general approach to problem solving [11].

Altshuller started by analyzing around 200,000 patents and he found that there were around 1,500 technical contradictions that could be solved easily by simply applying the discovered principles. He emphasized that one does not have to be born an inventor in order to be a good inventor, and he criticized the trial and error method that are normally used to make discoveries. Invention is nothing more than the removal of a technical contradiction with the help of certain principles and invention is certain if an inventor possesses knowledge of these principles [12].

Based on the theory or belief that "there are universal principles of invention that are the basis for creative innovations that advance technology, and that if these principles could be identified and codified, they could be taught to people to make the process of invention more predictable", there are eight different evolution trends that engineering system involve into. The eight trends are as follows (Gadd, 2011): increase in ideality; follows the S-curve; increase of controllability, flexibility, and dynamism; uneven development of parts; alternate simplification and increase of complexity; increase of segmentation; matching and mismatching parts; lesser human involvement [13].

A system can be following either one or combination of these trends. Also, these trends can be used in any type of application. Issac et al. (2012) proved that the trends in engineering education correlate with TRIZ's trend of evolution of Engineering Systems. In developing a more ideal engineering education course, universities could apply these evolution trends as a guide [14]. Other specific applications of TRIZ in Innovation Education such as in the curriculum design and innovation training were presented by Jiang (2010). They are useful as references to those who plan to implement Innovation Education with TRIZ problem-solving methodology [15].

Lepeshev et al. (2013) studied the "development of creativity in engineering education using TRIZ". TRIZ was applied intensively to creativity construction and development in engineering education, and the emphasis was in TRIZ's efficiency in producing innovative results [16]. In another paper, Jiang et al. (2012) introduced the use of TRIZ to innovative ability training for mechanical engineering's students. All problems in mechanical professional innovation ability's training of mechanical engineering students were also analyzed. Analyses were also done on the influencing factors from thinking characteristics of students and school innovation environment to the application of TRIZ to the Innovation Education [17].

## 3  Research Design

DEA method is applied to measure the relative efficiency of the decision-making units (DMU) in the organization. This research illustrates the application of non-parametric DEA models to evaluate the efficiency of eleven faculties from a public university in Romania. The gap between the best in the set DMU and the targeted DMU is quantified in relation to a set of parameters. This information is further converted into innovation challenges, which are tackled with TRIZ.

Efficiency is defined by DMU's inputs and outputs. For a correct choice of inputs and outputs in the analysis we took into consideration the faculties with the same field, in this case, the technical field. In DEA, the homogeneity of DMUs must satisfy three rules. First, the DMUs must have similar activities and the same objectives. Secondly, they should utilize similar inputs to produce the same outputs and, thirdly, they should operate within similar environments [18]. This application is tested in the case of a university, with faculties as homogeneous DMUs, because they use similar inputs and produce the same outputs. DEA investigation enables to know how efficient faculties can be in utilizing various resources comparing with their peers.

In this study, the constant returns to scale (CRS) model and the variable returns to scale (VRS) model (output oriented) is used to determine the output maximization of eleven faculties within the analyzed university. The next step was to calculate the value of scale efficiency (SE). Scale efficiency is the component of technical efficiency that can be attributed to the size of operations. Scale inefficiency represents deviations from the most productive scale size. It is the ratio of technical efficiency to pure technical efficiency [19]. In this study we have opted to use the software tool PIM-DEAsoft – V3.0 in order to apply the CRS and VRS models and to calculate SE [20]. Analysis has been done for five academic years (between 2013 and 2018) using data collected from the reports released by the university Rector.

The input and output variables used in this study are those contributing to performance and efficiency in higher education. The input variables taken into consideration are the number of academic staff (AS) and the number of non-academic staff (NAS). The academic staff includes the number of professors, lecturers, assistants who have contributed to teaching and research activities. The second input, non-academic staff, includes the number of persons which work for academic staff and students. These inputs were used in some other studies done by [10] and [21]. The output variables are the ratio between the number of students and the number of academic staff (ST) and the amount of research projects attracted by each faculty (RS). The first output was used in few studies done by [22] and [23]. The second output was used in other studies done by [9] and [24].

Analysis ends with the identification of variables that affect the results in the less efficient DMUs. In the attempt of improving these variables, some other variables might be affected. Here, TRIZ is introduced to tackle conflicts in an inventive manner.

## 4  Case Study

A case study was conducted in a Romanian higher education institution where the authors are employed. The Technical University of Cluj-Napoca, an "Advanced Research and Education University", is a tertiary educational institution having both tradition and national and international recognition. The data were collected from the Rector reports. Eleven faculties of Technical University of Cluj-Napoca from Romania were selected for this analysis (Table 1).

**Table 1.** The faculties analyzed in this study

| DMU | Description |
| --- | --- |
| DMU 1 | Faculty of Architecture and Urban Planning |
| DMU 2 | Faculty of Automation and Computer Science |
| DMU 3 | Faculty of Civil Engineering |
| DMU 4 | Faculty of Machine Buildings |
| DMU 5 | Faculty of Electronics and Telecommunications and Information Technology |
| DMU 6 | Faculty of Electrical Engineering |
| DMU 7 | Faculty of Mechanical Engineering |
| DMU 8 | Faculty of Materials and Environmental Engineering |
| DMU 9 | Faculty of Buildings Services |
| DMU 10 | Faculty of Engineering - CUNBM |
| DMU 11 | Faculty of Science - CUNBM |

Based on the CRS model of analysis (see Fig. 1), the results show that, out of eleven faculties, only one faculty (DMU9) is best positioned (most efficient during the five-year period).

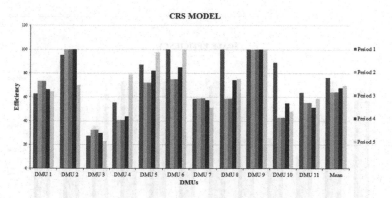

**Fig. 1.** Results from data analysis in CRS model

Specifically, for each period of analysis, the results show that three faculties (DMU6, DMU8 and DMU9) are efficient in the period 1 (2013/2014); two faculties (DMU2 and DMU9) are efficient in the period 2 (2014/2015), the period 3 (2015/2016) and the period 4 (2016/2017); and two faculties (DMU6 and DMU9) are efficient in the period 5 (2017/2018). The most inefficient faculty for all period analyzed is DMU3.

Using the VRS approach (see Fig. 2), two faculties (DMU2 and DMU9) look to be efficient during the period 2013–2018. Also, the results show that six faculties (DMU2, DMU6, DMU8, DMU9, DMU10 and DMU11) are efficient for period 1, four faculties (DMU2, DMU7, DMU9 and DMU11) for period 2, four faculties (DMU2, DMU6, DMU7 and DMU9) for period 3, three faculties (DMU2, DMU9 and DMU11) for period 4 and five faculties (DMU2, DMU5, DMU6, DMU9 and DMU11) are efficient for period 5. For this model, DMU3 is the most inefficient faculty in the period 2013–2018.

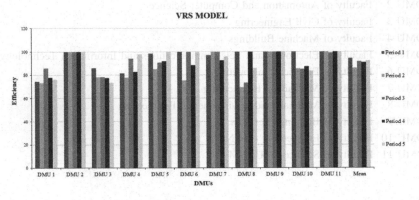

**Fig. 2.** Results from data analysis in VRS model

The scale efficiency (SE) is presented in Fig. 3 and shows that only one faculty (DMU9) is efficient for five academic years and the most inefficient faculty is DMU3.

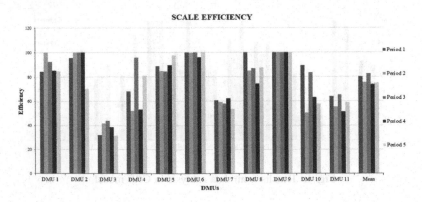

**Fig. 3.** Results from data analysis in SE

Analysis of efficiency with DEA indicates that DMU3 is in the worst position. According to the results, this unit has to improve its outputs with respect to the same amount of inputs as follows: O1 to increase income from research and development (R&D) projects with 179% in one year; O2 to increase the number of students with 170% in one year, such as to reach the same level of efficiency with the best positioned unit, DMU9. The level of growth for both outputs is significant in the case of DMU3. We can associate the targets for DMU3 as the "ideal final result" (IFR) according to TRIZ paradigm. The gap between current state and IFR for both performance indicators, as well as the need to reach the targets in a relative short period of time (one year) shows that inventive problem solving is the right approach, and not the traditional continuous improvement methodologies. Therefore, TRIZ has been considered to tackle the problem.

The first objective "to increase income from R&D projects with 179% in one year" is translated into operational alternatives as follows: either "O1.1 to double the number of projects, keeping the same value added of the project deliverables", or "O1.2 to keep the same number of projects, but doubling the value added (sophistication) of deliverables", or "O1.3 a combination of the first two operational alternatives. For identification of inventive solutions to these challenges, TRIZ inventive principles are considered in relation with O1.1 and O1.2. To be in the position to apply TRIZ, further investigations are necessary. Thus, it was searched for the roots where interventions could be applied, using a cause-effect analysis.

Due to space considerations, in this paper only the application of TRIZ for the first objective O1 is introduced. Thus, in the case of operational goal O1.1, the following roots have been found in the case of DMU3: R1.1 time allocated for various activities; R1.2 number of involved staff from the pool. In the case of operational goal O1.2, the following roots have been found: R2.1 skills of researchers (areas of professional interest); R2.2 infrastructure; R2.3 organization of teams; R2.4 target markets.

This information is organized such as to prepare the scene for TRIZ application. The following arrangements have been obtained: G1. How to allocate more time on research projects without affecting the quality of other activities (e.g. teaching, training for industry, consultancy for industry)? G2. How to make more people from the current pool of staff to be involved in research projects (e.g. doubling the current number)? G3. How to make people to contract new skills (better oriented to the hot subjects in the market) without relocating excessive additional time from other activities? G4. How to valorize the existent research facilities for more sophisticated research subjects? G5. How to reorganize the people with minimal interventions such as to double the value added of their deliverables? G6. How to make the current market to become interested on more sophisticated research subjects? (alternative: How to reach new beneficiaries, much more sophisticated than the current ones, with the same effort involved?).

Problem G1 becomes in TRIZ language: *improve* the time (speed) to execute the task (process) [TRIZ-9] *without damaging* stability of the other tasks (processes) [TRIZ-13]. This leads to the following innovation vectors: I1.1 replace of traditional system with a "softer" one; I1.2 make the system more sectional for easy aggregation and disaggregation; I1.3 exploit sensibility (resonance).

Problem G2 is deployed into TRIZ language as follows: *improve* the volume covered by the dynamic elements [TRIZ-7] *without damaging* effort to activate dynamic elements [TRIZ-19]. This is translated into the following innovation vector: I2.1 transformation of system properties (by changing conditions and degree of flexibility).

Problem G3 is converted in the TRIZ space as: *improve* the quantity of substance (know how) [TRIZ-26] *without damaging* area covered by the dynamic element [TRIZ-5]. The application of TRIZ indicates the following innovation vector: I3.1 make the system interchangeable; I3.2 think out-of-the-box (nonconventional approaches based on centrifugal effects); I3.3 reconfigurable construction.

Problem G4 is interpreted in TRIZ as: *improve* capacity (productivity) [TRIZ-39] *without damaging* shape (current infrastructure) [TRIZ-12]. Innovation vectors related to this problem are: I4.1 replace linear action with cyclic ones; I4.2 composite structures.

Problem G5 is reformulated in TRIZ as: *improve* quantity of substance [TRIZ-26] *without increasing* tension [TRIZ-11]. This leads to the following innovation vectors: I5.1 place parts in advance in a way they can go immediately intro action when required in a most convenient way; I5.2 replace linear actions with cyclic ones or use "centrifugal effects"; I5.3 increase local quality using transition to a heterogeneous structure.

Problem G6 is adapted for TRIZ application as: *improve* the complexity of the system [TRIZ-36] *without damaging* easiness to realize the system [TRIZ-32]. The associated innovation vectors are: I6.1 replace the current approach of targeting potential beneficiaries with several less-expensive approaches, even this comprises some of the properties (e.g. longevity); I6.2 increase the degree of segmentation; I6.3 instead of looking for beneficiaries in new markets make such as they will look for you.

As TRIZ results indicate, a bunch of simultaneous measures must be applied such as to jump into a new level of efficiency in the case of DMU3. Thus, generic innovation vectors have been translated into inventive solutions as follows:

- An upskilling program is initiated, each person focusing on a limited number of issues. In relation with projects, matrix form of organization is considered; thus, there is no need for each person to accumulate a big volume of new skills.
- In the research projects people will be organized in interdisciplinary teams, in structured that overpass departments, with the possibility to migrate from one team to another according to project context.
- Project opportunities will come first in a "node" where the project leader will have the freedom to invite and select the team from the overall pool of people, including the possibility to invite people outside the boarder of the DMU3.
- Current infrastructure will be reorganized such as to avoid underutilization (one of the situations identified in the root-cause analysis) and in the free space will be hosted equipment from some providers using a win-win partnership model.
- All people will be trained to approach market in a professional way and annual KPIs on the number and/or volume of R&D incoming projects will be associated to each person.
- An expo center will be promoted such as to increase the incidence of interaction with potential customers that come to visit your facilities (following some inspiring models from other universities – e.g. Technion).

# 5  Conclusions and Research Limitations

The value of this research stands in the combination of DEA and TRIZ for systematic analysis and innovation of decision-making units (DMUs) in organizations, in this case, in higher education institutions. The methodology has a general applicability in practice. A quantitative peer assessment of various DMUs is possible and areas that require intervention can be visualized. Information enables the formulation of conflicts; thus, systematic innovation is facilitated for defining appropriate directions of improvement.

For this analysis two inputs (AS and NAS) and two outputs (ST and RS) are used for the examination the possibility of measuring and comparing efficiency between faculties from a university by using CRS and VRS model (output oriented) to determine the output maximization and the value of scale efficiency (SE) for five academic years. The results of this study show that only one faculty (DMU9) is efficient during the period 2013–2018 and the most inefficient faculty is DMU3. The identification of variables that affect the results in the most inefficient DMU represents the next step. In the attempt of improving these variables, some other variables might be affected. In this case TRIZ is introduced to tackle conflicts in an inventive manner and to establish appropriate directions of intervention. At the end of this step, a set of innovative solutions have been generated. In addition, better use of budgets for institutional development, which is highly relevant in the case of public institutions must be considered.

The research in this paper is also subjected to some limitations which open new opportunities for further works. In this respect, calculation of relative efficiency scores with different models generates insight into the performance of DMUs on various dimensions and depends on managerial action. In this research we used only a performance model called "overall performance of faculties in higher education institution". The overall performance model is that universities employ people to produce enrolments and generate research output. There are several other possibilities to assess efficiency, depending on the sets of inputs and outputs or depending on the goals; for example: the performance model focuses on delivery of educational services, performance on fee-paying enrolments, teaching and research performance and so on.

# References

1. Bazrkar, A., Iranzadeh, S.: Prioritization of lean six sigma improvement projects using data envelopment analysis cross efficiency model. Qual. Access Success **18**(157), 72–76 (2017)
2. Jani, H.M.: Teaching TRIZ problem-solving methodology in higher education: a review. Int. J. Sci. Res. **2**(9), 98–103 (2013)
3. Thanassoulis, E., Dyson, R., Foster, M.: Relative efficiency assessments using data envelopment analysis: an application to data on rates departments. J. Oper. Res. Soc. **38**(5), 397–411 (1987). https://doi.org/10.1057/jors.1987.68
4. Charnes, A., Cooper, W., Rhodes, E.: Measuring the efficiency of decision making units. Eur. J. Oper. Res. **2**, 429–444 (1978)

5. Banker, R.D., Charnes, A., Cooper, W.: Some models for estimating technical and scale inefficiencies in data envelopment analysis. Manag. Sci. **30**(9), 1078–1092 (1984)
6. Fare, R., Lovell, C.: Measuring the technical efficiency of producation. J. Econ. Theory **19**, 150–162 (1978)
7. Coelli, T.: A Guide to DEAP V2.1 - A Data Envelopment Analysis (Computer) Program. CEPA - Centre for Efficiency and Productivity Analysis. https://economics.uq.edu.au/cepa. Accessed 20 Mar 2020
8. Selim, S., Bursalioglu, S.A.: Analysis of the determinants of universities efficiency in Turkey: application of the data envelopment analysis and panel Tobit model. Proc. - Soc. Behav. Sci. **89**, 895–900 (2013)
9. Aziz, N.A., Janor, R.M., Mahadi, R.: Comparative departmental efficiency analysis within a university: a DEA approach. Proc. - Soc. Behav. Sci. **90**, 540–548 (2013)
10. Avkiran, N.K.: Investigating technical and scale efficiencies of australian universities through data envelopment analysis. Socio-Econ. Plan. Sci. **35**, 57–80 (2001)
11. Glenn Mazur. http://www.mazur.net/triz/. Accessed 10 Mar 2020
12. Lerner, L.: Genrich Altshuller: Father of TRIZ. Russian Magazine Ogonek (1991)
13. Gadd, K.: TRIZ for Engineers. Wiley, London (2011)
14. Issac, L.S., Satesh, N.N., Kenny, T.B.: Application of TRIZ in the accreditation of engineering education. Int. J. Innov. Manag. Technol. **3**(2), 112–116 (2012)
15. Jiang, F.: Application idea for TRIZ theory in innovation education. In: 5th International Conference on Computer Science and Education (ICCSE), vol. 1535, no. 1540, pp. 24–27. IEEE, Hefei (2010)
16. Lepeshev, A., Podlesnyi, S., Pogrebnaya, T., Kozlov, A., Sidorkina, O.: Development of creativity in engineering education using TRIZ. In: Interdisciplinary Engineering Design Education Conference (IEDEC), pp. 6–9. IEEE, Santa Clara (2013)
17. Jiang, F., Xiao, Z., Wang, Y., Zhang, C.: Application TRIZ to innovative ability training in the mechanical engineering major. In: 7th International Conference on Computer Science and Education (ICCSE), vol. 1464, no. 1469, pp. 14–17. IEEE, Melbourne (2012)
18. Dyson, R.G., Allen, R., Camanho, A., Podinvoski, V., Sarrico, C., Shale, E.: Pitfalls and protocols in DEA. Eur. J. Oper. Res. **132**(2), 245–259 (2001)
19. Avkiran, N.K.: Productivity Analysis in the Service Sector with Data Envelopment Analysis. University of Queensland - Business School, Australia (2006)
20. Emrouznejad, A., Thanassoulis, E.: Performance Improvement Management Software: PIM - DEAsoft - V3.0 User Guide. UK: Performance Improvement Management Limited (2011)
21. Abott, M., Doucouliagos, C.: The efficiency of Australian universities: a data envelopment analysis. Econ. Educ. Rev. **22**, 89–97 (2003)
22. Sarrico, C.S., Dyson, R.G.: Using DEA for planning in UK universities. J. Oper. Res. Soc. **51**(7), 789–800 (2000)
23. De Witte, K., Hudrlikova, L.: What about excellence in teaching? A benevolent ranking of universities. Scientometrics **96**(1), 337–364 (2013). https://doi.org/10.1007/s11192-013-0971-2
24. Johnes, J.: Data envelopment analysis and its application to the measurement of efficiency in higher education. Econ. Educ. Rev. **25**, 273–288 (2006)

# Understanding and Overcoming the Low Utilization Rate of ARIZ in TRIZ Practices

Clément Acker[1], Antoine Braesch[1], Pierre Dumangin[1], Nathan Lauth[1], Amira Essaid[1], and Denis Cavallucci[2](✉)

[1] CESI Campus, Strasbourg, France
[2] INSA Graduate School of Applied Science, ICube Laboratory UMR7357, Strasbourg, France
denis.cavallucci@insa-strasbourg.fr

**Abstract.** It is well known that ARIZ constitutes the paradox of being the most powerful tool of TRIZ but also the least used. This lack of enthusiasm for its use is largely due to its apparent complexity and the feeling that this tool remains the prerogative of experts. Its algorithmic nature has questioned us to the point of investigating whether, today, modern numerical techniques could not, without distorting its structure, make it more accessible. This article presents our analysis of the state of the art on this subject, the methodology proposed for its evolution, its collaborative web development, how will be conducted its first tests and the way to measure its attractiveness rate to Internet users trained or not at TRIZ. Our hypothesis based on previous studies using classical ARIZ shows that the catch rate with an online collaborative application is potentially much higher than in a paper version and allows us to consider more serenely future usage of ARIZ in industrial situation or academic training curricula.

**Keywords:** ARIZ · TRIZ · IT implementation · Software

## 1 Introduction

### 1.1 ARIZ's Role in the History of TRIZ

From the earliest years of TRIZ's history [1], Altshuller sets out in his writings a methodical sequence of steps to accompany creative reasoning [2]. Without being named ARIZ, this sequence of steps land-marked the history of TRIZ from 1946 to 1985 [3]. The first appearance of the acronym ARIZ dates back to 1974, when the term algorithm was used for the first time. In total, more than 40 years of iterations have enabled ARIZ to evolve from a simple series of 4 steps to a complete algorithm of 40 steps divided into 3 phases [4]. The history of ARIZ is not the subject of this article, so we summarize this retrospective by the Fig. 1.

At the end of 1985, Altshuller announced that ARIZ had reached its ultimate version and that his research work to develop it had come to an end. ARIZ became then, in its 85C version, the standard for TRIZ academic training.

D. Cavallucci et al. (Eds.): TFC 2020, IFIP AICT 597, pp. 145–156, 2020.
https://doi.org/10.1007/978-3-030-61295-5_12

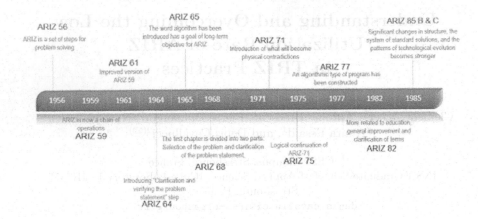

**Fig. 1.** Evolution of ARIZ.

## 1.2    The Attempts to Computerize ARIZ

The first software to computerize ARIZ has been developed in 1990 when, using the Prolog language, a version of Invention Machine was created [5]. It offers a human-machine interface that asks the user a simple question appearing in a window and then the user is invited to write down his answer in the next window [6]. Later, the first versions of Windows as an operating system let appear a more user-friendly interface with some graphics, but with the same logic. Thereafter, the computerization of ARIZ required the computerization of TRIZ, where the operationalization of some tools (like the Contradiction Matrix) was mixed with a particular effort in better addressing the analysis of the initial situation [7]. It was not only the object of numerous contributions of construction of various graphs [8], but also the means to get back to the parallel international research of the Value Analysis movement [9] where the first standards let appear a succession of steps supposed to formalize the design process. It is more the use of the Functional Analysis that interested the designers of methods and computer programs of TRIZ [10]. This appropriate alliance not only filled a methodological gap in TRIZ, but has allowed an harmony with the Functional Analysis which is already adopted in industry and engineering education [11].

The matrix representations and the construction of graphs are particularly suitable for computerization. For this reason, object-oriented programming has rapidly led to the emergence of various softwares implementing the TRIZ or some parts of it as well as a set of algorithms explaining which tool to use in which circumstances [12]. These alternatives for the use of TRIZ tools are often limited to asking the user questions about the nature of his problem and directing him in case of a simple problem to the matrix, to the SU-Fields for the physical problem, and to ARIZ when the problem is vaguely defined and complicated.

### 1.3  Review of Barriers to the Use of ARIZ in Education and Industry

These first attempts, which date back to the early 1990s, are still going on. We have still not gone beyond the stage of the annotations book, even though the functional package has grown considerably. The use of databases has enabled softwares to go online and to put to user's disposal a set of physical principles with pictorial or animated examples. At the same time, the beginning of the 2000s heralds a new era for TRIZ, which becomes the object of academic research and various challenges; one of them is to be hybridized with other methodological approaches, other societal purposes, and more recently to be subject to enriched development based on Artificial Intelligence.

Getting back to ARIZ, the situation is not changing. The resource document, which is often about 15 pages, is still given to TRIZ advanced learning candidates. They can read the names of the phases, observe a pictorial architecture in the form of a flow chart, and see the 40 steps with annotations (often Altshuller's original ones), each of them accompanied by one or more didactic or real-life examples to help the learner to understand the purpose of the step in question.

Consequently, we legitimately wonder what will allow ARIZ to benefit from new collaborative web development technologies, from a twofold perspective: making ARIZ more "user friendly" and thereby increasing the catch rate of novices to TRIZ rather than being limited to the Matrix for years before taking an interest in ARIZ. To achieve this, it is clear that ARIZ will have to operate more intuitively, more quickly and offer a permanent tracking of the progress of the questioning, particularly in its first phase. Our research through this article is therefore divided into three sections; the Sect. 2 aims to build a hypothetical continuum of steps that scrupulously take up the expected ARIZ-85C without distorting it. This continuum will be reconstructed online, according to contemporary UX/UI rules and in a collaborative mode. It will also benefit from all the power of case-based reasoning, where past cases will be capitalized to be eventually used in the context of ARIZ. The Sect. 3 focuses on building the online software prototype in order to conduct later experiments with groups of students. In this section, we present also the main advantages of using our proposed tool. In Sect. 4, we present the main metrics we will use in our future research to compare our tool to classical methods. Finally, Sect. 5 concludes the paper and presents the perspectives of our future research.

## 2  State of the Art

### 2.1  Invention Machine, the Prolog Beginnings of a Computerization of TRIZ

Invention Machine, also known two decades later as Goldfire Innovator, is a software developed by Invention Machine Corporation, a company acquired by IHS Markit in 2012. This software is a knowledge management engine and is intended to provide a structured process for ideation and creative problem solving to help engineers to innovate, to find new uses for old objects and to improve existing products. Goldfire Innovator is equipped with problem identification, analysis and resolution capabilities integrated with a patented syntaxic engine. The software relies on knowledge from internal and external knowledge bases, scientific patent databases and the Internet. All this knowledge is used to identify a problem area and then optimize a solution by applying the root cause analysis (a process that identifies the root causes of a problem in order to identify an appropriate solution), function modeling, or even TRIZ.

## 2.2    TechOptimizer the First Commercial Version of a Widely Distributed Tool

TechOptimizer is also a software developed by Invention Machine Corporation, released in 1998. It appears as a successor of Invention Machine software [13]. What makes TechOptimizer different from other attempts to operate TRIZ is that it has been widely distributed throughout highly industrialized countries and marketed a professional way. It is developed to be used by R&D professionals in order to define and to solve problems during the conceptual design phase of innovation. The software provides an access to a wide range of databases containing patent analyses, allowing the implementation of the TRIZ methodology. TechOptimizer consists of 5 different modules; the TechOptimizer module which defines, breaks down and analyzes the problem; the principle module gives examples of problem solving techniques; the prediction module gives examples of testing problem solving applications; the effects module explains the technical principles of TRIZ; and finally the function transfer module suggests transferring functions from one technical system to another. The efficiency of the software has been demonstrated through numerous tests, including its application to old cases. Thus it was shown that using TechOptimizer could have significantly accelerated the improvements of certain systems.

## 2.3    I-TRIZ Products and Their ARIZ Inclusion

I-TRIZ products are the property of Ideation company, another team originally rooted from ex-USSR founding members and established in 1992 in Michigan. Despite the fact that this team has both brought TRIZ to US market in the early times of TRIZ in USA, the proposed panoply of tools encompass Anticipatory Failure Determination, Directed Evolution and others, no one is clearly focusing on ARIZ. We could nevertheless observe many references to ARIZ steps in their ISQ (Innovation Situation questionnaire) which is both paper format and computer-based.

## 2.4    Enhanced Notebooks or Tutorials (TRISolver)

When TRIZ and ARIZ were sidelined by companies due to too much training requirements, a new type of innovation support software emerged. These tools come in the form of improved tutorials or online Notebooks. They allow the team in charge of the project to be assisted during the brainstorming, or the documentation concerning the project. They also make it possible to create a workspace shared with the entire team to work simultaneously on the same project remotely. TRISolver[1] is one of these solutions. It is developed in the form of a directory containing the project files as well as files adapted to the different stages of TRIZ, such as graphs with dots representing the implementation cost or the potential market for the innovation in progress. TRISolver also contains a toolbox to support the innovation team through the various stages of TRIZ. The development of notebooks and improved tutorials has helped to familiarize companies with TRIZ and innovation techniques, however their outdated interfaces and the training required to use them continue to hinder companies from using them.

## 2.5  TOP-TRIZ: The Asset of Experience

TOP-TRIZ is an approach developed by Zinovy Royzen, an expert in the field of TRIZ. His approach has given birth to a software assistance called TOP-TRIZ Problem Formulator and Solver [14]. TOP stands for Tool, Object, Product, because it is based on the modeling of the Tool - Object - Product function and it is presented as a solution to develop better products, at low cost, in a shorter time, while being more user-friendly (as intuitive as possible). The approach differs from the classic version of ARIZ-85C because it is based on the human experience of its creator, who taught ARIZ for years to various companies such as Boeing. The approach reduces also the number of steps required before obtaining a solution, improving then the efficiency of the remaining steps. These steps have also been reworked and enriched by templates to facilitate their completion.

## 2.6  The Versions After ARIZ-85C

In 1985, a final version of ARIZ was released, ARIZ-85C. After that, Altshuller decided to switch to a new topic of interest. Therefore the requests of the TRIZ methodology professors for a new version of ARIZ has to find another lead. He considered that this version had reached its ultimate state and that his research work to develop it had come to an end. But during a TRIZ conference held in 1989, the topic of improving ARIZ was raised. A number of TRIZ experts agreed that it would be a good idea to make a new version of ARIZ that focused on the following issues:

- Increase the reliability of the algorithm and make higher the probability of solving real-life problems with ARIZ.
- Improve learning methods to provide quality education in a reasonable amount of time by taking into account the increased demand which was ignored by Altschuler.

---

[1] http://www.trisolver.eu/index.html.

- Implement the new suggestions of the last five years.
- Prepare ARIZ to be computerized

After the endorsement of Altshuller, many versions of ARIZ have been proposed differing from the more classical versions of TRIZ in some aspects.

For example, based on ARIZ-2000, Pentti Soderlin proposed to drop the name ARIZ, so as not to confuse TRIZ and ARIZ, since the latter applies all the principles of TRIZ [15]. Therefore, he suggested to refer to the ARIZ algorithm as the Job plan of TRIZ. In addition to that, he considers that it is unnecessary to go through all the steps of the algorithm and proposes rather to go through the problem analysis phase which would determine the type of the problem we are dealing with. Depending on the result of this phase, it is possible then to find the part of the algorithm adapted to the resolution of this type of problem. For example, if our problem is described through a physical or technical contradiction, we will consider the part of the algorithm that leads to the resolution based on the problem-solving matrix.

A version adapted to a wider variety of problems has also been developed, named ARIZ-U-2010. ARIZ-U-2014 [16], being the latest proposal of an evolution of the algorithm that differs from the original because it can be applied not only to engineering problems, but also to other types of problems (such as biological or even legal, scientific or other problems). This version of ARIZ includes a phase of problem analysis, synthesis of the new system, but also a phase of evaluation and revision of the proposed ideas.

## 2.7    Analysis of the Uses of ARIZ Derivatives

These derivatives of ARIZ, not signed by Altshuller, have different advantages, depending on the version we take. In fact, Peter Soderlin's version, aims to speed up the use of ARIZ, and thus to make its use process much faster, encouraging then potential users of the method to apply the proposed version. ARIZ-U-2014, on the other hand, has the advantage to be used in more areas than the basic version of ARIZ, which considerably broadens the range of possibilities and makes it accessible to many experts in various fields.

# 3    Our Methodology

## 3.1    Towards the Use of New Technologies to Computerize ARIZ

In order to make ARIZ widely used, we need to make it more attractive to newcomers and easier for companies to use. We therefore study how valuable it would be to integrate levels of expertise into a new tool. This to allow both experienced users of ARIZ to use it quickly and easily, while to accompany novices at every stage of the problem solving process more didactically. In fact, a tool that is enriched by short texts and examples explaining how each step is carried out. As for the experts, they can easily ignore these additional information or even hide them in order to carry out the problem solving process quickly.

Another development direction we intend to evaluate, is to operate ARIZ using a true collaborative mode. Indeed some steps of the algorithm can potentially be performed independently from the previous ones. The possibility to work together on the same problem allows to involve all the project members in the progress of the problem solving process. It also allows the different project actors to review more easily the already completed steps, to detect potential errors more quickly, and thus to accelerate the progress of the project.

We also wanted to make the user experience as pleasant as possible, by considering an automatic backup function, allowing users to work without worrying about the sustainability of the data they are providing. In fact, they have only to enter a data in a field, leave the application and the data will be automatically saved in the project. This latter is also saved in an external database. We did not integrate a manual backup function in order not to mislead users, who might think that the automatic backup is not 100% efficient.

Working online is another potential promising direction for our tool. In order to allow different actors of the project to better work together and to make collaborative mode possible, we decided not to develop a desktop application but rather to use web technologies and make our application available on all operating systems. In addition to that, a mobile portability is also considered in order to make the application accessible and easy to use to everyone. For that purpose, we planed to develop the software by following some good practices to create a PWA (Progressive Web Application) which is a web application that adapts itself to mobile devices (Android or iOS).

### 3.2   Our Development Approach

As previously mentioned, for the objective of reducing time consuming and improve efficiency, our application is based on the use of web technologies that allow users to work online. For this, we have used HTML, CSS and JavaScript, in the form of TypeScript, since we have chosen, for the front-end of our application to use the Angular framework, developed by Google. This latter is one of the best framework to be used for developing web applications. In fact, it is well known allowing future developers to easily understand the code, and thus to modify or extend it. It also allows to make modifications possible in case a new version of ARIZ would be released and would require to adapt the application to this new version. On the server side, we decided to use a Node JS technology which allows us to use JavaScript to generate web pages. Since most of the tasks are done on the client side, Node JS was a perfect choice because it facilitates to create quick applications.

We used PostgreSql to build our database. This database management system is a good support for the Javascript language. In order to make the application work well, we also used Prisma, a tool that allows us to link a database with our server code very easily.

As Integrated Development Environment, we used IntelliJ and Visual Studio Code because they already support the sub-modules git which we used during the project in order to work more efficiently and at the same time on various parts of the application. We also used Postman, an HTTP request simulator, to check the behavior of our application.

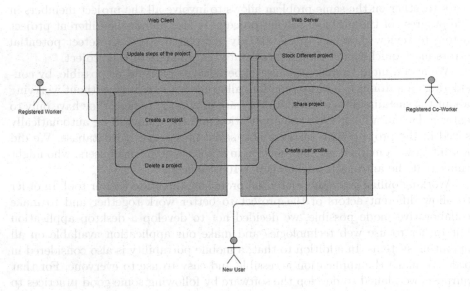

**Fig. 2.** Use case.

Figure 2 illustrates a user case of our solution:

As illustrated, the solution is organized in a client-server architecture that allows projects to be stored online and shared between project actors. User profiles are created and stored on the server. It is possible for the users, then to create projects, which will be stored on the server, and share them with the team members they work with. By this way, team members can make changes on the project they are working on and use projects already completed by other teams as a guide for completing the steps in their projects. It is also possible to delete projects that are no longer current or have not been completed.

### 3.3  Hypothetical Assessment of the Logic of Use of Our Approach

Our proposal can be summarized as a new collaborative environment for learning and practicing ARIZ online and collaboratively. It aims at being easy to handle. The descriptive parts of the different steps of ARIZ will allow users with different levels of experience to carry out their projects and to operate ARIZ in a faster and easier way compared to the current paper version of the algorithm present in most of the training sessions. The explanatory sections of our tool are written in such a way that even the most novice users can understand how to fill in the screens and progress through the ARIZ steps, while being optional for experts. To allow a better understanding of the solution and the work that is expected, the solution is translated into several different languages, with a simple means of changing languages. In this way, users can implement the application in their native languages and thus work more efficiently. The solution includes a graphical environment where it is easy for a user to navigate. A progress bar that evolves as the different stages of the project are completed, allows the user to evaluate its progress and the work remaining.

With a view to future developments, we have thought of emphasizing collaborative work and community support. The client-server architecture will allow projects to be stored on the server and help users to work together on the same project. The database will also make consulting previous projects possible in case there is uncertainty how to complete the current ARIZ step. More languages will be included in the future to facilitate the understanding of the ARIZ steps to a wider community.

## 4    Metrics to Compare Our Tool to Classical Methods

The proposed tool is in the coding phase. In a next step of this research, we will propose a test to a community of students. Our approach is then to evaluate the results of using the tool according to three criteria; the rate of use, the rejection rate and the duration of use. These three criteria will be explained below.

For the evaluation, we will isolate two groups of second year engineering school students, divided into several disciplines through one of their teaching modules over 24 h of tutorials. Two groups will then be made up of students of an equivalent level and three team exercises will be given to them, leaving them free to choose whether to use ARIZ, the Su-Fields Analysis or the Matrix. One of the groups will have to use our proposed tool and the other group will be given the paper version. Both groups will be registered for an E-learning course that will provide them the basics of these three tools.

The rate of use consists in comparing, in both groups, the prorate of choice of ARIZ compared to that of the Su-Field Analysis and the Matrix. Currently, surveys conducted on this topic indicate that ARIZ is used between 1 and 3% of the time compared to other TRIZ tools. Although we are aware that ARIZ integrates two steps that direct the user towards the use of Su-Field Analysis, we assume that the isolated use of Su-Field Analysis is also possible independently of ARIZ, just as it is possible in ARIZ to exit the algorithm with concepts without systematically using Su-Field Analysis.

The rejection rate consists of comparing the number of students starting an ARIZ study and the time they stop it. It should be noted that the two approaches that will be compared are the classic paper-based approach currently used at the Strasbourg engineering school INSA and this new online tool as illustrated in Fig. 3. We will therefore estimate both the number of students who have stopped and the moment when ARIZ was abandoned by a learner. The current use of ARIZ in the test school allowed us to observe a dropout in 40% of the cases. The rejection character is reached when the learner leaves ARIZ to move on to another TRIZ tool before a solution concept has been issued.

The duration of use is an important criterion to measure whether the tool is likely to be adopted by a large number of organisations (education and industry).

Thus we have observed that ARIZ classic version is driven by novice students over a period of about 7 h, with a quasi-systematic output at step 3.7 of the algorithm. In this situation, two outputs of the algorithm will be counted as not falling under the first criterion because three output paths of the algorithm are possible (at step 1.7; 3.7 and 4.1 and after). We hypothesize here that in numerical, collaborative and online mode, this score can easily be improved.

Obviously we are ignoring elements of evaluation linked with the performance of ARIZ to solve problems since this essential criteria is not an element of differentiation between a modern-computed version and a paper version.

Finally, it should be pointed out that the conditions of such an exercise require that it must be conducted without mentoring, after only one classical lecture (identical for both groups of students) on ARIZ. As one of the objectives of this research is to multiply the use of ARIZ among novices, it seems obvious that in both test groups, if expert mentoring takes place, the groups will complete ARIZ and it is then more the expert himself who would be evaluated, which is not our intention.

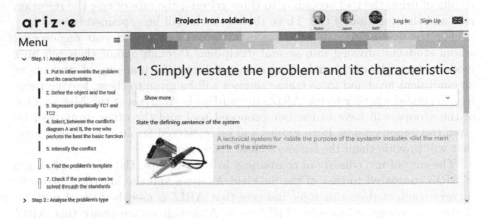

**Fig. 3.** Mock-up.

## 5   Conclusion

This paper was an opportunity to study the low level of use of ARIZ in education and industry. Why this tool, which is reputed to be so powerful, is so rarely used? Altshuller's three sentences accompanying the document version are a first sign: "don't start learning ARIZ without at least 80 h of TRIZ lessons". This simple sentence, probably legitimate when it was written by its author, no longer corresponds to the reality we are living through. Learning painfully is no longer the way to follow and the fact that knowledge only comes from a few, ever fewer experts over the years raises questions. If the TRIZ communities continue along this path, they will only end up seeing a lack of interest in Altshuller's work from

Generation Z. In this research, we are interested in resolving the contradiction of both acting in respect of Altshuller's latest developments, without distorting them, while reducing the difficulty of access to ARIZ both in terms of time and the performance of its use in real situations. A study has been conducted and an online collaborative tool has been created that grows richer as cases are shared and reassures the new user about his or her learning path to become more proficient in using ARIZ. This puts us in the perspective where shared and free, such a tool could help to ensure that the matrix is no longer the only popular tool for TRIZ with a wide audience, but that society finally discovers that TRIZ is not limited to the matrix and the associated inventive principles, but can, in complicated cases of analysis and resolution, serve industry and education in inventive performance. As a future work, we will conduct experiments with two groups of students (one group using our tool with a prior online training, another group using the classical method and its associated learning). The experience gathered from students needs also to be place in the perspective of acceptance by the new generation (also sometimes called Z generation) of a structured thinking approach. This has to be carefully observed in light of a rising consensus around the soft skills importance like intuition that might appear in opposition to a structured approach. An analysis and discussion of the measurement elements of the deliverable of this experiments will be proposed.

# References

1. Souchkov, V.: A brief history of TRIZ. TRIZ J. (2008). https://triz-journal.com/a-brief-history-of-triz. Accessed 28 Sept 2020
2. Altshuller, G.S., Shapiro, R.V.: About a technology of creativity. Quest. Psychol. **6**, 37–49 (1956)
3. Zlotin, B., Zusman, A.: ARIZ on the move. TRIZ J. **13**, 145–159 (1999)
4. Cameron, G.: ARIZ Explored: A Step-by-Step Guide to ARIZ, The Algorithm for Solving Inventive Problems (2015)
5. Hollingum, J.: Invention machine - a machine for making inventions? Assem. Autom. **18**(2), 112–119 (1998)
6. Marconi, J.: ARIZ: the algorithm for inventive problem solving. TRIZ J. **4**, 12–19 (1998)
7. Burgard, L., Dubois, S., De Guio, R., Rasovska, I.: Sequential experimentation to perform the analysis of initial situation. In: TRIZ Future, pp. 30–38 (2011)
8. Cavallucci, D., Rousselot, F., Zanni, C.: Initial situation analysis through problem graph. CIRP J. Manuf. Sci. Technol. **2**(4), 310–317 (2010)
9. Mao, X., Zhang, X., Abourizk, S.M.: Enhancing value engineering process by incorporating inventive problem-solving techniques. J. Constr. Eng. Manag. **135**(5), 416–424 (2009)
10. Liu, F., Jiang, P., Zhang, P., Tan, R.: Conceptual design process model for function and contradiction solving. In: 2008 IEEE International Conference on Management of Innovation and Technology, pp. 1–3, 1298–1302 (2008)
11. Leon-Rovira, N., Aguayo Téllez, H.: A new model of the conceptual design process using QFD/FA/TRIZ. In: 10th Annual Quality Function Deployment Symposium, USA (1998)

12. Ivashkov, M., Souchkov, V., Dzenisenka, S.: A TRIZ based method for intelligent design decisions. In: Applications of Digital Techniques in Industrial Design Engineering-CAID&CD, pp. 357–361 (2005)
13. Arel, E.T., Verbitsky, M., Devoino, I., Ikovenko, S.: TechOptimizer Fundamentals. Invention Machine Educational Services (2002)
14. Royzen, Z.: Solving problems using Top-TRIZ (2008)
15. Soderlin, P.: Thoughts on ARIZ - do we need to redesign the ARIZ 2000?. TRIZ J. (2003). https://triz-journal.com/thoughts-ariz-need-redesign-ariz-2000. Accessed 28 Sept 2020
16. Rubin, M.: On developing ARIZ-universal-2014. TRIZ J. (2014). https://triz-journal.com/on-developing-ariz-universal-2014. Accessed 28 Sept 2020

# Sustainable Development

# Excesses in Engineering Systems: A Helpful Resource

Oleg Abramov[✉]

Algorithm Ltd., Ruzovskaya Street 16, St. Petersburg 190013, Russia
Oleg.Abramov@algo-spb.com

**Abstract.** Excessiveness (redundancy) is often intentionally introduced in an engineering system (ES) in order to improve its reliability. In many cases, however, various types of excessiveness existing in an ES can be a good resource for improving the ES, whether by reducing its cost, minimizing its environmental impact, improving its compatibility with other systems, or something else. Yet modern TRIZ does not fully utilize this resource. For example, in Function Analysis (FA), although a useful function's excessive level of performance is seen as a disadvantage, this fact is normally ignored. Additionally, the cost and quantity of substances, energy and other useful resources spent in the system are evaluated subjectively and their excessive consumption is frequently classified as "acceptable" (this could be called "hidden excessiveness"), which in the analysis leads to a loss of some key problems and related solutions. In this paper, the author is trying to enhance TRIZ Resource Analysis and FA, by (1) introducing an objective approach to identifying different hidden excesses in the ES, which includes the excessive amount of energy, substances, and other resources (e.g. bandwidth, processing power, etc.) consumed by the system, and (2) by including these excesses in the TRIZ Resource Analysis. Four case studies demonstrate the practical application of this approach in the areas of machining operations, video displays, Wi-Fi systems and computer simulation algorithms.

**Keywords:** Excessiveness · Engineering system · Function analysis · Redundancy · Resource analysis · Trends of engineering systems evolution · TRIZ

## 1 Introduction to the Problem

Across different industries, introducing excessiveness or redundancy is a common and efficient way to improve the reliability of technical systems by utilizing excessive resources such as duplicating components, units or even by backing up the entire system in order to cope with failures [1–3].

Chybowsky and Matuszak [4] indicate the following types of redundancy: structural redundancy, functional redundancy, parametric redundancy, component surplus, strength surplus, time surplus, information surplus, and maintenance surplus.

In many cases, however, excessiveness is introduced into a technical system unintentionally and, as indicated by the author in an earlier conference paper [5], represents a great resource for improving the system by stripping off the excesses. Such

© IFIP International Federation for Information Processing 2020
Published by Springer Nature Switzerland AG 2020
D. Cavallucci et al. (Eds.): TFC 2020, IFIP AICT 597, pp. 159–171, 2020.
https://doi.org/10.1007/978-3-030-61295-5_13

improvement most frequently results in lowering the cost of the technical system without sacrificing performance, which is a frequent demand in TRIZ consulting projects.

The main TRIZ tools used for identifying and eliminating excesses are Function Analysis (FA) and Trimming [6]:

- FA identifies useful functions with excessive level of performance that partially addresses parametric and functional redundancies as well as strength surpluses;
- Trimming identifies unimportant but problematic components that can be eliminated from the system, which addresses component surplus and structural redundancy.

Unfortunately, these tools are not very reliable in terms of identifying excesses. For example, in the practical application of FA, the performance of useful functions is assessed subjectively, and the excessive performance of useful functions is frequently overlooked or neglected.

Additionally, some "hidden excesses" [5] are difficult to reveal because there are no clear criteria for evaluating excesses such as parametric redundancy, and time and information surpluses, especially when they are inherent to a principle of operation utilized in the analyzed system. For example, everyone usually overlooks the excessive energy consumption in an engine if the engine's efficiency is close to the theoretical limit for its engine type, and nobody worries about excessive use of computational power or bandwidth as long as the information is processed fast enough to satisfy the end consumer. On the other hand, using a more efficient engine or a more efficient data processing algorithm/software could significantly reduce the cost and/or increase the value of the engineering systems where these components are used.

In this paper, the author proposes a brief algorithm for (1) identifying excesses in a technical system and its components, and (2) for utilizing these excesses as a resource for improving the system and/or its components.

## 2   Method and Tools Utilized

The main tools utilized in the proposed algorithm are:

1. Function Analysis (FA) [6], which allows for identifying the useful functions in the entire technical system and all its components as well as the main parameters characterizing the performance of these functions; and
2. Analysis of physical limitations for the identified useful functions, which yields the minimum required values for the parameters of the useful functions, and then compares them with the actual values of these parameters.

## 3  Proposed Algorithm

The 11-step algorithm proposed for identifying and utilizing excessiveness in an engineering system and utilizing it as a resource for improvement is given in Table 1 below.

**Table 1.** Proposed algorithm for identifying and utilizing excesses in technical systems.

| Step # | Description | Comments |
|---|---|---|
| 1 | Select an engineering system to improve | This could be a product, technological process or equipment, or a component thereof |
| 2 | Perform component and interaction analyses for the system | Steps 2 and 3 are performed exactly as in classical Function Analysis [6] |
| 3 | Build a functional model of the system | |
| 4 | For each useful function, including the system's main function, determine its main parameters and their actual values | Parameters that characterize the performance of the function, e.g. speed, power, bandwidth, resolution, etc. |
| 5 | Generalize all useful functions | This step helps to mitigate psychological inertia imposed by the system's current operation principle. Generalization is done just as in Function Oriented Search (FOS) [7] |
| 6 | For each generalized function, determine the physical limits of its main parameters values | Physical limit means the minimum value of the parameter that would be enough to deliver the maximum performance that the object of the function can utilize |
| 7 | Compare physical limits for each parameter with its actual value; identify components that have functions with excessive parameters | At Steps 7 and 8, note that small excesses could represent a resource for an incremental improvement of the system, while utilizing very big excesses may require changing the operation principle – either of the entire system or of its component(s) – and result in a breakthrough innovation (which is not always good) |
| 8 | Evaluate how eliminating these excesses would benefit other components and the entire engineering system | |
| 9 | Select excesses that are the most promising to eliminate | Select the excesses whose elimination offers the highest benefits at reasonable challenges. QEA-screening [8] can be useful for this |
| 10 | Identify key problems to solve in order to eliminate selected excesses | This can be done using Cause and Effect Chains Analysis (CECA) [9] |
| 11 | Solve these key problems | At Step 11, any or all of the problem solving tools of TRIZ [6] can be employed |

As seen from Table 1, all steps, except Step 6 of the algorithm, are supported by existing TRIZ tools such as Function Analysis [6], FOS [7], QEA-screening [8] and CECA [9].

Since Step 6 is critical for the proposed algorithm, it deserves a more detailed explanation. At this step, it is important that the physical limit of the function parameter be determined independently of the action principle utilized to deliver the function. For this, it is frequently useful to employ the concept of the ideal final result (IFR) [6] – as was similarly suggested by Russo, Regazzoni and Montecchi [10] for eco-design.

For example, if we would like to identify the excess of energy used by a vehicle, we need to consider the vehicle's generalized function "to move an object". The minimum energy required to move the object from point A to point B is determined in Step 6 only as a difference in the potential energy of the object at these two points; that is, by the difference in elevation between the points. If point B is at a lower elevation than point A, then the energy required to move the object from A to B is negative and, theoretically, the vehicle could generate energy instead of consuming it when moving the object.

Step 6, however, is not always easy to do. For this reason and because it is so important, Step 6 is illustrated in more detail in the four quite different case studies below.

## 4   Case Studies and Discussion

### 4.1   Case Study 1: Drill Machines

It is well-known that machining operations such as the metal cutting processes employed, for example, in drill and lathe machines are among the largest energy consumers and carbon emitters in the world [11].

The cutting power used by these machines is spent mostly on the following [11]:

- Plastic deformation of the material that occurs during the machining (mostly – on deforming chips), which counts as a loss;
- Overcoming friction between the tool and work material as well as between the tool and shavings, which are also losses;
- Forming new surfaces on chips, which is yet another loss;
- Forming new surfaces on the work material, which is the only useful outcome of these processes.

The generalized main function of lathe and drill machines is "to remove extra material" from a workpiece, which is realized in current processes by cutting and removing chips from the workpiece. One of the main parameters of this function is energy consumption.

In order to identify the minimum energy (Step 6 of the algorithm in Table 1) required only for removing the extra material from a workpiece, it is helpful to consider the ideal final result (IFR) of the generalized function and compare it with the actual process. Figure 1 illustrates this with the process for making a hole in a metal workpiece.

As seen from Fig. 1, most of the energy in the current process is spent on generating chips (on forming their large surfaces, deforming them, etc.), while the ideal process involves only separating a single piece of material inside the hole from the workpiece and moving this piece out of the hole. Most of the energy consumed in the ideal process is spent on breaking molecular bonds on the surface of the hole, i.e. on forming only one surface.

This means that drilling consumes by a few orders of magnitude more energy than the ideal process of making holes, which indicates a huge energy excess in drilling.

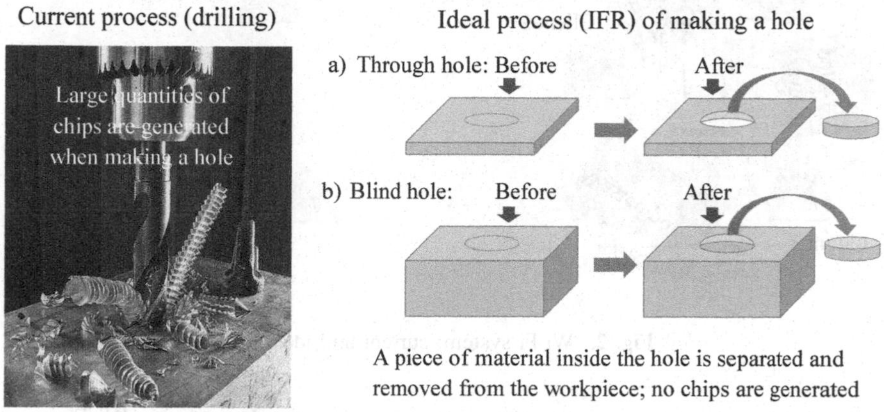

Current process (drilling)          Ideal process (IFR) of making a hole

Fig. 1. The process of making a hole in a metal workpiece: current and ideal.

**Comments.** Similar huge excesses of consumed energy exist in most machining operations such as those utilized in lathe and milling machines. Removing these excesses may lead to using alternative action principles: for example, holes in metal sheets are punched when possible, which is faster and requires much less energy per hole.

## 4.2    Case Study 2: Wi-Fi System

In a Wi-Fi system, which includes an Access Point (AP) or a Router connected to a number of client devices, the excessiveness of signal energy transmitted by the AP can be evaluated using the IFR approach just as in the previous case study.

Wi-Fi protocol requires all devices on the same network to be connected to the AP, which means that the AP needs to have an omnidirectional antenna that transmits and receives signal in all directions in order to maintain network functionality.

One of the critical parameters of any wireless communication system is the power of the transmitted signal. In order to determine how excessive this power is in the Wi-Fi network, it is necessary to compare how the generalized function "to transmit electromagnetic power" is performed in the current Wi-Fi system and in the ideal wireless network, in which signals are transmitted only between the AP and its clients with no transmissions in other directions.

The result shown in Fig. 2 shows a huge excess of transmitted power, which is wasted in the directions where there are no clients.

Current Wi-Fi system:
Signal is transmitted in all directions

Ideal Wi-Fi system (IFR):
Signal is transmitted only between the AP and its clients

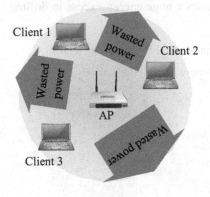
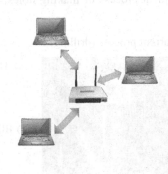

**Fig. 2.** Wi-Fi system: current and ideal.

**Comments.** It is possible to take advantage of this excess by using a Wi-Fi smart antenna system [12, 13]. This system has a switched-beam antenna and corresponding software able to determine the optimum direction for the AP to communicate with each client and always directs the antenna beam towards that client to which the AP is to communicate at the moment. This significantly improves the range and/or speed of the Wi-Fi network.

### 4.3  Case Study 3: Video Displays

In video devices such as computer monitors, TVs and virtual reality headsets, one of the most important parameters is screen resolution, so TV manufacturers offer higher and higher resolutions [14]: HD, then Full HD, then 4K, now – 8K, and there are plans for 16K and 32K, as shown in Table 2.

**Table 2.** TV resolutions.

| Resolution name | Horizontal × Vertical pixels | Total megapixels | Found in |
|---|---|---|---|
| 32K (32K UHD) | 30720 × 17280 | 530.84 | Long-term prospective |
| 16K (16K UHD) | 15360 × 8640 | 132.72 | Future TVs |
| 8K (8K UHD) | 7680 × 4320 | 33.18 | Hi-end TVs |
| 4K (Ultra HD) | 3840 × 2160 | 8.29 | Most modern TVs |
| 1080p (Full HD) | 1920 × 1080 | 2.07 | Inexpensive and older TVs |
| 720p (HD ready) | 1280 × 720 | 0.92 | Small and obsolete TVs |

A higher resolution implies a corresponding increase in the following parameters:

- Bandwidth needed to stream video content,
- Processing power and energy consumption required to generate high-resolution video, which is an especially big problem in gaming hardware delivering virtual reality (VR) and 3D experience, and
- Cost of the TV or a gadget.

Those who want to migrate from 4K to 8K TV may need to upgrade not only their Internet connection, but also their HDMI cables [14].

To assess whether such a high resolution is excessive, it is necessary to compare it with the maximum resolution that human eyes can perceive, which is easy to calculate if you know the field of view and the spatial resolution of the human eye. Thus, Clark [15] has estimated that the maximum resolution of the human eye is 576 megapixels.

This means that not only do current 4K and 8K resolutions not meet the eye's needs, but even the upcoming 16K (see Table 2) may also be too little. Therefore, only 32K would be able to deliver a video experience close to the maximum that our eye can perceive.

It has to be noted, however, that our eyes do not digest all visual information within the field of view equally well:

- In fact, we can fully digest only what is in our fovea (that is, within the central two degrees of our field of view), while most of what we see is actually blurry, and
- We all have a blind spot in each eye.

Taking this into account, Fraiman [16] estimated that at any given moment human eyes can see only 8 megapixels, which means that 4K already meets the maximum resolution that our eyes need, while 8K resolution is four times excessive, and 32K will be 64 times more than necessary.

**Comments.** To utilize this excess and make a 4K video device deliver a full 536-megapixel experience within the eye's entire field of view, the device has to display a crisp image only within a couple degrees around the center of the field of view. Since our eyes are constantly moving to scan the entire field of view, such device must track the eyeball movement and display a clear image exactly where the eyes are looking.

Such a device will provide the user with a 32K experience, the maximum that human eyes can digest, using a processing power and bandwidth that are virtually the same as in existing 4K devices. These features would be appreciated mainly in virtual reality headsets and in the gaming industry, which typically requires expensive and power-consuming high-end hardware to generate a crisp and smooth video.

### 4.4   Case Study 4: Algorithm for Numerical Calculation of Spin Echo Signals

The spin echo effect [17] relates to the magnetic resonance phenomenon. A spin echo occurs when a magnetic or paramagnetic substance located in an inhomogeneous magnetic field is subjected to a sequence of radio frequency (RF) pulses whose spectra are within the frequency range of the magnetic resonance of the substance, as shown in Fig. 3.

For a long time, spin echo was used in spin echo processors [18], which relate to functional electronic devices [19] for processing broadband RF signals. Another very important application of spin echo is magnetic resonance imaging (MRI) [20]. A similar phenomenon, photon echo, is used in cutting-edge quantum computers [21] to create quantum memory. Developing all these applications requires a fast computer simulation of spin echo signals, which the author researched in the 1990s.

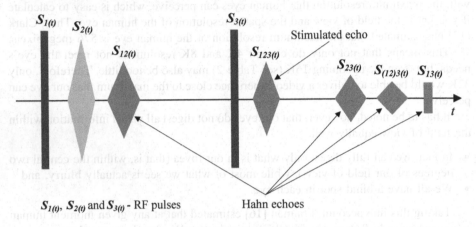

**Fig. 3.** Spin echo signals.

In order to numerically simulate spin echoes shown in Fig. 3, it is necessary to solve Bloch equations that describe magnetic resonance phenomena that include spin echo.

Let $M(t) = (M_x(t), M_y(t), M_z(t))$ be the nuclear or electron spin magnetization. Then the Bloch equations can be represented in matrix-vector notation as follows [22]:

$$\frac{d}{dt}\begin{pmatrix} M_x \\ M_y \\ M_z \end{pmatrix} = \begin{pmatrix} -\frac{1}{T_2} & \gamma B_z & -\gamma B_y \\ -\gamma B_z & -\frac{1}{T_2} & \gamma B_x \\ \gamma B_y & -\gamma B_x & -\frac{1}{T_1} \end{pmatrix} \begin{pmatrix} M_x \\ M_y \\ M_z \end{pmatrix} + \begin{pmatrix} 0 \\ 0 \\ \frac{M_0}{T_1} \end{pmatrix}, \quad (1)$$

where $\gamma$ is the gyromagnetic ratio and $B(t) = (B_x(t), B_y(t), B_0)$ is the magnetic field experienced by the nuclei or electron spins; $M_0$ is the steady state magnetization (it is in the z direction); $B_0$ is the z component of the magnetic field $B$, which in this particular case is constant in time.

In spin echo processors, $B_x(t)$ and $B_y(t)$ in Eq. (1) are magnetic field components created by RF pulses $S_1(t)$, $S_2(t)$ and $S_3(t)$ (see Fig. 3).

In order to simulate spin echo signals, it is necessary to solve Bloch equations for all isochromats (an isochromat is a microscopic group of nuclear or electron spins with the same resonant frequency) within the spectra of RF pulses.

The slowest part in the numerical simulation of spin echoes relate to solving Eqs. (1) on the time intervals of RF signals, which normally involves using the Galerkin method for spatial discretization and the explicit Runge-Kutta method for temporal discretization as, for example, Hazra, Lube and Raumer [23] did for MRI application.

This approach, however, requires large computational power, in particular because the Runge-Kutta method usually requires an accurate discretization of RF pulses - the smaller the sampling interval, the better, and at each sampling interval numerous arithmetic operations and trigonometric functions have to be calculated for each isochromat.

In the early 90s, when the author used an IBM PC/XT for simulating spin echoes in a spin echo processor, a single simulation using this method took about 20–30 h, which was completely impractical because the optimization of the processor required numerous iterations. So, the author tried to identify and eliminate redundant calculations in the simulations as follows [24].

First, taking into account that in reality the bandwidth of RF pulses in Fig. 3 is limited, and the isochromat spectrum in the spin echo processor is also limited, each RF pulse $S(t)$ creating $B_x(t)$ and $B_y(t)$ components in Eq. (1) can be represented by its samples using the Nyquist–Shannon-Kotelnikov theorem [25]:

$$S(t) = \sum_{n=-\infty}^{\infty} S(nT) \cdot sinc\left(\frac{t - nT}{T}\right), \tag{2}$$

where $T$ is sampling interval:

$$T \leq \begin{cases} \frac{1}{\Delta f_s} & \text{if } \Delta f_s > \Delta f_e \\ \frac{1}{\Delta f_e} & \text{if } \Delta f_s < \Delta f_e \end{cases},$$

where $\Delta f_s$ is the bandwidth of RF pulse; $\Delta f_e$ is the bandwidth of isochromat spectrum.

Second, interpolation function $sinc$ in Eq. (2) that provides the continuousness of signal $S(t)$ at the input of the spin echo processor, is redundant because the processor with its limited bandwidth works as a bandpass filter that itself restores a continuous signal.

Therefore, the author proposed substituting all continuous signals $S(t)$ in simulations with discrete signals $S_d(t)$ in the form of a Dirac comb function modulated by the signal samples:

$$S_d(t) = \sum_{n=-\infty}^{\infty} S(nT) \cdot \delta(t - nT), \tag{3}$$

where $T$ is the sampling interval as in formula (2).

The reaction of the spin echo processor to the discrete signal described by formula (3) is the same as the reaction to the original continuous signal, but, as shown by the author [24], the simulation of spin echoes for discrete signals is much simpler because

- For a signal in the form of a Dirac delta function, the Bloch Eq. (1) has a simple analytical solution and does not require employing the Runge-Kutta method;
- Each Dirac delta function in Eq. (3) just rotates the magnetization vector in the Bloch equation and the rotation matrix is the same for all isochromats.

This makes it possible to calculate the rotation matrix just once for each sample of the discrete signal (3), while for a continuous signal (2) using the Runge-Kutta method requires calculating the rotation matrix individually for each isochromat at each discretization interval.

As a result, the amount of processing power and time required for the simulations decreased by at least 20–30 times [24], which made the simulation of spin echoes practicable even on the slow PCs of the 90s.

**Comments.** Although on modern computers traditional simulation using the Runge-Kutta method would probably take no more than a few seconds, nevertheless, using the above-described approach can make it nearly in real-time.

The solution described in this case study uses the excessiveness of continuous signal implied by the ability of the simulated narrow-band system to restore the continuous signal from discrete signal. Therefore, this method can be useful for modeling various narrow-band resonance phenomena in different resonant media.

### 4.5    Discussion

**Excesses of Energy.** At first glance, the excess of energy used in various technical systems is the same as energy losses, elimination of which is a frequent objective of innovation projects. There is, however, a significant difference between these two concepts: energy losses are frequently considered with respect to a specific action principle utilized in the system, and eliminating these losses within the same action principle does not ensure that the energy excess will also be eliminated.

The proposed algorithm for identifying and utilizing excesses makes sure that all such excesses will be identified regardless of the action principle utilized, as shown in case studies 1 and 2. Generalizing functions and using the IFR approach help to do this.

**Excesses in Addressing Human Senses.** As shown in case study 3, the excessiveness of useful functions that address one of the human senses needs to be evaluated via assessing the maximum performance (e.g. sensitivity, resolution, etc.) of this sense.

**Excesses in Software.** Case study 4 shows that the proposed algorithm works exceptionally well for "non-material systems" such as computer models. With respect to this, it should be recognized that, despite the fact that many TRIZ tools are applicable for software development as Govindarajan, Sheu and Mann concluded [26], and, in particular, for speeding up different algorithms, as shown by Schlueter [27], the practical application of TRIZ tools in this area is still very limited.

Hartmann et al. [28] blame Moor's law, which often makes faster algorithms unnecessary because computing power increases so rapidly that it does not motivate software developers to improve the algorithms. Moor's law, however, gradually slows down and one can expect that the use of TRIZ tools in software development will eventually grow.

**General Applicability of the Proposed Approach.** As can be seen from all four case studies, the utilization of the excesses identified normally requires changing the action principle of the system, which often results in breakthrough solutions, assumes migration to a totally new system. Therefore, identifying excesses to utilize them as a resource for improvement makes sense mostly for mature engineering systems that are on the 3rd or 4th stage of their evolution, when all other resources for further improvement are exhausted.

Based on the results of successful practical applications of the proposed algorithm for identifying and utilizing excesses in technical systems, it seems fair to assume that using this tool may further improve the practical success rate of TRIZ projects above that reported by Abramov, Medvedev, and Rychagov in a recent paper [29].

## 5 Conclusions

The algorithm for identifying and utilizing excesses in technical systems disclosed in this paper is applicable to all engineering systems including "non-material systems" such as computer models and software algorithms.

This tool is best suited for mature systems that have already exhausted all other resources for further improvement. In this case, the use of identified excessiveness as a resource opens up new opportunities.

The use of this tool frequently leads to non-obvious breakthrough solutions, which, however, often requires changing the action principle of the system analyzed.

Overall, the proposed algorithm may further increase the success rate of TRIZ innovation projects, and, therefore, deserves to be included in the arsenal of TRIZ tools.

## References

1. Bauer, E.: Beyond Redundancy. How Geographic Redundancy Can Improve Service Availability and Reliability of Computer-Based Systems, 1st edn. Wiley, Hoboken (2011)
2. Dubrova, E.: Fault-Tolerant Design. Springer, New York (2013). https://doi.org/10.1007/978-1-4614-2113-9
3. Myers, A.: Complex System Reliability: Multichannel Systems with Imperfect Fault Coverage, 2nd edn. Springer, London (2014). https://doi.org/10.1007/978-1-84996-414-2
4. Chybowsky, L., Matuszak, Z.: Structural redundancy in an offshore vessel dynamic positioning system. Maint. Probl. **3**, 41–49 (2007)
5. Abramov, O.: Izbytochnost' v tekhnicheskih sistemakh (Excessiveness in engineering systems). [Publication in Russian]. In: Proceedings of the Scientific-Practical Conference "Creativity for a Decent Life", Velikiy Novgorod, Russia (2001). http://www.triz.natm.ru/articles/abram/abram01.htm. Accessed 02 May 2020

6. MATRIZ: MATRIZ – Level 1 Training Manual (2019). https://matriz.org/wp-content/uploads/2019/01/Level-1-Manual-Word.pdf. Accessed 09 May 2020
7. Litvin, S.: New TRIZ-based tool Function-Oriented Search (FOS). TRIZ J. (2005). https://triz-journal.com/new-triz-based-tool-function-oriented-search-fos/. Accessed 10 May 2020
8. Abramov, O., Markosov, S., Medvedev, A.: Experimental validation of quantum-economic Analysis (QEA) as a screening tool for new product development. In: Koziołek, S., Chechurin, L., Collan, M. (eds.) Advances and Impacts of the Theory of Inventive Problem Solving, pp. 17–25. Springer, Cham (2018). https://doi.org/10.1007/978-3-319-96532-1_2
9. Abramov, O.: TRIZ-based cause and effect chains analysis vs root cause analysis. In: Proceedings of the 11th International Conference TRIZFest-2015, Seoul, South Korea, pp. 283–291 (2015). http://matriz.org/wp-content/uploads/2012/07/TRIZfest-2015-conference-Proceedings.pdf. Accessed 09 May 2020
10. Russo, D., Regazzoni, D., Montecchi, T.: Eco-design with TRIZ laws of evolution. Proc. Eng. **9**, 311–322 (2011). https://www.sciencedirect.com/science/article/pii/S187770581100138X. Accessed 04 Aug 2020
11. Moradnazhad, M., Unver, H.: Energy efficiency of machining operations: a review. Proc. Inst. Mech. Eng. Part B: J. Eng. Manuf. 1–19 (2016). https://www.researchgate.net/publication/292213278_Energy_efficiency_of_machining_operations_A_review. Accessed 10 May 2020
12. Abramov, O. et al.: Switched Multi-Beam Antenna. US Patent 7,215,296, May 8, 2007 (2007)
13. 'Miniature Smart Antenna Wins Innovation Award'. Electronic Design (2007). http://electronicdesign.com/energy/miniature-smart-antenna-wins-innovation-award. Accessed 20 May 2020
14. Morrison, G.: 8K TV: What you need to know [Online article]. CNET Website (2020). https://www.cnet.com/news/8k-tv-what-you-need-to-know/. Accessed 11 May 2020
15. Clark, R.: Notes on the resolution and other details of the human eye [Online article]. Clarkvision Website (2005). https://clarkvision.com/imagedetail/eye-resolution.html. Accessed 11 May 2020
16. Fraiman, M.: What is the resolution of the human eye? [Online article]. PictureCorrect, Inc. (2014). https://www.picturecorrect.com/tips/what-is-the-resolution-of-the-human-eye/. Accessed 11 May 2020
17. 'Spin Echo' (2020). https://en.wikipedia.org/wiki/Spin_echo. Accessed 12 May 2020
18. Tarkhanov, V.: Operating principle of a spin-echo processor. [Publication in Russian] Nauchnoe Priborostroenie **13**(1), 51–57 (2003). http://iairas.ru/mag/2003/full1/Art7.pdf. Accessed 12 May 2020
19. Pleshakov, I.V., Popov, P.S., Dudkin, V.I., Kuz'min, Y.I.: Spin echo processor in functional electronic devices: control of responses in processing of multipulse trains. J. Commun. Technol. Electron. **62**(6), 583–587 (2017). https://doi.org/10.1134/S1064226917060171
20. Bushong, S., Clarke, G.: Magnetic Resonance Imaging: Physical and Biological Principles, 4th edn. Mosby, USA (2014)
21. Campbell, G., Ferguson, K., Sellars, M., Buchler, B., Lam, P.: Echo-based quantum memory. In: Bruss, D., Leuchs, G. (eds.) Quantum Information: From Foundations to Quantum Technology Applications, 2nd edn. Wiley-VCH, Weinheim (2019). https://arxiv.org/pdf/1902.04313v1.pdf. Accessed 12 May 2020
22. 'Bloch Equations' (2019). https://en.wikipedia.org/wiki/Bloch_equations. Accessed 14 May 2020

23. Hazra, A., Lube, G., Raumer, H.: Numerical simulation of Bloch equations for dynamic magnetic resonance imaging. Appl. Numer. Math. **123**, 241 (2018). https://www.sciencedirect.com/science/article/abs/pii/S0168927417302015?via%3Dihub. Accessed 14 May 2020

24. Abramov, O., Karpenkov, M.: Chislenniy raschet signalov spinovogo ekha (Numerical calculation of spin echo signals). [Publication in Russian]. In: LETI News, Collection of Scientific Papers, Leningrad Lenin Electrotechnical Institute, vol. 447, pp. 3–9 (1992)

25. 'Nyquist–Shannon Sampling Theorem' (2020). https://en.wikipedia.org/wiki/Nyquist%E2%80%93Shannon_sampling_theorem. Accessed 16 May 2020

26. Govindarajan, H., Sheu, D., Mann, D.: Review of systematic software innovation using TRIZ. Int. J. Syst. Innov. **5**(3), 72–90 (2019)

27. Schlueter, M.: Fast software by TRIZ. In: Proceedings of ETRIA World Conference TRIZ Future 2003, Aachen, Germany, 12–14 November 2003 (2003)

28. Hartmann, H., Vermeulen, A., Beers, M.: Application of TRIZ in software development. TRIZ J. (2004). https://triz-journal.com/application-triz-software-development/. Accessed 06 May 2020

29. Abramov, O.Y., Medvedev, A.V., Rychagov, V.Y.: Evaluation of the effectiveness of modern TRIZ based on practical results in new product development. In: Benmoussa, R., De Guio, R., Dubois, S., Koziołek, S. (eds.) TFC 2019. IAICT, vol. 572, pp. 36–44. Springer, Cham (2019). https://doi.org/10.1007/978-3-030-32497-1_4

# Learning Eco-Innovation from Nature: Towards Identification of Solution Principles Without Secondary Eco-Problems

Pavel Livotov[1(✉)], Mas'udah[2], and Arun Prasad Chandra Sekaran[1]

[1] Offenburg University of Applied Sciences, Badstr. 24, 77652 Offenburg,
Germany
pavel.livotov@hs-offenburg.de
[2] Politeknik Negeri Malang, Jl. Soekarno Hatta No. 9, 65141 Malang, Indonesia

**Abstract.** Environmentally-friendly implementation of new technologies and eco-innovative solutions often faces additional secondary ecological problems. On the other hand, existing biological systems show a lesser environmental impact as compared to the human-made products or technologies. The paper defines a research agenda for identification of underlying eco-inventive principles used in the natural systems created through evolution. Finally, the paper proposes a comprehensive method for capturing eco-innovation principles in biological systems in addition and complementary to the existing biomimetic methods and TRIZ methodology and illustrates it with an example.

**Keywords:** Eco-innovation · Biomimetics · Inventive principles · TRIZ

## 1 Introduction and Research Questions

Ecological requirements and demands of society for the conservation of nature force companies to apply eco-friendly technologies and equipment. Numerous approaches have been established to support sustainable and environmentally-friendly product and process development, such as the Eco-Design, which is defined by the International Standard Organization (ISO 14006:2011) as "integration of environmental aspects into product design and development, with the aim of reducing adverse environmental impacts throughout a product's life cycle". The eco-innovation focuses on the integration of environmental aspects and requirements in the early stages of the innovation processes for new product or technology development to provide significant environmental advantages. The ISO issued numerous norms, guidelines, and tools to maintain Eco-Design. For example, ISO14040:2006 describes the principles and framework for life cycle assessment (LCA), ISO14044:2006 provides LCA guidelines, and ISO14006:2011 provides guidelines to implement Eco-Design as part of an environmental management system (EMS) within companies.

The implementation of new technologies and eco-innovative solutions often lead to additional negative side effects and secondary problems, resulting in engineering contradictions. In accordance with VDI 4521 [1] the engineering contradiction can be defined as a situation in which the improvement of one parameter implies a worsening of another parameter within a system. In the context of eco-innovation, two types of eco-engineering contradictions can be defined – primary and secondary contradictions. A primary eco-engineering contradiction occurs when the improvement of a non-ecological engineering parameter (e.g. process yield) leads to a deterioration of an environmental characteristic (e.g. water consumption), or vice versa. A secondary eco-engineering contradiction is a situation where the improvement of one ecological parameter causes the worsening of another ecological parameter. For example, a method for preparing ceramic powders (US8765261B2) decreases the amount of carbon waste but may cause air pollution through dust. Especially the secondary eco-contradictions are not always evident for the engineers applying new technologies. The authors also advocate the hypothesis that different types of eco-engineering contradictions require individual approaches for their resolving.

Today, the biomimetics or biomimicry belongs to the established approaches to design for innovation and sustainability. A comprehensive literature review about this discipline including description of current biomimetic design methods for transferring design solutions from nature to technology is given in [2]. To the specific activities in bio-inspired design commonly belong abstraction, search, analysis and comparison, and transfer of analogies [3]. In this context, two opposite design approaches can be outlined: the problem-driven bio-inspired design approach and the solution-driven approach [4]. The more conventional problem-driven approach includes definition and reframing of engineering problem, followed by the search for biological solutions. Whilst the solution-driven design process starts with the identification of a biological solution and comprehensive analysis of the corresponding bio-system, continued by the search for engineering problem(s) to which the bio-solution could be applied. Helms [4] argues that both approaches are non-linear and dynamic in their nature. Thus, the later design process stages can influence previous stages causing iterative loops.

The biomimetic or bio-inspired design can be supported by the numerous analytical and creativity tools, and by the biomimetics databases, such as for example the AskNature database of the Biomimicry Institute [5]. Many of the bio-inspired design tools are based on or derived from the theory of inventive problem-solving TRIZ [2, 6]. The TRIZ methodology [1, 7] is currently an important part of the Knowledge-Based Innovation and belongs to one of the most comprehensive, systematically organized invention knowledge and creative thinking methodologies [8], as only TRIZ offers methods and abstract solution principles for identification and elimination of engineering contradictions and helps dramatically enhance the inventive skills of engineers. Moreover, the basic TRIZ principles of Ideality, resource-oriented and compromise-free problem-solving fit in perfectly with the strategy of sustainable eco-innovation. However, the systematic analysis of recent 60 scientific publications on eco-innovation applying TRIZ [9] shows that only very few of them rely on the biomimetics, such as, for example, the BioTRIZ method for eco-innovation [10]. The authors of BioTRIZ propose the following bio-inspired guidelines for eco-innovation: any waste should be a valuable resource; any product should be either inert/everlasting or easily degradable; products of degradation should be useful for the ecosystem; use of the resources that are already present or available in the eco-system. The paper [11] presents additionally general recommendations or "axioms" both for problem-driven and solution driven biomimetic design approaches:

- reduce the functionality of a biological prototype,
- interpret a biological solution instead of direct copying,
- use the final outcomes of a bio-solution but not the means,
- identify contradicting requirements.

According to [12] a trade-off between two contradicting requirements belongs to a central concept of biomimetics. The recent study postulates that the ontology of biomimetics based on the TRIZ contradiction matrix, also called as Altshuller matrix, will enable the identification of these contradictions, thus connecting a problem in engineering with its solution in biology [13]. In accordance with TRIZ the engineering contradictions can be solved with the help of the 40 Inventive Principles [7]. The paper [12] demonstrates an original ontology-based approach to *hierarchical* extension of 40 Inventive Principles with additional sub-principles derived from the living nature. For example, the TRIZ inventive principle *N.15 Dynamism or Adaptability* is extended to 6 sub-classes with totally 26 sub-principles incorporating biological terms. For instance, to the sub-principles with a lower hierarchy level belong *dynamic equilibrium, acclimatization,* or *genotypic change.* Interestingly, the previous analysis shows that 95% of the solutions created by nature and evolution match the TRIZ inventive principles known from engineering [14]. Most of the TRIZ-related biomimetic design methods apply the principles of the Altshuller matrix or rely on its extended, reduced or adapted versions but keep the TRIZ Inventive Principles unchanged [15]. The illustration of the inventive principles with biological examples can reduce the level of TRIZ abstractness and enhance engineering creativity [16].

On the contrary, our recent study on eco-innovation in process engineering [9] uses the substantially extended version of 40 TRIZ Innovation Principles with 160 sub-principles and identifies 23 strongest inventive sub-principles for resolving eco-contradictions. This suggestion is based on analysis of 100 eco-patents, 58 process intensification technologies and literature. However, most of the new eco-solutions contain secondary eco-contradictions.

In conclusion it may be well assumed that the existing biological systems should show a lesser additional environmental impact, if it exists at all, as compared to the human-made products or technologies. Indirect confirmation of this hypothesis can be also found in life sciences and biotechnologies [17]. Thus, the extraction of underlying abstract eco-inventive principles used in the nature could be helpful for problem solving not only in environment engineering. Such biological inventive principles which can be found in biological systems, are termed here as "natural inventive principles". Their identification appears to be particularly challenging, as nature has not filed any patents which could be analyzed in search for inventive principles as done by the TRIZ creators [7].

Since biological systems, defined here as systems of/with living biological organisms created by evolution, are more complex than engineering systems, the technology transfer from nature to engineering requires not only the significant efforts and interdisciplinary skills and knowledge of the researchers and engineers but also the advanced approaches and tools. In this context, the presented paper puts forward the following research questions:

1. Which natural inventive principles known from literature can be used for eco-innovation?
2. Which natural inventive principles can be used for extension of the 40 Inventive Principles or other TRIZ tools [1], which practically do not contain any biological operators?
3. Are there any natural inventive principles which cannot be assigned to the existing inventive tools of TRIZ?
4. How the systematic inventive thinking and problem solving can be enhanced by nature going beyond the application of the biomimetic for function or technology transfer from nature to engineering?
5. Which approaches or algorithms can be proposed for the identification of the natural eco-inventive principles in biological systems adapted to the environmental challenges?
6. How to find in nature solutions for specific eco-problems or "non-natural" phenomena, faced or created by humans?
7. Do different types of eco-engineering contradictions, primary and secondary, require specific inventive principles and approaches for their resolving?

## 2   Identification of the Nature-Inspired Eco-Innovation Principles

Besides the literature analysis, the identification of the *natural* principles for eco-innovation can be performed by combining different complementary approaches:

 I. Retrieval and analysis of existing bio-inspired eco-friendly technologies and of the corresponding biological solutions, for example in the *AskNature* database of the Biomimicry Institute [5], followed by identification of the abstract natural solution principles,
 II. Problem-driven approach: search for biological solutions for existing environmental problems using various algorithms, for example the Function-Oriented Search for bio-inspired design [15] or the Unified problem-driven process of biomimetics [18],
III. Solution-driven approach: identification of the eco-systems existing in unfavourable environment and under temporary environmental stress, identification of a biological solutions, and selection of the eco-engineering problem to which the bio-solution could be applied.

The approaches I, II and III can be preferably applied for the pre-defined groups or categories of essential ecological requirements and critical eco-problems. For example, in their recent study [9] the authors propose to use 14 environmental impact categories in accordance with the international Life Cycle Assessment (LCA) norms ISO 14040:2006, ISO 14044:2006 and Guidelines for Incorporating Eco-Design ISO 14006:2011: Acidification, Air pollution, Chemical waste disposal, Depletion of abiotic resources, Energy consumption, Eutrophication, Ozone layer depletion, Photochemical oxidation, Radioactivity, Raw material intensity, Safety risks, Solid Waste,

Toxicity, Water pollution and others. These categories not only describe the initial eco-problem domains but can be used for identification of probable secondary eco-contradictions in the field of analysis. Table 1 presents a fragment of correlation matrix of interactions with 10 environmental categories, most relevant in the process engineering [9]. This correlation matrix has been extracted from 100 patent documents with ecological goals of inventions. It helps to see how one improved eco-parameter can affect the other eco-parameters either positively or negatively, and to check if a biological system provides the same properties as the engineering one. For instance, reduction of *Acidic gases emissions* (3) has a positive impact on *Air pollution* (2) but can negatively affect *Energy consumption* (1).

**Table 1.** Correlation matrix of ecological requirements with identified secondary eco-contradictions: "−1" negative impact (eco-contradiction); "+1" positive impact; "0" – neutral.

| Eco-parameters to be improved: | Eco-parameter changed for the worse (secondary impact) | | | | | | | | | |
|---|---|---|---|---|---|---|---|---|---|---|
| | 1 | 2 | 3 | 4 | 5 | 6 | 7 | 8 | 9 | 10 |
| 1 Energy consumption | | −1 | +1 | −1 | −1 | −1 | +1 | +1 | +1 | −1 |
| 2 Air pollution | −1 | | +1 | −1 | −1 | −1 | −1 | +1 | +1 | −1 |
| 3 Acidification | −1 | +1 | | −1 | 0 | −1 | −1 | +1 | +1 | 0 |
| 4 Safety risks | −1 | −1 | 0 | | −1 | −1 | +1 | +1 | 0 | −1 |
| 5 Chemical waste disposal | −1 | −1 | 0 | +1 | | +1 | +1 | +1 | 0 | 0 |
| 6 Depletion of abiotic resources | −1 | −1 | +1 | 0 | +1 | | +1 | +1 | +1 | −1 |
| 7 Toxicity | +1 | −1 | 0 | +1 | +1 | +1 | | +1 | 0 | +1 |
| 8 Eutrophication | +1 | +1 | +1 | +1 | +1 | +1 | +1 | | +1 | 0 |
| 9 Photochemical oxidation | +1 | −1 | +1 | 0 | −1 | −1 | 0 | +1 | | 0 |
| 10 Water pollution | +1 | +1 | 0 | 0 | 0 | +1 | +1 | 0 | 0 | |

There are different approaches for problem-driven identification of biological solutions for existing engineering problems. As illustrated in Table 2, these approaches differ in terms of specific details but show clear similarities in their logic independently whether they are related or not related to TRIZ. The algorithms have as a rule a non-linear and iterative character with feedback and refinement loops. At the initial research phase, it is rather difficult to prefer one or another algorithm, as the limited amount of critically reviewed case studies does not allow to objectively judge or compare their efficiency in the field of eco-innovation. One can also consider a combined problem-driven bio-inspired design approach which will bundle the strong points of different methods. In this context, the extraction of abstract biological solutions principles for eco-problems constitutes one of the most important questions of the research agenda proposed in this paper. Generally, the methods applying the function-oriented search appear to be more efficient and promising for the automated data processing.

**Table 2.** Comparison of some problem-driven bio-inspired design processes.

| Helms, 2009 [4] | Savelli & Abramov, 2017 [17] | Fayemi et al., 2018 [18] | The Biomimicry Institute, 2020 [19] |
|---|---|---|---|
| 1. Problem definition incl. functional decomposition and optimisation<br>2. Reframing the problem in universally applicable biological terms<br>3. Biological solution search with a set of heuristics<br>4. Definition of the biological solution<br>5. Extraction of solution principle in an abstract form<br>6. Application of solution principle | 1–4. Problem definition incl. target parameters, key problem and function<br>5. Formulation of parameters/conditions for performing the key function.<br>6. Generalization of function and object<br>7–8. Identification of natural environments for generalized object and of natural phenomena with similar generalized function<br>9–11. Selection and adaptation of bio-solution | 1. Problem analysis<br>2. Abstract technical problem definition<br>3. Problem transposition to biology<br>4. Identification of potential biological models<br>5. Selection of appropriate biological models<br>6. Extraction of abstract biological strategies<br>7. Transposition of the biological solution to technology<br>8. Solution implementation and test in initial context | 1. Define the challenge, incl. criteria and constraints that determine success<br>2. Biologize function and context<br>3. Discover biological strategies<br>4. Abstract design strategies: translating the biological strategies into design strategies<br>5. Emulate nature's lessons: creation of bio-inspired concepts<br>6. Evaluation of bio-inspired concepts |

Table 3 presents the general *solution-driven* process of biomimetic design with the proposed modifications for identification of the *natural* principles for eco-innovation. The iterative algorithm starts with systematic search for the biological eco-systems operating under constant or temporary environmental stress, such as for example, high or low temperatures, extreme sun radiation or other harmful energy fields, toxic substances or dangerous living organisms in the environment etc.

Considering high complexity of any eco-system, the second phase of the solution-driven process must help to clarify and specify all essential biocomponents, Then, using the Function Analysis, it is necessary to comprehensively identify all functions of biocomponents and the strategies how they adapt themselves to unfavourable environment and counteract threads. Similar to the engineering systems, opposing functions or conflicts of goals can be identified also in the biological systems. Such situations should be thoroughly explored to extract possible concealed bio-solutions. For example, for a plant leaf, the reduction of water loss and higher surface area for photosynthesis build a pair of contradictory requirements. The surface structure, form, position, colour, biochemistry, or other properties of the plant leaf could give an answer, how a bio-system answer to this challenge. In other words, the identification of such conflicts of objectives is often a key to extraction of biological solutions.

**Table 3.** Modified solution-driven process of bio-inspired design.

| Phase | Description (after Helms, [4]) | Modification for extraction of abstract natural principles for eco-innovation |
|---|---|---|
| 1 | Identification of biological solutions | 1.1. Definition and classification of environmental stress factors<br>1.2. Systematic search for biological eco-systems exposed to environmental stress |
| 2 | Analysis and definition of the biological solution | 2.1. Component and function analysis for the eco-system, its sub-systems (bio-components) and super-system<br>2.2. Identification of contradictory functions and eco-requirements. Formulation of eco-contradictions<br>2.3. Identification of the eco-system components responsible for resolving of eco-contradiction between opposing functions or requirements |
| 3 | Extraction of biological solution principles | 3.1. Extraction of concrete biological eco-solutions in the biocomponents identified in step 2.3<br>3.2. Formulation of abstract biological eco-solution principles in biological terms |
| 4 | Reframing biological solution principles in universally applicable engineering terms | 4.1. Transformation of abstract biological solution to eco-engineering using universally applicable technical terms<br>4.2. Extraction of the underlying abstract engineering principles and their assignment to the TRIZ Tools, such as 40 Inventive Principles (Sub-Principles), Standard solutions, Separation principles<br>4.3. Identification of new natural inventive principles or sub-principles<br>4.4. Assignment of all inventive principles and sub-principles to the corresponding eco-contradictions |
| 5 | Search for engineering domains and problems for application of biological solution principles | 5.1. Search for eco-engineering problems or problem clusters in different technical domains (for example, in process engineering with the help of environmental impact categories)<br>5.2. Search for the eco-contradictions in engineering domains similar to the natural eco-contradictions defined in step 2.2 (for example, with the Correlation matrix of eco-categories, s. Table 1) |
| 6 | Definition of engineering problem | 6.1. Definition of a specific-engineering problem incl. possible primary and secondary eco-engineering contradictions |
| 7 | Application of the biological principles and development of the bio-inspired engineering solution. | 7.1. Development of bio-inspired eco-solution (product or process)<br>7.2. Anticipation of possible new secondary problems and eco-contradictions<br>7.3. Optimization of existing eco-solution or application of other biomimetic inventive principles and solutions |

Generally, the phases 2, 3 and 4 of the proposed solution-driven process are most relevant in the context of the research objectives defined in this paper, namely, the identification of new abstract biological inventive principles or sub-principles for eco-innovation. Therefore, each biological eco-system, regardless of the approach used to select it, must undergo a thorough analysis in accordance with the procedures of the process phases 2, 3 and 4.

## 3   Illustrating Case Study

Figure 1 shows a colony of grey mangroves, a natural maritime marsh eco-system. Mangroves are salt-tolerant trees, also called *halophytes*, and are adapted to life in harsh coastal environment under the low oxygen conditions of waterlogged mud. They contain a complex salt filtration system and complex root system to cope with saltwater immersion and wave action [20]. Living in such hostile environment poses some serious challenges and requires some adaptations. Dead mangrove leaves and branches add nutrients to the tidal creek. Most debris is broken down by microorganisms (bacteria and fungi) before it is made available to the food chain. Mangrove roots trap plant material such as seagrass which adds more nutrients to the system. Some crabs graze directly on leaf littler, prawns and small fish feed on decomposed littler and fish feed on small crustaceans. The remaining organic matter is taken up by the roots of the mangroves. The algae that collects on the surface of mangrove roots is look for snails and crustaceans which are in turn eaten by wading birds. Furthermore, mangroves are highly productive ecosystem, a vital habitat for juvenil fish and home to many bird species. Mangroves colonies also anchor shorelines and act as a coastal buffer zone between land ecosystems and see.

**Fig. 1.** Colony of grey mangroves *Avicennia marina* in Western Australia.

Table 4 presents an incomplete fragment of the component and function analysis of the mangroves eco-system, corresponding to the phase 2 of the proposed solution-driven approach to bio-inspired design. Each function is a subject of further analysis, which results in the identification of biological solution principles. Additionally, a correlation matrix of the identified function, similar to the matrix presented in Table 1, will allow to systematically identify resolved contradictions and synergies between the functions in the eco-system. For instance, the extraction of the salt takes place

**Table 4.** Fragment of the component and function analysis of the mangroves eco-system.

| System level | | Eco-function | Examples of eco-innovation principles in biological terms |
|---|---|---|---|
| Super system | Mangroves colony | Buffer zone between land and see; anchoring shorelines; protecting coral reefs from sedimentation; capturing carbon dioxide | Roots reduce turbulences in coastal barrier structures [21] |
| System | Mangrove tree | Nurseries and food source for marine life Attracting living organisms to the eco-system | Increase the level of biodiversity Attract bio-resources Use microorganisms in hostile environment |
| Sub-systems | Pneumatophores | Absorbing oxygen from the air and water (pipe-like structures sticking out of the mud act like snorkels) | Simultaneous absorption of substances from gas and fluid |
| | Roots and stems | Mangrove roots and stems have special tissues which act as a barrier to salt | Use in parallel different technologies (in root and leaves) to block or extract harmful agent |
| | Fresh leaves | Extraction of the salt underneath the mangrove leaves (special glands concentrate salt and excrete it to the surface) | Use different sides or parts of an object for competing operations: extraction of salt and photosynthesis |
| | Leaves, flowers, fruits | Concentrating and removal the salt: salt can be moved to old leaves, flowers, tree bark or fruits which then drop off, taking the concentrated salt with them | Apply biodegradable waste to remove harmful substances |
| | Seeds | Protect reproductive function from environment: seedlings germinate, and start developing on the tree and can survive in seawater for year or more | Isolate sensitive biological processes from hostile environment |

underneath the mangrove leaves and does not affect the photosynthesis. As already mentioned earlier, such balanced separation of opposing functions "invented" by nature provides clues about new bio-solution principles. Some examples in Table 4 illustrate possible eco-innovation principles, which are the subject of further analysis.

## 4   Concluding Remarks and Outlook

Since the development of new environmentally-friendly technologies and products often results in technical and environmental negative side effects, additional methodological efforts are required to reduce secondary environmental problems in eco-innovation. The paper proposes a research agenda and conceptualizes a comprehensive approach for identification of new biomimetic abstract innovation principles in addition and complementary to the existing biomimetic methods and TRIZ methodology. The authors argue that the enormous potential of biomimetics for eco-innovation is not yet fully exploited. Therefore, the presented paper advocates the need for identification of new abstract biological inventive principles or sub-principles for eco-innovation. The future research should be focused on

- selection of the biological eco-systems under environmental stress as research object and source of information and inspiration,
- comprehensive identification of natural abstract innovation principles and sub-principles,
- classification of the natural innovation principles and their assignment to the eco-engineering contradictions and eco-innovation domains for the sharing and reuse of innovation knowledge.

Even if the research scope is limited to the domain of eco-innovation, its basic outcomes, innovation principles and tools can be recommended for the other domains.

## References

1. VDI Standard 4521: Inventive problem Solving with TRIZ. Fundamentals, Terms and Definitions. The Association of German Engineers (VDI), Beuth Publishers, Duesseldorf, Germany (2016)
2. Cohen, Y.H., Reich, Y.: Biomimetic Design Method for Innovation and Sustainability. Springer, Cham (2016). https://doi.org/10.1007/978-3-319-33997-9
3. Hashemi Farzaneh, H., Lindemann, U.: A Practical Guide to Bio-inspired Design. Springer, Heidelberg (2019). https://doi.org/10.1007/978-3-662-57684-7
4. Helms, M.: Biologically inspired design: process and products. Des. Stud. 30, 606–622 (2009)
5. AskNature database of the Biomimicry Institute. https://asknature.org/. Accessed 22 July 2020
6. Vincent, J.: Biomimetics - a review. Proc. Inst. Mech. Eng. Part H: J. Eng. Med. 223(8), 919–939 (2009)
7. Altshuller, G.S.: Creativity as an Exact Science. The Theory of the Solution of Inventive Problems. Gordon & Breach Science Publishers, New York (1984)

8. Cavallucci, D., Cascini, G., Duflou, J., Livotov, P., Vaneker, T.: TRIZ and knowledge-based innovation in science and industry. Proc. Eng. **131**, 1–2 (2015)
9. Livotov, P., et al.: Eco-innovation in process engineering: contradictions, inventive principles and methods. Therm. Sci. Eng. Prog. **9**, 52–65 (2019)
10. Bogatyrev, N., Bogatyreva, O.: BioTRIZ: a win-win methodology for eco-innovation. In: Azevedo, S.G., Brandenburg, M., Carvalho, H., Cruz-Machado, V. (eds.) Eco-Innovation and the Development of Business Models. GINS, vol. 2, pp. 297–314. Springer, Cham (2014). https://doi.org/10.1007/978-3-319-05077-5_15
11. Bogatyrev, N., Bogatyreva, O.: TRIZ-based algorithm for biomimetic design. Proc. Eng. **131**, 377–387 (2015)
12. Vincent, J.: The trade-off – a central concept for biomimetics. Bioinspired Biomimetic Nanobiomater. **6**(2), 67–76 (2017)
13. Vincent, J., Cavallucci, D.: Development of an ontology of biomimetics based on Altshuller's matrix. In: Cavallucci, D., De Guio, R., Koziołek, S. (eds.) TFC 2018. IAICT, vol. 541, pp. 14–25. Springer, Cham (2018). https://doi.org/10.1007/978-3-030-02456-7_2
14. Mann, D.: Natural world contradiction matrix: how biological systems resolve trade-offs and compromises. Proc. Eng. **9**, 714–723 (2011)
15. Savelli, S., Abramov, O.Y.: Nature as a source of function-leading areas for FOS-derived solutions. TRIZ Rev.: J. Int. TRIZ Assoc. MATRIZ **1**(1), 86–98 (2019)
16. Weaver, J., Kleinke, D.: Extending the TRIZ methodology to connect engineering design problems to biological solutions. In: NCIIA 16th Annual Conference (2012)
17. Williamson, E.D.: Life sciences today and tomorrow: emerging biotechnologies. Crit. Rev. Biotechnol. **37**(5), 553–565 (2017)
18. Fayemi, P.-E., Gilles, M., Gazo, C.: Innovative technical creativity methodology for bio-inspired design. In: Cavallucci, D., De Guio, R., Koziołek, S. (eds.) TFC 2018. IAICT, vol. 541, pp. 253–265. Springer, Cham (2018). https://doi.org/10.1007/978-3-030-02456-7_21
19. The Biomimicry Design Process. https://toolbox.biomimicry.org/methods/process/. Accessed 22 July 2020
20. Flowers, T.J., Colmer, T.D.: Plant salt tolerance: adaptations in halophytes. Ann. Bot. **115** (3), 327–331 (2015)
21. Van de Riet, K.: Biomimicry of Mangroves Teaches How to Improve Coastal Barriers. https://www.ansys.com/blog/biomimicry-mangroves-improve-coastal-erosion-coastal-barriers. Accessed 22 July 2020

# A Future Eco-Design Framework Based on TRIZ's Contradictions and Bio-Inspired Design Process

Marouane Mouatassim[1,2(✉)], Mickael Gardoni[1,3], Arlindo Silva[2], Denis Cavallucci[3], Houcine Dammak[1], and Abdellatif Dkhil[1]

[1] École de Technologie Supérieure, Montréal, Canada
{marouane.mouatassim.1,houcine.dammak.1,
abdellatif.dkhil.1}@ens.etsmtl.ca,
mickael.gardoni@etsmtl.ca
[2] Singapore University of Technology and Design, Singapore, Singapore
arlindo_silva@sutd.edu.sg
[3] Institut National des Sciences Appliquées, Strasbourg, France
denis.cavallucci@insa-strasbourg.fr

**Abstract.** In the products development process, innovation is prescribed as a key parameter for technological evolution. It describes itself as a complex process that exploits different ways of transforming an idea into a reliable product. However, its way of resolution tends to amplify the conflicts of technical systems called technological contradictions. In this paper, was used the contradiction solving methods based on TRIZ Matrix in order to extract an ideal inventive principle which basically requires the existence of at least one contradiction to be eliminated. Then we will explore the potential of Bio-Inspired Design process that seeks, from ecosystem elements to extract conflicting functions that can be technologically transferable. Taking in account the aforementioned reasoning, we will discuss how the technical contradictions and their causalities can interrogate biomimetic databases to improve the innovation process by designing new environmental-friendly products that are more reliable. The aim of this work is to introduce new "eco-principles" by analyzing analogies between technical and biological solutions. The main objective is to analyze the possibilities to optimize an eco-inventive process for the next new technological generations. Based on this vision, the endpoint is to provide designers and engineers with the ideal eco-inventive methodology.

**Keywords:** Contradiction · TRIZ matrix · Bio-inspired design · Biomimetics · Eco-design

## 1 Introduction

At the development stage of a new or improved product (new technology, device or industrial process), innovation is often a complex parameter to manage. As a process, it requires several dimensions of apprehension (economic, operative, cognitive, etc.). Among these, systemic approach is defined as a complex multidimensional space used

© IFIP International Federation for Information Processing 2020
Published by Springer Nature Switzerland AG 2020
D. Cavallucci et al. (Eds.): TFC 2020, IFIP AICT 597, pp. 183–195, 2020.
https://doi.org/10.1007/978-3-030-61295-5_15

to opportunistically find strategic spaces to design new or improved products [1, 2]. Biological dimension refers to the likely analogies between technological and living systems [1]. In this paper, the innovation process will be discussed in both dimensions. In this context, we will discuss the interactions of technical systems to create system conflicts called contradictions. According to TRIZ[1], these contradictions are considered fundamental to any inventive design process. However, they are based on a limited set of knowledge and governed by old unsustainable technical solutions. Hence the interest in developing new sources of knowledge. We believe that biomimetics could make a significant contribution not only to redefining innovative design, another equally important aspect is to develop new tools that help in designing systematically green products. In order to identify the difficulties inherent in implementing a methodological structure adopting TRIZ and biomimetic approach, we present a brief state of art of methodological tools and the difficulties encountered. We will then present our methodology and the experimental protocol where the objective is to optimize an eco-design framework based on technological contradictions and Bio-Inspired Design process.

## 2   State of Art and Research Background

### 2.1   Innovation Process and Technological Evolution

There are many approaches and methodologies to structure the innovation process within organizations and companies. The interest in innovating differently has steadily increased and has continued to grow in recent decades [1, 2]. On the one hand, scientific and technical progress has made it possible to understand structures ranging from the microscopic to the ecosystem scale and satellites. On the other hand, this exploration has enabled us to systematically combine technology with all capitalized knowledge. According to many historians [3, 4], technological evolution is only the result of technical and social systems interactions that allow, not only to continually expand the fields of knowledge, but also to improve, substitute or even eliminate existing technologies. This interaction of technical systems has been extensively studied in order to prevent technological trends [2, 5].

The inventive problems are manifested by the emergence of conflicts in technical systems called contradictions. Integration this concept, as a main basis of TRIZ theory, illustrates that the technological evolution is governed by these contradictions in all existing entities or systems. According to [6], technology is a result of combination of several functionalities from different areas (domains, applications, industrial processes, new knowledge etc.). The mechanisms of technological evolution are focused on a self-creation process (*autopoietic proliferation*) which every technology is built from other ones, and so on. Suppose as an example, digital systems are designed and organized to mange data and information (storing, communicating, selecting etc.) in a binary way. A new or improved security system is built to perform alarm system, as proto-system (crowd), but impose conflicting requirements in the digital system (transition from

---

[1] Theory of inventive problem solving.

proto-system to integrated system). The ideal technological system concept was created to perform system functionalities (useful functions) and to decrease the harmful side effects (harmful functions). The contradiction can be extracted when new or improved function causes an unacceptable situation of the whole system being under development [2].

## 2.2  Theory of Inventive Problem Solving

TRIZ, invented by a russian scientist *Genrich Altshuller* (1926–1998) and also known as Teorija ReshenijaIzobreteliskih Zadatch, was developed on the basis of analysis of several hundred thousands of patents [5]. According to [7–9], any technology (product, service or process) evolves along an evolutionary curve adopted by technical systems (sometimes called technological systems) [2]. This curve is similar to that of the development of a biological systems (birth, growth, maturity, decline and extinction) [7].

In order to solve an inventive problem, from the technical problem to the technical solution, TRIZ focuses mainly on three fundamental principles (Fig. 1): **ideality** which use the Ideal Final Result (IFR) to increase the ratio between useful and harmful functions, **patterns of evolution** of technical systems and **contradiction**, negative interaction of pair tool/object, that is defined as a main axis. TRIZ's knowledge database is a toolbox containing rules and resolution standards: 39 EP (Engineering Parameters), 40 IP (Inventive Principles), separation principles, standard solutions, ARIZ[2], 9 screens concept etc. [10].

As part of this paper, we will focus on the fundamental and axial concept: contradiction principle (Fig. 1.a).

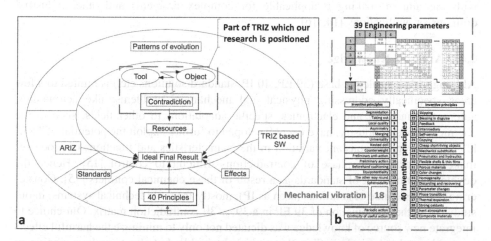

**Fig. 1.** Inventive problem-solving process of TRIZ adapted from [11]

---

[2] Algorithm for inventive problem solving: [A problem-solving tool that transform a complex inventive situation into a well-defined model of the problem, which can be solved effectively using a wide spectrum of TRIZ tools]. TRIZ Glossary of Vladimir Petrov.

## 2.3    Contradiction Principle

In dialectical thinking, contradiction is the basic concept [12]. It consists of two mutually dependent aspects, but at the same time opposite to each other [13, 14]. Knowledge and analysis of contradiction are considered as main basis of dialectical thinking. According to the latter, the presence of contradiction between two elements does not constitute a barrier, contrary this contradiction is even considered the essence of existance. It cannot independently exist, it is mutually connected and expresses itself in different areas [12].

In the technological and industrial world, the contradiction is the expression of a form of technical system conflicts: when one of its parameters or functionalities is improved, another is damaged. Several problems have been solved through the contradictions that must be overcome without compromise. However, this resolution remains perplexing to ourdays. According to [13], considering evolution of technology and consumers needs, technical systems become more complex and form several hundred contradictions. Indeed, when a technical system presents a large number of contradictions, the central problem formulation becomes difficult to solve. The representation of a contradiction is done by combining two of 39 EP, one to preserve and the other to improve. The result of the combination is inventive principles, illustrated as ideal solutions, that must be analyzed to eliminate the contradiction [15]. For example, the IP 18. *Mechanical vibration* can be proposed to solve 158 (1/10, 1/14, 1/21, 1/26… 39/31, 39/37) types of system conflicts or contradictions (Fig. 1.b).

However, TRIZ often focuses on problems with a limited number of contradictions. Moreover, the interpretation of the IP derived from the contradiction matrix is still not easy to be understood because of the high level of abstraction of the solution. It is for this reason that several research and studies have been started to computerize TRIZ with the aim of making it applicable for complex problems and other industrial domains or applications [14, 16].

## 2.4    Areas of Knowledge

Although it's knowledge base (39 EP, 40 IP, standard solutions etc.) is limited to a few areas specifically addressing physical and mechanical problems, like aeronautics, automotive industry and electronics, specific adaptations to other fields, such as the chemical process industry, have been developed to further exploit the potential of TRIZ [17]. However, the constant variation in the characteristics and functions of processes makes the extraction phase of contradictions difficult to control [15]. Hence the development of a set of standards as a result of these chemical conflicts [15]. Considering the abundance of solutions (seen as IP), mostly from old technical systems, in our study, from the combination of 39 EP in a 39 × 39 contradiction matrix. Our choice to integrate new source of knowledge was dictated not only to minimize the harmful effects caused by technological conflicts that are unsustainable, but also to make a significant contribution for developping new eco-principles until their computerization.

We support the statement in the 85-B version of ARIZ, which was developed specially to solve complex problems [18, 19]. According to the latter, biological knowledge can be categorized, codified and capitalized for technological and industrial twinning purposes [20]. In this context, [13, 14] stated the importance of standardizing vocabulary through the development of complete ontologies[3] to facilitate the process of transforming and transfering biological knowledge into information that can be used in technology. This transfer phase represents the main focus of BID practices as a new «creative» innovation approach as well as an «eco-responsible» to rethink our engineering design processes.

## 2.5 Bio-Inspired Design

The choice to use contradiction principle was dictated by the presence of conflicting functions (seen as standard conflicts) in living organisms which are the subject of several research works. In biomimetic architecture, as a subset of engineering design, biology is used to increase technical functions. As an example of this thinking level (Fig. 2), the biological cell structure (a. Phragmocone of the cuttlefish) represents a series of sub-parallel plates called pillars (b) representing a typical fractal dimension which can be usable in architectural design. Its geometric model (c) illustrates the gaps between the supporting pillars from conduits. These can give [...the sandwich structure extra functionality as ducting, or support of wiring or piping.] [19]. This cell structure can inspire designers to resolve technical conflicts by transposing the identified characteristics (biological functions), that are conflicting (rigidity, lightness, resistance and flexibility), to the technology.

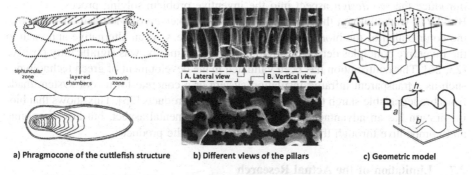

a) Phragmocone of the cuttlefish structure    b) Different views of the pillars    c) Geometric model

**Fig. 2.** Biological cell structure with conflicting functions, adapted from [19]

The literature review has shown that, generally, the Bio-Inspired Design (BID) practice takes two ways of problem solving: the *solution based* approach where the solution can be identified in a biomimetic database [21], or potentially observable solution in nature and the *problem-driven* approach that follows the path of a technical and/or inventive problem-solving process. The first focuses on the analysis of a natural products

---

[3] Ontology is a standardized language. In biomimetics, ontology can be used to develop digital systems of design information in different areas (medicine, engineering, architecture, materials science etc.). Thus, it can help to built an artificial intelligence system for inventive problems [12].

or processes with the aim of extracting, through a basic research process, transferable biological knowledge in technology and subsequently mimicking the characteristics leading to this biological function *(nature to design)*. The second is described as a bio-mimetic process that use a standard engineering methods to solve inventive problems: identification (analysis of technical knowledge), formulation of technical problem (system conflicts formulation) and solution concepts generation and selection. The methodological approach combines at least two distinct areas: design engineering and life sciences [22]. Through this fusion field, several tools, methods and theories have been wrapped up in order to structure biomimetic process.

## 2.6 Methodological Tools

Among the methods introduced in design engineering, from creating rational problem-solving approaches, to technical design models, analysis tools in order to set up creative processes, decision support standards, visualization tools and structuring ideas, etc. TRIZ has been extensively studied with the aim of facilitating the transfer process of biological knowledge: capitalization, codification and conversion of functions at all levels (structure, materials, living systems, etc.) [23]. However, this hybrid methods (Eca-TRIZ, Eco-TRIZ, Bio-TRIZ etc.) was considered to be devoid of biological data (categorized as inventive principles) despite the development of other matrix such as 6X6 from Bio-TRIZ methodology. The latter was created with the aim of providing an alternative solution in the event of a failure to resolve technical contradictions [24, 25].

Alongside to the TRIZ principles, Bio-TRIZ axioms have been developed to introduce the *eco-design* aspect into the inventive problem-solving process. Through Bio-TRIZ methodology, the research team at the University of Bath demonstrated that the contribution of the biomimetic development process, as an alternative approach to the inventive principles derived from the Altshuller's matrix, was significantly positive [25, 26]. This contribution has been validated in the development of green technologies such as a transparent infrared insulation system or a concrete formwork system made from biodegradable starch to extend the life cycle of products [25]. This shows that bio-inspiration has an advantage other than the environmental aspect, but also economic and competitive through the quality and lifespan of the products.

## 2.7 Limitation of the Actual Research

The core problem being the complexity of living systems and the dissimilarity between the living and the artificial, the major disadvantage of transforming biological knowledge into a technical language boils down to the difficulty of implementing new transfer tools that enable to translate, capitalize and codify biological and technical information. Under current conditions, the biological knowledge transfer can be only partial [14]. Consequently, implementing a functional biomimetic process will require firstly access to the world of living organisms, in particular through biological databases available for the technology. Secondly, it is important to structure methodological tools that enable to convert and transfer biological knowledge into a designers-readable informations. The use of TRIZ in biomimetic development process has been the subject of a wide list of scientific research and publications [13, 19, 23, 26] etc.

It has been shown that the biomimetic approach requires a deep understanding of complex biological codes and features: abundant functionalities, and therefore a large number of contradictions. According to [13], among the difficulties of formulating an inventive problem is the presence of a large number of contradictions. However, this disadvantage could be overcome by the introduction of new computerized methods adapted to complex problems. In this context, [13, 14] declare a need to standardize the biomimetic vocabulary by introducing new ontologies to facilitate the BID process. Thus, the 39 EP and 40 IP can be linked to a possible biological strategies (immune system, growth, fecundity etc.). According to [14], the ontology is built but still under process, especially proof of concept, data collection and computing development. There are actually two potential tools to studying the concept of ontology modeling: SimplySolve matrix and Bonsai database dedicated to biomimetics.

Furthermore, biomimetic aspects are seen as key elements in rethinking the eco-logical and environmental dimension in engineering design process. As far as TRIZ is concerned, the integration of biomimetic development process will mainly make it possible to systematize eco-design and facilitate its appropriation on the technological and industrial scale. [27] pointed out that technology and industrial companies still face many difficulties, particularly in terms of the appropriation of eco-design methods. According to [28], two criteria, systematization and appropriation, are considered central in the eco-innovation process.

## 3 Proposed Methodology to Optimize an Eco-Design Process

The complexity of the biomimetic process can be facilitated by creative engineering methods. This paper focuses on the initial step of the inventive problem solving process of TRIZ using Altshuller's matrix to extract the inventive principles. As part of our research, we will use the analysis of IP extracted from $39 \times 39$ contradictions matrix with the aim of transposing them to biological solutions.

In order to exploit other research works, we will use the unified *problem-driven* process of biomimetics (Fig. 3). The latter contains two sections structured in stages: section 1 corresponding to the transposition of technology to biology (stage 1 to 4) and section 2 corresponding to reverse transposition (stage 5 to 8).

In the methodological approach, we propose two main axes. The first is the identi-fication of indicators to be considered in the combined approach (*Putting biology in TRIZ*) through the research of [25, 29] which showing the link between technical systems and biological systems. The Bio-TRIZ methodology that was developed with the aim of introducing biomimetic parameters, through a $6 \times 6$ matrix, by bringing 6 operational fields: substance, structure, energy, information, space and time, in the knowledge base of TRIZ. The second axis experiments with the research of [14, 17, 30, 31] on developping new ontologies as part of a likely analogy between at least three different fields: computer science, biology and innovative design engineering. The results of [14, 18, 21] research work allowed us to ask a fundamental question around the formulation, extraction and elimination of contradictions:

How to solve the technical contradictions with the support of Bio-Inspired Ideation Process? Our methodological approach is structured in five phases:

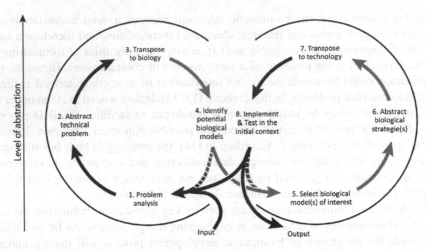

**Fig. 3.** The unified *problem-driven* process of biomimetics [21]

## 3.1    Phase 1: Conceptualization of Contradictions

The most critical step in TRIZ resolution process is the formulation of a contradictions. In order to decipher the codes of a technical problem, a structure of inventive problem solving proposed in four steps by [30] will be used to extract technical contradictions. During the first phase, from the problem graph situation (inventive situation analysis, problem analysis) to contradiction formulation (abstract technical problem), we will focus only on the first two steps using mainly the contradiction matrix of SimplySolve tool [32]. The latter will allow us to extract, from the 39 × 39 matrix, the IP corresponding to the initial situation that presents itself in the form of technical contradiction to be solved (Fig. 4).

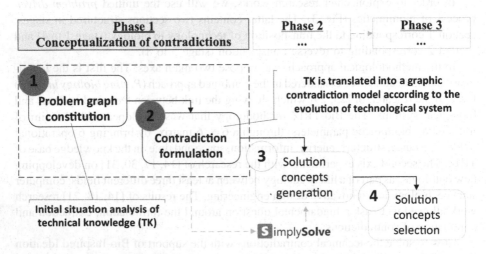

**Fig. 4.** Conceptualization of contradictions phase

Then comes the ideation phase by conceptualizing the desired functions. A function is the result of an interaction between a tool that controls physical parameters and an object that performs the desired function. This phase will focus on identifying causal links between technical and biological functions. Two steps will be considered: the first corresponds to a decomposition of the technical system in order to expose the links between tool, object, function and contradiction (Fig. 5).

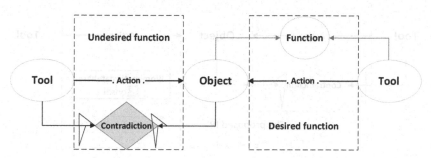

**Fig. 5.** Interraction, tool, object, function, contradiction

The second step is the transposition of causal elements to phenomena or processes identified in Bonsai database for scientific research in biomimetics and artificial intelligence [33].

### 3.2 Phase 2: Bio-Inspired Ideation Process

This phase corresponds to the conceptualization of desired functions based on technical causal links and biological functionalities. The aim of this phase is to transpose functions, resulting from technical contradictions, to biology. This phase is in stage 5, 6 and 7 of the unified *problem-driven* process. This step would be linked to a semantic dictionary in order to categorize and capitalize keywords consistent with the desired functions, supposed to eliminate a contradiction in the technical system (Fig. 6).

To illustrate, the IP.18 *Mechanical vibration* derived from SimplySolve matrix could correspond to a list of keywords intended for the categorization of natural processes or strategies derived from the living organisms. For example, on Bonsai database, the EP.1 weight of moving object and EP.10 power/intensity can be linked to keywords that allow to extract a list of corresponding natural strategies or processes. In the matrix, these two keywords are corresponding to the first system conflict (1/10) of 158 possible contradictions which the IP.18 proposes.

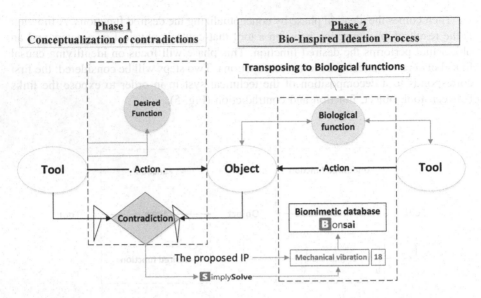

**Fig. 6.** Bio-Inspired Ideation Process

### 3.3   Phase 3: Experimental Protocol

The experimental phase will allow us to measure the association impact of the two sections of the unified *problem-driven* process by following contradiction solving structure. First, phase 1 of our methodology will suggest the use of the concept of contradiction to develop innovative solution concepts. Then, phase 2 will allow us to analyze the contribution of the Bio-Inspired Ideation Process. The aim of this experiment is to statistically measure the potential of the approach. On that premise, to prepare the implementation of tools structuring eco-inventive resolution, and to guide our thinking on the development of new principles of eco-design and eco-innovation. In this context, a previous study has been conducted based on similar study protocol in Canada, Montreal, during an international creativity competition "*24 h of innovation*". During this event, local students went through a team design for total of roughly 30 min, in which they had 24 consecutive hours to find creative solutions to challenges put forward by businesses and research labs. Local and international committees examine solved problems and choose, using an identical evaluation grid, the three best proposed inventive solutions. After that, different prizes are given to the local and international winers. However, our local teams were not numerous, and the results of this preliminary research were not enough to confirm our hypothesis.

In order to measure the contribution of the Bio-Inspired Ideation Process, participants (designers, architects and engineers) will be recruited from Singapore University of Technology and Design. They will be invited to participate in this research study (study case will be chosen) by faculty members. Participants are expected to participate one time, on the day of the experiment only. The total experiment period is estimated to last around 4 h. Participants will be invited to use 4 methodological tools: SimplySolve matrix, Bio-TRIZ matrix, simplified Bio-Inspired Ideation Process using Bonsai database and a simple brainstorming session which will be considered as a group control.

Subsequently, participants will be split into groups of 4 or 5 people, depending on class size. The experimental protocol takes place around four ideation sessions. Different classes will receive slightly different methodological supports, with varying stimuli such as accompanying videos, physical items, technical images, etc. Once the experiment is completed, the results will be submitted to the jury members (members of the faculty team in SUTD). They will be tasked with rating solutions on a 5-point likert scale on three dimensions: novelty, usefulness and eco-originality. The judge scores will be used to analyze the contribution of this study.

### 3.4    Phase 4: Data Collection and Analysis

The fourth phase would therefore be devoted to collecting data and qualitative informations to designing biomimetic transfer tools. These tools will potentially be modelled using a computer program to connect SimplySolve with existing biomimetic knowledge bases, virtually Bonsai.

In this context, collaboration for the development of a functional bio-inspired tool would be desirable in the context of this work. This phase will focus on the second axis of the methodological approach, the analysis and research work experimentation of [17, 30, 31] for developping a new ontologies.

### 3.5    Phase 5: Synthesis

The synthesis phase will be devoted to the analysis of the protocol and the expected results in addition to the evaluation of transfer tools with the aim to integrate them into the optimization of an eco-design framework. The goal is to propose a structure to streamline our process.

## 4    Next Step

This paper present the possibility to solve technical problems in the evolutionary context. TRIZ methodology has studied the inventive problem solving process that enables to increase the useful functions and decrease the harmful functions of new technological generations. Through a critical literature review, we have identified the potential of TRIZ approach as a promising tool for transferring biological knowledge. However, the limitations of this approach boil down to the disparity between technical and biological systems. Research work proposed as part of this article focuses on the development of tools to facilitate the transfer between two fields of knowledge: technical and biological. This leads us to direct the research problem for the development of tools facilitating eco-innovation and eco-design. In view of this observation, our main objective is to develop tools, both structuring the eco-inventive resolution phases and increasing the knowledge space of TRIZ toolbox.

In order to carry out this research project, a methodology has been proposed and structured in 5 phases. The first focuses on the use of TRIZ to formulate an inventive problem, thus extracting contradictions and corresponding inventive principles. The second allows, via a semantic dictionary, to transpose the elements of the inventive situation to natural processes. The third would be an experimental phase to measure the impact of our Bio-Inspired Ideation Process. The fourth phase will be dedicated to design transfer tools with the aim of optimizing an eco-design framework. Finally, the fifth phase will analyze the protocol as well as the results and evaluate the transfer tools in the hope of streamlining the process.

# References

1. Reyne, M.: Maîtriser l'innovation technologique: méthodes et outils pour concevoir des produits nouveaux: intelligence économique, démarches de créativité, prévisions technologiques, p. Vii. Dunod: L'Usine nouvelle, Paris (2002)
2. Inc, B.X., Fey, V., Rivin, E.I.: Innovation on Demand. Cambridge University Press, Cambridge (2005)
3. Flichy, P.: L'innovation technique: récents développements en sciences sociales: vers une nouvelle théorie de l'innovation. Nouv. éd. ed. Éditions La Découverte, Paris (2003)
4. DeBresson, C.: Comprendre le changement technique. Understanding technological change. Presses de l'Université d'Ottawa, Ottawa (1993)
5. Petrov, V.: TRIZ. Theory of Inventive Problem Solving: Level 1. Springer, Cham (2019). https://doi.org/10.1007/978-3-030-04254-7
6. Arthur, W.B.: The Nature of Technology: What it is and How it Evolves. Free Press, New York (2009)
7. Terninko, J., Zusman, A., Zlotin, B.: Systematic Innovation: an Introduction to TRIZ: Theory of Inventive Problem Solving, p. xiii. St. Lucie Press, Boca Raton (1998)
8. Orloff, M.A.: Inventive Thinking Through TRIZ: A Practical Guide. Springer, New York (2003). https://doi.org/10.1007/978-3-662-08013-9
9. Rantanen, K., Domb, E.: Simplified TRIZ (2002)
10. Mayda, M., Börklü, H.R.: An integration of TRIZ and the systematic approach of Pahl and Beitz for innovative conceptual design process. J. Braz. Soc. Mech. Sci. Eng. 36(4), 859–870 (2013). https://doi.org/10.1007/s40430-013-0106-y
11. Rantanen, K., Domb, E.: Simplified TRIZ New Problem-Solving Applications for Engineers and Manufacturing Professionals. TRIZ. St. Lucie Press, Boca Raton (2002)
12. Savransky, S.D.: Engineering of Creativity: Introduction to TRIZ Methodology of Inventive Problem Solving. CRC Press, Boca Raton (2000)
13. Rousselot, F., Zanni-Merk, C., Cavallucci, D.: Towards a formal definition of contradiction in inventive design. Comput. Ind. 63(3), 231–242 (2012)
14. Cavallucci, D., Vincent, J.F.V.: Development of an Ontology of Biomimetics Based on Altshuller's Matrix (2018)
15. Pokhrel, C., et al.: Adaptation of TRIZ contradiction matrix for solving problems in process engineering. Chem. Eng. Res. Des. 103, 3–10 (2015)
16. Cavallucci, D.: TRIZ – The Theory of Inventive Problem Solving: Current Research and Trends in French Academic Institutions. Springer, Cham (2017). https://doi.org/10.1007/978-3-319-56593-4

17. Yan, W., et al.: An ontology-based approach for inventive problem solving. Eng. Appl. Artif. Intell. **27**, 175–190 (2014)
18. Chechurin, L., Borgianni, Y.: Understanding TRIZ through the review of top cited publications. Comput. Ind. **82**, 119–134 (2016)
19. Vincent, J.F.V.: Biomimetics in architectural design. In: Intelligent Buildings International, pp. 1–12 (2014)
20. Vincent, J.F.V.: Biomimetics in architectural design. Intell. Build. Int. **8**(2), 138–149 (2016)
21. Fayemi, P.-E., Gille, M., Gazo, C.: Innovative Technical Creativity Methodology for Bio-Inspired-Design, pp. 253–265. International Federation for Information Processing (2018)
22. Fayemi, P.E., et al.: Biomimetics: process, tools and practice, p. 011002 (2017)
23. Vincent, J.F.V.: Biomimetics—A review. Proc. Inst. Mech. Eng. Part H: J. Eng. Med. **223** (8), 919–939 (2009)
24. Badarnah, L., Kadri, U.: A methodology for the generation of biomimetic design concept (2014)
25. Bogatyreva, O.: A win-win methodology for eco-innovation. In: Eco-Innovation and the Development of Business Models: Lessons from Experience and New Frontiers in Theory and Practice (2014). http://biotriz.be/data/documents/Win-win-methodology-for-eco-innovation. pdf. Accessed 21 Mar 2020
26. Bogatyreva, O., Nikolay, O.: TRIZ based algorithm for biomimetic design. In: Conference at ETRIA, Lisbon. http://biotriz.be/data/documents/BioTRIZ_Biomimetic-Design.pdf. Accessed 21 Mar 2020
27. Cherifi, A., Dubois, M., Gardoni, M., Tairi, A.: Methodology for innovative eco-design based on TRIZ. Int. J. Interact. Des. Manuf. (IJIDeM) **9**(3), 167–175 (2015). https://doi.org/ 10.1007/s12008-014-0255-y
28. Bossle, M.B., et al.: The drivers for adoption of eco-innovation. J. Clean. Prod. **113**, 861–872 (2016)
29. Sunguroğlu Hensel, D., Vincent, J.F.V.: Evolutionary inventive problem solving in biology and architecture: ArchiTRIZ and Material-Ontology. Intell. Build. Int. **8**(2), 118–137 (2016)
30. Cavallucci, D., Rousselot, F., Zanni, C.: Initial situation analysis through problem graph. CIRP J. Manuf. Sci. Technol. **2**(4), 310–317 (2010)
31. Houssin, R., Renaud, J., Coulibaly, A., Cavallucci, D., Rousselot, F.: TRIZ theory and case based reasoning: synergies and oppositions. Int. J. Interact. Des. Manuf. (IJIDeM) **9**(3), 177–183 (2014). https://doi.org/10.1007/s12008-014-0252-1
32. SimplySolve: Contradiction matrix & substance-field combination. https://simplysolve. inventivedesign.unistra.fr/. Accessed 21 Mar 2020
33. BONSAI: Bridging biOlogy & eNgineering uSing AI. https://api.inventivedesign.unistra.fr/ bonsai/. Accessed 21 Mar 2020

# TRIZ to Solve Challenges for Designing Sustainable, Intelligent and Inclusive Buildings

Emilia Brad and Anca Stan(✉) ⓘ

Technical University of Cluj-Napoca, Bdul Muncii 103-105,
Cluj-Napoca, Romania
sarb_anca@yahoo.com

**Abstract.** Concurrent Multi-Function Deployment method is used to study a multitude of criteria that give the performance of a building. Performance criteria such as costs, health and comfort of the inhabitants are weighted. They are in relation with target functions, such as sustainability, intelligence and inclusivity. TRIZ is included to solve several conflicts in relation with these target functions. An iterative process of combining target functions for solving conflicts is included. The methodology was tested for the case of a residential house. The beneficiary was questioned regarding his expectations on the building's sustainability, smartness and inclusiveness. Beneficiary's expectations are deployed into weighted engineering specifications. This information is relevant with respect to those specifications that are negatively correlated. With TRIZ, the generic directions of innovation have been identified. Following the iterative algorithm for combining target functions, generic directions of innovation have been converted by the architect into practical solutions, allowing the authors to demonstrate that such design of buildings is possible. The novelty of this paper is that it focuses on using CMFD and TRIZ on the entire design of a building, not just certain materials or parts of a building.

**Keywords:** Sustainability · Smart house · Inclusive building · TRIZ · Cost management · Problem solving · Performance planning

## 1 Introduction

Since the 20th century, a need has developed to create buildings that are able to function to their full potential for the purpose for which they were created. Into these buildings there have been incorporated new technologies with a decisive role in their sustainability, aesthetics, productivity, accessibility and safety, but also in cost reduction [1].

In general, a building is considered to be efficient if at the time of the design a multitude of criteria were taken into account for the development of a functional and comfortable building. A high-performance building must incorporate the following characteristics: interior comfort, high durability, high energy efficiency, high productivity and well-being for residents [2].

A concept that supports this view is the concept of "Whole Building Design Approach". This approach considers that in the field of construction there are two

© IFIP International Federation for Information Processing 2020
Published by Springer Nature Switzerland AG 2020
D. Cavallucci et al. (Eds.): TFC 2020, IFIP AICT 597, pp. 196–206, 2020.
https://doi.org/10.1007/978-3-030-61295-5_16

extremely important conditions that must be implemented: the approach of an integrated design and the integration of all team members in the creation process (community, beneficiaries, investors, specialists in the field, etc.) [3]. The concept of high-performance building was introduced in the approach as a whole to the design and construction of buildings, and must include features such as: accessibility, aesthetics, cost efficiency, functionality, productivity, occupational health, history, safety and security, sustainability [4].

Figure 1 highlights the characteristics of a sustainable, intelligent and inclusive building with high performance: smart technologies, low costs, sustainable, productive, accessible, functional, aesthetic and offering a high degree of safety.

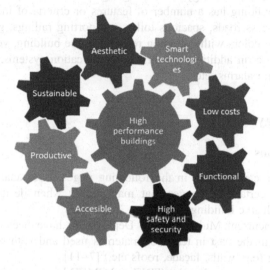

**Fig. 1.** The characteristics of a sustainable, intelligent and inclusive building with high performance.

When we talk about sustainability, we take into account a number of characteristics that a building must have. These characteristics include [5]: minimum operating costs, protection of residents' health, the environment and natural resources, protection of the land on which it was built, groundwater protection, use of rainwater in the household, decontamination of contaminated soil, low level noise emissions, lowering air and greenhouse gas pollutants, durability and usability for the purpose for which it was created, reuse and recycle of the building's materials after demolition, low energy use, its ability to be ventilated, the use of natural light to its full potential, the existence of equipment for producing energy from renewable sources, etc.

The criteria for determining the performance of buildings in terms of sustainability are: recyclable furniture, economical household appliances, economical electrical equipment, water purification system used in the household and which is discharged, and the materials from which the building is built be recyclable.

There are a number of criteria that show us that a building is intelligent. These criteria include [6]: flexible design, energy efficient design, Wi-Fi networks, VOIP networks (voice over internet protocol), video monitoring, building access monitoring, suppression automatic fire, built-in support (for lighting, signaling, smoke control, etc.), attention to traffic in the building and social spaces, modes of transport in the vicinity of the building, etc.

The main criteria that give the performance of a building are: incorporation of a light control system, incorporation of light and hearing warning systems, installation of a heating control system, an audio control system and a building access system. In addition, one can include: integration of all building systems, remote operation and optimization, maintenance monitoring management, energy management systems, continuous monitoring and feedback, energy efficient equipment, thermal energy storage, thermal water and energy monitoring, light control etc. [6].

An inclusive building has a number of features or criteria of inclusiveness: wide doors and wide access roads, spacious toilets, supporting railings, good lighting, the use of eye-pleasing colors with a guiding role inside the building, vertical traffic with ramps, elevators, etc. in addition to stairs, communication systems, emergency exits accessible to all, fire alarms, etc.

## 2  Methodology

### 2.1  Fundamentals

The aim of this research paper, in the following pages, is to analyze whether it is possible to solve certain challenges that may appear when designing sustainable, intelligent and inclusive buildings.

TRIZ and Concurrent Multi-Function Deployment have been used in the construction industry in the past in terms of materials used and with regards to specific parts of a building (e.g. walls, façade, roofs etc.) [7–11].

The novelty of this research is that TRIZ and CMFD have never been applied on an entire construction/building, much less on an intelligent, sustainable, intelligent one.

For multi-criteria performance planning, the method entitled Concurrent Multi-Function Deployment (CMFD) was adopted [12], which allows the concurrent approach of several objective functions and the inclusion of structured innovation in the design process of the solution.

The research path on the performance of sustainable, intelligent and inclusive buildings is highlighted in Fig. 2.

According to the methodology of the CMFD algorithm, a series of steps must be followed [12]:

1. Defining the objective set of functions and organizing specialized teams for each of these objective functions
2. Identification and classification, by importance, of the requirements related to the objective and business functions in general
3. Objective function planning - the objective functions are analyzed in relation to the investment plans
4. Determining and classifying the value characteristics that define each objective function

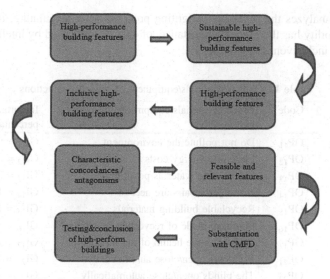

**Fig. 2.** The route and associated methods to CMFD

5. Generation of local solutions for the entire architectural system and its subsystems
6. Local solution planning
7. Generating the complete solution with the help of aggregation and innovation
8. Analysis of the complete general solution in relation to the value characteristics
9. Defining the constituent parts of the whole solution and the processes that support the execution
10. Concurrent planning of the parts of the solution and their corresponding processes
11. Execution operations planning

Based on the CMFD framework, the most important criteria of sustainability, intelligence and inclusiveness will be analyzed.

## 2.2 Testing

To test the CMFD method, the objective functions of a sustainable, intelligent and inclusive building (FO) and their requirement-functions (FR) are chosen as follows:

FO = {sustainability, intelligence, inclusiveness}
FR = {costs, health and comfort of the inhabitants}

In order to test this method a client/beneficiary of a house was chosen, this client has the following particular perspective on the building: he considers that the initial investment should cost a maximum of 130,000 euros (FR1) with an importance of $I = 25\%$, the maximum total investment will cost 400,000 euros (FR2) with an importance $I = 25\%$, the house's floors will have a surface of maximum 250 m$^2$ (FR3) with an importance $I = 10\%$, the ease of operation (FR4) has an importance $I = 10\%$, the protection of the health of the residents (FR5) has an importance $I = 15\%$, and the protection of the environment (FR6) has an importance $I = 15\%$.

Table 1 analyzes the objective weighting process. After calculating, it was found that sustainability has the highest importance, of 45.12%, followed by intelligence with 31.71% and inclusiveness with 23.17%.

**Table 1.** Objects/materials/equipment of objective functions

| Objective function | Code | Objects/materials/equipment that meet the objective | Importance percentage (%) |
|---|---|---|---|
| Sustainability | $OP_{11}$ | Do not pollute the environment | $GI_{11} = 9\%$ |
| | $OP_{12}$ | Have low energy costs | $GI_{12} = 23\%$ |
| | $OP_{13}$ | Use as little water as possible | $GI_{13} = 20\%$ |
| | $OP_{14}$ | No major repairs are needed | $GI_{14} = 10\%$ |
| | $OP_{15}$ | Recyclable building materials | $GI_{15} = 17\%$ |
| | $OP_{16}$ | Furniture made of recyclable materials | $GI_{16} = 5\%$ |
| | $OP_{17}$ | To protect the health of the inhabitants | $GI_{17} = 16\%$ |
| Intelligence | $OP_{21}$ | Windows open/close automatically | $GI_{21} = 11\%$ |
| | $OP_{22}$ | The blinds open/close automatically | $GI_{22} = 11\%$ |
| | $OP_{23}$ | The front door opens/closes automatically | $GI_{23} = 7\%$ |
| | $OP_{24}$ | Heating monitoring system | $GI_{24} = 20\%$ |
| | $OP_{25}$ | Light monitoring system | $GI_{25} = 19\%$ |
| | $OP_{26}$ | Danger warning alarm | $GI_{26} = 9\%$ |
| | $OP_{27}$ | The light turns on/off automatically | $GI_{27} = 7\%$ |
| | $OP_{28}$ | Integrated audio system | $GI_{28} = 4\%$ |
| | $OP_{29}$ | Building security and protection system | $GI_{29} = 12\%$ |
| Inclusivity | $OP_{31}$ | Large rooms | $GI_{31} = 13\%$ |
| | $OP_{32}$ | Large hallways | $GI_{32} = 13\%$ |
| | $OP_{33}$ | Large bathrooms | $GI_{33} = 13\%$ |
| | $OP_{34}$ | Non-slippery floor | $GI_{34} = 12\%$ |
| | $OP_{35}$ | Lights open easily | $GI_{35} = 7\%$ |
| | $OP_{36}$ | Doors open easily | $GI_{36} = 9\%$ |
| | $OP_{37}$ | No level differences | $GI_{37} = 4\%$ |
| | $OP_{38}$ | Easily accessible alarm system | $GI_{38} = 12\%$ |
| | $OP_{39}$ | Warning signs | $GI_{39} = 10\%$ |
| | $OP_{310}$ | Well-lit rooms | $GI_{310} = 7\%$ |

Table 2 shows the value characteristics related to sustainability, inclusivity and intelligence.

**Table 2.** Objective function planning

| | | Sustainability | | |
| --- | --- | --- | --- | --- |
| | | Intelligence | | + |
| | | Inclusivity | + | - |
| | | Optimization trends | ↑ | ↑ | ↑ |
| Links:<br>● powerful link<br>☺ medium link<br>℗ possible link<br>+ positive correlation<br>- negative correlation<br>↑ positive trend<br>↓ negative trend | Importance | Inclusivity | Intelligence | Sustainability |
| Initial investment max 130.000 euro | 25% | ℗ | ● | ● |
| Total investment max 400.000 euro | 25% | ℗ | ● | ● |
| House floors max 250 m² | 10% | ● | ℗ | ℗ |
| Easy to operate | 10% | ● | ☺ | ℗ |
| Protects residents' health | 15% | ● | ℗ | ● |
| Protects the environment | 15% | ℗ | ℗ | ● |
| Value share (PV) | | 23.17% | 31.71% | 45.12% |

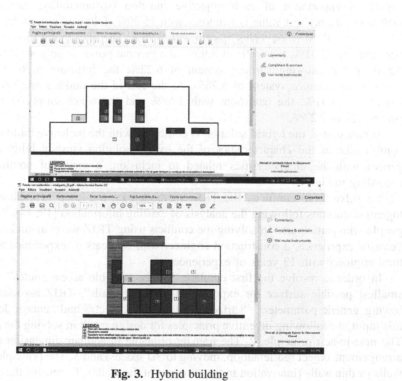

**Fig. 3.** Hybrid building

Based on the application of the CMFD method, a hybridization of the three concepts follows. According to the actual algorithm and data, it starts with the combination of the first two buildings - the sustainable building and the smart building - resulting in a hybrid building.

The designed hybrid building in Fig. 3 has 249 $m^2$ and two floors. It is covered with 15 cm thermal insulation made of recyclable materials. The window glass reflects sunlight. Ventilation is achieved through a ventilation and air purification plant. The ventilation and purification system is doubled by the possibility of natural ventilation. The heating of the building is done with the help of a geothermal pump. Domestic hot water is produced by means of a bivalent boiler through solar panels located on the roof of the terrace. The existing voltaic panels supply a battery system. The windows have a system of embedded blinds. This building can be controlled remotely in terms of: heating, lighting, safety, monitoring, energy and water consumption. The doors open from the remote control, close automatically if they are left open, and after a period of vacancy, the heating agent, ventilation and microsystem in the respective room stop. The doors to the main access are activated by a fingerprint reader for pedestrian access and based on remote control or intelligent vehicle recognition for cars. In the event of damage to the installation systems, the smart central panel interrupts the power supply with the respective agent or activates the automatic extinguishing system of all. The occupants of the building have a "carrier" switch/phone/tablet with which they can control the lights throughout the house.

Taking into account the relative weight of each subcomponent in relation to the degree of importance of each objective function (sustainability, intelligence and inclusion), the highest value is windows with 15.29%, followed closely by doors with 12.37% and HVAC monitoring system with 9.96%. The light monitoring system has a percentage of 8.01%, the walls of 7.95%, the thermal power supply system of 6.97%, the danger monitoring/warning system of 6.22%, the furniture of 6.03% and the building surveillance system of 5.78%. At the end of the ranking are: vertical circulation with 1.91%, the bathroom with 1.68% and the water supply system with a percentage of 1.27%.

Subsequently, the hybrid solution is combined with the inclusive building. When a combination of the characteristics of the hybrid solution (sustainability and intelligence) with the characteristics related to inclusion, a series of conflicts appear, according to Fig. 4.

To solve these conflicts, the TRIZ methodology was used, a method based on logical deductions following the analysis of existing information [13, 14]. The panel of people who participated in solving the conflicts using TRIZ were: an architect with 10 years of experience, a construction engineer with 37 years of experience and a structural engineer with 13 years of experience.

In order to resolve the first conflict: "widest possible access routes" versus "the smallest possible surface for exposing the exterior walls", TRIZ associates the following generic parameters: "surface of stationary objects" and "energy loss". Given this input, the following inventive principles for design result in solving the problem: 1. The nest-in-nest principle, 2. The transfer principle in another dimension (multi-level arrangement, object reorientation, moving to 3D spaces) and 3. The principle of flexible walls or thin walls (innovation in the structure of the walls). To resolve the conflict, the

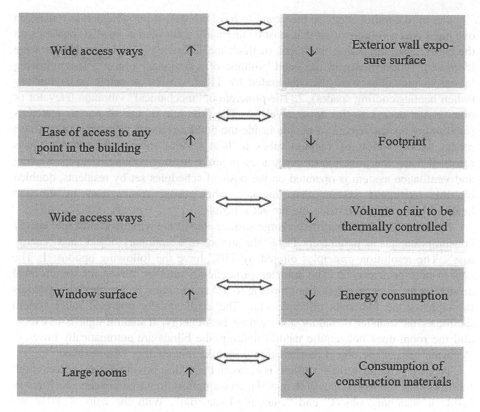

**Fig. 4.** Conflict list inclusive building vs. hybrid building

nest-in-nest principle was chosen, in the sense that all rooms are structured around a central hall, and access is made in all rooms through it, it being dimensioned according to the rules and, thus, avoiding, as far as possible, the existence of a large exposure area of the exterior walls.

To resolve the second conflict: "as easy as possible access to any point in the building" and "as little footprint as possible on the ground" the following generic TRIZ parameters were selected: "surface of stationary objects" and "convenience in use -It has". The principles offered by TRIZ for solving this conflict are: 1. The principle of partial or excessive actions and 2. The principle of asymmetry (building the building on two levels, but asymmetric). In resolving this conflict, a combination of the two principles was chosen, in the sense that the principle of asymmetry was used, the floor has a smaller surface than the ground floor, ensuring the necessary dimensions for the rules in force for people with disabilities. Also, for the principle of "excessive actions" the following solutions were implemented: a platform lift, hydraulic, was installed, which ensures the access of all residents of the building to the upper floor. However, the ingenuity of the professional who recommended this solution is noticeable, as the costs with this platform lift are much lower than the costs of foundations and earthworks on the entire surface, of 249 m$^2$, if it had been carried out on a single level.

The third conflict is due to the desire to have the widest possible access routes, on one hand, and a volume of air that must be thermally controlled as small as possible, on the other hand. Based on the TRIZ method, the following generic parameters were identified: "convenience in use" and "volume of a stationary object". The following inventive principles were then generated by TRIZ: 1. The principle of asymmetry (when heating/cooling spaces), 2. The principle of "mechanical" vibration (elevator or other easier access to the upper level), 3. The principle of use of porous materials (facilitating the movement of people inside the building) and 4. The principle of inert media (incorporation of vacuum tubes to heat several rooms). This conflict was resolved using the principle of asymmetry in space heating/cooling: both the heating and ventilation system is operated on the basis of schedules set by residents, doubled by the intelligent system that operates when using rooms and in function heating/cooling needs outside the pre-set schedule.

The fourth conflict identified: a large surface area of the windows and a low energy consumption, has as parameters TRIZ "the surface of a stationary object" and "energy loss". The resolution principles offered by TRIZ have the following options: 1. The nest-in-nest principle, 2. The transfer principle in another dimension (multi-level arrangement, object reorientation, moving to 3D spaces) and 3. The flexible materials principle or the materials principle thin. The automatically operated roller system facilitates the transfer of indoor and outdoor heat energy. If natural light is in excess and the room does not require natural lighting, the blinds are automatically lowered. With the help of the object reorientation principle, this conflict was resolved.

The last of the identified conflicts is between the widest possible access routes (high mobility) and the lowest possible material consumption. Input parameters are: "moves inside a stationary object" and "amount of material". With the help of TRIZ we identified the following solving principles: 1. The principle of local quality (choice of differentiated materials for different spaces), 2. The principle of changing parameters and 3. The principle of composite materials (use of recyclable materials, waste, etc.). The third principle, the principle of composite materials is the one on which this conflict was resolved. Recycled materials were used in the construction of the building: recycled brick, recycled wood, thermal system made of recyclable material, recycled parquet, furniture made of recycled materials, etc., and the load-bearing masonry walls of the building, plus the positioning of door and window openings are dimensioned and positioned according to the brick modules specified by the manufacturer, so the losses that may occur in the construction process are almost non-existent.

Taking into account all of the above, a sustainable, intelligent and inclusive building was designed (see Fig. 5).

This building has 255 m$^2$ and is developed on two floors, the ground floor having an area of 137 m$^2$, and the floor having an area of 118 m$^2$. It is covered with 15 cm thermal insulation made of recyclable materials. The exterior finishes are made of recycled brick from demolition and recycled and treated plywood. The heating of the building is done with the help of a geothermal pump, the heating is through the floor. This pump heats up in winter and cools the walls in summer.

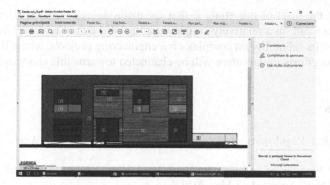

**Fig. 5.** Sustainable, intelligent and inclusive building

Domestic hot water is produced by means of a bivalent boiler, solar panels were placed on the roof terrace. The windows have a system of masked roller shutters in thermal insulation with automatic operation from the switch/remote control/telephone, etc. This building can be controlled remotely in terms of: heating, lighting, safety, monitoring, energy and water consumption. The garage door opens from the remote control, closes automatically if left open. In the event of damage to the installation systems, the intelligent central panel interrupts the power supply with the respective agent or activates their automatic extinguishing system. The hydraulic elevator in the building is provided with perimeter railings, and in case of calamity, will not be disconnected to facilitate evacuation from the upper floor. The occupants of the building have a "carrier" switch/phone/tablet with which they can control the light throughout the house.

The sustainable, intelligent and inclusive building has sized flows for persons with disabilities, access ramps to the main entrance and on the terrace. It has warning signs at the beginning and end of the ramps and in front of the steps. On ramps and terraces the current hand is doubled (at 90 and 60 cm). The main ramp is covered, but has non-slip floors. The halls and rooms allow the simultaneous passage of two wheelchairs. The switches and sockets are at a maximum height of 90 cm.

## 3 Conclusions

In the context of world trends for finding sustainable solutions to energy and climacteric challenges, as well as to more inclusive communities, this research provides insights on how to approach such issues for building construction.

The purpose of this paper is to formulate a methodology for handling qualitative optimization of buildings when several target-functions are considered, such as smartness, green design and inclusiveness.

This paper demonstrates that it is possible to formulate a balanced solution in designing a building where several target functions, such as sustainability, inclusiveness and smartness are taken into account. The proposed methodology is applicable in any civil engineering project, where we need to tackle design from multiple angles.

However, the limit of this study is that the methodology was tested only on three target functions and on a relatively simple building. We do not have yet a clear understanding about its reliability on complex civil engineering projects, where the entropy is very high. Our efforts in the future will be channeled towards this shortcoming.

# References

1. The Building Regulations, Buildings and buildings, England and Wales, Great Britain (2010)
2. Zafar, S.: Features of a Green Building. https://www.ecomena.org/salient-features-of-a-green-building/. Accessed 15 May 2020
3. Powler, D.: Whole Building Design - The Role of Buildings and the Case for Whole Building Design. https://www.wbdg.org/resources/whole-building-design. Accessed 15 May 2020
4. http://www.enil.eu/news/the-worlds-most-accessible-building/. Accessed 15 May 2020
5. Guideline for Sustainable Building. Federal Office for Building and Regional Planning edn. Ministry of Transport, Building and Housing, Germany (2001)
6. Edgar, A.: Intelligent Building Processes for Intelligent Buildings, Intelligent Building Concepts Intelligent Design & Construction Concepts, A SMART Proposal, Building Smart Alliance, online edition (2016)
7. Ding, Z., Jiang, S., Wu, J.: Research on Construction Technology Innovation Platform Based on TRIZ. In: Wen, Z., Li, T. (eds.) Knowledge Engineering and Management. AISC, vol. 278, pp. 211–223. Springer, Heidelberg (2014). https://doi.org/10.1007/978-3-642-54930-4_21
8. Wu, C.M., Yu, W.D., Cheng, S.T.: A model used for the generation of innovative construction alternatives. J. Chinese Inst. Civ. Hydraulic Eng. 25(2), 123–136 (2013)
9. Coskun, K., Cem Altun, M.: Applicability of TRIZ to in-situ construction techniques. In: 2nd International Conference on Construction and Project Management, in International Proceedings of Economics Development & Research, IPEDR, vol. 15, IACSIT Press, Singapore (2011)
10. Sen Chiu, R., Cheng, S.T.: The improvement of heat insulation for roof steel plates by triz application. J. Marine Sci. Technol. 20(2), 122–131 (2012)
11. Lee, D., Shin, S.: Advanced high strength steel tube diagrid using TRIZ and nonlinear pushover analysis. J. Const. Steel Res. 96, 151–158 (2014)
12. Brad, S.: Concurrent multifunction deployment (CMFD). Int. J. Prod. Res. 47(19), 5343–5476 (2009)
13. Brad, S., Ciupan, C., Pop, L., Mocan, B., Fulea, M.: Manualul de bază al managerului de produs în ingineria şi managementul inovaţiei. Editura Economica, ISBN 978-973-709-265-6, Bucharest (2006)
14. Russo, D., Carrara, P.: Innovation lab: new TRIZ tools for fast idea triggering. In: Benmoussa, R., De Guio, R., Dubois, S., Koziołek, S. (eds.) TFC 2019. IAICT, vol. 572, pp. 16–25. Springer, Cham (2019). https://doi.org/10.1007/978-3-030-32497-1_2

# Tools and Techniques of TRIZ for Enhancing Design

# Application of TRIZ Substance-Field Analysis and Situational Analysis for Risk Analysis and Development of Common Language Among Stakeholders

Tony Tanoyo[1](✉), Iouri Belski[2], and Jennifer Harlim[3]

[1] Leica Biosystems, Melbourne, Australia
tony.tanoyo@gmail.com
[2] Royal Melbourne Institute of Technology, Melbourne, Australia
[3] Monash University, Melbourne, Australia

**Abstract.** The aim of this research is to explore the application of Substance-Field Analysis and Situational Analysis for system modelling, risk analysis and for development of common language among stakeholders. To establish the abovementioned influence of Substance-Field and Situational Analysis this research considered a product in the sustaining product life-cycle phase.

Non-TRIZ tools such as FMEA (Failure Modes and Effects Analysis) are often used for risk analysis when assessing the impact to any changes introduced to the design.

Substance-Field Analysis and Situational Analysis were introduced to complement FMEA. The benefits and value of both TRIZ tools added to current approaches were evaluated and explored. The research shows that using both tools can work together and complement existing problem-solving methods applied within an engineering organization.

Firstly, Substance-Field Analysis tool was found particularly useful for modelling the system, risk analysis and idea generation and very effective for development of common language among stakeholders (such as project/ program management, director, etc.)

Secondly, Situational Analysis was found exceptionally functional for prioritizing and identifying the appropriate level of actions to respond to a problem. It also helped improving communication among stakeholders.

There are several limitations of this research. This study was conducted within a single engineering firm. Also, it considered a product only in the sustaining product life-cycle phase. Therefore, the research findings of this study cannot be generalized for all companies and for a complete product life-cycle. Additional investigations are required for further generalization of the findings.

**Keywords:** Substance-Field analysis · Situational analysis · Risk analysis · System modelling · Design improvement · Problem solving process

© IFIP International Federation for Information Processing 2020
Published by Springer Nature Switzerland AG 2020
D. Cavallucci et al. (Eds.): TFC 2020, IFIP AICT 597, pp. 209–220, 2020.
https://doi.org/10.1007/978-3-030-61295-5_17

# 1 Introduction

Engineering profession is responsible for development of artefacts that, most of the time, make human's life more enjoyable. On occasions, though, products and processes developed by engineers fail. To establish the reasons for the failures, engineers use numerous Failure Analysis (FA) procedures. The most commonly used FA procedures include Failure Modes and Effects Analysis (FMEA) [1], also known as Failure Mode Effect Cause Analysis (FMECA), Fault Tree Analysis (FTA) [2], Problem Analysis [3], Event Tree Analysis (ETA) [4], Root-Cause Analysis (RCA) [5], cognitive map-based system analysis [6] and the Anticipatory Failure Determination (AFD) [7, 8].

Systematization of Substance-Field Analysis (Su-Field Analysis) [9] not only simplified modelling of engineering systems and made idea generation more systematic [10], but also permitted Su-Field Analysis use in FA [11]. Belski et al. presented two small case studies and showed that the FA procedure based on Su-Field Analysis can be helpful in establishing numerous failure scenarios systematically. This study investigates whether the Su-Field Analysis-based FA procedure can effectively complement the FMEA.

The above-mentioned FA procedures are usually deployed for establishing technical reasons of failures. Human-related reasons are not covered much by these procedures. This study explores whether the other TRIZ tool – the heuristic of Situational Analysis (SA) [12] can help in identifying reasons for failure that can be avoided with help of human interaction.

# 2 Research Questions

The aim of this research is to explore the application of Su-Field Analysis and SA for system modelling, risk analysis and for development of common language among stakeholders. The research questions explored in this paper are:

1. Can the procedure of SA be more effective in the problem identification process, pinpointing reasons for failure that is beyond the technical causes?
2. Can the Su-Field-based FA procedure effectively complement the FMEA procedure?

# 3 TRIZ Tools Investigated - Situational Analysis and Substance Field Analysis

The heuristic of SA [9, 13] is intended to help a user to understand a problematic situation more clearly and to separate technical challenges embedded in the situation from human-related issues. The tool requires a user to answer a set of questions, prompting the user to scrutinize the problem beyond the original problem statement. The process of answering these questions is not linear. A practitioner usually moves back and forth between the questions numerous times before the problematic situation is clarified. This process assists a user to consider the problem from different perspectives and fully appreciate the cyclic nature of engineering problem solving. Due to engagement of a user in the cyclic process of questioning assumptions, SA can be very effective during the problem definition process [14]. The series of questions require a user to consider the Main Useful Function (MUF) to improve, the needs outside the technical nature of the problem and establish ways these needs can be met beyond the traditional design changes approach.

Su-Field Analysis is a TRIZ heuristic that is based on modelling [9, 13]. It represents technical systems as a set of interconnected components – a set of substances interacting with each other by means of fields, which, in turn, are generated by the substances. By breaking down the model components, it helps the practitioners to break down the complex problem into manageable elements and facilitates the clarification of problem structure [14]. Effective for problem finding, Su-Field Analysis is also useful to generate solution ideas. It expects a user to follow the 5 Steps process and to utilise 5 Model Solutions. Su-Field Analysis uses eight fields of MATCEMIB (Mechanical, Acoustic, Thermal, Chemical, Electric, Magnetic, Intermolecular and Biological) to generate ideas [15].

## 4  Background

The organization involved in the investigation is a large size, global medical devices company based in Melbourne, Australia. The company focusses on both new products and product sustainment. The company has a very strong focus on problem solving.

Within the organization, Problem Solving Process (PSP) is part of the organizational culture. The company's PSP involves four stages: 1) Problem Definition, 2) Investigation, 3) Verification, 4) Ensuring Sustainment [16, 17]. The organization acknowledges that for efficient problem-solving process, substantial time needs to be devoted to the problem definition stage. The importance of proper problem definition is also well-covered in literature [14, 18].

Simple and systematic problem definition process helps in narrowing down the focus of engineering investigation and verification efforts, hence cutting down time and resources required to solve the problem. Based on the current practice, the organization's approach to the definition of the problem begins with the Pareto analysis of the data with three distinct measures: TAG (Trend, Actual, Gap) and ends with a FA using 5-Whys technique. If the problem is linked to an actual design issue, this approach often fails to identify important aspects of human interactions that can help in significantly simplifying the problem and result in minimizing changes to the actual design itself.

The organization develops and manufactures medical equipment, including pathology and cancer diagnostics machines. It is a global leader in the clinical diagnosis workflow solutions and automation, integrating each step in the workflow from biopsy to diagnosis. All products manufactured by the organization has to meet the U.S Food and Drug Administration (FDA) standards [19].

To establish the influence of Su-Field Analysis and SA on the problem-solving process, this research considered a product in the sustaining product life-cycle phase. This product has been on the market for several years and has been reported to have high number of heater failures when used in the field. Therefore, Su-Field Analysis and SA were used to determine the root-cause of the problem and to establish effective countermeasures to eliminate the problem.

As the organization is in the medical field, FMEA is the recommended risk analysis tool for both product development and sustaining product life-cycle stages. FMEA is often used by the companies that develop medical equipment [20]. There are well-known limitations of FMEA published by FMEA scholars and acknowledged by engineering experts. Some of these limitations relate to the reliance of FMEA assessment of the potential failures on the individual's or team's experience and knowledge. Therefore, there is always concerns on the validity of conclusions attained by this process [20]. It has also been reported that FMEA assumes existence of a linear relationship between the severity, probability and detection ranking. These parameters, though, usually do not have linear relationship [21]. This study investigates whether pairing TRIZ tools of Su-Field Analysis and SA with FMEA can address some limitations of FMEA.

## 5  Methodology

As the investigation is unique to the organization, a case study approach was undertaken. The case study approach is suitable in this situation as it enables investigation of a real-life phenomenon within a specific context [22]. It also allows for a smaller sample to be analyzed in depth longitudinally [22] which suits the application in the context of this research. Chetty suggested that the use of the case study method is effective for research investigations within businesses and large organizations [23].

A single case approach, which is deployed by this study, focuses the investigations on the specific organizational needs. This research involved multiple sources of data which include information on the problem-solving tools used within the company, the engineer's perspective, informal and formal feedback from stakeholders. Information about the problem-solving tools used within the organization was briefly presented in the previous section. For the purpose of this paper, only the engineer's experience is discussed. Informal feedback was continuously sought from the stakeholders throughout the process, while the design of formal feedback is currently being planned and considered. The reflection of the benefits and value that both TRIZ tools added to current organizational procedures are evaluated and explored.

## 6  Results

### 6.1  Establishing Proper Problem Definition by Means of the Situational Analysis

TRIZ SA tool was used to demonstrate a clear breakdown structure of the problem of heater failures that was mentioned in the previous section of the paper. While conducting the SA procedure, the researchers used inputs from the data supporting the contention of the problem and FA data. It was concluded that the MUF of the system to be improved is *controlling the heat*. The next section of the paper shows how Su-Field Analysis was used to systematically identify the MUF for the *heating control system*. After completion of SA, it was observed that:

1. Initially, the problem was focused on the reliability improvement of the heater, which can be achieved by making appropriate design changes. After conducting the SA procedure, it was concluded that the problem of heater failures was not just technical. Some non-technical requirements, such as customer needs, safety standards and FDA regulations put significant constraints on the heater design.
2. SA identified that design improvements are not viable until some other tasks, such as liaising with stakeholders on the possibility of removing a thermal fuse from the existing heater and adjusting the heater specification are completed. These tasks are not explicitly technical. Therefore, for younger engineers, the existence of these non-design (non-technical) tasks were unexpected. Clearly, non-attendance to such 'non-technical' tasks may have caused delays in improvements of the heater and even may have failed any improvements.

### 6.2  System Modeling

Su-Field modelling was used to model the *heating control system*, which is the system to be improved. Having completed this model helped in understanding the problem and especially its MUF. Figure 1 presents the Su-Field model of the *heating control system*.

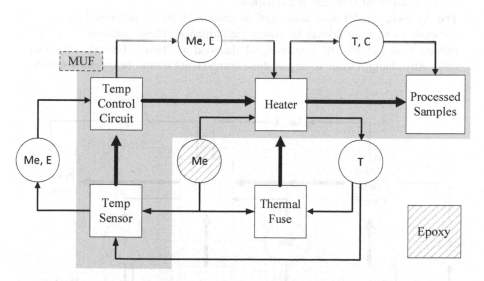

**Fig. 1.** The Su-Field model of the heating control system

In the Su-Field model shown in Fig. 1, the square boxes depict the elements of the *heating control system* (substances). The circles with the letters inside represent the fields of interaction (Me – mechanical, E – electrical, T – thermal, C – chemical). The thick arrows identify the intended outcomes and the thin arrows identify the means of achieving these outcomes.

The operation of the *heating control system* can be explained in the following way. The temperature sensor that is mechanically attached to the temperature control circuit by wire and solder joints delivers an information on the temperature electrically by changing the electrical resistance. The temperature control circuit that is mechanically affixed to the heater by wire and solder joints adjusts the heat produced by the heater by increasing or decreasing the amount of current supplied (electrical). The heater changes the chemical properties of the sample placed on top of it by increasing the heat. A processed sample is produced as a result.

The heater also heats up the thermal fuse, that expands and, in case of overheating (150 °C), breaks the heater current supply. The heater, thermal fuse and temperature sensor are all encapsulated by epoxy (mechanical). For simplicity purposes, the epoxy is shown in Fig. 1 on the bottom right side corner with its box as well the circle representing the mechanical field applied to the temperature sensor, the heater and the thermal fuse filled with stripes.

Analysis of the system's Su-Field model shown in Fig. 1 resulted in the following discoveries:

1. The MUF of the system is to control the heater temperature and produce a processed sample. It does not include the thermal safety protection.
2. The Su-Field model was well understood by the members of the improvement team, who had different technical backgrounds.
3. The Su-Field model was also used to communicate to other stakeholders the components that are critical to system performance. These components are highlighted by the checkered area in Fig. 2 (labelled as "Heater Intrinsic Characteristic"). Any changes made to any of these components should be carefully reviewed.

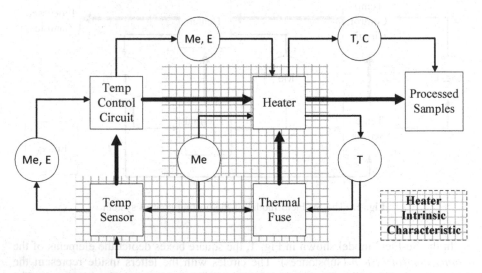

**Fig. 2.** The Su-Field model of the "Heater Intrinsic Characteristic" area

## 6.3    Risk Analysis

The Su-Field model of the current system was used to perform risk analysis. The approach of using Su-Field model for risk analysis is to consider the scenario where input/s to the system has failed. For this *heating control system*, these inputs are coming from the temperature control circuit, the temperature sensor and the thermal fuse. As an example of the outcomes of the Su-Field modelling, only component type of failures within the electric field is considered in this paper. Failure scenarios within the temperature control circuit itself were excluded due to lack of space. Failures of the thermal fuse, which is outside of the MUF area was also excluded from this example.

The process that is followed for this analysis is described below.

Step 1: Replace the system's input component with one of the symbols shown in Table 1.

**Table 1.** The symbols used to represent the type of component failures

| Symbols | I | \\ | ☐ |
|---|---|---|---|
| Description | Component is shorted | Component is open | Component is missing |

Step 2: From the list of negative effects presented in Table 2, decide the appropriate negative effects generated on the next interactions between different substances. Replace the impacted thick arrows by the appropriate line type shown from Table 2.

**Table 2.** Types of lines used to represent the negative effects

| Line Type | – – – – ▶ | —⊗▶ | ⟹ | ————— |
|---|---|---|---|---|
| Negative Effects | Insufficient action | Harmful action | Excessive action | Missing action |

The first failure scenario established by the process is short circuiting of the temperature sensor. Its model is shown in Fig. 3. Because of short circuiting, the temperature control circuit will 'order' the heater to deliver too much heat to the samples. This will cause incomplete sample processing. The thermal fuse will prevent the heater temperature to exceed 150 °C.

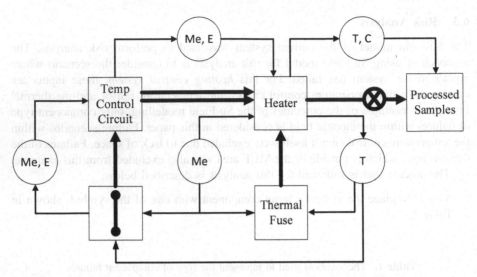

**Fig. 3.** Failure scenario 1 - temperature sensor is shorted

The second failure scenario is an open-circuited temperature sensor (see Fig. 4). This will result in the temperature control circuit 'order' for the heater to deliver insufficient heat to the sample and will cause incomplete sample processing.

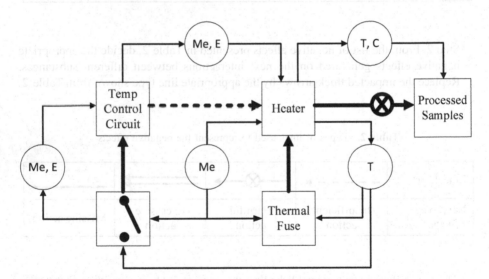

**Fig. 4.** Failure scenario 2 - temperature sensor is open-circuited

The third failure scenario is when the temperature sensor is missing (see Fig. 5). This will result in the temperature control circuit not being able to generate additional power to the heater and causes incomplete sample processing result.

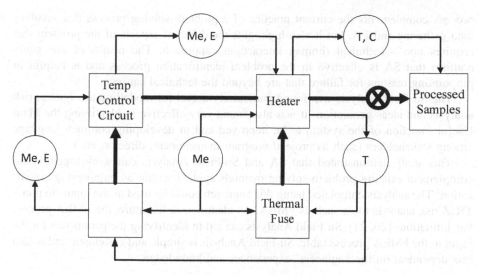

**Fig. 5.** Failure scenario 3 - temperature sensor is missing

Table 3 shows how the three types of failure scenarios are captured as the inputs to the FMEA. Note that Table 3 does not include the severity, probability and prevention/detection control rating columns.

**Table 3.** Summary of potential failure modes identified as inputs to FMEA

| Item | System/Subsystem/Component | Item/Function | Potential Failure Mode | Potential Effect(s) of Failure | Potential Causes/Mechanism of Failure |
|---|---|---|---|---|---|
| 1 | Heater | Generates heat for chemical reaction | Too much heat generated | Incomplete sample processing | Temperature sensor is shorted. |
| 2 | Heater | Generates heat for chemical reaction | Too little heat generated | Incomplete sample processing | Temperature sensor is open. |
| 3 | Heater | Generates heat for chemical reaction | No heat generated | Incomplete sample processing | Temperature sensor is missing |

## 7  Discussion

This study reiterates the importance of proper problem definition and supports literature findings that proper understanding of the problem is the most important step of problem solving [18]. This study also illustrates the usefulness of SA for proper problem definition, which also is supported by earlier publications [14]. Not only that the SA process complements the current practice of a problem-solving process that involves data gathering and FA, but it also highlights the different aspects of the problem that requires non – technical (human interactions) approach. The results of this study confirm that SA is effective in the problem identification process and is helpful in pinpointing reasons for failure that are beyond the technical causes.

The Su-Field analysis was found particularly useful for modelling the system, risk analysis and ideas generation. It was also found very effective in identifying the Main Useful Function of the system to be improved and in developing common language among stakeholders (such as project/ program management, director, etc.).

This study demonstrated that SA and Su-Field Analysis can work together and complement existing problem-solving methods applied within an engineering organization. The analysis completed using this approach could be used as the inputs to non – TRIZ risk analysis tools such as FMEA. As identified in literature, the FMEA process has limitations [20, 21]. Su-Field Analysis can aid in identifying the parameters for the input to the FMEA process table. Su-Field Analysis is simple and systematic and is also less dependent on the engineers' experiences and knowledge.

## 8    Implications, Research Limitation and Future Research Direction

The outcomes of this study demonstrate that Su-Field analysis and SA can be applied together and complement existing problem-solving methods used within an engineering organization. Firstly, SA is useful for effective problem definition, prioritization and identification of the appropriate level of actions (technical/non-technical/long-term/short-term) to a problem. The SA process is not intended to replace the current practice of problem solving that involves data gathering and FA. Instead it takes on the inputs from these two processes with the additional step in identifying the MUF of the system to be improved.

The Su-Field modelling can be used to identify the MUF of the system to be improved and for risk analysis – to systematically generate a list of possible failure scenarios. The output of the Su-Field modelling can be incorporated as the input to the risk analysis tool such as FMEA. The process of generating the list of possible failure scenarios with Su-Field modelling is more systematic, and, therefore, is less dependent on the engineers' experiences and knowledge. Furthermore, the Su-Field models of the system to be improved can be well understood by people from different background. This is likely to improve communication within the organization and remove the level of abstraction in the actual information presented.

Su-Field and SA are normally applied during new product development phase. This study has demonstrated the use of this tool in the sustaining phase of product development and the real business impacts of using this tool. This study was carried out in a single engineering firm and considered a product only in the sustaining product life-cycle phase. Therefore, the research findings cannot be generalized for all companies and for the complete product life-cycle. Further investigations are required for generalization. Nonetheless, the results presented in this study have significant practical implications not only for the engineering personnel, but also for company managers.

# References

1. U.S. Department of Defense: MIL–STD–1629A. U.S. Department of Defense: Washington DC. p. 54 (1980)
2. Vesely, W.E., Roberts, N.: Fault tree handbook. Nuclear Regulatory Commission (1981)
3. Kepner, C.H., Tregoe, B.B.: The New Rational Manager: An Updated Edition for a New World. Princeton Research Press, Princeton (1997)
4. Papazoglou, I.A.: Mathematical foundations of event trees. Reliab. Eng. Syst. Saf. **61**(3), 169–183 (1998)
5. Mobley, R.K.: Root cause failure analysis: Butterworth-Heinemann (1999)
6. Augustine, M., et al.: Cognitive map-based system modeling for identifying interaction failure modes. Res. Eng. Des. 1–20 (2011)
7. Kaplan, S., et al.: New tools for failure and risk analysis: an introduction to anticipatory failure determination (AFD) and the theory of scenario structuring. Ideation International (1999)
8. Chybowski, L., Gawdzińska, K., Souchkov, V.: Applying the anticipatory failure determination at a very early stage of a system's development: overview and case study. Multidiscipl. Aspects Prod. Eng. **1**(1), 205–215 (2018)
9. Belski, I.: Improve your Thinking: Substance-Field Analysis. TRIZ4U, Melbourne (2007)
10. Dobrusskin, C., Belski, A., Belski, I.: On the effectiveness of systematized substance-field analysis for idea generation. In: Tucci, C., Vaneker, T., Nagel, T. (eds.) Proceedings of the TRIZ Future Conference: Global Innovation Convention (TFC 2014). The European TRIZ Association: Freiburg, Germany, pp. 123–127 (2014)
11. Belski, A., et al.: Application of substance-field analysis for failure analysis. In: Aoussat, A., et al. (eds.) Proceedings of the 13th ETRIA world TRIZ Future Conference 2013, pp. 483–490. Arts Et Metiers ParisTech, Paris (2013)
12. Belski, I., Chong, T.T., Belski, A., Kwok, R.. TRIZ in enhancing of design creativity: a case study from Singapore. In: Chechurin, L. (ed.) Research and Practice on the Theory of Inventive Problem Solving (TRIZ), pp. 151–168. Springer, Cham (2016). https://doi.org/10.1007/978-3-319-31782-3_9
13. Educating the Edisons of the 21st Century, https://emedia.rmit.edu.au/triz/. Accessed 23 May 2020
14. Harlim, J., Belski, J.: On the effectiveness of TRIZ tools for problem finding. Procedia Eng. **131**, 892–898 (2015)
15. Belski, I., et al.: Engineering creativity: the influence of general knowledge and thinking heuristics. In: Chechurin, L., Collan, M. (eds.) Advances in Systematic Creativity, pp. 245–263. Palgrave Macmillan, Cham (2019)
16. Iverson, S., Search marketing: using root cause analysis tools on PPC campaigns. In: Sean Iverson: Digital Marketing (2016)
17. VideoJet, Problem solving through root cause analysis: choosing effective processes and tools (2014)
18. Harlim, J., Belski, I.: Long-term innovative problem solving skills: redefining problem solving. Int. J. Eng. Educ. **29**(2), 280–290 (2013)
19. U.S. Food and Drug Administration. Premarket Notification 510(k), https://www.fda.gov/medical-devices/premarket-submissions/premarket-notification-510k. Accessed 23 May 2020

20. Shebl, N.A., Franklin, B.D., Barber, N.: Failure mode and effects analysis outputs: are they valid? BMC Health Serv. Res. **12**(1), 150 (2012)
21. Shahin, A.: Integration of FMEA and the Kano model. Int. J. Qual. Reliab. Manag. **21**(7), 731–746 (2004)
22. Zainal, Z.: Case study as a research method. J. Kemanusiaan **5**(1) (2007)
23. Chetty, S.: The case study method for research in small-and medium-sized firms. Int. Small Bus. J. **15**(1), 73–85 (1996)

# How to Organize a Knowledge Basis Using TRIZ Evolution Tree: A Case About Sustainable Food Packaging

Davide Russo[1]([✉]) [iD], Christian Spreafico[1] [iD], and Paolo Carrara[2]

[1] University of Bergamo, Viale Marconi 5, 24044 Dalmine, BG, Italy
davide.russo@unibg.it
[2] Warrant Innovation Lab, Correggio, RE, Italy

**Abstract.** This paper proposes a system of knowledge organization based on TRIZ-derived evolutive trends. The organization is operated by adopting the Macro to Micro TRIZ law as a trigger for defining search targets and as a backbone to build the knowledge evolutive tree. This approach was applied to classify thousands of documents from worldwide Patent database and papers from international journals according to a high-level classification. The goal of this work is to helps to find high-level ranking strategies, allowing a hierarchy of information and better organization to build a knowledge base perfectly matching with the terms of research during problem-solving in the most suitable manner in relation with the specific purposes. This method was applied to practical case study dealing with food packaging during an activity that has been carried out in collaboration with the consultancy firm Warrant Innovation Lab, as part of the program that offers small and medium-sized Italian companies on the topic for supporting TRIZ-based innovation activities. The contribution of this work is to provide novel and intuitive approach to SMEs where the organization of knowledge is of immediate reading and execution for experts in the field.

**Keywords:** Evolutive tree · TRIZ · Food packaging

## 1 Introduction

Information management is a fundamental problem for problem solving. There are different methods of classifying knowledge: conceptual and mental maps, morphological matrices, graphs and graphs, etc.

A well-organized knowledge base is the resource that allows you to correctly understand the evolution of phenomena. The evolution of knowledge can also be mapped. There are several approaches related to this purpose: bibliometric analysis and knowledge mapping [1], content analysis through known clustering algorithms [2], clustering ensembles [3], knowledge mining approaches [4, 5] and ontological mapping methods [6] more dedicated to the integration of multiple knowledge bases.

TRIZ can also be used to organize information, although only very few applications have shown consistent evidence [7]. In this context, we believe that the part of TRIZ relating to the theory of evolutive trees [8] is particularly suitable for framing

© IFIP International Federation for Information Processing 2020
Published by Springer Nature Switzerland AG 2020
D. Cavallucci et al. (Eds.): TFC 2020, IFIP AICT 597, pp. 221–230, 2020.
https://doi.org/10.1007/978-3-030-61295-5_18

theoretical information in a framework useful for problem solving. In one of our previous articles [9], we proposed the use of evolutive trees to organize information for problem-solving in the case of improving a pyrolysis reactor and we showed practically how to use these information to reformulate TRIZ physical contradictions.

In this paper we present a structured approach to research and organize information for problem-solving based on evolutive trees and a case study on food packaging, carried out by the authors in collaboration with WIL - Warrant Innovation Lab, a firm devoted to facilitate and diffuse the systematic innovation in SMEs, through technology transfer and sharing of knowledge, ideas, technologies and methodologies, in order to establish cooperation and partnership with suitable research teams.

The choice to base our analysis on evolutive trees of Shpakovsky is due to their ability to organize and at the same time hierarchize information according to specific criteria that can trace a trend of evolution of technologies, contrary to other classification methodologies which, although since the information on different levels of detail they cannot suggest a scale to order it.

We also suggest a criterion for creating research targets with which to build the super level of hierarchy.

The results obtained from the application in the field tested together with Warrants Innovation Lab within the standard perimeter of application for what the method was conceived, or the local companies, are promising. The type of approach was accepted with enthusiasm due to its perceived novelty and the expert in the field considered the organization of the knowledge suitable and ready for supporting problem solving activities.

## 2   State of the Art

The evolutive trees of Shpakovsky are based on the Laws of Technical System of Evolution [10] and the related patters: The Evolution Toward In-creased Ideality pattern explains that technical systems evolves by maximizing their ratio of useful to harmful effects and approaching ideality. The Stages of Technology Evolution pattern maps the technological maturity of the systems through an S-curve. The Non-Uniform Development of System Elements pattern explains that different systems could evolve by their different schedules, since they are affected by different constraints during different period. The Evolution Toward Increased Dynamism and Controllability pattern hierarchizes the technical systems in relation to the increasing of their dynamism and controllability. The Increased Complexity and Simplification pattern states that an initial tendency to add functionalities to the systems is generally followed by an increasing in their complexity that causes their segmentation into multiple simpler systems with more functionalities. The Evolution with Matching and Mismatching Elements pattern explains that system elements are matched or mismatched to improve performance or compensate for undesired effects. The Evolution Toward the Micro-level and Increased Use of Fields pattern stresses the idea that the evolution of technical systems moves from macro to micro level where energy fields are exploited to increase the performances and controls. The Evolution Toward Decreased Human Involvement pattern states that the decreasing of the human involvement is related to the increasing of the evolution of the technical system.

During the years, different authors improved the patterns by founding hidden patterns for describing the technological evolution emerging from new information technologies such as semantic web, data mining, text mining, theory of chaos and evolutive algorithms [11]; proposing algorithms supporting functional analysis involving evolutive trend and models for function representation [12, 13]; integrating technology road-maps to describe the life curves of a considered technical system [14].

Among all these approaches, the evolutive trees proposed by [8] are one of the most simple and immediate way to organize and to structure technical and patent information. His work hierarchizes the evolution patterns considering the following actions: (i) Introducing a new existing object or segmenting the existing ones by also involving fields and forces. (ii) Coordinating the shape, size, and properties of the surfaces with the internal structure of the system's elements, process parameters, fields, and forces; (iii) Dynamizing the sets of objects, processes, fields, and forces; (iv) Increasing the controllability of the system and (v) coordinating the actions of the components of the system.

We propose an approach like that of Shpakovsky, based on a vertebral column in which the macro-micro pattern exclusively appear.

## 3 Methodology

In this article we propose a knowledge organization system for the construction of a knowledge base organized in function of a future problem-solving or decision-making activity.

The evolutionary tree offers the organizational structure suitable for creating the hierarchy of content, allowing a high-level strategic vision within which to organize any other classification (Fig. 1).

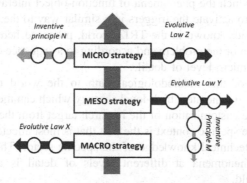

**Fig. 1.** The adopted evolutive tree with the vertebral column based on macro-micro pattern of evolution.

The mechanisms on the main branch are ordered on the basis of the TRIZ pattern "Evolution toward the Micro-level and Increased Use of Fields" explaining that technological systems tends to perform its main function by going from a macroscopic to a microscopic level, increasing the use of energy fields, to improve performance and increase control of its operating mode.

The following flow chart summarizes the steps of the proposed method (Fig. 2).

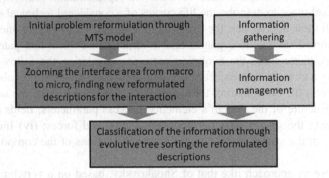

**Fig. 2.** Flow chart of the method

In the following, each step of the method is explained in detail.

The starting point is the MTS models, which requires establishing the main function, who receives the action and the tool entering into contact with the object to perform the function. The interface between tool and object is therefore considered, analyzing the way in which the main function is exchanged. In the case of multiple functions, the model repeats several times.

Once the interface has been identified, you try to change the level of detail between function and object, gradually changing the same interface area, decreasing it until it disappears. The process is accompanied by a change in the level of detail and the physical scale with which the phenomena of function-object interaction are explained. This process is able to activate the triggers in a similar way to the STC technique, i.e. Size-Time-Cost, already known in the TRIZ world, proposed here in a very targeted way on a specific area of the problem and according to a sequence of investigation that goes from macro to micro level of detail.

The application of this methodological path to the world of research can be effective if exploited to generate a high-level strategy which can then be translated into a research target. The customization of the research target from the general strategy to its translation into the specific context is the part that is most affected by the operator's subjectivity and his technical knowledge of the specific sector. The description of the physical-chemical phenomena at different levels of detail is also related to the knowledge of the field.

The methodological path involves zooming the interface area from macro to micro, trying to reformulate the description of this interaction and imagining the consequences that this entails at the tool level:

*If I decrease the interface, how should I modify the tool so that it can still reach its goal?*
*As consequence, how is the function changed?*

Normally, descending the dimensional scale, the technology used for the tool, i.e. the operating principle, at a certain point stops working or being optimal, and it is necessary to radically change the way and the physical principle with which the instrument works. By adopting this technique, we can formulate different strategies to achieve the same goal, by simply changing the different interfaces and the dimensional representation scales. These strategies represent the macro-classifications of our knowledge base.

### 3.1 Applying the Methodology to Packaging

The exemplary case of the methodology considers a food product that must be protected by packaging. In this case, protection is a fairly broad concept that includes both physical protection from external agents (whether they are gaseous, liquid and solid), i.e. a physical barrier against the outside to guarantee hygiene, and the containment functions of the internal atmosphere with which to control the processes of product deterioration and charger proliferation, where the goal is to preserve the organoleptic qualities of the product.

According to what described in the previous chapter, our goal is to apply the rules of macro micro to identify a macro classification of the operating strategies of a food packaging. In this specific case, the hierarchy that is created with this trend should lead to an increase in the sustainability of food packaging. The MTS model suggests to focus the attention directly on the food product and considering the above functions ensured by the instruments in contact with it, namely the air and the contact surface with the packaging film.

The first step consists in traditional packaging typically filled with air without hermetic sealing. An example of this can be the classic fruit paper bag. The documents that work in this area increase the sustainability of the packaging by changing the material with which it is made or minimizing the mass of the packaging, both by reducing thickness and modifying its shape by optimization. In macro-level analysis the food product is typically described as surrounded by a volume of air. By reducing this interface, the first step concerns the reduction elimination of air. Consequently, any expert will translate this concept into vacuum packaging.

The second step works on the same eco-improvement strategy as the second but with the total removal of the internal atmosphere, creating vacuum packaging, consequently eliminating the industrial process of generating the modified atmosphere during the production phase in favor of a more simple and less impacting vacuum mechanism. In addition, vacuum packaging can also significantly increase the shelf life of some types of food compared to modified atmosphere packaging. Going down a step, the volume of air is no longer considered, but the description moves to its chemical composition, with the interaction between the product and nitrogen or oxygen. In the case of contact with nitrogen, there are no contraindications, while the presence of oxygen triggers unwanted oxidation phenomena of the product. The STC approach suggests reducing the percentage of oxygen up to eliminating it, thus replacing it with a "modified atmosphere". Con-text research tries to establish how many alternative ways exist to achieve this goal and with what types of gas.

The third step concerns the modified atmosphere packaging, in which it acts on the internal atmosphere, changing the concentration of the gases contained, typically with the increase of nitrogen and the decrease of oxygen or with the insertion of $CO_2$, at the in order to improve the conservation of food content by avoiding waste and postponing the expiry date. This strategy has significant environmental benefits since the over-production of food and the greater management of food waste are reduced. The next step deals with the descend to an even smaller level of detail. In this case, we imagined the degradation process of the food product due to the proliferation of small bacteria, continuing to analyze the description of their behavior no longer in the environment in which they are immersed. Any action that can be taken to inhibit their growth or to extinguish them rather than help the proliferation of those desired belongs to this dimensional scale. On the other hand, the strategy that can be adopted by the tool is a packaging capable of activating targeted actions directly against them. Contextual research has shown that the combination of these techniques passes under the generic name of active packaging.

Finally, the fourth step concerns active packaging, which are vacuum packaging in which the packaging material is doped with particles of metallic bactericidal material or of vegetable or animal origin. In this case, despite its addition entails an increase in environmental impacts, it is in almost all cases more than compensated by the further increase in food conservation and therefore by the even more marked minimization of waste.

In this way, we have created at least 4 strategies to rearrange knowledge base information and populate it with subclassifications (Fig. 3).

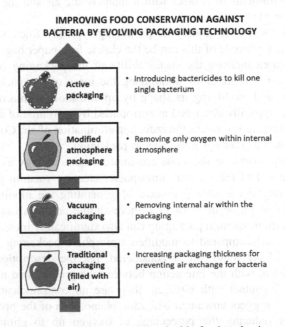

**Fig. 3.** Evolutive tree of sustainable food packaging.

Searching for information already organized by high-level strategy allows a better understanding of the data for problem solving or decision-making. High granularity helps to filter the data making it more consistent and more accurate for the proposed objectives. For example, according to classical approach we can collect all materials suitable to treat a certain type of cheese, while in the new organization we are able to collect only those allowing an active control to the same set of cheese in order to increase its duration.

For reasons of brevity, only the first branch tree is shown. For a more detailed analysis it is then possible to operate a patent/literature intelligence in order to extrapolate technological trends and trends.

# 4  Case Study

During the case definition of the case study, the TRIZ evolution tree and evolution and the classification basis of knowledge laws were applied to obtain the scheme explained in Sect. 3.1. In the following, the method is presented step-by-step by focusing in detail on the more applicative aspects.

## 4.1  STEP 1: Information Gathering

The information is collected from databases of scientific articles (e.g. Google Scholar and SCOPUS) and patents (ESPACENET).

The case study presented in this paper concerns the collection of information relating to sustainable food packaging, with the aim of improving the protective function of the food it contains.

The collection of relevant documents to be analyzed was carried out by collecting all the documents related to cheese packaging from SCOPUS and ESPACENET, by using, as keywords, the roots of the main terms "pack +" OR "envelop+" AND "food +"). The identified documents are more than 4000 papers and 7000 patents. Then, title, abstract and keywords of the documents have been manually analyzed to investigate their adherence with the argument of the analysis and with environmental sustainability. As a result, the considered set of documents counts about 400 scientific papers, of which approximately 70% consist of journal articles and 2000 patents, of which approximately 60% are still alive.

## 4.2  STEP 2: Information Management

The pool of documents is analyzed according to taxonomic criteria. Taxonomy is the discipline of classification in the hierarchy on a scientific basis.

In the specific case, this means collecting the different types of food product. In particular, in the case of cheese packaging, we are not only looking for the keyword "cheese", but we can divide it into macro-categories (hard, medium or soft) and for each of these lists all product types, as shown in Table 1.

**Table 1.** Types of products classified into macro-categories, example of cheeses.

| Hard cheeses | Medium cheeses | Soft cheeses |
|---|---|---|
| Cheddar, Grana, Parmigiano, Kashar, Rumi, Asiago, Manchego, Graviera, etc. | Gouda, Edam, Emmental, Provola, Provolone, etc. | Mozzarella, Stracchino, Burrata, Gorgonzola, Blue cheese, Nabulsi, Kalari, etc. |

On the other hand, if we consider the product of the packaging, we can do the same for the macro-categories of materials and for the specific types, as shown in Table 2.

**Table 2.** Types of materials, example from cheese packaging.

| Bioplastics | Plastics | Metals |
|---|---|---|
| Polylactic Acid (PLA), Polycaprolactone (PCL), Starch blends, Cellulose, Algae, etc. | Polythylene, Polyamide, Nylon PVC, Polypropylene, Polystyrene, etc. | Aluminum foils, silicon oxide, etc. |

### 4.3   STEP 3: Classifying the Information with the Evolutive Trees

On the basis of the presented evolutive tree, all documents relating to sustainable food packaging and their information have been classified and sorted. The final step is to organize the information found so far according to the organizational scheme suggested by the evolutionary tree as shown in Fig. 4.

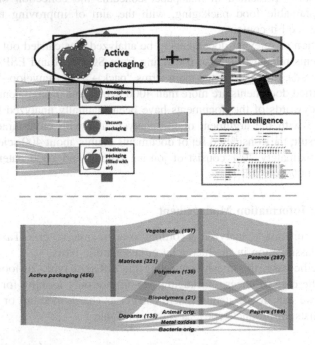

**Fig. 4.** Evolutive tree of sustainable food packaging with patent intelligence and detail on active packaging.

The Sankey diagram represented in the bottom part of Fig. 5 shows the distribution of the most used materials to increase the sustainability of active food packaging among the papers and patents. As can be seen from the first subdivision starting from the left, of all the documents (456) a good part describes materials for making the matrices (321), while the others for the dopants (135). The second subdivision allows instead to divide the materials of the matrices and dopants according to their typology. In this way vegetal-origin materials are the most popular for both matrices and dopants, while polymers are used only for matrices. Finally, the subdivision of the third level leads the materials to the respective documentary source or patents (287) and papers (169). The analysis of the active packaging can be further refined by studying the specific types of materials with the bubble chart, also by comparing them with their temporal distribution, which can be particularly useful to highlight temporal trends.

This specific analysis on a certain strategy, e.g. active food packaging can be strategic for a decision-making activity in which an entrepreneur is suggested, which path to take to innovate his product.

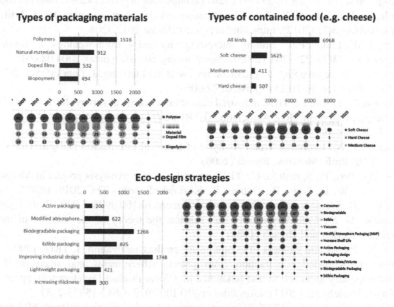

**Fig. 5.** Specific patent intelligence about active packaging.

## 5   Conclusions

This paper presents a methodology for analyzing patents and scientific literature for building a knowledge base. TRIZ law Macro to Micro is used for formulating queries to db to create a high-level hierarchy for organizing documents by strategies.

All information follows this hierarchy and can be visualized by the evolutive tree introduced by Shpakosky.

A case study relating to sustainable food packaging illustrates its execution.

The results in the field tested together with Warrants Innovation Lab with local companies are giving promising results, because the type of approach is perceived by SMEs as new, and the organization of knowledge is of immediate reading and execution for experts in the field.

The methodology was born from the impossibility of using experts to organize the database but it has proved effective to replace them. It will be tested in the near future in other applications to better define its limits and open problems.

# References

1. Hirsch, J.E.: An index to quantify an individual's scientific research out-put. Proc. Natl. Acad. Sci. U.S.A. **102**(46), 16569–16572 (2005)
2. Xu, D., Tian, Y.: A comprehensive survey of clustering algorithms. Ann. Data Sci. **2**(2), 165–193 (2015). https://doi.org/10.1007/s40745-015-0040-1
3. Vega-Pons, S., Ruiz-Shulcloper, J.: A survey of clustering ensemble algorithms. Int. J. Pattern Recogn. Artif. Intell. **25**(3), 337–372 (2011). https://doi.org/10.1142/S0218001411008683
4. Korde, V., Mahender, C.N.: Text Classification and classifiers: a survey. Int. J. Artif. Intell. Appl. (IJAIA) **3**(2) (2012). https://doi.org/10.5121/ijaia.2012.3208
5. Facca, F.M., Lanzi, P.L.: Mining interesting knowledge from weblogs: a survey. Data Knowl. Eng. **53**(3), 225–241 (2005). https://doi.org/10.1016/j.datak.2004.08.001
6. Chen, C.: Science mapping: a systematic review of the literature. J. Data Inf. Sci. **2**(2), 1–40 (2017). https://doi.org/10.1515/jdis-2017-0006
7. Spreafico, C., Russo, D.: TRIZ industrial case studies: a critical survey. In: 15th TRIZ Future Conference, European TRIZ Association (ETRIA eV), 26.-29 October 2015, Berlin, vol. 39, pp. 51–56. Elsevier (2016)
8. Shpakovsky, N.: Evolution Trees. Analysis of technical information and generation of new ideas. TRIZ Profi, Moscow, Russia (2006)
9. Russo, D., Peri, P., Spreafico, C.: TRIZ applied to waste pyrolysis project in Morocco. In: Benmoussa, R., De Guio, R., Dubois, S., Koziołck, S. (eds.) TFC 2019. IAICT, vol. 572, pp. 295–304. Springer, Cham (2019). https://doi.org/10.1007/978-3-030-32497-1_24
10. Altshuller, G. S.: Creativity as an exact science: the theory of the solution of inventive problems. Gordon and Breach (1984)
11. Leon, N.: Trends and patterns of evolution for product innovation. J. TRIZ. (2006)
12. Russo, D.: Knowledge extraction from patent: achievements and open problems. a multidisciplinary approach to find functions. In: Global Product Development, pp. 567–576. Springer, Heidelberg. (2011). https://doi.org/10.1007/978-3-642-15973-2_57
13. Russo, D., Spreafico, C.: TRIZ 40 inventive principles classification through FBS ontology. Procedia Eng. **131**, 737–746 (2015)
14. Slocum, M.: Use the eight patterns of evolution to innovate. TRIZ J. (2014)

# An Approach of Product-Type Process Trimming

Fanfan Wang[1,2(✉)] , Runhua Tan[1,2(✉)] , Lulu Zhang[1,2] ,
Jianguang Sun[1,2], Zhitao Song[1,2] , and Yu Wang[1,2]

[1] School of Mechanical Engineering, Hebei University of Technology,
Tianjin, China
wangfanfan8888@163.com, rhtan@hebut.edu.cn
[2] National Engineering Research Center for Technological Innovation Method
and Tool, Hebei University of Technology, Tianjin, China

**Abstract.** The product-type process is a kind of process in which raw materials go through multiple processing steps in a production facility and become a product for users. Due to the many process steps and long accumulated time, the raw materials often need to undergo complex and lengthy processing, resulting in complex systems and low efficiency. This paper defined the process efficiency as the ratio of "unit capacity" to "time" and "space", and trimmed the process from the perspective of time and space. Summarized a set of trimming rules applicable for product-type process trimming. Transformed the function missing problem formed after trimming into technical and physical conflicts, solved them using the tools in TRIZ, and finally designed the principle solutions into specific solutions. Product-type process trimming is a full-time cycle analysis system from raw materials to product, which avoids the disadvantage of traditional substance-field model based on the instantaneous operation of the system. Finally, example demonstrated the feasibility of this method.

**Keywords:** TRIZ · Trimming · Product-type process · Innovation design

## 1 Introduction

Innovation is an important part of an enterprise's core competitiveness [1]. According to the different objects, innovation can be divided into product innovation and process innovation. Product innovation is the development of new products or services through technological innovation, that is, the innovation that changes the product or service itself. Process innovation includes new processes, new equipment and new organizational management methods, which can reduce the production cost of products and services [2].

Trimming is an auxiliary invention process derived from the classic TRIZ. The application of trimming method can achieve different design objectives, such as simplifying structure, reducing cost, eliminating conflicts, improving performance, etc. [3]. Both product trimming and process trimming involve two important steps: trimming component determination and functional restructuring. Many experts and scholars have studied these two steps.

© IFIP International Federation for Information Processing 2020
Published by Springer Nature Switzerland AG 2020
D. Cavallucci et al. (Eds.): TFC 2020, IFIP AICT 597, pp. 231–242, 2020.
https://doi.org/10.1007/978-3-030-61295-5_19

Mann D L gave priority to remove components with harmful, excessive and insufficient functions [4]. Lin Yunman, Sheu D D et al. introduced harmful function analysis, causal chain analysis and other tools to determine the target of product trimming [5]. Yu Fei et al. put forward the quantitative calculation method of component trimming priority [6]; Li Miao decomposed the process into sub-processes to establish a process functional model [7], and analyzed the root cause of the problem sub-process.

System function reorganization is accompanied by trimming implementation, and the essence is the mining and utilization of system resources [8]. The trimming rules are used to guide the trimming operator to find a solution to the missing function elements. Yeoh has proposed three rules for the distribution of useful functions of the system based on the interaction of components [9]. Sheu D D extended six trimming rules based on the existing rules [8]. Grawatsch analysed from the perspective of technological evolution to get heuristic questions that guide designers to assign useful functions of the system, and guide designers to determine trimming components and redistribute the useful functions of the system [10].

Most of the previous studies only focused on one of the product or process trimming, ignoring the situation where the two overlap. There is a special process, its exterior is a product, but its interior is an automated process. The system processes the input raw materials and outputs products for users. This special process is defined as product-type process. The trimming methods produced by the previous research has certain difficulties in the implementation of the product-type process, so further research on the method of product-type process trimming is needed.

## 2 Basic Conception

### 2.1 Trimming

Trimming is a tool for problem analysis in TRIZ theory. It is an evolutionary route in TRIZ, which makes the system evolve towards a more simplified and lower cost direction, while the performance remains the same or better. Trimming makes the product or process closer to the ideal solution [11]. Cutting out the components that caused the problem can often solve the problem at the root, resulting in a higher level of innovation.

Trimming is one of the important methods to realize system functions at a low cost in TRIZ. The purpose of general application of function trimming is as follows [12]:

(1) Cost reduction;
(2) Eliminate excessive, harmful and repetitive effects, and realize system improvement and system ideality improvement;
(3) To simplify the system functions, reduce the complexity of the product or system, improve the maintainability and reduce the operation difficulty on the premise of ensuring the main functions of the system;
(4) Eliminate or reduce the harmful effect in the system, reduce the system cost, and guarantee the high product function and performance at the same time;
(5) Design for patent design around.

## 2.2    Product-Type Process Concept

**Technological Process.** The process in the field of mechanical engineering refers to the arrangement of processes from raw materials to finished products. The process is divided into technical process and non-technical process, which is a way to convert the input of resources or raw materials into a valuable product or service for customers [13].

The process or flow in this paper belongs to the technical process, is from the raw material to the product of the procedure arrangement or the operation object from the work blank to the finished product of the conversion process. The operation is composed of the material objects in the process flow system and their interactions. The purpose is to change the properties, parameters and relationships of the operating objects.

The operation is the decomposition of the process flow, which is equivalent to a functional element, including the effect, function carrier and target object. Operations are not independent of each other, because of the existence of input, output and material flow, adjacent operations will affect each other. The operation flow is a collection of operations arranged in the order in which they are executed.

**Product.** The essence of the product is a carrier of function that fulfills the specific needs of users by completing its own functions. There are various forms of products, including tangible items such as mobile phones and desks, as well as intangible services such as telecommunications services and legal consulting. The products discussed here refer specifically to tangible products.

In TRIZ theory, function models are used to describe the composition and relationship of product systems. A function model is a model with no time dimension, which can only represent the interaction between components in a certain state. This makes the function model flawed: when certain components of the system or super system that participate in the work have different effects at different times and other components, it is difficult for a single function model to fully express the working status of these components. As shown in the Fig. 1, this will make the analysis process complicated.

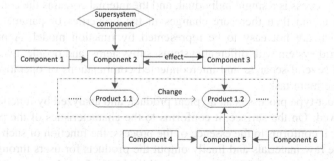

**Fig. 1.** The state of component changes in the function model.

**Product-Type Process.** There is no clear boundary between the product and the process, and there is an intersection between the two. The intersection area is the product-type process. The following Table 1 lists some examples of single product, product-type process and typical process to illustrate the difference between the three.

**Table 1.** Examples of single product, product-type process and typical process.

| Single product | Product-type process | Typical process |
|---|---|---|

As can be seen from the above table, the functions of a single product are relatively few, and the relationship between system components in the function model is fixed. Product-type process is a single individual, and the internal contains the components of single product, and then there are changes in the properties or parameters of flow material, which are not easy to be represented by function model. A process is a complex hybrid system with different systems, subsystems, and people involved that is composed of several separate and interconnected combinations of operations to complete the same main task.

The product-type process is an atypical product, and analyzed by function model is naturally flawed. On the surface, it conforms to the characteristics of the product, but on the inside, it conforms to the essence of the process: the function of such products is to process the raw materials and finally output the products for users through multiple processes. To sum up: product-type process is a kind of production process which exists in consumer products, operates mainly on material flow and has a high degree of automation (Fig. 2).

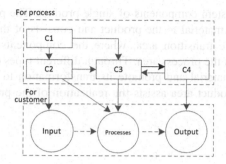

**Fig. 2.** Schematic of product-type process

# 3 Product-Type Process Model and Trimming Method

## 3.1 Process Function Classification

Process functions are divided into Useful Function and Harmful Function. The Useful Function is divided into Productive Function, Providing Function and Corrective Function, among which the Providing Function includes Supporting Function, Transporting Function and Measurement Function [14], as shown in the Fig. 3.

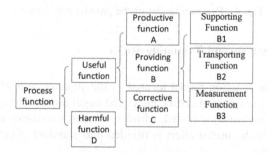

**Fig. 3.** Classification of process functions

The Productive Function is a useful function that changes the attributes or parameters of the flow material to the product; the Providing Function provides the necessary auxiliary functions for the smooth progress of the process, such as changing the position of the flow material, detecting parameter changes, and fixing the position. Productive Function and Providing Function may introduce Harmful Function in the process of action. At this time, Corrective Function is needed to prevent or correct harmful effects.

## 3.2 Product-Type Process Modeling

The Fig. 4 shows the function model of the product-type process. The upper part is the product area, the lower part is the process area. The product area describes the function model composed of system components of single product. The process area describes the flow from the raw material to the product and consists of the flow of operations. The shaded area is the transition area, where the components of the product area operate the materials in the process area. Through different types of operations, change the properties of the material and promote its transformation to the finished product. The function of the product area assists the realization of the process function of the process area.

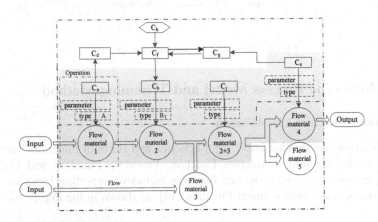

**Fig. 4.** Function model of the product-type process

## 3.3    Function Analysis and Trimming Rules

**Product Area.** The function model located in the product area of the product-type process is composed of function carrier, effect and target object. The type of effect is the same as the traditional function model, which is divided into useful effect and harmful effect, among which the useful effect is divided into standard effect, excessive effect and insufficient effect.

Trimming rules are the guiding principles of trimming, which are used to guide designers how to delete objects correctly and ensure the normal execution of useful functions at the same time. Sheu D D [8] formulated six trimming rules for product trimming. Whether the correct rules are selected will directly affect the quality of the final plan, so based on those six rules, four rules that are suitable for the function trimming of the product area in the product-type process are integrated. The cropping rules are shown in Fig. 5.

**Rule A:** If the target object of the function is no longer needed, both the function carrier and the useful effect can be deleted.

**Rule B:** When the useful effect on the target object is no longer needed, the function carrier and its effect can be removed.

**Rule C:** If the target object can perform the useful effect on its own, the function carrier that performs the useful effect can be deleted.This is usually a tailoring opportunity for new discoveries and technologies.

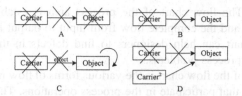

**Fig. 5.** Trimming rules of product area

**Rule D:** If there is a new function carrier that can produce the same effect on the target object, and it is more beneficial to adopt this function carrier than before, then the original function carrier and effect can be deleted. The new effect can be the same as before, or it can be a different effect but the same result.

**Transition Area.** A special function area in the product-type process model is the transition area between the product area and the process area. The flow material is gradually transformed into product with the aid of the transition area function. The transition area is a relatively important and complex area in the product-type process, because the target object of the effect is also the function carrier of the process area. Therefore, the integrity of the useful functions of the flow material should be considered when formulating the trimming rules. The function trimming rules of transition area is shown in Fig. 6.

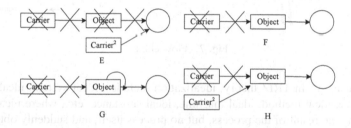

**Fig. 6.** Trimming rules of transition area

**Rule E:** After trimming according to the rule A, the function carrier of subsequent operation will lose the useful effect of flow material, so it is necessary to re-find the function carrier for the flow material on the basis of rule A. New function carrier can be found from inside and outside the system.

Rules F, G, and H are equivalent to rules B, C, and D, respectively.

In order to facilitate the use of trimming rules, the product area and the transition area are unified into non-process area, and similar rules are removed. The trimming rules of non-process area are summarized as rules A, B, C, D, and E.

**Process Area**

*Flow Chart.* The description of the process area by the function model has defects in timing, and using the flow chart to describe the working state of the process area can avoid such defects. The flow chart of the process area is established by means of horizontal swimlane, and the complete flow from input to output is shown in the flow chart. Using flow chart can help designers to find defects in the process, so as to effectively deal with process problems.

The first column of the flow chart is the various forms of flow material, and the first row are the elements that participate in the process operations. The intersection of the flow material and the element is the effect. The element, the flow material and the effect form an operation. The arrow indicates the direction of change of the operation flow and the flow material. On the left is the change of the parameters of the flow material, indicating that the useful function changes the parameters or attributes of the flow material. Take a certain type of water heater as an example to establish a flow chart, as shown in the Fig. 7.

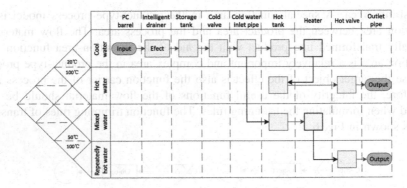

**Fig. 7.** Flow chart

*Process Efficiency.* In TRIZ theory, idealization includes: ideal system, ideal process, ideal resource, ideal method, ideal machine, ideal substance, etc., where ideal process refers to only the result of the process, but no process itself, and suddenly obtained the result [15]. Inspired by the ideality formula, the product-type process efficiency is:

$$E = \left( \frac{Q}{T_1 + V_1 a_1} - \frac{H}{T_2 + V_1 a_2} \right) \times 100\% \tag{1}$$

Which:

E: Efficiency, the efficiency with which raw material input is converted into finished product;
Q: Quantity, the amount of raw materials or semi-finished products in the system that are all converted into finished products;
H: Harmful, the amount of waste produced during the conversion of raw materials or affected by harmful effects;
T: Time, time consumed in each step;
V: Volume, volume per unit of material;
a: Constant, the number of times materials are transferred between operations.

According to the formula, the minimization of $T_1$ and $a_1$ should be pursued, the H should be eliminated. After the component is deleted, resources should be sought from the nearby operations or components in the product area or outside the system to make up for the lack of function. It is better if the principle can be changed so that the operation is no longer needed. Reflected in the flow chart are:

**Rule I:** Remove harmful flow, harmful operations and their ancillary operations;

**Rule J:** The providing functions between input, productive functions and output are as short as possible, and removing unnecessary providing functions;

**Rule K:** Remove the corrective function as much as possible, the basic method is to remove the operation that produces the corresponding harmful effect;

**Rule L:** Reduce the vertical distance in the flow chart between the input and output as much as possible, and remove the operation that causes the vertical transfer of the process.

### 3.4   Functional Restructuring

After trimming, the functions of the product area and process area will be incomplete. According to the guidance of the trimming rules, the knowledge base or function-oriented search (FOS), resource analysis and other methods to determine new operations that have the same or similar effects as the removed operations. Draw a conceptual solution of the trimming model. If there still have problem with the solution, describe the problem as a conflict.

Select the appropriate TRIZ resolution tool according to the type of conflict. If the described conflict is a technical conflict, then using the invention principle to resolve; if the described conflict is a physical conflict, then using separation principle to resolve, and obtained conceptual solution. Convert the obtained conceptual solution into a concrete solution. Iterate repeatedly to get the final solution.

## 4   Case Study

In China, people are used to drinking hot water, which is considered a healthy lifestyle. The invention of the automatic drinking water dispenser meets the needs of people to drink water at any time [16]. A certain type of water dispenser has the structure of water intake, water storage, heating, heat preservation, etc. It is a product-type process for heating cold water. Because the water in the storage device is repeatedly cooled down and heated, it will produce harmful substances to the human body after a long time. This kind of water is called "thousand-boiling water" [17]. Analyze the water dispenser with the above product-type process analysis method.

### 4.1   Building Function Model

Through the function model analysis (see Fig. 8), it is found that the functions of the product area include "intelligent drainer to obstruct dirt", "steam enters into ventilated device", " ventilated device hold pressure of water storage tank", "sponge insulation hot tank" and so on. These functions are providing functions and have no obvious harmful effects, so it is impossible to determine who caused the "thousand-boiling water" problem. The following is a flow chart of the establishment of the process area for further analysis.

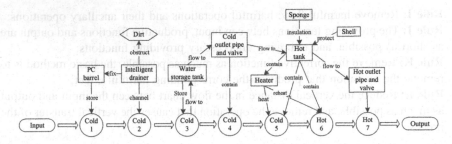

**Fig. 8.** Function model of water dispenser

## 4.2 Build Flow Chart

From the Fig. 9, it can be seen that the hot tank contains cold, hot and mixed water at the same time. The cold water enters the hot tank from the cold water inlet pipe and is heated. After the water level drops, the cold water comes in again and the temperature of the water drops, thus, it is heated again. Such a cyclical reciprocation produced the "thousand-boiling water".

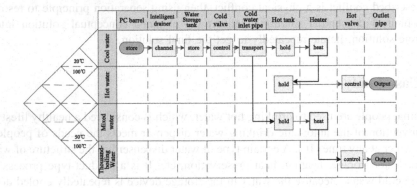

**Fig. 9.** Flow chart of water dispenser

## 4.3 Implementation of Trimming

According to the trimming rule I: Remove harmful flow, harmful operations and their ancillary operations. Remove the flow that produces "Thousand-boiling Water", that is, remove the flow from "cold water inlet pipe-transport-cold water" to "outlet pipe-output-Thousand-boiling Water" in the flowchart. The specific operation is to remove the flow of cold water into the hot tank or remove the hot tank, as show in the Fig. 10.

After being removed, the cold water no longer enters the heat tank through the cold water inlet pipe, but there must be water in the heat tank, thus creating a physical conflict: There must be water and no water in the hot tank.

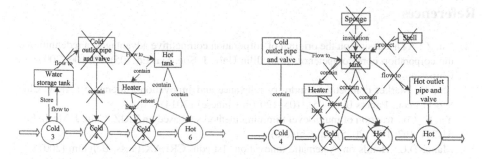

**Fig. 10.** Function models after trimming

Four separation principles are used to resolve physical conflicts, namely: spatial separation, time separation, conditional separation, and overall and partial separation. Since there should be hot water in the hot tank when drinking water, there is no need to have hot water at other times, therefore, using time separation.

According to the principle of time separation and the combination of 40 invention principles, the following solutions are obtained:

1) Heat the water at the cold water inlet pipe, so that the water that enters the hot tank is always boiled. The hot tank only stores hot water and keeps warm, no longer heats the water.
2) Remove the hot tank and use the heating method at any time to heat the water in the outlet pipe while opening the outlet valve.

Both schemes eliminate the H of "thousand-boiling water" and reduce the length of the operation flow, that is, $T_1$ and $a_1$. Therefore, compared with the original scheme, the Efficiency has been improved.

## 5 Conclusion

First put forward the concept of product-based process, then put forward a set of analysis process and trimming rules according to the characteristics of product-based process. According to the process function model, the product-type process is divided into product area, transition area and process area. The product area and transition area use the function model to sort out the component trimming rules. The process area proposes the process trimming rules by analyzing the flowchart. This method supplements the original trimming methods, and the feasibility of the method has been verified by the design of the water dispenser.

**Acknowledgements.** This research is supported by National Innovation Method Fund of China (2017IM040100), National Natural Science Foundation of China (Grant No. 51675159), and the National Special Project for Local Science and Technology Development (Grant No. 18241837G).

# References

1. Xu, Z.: A Discussion on the original of corporation competitive advantages: a redefinition of the corporation core competence. Chin. Jilin Univ. J. Soc. Sci. Ed. (05), 99–106 (2003). (in Chinese)
2. Zhi, Y.: Market competition, industry relevance and innovation-a literature review. Chin. World Econ. Papers 000(005), 105–120 (in Chinese) (2014)
3. Yu, F.: Construction of multi-level trimming method set based on TRIZ. Chin. J. Mech. Eng. **51**(21), 162–170 (2015). (in Chinese)
4. Mann, D.L.: Hands on systematic innovation, 1st edn. CREAX Press, Belgium (2007)
5. Lin, Y.: Triz-based computer aided pruning process and tools. China: National Tsing Hua University, Taiwan (2010). (in Chinese)
6. Yu, F.: Study on trimming priority based on system functional model. Chin. Comput. Integr. Manuf. Syst. **19**(2), 338–347 (2013). (in Chinese)
7. Li, M.: An integrated TRIZ approach for technological process and product innovation. Proc. Inst. Mech. Eng. Part B J. Eng. Manuf. **231**(6), 1–16 (2015)
8. Sheu, D.D.: TRIZ-based trimming for process-machine improvements: slit-valve innovative redesign. Comput. Ind. Eng. **66**(3), 555–566 (2013)
9. Yeoh Teong, S.: TRIZ - Systematic Innovation in Manufacturing. firstfruits sdn bhd, 43–49 (2013)
10. Grawatsch, M.: Module 3 of the support training course. Montanuniversita ïLeoben (2005)
11. Mann, D.L.: Trimming evolution patterns for complex systems. LNCS. http://www.systematic-innovation.com/assets. Accessed 10 May 2020
12. Tan, Y.: Process function analysis and process trimming of process-oriented problem solving. China, Hebei university of technology (2017). (in Chinese)
13. Tsung-I, H.: A process improvement model for non-technical system using TRIZ methods. China: I-Shou University, Taiwan (2013). (in Chinese)
14. Denny, C.: TRIZ-based Process Analysis and Trimming Method. China: National Tsing Hua University, Taiwan (2013). (in Chinese)
15. Zhang, H.: Innovative Design-Systematic Innovation based on TRIZ. 1st edn. China Machine Press, 22 Baiwanzhuang Street, Xicheng District, Beijing, China (in Chinese) (2017)
16. He, X.: Application of TRIZ contradiction solving principles in water dispenser design. Chin. Packag. Eng. **36**(14), 60–63 (2015). (in Chinese)
17. Yu, F., Zhang, H.: Trimming-based conflict discovery and problem-solving process model. https://doi.org/10.1109/icmit.2012.6225882 (2012)

# High Power Density Speed Reducers: A TRIZ Based Classification of Mechanical Solutions

Lorenzo Maccioni[✉] ⑩, Yuri Borgianni⑩, and Franco Concli⑩

Faculty of Science and Technology, Free University of Bozen-Bolzano,
39100 Bolzano, Italy
lorenzo.maccioni@unibz.it

**Abstract.** This paper aims to create a conceptual map of problems and solutions concerning High Power Density Speed Reducers (HPDSRs), i.e. planetary gearboxes, cycloidal gears and harmonic drives. The existing designs of HPDSRs are explored and classified through the Problem Solution Network (PSN), i.e. a method based on the Network of Problems from the TRIZ base of knowledge that considers different levels of abstraction. Through the PSN, it was possible to highlight conceptual design differences and communalities among the various HPDSRs in order to clarify the working principles of existing solutions. HPDSRs carry out the speed reduction through components that perform planetary motions. Therefore, a first distinction has been made based on input and output motions. Cycloidal and harmonic solutions have as output the rotation motion of the planet while planetary gear trains have as output the revolution motion of the planetary pinion. A second classification has been made on the strategy for avoiding the secondary path of contact, i.e. the unwanted contact between two components outside of the expected contact area. Cycloidal solutions modify the tooth profile while harmonic solutions deform the planetary pinion. Further considerations have been made on multi-stage solutions that take into account differential principles to multiply the useful function.

**Keywords:** TRIZ · Conceptual design · Problem solution network · Planetary gearbox · Harmonic drive · Cycloidal gears

## 1 Introduction

Many generations of engineers have contributed to the development and the fine-tuning of technical systems capable of transmitting mechanical power efficiently by reducing rotational speed and increasing torque. The working principles and the design criteria of the acknowledged solutions developed over the years, e.g. ordinary gearboxes and worm gear reducers, belong to the background of every mechanical designer. Therefore, in order to innovate in this field, it is important to overcome the psychological inertia inevitably induced by the study of these consolidated topics. Indeed, designers usually tend to fixate on existing solutions and optimize their firstly conceived ideas, thus neglecting a comprehensive design space exploration and failing to innovate the technical systems in play [1].

© IFIP International Federation for Information Processing 2020
Published by Springer Nature Switzerland AG 2020
D. Cavallucci et al. (Eds.): TFC 2020, IFIP AICT 597, pp. 243–253, 2020.
https://doi.org/10.1007/978-3-030-61295-5_20

Nowadays, the market pushes for the development of new reduction systems that have to be devised for limited spaces and/or with few mechanical components. An example can be the robotics industry, where it is necessary to use mechanical solutions with a very high Gear Ratio (GR) in relatively small dimensions to exploit the potential of electric motors in terms of efficiency and control [2]. In this context, ordinary gearboxes are not able to meet the requirements of compactness, and the main solutions that allow reaching certain power concentration nowadays can be grouped into three families, i.e. planetary gearboxes, cycloidal gears and harmonic drives [3]. All these are conventionally designated as High Power Density Speed Reducers (HPDSRs). As opposed to ordinary gearboxes, which are made with rigid components and/or have fixed axes, these systems perform their function exploiting components that have planetary motions [4]. This means that at least one component of the HPDSRs has a revolution motion and a rotation motion. The motion and torque transmission is made possible by the synchronous meshing of "teeth" with specific profiles. In the case of cycloidal gearboxes, the meshing takes place between the cycloidal lobes and rollers [5]. The latter can be located either outside or inside the cycloidal profile (hypocycloid) [6]. In addition, the rollers can be integrated (fixed) to or can be made with rolling elements to reduce power losses [7]. On the other hand, in the case of harmonic drives, the planetary pinion (flexspline) is flexible and the revolution motion can be imposed by a cam (also called wave generator) [8]. To reduce wear on this particular cam, bearings with flexible races, which are the most critical components, are often used [9]. However, many other solutions have been developed and there are many architectures and many variants among HPDSRs. Then, it is easy to understand the high complexity and variety of these solutions.

In this context, a design instrument could be useful with the dual purpose of managing the complexity of these technical systems and supporting the abstraction of the various problems that emerge during the design of new solutions (and therefore to overcome psychological inertia). The Problem-Solution Network (PSN) [10] is here used and tested as a tool to make order on the HPDSRs' pros/cons and conceptual features. The PSN is based on the co-evolution of problems and solutions [11]. It allows designers to decompose the overall problem by keeping track of the different possible solutions at different abstraction levels [12]. Through processes of analysis, synthesis and evaluation, the PSN makes it possible to analyze existing solutions and to identify the fundamental aspects that characterize them in terms of commonalities and differences. The relation between TRIZ and the PSN is widely described in [13]. In the present paper, the PSN is used to describe the existing design of HPDSRs that are presented in Sect. 2. A brief theoretical overview of the PSN and its application to the case study is presented in Sect. 3. Discussions and conclusions are presented in Sect. 4.

## 2   High Power Density Speed Reducers

### 2.1   Cycloidal Gears

A cycloidal speed reducer includes four main components, as illustrated in Fig. 1: an input shaft with an eccentric cam, a cycloidal disk, the ring gear pin with rollers on which the cycloidal disk meshes, and an output shaft connected with a mechanism that extracts the rotation motion of the cycloidal disk (usually hole-pin). The input shaft moves the center of the cycloidal disk along a circular trajectory, providing the revolution motion. Following this trajectory, the cycloidal disk meshes on the rollers located on the casing, rotating in the opposite direction to that of the shaft. Usually, holes realized inside the cycloidal disk drag pins during the rotation motion, allowing the output shaft to extract this motion and transmit it as the output motion.

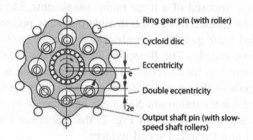

**Fig. 1.** Cycloidal gear [14]

This system is dynamically unbalanced since the center of mass moves eccentrically. There are three solutions to balance it:

- By adding mass, using a counterweight to be mounted on the shaft [15];
- By subtracting mass, for example from the eccentric cam;
- By exploiting another cycloidal disk 180° out of phase with respect to the first one [16].

The Gear Ratio (GR) can be expressed as in Eq. 1 [17]. Here, Z1 is the number of teeth of the planetary pinion (in the case represented in Fig. 1, the number of lobes of the cycloidal disk) and Z2 is the number of teeth of the ring gear (in the case represented in Fig. 1, the number of rollers).

$$GR = \frac{\omega_{input}}{\omega_{output}} = \frac{Z_1}{Z_2 - Z_1} = \frac{Z_1}{\Delta} \tag{1}$$

It is therefore easy to infer that the highest GR is obtained when the difference Z2–Z1 ($\Delta$) is minimal, and in the case of cycloidal gearboxes, it is possible to reach the difference of one tooth only [17].

The rolling contact between the cycloidal disk and the rollers is the main factor influencing the efficiency of the gearbox [18]. The various sources of power loss in a cycloidal gearbox are:

- The rolling friction between the rollers and the disk;
- The friction in the bearings;
- The friction between holes and pins.

If the rollers are not free to rotate, the cycloid efficiency is a function of the circumference of the cycloid disk [7]. The rollers can be made with sliding or ball bearings (non-compact solution) in order to reduce any tangential force due to friction and machining errors (increasing the efficiency) or they can be made integral to better resist shocks and overloads [7].

## 2.2  Harmonic Drive

A Harmonic Drive is composed of a three main components, identifiable in Fig. 2; a fixed ring gear (circular spline), in which a flexible planetary pinion (flexspline), and a camshaft (the so-called wave generator) mesh, which deforms the flexspline and allows the system to engage correctly. The flexspline has generally two teeth less than the circular spline and, therefore, for each turn of the wave generator in a direction the flex spline moves two teeth in the opposite direction. Also in this case, the GR can be described by the Eq. 1 but the minimum $\Delta$ that can be achieved by a Harmonic Drive is 2. However, as can easily be seen from Fig. 2, the Harmonic Drive is dynamically balanced, as opposed to a cycloidal speed reducer.

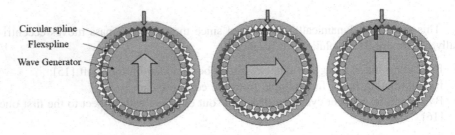

Circular spline
Flexspline
Wave Generator

**Fig. 2.** Harmonic drive

The performance of a harmonic gearbox is mainly affected by the kinematic error [19]. This error gives rise to vibrational effects with consequent torque losses and output speed fluctuations. To ensure correct operation and maximize performances, the kinematic error has to be limited by using tight dimensional tolerances and additional components to ensure the necessary geometric tolerances between the main components.

The efficiency of a Harmonic Drive is influenced by the flexspline deformation (dissipated deformation energy) and tooth meshing (energy dissipated by friction).

Usually, the teeth of the flexspline are manufactured with an involute profile. This is because the technologies used to make them are nowadays reliable and relatively cheap. The wave generator is realized with an elliptical shape. This shape allows generating the lowest tensional state on the flexspline during its deformation. When these two solutions are coupled, problems arise because, due to the elliptical wave generator, the involute profile is not a conjugated profile over the entire meshing area, thus causing unwanted crawling that reduces the performance and integrity of the teeth [20]. In order to reduce the probability of secondary paths of contact, the teeth can be corrected by modifying the addendum coefficients and/or changing the pressure angle.

Two ways can be chosen to improve the performance of the meshing area:

- By keeping the elliptical shape of the wave generator and changing the shape of the tooth profile;
- By keeping the involute profile and changing the shape of the wave generator.

When the former applies, it is possible to create teeth with double arc profile [21]. When the latter is adopted, the wave generator has to be modified in order for the flexspline to take on an arched circle shape in the area of engagement [20]. To achieve this condition, a possible solution, theoretically investigated in [22], is to use two "rigid cylindrical" bearings mounted on two eccentric pins offset by 180° instead of a flexible bearing mounted on the elliptical wave generator. In this way, the forces on the bearings are advantageously distributed and it is possible to avoid the introduction of flexible bearings. An alternative solution is the one proposed in [20], which suggests modifying the shape of the wave generator to have two circular arc zones and two elliptical zones. In [20], the theory for the generation of the wave generator profile is also developed in order to avoid secondary paths of contact with involute teeth. With this design, the kinematic error in Harmonic Drives is reduced. In addition, because the gears are circular in the meshing arc, the involute profiles are conjugated.

## 2.3   Planetary Gearboxes

Planetary gearboxes can be designed in different configurations. Usually, the ring gear is fixed; the input motion is assigned to the sun gear, which transfers the rotation motion to the planetary gear(s), which, in turn, undertake(s) a revolution motion that is extracted as an output motion usually by the planetary carrier (See Fig. 3).

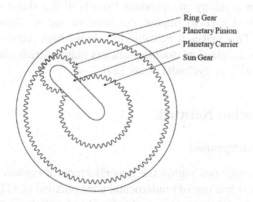

Ring Gear
Planetary Pinion
Planetary Carrier
Sun Gear

**Fig. 3.** Planetary gearbox

To achieve GR higher than 100, with size and efficiencies comparable to cycloidal and harmonic gearboxes, two stages in series have to be used. An interesting "double" stage of planetary gearbox configuration consists in the Wolfrom solution [23], topologically shown in Fig. 4. Instead of extracting the motion from the first stage through a planetary carrier, a second planetary pinion is created and joined with the first planetary pinion, which meshes with a second ring gear. This second stage, composed by planetary pinion(s) and a second ring gear, has a different number of teeth than the first stage to exploit a differential principle to reduce the output speed. In other words, this second stage receives as an input a planetary pinion, which already has its rotation and revolution motion, and it moves a ring gear with an appropriate number of teeth.

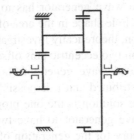

**Fig. 4.** Wolfrom solution

It is interesting to notice that the rotation and revolution motion of the planetary pinion of the second stage does not necessarily have to be imposed by a first stage of a planetary gearbox [24]. This speed reduction method is based on a differential system, which exploits small differences in the number of teeth between the first and second stage. Since the motion of the first stage is univocally defined and has only one degree of freedom at the second stage, it is possible to extract the rotation motion of the second ring gear (movable in this case), whose displacement is due to the different number of teeth compared to the first stage. It is interesting to notice that the Wolfrom solution proposes a reduction topology independent from both the shape of the transmission profile and the method used to impose the rotation and revolution motions on the planetary pinion(s). This makes it possible to achieve high reduction ratios with performances similar to the classical double planetary stage, which allows the designer to use different solutions, e.g. cycloidal gears [24].

## 3   Problem Solution Network

### 3.1   Theoretical Background

The PSN has been developed within the general scope of considering multiple problems contextually, which is one of fundamental aims pursued by OTSM-TRIZ [25, 26]. It differs from other models belonging to this family (details are out of the scope of the present paper) and its logic is recognized as a valuable support to systematic conceptual design [27].

Specifically, the PSN foresees the creation of a conceptual map in the form of a network of problem-solution sequences ordered hierarchically. The problems are represented with yellow boxes and the solutions with green boxes [10]. The logic behind the approach is the concept that several alternative solutions can be associated to a problem, which are characterized by different sub-problems. The representation of a problem, even if already solved with existing solutions, is fundamental to stimulate the exploration of possible alternative solutions characterized by different and, possibly easier to solve, sub-problems. Both in formulating problems and in generating solutions, it is fundamental to be as much general as possible, to examine the system exhaustively and to limit the negative effects due to psychological inertia or preconceptions.

In the PSN, a problem is considered as any 'question' that can be expressed in the form 'How to verb – noun?' (e.g. 'How to transmit torque?'). The 'verb – noun' form does not necessarily express a function but may refer to a desired result, effect, property and/or quality/performance that the system should provide according to the design requirements (e.g. 'ensure system adaptability' expresses a technical problem that is not a function).

The first box that has to be made in the PSN network is yellow, therefore related to a problem. This problem has to represent the design task. In other words, it represents the most abstract problem that can be formulated from the requirements list. The first level of problems is related to the main functionalities of the system, to be implemented in any case and regardless of any specific solution. It is possible to see in Fig. 5 the design task and the main problems of the case study illustrated in this paper.

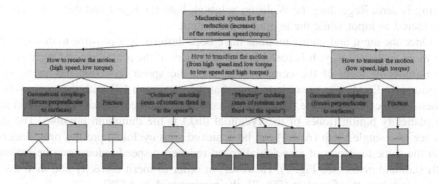

**Fig. 5.** Design task in problem-solution network

After the first level of problems, a level of solutions follows, followed by another level of problems and so on. This is because, apart from the direct link between the first level and design tasks, the sub-problems are dependent on the type of solution adopted. The different levels of problem and solution then represent the different levels of abstraction to which the main problem has been broken down. To do this, there are appropriate guidelines to be followed [10].

## 3.2   Application to the Case Study

By focusing on the branch of the PSN that concerns the design of "Planetary meshing", it is possible to individuate three main design problems, see Fig. 6.

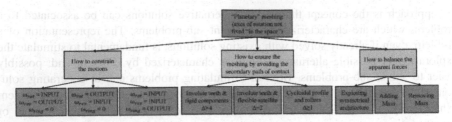

**Fig. 6.** Planetary meshing

The first problem that arises when a designer wants to reduce rotational speed through planetary motions is to define how to constrain the motions. In other words, the designer should define the input and output motions so that the rotation speed is reduced. Generally, the parameters that can be controlled are the rotational speed of:

- Rotation of the planetary pinion ($\omega$_rot)
- Revolution of the planetary pinion ($\omega$_rev)
- Ring gear ($\omega$_ring)

For example, in case of Cycloidal and Harmonic architectures, the $\omega$_rot is the input, the $\omega$_rev is the output and the $\omega$_ring is zero. In case of planetary gearboxes, the $\omega$_rev can be considered the input, the $\omega$_rot is the output and, in this case too, the $\omega$_ring is zero. Regarding the Wolfrom solution, both the $\omega$_rot and the $\omega$_rev can be considered as input while the $\omega$_ring is the output.

Once the input and output motions have been defined, it is possible to describe the GR in an analytical way. It is based on the diameters of the primitives and therefore on the number of teeth of the components, since the speed reduction has to be synchronous. In Eq. 1, it is possible to note that the maximum GR with the same overall dimensions occurs when the difference in teeth between the external ring (rollers) and the planetary pinion (lobes of the cycloidal disk) is the minimum possible. The difference of a single tooth ($\Delta = 1$) can be achieved with cycloidal profiles only. Indeed, with the same topology of a cycloidal speed reducer, a speed reducer can be realized with standard gears (see Fig. 7). However, in order to mesh correctly and then avoid the secondary path of contact (Fig. 7), the minimum $\Delta$ is 4 [28].

At this point, the following problem can easily be expressed through a contradiction. On the one hand, the difference between teeth ($\Delta$) has to be minimal to allow a high GR. On the other hand, the smaller the $\Delta$, the greater the risk of secondary path of contact. Therefore, the resulting problem is how to ensure the meshing with the minimum $\Delta$ avoiding the secondary path of contact. On the one hand, the solution is to modify the tooth shape (cycloidal profile). On the other hand, by exploiting the principle of macro-micro separation and the dynamization, it is possible to achieve the solution proposed by the Harmonic drive. Indeed, by using involute or similar teeth profiles, the diameter of the motion primitive should be overall large to generate high reduction ratios and locally small to avoid secondary interference. Harmonic Drive solves this physical contradiction by deforming the flexspline to have a large overall diameter and a small one in the meshing area. In this way, the Harmonic drive could

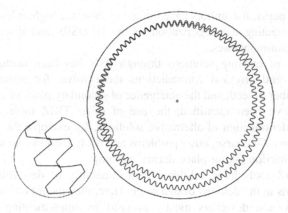

**Fig. 7.** Secondary path of contact

achieve a $\Delta$ equal to 2. Another aspect to take into account is how to balance the system, and often, the balancing solutions can be exploited to improve the performance of the system. For example, by balancing the cycloidal gearbox with an additional cycloidal disk, it is possible to exploit this new disk to increase the GR as in the Wolfrom solution [16]. Another example is the use of a symmetrical wave generator in the harmonic drive. This solution increases the transmissible torque because many more teeth (and diametrically opposed teeth) can mesh at the same time. More detailed ramifications of PSN can be realized and parts of these have been presented in [29].

## 4 Discussion and Conclusion

Through the PSN, it was possible to describe the co-evolution of problems-solutions that can be addressed in the design of a HPDSR from the maximum level of abstraction to a more detailed level. The hierarchical structure of the PSN has been fundamental to map the similarities and divergences between the existing solutions. The ordered sequence of problem-solutions has made it possible to understand and trace how a problem was solved by one or more solutions and how different solutions present in the literature were ascribable to a single problem. The independence between the branches has made it possible to abstract from the technical solutions found in the literature in order to think about design changes at different levels of abstraction.

This description allows understanding that, at a high level of abstraction, the Harmonic and Cycloidal solutions are similar as of how the motions are constrained. Moreover, it was possible to understand that these two solutions differ in terms of how to avoid the secondary path of contact by trying to minimize $\Delta$. The use of the PSN has also been useful to map Wolfrom solutions, which, although they were initially conceived for planetary gearboxes, were applied also to cycloidal solutions.

The case study analyzed is extremely vast and complex and, through the PSN, it was possible to synthesize its variety and manage its complexity. However, in order to represent all the existing solutions exhaustively, the branches of PSN should be manifold. In this paper, the authors have limited to show the highest level of abstraction only. It allows creating a categorization of the HPDSRs and discussing the main differences and commonalities.

The analysis of existing solutions through PSN has been useful to understand which technical and physical contradictions these solve, for instance the conflict between the number of teeth and the emergence of secondary paths of contact. Once the contradictions have been identified, the use of other TRIZ tools can support the designer to the identification of alternative solutions, for example the dynamization in harmonic solutions. Of course, other problems and contradictions are still to be solved, for instance the friction taking place during meshing.

Overall, TRIZ tools have exhibited their capability of describing conventional technical solutions at the detailed design stage. Here, the amount of involved creativity is generally low and designers mostly proceed by implementing and combining existing and acknowledged solutions. However, the fact that many problems are in play, as shown by the PSN, indicates the ample margins of inventiveness are still present also where solutions are seemingly standardized.

# References

1. Youmans, R.J., Arciszewski, T.: Design fixation: classifications and modern methods of prevention. AI EDAM **28**(2), 129–137 (2014)
2. Sensinger, J. W., Lipsey, J. H.: Cycloid vs. harmonic drives for use in high ratio, single stage robotic transmissions. In: 2012 IEEE International Conference on Robotics and Automation, pp. 4130–4135. IEEE (2012)
3. Concli, F., Maccioni, L., Gorla, C.: Lubrication of gearboxes: CFD analysis of a cycloidal gear set. WIT Trans. Eng. Sci. **123**, 101–112 (2019)
4. Olson, D.G., Erdman, A.G., Riley, D.R.: Topological analysis of single-degree-of-freedom planetary gear trains. J. Mech. Des. **113**(1), 10–16 (1991)
5. Chen, B., Fang, T., Li, C., Wang, S.: Gear geometry of cycloid drives. Sci. China Ser. E: Technol. Sci. **51**(5), 598–610 (2008)
6. Gorla, C., Davoli, P., Rosa, F., Longoni, C., Chiozzi, F., Samarani, A.: Theoretical and experimental analysis of a cycloidal speed reducer. J. Mech. Des. **130**(11) (2008)
7. Sensinger, J.W.: Efficiency of high-sensitivity gear trains, such as cycloid drives. J. Mech. Des. **135**(7) (2013)
8. Zigmond, E.J.: Harmonic Drive Development, vol. 412. Pratt & Whitney Aircraft Division, United Aircraft Corporation, CANEL Operations (1964)
9. Ostapski, W.: Analysis of the stress state in the harmonic drive generator-flexspline system in relation to selected structural parameters and manufacturing deviations. Bull. Polish Acad. Sci. Tech. Sci. 683–698 (2010)
10. Fiorineschi, L., Rotini, F., Rissone, P.: A new conceptual design approach for over-coming the flaws of functional decomposition and morphology. J. Eng. Des. **27**(7), 438–468 (2016)
11. Fiorineschi, L., Frillici, F.S., Rotini, F.: Enhancing functional decomposition and morphology with TRIZ: literature review. Comput. Ind. **94**, 1–15 (2018)
12. Fiorineschi, L.: Abstraction framework to support students in learning creative conceptual design. J. Eng. Des. Technol. **16**, 616–636 (2018)
13. Fiorineschi, L., Frillici, F.S., Rotini, F., Tomassini, M.: Exploiting TRIZ tools for enhancing systematic conceptual design activities. J. Eng. Des. **29**(6), 259–290 (2018)

14. PDTA. https://www.ptda.org/resources/product-training/pt-mc-tech-tips/gears.aspx. Accessed 11 June 2020
15. Thube, S. V., Bobak, T.R.: Dynamic analysis of a cycloidal gearbox using finite element method. AGMA Technical Paper, pp. 1–13 (2012)
16. Blagojevic, M., Marjanovic, N., Djordjevic, Z., Stojanovic, B., Disic, A.: A new design of a two-stage cycloidal speed reducer. J. Mech. Des. **133**(8), 085001 (2011)
17. Sensinger, J.W.: Unified approach to cycloid drive profile, stress, and efficiency optimization. J. Mech. Des. **132**(2), 024503–024508 (2010)
18. Malhotra, S.K., Parameswaran, M.A.: Analysis of a cycloid speed reducer. Mech. Mach. Theory **18**(6), 491–499 (1983)
19. Ghorbel, F.H., Gandhi, P.S., Alpeter, F.: On the kinematic error in harmonic drive gears. J. Mech. Des. **123**(1), 90–97 (2001)
20. Maiti, R.: A novel harmonic drive with pure involute tooth gear pair. J. Mech. Des. **126**(1), 178–182 (2004)
21. Chen, X., Liu, Y., Xing, J., Lin, S., Xu, W.: The parametric design of double-circular-arc tooth profile and its influence on the functional backlash of harmonic drive. Mech. Mach. Theory **73**, 1–24 (2014)
22. Kosse, V.: Analytical investigation of the change in phase angle between the wave generator and the teeth meshing zone in high-torque mechanical harmonic drives. Mech. Mach. Theory **32**(5), 533–538 (1997)
23. Tuplin, W.A.: Designing compound epicyclic gear trains for maximum speed at high velocity ratios. Mach. Des. **29**(7), 100–104 (1957)
24. Lin, W.S., Shih, Y.P., Lee, J.J.: Design of a two-stage cycloidal gear reducer with tooth modifications. Mech. Mach. Theory **79**, 184–197 (2014)
25. Cavallucci, D., Khomenko, N.: From TRIZ to OTSM-TRIZ: addressing complexity challenges in inventive design. Int. J. Prod. Dev. **4**(1–2), 4–21 (2007)
26. Khomenko, N., De Guio, R.: OTSM network of problems for representing and analysing problem situations with computer support. In: León-Rovira, N. (ed.) CAI 2007. ITIFIP, vol. 250, pp. 77–88. Springer, Boston, MA (2007). https://doi.org/10.1007/978-0-387-75456-7_8
27. Lin, H.H.: Application of a fuzzy decision model to the design of a pillbox for medical treatment of chronic diseases. Appl. Sci. **9**(22), 4909 (2019)
28. Maiti, R., Roy, A.K.: Minimum tooth difference in internal-external involute gear pair. Mech. Mach. Theory **31**(4), 475–485 (1996)
29. Fiorineschi, L., Papini, S., Pugi, L., Rindi, A. Rotini, F.: Systematic design of a new gearbox for concrete mixers. J. Eng. Des. Technol. (2020)

# TRIZ and System Engineering

# A Systematic Innovation Process Oriented to Inter-discipline

Jianguang Sun[1,2](✉), Hao-Yu Li[1,2] (iD), Yu-Juan Du[3] (iD),
Zhitao Song[1,2] (iD), and Runhua Tan[1,2] (iD)

[1] Hebei University of Technology, Tianjin 300401, China
sjg@hebut.edu.cn
[2] National Engineering Research Center for Technological Innovation Method
and Tool, Tianjin 300401, China
[3] China North Engine Research Institute, Tianjin 300401, China

**Abstract.** The method of achieving remarkable interdisciplinary innovation is a challenging topic for industrial innovation and technological development. Interdisciplinary innovation is recognized as an effective way to achieve high level and radical innovation. In the process of solving the invention problem, the classical TRIZ simplifies the complex problem into a standard problem. In the standard form, some standard solutions are matched to solve these problems, and finally transformed into specific solutions. It shows that TRIZ can deal with interdisciplinary problems. With the increasing complexity of scientific research and technical problems, the Network of Problem of OTSM derived from TRIZ is difficult to achieve collaboration. The interdisciplinary problem is firstly analyzed by function model and cause analysis. Then multiple solutions can be obtained by comprehensive application of effective tools such as design-by-analogy, multi-contradiction problem solving and patent design around. The two paths of interdisciplinary innovation are incremental innovation and disruptive innovation. Finally, a systematic innovation process oriented to inter-discipline is initially established based on patent database, OTSM and QFD. The case study of tire breaker briefly illustrates this systematic innovation process.

**Keywords:** Systematic innovation · Interdisciplinary research · TRIZ · Network of problem

## 1 Introduction

Compared to optimization, the indispensable elements of innovation are more abundant, to which relationship of many stakeholders related are more complicated [1]. The main purpose of innovation is to meet current or prospective needs, and to successfully create new products and services by adjusting and upgrading existing technologies [2]. The complexity and uncertainty of innovation are not only be restricted to technological achievements, but also the design process of the former [3]. It's worth thinking about how to fulfill high quality innovation, rather than optimizing existing technology [4]. However, large-scale innovations often involve the mind, process and organization of interdisciplinary research (IDR) [5].

© IFIP International Federation for Information Processing 2020
Published by Springer Nature Switzerland AG 2020
D. Cavallucci et al. (Eds.): TFC 2020, IFIP AICT 597, pp. 257–267, 2020.
https://doi.org/10.1007/978-3-030-61295-5_21

As a promising way for radical innovation, IDR is favorable to explore new technology through collaboration among multiple disciplines [6]. In recent decades, scientists, engineers, social scientists and humanities scholars have provided insights into complex innovation problem from different perspectives, thus facilitating the scientific knowledge and technology [7]. Gooch argued that IDR offers a unique opportunity to create impact on different levels, but also brings obstacles to research in the absence of collaboration [8]. Arroyave indicated that IDR requires an understanding of general principles of design frameworks [9]. It is a quite complex process to create new products or services to across the boundaries of disciplines [7]. Therefore, it is a new topic worthy of thinking to explore a method applicable to interdisciplinary problems, especially those involving engineering technology.

This paper proposes an integrated framework of system innovation which are used to solve interdisciplinary problems. The rest of this paper is organized as follows. Section 2 presents the related concept and the literature review about IDR, and the limitations of TRIZ & OTSM in solving interdisciplinary problems. Section 3 describes the process of analyzing interdisciplinary problems, which related to network of problem (NoP). Section 4, two alternative routes, the incremental innovation and disruptive innovation, are suggested by the systematic innovation process oriented to inter-discipline. In Sect. 5, a case study briefly illustrates the proposed framework. Section 6 discusses the findings and limitations of our research.

## 2  Literature Review

### 2.1  Related Concepts About IDR

Compare to general problems, the main characteristic of interdisciplinary problems is that it can't be satisfactorily understood and addressed with knowledge of single discipline [10]. It is embodied in the difficult function elements or factors excavated by problem analysis tools. Due to the limitation of their own knowledge, it is hard for engineers in a certain field to deal with them [11]. Therefore, integrating the views of different disciplines is imperative.

At present, there are three approximate approaches. However, many academics did not make a distinction. It is necessary to clarify the terminology of multidisciplinary, interdisciplinary and transdisciplinary research [7]. Similarities and differences between them are explained as follows, as the guiding ideology of the framework of this article.

- Multidisciplinary research adds breadth and available resources by combining disciplinary or domain perspectives. Due to the limitation of their own perspective, they failed to reach a consensus on complex problems.
- Interdisciplinary research is characterized by collaborating separate resources from various domains which includes methods, tools, data and so on. Nothing is more important than communication and consensus building in this research. Therefore, a dynamic network is needed to maintain the internal and external interactions between various teams.
- Transdisciplinary research focuses on a comprehensive framework involving a wide range of stakeholders, such as practitioners, the public and government. It

transcends the narrow scope of IDR, which is restricted in related field, including politics, economics, ecology, sociology.

More vivid term, cross-disciplinary research, is often seen in related literatures. It usually emphasizes an action that researchers mutually cross boundaries of disciplines and exchange information, both of which are involved in interdisciplinary and trans-disciplinary research. To make differences clear, the comparison graph related to above concepts is shown in Fig. 1. Considering the scope and advantages of the three types, this paper adopts IDR as the guidance of system innovation process.

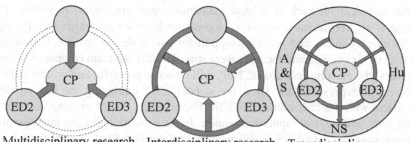

Multidisciplinary research   Interdisciplinary research   Transdisciplinary research
ED: Engineering Discipline; CP: Common Problem; NS: Natural Science;
A&S: Art & science; Hu: Humanities

**Fig. 1.** Similarities and differences of three types (adapted from literature [7])

## 2.2 Triz and Otsm

To gain or protect market share, it is of paramount importance to enhance competitiveness by core technology with innovation. The systematization of R&D has been an inevitable trend rather than the traditional trial and error procedure [12]. TRIZ has provided a reliable systematic method for innovation during the design process, as shown in Fig. 2. It seems that TRIZ has the ability to implement IDR by closing the gap between disciplines. As the technical problems get more complex and interdisciplinary, TRIZ often filed to solving multi-contradiction which grow dynamically, but solving them one by one has little relevance.[13]

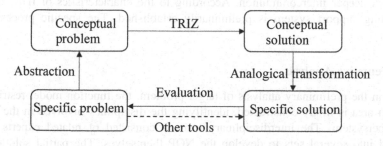

**Fig. 2.** TRIZ routes to problem solving

Because the classic TRIZ is limited to solving single engineering problems, majorly mechanical field, the general theory of problems solving (Russian acronym OTSM) was studied by Altshuller in the middle of the 80s [5]. Up to now, most of the literature on OTSM focuses on the management of contradictions. A lot of research on Network of Contradiction has contributed to multi-contradiction management and solving, which are moving in the direction of analyzing the dynamic influence and programming solving path based on complex network theory. By comparison, few studies have been done on NOP, especially in the analysis of initial problems, and its application in IDR is still limited.

The NoP has three defects. Firstly, considering the limitation of team knowledge and the technical bulwark in related industries, open innovation inevitable. Patent database is an irreplaceable source of significant knowledge, which greatly inspires interdisciplinary teams and provides support for patent design around. Therefore, if a great deal of views, data and methods were shared within the team composed of various disciplines, the existing instrument, NoP, will be more powerful and will be embodied in knowledge representation. Then, the standards for extracting the key problem is inconsistent with the characteristic of IDR. For instance, one of existing standards is a priority node with several inputs and outputs. In the network including interdisciplinary problems, many so-called key problems may be determined but most of them have no relationship. Last but not least, the NoP of OTSM does not pay attention to generalizing the parameters which are very personalized. Although the OTSM itself can be applied to many disciplines and even non engineering disciplines, personalized parameters are certainly not conducive to information sharing.

Therefore, exactly as classical TRIZ is good at solving problems and modern one is excelled at discovering right them, we should also turn our attention to correctly determining common problems faced by different disciplines, ensuring that resources and efforts focus on one same goal. To compensate for these shortcomings, Sect. 3 describes the process of constructing the network of interdisciplinary problem which supports to the collaborative innovation in IDR.

# 3  The Process of Analyzing Interdisciplinary Problems

In order to effectively implement interdisciplinary innovation, it is necessary to study the systematic innovation process supported by large-scale knowledge database, which facilitates deeper intercommunion. According to the characteristics of IDR, the corresponding support system is preliminarily established. The specific process is as follows.

## 3.1  Tentative Analysis

Based on the preliminary analysis of target problem, the function model restricted in problem area is firstly constructed, identifying the disciplines involved in the system and supersystem. The interdisciplinary team is consisted of related experts and is grouped into several sets to develop the NOP themselves. The partial solutions are primarily obtained by exporting available resources which are analyzed with 9-windows and classified according to their disciplines. The management of interdisciplinary teams was already studied by Khomenko [5]. On this basis, analysis tools should be introduced to team communication in the next phase.

## 3.2 Construction and Transformation of a Network of Interdisciplinary Problem

Identifying the right problem is far more significant than solving it forever. It is just a multidisciplinary research, although it has a massive viewpoint from various discipline in Sect. 3.1. The analysis tools, failure analysis, root cause analysis and anticipatory failure determination, can be used to construct the top network, zooming in the common root cause of the teams. Only in this way can this process be consistent with collaborative research. In fact, constructing the top network reveals that the parameter has unsatisfying value, named evaluation parameter. Changing the value of parameter of root cause, known as the action parameter, provides partial solution [14].

Aiming at the root cause, the middle networks composed of partial solution are developed by each sub-team through retrieving related patents. Patent and resource analysis complement each other. As mentioned in Sect. 2, derivative problems continuously arise at the bottom network. Problem flow network of OTSM is presented as a fractal structure which converges top-down [15]. For solving interdisciplinary problem effectively, priority will be given to those nodes of network involved in two or more disciplines, making integrated solutions. These key nodes are connected by action parameters and evaluation parameters, then transforming into net of contradiction based on element-name-value (ENV) model.

## 3.3 Design-by-Analogy for Closing the Gap During the IDR

The more important difficulty is to close the gap between disciplines. Due to the complexity of interdisciplinary problem, most of views are deeply rooted in in their own domains and there is no bridge to connect them [9]. It is quite important to convert the specific problems and partial solutions into general format, namely abstraction.

According to the principle of using same innovation method to deal with similar problem situations, the problem of a certain discipline is abstracted as standard scenario and matched with one or more conceptual solutions. The designers are stimulated to conceive solutions by analogizing and transferring knowledge of other disciplines. While solving interdisciplinary problem, the gap between different cognitive domains can be closed by analogy, a basic way of thinking of human beings who reuse the existing solutions in terms of similarity degree [16]. As shown in Fig. 4, the whole process is consisted of abstraction, retrieval, mapping and generating new solutions. Owing to the complexity of interdisciplinary problem, design-by-analogy plays an important role, but it is not enough to solve the problem thoroughly. Due to multiple and interrelated sub problems, solving one by one will lead to less relevant solutions and derivative problems. Therefore, it is necessary to intuitively explain the relevance by NoP, so as to solve the multi-contradiction and even multi-parameter contradiction.

In the framework, the problem in a certain field is firstly reduced to a standard problem expressed by the conceptual model. Among many design models, the function-behavior-structure (FBS) model is recognized as an engineering design community, through which we can powerfully abstract the products and processes at a higher level [17]. Extracted features at three levels are mapped to some standard solutions with TRIZ tools or used as key words for patent retrieval. In far and near domains, the relevant knowledge is migrated and finally transformed into specific solution for practical matters.

To illustrate the process mentioned above more directly, a network of interdisciplinary problem network is constructed, as shown in Fig. 3.

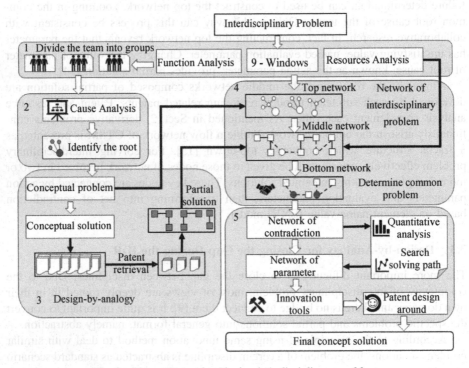

**Fig. 3.** The process of analyzing interdisciplinary problems

## 4   System Innovation Based on Inter-discipline

Due to existing innovative methods can hardly play a huge role in cross domain, constructing an integrated innovation platform is urgent for products entering the market from the fuzzy front end and making the best of interdisciplinary knowledge. In addition, some effective tools oriented inter-discipline can be selected at the framework front-end, such as incremental innovation and disruptive innovation.

The core of incremental innovation is to discover and solve contradictions constantly, increasingly better performance of products along the similar or same S-curve [2]. The difference between design results and existing results is not particularly large. Supposing external knowledge were adopted into final solution, high quality innovation could be realized. The original intention of OTSM to realize interdisciplinary innovation is hardly reflected in actual cases which are studied from single perspective.

The incremental innovation process consists of the problem flow network of OTSM, the tools of TRIZ, design-by-analogy, the patent database and so on. Afterward, the above tools are integrated to solve complex and interdisciplinary problems. Lastly, multiple partial solutions from different domains are mapped and merged into final solution. The incremental innovation process oriented to Inter-discipline is as shown in Fig. 4.

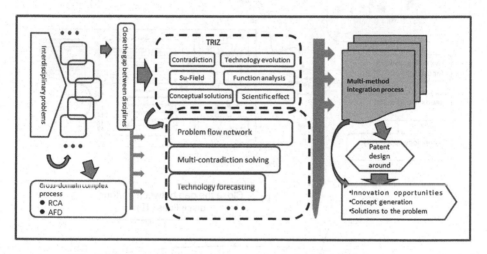

**Fig. 4.** The incremental innovation process oriented to inter-discipline

Mining opportunities for disruptive innovation as the key step of the second route, it is mainly targeted at mature products whose main function has been satisfied [18]. The new-market disruption is achieved by reducing over satisfied needs and strengthening some auxiliary functions, orienting to inter-discipline. QFD can be used as an effective analysis tool to find technology opportunities. The systematic innovation process oriented to inter-discipline is as shown in Fig. 5.

The final innovation results are characterized with multi-technology route, fire-new concept and factual solution.

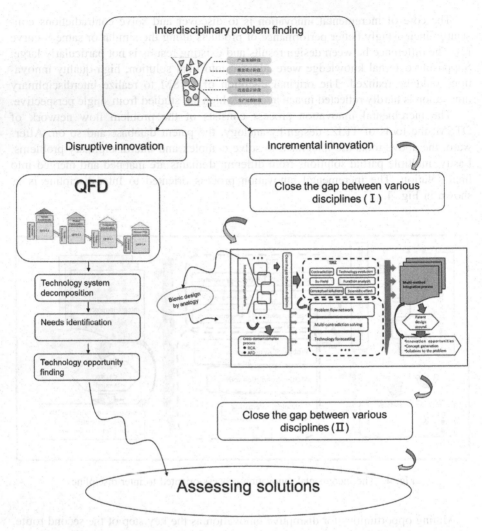

**Fig. 5.** The systematic innovation process oriented to inter-discipline

# 5   Case Study

As shown in Fig. 6, Tire breaker is a kind of roadblock with sharp barbs. If tires were slashed, the gas in tire would be discharged immediately along the vent. The vehicle loses its ability to run. Therefore, it is a necessary anti-terrorism equipment for safety purposes. However, this existing product are mostly this type that fixed on the ground and bulky as a whole. In response to some unexpected events, a portable tire breaker is often needed.

**Fig. 6.** Tire breaker

## 5.1 The Incremental Innovation

Analyze this problem from different discipline perspectives. For example, the problem can be abstracted into physical contradiction in mechanical engineering areas. For obstructing the vehicle, tire breaker should be designed as long as possible, so that road is cut off completely. Paradoxically, the length of tire breaker shall not be more than 1 m, for the convenience of carrying. In other words, we hope that the size of tire breaker will be both long and short, namely, a physical contradiction. Then, the conceptual problem can be solved by separation principles. Those conceptual solutions of various domains are transformed into partial solutions. Ultimately, the final concept solution is formed by fusion of partial solutions. Take time separation as an example, small size when carrying and large size in deployment. The expansion and deformation of equipment can be realized by many effects from various disciplines, such as explosive gas produced by chemical energy, expansion by electric and mechanical energy, as shown in Fig. 7.

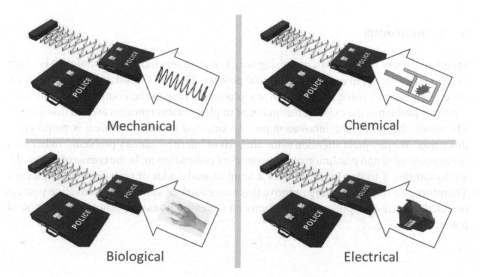

**Fig. 7.** Portable tire breaker

## 5.2    The Disruptive Innovation

The user's requirements can be identified by QFD in which the core tool, house of quality, is used to transform requirements into design parameters. The results show that users have very low expectation for service life, because of few opportunities for move operation. Therefore, the recovery function of the product can be abandoned, namely, disposable products. Three kinds of disposable and portable tire breakers can also be driven by chemical, electric and mechanical energy, which greatly reduces the design difficulty, as shown in the Fig. 8.

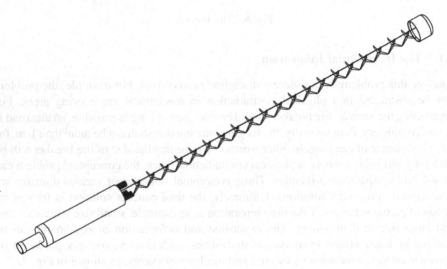

**Fig. 8.**  Disposable tire breaker

## 6    Conclusions

Interdisciplinary research as a promising way to realize remarkable innovation, it is worth making great efforts to explore the specific process. TRIZ & OTSM as effective methods have been used to solve interdisciplinary problems. Due to the complexity of interdisciplinary problems, the existing methods and implementation process are still insufficient. Therefore, the systematic innovation process oriented to inter-discipline is proposed in this paper. We pay great attention to the analysis of interdisciplinary problems, rather than the management and resolution of the network of contradiction. In the course of this study, we found that it took a lot of time for a team to study a lot of texts, especially patents. Therefore, we should not only improve this framework of systematic innovation process oriented to inter-discipline, but also focus on the extraction of structural information of patent.

**Acknowledgements.** This research is supported by the National Innovation Method Fund of China (2017IM040100), Erasmus + Program of European Union (586081-EPP-1-2017-1-FI-EPPKA2-CBHE-JP) and the Natural Science Foundation of Hebei province of China (Grand No. E2017202260).

# References

1. Khomenko, N., De Guio, R., Cavallucci, D.: Enhancing ECN's abilities to address inventive strategies using OTSM-TRIZ. Int. J. Collaborative Eng. **1**(1–2), 98–113 (2009)
2. Runhua, T.A.N., Guozhong, C.A.O., Wei, L.I.U.: Concepts and methods of innovative design. J. Mach. Des. **36**(09), 1–6 (2019)
3. Czinki, A., Hentschel, C.: Solving complex problems and TRIZ. Procedia CIRP **39**, 27–32 (2016)
4. Cavallucci, D., Khomenko, N.: From TRIZ to OTSM-TRIZ: addressing complexity challenges in inventive design. Int. J. Prod. Dev. **4**(1–2), 4 (2007)
5. Khomenko, N., Avci, N., Kaikov, I., et al.: Innovation management of interdisciplinary team: contribution of OTSM-TRIZ network of problems approach[EB/OL] (2008). https://otsm-triz.org/sites/default/files/ready/080619_otsm-triz_for_managment_of_innovation.pdf
6. Porter, A.L., Roessner, J.D., Cohen, A.S., et al.: Interdisciplinary research: meaning, metrics and nurture. Res. Eval. **15**(3), 187–196 (2006)
7. Atila, E.: Transdisciplinary Engineering Design Process. John Wiley & Sons, Hoboken (2018)
8. Gooch, D., Vasalou, A., Benton, L.: Impact in interdisciplinary and cross-sector research: Opportunities and challenges. J. Assoc. Inf. Sci. Technol. **68**(2), 378–391 (2017)
9. Arroyave, R., Shield, S., Chang, C.N., et al.: Interdisciplinary research on designing engineering material systems: results from a national science foundation workshop. J. Mech. Des. **140**(11), 110801 (2018)
10. Khomenko, N., Ashtiani, M.: Classical TRIZ and OTSM as a scientific theoretical background for non-typical problem solving instruments. In: Frankfurt Etria Future (2007)
11. Repko, A.F.: Interdisciplinary Research: Process and Theory, p. 17. Peking University Press, Peking (2016)
12. Runhua, T.A.N.: C-TRIZ and Its Applications: Theory of Inventive Process Solving, p. 282. Higher Education Press, Beijing (2016)
13. Cavallucci, D., Khomenko, N., Morel, C.: Towards inventive design through management of contradictions. In: 2005 CIRP International Design Seminar (2005)
14. Cavallucci, D., Eltzer, T.: Parameter network as a means for driving problem solving process. Int. J. Comput. Appl. Technol. **30**(1–2), 125–136 (2007)
15. Khomenko, N., De Guio, R., Lelait, L., et al.: A framework for OTSM? TRIZ-based computer support to be used in complex problem management. Int. J. Comput. Appl. Technol. **30**(1–2), 88–104 (2007)
16. Lizhen, J.I.A., Fei, Y.U., Runhua, T.A.N., et al.: Research on design-by-analogy based on refined SBF model. J. Mach. Des. **35**(11), 22–30 (2018)
17. Gero, J.S.: Representation schema for design. AI Mag. **11**(4), 26 (1990)
18. Christensen, C.M.: The Innovator's Dilemma: When New Technologies Cause Great Firms to Fail. Harvard Bussiness School Press, Boston (1997)

# Eliminating Disadvantages by Changing Transitions in a State Machine Cause-Effect Model

Jerzy Chrząszcz[1,2]($\boxtimes$) (iD)

[1] Warsaw University of Technology, Institute of Computer Science,
Warsaw 00-665, Poland
jch@ii.pw.edu.pl
[2] Pentacomp Systemy Informatyczne S.A., Warsaw 02-222, Poland

**Abstract.** The typical TRIZ approach to system improvement is to remove key disadvantages identified in a structural cause-effect model. Using the behavioral state machine model we may try to develop other strategies. The basics of state machine causality models, such as building and simplifying a model as well as converting it to a regular expression representation, have been presented in the previous author's papers. This paper aims at developing a methodical approach to system improvements by changing transitions between the states in a state machine model. It addresses the analogy between the states-transitions structure of a state machine model and the hardware-software duality, as well as conceptual connections between the cause-effect analysis and Standard Inventive Solutions and other TRIZ tools.

**Keywords:** TRIZ · CECA · Cause-effect analysis · State machine · Vulnerability · Substance-Field model · Standard Inventive Solutions

## 1 Introduction to State Machine CECA Model

The Cause-Effect Chains Analysis (CECA) is a method developed in the 1990s for supporting systematic identification of the problems to be solved in order to achieve required improvements to the analyzed system [1, 2]. First, the goal of the project at hand is used to define one or more *target disadvantages* that should be eliminated. Then, subsequent causes are investigated one by one, which results in building chains of *intermediate disadvantages*, until finding a cause which either remains beyond control (like laws of nature or geometrical properties) or reflects a project requirement or a constraint. Such *root cause* stops the expansion of a given chain of the causality model and it is considered irremovable, as a rule. Linear chains may have common causes and may connect through logical operators (AND, OR), indicating how the input causes trigger the effects.

The above procedure results in a structural model of cause-effect relations within the analyzed system, which is further explored to identify the *key disadvantages*, reflecting the most impactful causes of the target disadvantages. Finally, the most promising set of key disadvantages is selected, so that solving the *key problems* derived from the key disadvantages is expected to eliminate the target disadvantages.

D. Cavallucci et al. (Eds.): TFC 2020, IFIP AICT 597, pp. 268–279, 2020.
https://doi.org/10.1007/978-3-030-61295-5_22

The rules and guidelines originally stated for this method are generic, which makes them universal. On the other hand, the main technique for discovering the causes of a particular effect is answering the question *why?* or *why did it happen?* Asking such open questions implies that the answers will depend on the knowledge and experience of the analysts. Therefore the models developed for the same problem by different teams may differ, and building cause-effect diagrams remains a matter of experience and specific "best practices" or "style", to a great extent.

Among several enhancements proposed to introduce more order into the original CECA method, especially important for further considerations, is the concept of the *parameter-function nexus chain* [3], indicating that because of the nature of interactions between system components, a properly built chain of causes should reflect conditions interleaved with actions. Conditions refer to parameters, while actions refer to functions, and such an interleaved sequence describes the development of the last disadvantage in the chain (in particular − a target disadvantage).

The parameter-function paradigm (also dubbed *condition-action*) paved the way for the state machine approach to CECA modeling presented in [4]. The state machine model consists of *states* describing interactions and *transitions* between states, which are executed upon satisfying specific conditions, inherited from the condition-action model. A set of building blocks was proposed for all basic structural elements found in a CECA diagram obeying the parameter-function paradigm, together with rules for converting a diagram into a state machine model. The original method was later enhanced by providing guidelines for simplification and further transformations using formal grammars and regular expressions, as described in [5].

The state machine model is behavioral rather than structural and it reflects causality relations as collections of concurrent processes represented by connected state machines derived from respective linear chains of the original model. Each of the processes starts from a state representing a particular root cause and progresses through the following states when subsequent conditions are satisfied until a target disadvantage is reached. A sample CECA diagram is shown in Fig. 1, along with a corresponding state machine model ($t1 \div t3$ reflect target disadvantages).

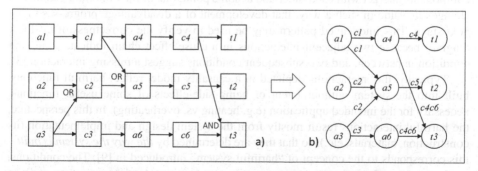

**Fig. 1.** A sample CECA diagram (a) and its counterpart state machine model (b). The $a_i$ nodes describing interactions become states and $c_i$ nodes describing conditions become conditional transitions between the states. AND operator modifies original conditions, while OR operators are converted into "parallel" transitions indicating alternative paths leading to a given state [5].

To conclude this section, let us briefly recall the main features of the various models. The classic structural CECA model [1, 2] shows the *structure of impact* – how linear chains are interconnected, and the *order of impact* – in what sequence particular causes in a linear chain contribute to a target disadvantage. A cause in a linear chain may also be active before and after the moment indicated by its position in a sequence, but it is only evaluated in a specific context defined by the position.

The basic combinational CECA model [6] only shows the structure of impact. The linear chains of intermediate causes are modeled with logical repeaters, as they just propagate causality and do not introduce any logical functions into the model. Consequently, the input values are repeated at the outputs and there is no way to analyze linear chains in finer detail, so they are compacted.

The enhanced combinational CECA model [7] proposes linear chains to be extended by explicit indication of *vulnerabilities*, which trigger the effects jointly with *hazards* through logical AND operators. This change is essential because vulnerabilities are not caused by hazards, which is indicated by serial connections in classic linear chains. Actually, despite being present in the system, a vulnerability cannot trigger the effect without a hazard, which appears due to the activation of deeper causes in a chain. This approach was further explored in [8] to show correspondence with the appropriate quadrants of the SWOT (Strengths, Weaknesses, Opportunities, Threats) matrix.

The sequential CECA model [4, 5] uses state machine notation to reflect both the structure of impact and the order of impact, and therefore its content may be seen as equivalent to the classic model, structured by applying the condition-action paradigm. Changing the perspective from structure to process view brings an additional benefit of recognizing transitions with equivalent conditions in different chains as synchronization points, which may give a better understanding of time relations important for the development of disadvantages.

## 2  State Machine Model and Hardware-Software Duality

The condition-action approach reflects the nature of changes in the real world: system components interact with each other and at some point, one of the important parameters changes its value in such a way, that development of a disadvantage progresses to the next stage. This interleaved pattern may be used to verify the correctness of a CECA diagram because two adjacent interactions in a cause-effect chain indicate a missing condition in between, and two subsequent conditions suggest a missing interaction [3].

Typically, the interactions depicted in a causality model reflect harmful functions, built into the system without intent or being side-effects of some useful functions, necessary for the intended application (e.g. heating vs. overheating). In this perspective, the harmful interactions result mostly from the system design and implementation (its construction, materials, etc.), so that they are determined by *the way the system is built* – this corresponds to the concept of "harmful system" introduced in [9]. The conditions, on the contrary, depend on the operating situation (settings, load, temperature, etc.), so that they are mostly determined by *the way the system is used*.

This may be summarized as follows:

- harmful interactions take place because the world and the system works like that, so they result from the laws of nature, or operation principle, construction, materials, etc. used in the system,
- therefore to change unwanted interactions we should change the operation principle or construction or materials, etc. – this is the *structural perspective*,
- on the contrary, the conditions depicted in the CECA model refer to values of control parameters – this is the *parametric perspective*,
- consequently, changing the system structure is like redesigning, while changing the system parameters is like configuring or tuning.

The discussion regarding these differences leads to the allegory of a production plant, with interactions reflecting machinery or production means and conditions representing production instructions, which describe a specific sequence of interactions required to "produce" the target disadvantages [5]. This decomposition was found to be similar to the hardware-software duality in the IT industry, where hardware units (processors) are used under the control of software. A computer program contains instructions describing which particular operations and in which order they should be executed by hardware to obtain the intended results.

In a state machine model, the states represent interactions and the transitions indicate which interactions are involved in the development of a target disadvantage as well as when (i.e. upon which conditions) the development may progress from one state to another. Using the above-mentioned allegory, we may perceive states as equivalent to hardware and the transitions as equivalent to the software. This analogy encourages us to explore the essential differences between the nature of interactions and conditions beyond the interleaved pattern supporting the proper construction of CECA diagrams.

The possibility of achieving different results using the same hardware controlled by modified software is a distinctive advantage of computers. Changes in the software are in general faster, cheaper, and safer than changes in hardware, because they are easier to design, develop, and test. Due to the non-material nature of software, such changes are also non-destructive and reversible. These advantages became the foundation of the unparalleled success of computers in numerous areas of human activity.

Taking this into account, it seems interesting to check if the paradigm of changing instructions to alter operations of the same hardware may also be applied to the state machine CECA models with noteworthy benefits. In the following sections, we will explore which useful effects may be achieved by changing the structure of interconnections and conditions assigned to the transitions in state machine CECA models.

# 3 State Machine Model and System Operator

The System Operator is known in TRIZ to be a useful tool for breaking the psychological inertia by applying multiple perspectives to describe a problem situation. It is usually shown as a $3 \times 3$ matrix, with the rows reflecting super-system, system, and sub-system level of the hierarchy and the columns reflecting the past, present, and future.

Each of the cells, traditionally called windows, may be used to provide a specific view of a problem or a solution. The structure is generic and so it may be easily expanded to accommodate particular needs or merged with other tools, as shown in [10]. The description of System Operator given in [11] goes even further, indicating that the views in the same row are connected by cause-effect relations. Although it may look similar to a state machine model, which also represents changes in time as states connected by transitions, deeper inspection reveals more differences than similarities.

The purpose of the System Operator is to model the analyzed system at different levels of hierarchy and in different moments in time, including the future. The purpose of a CECA model – also in the state machine notation – is to represent underlying causes of the target disadvantages, so the analysis is focused on the past moments in time and the future behavior of the system is not covered.

Moreover, the columns of the System Operator are like snapshots of different system hierarchy levels taken at the same time, with no support for differentiating the time axes for different levels, and the interconnections are predetermined by the matrix structure. In a state machine CECA model, the structure of interconnections may be arbitrary because the states and transitions are added as needed during the analysis, and transitions are executed upon satisfying conditions, not just because of the time passed.

Therefore it should be noted, that the System Operator (regularly structured and synchronously time-sliced) has a different purpose and properties than a state machine CECA model (with unrestricted structure and many asynchronous time axes).

# 4   State Machine Model and Inventive Principles

Whether the original CECA diagram correctly models system vulnerabilities, or the vulnerabilities are identified during an additional analysis [8], they would presumably be reflected by transitions in the state machine model. To justify this statement, let us remind ourselves that interactions cause changes in control parameters, which are in turn tested by the conditions to decide if the "production" process should proceed to the next stage. Therefore the conditions operate like gates, which enable or disable the development of disadvantages depending on the properties of the system, which characterizes vulnerabilities. To emphasize this behavior, some publications describe transitions as *being guarded* by respective conditions.

Perceiving transitions as conditional gates inspires us to consider some mitigation strategies, such as *blocking* – if we do not allow to satisfy a particular condition, then the transition will not happen, and the development of a disadvantage will not progress. We might also force another condition to be fulfilled before or instead of the one we want to skip, to move the process to another state resulting in:

- *warning* – if the interaction in the achieved state may generate an alert signaling detection of abnormal and potentially dangerous system behavior,
- *avoiding* – if the interaction in the achieved state may prevent further development of unwanted effect by staying in a safe context or applying an "emergency brake",
- *counteracting* – if the interaction in the next state may act as an "emergency valve" correcting or compensating the unwanted changes in the system.

It should be noted, however, that these strategies rely on the availability of the states related to specific interactions to be used for creating required enhancements. In an optimistic scenario, these "useful" states might be discovered during analysis and incorporated into the model. In such a case, the only missing link is a new transition, which should be added into the model and eventually implemented in the analyzed system. Unfortunately, the original CECA method is restricted to revealing system disadvantages, so that interaction or property is documented in a CECA model if and only if it contributes to any of the target disadvantages. This implies that in a realistic scenario some states delivering useful interactions required by the mitigation strategies are probably not present in the model. In such a situation we should add these missing states, which seems to violate the assumption of focusing on the transitions, as the software-like layer of a state machine causality model. We will address this in Sect. 6.

As it was indicated above, changing transitions in a state machine CECA model is like spoiling the recipe for target disadvantages. To approach this task systematically, we may use Inventive Principles as a list of strong generic solutions to choose from:

- for *blocking* the most promising seem *prior anti-action* or *cushion in advance*,
- for *warning* – *copying* or *intermediary*,
- for *avoiding* (by changing order or duration or rhythm of the harmful interactions) – *dynamicity, remove stress, rushing through* or *periodic action*,
- for *counteracting* (by compensating effects of the ongoing harmful interactions) – *feedback, self-service,* or *anti-weight*.

## 5   State Machine Model and Standard Inventive Solutions

In addition to Inventive Principles, another collection of TRIZ "best practices" are Standard Inventive Solutions, which uniformly represent patterns of problems as well as patterns of solutions using Substance-Field (Su-Field) models. To use these solutions, a specific problem identified in the system must be transformed into a Su-Field model first. Then a model of an appropriate solution should be selected. Finally, the chosen Su-Field model of a solution must be converted back into a concept of a specific solution, applicable in a particular problem situation. The original set of 76 solutions developed within classic TRIZ has been expanded with additional items [12] and also transposed from the technical domain into the business and management area [13].

A complete Su-Field model usually reflects two substances participating in the analyzed interaction, and a field of energy involved in this interaction. Standard Inventive Solutions provide an extensive catalog of remedies for typical problems, such as missing substance, missing field, harmful interaction, excessive useful interaction, and insufficient useful interaction. A structured set of solutions is provided for each category of problems, typically in the form of graphical Su-Field models accompanied by guidelines for their application. For example, one of the solutions for eliminating a harmful interaction between two substances is to introduce a protective shield using another substance (standard 1.2.1), as it is shown in Fig. 2.

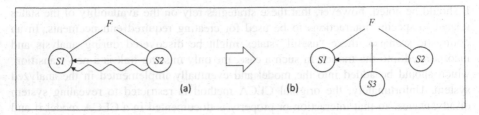

**Fig. 2.** A Su-Field model of a problem: besides a useful interaction between substances *S2* and *S1* through a field *F*, there is also a harmful interaction – indicated with a weaved line (a) and a model of a solution with additional substance *S3* protecting *S1* against the harmful action (b).

It seems that Standard Solutions could be useful for developing a state machine CECA modeling approach in two ways:

- by applying the concept of confronting models of problems with a structured catalog of solutions defined in the model space,
- by adapting selected models from the Standard Solutions collection to be used for extending state machine causality models.

The crucial difference, though, is that a Su-Field model reflects specific interaction(s) performed in the analyzed system (before or after the improvement), while a CECA model represents the development of specific disadvantages, and in the original version of the method does not allow for representing the proper operation of the system. Hence, these methods use different perspectives of the system for different purposes.

The limited scope of CECA models is usually justified in discussions by indicating, that CECA is a dedicated analytical tool, aiming to identify key disadvantages. Period. On the other hand, a typical goal of a TRIZ project is to find a feasible solution to a given problem, and therefore using different tools for analysis and solution generation comes from the limitations of the existing tools rather than methodical advantages. In other words – we need key disadvantages solely as a useful outcome to be taken from one island-like tool to another. From this point of view, any attempt to expand the boundaries of applicability or to integrate existing TRIZ tools appears desirable, or at least interesting.

A well-known CECA extension is the Root Conflict Analysis (RCA+) method [14]. It identifies and documents negative as well as positive effects brought into the system by particular causes, expanding the picture of a problem situation. The causes triggering both positive and negative effects reflect conflicting requirements to remove and to retain particular characteristics of a system. Thus the main added value of RCA+ with respect to CECA is a more complete model of causality with direct support for problem formulation. The RCA+ approach and its visual representation have been further developed as the CECA+ method [15], offering additional annotations to the basic diagram, which may be useful for extending the analysis towards the solution generation.

Taking this into account, let us follow the Standard Inventive Solutions approach and find out which extensions should be introduced into the state machine CECA model to benefit from this paradigm.

# 6   Extending State Machine CECA Model

We will start by reconsidering the interpretation of boxes in a structural CECA diagram. The target disadvantages are, by definition, unwanted in the context of a given project. The root causes, on the contrary, reflect common factors, such as gravity or law. They are neutral by nature and the negative impact of these conditions comes from specific properties of the system, which make it vulnerable to certain root causes.

From the behavioral perspective, a target disadvantage reflects a terminal state, while a root cause reflects an initial state of a particular state machine. Each transition in a cause-effect model advances the disadvantage development process to a "worse" state of the system, since with each "bad" transition we move closer to a target disadvantage. Consequently, the initial state represents the "best" possible system state in a given state machine, before triggering any of the "bad" transitions – i.e. none of the intermediate disadvantages are active yet.

Nonetheless, the root causes have been identified as contributing to disadvantages, so if we would like to represent a proper system operation in the same model, we should add a new state as a common predecessor of all root causes. Because the factors modeled by root causes always apply, the transitions between such primary state and the root causes should be unconditional, and therefore immediate. Although the additional primary state looks to be a rational extrapolation of the system's health status inferred from the root causes, it does not seem to bring any extra value to the model.

The first one of the described strategies is *blocking* i.e. stopping the development of a disadvantage by not allowing it to satisfy the condition guarding transition to the next "worse" state. This equals to virtually removing a respective transition from a state machine model. Taking the risk-based approach we might say, that despite an incident hazard, the unwanted effect does not appear. Such a scenario is equivalent to removing a vulnerability, making the system resistant to a specific interaction modeled by a respective state. For instance, a self-sealing tire remains pressurized despite being pierced by a sharp object. The described situation is shown in Fig. 3a.

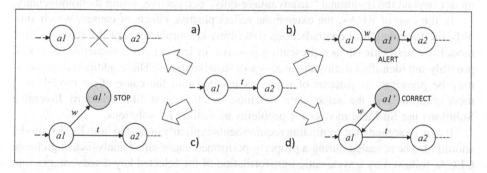

**Fig. 3.** Illustration of changes in a state machine CECA model recommended by the mitigation strategies: *blocking* (a), *warning* (b), *avoiding* (c), and *counteracting* (d). Transition *t* is guarded by a triggering level and transition *w* is guarded by a warning level of the same control parameter.

The *warning* strategy relies on transiting to a state, which can provide an alert signal before an unwanted transition to the next stage of a harmful process, i.e. a different level of the same control parameter is used in the condition guarding respective transitions. Despite activating an alert, the additional state continues previous interaction, so if after crossing the warning level the system operation is not changed, the control parameter will eventually cross the triggering level and the development of a disadvantage will advance to the next stage. For instance, if a driver ignores alerts from proximity parking sensors, the car will keep moving towards an obstacle. This situation is depicted in Fig. 3b.

As was indicated before, the *avoiding* strategy involves choosing "lesser evil" by transiting to a state, which changes the system operation in such a way, that it switches to a safe context. In a state machine CECA model, it is reflected by a transition to another state or a sequence of states, which does not end up with a target disadvantage, and it does not reflect a proper operation either. To remain within automotive examples, this strategy may be seen as turning to a pit stop upon detecting a malfunction instead of continuing driving towards a crash. Such a scenario is pictured in Fig. 3c.

Finally, the *counteracting* strategy employs transiting to a state providing an interaction capable of reverting the control parameter, previously deviated towards dangerous values, back into a safe range. Similarly to *warning* and *avoiding*, this also requires an additional condition which will be satisfied before the "bad" transition is executed. For example, the Anti-lock Braking System (ABS) measures tires skidding and pulses particular brakes respectively, so that vehicle controllability is retained. This strategy is schematically shown in Fig. 3d.

As can be seen, *blocking* is yet another name for the usual approach to eliminating disadvantages, i.e. it aims at removing a cause from a sequence [16]. Consequently, there is no need for any model extensions. The remaining strategies, on the contrary, need additional transitions and, presumably, additional states providing specific interactions required for signaling, skipping, or neutralizing unwanted changes of a specific control parameter. So that the situation seems similar to switching from CECA to RCA+: to increase the functionality of the basic method, we have to extend the model beyond the traditional "disadvantage-only" perspective, losing its homogeneity.

In the case of RCA+, the extensions reflect positive effects of causes, which simplify the formulation of contradictions describing key problems. For the state machine model, we need extensions representing positive (or less negative) sequences of states, possibly not identified during the analysis of disadvantages. These additional elements may be perceived as patterns of solutions inserted into the cause-effect model. And these patterns use the same state machine notation, just like Standard Inventive Solutions use Su-Field models for problems as well as for solutions.

It may be argued, that conflicting requirements explicitly indicated in an RCA+ model should also be revealed during a properly performed cause-effect analysis using classic CECA, followed by a systematic transformation of the selected key disadvantages into key problems formulated as contradictions. This situation appears similar to selecting a regular (though longer) way or a shortcut, depending on personal experience and preferences – and the same may hold true for considered extensions of state machine CECA models.

# 7 Example

To illustrate the proposed approach, we will use a simple cause-effect model adapted from [8], with the description given in the table form to keep Figs. 4 and 5 legible.

**Table 1.** A sample cause-effect chain described using the condition-action approach

| | |
|---|---|
| Action a1 | Vehicle moves along a road |
| Condition c1 | Driver allows tire to ride onto a sharp object lying on the road |
| Action a2 | Tire rides onto a sharp object |
| Condition c2 | External tire layer allows sharp object to penetrate |
| Action a3 | Sharp object thrusts into the tire |
| Condition c3 | Tire body allows sharp object to penetrate |
| Action a4 | Sharp object penetrates the tire body |
| Condition c4 | Internal tire layer allows the object to penetrate |
| Action a5 | Sharp object makes a hole across the tire body |
| Condition c5 | Pierced tire allows pressurized air to come out |
| Action a6 | Pressurized air comes out of the tire |
| Condition c6 | Depressurized tire allows the walls to collapse |
| Action a7 | Depressurized tire collapses under vehicle's weight |
| Condition c7 | Flat tire incurs excessive friction |
| Target disadvantage t1 | Vehicle stops because of a flat tire |

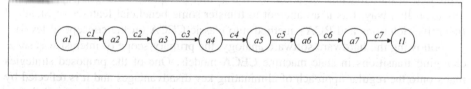

**Fig. 4.** The state machine diagram of the cause-effect chain described in Table 1.

As a rule, all conditions (supposedly reflecting system vulnerabilities) are potential candidates for elimination using the *blocking* strategy. We may, for instance, harden the external layer of the tire to protect it against the sticking of sharp objects.

Reinforcing the tire body or its internal layer could protect the tire against puncture, despite the sticking of sharp objects, while self-sealing tires would minimize the pressure drop and run-flat tires would allow for driving despite a substantial pressure loss. All these approaches fall into the *avoiding* strategy, as we stop the development of a disadvantage at the acceptable level of harm.

We might also think about self-inflating tires, an example of using the *counteracting* strategy, as we actively revert the harm. We could also use a pressure monitoring system, to generate an alert in case of decreased pressure, allowing for early remediation (repairing the puncture before severe tire failure due to collapsed walls), which falls into the *warning* strategy. The state machine model illustrating the mentioned extensions is shown in Fig. 5 along with the labels indicating described solution ideas.

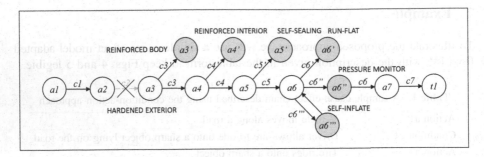

**Fig. 5.** Extended state machine model from Fig. 4 with examples of using mitigation strategies: *blocking* (removed *c2*), *avoiding* (*a3'*, *a4'*, *a5'*, *a6'*), *warning* (*a6''*), and *counteracting* (*a6'''*).

## 8   Conclusions and Further Work

The goal of this research was to extend the state machine CECA approach towards the solution generation stage. It was inspired by the hardware-software duality and unified modeling of problems and solutions used by Standard Inventive Solutions. The former resulted in the analysis of differences between approaches to the elimination of disadvantages represented by states and transitions (redesigning vs. configuring). The latter was used for developing models of solutions for mitigation strategies.

The key outcome of this work is the idea of extending state machine CECA models reflecting the development of disadvantages to represent patterns of generic solutions expressed in state machine notation, as well as four mitigation strategies substantiating this idea. In a way, this is an attempt to transfer some beneficial features of Standard Inventive Solutions and RCA+ method into classic CECA (at the conceptual level).

Following the hardware-software analogy, the primary scope of interest was set at changing transitions in state machine CECA models. One of the proposed strategies maps onto the regular approach of eliminating key disadvantages and it is reflected by removing transitions. The other strategies require adding extra transitions to existing or (more likely) to additional states, reflecting generic solutions.

Further research may address:

- identifying other strategies and developing respective state machine models,
- finding a mapping between mitigation strategies and Standard Inventive Solutions,
- expanding the scope of interest to cover states in addition to transitions,
- developing guidelines for using the proposed approach in specific application areas.

**Acknowledgements.** The author gratefully acknowledges Dr. Oleg Abramov for inspiring discussions about the CECA method and its extensions. Mr. Dariusz Burzyński should be credited for proofreading and enhancing the correctness and clarity of this paper.

# References

1. Litvin, S.S., Akselrod, B.M.: Cause-effects chains of undesired effects, methodical theses. CPB (1996). in Russian
2. Abramov, O.: TRIZ-based cause and effect chains analysis vs root cause analysis. In: Souchkov, V., Kässi, T. (eds.) Proceedings of the TRIZfest-2015 International Conference, Seoul, South Korea, pp. 288–295. MATRIZ (2015)
3. Yoon, H.: Occasion axis and parameter-function pair nexus for effective building of cause effect chains. In: Souchkov, V., Kässi, T. (eds.) Proceedings of the TRIZfest-2014 International Conference, Prague, Czech Republic, pp. 184–194. MATRIZ (2014)
4. Chrząszcz, J.: Modelling CECA diagram as a state machine. In: Cavallucci, D., De Guio, R., Koziołek, S. (eds.) TFC 2018. IAICT, vol. 541, pp. 302–314. Springer, Cham (2018). https://doi.org/10.1007/978-3-030-02456-7_25
5. Chrząszcz, J.: Exploring state machine CECA model. In: Benmoussa, R., De Guio, R., Dubois, S., Koziołek, S. (eds.) TFC 2019. IAICT, vol. 572, pp. 388–399. Springer, Cham (2019). https://doi.org/10.1007/978-3-030-32497-1_31
6. Chrząszcz, J., Salata, P.: Cause-effect chains analysis using Boolean algebra. 16th International TRIZ Future conference TFC 2016. In: Koziołek, S., Chechurin, L., Collan, M. (eds.) Advances and Impacts of the Theory of Inventive Problem Solving, pp. 121–134. Tools and Case Studies, The TRIZ Methodology (2018). https://doi.org/10.1007/978-3-319-96532-1_12
7. Chrząszcz, J.: Quantitative approach to cause-effect chains analysis. In: Souchkov, V. (ed.) Proceedings of the TRIZfest–2017 International Conference. Krakow, Poland, pp. 341–352. MATRIZ (2017)
8. Chrząszcz, J.: Indicating system vulnerabilities within CECA model. In: Mayer, O. (ed.) Proceedings of the TRIZfest-2018 International Conference, Lisbon, Portugal, pp. 31–37, MATRIZ (2018)
9. Lenyashin, V., Kim, H.J.: Harmful System – using this concept in modern TRIZ (2006). in Russian. http://www.metodolog.ru/00859/00859.html. Accessed 20 Apr 2020
10. Mann, D.: Hands-On Systematic Innovation for Business and Management. IFR Press, Clevedon, UK (2014)
11. Frillici, F.S., Rotini, F., Fiorineschi, L.: Re-design the design task through TRIZ tools. In: Marjanović, D., Štorga, M., Pavković, N., Bojčetić, N., Škec, S. (eds.) Proceedings of the DESIGN 2016 14th International Design Conference, Dubrovnik, Croatia, pp. 201–210 (2016)
12. Russo, D., Duci, S.: From Altshuller's 76 Standard solutions to a new set of 111 standards. In: Aoussat, A., Cavallucci, D., Trela, M., Duflou, J. (eds.) 13th ETRIA TRIZ Future Conference TFC 2013, Paris, France, pp. 305–315 (2013)
13. Souchkov, V., Roxas, B.: A system of standard inventive solution patterns for business and management. In: Souchkov, V. (ed.) Proceedings of the TRIZfest-2016 International Conference, Beijing, China, pp. 22–34. MATRIZ (2016)
14. Souchkov, V.: Root conflict analysis (RCA +): structuring and visualization of contradictions. In: Proceedings of the ETRIA World Conference TRIZ Future 2005, Graz, Austria, pp. 474–483. Leykam Buchverlag (2005)
15. Lee, M.-G., Chechurin, L., Lenyashin, V.: Introduction to cause-effect chain analysis plus with an application in solving manufacturing problems. Int. J. Adv. Manuf. Technol. 99, 2159–2169 (2018). https://doi.org/10.1007/s00170-018-2217-1
16. Ponomarenko, A.I.: Selecting tasks using the operator of negation of unwanted action. J. TRIZ, 1, 51–53 (1995). in Russian

# Contribution to TRIZ in Combining Lean and Inventive Design Method

Masih Hanifi[1,2,3(✉)], Hicham Chibane[2,3], Remy Houssin[1,3], and Denis Cavallucci[2,3]

[1] Strasbourg University, 4 Rue Blaise Pascal, 67081 Strasbourg, France
[2] INSA of Strasbourg, 24 Boulevard de la Victoire, 67000 Strasbourg, France
Masih.hanifi@insa-strasbourg.fr
[3] ICUBE/University of Strasbourg, 4 Street Blaise Pascal, 67081 Strasbourg, France

**Abstract.** Inventive Design Methodology (IDM) has been developed to provide formalism to classical TRIZ. However, this methodology is perceived as long and tedious by its users with lots of questionable internal activities. Besides, the ability of IDM to give the best result depends on individual knowledge and experiences to provide an accurate initial situation analysis. In parallel to this, lean philosophy is known for combining tools and long-term vision for continuous improvement. It also focuses on removing the non-valuable activities during the process and maximizing the quality of the results. The integration of Lean with the IDM framework led us to propose a new process, which is called Agile Inventive Design Approach (AIDA). In this article, we introduce the initial phase of this new process, and we discuss its differences with other existing methods related to the initial analysis phase of inventive design through a case study.

**Keywords:** Inventive design · Complex problem · Problem Graph · Root contradiction analysis · Network of Problem

## 1 Introduction

Nowadays, companies permanently look for methods to assist problem formulation in the early stage of inventive design due to its impact on the overall success of the process. Among these methods, Network of Problem, Problem Graph, and Root Conflict Analysis play an important role due to their ability to assist contradictions disclosure. Nevertheless, the agility of these methods, particularly Network of Problem, could not meet the needs of today's market. Thus, it was necessary to combine them with other methodologies that give them the characteristics of an agile method-ology, which are the capability of iterative and evolutionary development, the ability to produce a rapid and flexible response to change, the capacity of promoting communication and adaptive planning ability [1]. One of these methodologies, namely Lean, was chosen in [2] to apply its principles to the phases of the Inventive Design Method.

Lean was introduced by Toyota company in the 1950s. It provides principles and tools to decrease time, maximize value, and reduce cost within a process [3].

© IFIP International Federation for Information Processing 2020
Published by Springer Nature Switzerland AG 2020
D. Cavallucci et al. (Eds.): TFC 2020, IFIP AICT 597, pp. 280–291, 2020.
https://doi.org/10.1007/978-3-030-61295-5_23

In our research, we apply Lean principle, particularly the third principle of lean, which is to make the stream of information flow, and to create a pull stream of information, to an integration of the best features of existing methods possessing the ability to formulate problems. Consequently, we built a new method with a suitable agility to improve the initial analysis phase. This proposed method also integrate some solution phase features into the initial analysis phase in order to develop chains of problems only limited to the needs. The paper introduces this lean-based method. Furthermore, it discusses its differences with Network of Problem through a case study. The overall structure of the paper is organized as follows. In Sect. 2, we present the relevant literature. Section 3 presents the steps of our proposition (Inverse Problem Graph). In Sect. 4, a case study is presented in which the proposed method is applied to "Biogas Power Plant". The paper finishes with the discussion and the conclusion in Sect. 5.

## 2 Literature Review and Background

### 2.1 Inventive Design Methodology (IDM)

Before we describe the existing methods to formulate the problems, it is necessary to briefly remind the four phases of the Inventive Design Methodology (IDM) framework [4, 5]. These phases are as the following:

1. Initial Analysis: This phase is to collect all the related knowledge, which comes from tacit know-how of experts, patent and internal documents of the company, and other existing data relating to the subject. Subsequently, this collected knowledge should be converted to a graphical model to facilitate decision-making [6, 7]. Among the applied methods in this phase, Network of Problem (NoP), Problem Graph, and Root Conflict Analysis (RCA+) play a vital role because of their capacity to show the contradictions.
2. Contradictions Formulation: It is the time of formulating the contradictions, which are physical and technical issues in a system [7]. These contradictions are considered as bottlenecks in the development of the system [6]. In the following, the extracted contradictions are applied as an input point to use TRIZ tools.
3. Solution Concept Synthesis: The designers could apply different TRIZ methods and techniques, such as contradictions matrix related to inventive principles to solve technical contradictions, the substance-field modeling related to inventive standards to solve the physical contradictions, and ARIZ-85C [7–12].
4. Solution Concept Selection: Finally, the impact of each solution concept on problem formulation in the Initial Analysis phase should be measured. For this purpose, the external experts should weigh the impact of each concept on the evaluation parameter by filling out an evaluation grid [6].

Our concentration in this article is on the first phase of IDM, which is the first step of "Agile Inventive Design Approach (AIDA)". We will describe other phases in our future papers, which will introduce other steps of AIDA. In the next, we will describe in detail the existing methods to formulate problems in the first phase.

## 2.2    Existing Methods for Formulating a Problem in Initial Situation Analysis Phase

As we explained before, Initial Analysis in the IDM framework is a phase to collect all the existing knowledge related to a subject. Subsequently, designers use a wide range of methods to formulate problems. Here, we describe just the methods with the ability to illustrate the contradictions. According to state of the art, these existing methods, applied for analyzing problems in innovation projects, could be divided into two groups, first methods based on searching for causes, and second methods based on looking for the effects.

Among the methods in the first group, it is possible to indicate Root Conflict Analysis and Cause-Effect Chain Analysis Plus, described in the following.

Introduction of Root Conflict Analysis (RCA+) could facilitate the extraction of contradictions [13–15]. Its process starts with a general problem, placed on top of the diagram [16]. In the following, designers use what-question to discover the causes related to the general problem [16]. The appeared cause could only have a negative effect, which means the chain of cause should be continued until illustrating of a contradiction. The cause could also lead to a positive effect. This type of cause shows contradictions [14]. After completing the first chain, the designers should continue the process until exploring all the causes [17]. RCA(+) could show the contradictions. Nevertheless, this method does not pay attention to partial solutions, which partially solve a problem. Besides, a designer should complete all chains of causes at the beginning of the project without paying attention to their usefulness in the solution step.

Another existing method in the first group is Cause-Effect Chain Analysis Plus [18]. Lee et al. introduced this method, which has a development trend quite similar to RCA+. Indeed, its process starts with a general problem. Subsequently, designers complete the chains of causes related to the first problem until discovering the cause with positive and negative effects in each chain. This method could illustrate the contradictions. Besides, it shows the solving directions to solve them. However, the waste of time for creating unusable chains of causes has been ignored. Furthermore, this method could not show solutions, which could partially solve a problem. It is the reason that the designers need the methods in the second group.

The second group, it includes methods such as Network of Problems (NoP), and Problem Graph, which is an improved version of NoP.

Nikolai Khomenko introduced the Network of Problem (NoP) method to disintegrate an overall problem into a set of sub-problems, which are easier to solve [19–21]. The sub-problems, forming the body of NoP, could be a problem or a partial solution. Development of NoP begins with a collection of the most critical problems and their potential partial solutions, related to the main problem. Then, this collected I formation should be transformed into the network of the problem [22, 23]. In the last step, the most significant problems, creating the bottlenecks in the system, should be extracted. These bottlenecks consist of a series of contradictions, applied to construct the network of contradiction [22, 23]. Nevertheless, a supper problem, selected by the designer according to the guide of NoP, is most of the time too general, which makes the network of problems too large and complex. Furthermore, NoP did not provide a clear definition of the problem and partial solution [20]. Accordingly, Problem Graph was proposed to solve some drawbacks related to NoP.

D. Cavallucci proposed Problem Graph, which is another method in the second group. This method is an improved version of NoP [24–26]. The process of Problem Graph, such as other discussed methods, starts with a general problem. Then, the designers search for the effects of the general problem, which could be a partial solution or another problem. After creating a network of problems and partial solutions, the related parameters should be derived. These parameters are applied in the formulation of contradictions. A problem graph could illustrate the contradictions. However, a designer needs to devote a lot of the time to collect the problems and partial solutions, without paying attention to their effectiveness in the solution phase of inventive design.

As we considered in all the discussed methods, which they could illustrate the contradictions in the Initial Analysis step of inventive design, the waste of time to develop the useless chains of causes has been ignored. Further, the methods do not have suitable agility to respond to the needs of today's market. Accordingly, it was necessary to apply Lean to improve the agility and effectiveness of the process. The result of this application, it was a new agile method to formulate the problems. In the next section, we introduce this method.

## 3  Proposed Method: Inverse Problem Graph

### 3.1  Notions of Components of Inverse Problem Graph (IPG)

The Inverse Problems Graph is constructed with the following types of entities, which are shown graphically in Fig. 4:

1. Problem: In Inverse Problem Graph, a problem is defined as a barrier that restricts the realization of what has to be done. There are 5 types of problems in IPG:
   a. Initial problem: A problem that is located on the first level of the graph, and it is defined by considering the objective of the project.
   b. Harmful problem: A problem that has a harmful effect on the system.
   c. Source of partial solution: A problem, that leads to the partial solution.
   d. Harmful-Useful problem: A problem that has harmful and useful effects on the system. This problem should be converted to a partial solution.
   e. Out-of-capacity problem: A problem that the company does not have the essential capacity to solve it.
2. Partial solution: A phrase that represents knowledge of members of the design team about a patent by the company or its competitors and their experience.
3. Parameters: In an Inverse Problem Graph, there are 2 types of parameters:
   a. Evaluation parameters: the parameters that contribute the designers to evaluate their design choice.
   b. Action parameters: the parameters that their nature lies in the capacity of state modification.
4. Level: the level shows the position of the problem and partial solution in the IPG.
5. Iteration: The number of entries to IPG, to select a contradiction. This notion is added to the structure of the method to create a flow of information.

### 3.2 Process of Inverse Problem Graph

1. Step1: Define the objective of the project : In this step, the objective of the project should be defined according to the problem situation in the system.
2. Step 2: Write the initial problem of Inverse Problem Graph (IPG): Write the initial problem by considering the objective of the project in the first step of the Inverse Problem Graph method.
3. Step 3: Find related problems to initial problems: To find all the problems and partial solutions, it should be asked "what in the Selected-Level cause the initial problem?" "This problem is the effect of what in the Next-level of the graph".
4. Step 4: Grade problems in terms of importance: For all problems in the Selected-Level of the graph, it should be verified, "Which problem is in the border of company's activities?". Besides, it should be asked, "Which problem can bring the most profit with minimal cost to the company?". In each iteration, we should choose the most important problem, by considering the answer to questions.
5. Step 5: Determine the type of the selected problem: For each second-level problem, it should be asked if it is a Harmful-Useful problem, or it is just a Harmful problem. This step includes the following sub-steps:
   a. For a Harmful-Useful problem, it should be converted to a partial solution.
      i. Determine the source of the contradiction: ask the question "What problem in the Next-level of graph cause this partial solution?" "This partial solution is the effect of which problems in the Next-level of the graph?". The result of this sub-step determines the source of contradiction.
      ii. Determine the cause of the source of the contradiction: Ask this question "What problem in the Next-level of graph cause the source of the question?". This step might be done if a designer needs to explore the root conflicts of the source of contradiction after evaluating the concept.
   b. For a Harmful problem, it should be asked this question "What problem in the Next-level of graph causes this problem?".
6. Step 6: Extract the illustrated contradiction from the graph: extract the contradiction of the most important problem to solve. We should consider that each iteration designer can select just one contradiction to receive a flow of information.
7. Step 7: Allocate appropriate parameters: For the problems and partial solution in the selected contradiction, allocate the appropriate evaluation parameter, and the appropriate action parameter. These parameters are applied in the contradiction formulation of inventive design.

## 4 Implementation and Case Study of the Proposed Method

In this section, the proposed method "Inverse Problem Graph" has been applied to a school case study to provide more information that is practical and to evaluate its advantages and limits. However, it is worth noticing that NoP was applied before this case study in [22]. The reason for choosing this subject to highlight the differences between our proposal and NoP.

The considered case study concerns a "Biomass Power Plant" that uses renewable organic waste to produce electricity. Indeed, this plant burns wood waste or other waste to produce steam running the turbines to make electricity. The case study refers to the increase in the efficiency of the power plant. Therefore, the designers should find the causes, which decrease the efficiency of the system. For this purpose, they apply "Inverse Problem Graph", the proposed method in this article. In the following, we explain the application of the steps of the method to this case study.

Step1: According to the process of the Inverse Problem Graph method, in the beginning, the designers should define the objective of the case study. In this case study, the power plant does not have enough efficiency. As a result, designers needed to increase the efficiency of the system, which was defined as the objective of the project, as Fig. 1 shows.

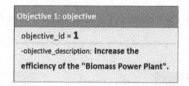

**Fig. 1.** Definition of the objective

Step2 : In the following, the designers should define the initial problem by considering the objective in the first step. In our case, this problem was defined as "The efficiency of the power plant has been reduced". Subsequently, the problem should be written on the left side of the working page.

Step3: After defining the initial problem, it was the time of finding its all the related problems and partial solutions in the second-level of the diagram by applying the question "What in the Selected-Level cause the initial problem?". In the case study of the power plant, the problems "Heat exchanger is used" and "Biogas should be burnt" were illustrated in the diagram of the "Inverse Problem Graph". Figure 2 shows these problems.

Step4: Then, the designers should grade the defined problems in the last step, and select the one, which was the most important with the most profit for them. Accordingly, they selected "Heat exchanger is used", as Fig. 2 shows.

Step5: In the next step, the type of the selected problem should be determined. This problem was a Harmful-Useful problem, which its positive effect was its ability to cooling the biogas, and its harmful effect is the reduction of the efficiency of the power plant. Consequently, this Harmful-Useful problem should be converted to a partial solution. The Fig. 3 shows this conversion. In the following, the source of the partial solution was defined, which was "Biogas should be cooled". Figure 4 shows the Inverse Problem Graph in the first iteration of our case study.

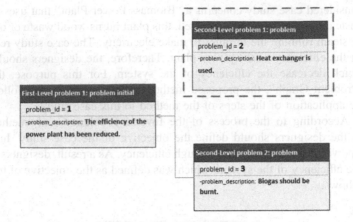

**Fig. 2.** Selection of the most important problem

**Fig. 3.** Conversion of the problem to partial solution

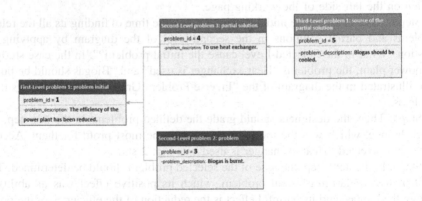

**Fig. 4.** Inverse Problem Graph of the example in the first iteration

Step6: Then, the illustrated contradiction of the most important problem in the diagram should be extracted, as Fig. 5 shows.

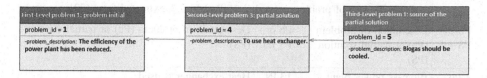

Fig. 5. Extraction of the contradiction

Step7: At the end of the method, the appropriate parameters were allocated to the problems and partial solution of the last step. Figure 6 shows this allocation.

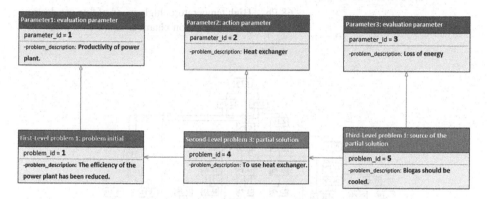

Fig. 6. Allocation of the parameters

## 5 Discussion and Conclusion

As we explained before, NoP was applied to illustrate the related problems to the "Biogas Power Plant" case study, as Fig. 7 and Table 1, which are a proof for Table 2, show. Indeed, Table 1 shows that the phrases, representing problems and partial solutions, do not have the same structure. For example, it is possible to mention the difference between the expressions, illustrating problem one and problem eight, the first one is a sentence, and the second one is a question. The drawback related to the formulation of the phrases of problems and partial solutions has been solved in Inverse Problem Graph. Besides, Table 1 shows that the designers, by applying NoP, need to collect all problems and partial solutions to arrive at a problem in the lower level of a problem situation. For instance, the designers have collected about sixty problems and partial solutions to illustrate contradictions related to problem 68. In Inverse Problem Graph, this shortcoming has been resolved by providing the possibility to start directly from a lower level of a problem situation.

**Table 1.** List of problem related to NoP of Fig. 7, extracted from [23]

| Pb or PS ref. | Description of problem (Pb) or partial solution (PS) | Pb or PS ref. | Description of problem (Pb) or partial solution (PS) |
|---|---|---|---|
| 1.Pb | Biomass power plant should be improve | 13.Ps | Heat exchanger is used |
| ... | ... | ... | ... |
| 5.Ps | Produce clean biogas | 19.Pb | Heat exchanger decreases efficiency of power plant |
| ... | ... | ... | ... |
| 8.Pb | How can one eliminate tar vapour from the biogas? | 22.Pb | It is not so efficient to burn biogas to heat water |
| ... | ... | 68.Pb | High temperature, high speed of flue gas destroy post combustion chamber in the turn place |

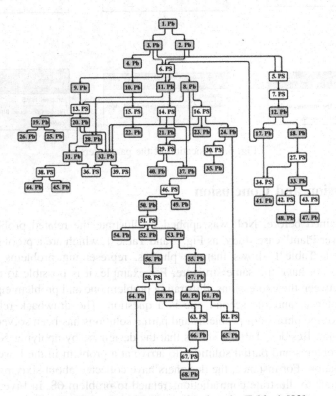

**Fig. 7.** Network of Problem related to the Table 1 [23]

**Table 2.** Comparison of Network of Problem and Inverse Problem Graph

| Criteria | Network of Problem | Inverse Problem Graph |
|---|---|---|
| Structure of problem and partial solution | No specific structure is provided for the problems and the partial solutions | Problems and partial solutions have a specific structure |
| Initial problem | The initial problem is defined too general | The initial problem is defined according to a specific objective |
| Development of the chains of problem and partial solution | Multiplicity of chains because the initial problem is too general | Development of chains according to a specific initial problem |
| Movement to develop the chains | Movement is done from upper-level to lower-level | Movement is done from lower-level to upper-level |
| Impact of final solutions on development of the chains | The final solutions could not be considered during the development of the chains | The final solutions have direct impact on the development of the chains |
| Consideration of usability of the developed chains in the next phase of inventive design | Usability of the developed chains is not considered | Development of the chains should be done according to the need of designer in solution phase |
| Agility of the process in the presence of a contradiction to the next phase of inventive design | The method does not have the essential agility to respond the need of market | Agility of the method has been increased by developing the chains according to the needs and objective |

In this article, we reviewed the existing methods with the ability to demonstrate the contradictions. We concluded that all of them ignored the time spent to collect useless information. Subsequently, we combined the best characteristics of reviewed methods into a new method called Inverse Problem Graph. Additionally, to increase the agility of this proposal, we applied Lean principles to it. Finally, we applied the proposed method to a case study and compared it with Network of Problem, discussed in the literature section.

To summarize we proposed three important contributions to the inventive design process. First, our proposal improve the readability of the created chains by added iteration notion. Second, it supports the contradiction use at the heart of the process. Third and important contribution, our work increase the agility of the inventive design process. Indeed, in all of the reviewed methods, designers need to start with a too general problem, located in upper-level of a problem situation, and construct a complete map of the problem situation by interviewing each expert to extract all of his knowledge, without considering how effective it is in solving the problem, to clarify the situation. This generate time-consuming hours of questionings that often come up against opposition between experts. In Inverse Problem Graph, the process starts from a lower level problem by concentrating on the most significant problem. Then, the designers develop the chains of contradictions according to the needs that come from the solution phase of inventive design.

One of our future investigations is focusing on incorporating our proposal in a process that, along with TRIZ tools, could connect faster the solution phase to the extracted contradiction. The other investigation focuses on automatic extraction of essential information of Inverse Problem Graph by applying machine learning and NLP to make the proposed approach "Agile Inventive Design Approach" more automatic and less depending on human experts.

# References

1. Kumar, G., Bhatia, P.K.: Impact of Agile Methodology on Software Development Process. Int. J. Comput. Technol. Electron. Eng. (IJCTEE), **2**(4), p. 5 (2012)
2. Hanifi, M., Chibane, H., Houssin, R., Cavallucci, D.: Improving inventive design methodology's agility. In: Benmoussa, R., De Guio, R., Dubois, S., Koziołek, S. (eds.) TFC 2019. IAICT, vol. 572, pp. 216–227. Springer, Cham (2019). https://doi.org/10.1007/978-3-030-32497-1_18
3. Chen, H., Taylor, R.: Exploring the impact of lean management on innovation capability. In: PICMET 2009–2009 Portland International Conference on Management of Engineering & Technology, Portland, OR, USA, Août 2009, pp. 826–834 (2009). https://doi.org/10.1109/picmet.2009.5262042
4. Chinkatham, T., Cavallucci, D.: On solution concept evaluation/selection in inventive design. Procedia Eng. **131**, 1073–1083 (2015). https://doi.org/10.1016/j.proeng.2015.12.425
5. Zanni-Merk, C., Cavallucci, D., Rousselot, F.: Use of formal ontologies as a foundation for inventive design studies. Comput. Ind. **62**(3), 323–336 (2011). https://doi.org/10.1016/j.compind.2010.09.007
6. Cavallucci, D., Strasbourg, I.: From TRIZ to inventive design method (IDM): towards a formalization of Inventive Practices in R&D Departments, p. 2 (2012)
7. Cavallucci, D.: Designing the inventive way in the innovation era. In: Chakrabarti, A., Blessing, L.M. (eds.) An Anthology of Theories and Models of Design, pp. 237–262. Springer, London (2014). https://doi.org/10.1007/978-1-4471-6338-1_12
8. Childs, P.R.N.: Mechanical Design Engineering Handbook. Butterworth-Heinemann, Amsterdam (2014)
9. Ilevbare, I.M., Probert, D., Phaal, R.: A review of TRIZ, and its benefits and challenges in practice. Technovation **33**(2–3), 30–37 (2013). https://doi.org/10.1016/j.technovation.2012.11.003
10. Zhang, X., Mao, X., AbouRizk, S.M.: Developing a knowledge management system for improved value engineering practices in the construction industry. Autom. Constr. **18**(6), 777–789 (2009). https://doi.org/10.1016/j.autcon.2009.03.004
11. Gadd, K.: TRIZ for Engineers: Enabling Inventive Problem Solving, pp. i–xviii. John Wiley & Sons Ltd, Chichester (2011)
12. Chou, J.R.: An ARIZ-based life cycle engineering model for eco-design. J. Clean. Prod. **66**, 210–223 (2014). https://doi.org/10.1016/j.jclepro.2013.11.037
13. Dobrusskin, C.: On the identification of contradictions using cause effect chain analysis. Procedia CIRP **39**, 221–224 (2016). https://doi.org/10.1016/j.procir.2016.01.192
14. Souchkov, V.: Application of root conflict analysis (RCA+) to formulate inventive problems in the maritime industry. 51 Sci. J. Marit. Univ. Szczec. **123**(51), 9–17 (2017). https://doi.org/10.17402/225

15. Souchkov, V.: A guide to root conflict analysis (RCA+), p. 26 (2011). http://www.xtriz.com/publications/RCA_Plus_July2011.pdf
16. Abramov, O.Y.: TRIZ-based cause and effect chains analysis vs root cause analysis. In: Proceedings of The TRIZfest-2015 International Conference, 10–12 September 2015, Seoul, South Korea, pp. 283-291 (2015)
17. Gîfu, D., Teodorescu, M., Ionescu, D.: Design of a stable system by lean manufacturing. Int. Lett. Soc. Humanist. Sci. **28**, 61–69 (2014). https://doi.org/10.18052/www.scipress.com/ILSHS.28.61
18. Lee, M.-G., Chechurin, L., Lenyashin, V.: Introduction to cause-effect chain analysis plus with an application in solving manufacturing problems. Int. J. Adv. Manuf. Technol. **99**(9–12), 2159–2169 (2018). https://doi.org/10.1007/s00170-018-2217-1
19. Fiorineschi, L., Frillici, F.S., Rissone, P.: A comparison of classical TRIZ and OTSM-TRIZ in dealing with complex problems. Procedia Eng. **131**, 86–94 (2015). https://doi.org/10.1016/j.proeng.2015.12.350
20. Becattini, N., Cascini, G., Rotini, F.: OTSM-TRIZ network of problems for evaluating the design skills of engineering students. Procedia Eng. **131**, 689–700 (2015). https://doi.org/10.1016/j.proeng.2015.12.356
21. Becattini, N., Cascini, G., Rotini, F.: An OTSM-TRIZ based framework towards the computer-aided identification of cognitive processes in design protocols. In: Gero, J.S., Hanna, S. (eds.) Design Computing and Cognition '14, pp. 99–117. Springer, Cham (2015). https://doi.org/10.1007/978-3-319-14956-1_6
22. Khomenko, N., De Guio, R.: OTSM network of problems for representing and analysing problem situations with computer support. In: León-Rovira, N. (ed.) CAI 2007. ITIFIP, vol. 250, pp. 77–88. Springer, Boston, MA (2007). https://doi.org/10.1007/978-0-387-75456-7_8
23. Khomenko, N., Guio, R.D., Lelait, L., Kaikov, I.: A framework for OTSM TRIZ-based computer support to be used in complex problem management. Int. J. Comput. Appl. Technol. **30**(1/2), 88 (2007). https://doi.org/10.1504/IJCAT.2007.015700
24. Cavallucci, D., Rousselot, F., Zanni, C.: Initial situation analysis through problem graph. CIRP J. Manuf. Sci. Technol. **2**(4), 310–317 (2010). https://doi.org/10.1016/j.cirpj.2010.07.004
25. Howladar, A., Cavallucci, D.: Analysing complex engineering situations through problem graph. Procedia Eng. **9**, 18–29 (2011). https://doi.org/10.1016/j.proeng.2011.03.097
26. Souili, A., Cavallucci, D., Rousselot, F., Zanni, C.: Starting from patents to find inputs to the problem graph model of IDM-TRIZ. Procedia Eng. **131**, 150–161 (2015). https://doi.org/10.1016/j.proeng.2015.12.365

# Quantification of Influences Between Components, Functions and Process Usage Stages by Linking TRIZ Methods and Systems Engineering

Ovidiu Bielefeld[1]($^{(\boxtimes)}$), Vladimir Sizikov[2], Nadine Schlüter[1],
Manuel Löwer[1], Tim Katzwinkel[3], and Arthur Schleicht[2]

[1] Research Group Product Safety and Quality Engineering,
University of Wuppertal, Gaußstraße 20, 42119 Wuppertal, Germany
bielefeld@uni-wuppertal.de
[2] Robert Thomas Metall- Und Elektrowerke GmbH & Co. KG, Hellerstraße 6,
57290 Neunkirchen, Germany
[3] Institute for Product Innovation, University of Wuppertal, Bahnhofstraße 15,
42651 Solingen, Germany

**Abstract.** Due to globalization, individualization, and other global trends, the variety of new functionalities for technical products is constantly increasing, which leads to a complexity that is almost impossible to master. Especially the systematic identification of influences (negative or positive) between functions, components, and process usage stages in a complex technical system is a major challenge for companies particularly in the early phases of (new) product development. At the last ETRIA TRIZ Future Conference 2019, a presented model-based approach showed how using the combination of Systems Engineering (SE) and TRIZ, leads to a quick identification of influences between different types of elements and engineering contradictions. The goal of this research paper is to depict how the systematic identification of influence types (negative or positive) between different types of elements extended the introduced approach. The paper also presents newly developed specific metrics and scales that aim to ensure a representative quantification and to facilitate the identification and prioritization of engineering contradictions in complex products. For the validation of the developed approach, a modern vacuum cleaner with a technically advanced filtering technology (technical functions) is examined and the engineering contradictions in its design are also identified and prioritized. The approach and findings are discussed and further research steps are pointed out.

**Keywords:** System engineering (SE) · System model · Influences · Vacuum cleaner · Function model · TRIZ · Engineering contradiction

© IFIP International Federation for Information Processing 2020
Published by Springer Nature Switzerland AG 2020
D. Cavallucci et al. (Eds.): TFC 2020, IFIP AICT 597, pp. 292–303, 2020.
https://doi.org/10.1007/978-3-030-61295-5_24

# 1 Introduction

Technical innovations since the 1990s, especially information and communication technologies, have allowed technically advanced products with highly integrated functionalities to be offered on the market in series production [1]. This increases product complexity and invokes more engineering contradictions in the product system. With the help of function modeling, different functional models with defined useful and harmful functions are created to visualize engineering contradiction. However, the focus of these function models is on specific aspects (e.g., different target components, harmful functions, etc.). There is no holistic view on the overall system.

Consequently, the overall system or overall model is described using various functional models, neglecting that individual functional models can also influence themselves reciprocally [2]. Therefore, the consideration of several functional models in an overall model and their reciprocal influences represent a present research gap in the research field of TRIZ. Furthermore, there is a lack of a procedure to identify the types of reciprocal functional influences (positive or negative) as well as to evaluate their influence on the overall system quantitatively. This results in the second desideratum in the research field of TRIZ. Evaluation and quantification of reciprocal influences can also help to identify and prioritize the types of influences, e.g., according to critical consequences for the overall system. The initial problems described above and the research gaps mentioned give rise to the following research questions, which will define the content of this paper:

1. Is there an overall model by which all functional models according to TRIZ can be visualized with several target components and also under consideration of the processes (temporal sequences)?
2. Which TRIZ tools are there to prioritize influences or engineering contradictions?
3. How can reciprocal influences (positive or negative) be evaluated or quantified so that enables the prioritization and thus the identification of "weak points" in the overall system?
4. How do these influences affect the overall system? Which influences can have critical consequences on the overall system?

The first research question was answered at the last TRIZ Future Conference in 2019 by presenting an approach for combining SE and TRIZ. With this approach, it could be shown how several functional models have been integrated into an overall model, which is modeled according to the SE fundamentals [2]. In addition to the linked functional models, the overall system contains further relevant aspects for the problem analysis according to TRIZ: target components, components hierarchies, and usability, or process usage stages. Based on the overall model, a goal-oriented analysis could be performed to identify and formulate engineering contradictions [2]. The remaining research questions will be answered in this paper with the aim to systematically identify the positive and negative influences in the overall model, to quantify them, and subsequently prioritize them using a newly developed scaling. To achieve this aim, it is examined if the research questions can be answered with the help of the state of the art in the next chapter. In Sect. 2.1, TRIZ tools for weighting and prioritizing are examined (research question 2). In the research field of SE (Sect. 2.2) it is investigated how influences can be evaluated and quantified as relationships between system elements (research question 3). In the context of SE, system elements are the functions, components, and process usage stages [2]. Besides, it will be investigated if - with the help of the evaluations of the influences - their consequences on the overall system can also be determined (research question 4). In Sect. 3, the extended approach for linking SE with TRIZ will be presented using the Aqua-FreshAir-Box of a vacuum cleaner as an example. Finally, in the last section, the results are discussed and an outlook regarding further research work is given.

## 2  State of the Art

### 2.1  TRIZ Methods for Weighting and Prioritizing of Engineering Contradictions

In this section, it is examined whether the currently available TRIZ methods can be used to weight and prioritize influences between system elements in a technical system (research question 2). Functional analysis (FA), cause and effect analysis (CECA), and root conflict analysis (RCA) are the appropriate methods for analyzing and visualizing the interactions of a technical system [3]. The advantages and disadvantages of FA and CECA have been considered in detail in previous work [2]. Compared to CECA, which describes problem chains, RCA also formulates and analyses engineering contradictions. Besides, the problem to be solved is selected (prioritized) according to two procedures [4]:

1. Elimination of negative causes at the lowest level and
2. Elimination of engineering contradictions at the lowest level.

The procedures have different approaches for the evaluation of the elements. In FA a ranking of the functions is carried out according to their relation to the target component [5]. CECA and RCA divide the problems/causes into levels, with the lowest level (root cause) having the highest importance [4, 5]. However, these approaches do not allow the consideration of several target components and do not allow visualization of the overall model. Further methods have been developed for the holistic consideration of reciprocal influences in a technical system. Here, the General Theory of Powerful Thinking (OTSM) and especially the Inventive Design Method (IDM) are of importance [6, 7]. The methods analyzed how new solutions influence the whole problem model. The assessment of influences in the problem analysis phase, before the solutions are developed, is investigated in further research. Two of them are related to this work:

1. Renauld et al. address the issue of usability with a multi-user approach, in which the relation to several users of a product in different phases of the product life cycle, or with different types of use of the product is examined. Here, the functions, users, and process steps are analyzed. Prioritization of the engineering contradictions is done according to the complementarity with various users [8].

2. Wessner et al. developed a new tool from a combination of three TRIZ tools (FA, RCA, and process analysis) to better understand the hierarchies and interactions in the technical system [9]. A major advantage is the temporal view of the functions through integrated process analysis. Additionally, all findings are integrated into a graphical model, which makes it easier to select the problems to be solved.

In summary, it can be pointed out that the last two research questions (research questions 3 and 4) cannot be answered with the methods examined above. Therefore, in the research field of SE and graph theory, it will be researched how influences can be evaluated and quantified as relations between system elements.

## 2.2 Systems Engineering and Graph Theory for Weighting and Prioritizing of Engineering Contradictions

SE is used to model complex technical products by "decomposing" them, to systematically analyze the relationships between the individual elements, also called system elements. SE helps to better describe and understand technical products because they are transparently visualized in a transdisciplinary model [10]. A characteristic feature of SE is the system description according to Häuslein [11]. A system is described through five characteristics: System-Input and System-Output, Environment element, System boundary, Elements (system elements) and Relations between the elements (see Fig. 1).

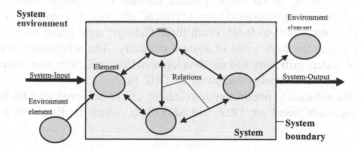

**Fig. 1.** System description according to the principles of the SE (based on [11])

Model-based system engineering (MBSE) is the extended form of the SE. MBSE is used to create a formalized system model, which usually requires a modeling approach and a tool [12]. In the preceding research, Demand Compliant Design (DeCoDe) was selected as the modeling approach [2]. DeCoDe has a standardized description of the elements and relations based on the principles of the SE. In addition, the DeCoDe views (e.g., process, functions, or components) on a technical system have resulted from the domains of classical product development. These views or domains are matrix-based opposed and analyzed. Consequently, DeCoDe has a matrix-based modeling structure that uses the three types of matrices:

- Domain Structure Matrix (DSM): describes the relationship/relation within one view, e.g., functions or features
- Domain Mapping Matrix (DMM): describes the relationship/relation within two views, e.g., components and functions)
- Multi-Domain Matrix (MDM): describes the relationship/relation of more than two views, e.g., components, functions, and processes [13].

The tool for implementing DeCoDe modeling is the LOOMEO® software, which was developed for complexity management. With LOOMEO®, both matrix- and graph-based modeling are possible. The graphical representation in LOOMEO® is based on graph theory [13]. Also, nodes and edges known from graph theory are translated into the language of SE or DeCoDe as follows: nodes as the elements of a system and edges as the relations or relationships between the elements. With LOOMEO® it is possible to weight or evaluate the influences in the form of relations (edges) between the elements. With the help of weighting or evaluation, active and passive sums can be formed. In principle, it can be concluded from the active and passive sums if elements are active or passive in the system. Active means that an element influences another element, passive elements are only influenced by other elements. From the multiplication of the active and passive sum, the so-called "criticality" index is calculated. An element with high criticality is called "critical" [13]. The evaluation of the relations is carried out depending on the purpose of the modeling. The evaluations result in active and passive sums as well as criticality. Regarding the aim of this paper, the influences (positive or negative) can be evaluated and quantified. Furthermore, criticality can be used to identify "weak points" in the overall system. Besides, it can be systematically investigated which influences (relations) have a "critical" effect on the overall system and the "critical" elements linked to them. From these findings, appropriate measures can be derived to reduce the high value of system criticality. The relationship between the reduction of system criticality and the development time and effort also corresponds to the increase of system ideality according to TRIZ [4].

A possible solution to obtain a system ideality can be achieved with the help of the extended approach based on TRIZ and SE/MBSE, which is discussed in the next section.

## 3   Presentation of the Extended Approach for Using and Linking TRIZ and Systems Engineering

In the last TRIZ Future Conference 2019, an approach for linking TRIZ with SE has been presented. The aim was to use the potential of SE/MBSE for TRIZ to transfer different functional models according to TRIZ into an overall model, modeled with SE/MBSE [2]. In addition to the function models, the overall system also includes harmful functions, process usage stages, hierarchy of components, and target components. This enables a comprehensive problem analysis according to TRIZ. It has been shown that the overall model can be used to identify engineering contradictions more quickly and in a problem-specific context [2]. The approach for using and linking TRIZ with SE includes three steps:

(1)  Modeling of the functional model based on TRIZ,
(2)  Modeling of the overall model based on MBSE/SE, and
(3)  Findings from the overall model.

Since the overall system is already provided and also the sufficient information on the system elements (functions, components, target components, and process usage stages) is available in the form of an MDM (steps 1 and 2), the analysis can be enhanced in step 3 [2]. In the previous work, the problem analysis in the third step resulted in the identification of engineering contradictions [2]. Those are considered, in this context, as negative influences on the overall system. But what about the positive influences on the system, which have a positively reinforcing effect, for example on the functions? How can these be identified? How can both reciprocal influences, positive and negative, be identified and quantified in an MDM (see research question 3)? How do positive and negative influences affect the overall system (see research question 4)? With the enhancement of the third step (Findings from the overall model), these questions will be answered.

First of all, it is necessary to develop a scaling or ranking system. This should evaluate or weight the relations (edges) between the system elements so that they can be transparently identified in an MDM as positive or negative influences (*Step 3.1 Evaluation of the relations between the elements*). Based on this evaluation, influences can be visualized in an MDM depending on their type. The focus here is primarily on the engineering contradictions. In particular, the "critical" system elements involved in the engineering contradictions should be identified and prioritized (*Step 3.2 Identification and prioritization of critical elements based on the assessment*). Next, the identified critical elements will be separately analyzed to identify similarities (*Step 3.3 Analysis of the critical elements*). Then, the results should be evaluated (*Step 3.4 Evaluation of the results of the analysis*), so that measures for product development can be derived, for example, to reduce the value of system criticality and thus increase system ideality (see Sect. 2.2). The entire, extended approach is illustrated in the Fig. 2.

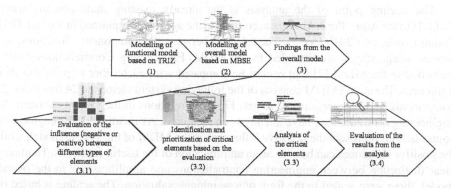

**Fig. 2.** Extended approach for quantification of influences between components, functions and process usage stages by linking TRIZ with SE

For a better understanding, the approach is presented using the Aqua-FreshAir-Box product as an example. The individual, new steps of the approach (3.1 to 3.4) are described below as individual Sects. (3.1 to 3.4) of this chapter.

## 3.1 Evaluation of the Influence (Negative or Positive) Between Different Types of Elements

As a product example, a vacuum cleaner of the brand THOMAS, which uses water as a filter medium, was taken. The primary useful function of a vacuum cleaner is to suction up dirt (coarse and fine particles, as well as hair). Other special functions are: Binding of dry dirt in the water (an advantage for allergy sufferers), wet vacuuming of various surfaces (hard floor, carpet, upholstery, and car seats), and trapping of odor molecules in the water and air refreshment. Using the vacuum cleaner consists of three process usage stages: (1) preparation, (2) vacuuming, and (3) cleaning the filter. Figure 3 shows an example of the filter unit of the Aqua-FreshAir box.

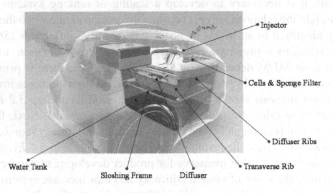

**Fig. 3.** Aqua-FreshAir-Box (selected components of the filter unit)

The starting point of the analysis is the already existing multi-domain matrix (MDM) to the Aqua-FreshAir-Box according to the approach explained in the last TRIZ Future Conference 2019 [see 2]. The relations between the components, functions, and process usage stages are modeled in the MDM. Engineering Contradictions can be identified in the MDM [2], but cannot be compared with each other to prioritize their influences. The actual MDM consists of the following system elements: 24 functions, 23 components, and 3 process usage stages. From the relations of the system elements, 92 engineering contradictions have already been identified. As mentioned, the engineering contradictions represent the negative influences in the MDM of the system model, while the positive influences can be seen as an amplification of the useful functions. To make a clear distinction between engineering contradictions and amplifications in the overall model, these were scaled in the form of a weighing/evaluation. The scaling is based on empirical tests. Several scales have been tested. The following evaluation system is best suited for the aim of the research:

- Negative influence (contradiction between the elements): Value = 10

- Positive influence (amplification of useful functions): Value = 1
- If there is no influence, the relation remains without evaluation: Value = 0

Not only the relations between functions and components are evaluated as in classical TRIZ, but also the relations from the following matrices: function-function, component-functions, process-process, process-component, and process-function. An example of these matrices is the process-process matrix in Fig. 4, which represents the three process usage stages. This shows that the "P3 Cleaning" process step amplifies the "P2 Dirt Suction" process step by emptying the filter unit and returning it to full functionality. Conversely (influence of P2 on P3), an engineering contradiction occurs: When dust is sucked in, cleaning is required.

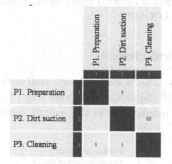

**Fig. 4.** Evaluation of the relations in process-process-matrix for the process usage stages (illustration from LOOMEO®)

Based on the evaluation of the relations (edges) between the system elements, the next step is to identify critical elements by calculating active and passive sums, and criticality of the overall system model.

## 3.2 Identification and Prioritization of Critical Elements Based on the Evaluation

As described in Sect. 3.1, the individual values or weightings influence the overall system. The critical elements are identified based on the active sum and criticality (see Fig. 5).

For the overall system, the criticality has the value 12,060 and the active sum 134. The ranking for criticality (right in Fig. 5) results in a list of critical elements, which are the following functions: F. Dirt suction (Primary useful function), SF. Dirt deposition (primary harmful function), F1.1.4 Dirt stopping, F1.1.5 Dirt transportation, 2.4.1 Water transportation and F2.5.2 Dirt cleaning.

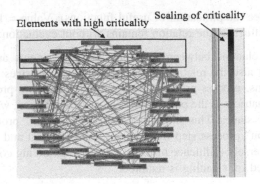

**Fig. 5.** Identification and of critical elements based on the evaluation from criticality in MDM (principle representation from LOOMEO®)

### 3.3   Analysis of the Critical Elements

After being determined, the critical elements are analyzed using the software's focus function. All connections of individual functions (e.g., to components) are analyzed without losing view of the interactions in the overall system (see Fig. 6).

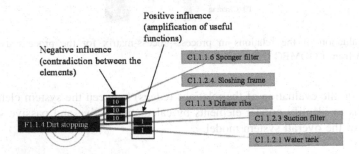

**Fig. 6.** Analysis of the critical element (function: F1.1.4 Dirt Stopping) using the software's focus function (illustration based on LOOMEO®)

As a further step, two procedures, similar to RCA (see Sect. 2.1 and detailed theoretical description in [4]), can be used:

1. Modification of the critical element itself, taking into account all related engineering contradictions. However, this procedure does not solve the complexity of the problem and does not give any indication of the necessary changes. Furthermore, the critical elements listed in Sect. 3.2 are useful functions, which according to classical TRIZ, cannot be modified without consequences.
2. Search and identification of several system elements (functions and components) that are in contradiction with the same critical element. The intention behind this is to ensure that, if the criticality of this critical element is reduced, then the engineering contradictions of several system elements will be reduced as well and thus

the criticality in the overall system model. For this reason this approach seems to be more effective. The engineering contradictions can be quickly identified in the detailed view using the component-functions Matrix. For example function F1.1.4 (see Fig. 4) has engineering contradictions with components C1.1.1.3, C1.1.1.6, and C1.1.2.4.

3. When a new solution for a defined engineering contradiction found, it can have negative influence(s) at any other element. This possibility can be checked, using the MDM-model with integration of new solution.

Compared to RCA and functional analysis, all dependencies in a model are considered with the possibility of zooming or focusing on the critical elements. The detailed view on the functions from the list (see Sect. 3.2) results in 24 engineering contradictions with a total of nine components (see Table 1). Each location with a contradiction is marked with "10" (Negative influence or contradiction between the elements).

**Table 1.** Engineering contradictions of critical elements (functions) with components.

| | F<br>Dirt<br>Suction | SF<br>Dirt<br>deposition | F1.1.4.<br>Dirt<br>stopping | F1.1.5.<br>Dirt<br>transportation | F2.4.1.<br>Water<br>transportation | F2.5.2.<br>Dirt<br>cleaning |
|---|---|---|---|---|---|---|
| C1.1.1.5 Cells | 10 | | | | | |
| C1.1.1.3 Diffuser Ribs | 10 | 10 | 10 | | | 10 |
| C1.1.1.6 Sponge Filter | 10 | 10 | 10 | | | 10 |
| C1.1.2.1 Water Tank | 10 | | | | | |
| C1.1.1.10 Transverse Rib | 10 | 10 | | | | 10 |
| C1.1.1.2 Diffuser | 10 | 10 | | | | 10 |
| C1.1.2.4 Sloshing Frame | 10 | 10 | 10 | | | 10 |
| C1.1.1.1 Injector | 10 | | | | | |
| C1.1.2.3 Suction Filter | | 10 | | | 10 | 10 |

From the table, it can be concluded that three components (C1.1.1.3, C1.1.1.6, and C1.1.2.4) contradict all critical elements (in this case the 6 functions) identified from criticality in step 3.2 (see Table 1). This means, according to the second procedure similar to RCA, that if a solution of the engineering contradictions at these three components is found, at the same time most of the engineering contradictions of the critical elements (6 functions) are solved. This procedure is comparable to the Pareto principle because many engineering contradictions can be solved with low effort.

### 3.4 Evaluation of the Results from the Analysis

Using the new steps above (3.1 to 3.3), the problem analysis focused on the three most important components that have a total of 12 engineering contradictions with critical elements (see 23 components and 92 engineering contradictions for all elements in the whole system). The results of the analysis have the following significance for product development:

- Quantification of the important influences (e.g., of useful and harmful functions) to realize a simple and transparent prioritization of engineering contradictions
- Improvement of functionality and usability while changing the minimum number of components (see the second procedure from step 3.3)
- The most important problems are focused and solved, thus reducing the value of the criticality of the overall system
- Proving of new solution, if it has negative influences (as described in 3.3)
- Once the search for solutions to identified problems is complete, the entire system is modified. The analysis can be repeated for new framework conditions to define new development directions for the future.

## 4   Conclusion and Outlook

The approach presented is based on earlier research in which TRIZ was successfully combined with SE. With the help of the system model, it was possible to identify and analyze engineering contradictions that were, until now, not recognizable in the context of TRIZ problem analysis [2]. In this research, the aim was to systematically identify positive and negative influences in the overall model and to quantify and prioritize them using a newly developed scaling. To achieve this aim, the original approach was extended by four additional steps which were successfully tested using the example of the Aqua-FreshAir-Box in Sects. 3.1–3.4. The following new aspects result from the application of the approach:

- Consideration of all problems in one model: technical functions, components, and usability (process usage stages)
- Identifying the critical elements in the system quickly and systematically, resulting in the prioritization of then for change in product development
- Holistic consideration of all relations in the system: e.g., function-component, function-function, function-process and process-component with their reciprocal interactions considered
- Tracing of changes throughout the system. Positive influences (e.g., useful functions) are also taken into account in the analysis and search for solutions to engineering contradictions
- Information from an MDM can be used, specifically for long-term planning of subsequent steps in product development.

These work results are important for product development because of the focus on the essential problems (engineering contradictions and influences) and the quick identification of potential weaknesses in the product system which help saving time and resources. These positive results encourage future work on the approach to linking SE with TRIZ. A focus of further research work is the presented evaluation or weighting of the influences (relations) between the system elements.

That should be more detailed, e.g., to assess the engineering contradictions (negative influences) between each other. Based on this, a faster prioritization between the contradictions can be carried out, because until now all engineering contradictions in the system have the same priority.

Furthermore, it is to be examined whether the approach presented is also suitable for the manufacturing processes. This is because of the purchase of raw materials and semi-finished products generates costs, especially when the product becomes more complex. These costs can be taken into account in the problem analysis if manufacturing processes are modeled in MDM.

# References

1. Schmidt: Ein systemdynamischer Ansatz, S.: Die Diffusion komplexer Produkte und Systeme. Gabler Verlag, Wiesbaden (2009)
2. Bielefeld, O., Sizikov, V., Schlüter, N.: Research of the possibilities for using and linking TRIZ methods with systems engineering. In: Benmoussa, R., De Guio, R., Dubois, S., Koziołek, S. (eds.) TFC 2019. IAICT, vol. 572, pp. 174–186. Springer, Cham (2019). https://doi.org/10.1007/978-3-030-32497-1_15
3. Verein Deutscher Ingenieure (VDI)-Standard 4521 Sheet 1, VDI, Düsseldorf (2016)
4. Verein Deutscher Ingenieure (VDI)-Standard 4521 Sheet 2, VDI, Düsseldorf (2018)
5. Ikovenko, S., et al.: State-of-the-Art-TRIZ, Theory of Inventive Problem Solving, A Guide for Level 1 certification by the International TRIZ Association. MATRIZ, Novismo, Warsaw (2019)
6. Cavallucci, D., Fuhlhaber, S., Riwan, A.: Assisting decisions in Inventive Design of complex engineering systems. Procedia Eng. **131**, 975–983 (2015)
7. Chibane, H., Dubois, S., De Guio, R.: Automatic Extraction and Ranking of Systems of Contradictions Out of a Design of Experiments. In: Cavallucci, D., et al. (eds.) TFC 2018. IAICT, vol. 541, pp. 154–164. Springer, Cham (2018). https://doi.org/10.1007/978-3-030-02456-7_23
8. Renaud, J., Houssin, R., Gardoni, M., Nour, M.: Multi-users of a product: emergence of contradictions. In: Cavallucci, D., et al. (eds.) TFC 2018. IAICT, vol. 541, pp. 154–164. Springer, Cham (2018). https://doi.org/10.1007/978-3-030-02456-7_13
9. Wessner, J.: TRIZ - time and fault tree analysis with function analysis. In: Souchkov, V., Mayer, O. (eds.) The 15th International Conference TRIZfest-2019, September 11–14, 2019, Heilbronn, Germany, Conference Proceedings, pp. 391–398 (2019)
10. Winzer, P.: Generic Systems Engineering - Ein methodischer Ansatz zur Komplexitätsbewältigung. Springer Vieweg Verlag, Heidelberg (2016). https://doi.org/10.1007/978-3-642-30365-4
11. Häuslein, A.: Systemanalyse: Grundlagen, Techniken, Notierungen, p. 29. VDE-Verlag, Berlin (2004)
12. Echterhoff, O.: Systematik zur Erarbeitung modellbasierter Entwicklungsaufträge; Dissertation; Verlagshaus Monsenstein und Vannerdat OHG; Paderborn (2016)
13. Lindemann, U., Maurer, M., Braun, T.: Structural Complexity Management. Springer-Verlag, Berlin Heidelberg (2009)

# TRIZ and Complexity

# Network of Contradictions Analysis in Marketing Information Quality Management

Joanna Majchrzak[✉] and Marek Miądowicz

Poznan University of Technology, 5 M. Skłodowska-Curie Square,
60-965 Poznan, Poland
joanna.majchrzak@put.poznan.pl

**Abstract.** The aim of this paper is to develop the method for network of contradiction analysis and improve the marketing information quality management. The issue of information is discussed. The information is considered as an abstract system and the marketing information is the variant form of this system. The reference to the basis of Classical Theory of Inventive Problem Solving (TRIZ) and General Theory of Powerful Thinking (OTSM) is made. The method of representing and selecting appropriate subset of contradictions among a complete set of contradictions within technical systems is presented. The principles and operations of Qualitology, Grey System Theory and Statistics are applied to adjust the method to guide the problem solver in choosing the most important contradictions within the abstract system of marketing information. The developed method for network of contradiction analysis in marketing information quality management was applied in the sales department of a manufacturing company. It is noticed that the selected subset of contradiction is to be further faced with ARIZ85-C. The analysis of the possibilities of the concept of the ARIZ85-C algorithms application to provide the best approach to be followed in solving the inventive problems in abstract system of information is the objective for the future studies.

**Keywords:** TRIZ · Contradiction cloud · Marketing information · Quality management

## 1 Introduction

Information is a complex concept, occurring in various fields so it is difficult to find one joint mapping of the interpretations of this concept. In the most general terms, the concept of information is understood as a basic element of our mental activity. We create information, distribute it remotely, and receive it from everywhere [20]. In the study of information, two different perspectives can be distinguished, the first, proposed by two Swedish specialists, is the infological perspective related to the person who created or received the information [21, 28]. The second datalogical, in which information is assumed to be independent of the recipient's mind. This work adopts an infological approach. We assume that the observer, $U$, deals with some fragment of reality, $R$, which in consequence causes that in his mind a specific mapping (reflection,

© IFIP International Federation for Information Processing 2020
Published by Springer Nature Switzerland AG 2020
D. Cavallucci et al. (Eds.): TFC 2020, IFIP AICT 597, pp. 307–320, 2020.
https://doi.org/10.1007/978-3-030-61295-5_25

content, description) of this fragment arises, the so-called infological model of $R$ reality in $U's$ consciousness [27].

Marketing information is treated as a distinctive piece of information, considering the objective and subjective criterion. Referring to the objective criterion for determining marketing information, it is assumed that this is a kind of information that maps individual elements of the marketing mix. The marketing mix model has been developed in numerous studies, shaping various models of marketing composition [14]. In subject literature and practice of marketing activities, the most often referred to is the marketing mix model proposed by McCarthy [26], the so-called four $Ps$ of marketing: product, price, promotion, and place. The marketing mix model proposed by McCarthy [26] is adopted as the objective criterion for marketing information classification. Referring to the criterion of subjective determination of marketing information, it is assumed that this is a kind of information that is created, transmitted, or received by entities in the structure of marketing relations. Evert Gummesson [15], one of the creators of the concept of relationship marketing, specifies thirty types of relationships in the structure of marketing relationships, e.g., the relationship between the supplier and the customer, the interaction between the customer and front line personnel, the relationship between internal and external customers, internal marketing relationships with the "employee market", the non-commercial relationship, quality providing a relationship between production and marketing, the relationship to the customer's customer, the green relationship, the knowledge relationship etc. In the subject criterion, the collection of thirty types of relationships in the structure of marketing relationships is applied.

In the following chapters, referring to the basics of Classical Theory of Inventive Problem Solving (TRIZ) and General Theory of Powerful Thinking (OTSM) which develops Classical TRIZ [17], it is presented how to improve marketing information quality management. The aim of the works is to adapt and apply the method for representing and selecting problems through contradictions clouds [11, 12] at the planning stage, i.e., research, analysis and design of the intangible (abstract) marketing information system. Referring to the quite simple statement "the inventor must find and remove the technical contradictions" [3] to present an inventive solution. Theory for solving problems, Classical TRIZ and OTSM, is primarily intended for engineers. However, it is indicated that it will be available and understandable to people who do not deal with technology [13]. The set of principles of thinking management in solving inventive principles (just principles rather than specific formulas and rules) developed within the theory should then be referred to other fields and used to organize creative thinking related to any area of human activity [2]. In order to refer to the selected method for representing and selecting problems through contradictions clouds in marketing information quality management the need to use methods and instruments to model abstract systems is noticed. In this work, reference is made to the selected methods and instruments of such as theories as: Marketing Management, Qualitology, AIMQ methodology, Grey Systems Theory and Statistics.

# 2 The Concept of Contradiction Cloud

TRIZ is a theory for solving problems during the inventive process which was developed by Genrich Saulovich Altshuller between 1946 and 1998. It provides methodology and set of instruments to guide and support creative technical activities with systematic means [10, 17]. The classic theory of TRIZ is based on three postulates, i.e., the postulate of objective laws of system evolution, the postulate of contradiction, the postulate of specific situations [18]. The adoption of the above postulates constituted the basis for the development of individual methods and set of instruments, such as: a System of 8 Laws of Engineering System Evolution and the TRIZ System of Standard Solutions for Inventive Problem Solving, instruments for dealing with contradictions (ARIZ85C - a meta-method using most of the basic TRIZ instruments), the TRIZ System of Standards (typical solutions), the analysis of available resources of the specific situation in order to study the situation and to construct a satisfactory solution. OTSM develops Classical TRIZ ideas further to propose instruments, to deal with non-typical complex interdisciplinary problem situations, which refer to the four main technologies: New Problem technology, Typical Solution technology, Contradiction technology and Problem Flow technology. These technologies are integrated into the Problem Flow Networks approach (PFN), including four kinds of networks: Network of Problems, Contradiction Network, Parameter Network (Specific) and Parameter Network [17, 18].

In this paper, we present a method for adaptation and application of the concept representing and selecting problems through contradictions clouds [11] in Contradiction Network. The method guides the problem-solving process in eliciting a set of technical contradictions [7, 8, 12]. In the concept of contradiction cloud, the acquisition of contradictions (i.e., the specific processes allowing the emergence of parameters related with the studied system) can be specified. Here, the three principal stages are identified, such as the description of a first set of parameters by the comprehension of past-present evolution dynamics of a given system (reference to the Multi-Screen Analysis), description of a second set of parameters by studying the positioning of the system through Laws of Engineering Systems Evolution, and differentiating the Active Parameters (APs) from the Evaluating Parameters (EPs). Following these stages, the APs are associated with the EPs by means of their respective Values (Va and Vā). Then, the contradictions are differentiated by referring to particular characteristics associated to values, and finally to a graphical representation. Three elements of contradiction characteristics are distinguished, i.e., Importance, Universality and Amplitude. In the differentiation of contradiction by the importance, it is assumed that the contradictions components, i.e., an Active Parameter and a pair of Evaluating Parameters, do not have the same importance. The several Evaluating Parameters might characterize the essentials of the problem more than the others, thus, the qualitative value is associated to each Evaluating Parameters which compose a group of contradictions. As a result, the EPs are placed in a relative scale of importance (for example, from 1 to 3, [8]). Then, the role of the Active Parameter within a contradiction is differentiating referring to the potential impact that this $AP_i$ (set at Va and Vā) will have on the problems to which it is related. The range form 0.5 (weak impact) to 2 (strong impact) is used. Importance of contradiction, $X$, which stands for the association of an $AP$ and its pair of opposite $EPs$, is calculated according to the following formula:

$$X = \alpha AP_x(Coef.EP_n + Coef.EP_m).$$  (1)

Where:

$\alpha$: the multiplying coefficient applied to the concerned $AP$,

$Coef.EP_n$ and $Coef.EP_m$: the two values of relative importance for each $EP$ simply added.

In the differentiation of contradiction by the universality, it is noticed that $EPs$ seem to appear in a recurring way in a large amount of contradictions. The universality, $Y$, is measurement of the occurrences, $QEP_x$, of the $EP$ in a set of contradictions. The universality criterion, $Y$, takes the following form:

$$Y = QEP_n + QEP_m.$$  (2)

Where:

$QEP_n$ and $QEP_m$: correspond to the quantity of occurrence the $EP$ has in a set of contradictions.

In the differentiation of contradiction by the amplitude the sum of $EPs$ pairs each $AP$ is attached to within a contradiction group is calculated. The following formula is proposed for, $Z$, the criterion of amplitude:

$$Z = \sum C[EP_n; EP_m] \in AP_x.$$  (3)

Where:

C: represents any couple $EP_n$, $EP_m$.

The computed value of the $X$ and $Y$ is placed in Cartesian coordinate system, and the value, $Z$, corresponds to the length of diameter of a $XY$ dots (circles).

In order to apply the above procedure for the purposes of representation and classification of contradictions in marketing information system (intangible, abstract system) the need to introduce additional actions and tools is noted. In the next chapter the set of actions and tools will be proposed to enable the adaptation and application of the concept representing and selecting problems through contradictions clouds in information quality management.

## 3   The Concept of Contradiction Cloud in Abstract System

In order to adjust the method for representing and selecting problems through contradictions clouds in marketing information quality management the selected methods and instruments to model abstract systems are used. At the stage of determining active parameters ($APs$) and evaluation parameters ($EPs$), in the abstract system of marketing information, the reference to the basics of qualitology is made. In this theory, it is assumed that the category of quality can fulfil a general, relevant, and universal cognitive (epistemological) function in relation to each subject [9, 19, 25]. The theoretical foundations for the quantitative (numerical) method of quality assessment, i.e., the "science of quality measurement" are developed within an independent scientific discipline which is called qualimetry [4–6]. At the stage of determining parameter values, AIMQ [22] is used, i.e., a methodology for information quality assessment. In the AIMQ methodology information quality (IQ) is represented by the product quality and service quality. Product quality includes dimensions related to product features (involves the tangible measures of accuracy, completeness, and freedom from errors). Service quality includes dimensions related to the service delivery process (addressing the intangible measures of ease of manipulation, security, and added value of the information to consumers). The AIMQ instrument measures IQ for each of the IQ dimensions [16, 22, 29]. At the research stage, the association between *APs* Values (*Va* and *Vā*) with the *EPs* refers to the Statistical Correlation Analysis, i.e., the measure of the linear relationship between two variables [1]. At the stage of calculating differentiation characteristics, i.e., Importance, the reference is made to Grey Incidence Analysis of Grey Systems Theory. Grey Systems Theory was created in China by a Chinese scholar, Professor Deng Julong. What distinguishes grey methods is the fact that they entitle to inference based on incomplete ($n \geq 4$), uncertain and few information about the systems being studied. The fundamental idea of grey incidence analysis is that the closeness of a relationship is judged based on the similarity level of the geometric patterns of sequences curves, which map the variables values (parameters) [23, 24]. The sequence of actions proposed to represent and classify technical contradictions in abstract system is presented below.

## 1. The Acquisition of Contradictions

**Stage 1.1. The description of a set of parameters by the category of quality.**
The system of information quality, *IQ*, is expressed as a set of features belonging to it.

$$\mathrm{IQ} = \{c_1, c_{...} c_n\}. \tag{4}$$

Where:

$c_1, c_{...} c_n$: *a set of features belonging to the information.*

**Stage 1.2. The differentiation of the *APs* from the *EPs* and measuring their value.**

The commonly observed phenomenon of the relationship between features justifies the division of features into explanatory ($IQ^{AP}$, Active Parameters) and explanatory ($IQ^{EP}$, Evaluation Parameters) sets of features.

$$IQ^{AP} = \{c_1^{AP}, c_{...}^{AP}, c_n^{AP}\}, IQ^{EP} = \{c_1^{EP}, c_{...}^{EP}, c_n^{EP}\}. \tag{5}$$

Where:

$c_1^{AP}, c_{...}^{AP}, c_n^{AP}$: set of features taking the form of Active Parameters belonging to the information.

$c_1^{EP}, c_{...}^{EP}, c_n^{EP}$: a set of features taking the form of Evaluation Parameters that belong to information.

The information quality model of AIMQ methodology is applied to determine the above sets of features. In this model, for specific features of information, Cronbach alphas were computed, factor analysis was performed, and features that did not add to the reliability of the scale or did not measure the same construct were eliminated. A questionnaire for assessing the actual state of the parameters was prepared, including a set of questions to assess the state of the fifteen adopted features that belong to the information, and a 0 to 10 scale where 0 is not at all and 10 is completely [16, 22].

**Stage 1.3. Measuring values and determining association of *APs* with the *EPs* by means of their respective Values (*Va* and *Vā*).**

In order to identify the association of *APs* values (*Va* and *Vā*) with the *EPs* the analysis of correlation is applied. The analysis of phenomena correlations using the Pearson's linear correlation coefficient is used:

$$X_i = (x_i(1), x_i(1), \ldots, x_i(n)),$$

$$Y_j = \left( y_j(1), y_j(1), \ldots, y_j(n) \right).$$

$$r = \frac{SS_{XY}}{\sqrt{SS_X SS_Y}}. \tag{6}$$

*Where:*

$X_i$: *the behavioral sequence of the active parameter (AP_i)* with the *k*th observation values being    $x_i(k)$, $k = 1, 2, \ldots, n$.

$Y_j$: *the behavioral sequence of the active parameter (EP_j)* with the *k*th observation values being    $y_i(k)$, $k = 1, 2, \ldots, n$. The observation value may refer to observation system at time moment $k$, at the criterion $k$, or observation of the parameters of the *k*th system [23].

$SS_X SS_Y$: standard deviation of independent variables $x$ and dependent variables $y$.

The Pearson correlation coefficient $r$ takes values in the range of variability from -1 to 1. Depending on the practical situation involved, the value of the correlation coefficient is determined, $r'$, which is considered significant, i.e., indicating a significant, for reasons of the study, relationship between two variables. The sign of the $r$ Person correlation coefficient informs about the direction of correlation. The recognized character of features put together allows for identification of the Network of Contradictions. The existence of a correlation between two variables does not in itself mean that one variable is the cause of another. Determining causality will be recognized by using Grey Incidence Analysis.

## 2. The Differentiation of Technical Contradictions
## 2.2. First Differentiation: Importance

Knowledge of importance of individual evaluation parameters, *EPs*, and the strength of the impact of individual active parameters *APs* on *EPs* values, in the case of an abstract information system, is incomplete and uncertain. The Grey Incidence Analysis method is used to analyse relationships in such systems. The axioms of the Degree of Grey Incidence imply that any two sequences of a system (*APs* sequence and *EPs* sequence) cannot be absolutely not related. The property of wholeness reflects the influence of the environment on comparison of the grey incidence. When the environment (other parameters within the system, or supersystem) changes, the degree of grey incidence also changes [23, 24]. The steps of Grey Incidence Analysis are presented below.

**Step 2.2.1.** Find the initial image (or average image) of each sequence.

$$X_i D_1 = (x_i(1)d_1, x_i(1)d_1, \ldots, x_i(n)d_1), \quad Y_j D_1 = \left( y_j(1)d_1, y_j(1)d_1, \ldots, y_j(n)d_1 \right),$$

$$x_i(k)d_1 = \frac{x_i(k)}{\bar{X}_i}, \quad y_j(k)d_1 = \frac{y_j(k)}{\bar{Y}_j}. \tag{7}$$

**Step 2.2.1.** Find difference sequence. Denote:
$$\Delta_i(k) = \left| x_i(k)d_1 - y_j(k)d_1 \right|,$$

$$\Delta_i = (\Delta_i(1), \Delta_i(2), \ldots, \Delta_i(n)), \tag{8}$$

for $i, j = 0, 1, 2, \ldots m$.

**Step 2.2.3.** Find the maximum and minimum differences. And write:

$$M = max_i max_k \Delta_i(k), \quad m = min_i min_k \Delta_i(k). \tag{9}$$

**Step 2.2.4.** Find incidence coefficients.

$$\gamma_{ij}(k) = \frac{m + \zeta M}{\Delta_i(k) + \zeta M}, \tag{10}$$

for $\zeta \in (0, 1)$, $k = 1, 2, \ldots, n$; $i, j = 1, 2, \ldots, m$.

**Step 2.2.5.** Compute the degree of incidence.

$$\gamma_{ij} = \frac{1}{n} \sum_{k=1}^{n} \gamma_{ij}(k) \tag{11}$$

for $i, j = 0, 1, 2, \ldots, m$.

**Step 2.2.6.** Calculate the value of first contradiction differentiation: Importance (see Formula 1, here indicated by the symbol *Imp*).

$$\text{Imp.} = \alpha AP_i \left( \text{Coef.EP}_{j1} + \text{Coef.EP}_{j2} \right), \tag{12}$$

$$\alpha AP_i = \frac{1}{m} \sum_{j=1}^{m} \gamma_{ij},$$

$$\text{Coef.EP}_j = \gamma_{ij}.$$

$\alpha$: the multiplying coefficient applied to the concerned *AP* calculated as **the sum of the degree of incidence coefficients $\gamma_{ij}$ between $AP_i$ and $EPs$ occurring in a given set of contradictions**. Here, the property of wholeness is considered, i.e., the strength of $AP_i$ impact on each of $EPs$ (for which a significant correlation value has been identified (see Stage 1.3) is computed.

Coef.EP$_j$: *the value of degree of incidence coefficient* $\gamma_{ij}$ between *EP$_j$* and *AP$_i$*.

*Coef. EP$_{j1}$* and *Coef. EP$_{j2}$*: the two values of degree of incidence of *EPs* with *AP$_i$* simply added.

**2.2. Second differentiation: Universality** (see Formula 2), where *Y* is referred to as *Univ.*.

**2.3. Third differentiation: Amplitude** (see Formula 3), where *Z* is specified as *Amp.*

**3. Graphical Representation of Technical Contradictions**

The computed value of the *Imp.* and *Univ.* is placed in Cartesian coordinate system, and the value, *Amp.*, corresponds to the length of the diameter of *Imp.* and *Univ.* dots (circles).

The developed method of representing and classifying contradictions was used in marketing information in the sales department of a manufacturing company operating in the medical products and equipment industry. Referring to the characteristics of information adopted in this work, it is pointed out that it is information about the company's product, transferred within relationship between production and marketing department.

# 4    Application: Case Study of Products and Equipment Industry

The questionnaire of AIMQ methodology was delivered to the sales department of a manufacturing company operating in the medical products and equipment industry. The sales department consists of domestic sales department, export sales department and sales support department. Export department currently hires 8 area managers, and these are the individuals who were asked to participate in the survey. The sales department in the given company participates in information exchange between virtually all other company's departments. In this specific case, however, the evaluation of information quality pertains to information received from one of the company's project groups responsible for designing and launching a new version of a product that best responds to the needs of medical facilities in the time of a Covid19 pandemics. Due to the urgency of product's delivery to final users, the project group was working under tremendous time pressure, which naturally resulted in less detailed and less profound description of the product in materials presented to the sales department, however, the questionnaire respondents were well aware of the circumstances and therefore should be considered less demanding than in normal cases. The information provided by the project team was of various nature, including technical documentation, product specification, production costs valuation, detailed product training, benefits compared to competitive solutions, answering specific technical questions received from potential customers, delivery time, technical requirements on site, etc. The general perception of the sales department members was that the information provided by the project group was in majority insufficient and incomplete, which largely hindered their ability to perform professionally in front of their customers and business partners and altogether made them feel uneasy, however this perception also varied between individuals. The latter could have been the product of the learning curve phenomenon in the project team, whose members used the experience, gained in handling initial inquiries from sales department and quickly supplemented and improved the information and materials they were sharing later. Altogether a total of 8 questionnaires were distributed among export department employees, which covered the entire population in this research group. All of them returned the properly filled in questionnaires within one week.

**Result 1. The acquisition of contradictions**
**Result 1.1. The description of a set of parameters by the category of quality.**

IQ = {Appropriate Amount, Interpretability, Objectivity, Relevancy, Understandability, Completeness, Concise Representation, Consistent Representation, Free of Error, Security, Timeliness, Accessibility, Believability, Reputation, Ease of Operation}.

**Result 1.2. The differentiation of the *APs* from the *EPs* and measurement of their value.**

$IQ^{AP} = \{c_1^{AP}$ : Security, $c_2^{AP}$ : Timeliness, $c_3^{AP}$ : Accessibility, $c_4^{AP}$ : Believability, $c_5^{AP}$ : Reputation, $c_6^{AP}$ : Ease of Operation$\}$, $IQ^{EP} = \{c_1^{EP}$ : Appropriate Amount, $c_2^{EP}$ : Interpretability, $c_3^{EP}$ : Objectivity, $c_4^{EP}$ : Relevancy, $c_5^{EP}$ : Understandability, $c_6^{EP}$ : Completeness, $c_7^{EP}$ : Concise Representation, $c_8^{EP}$ : Consistent Representation, $c_9^{EP}$ : Free of Error$\}$.

The assess of actual state of each *APs* and *EPs* calculated as an average rating of individual items:

$$c_1^{AP} = AP_1 = (7.5, 7.3, 8.5, 7.3, 8.3, 7.5, 8.0, 6.8),$$

$$c_2^{AP} = AP_2 = (7.2, 7.8, 7.8, 7.2, 7.8, 6.8, 7.2, 7.2),$$

$$c_3^{AP} = AP_3 = (6.0, 6.0, 7.0, 6.7, 5.2, 5.5, 7.2, 6.5),$$

$$c_4^{AP} = AP_4 = (5.0, 5.5, 6.0, 5.8, 5.3, 5.5, 5.3, 6.3),$$

$$c_5^{AP} = AP_5 = (3.3, 3.8, 3.8, 3.5, 3.5, 4.0, 3.5, 3.5),$$

$$c_6^{AP} = AP_6 = (5.0, 5.8, 5.2, 4.8, 5.0, 5.4, 5.0, 4.8),$$

$$c_1^{EP} = EP_1 = (5.5, 5.0, 7.3, 4.8, 4.8, 6.0, 6.5, 6.3),$$

$$c_2^{EP} = EP_2 = (6.2, 8.0, 7.4, 6.6, 7.6, 6.6, 7.4, 6.6),$$

$$c_3^{EP} = EP_3 = (8.0, 8.5, 8.0, 7.5, 9.3, 8.5, 8.0, 8.5),$$

$$c_4^{EP} = EP_4 = (8.5, 9.5, 9.0, 9.3, 9.3, 8.5, 8.5, 8.3),$$

$$c_5^{EP} = EP_5 = (8.3, 8.8, 8.5, 8.3, 8.5, 8.5, 8.8, 9.0),$$

$$c_6^{EP} = EP_6 = (3.5, 4.5, 3.7, 4.3, 3.7, 3.0, 3.8, 4.3),$$

$$c_7^{EP} = EP_7 = (6.3, 7.3, 7.8, 6.8, 7.5, 7.5, 6.8, 7.0),$$

$$c_8^{EP} = EP_8 = (7.8, 8.0, 8.0, 8.3, 8.3, 7.3, 8.8, 7.8),$$

$$c_9^{EP} = EP_9 = (5.8, 6.3, 6.8, 6.5, 6.5, 6.8, 6.8, 6.3).$$

The association of $APs$ values ($Va$ and $V\bar{a}$) with the $EPs$ computed based on the results of the analysis of phenomena correlations using the Pearson's linear correlation coefficient is presented in the Table 1.

**Table 1.** The results of the correlations analysis between $AP_i$ values with the $EP_j$.

| $r$ | $EP_1$ | $EP_2$ | $EP_3$ | $EP_4$ | $EP_5$ | $EP_6$ | $EP_7$ | $EP_8$ | $EP_9$ |
|---|---|---|---|---|---|---|---|---|---|
| $AP_1$ | 0.321 | 0.448 | 0.131 | 0.131 | −0.296 | −0.473 | 0.446 | 0.380 | 0.486 |
| $AP_2$ | −0.105 | 0.776 | 0.249 | 0.329 | 0.092 | 0.377 | 0.432 | 0.385 | −0.014 |
| $AP_3$ | 0.567 | 0.012 | −0.296 | −0.743 | 0.182 | 0.377 | −0.235 | 0.537 | 0.262 |
| $AP_4$ | 0.401 | −0.041 | −0.473 | −0.132 | 0.455 | 0.415 | 0.397 | −0.193 | 0.277 |
| $AP_5$ | 0.258 | 0.309 | 0.446 | 0.195 | 0.188 | −0.275 | 0.772 | −0.440 | 0.646 |
| $AP_6$ | −0.047 | 0.558 | 0.380 | 0.257 | 0.143 | −0.045 | 0.430 | −0.287 | 0.076 |

The value of the coefficient, $r'$, is assumed as $r' = 0.3$ (i.e., presence of a relatively weak correlation). In Network of Correlation, only those association of $APs$ values ($Va$ and $V\bar{a}$) with the $EPs$ is considered, for which value $|r| > r'$. Thus, the recognized character of the Network of Contradictions is presented in Table 2.

**Table 2.** The Network of Contradiction in IQ system

| $|r| > r'$ | $EP_1$ | $EP_2$ | $EP_3$ | $EP_4$ | $EP_5$ | $EP_6$ | $EP_7$ | $EP_8$ | $EP_9$ |
|---|---|---|---|---|---|---|---|---|---|
| $AP_1$ | ↑$Va$ | ↑$Va$ | | | | ↓$V\bar{a}$ | ↑$Va$ | ↑$Va$ | ↑$Va$ |
| $AP_2$ | | ↑$Va$ | | ↑$Va$ | | ↑$Va$ | ↑$Va$ | ↑$Va$ | |
| $AP_3$ | ↑$Va$ | | | ↓$V\bar{a}$ | | ↑$Va$ | | ↑$Va$ | |
| $AP_3$ | ↑$Va$ | | ↓$V\bar{a}$ | | ↑$Va$ | ↑$Va$ | ↑$Va$ | | |
| $AP_5$ | | ↑$Va$ | ↑$Va$ | | | | ↑$Va$ | ↓$V\bar{a}$ | ↑$Va$ |
| $AP_6$ | | ↑$Va$ | ↑$Va$ | | | | ↑$Va$ | | |

The contradictions occurred then the value of the Active Parameters $AP_1$, $AP_3$, $AP_4$ and $AP_5$ is considered. For the $AP_2$ and $AP_6$ it is recognized that, to improve the state of the $EPs$ within the system, their value needs to be increased (↑).

**Stage 2. The differentiation of technical contradictions.**

The computed value of the contradictions Importance (*Imp.*), Universality (*Univ.*) and Amplitude (*Amp.*) is presented in Table 3.

**Table 3.** The differentiation of technical contradictions.

| No. | $TC_{ij}$ | | | Importance | Occurrence | Amplitude |
|---|---|---|---|---|---|---|
| 1 | $AP_i$ | $EP_{j1}$ | $EP_{j2}$ | *Imp.* | *Univ.* | *Amp.* |
| 2 | $AP_1$ | $EP_1$ | $EP_6$ | 0.896 | 10 | 5 |
| 3 | $AP_1$ | $EP_2$ | $EP_6$ | 0.892 | 9 | 5 |
| 4 | $AP_1$ | $EP_7$ | $EP_6$ | 0.895 | 10 | 5 |
| 5 | $AP_1$ | $EP_8$ | $EP_6$ | 0.941 | 13 | 5 |
| 6 | $AP_1$ | $EP_9$ | $EP_6$ | 0.884 | 9 | 5 |
| 7 | $AP_3$ | $EP_1$ | $EP_4$ | 0.942 | 6 | 3 |
| 8 | $AP_3$ | $EP_6$ | $EP_4$ | 0.939 | 10 | 3 |
| 9 | $AP_3$ | $EP_8$ | $EP_4$ | 0.936 | 9 | 3 |
| 10 | $AP_3$ | $EP_1$ | $EP_3$ | 0.910 | 8 | 4 |
| 11 | $AP_3$ | $EP_5$ | $EP_3$ | 0.889 | 6 | 4 |
| 12 | $AP_3$ | $EP_6$ | $EP_3$ | 0.887 | 12 | 4 |
| 13 | $AP_3$ | $EP_7$ | $EP_3$ | 0.862 | 12 | 4 |
| 14 | $AP_5$ | $EP_2$ | $EP_8$ | 1.129 | 8 | 4 |
| 15 | $AP_5$ | $EP_3$ | $EP_8$ | 1.112 | 11 | 4 |
| 16 | $AP_5$ | $EP_7$ | $EP_8$ | 1.250 | 9 | 4 |
| 17 | $AP_5$ | $EP_9$ | $EP_8$ | 1.124 | 8 | 4 |

Source: own studies

**Stage 3.** Graphical representation of technical contradictions, which occurred in the marketing information system of selected company, is presented in Fig. 1.

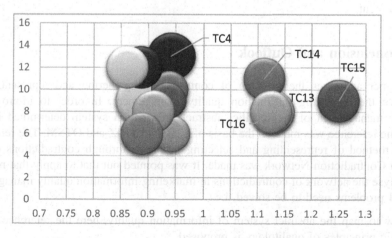

**Fig. 1.** Graphical representation of technical contradiction.

The seventeen contradictions are identified in the marketing information system. Five contradictions are placed in the zone of the high consideration, such as:

- TC4: $AP_1$ [Security] must be both $(Va)$ [information] for $EP_7$ [Concise Representation] AND $(V\bar{a})$ [information] for $EP_6$ [Completeness],
- TC13: $AP_3$ [Accessibility] must be both $(Va)$ [information] for $EP_7$ [Concise Representation] AND $(V\bar{a})$ [information] for $EP_3$ [Objectivity],
- TC14: $AP_5$ [Reputation] must be both $(Va)$ [information] for $EP_2$ [Interpretability] AND $(V\bar{a})$ [information] for $EP_8$ [Consistent Representation],
- TC15: $AP_5$ [Reputation] must be both $(Va)$ [information] for $EP_3$ [Objectivity] AND $(V\bar{a})$ [information] for $EP_8$ [Consistent Representation],
- TC16: $AP_5$ [Reputation] must be both $(Va)$ [information] for $EP_7$ [Concise Representation] AND $(V\bar{a})$ [information] for $EP_8$ [Consistent Representation].

Here, the Active Parameters, such as, $AP_1$, Security of information (i.e., the extent to which access to information is restricted), $AP_3$, Accessibility of information (i.e., the extent to which information is available, or easily and quickly retrievable) and $AP_5$, Reputation of information (i.e., the extent to which information is highly regarded in terms of its source or content) and their value need to be analysed first in order to improve the state of the significant Evaluation Parameters. The improvement of the Evaluation Parameters identify within the best ranked contradictions, such as: $EP_7$, Concise Representation (i.e., the extent to which information is compactly represented), $EP_6$, Completeness (i.e., the extent to which information is not missing and is of sufficient breadth and depth for the task at hand), $EP_3$, Objectivity (i.e., the extent to which information is unbiased, unprejudiced, and impartial), $EP_2$, Interpretability (i.e., the extent to which information is in appropriate language, symbols, and units, and the definitions are clear), $EP_8$, Consistent Representation (i.e., the extent to which information is presented in the same format), reflect the improvement of the marketing information quality management. The proposed and applied method enable to reflect the problems of contradiction and identify the substantial contradiction which need to be approach in the first place to improve the marketing information quality management.

# 5   Conclusion and Outlook

The paper addresses the problem of contradictions gathering and representing to improve the marketing information quality management. In order to improve the quality management of the specific, abstract information system determined in this way, the reference was made to the basis of Classical TRIZ and OTSM. The reference to the method of representing and selecting problems through contradictions clouds [11] in Contradiction Network was made. It was pointed out that to apply that method to analyse the network of contradictions in marketing information quality management several problems need to be solved, i.e.:

1. how to map the abstract system of information quality, here the reference to the basic principles of qualitology is proposed,

2. how to identify the active and evaluation parameters the information system and evaluate their value, here the reference to the methodology for information quality assessment (AIMQ) is proposed,
3. how to determine the relations between the active parameters and evaluation parameters, i.e., to recognize how the change (increase/decrease) of active parameter value is accompanied by the change (increase/decrease) of evaluation parameters value, here the reference to correlation analysis is proposed,
4. how to evaluate the strength of the impact of individual active parameters on evaluation parameters values and the importance of the evaluation parameters, here the reference to the method of grey incidence analysis (GIA) is proposed.

Finally, the procedure for the acquisition of contradictions and the differentiation of contradictions in terms of its Importance was proposed. The procedure was applied to the method of representing and selecting problems through contradictions clouds in Contradiction Network analysis to improve the Marketing Information Quality Management. The potential of the proposed concept has been shown through its application in the sales department of the selected manufacturing company. The promising results obtained so far suggest extending the analysis of the selected subset of contradiction. The application of other methods and instruments developed within Classical TRIZ and OTSM, the application of the ARIZ85-C to provide the best approach to be followed in solving the inventive problems in abstract system of information is the objective for further studies.

# References

1. Aczel, A.D., Sounderpandian, J.: Statistics in management. Wydawnictwo Naukowe PWN (2018)
2. Altshuller, G.S.: Elementy teorii twórczości inżynierskiej. Wydawnictwa Naukowo-Techniczne, Warszawa (1983)
3. Altshuller, G.: And suddenly the inventor appeared: TRIZ, the theory of inventive problem solving. Technical Innovation Center, Inc. (1996)
4. Azgaldov, G.G.: Kwalimetrija – nauka ob izmerenii kaczestwa produkcii, Standardy i Kaczestwo, 8 (1968)
5. Azgaldov, G.G., Kostin, A.V.: Applied qualimetry: its origins, errors and misconceptions. Benchmarking Int. J. 18(3), 428–444 (2011)
6. Azgaldov, G.G., Kostin, A.V., Padilla Omiste , A.E.: The ABC of Qualimetry: Toolkit for Measuring the immeasurable, Ridero, Ekaterinburg (2015)
7. Baldussu, A., Becattini, N., Cascini, G.: Network of contradictions analysis and structured identification of critical control parameters. Procedia Eng. 9, 3–17 (2011)
8. Becattini, N., Borgianni, Y., Frillici, F.S.: Employing customer value criteria to address networks of contradictions in complex technical systems. In: ScienceDirect (2015)
9. Borys, T.: Kategoria jakości w statystycznej analizie porównawczej. Wydawnictwo Uczelniane Akademii Ekonomicznej, Wrocław (1984)
10. Cascini, G.: TRIZ-based anticipatory design of future products and processes. J. Integr. Des. Process Sci. 16(3), 29–63 (2012)

11. Cavallucci, D., Rousselot, F., Zanni, C.: Representing and selecting problems through contradictions clouds. In: Cascini, Gaetano (ed.) CAI 2008. TIFIP, vol. 277, pp. 43–56. Springer, Boston, MA (2008). https://doi.org/10.1007/978-0-387-09697-1_4
12. Cavallucci, D., Rousselot, F., Zanni, C.: On contradiction clouds. Procedia Eng. **9**, 368–378 (2011)
13. Chechurin, L., Borgianni, Y.: Understanding TRIZ through the review of top cited publications. Comput. Ind. **82**, 119–134 (2016)
14. Goi, C.L.: A review of marketing mix: 4Ps or more? Int. J. Mark. Stud. **1**(1), 2 (2009)
15. Gummesson, E.: Relationship marketing operational. Int. J. Serv. Ind. Manage. **5**(5), 5–20 (1994)
16. Kahn, B.K., Strong, D.M., Wang, R.Y.: Information quality benchmarks: product and service performance. Commun. ACM **45**(4), 184–192 (2002)
17. Khomenko, N., De Guio, R.: OTSM network of problems for representing and analysing problem situations with computer support. In: León-Rovira, N. (ed.) CAI 2007. ITIFIP, vol. 250, pp. 77–88. Springer, Boston, MA (2007). https://doi.org/10.1007/978-0-387-75456-7_8
18. Khomenko, N., Ashtiani, M.: Classical TRIZ and OTSM as a scientific theoretical background for non-typical problem solving instruments. ETRIA Future, Frankfurt (2007)
19. Kolman, R.: Kwalitologia: wiedza o różnych dziedzinach jakości. Wydawnictwo Placet, Warszaw (2009)
20. Kowalczyk, E.: O istocie informacji. Wydawnictwa Komunikacji i Łączności, Warszawa (1981)
21. Langefors, B.: Infological models and information users view. Inf. Syst., 5, 17–32 (1980)
22. Lee, Y.W., Strong, D.M., Kahn, B.K., Wang, R.Y.: AIMQ: a methodology for information quality assessment. Inf. Manag. **40**(2), 133–146 (2002)
23. Liu, S., Lin, Y.: Grey Information Theory and Practical Application. Springer, London (2006). https://doi.org/10.1007/1-84628-342-6
24. Liu, S., Yang, Y., Forrest, J.: Grey Data Analysis. Springer, Berlin, Germany (2016). https://doi.org/10.1007/978-981-10-1841-1
25. Mantura, W.: Zarys kwalitologii. Wydawnictwo Politechniki Poznańskiej, Poznań (2010)
26. McCarthy, E.J.: Basic Marketing. Richard D. Irwin, Homewood (1964)
27. Stefanowicz, B.: Informacja, Oficyna Wydawnicza. SGH, Warszawa (2004)
28. Sundgren, B.: An Infological Approach To Data Bases. Skriftsene Statistika Centralbyran, Stockholm (1973)
29. Wang, R.Y.: A product perspective on total data quality management. Commun. ACM **41**(2), 55–61 (1998)

# Feature Selection-Based Approach for Generalized Physical Contradiction Recognition

Naser Ghannad[1] ⓘ, Roland De Guio[1](✉) ⓘ, and Pierre Parrend[2] ⓘ

[1] Icube INSA de Strasbourg, Strasbourg, France
{naser.ghannad, roland.deguio}@insa-strasbourg.fr
[2] ECAM Strasbourg-Europe, Schiltigheim, France
pierre.parrend@ecam-strasbourg.eu

**Abstract.** The objective of this paper is to improve a machine learning based methodology for recognizing the features of a Generalized Physical Contradictions (GPC) before knowing the contradiction itself when the system to be improved can be described by a simulated model based on design parameters and performance parameters. The paper starts with the background about identifying contradictions from data. It focuses on physical contradiction parameters identification with quantitative data and machine learning techniques. Although previous approaches are promising, they still have several drawbacks that require to be fixed. For instance, they do not propose any metric to inform the user about the quality of the result, which depends, among others, on the sample size. These drawbacks mainly appear in case of imbalanced data or complex relation between variables. To address these issues, we first tested different feature importance variable provided by decision tree methods (with the XGBOOST library) and retain the total gain. Second, we compared the XGBOOST methods with the previous proposed SVM based approach to see which one better describes the feature importance of variables involved in a GPC. As result XGBOOST was more robust to the noise from non-important variables. Third, we defined a set of measures for helping the user to know which is the sample size required to get good results with the tested methods.

**Keywords:** Inventive problem solving · Feature selection algorithm · Generalized physical contradiction · XGBOOST

## 1 Introduction

The notion of contradiction is a cornerstone of the TRIZ [1]. Multiple tools and methods deal with how to solve invention problems formulated with the help of contradictions [2–13]. Fewer works attempt to identify the contradictions underlying an invention problem. Identifying contradictions is an important, but sometimes tricky step in the problem formulation-solving process. The difficulty may be such that one sometimes observes in problem-solving seminars the inability of some people to formulate a contradiction. However, more often an inverse situation is observed, i.e. The expression of numerous contradictions among which one has to choose the

D. Cavallucci et al. (Eds.): TFC 2020, IFIP AICT 597, pp. 321–339, 2020.
https://doi.org/10.1007/978-3-030-61295-5_26

contradiction(s) to be dealt with. To respond to this last practical situation, some authors and experts propose concepts of classification of contradictions (core contradiction, system contradiction, etc.) or classification criteria relating to a set of expressed contradictions. In the vast majority of cases, the search for contradictions is a qualitative process carried out by experts. The difficulties mentioned above and the increasing complexity of the representation and behaviour of certain systems have led us to seek digital alternatives.

The research presented in this paper is part of a research that aims at improving the theoretical and practical continuum between design approaches based on optimization and those based on invention [14]. It enriches the work concerning the automated or semi-automated expression of a constraint system based on the results of physical experiments or numerical simulations whose interest has been validated by previous work [15–17].In this paper, we focus on the development of numerical tools and algorithms facilitating the identification of the design parameters involved the concepts and contexts of generalized physical contradictions associated with a system of technical contradictions with the aim of constituting a generalized system of contradictions.

In the following at first, we describe how finding the important action parameters that are involve in the contradiction helps the expert to understand the problem inside of the system and give him a clue to improve the process of the system with add or remove the action parameters that are involve in contradiction. Second, we describe the algorithms that can helps us to find the most important action parameters. Third, we test different feature importance of different algorithm to see which one can give better and more robust results to find the important variable. Fourth, by doing some experiments, we showed that, how we can get the right number of sample size based on the accuracy of the model.

## 2    Background

### 2.1    TRIZ System of Contradictions

Commonly, the TRIZ identifies 3 types of contradictions: the administrative contradiction, the technical contradiction and the physical contradiction. The OTSM-TRIZ has made explicit a form of link between technical contradictions and a physical contradiction which is called a system of contradictions. In the research related to this paper, we are interested in the identification of systems of contradictions by using numerical tools and experimental or simulation data. To deal with this issue, it was necessary to represent the concepts of technical, physical and system of contradictions so that these identifications could be made. The following paragraphs recall the definitions and representations of the TRIZ contradictions in a data table.

Consider a system whose performance is evaluated using two evaluation parameters (EP) y1 and y2. To do so, 8 experiments or simulations were performed by acting on the design parameters x1 to x5 of the considered system, which we will henceforth call Action Parameters (AP) in the remainder of the paper. We give the value 1 to the evaluation parameter, for a given experiment if the simulated system meets the objectives for the evaluation parameter. Otherwise, the evaluation parameter takes the value 0. The result is given in Fig. 1 (a) below. When analyzing it, it can be seen that sometimes one objective can be satisfied but never both objectives at the same time. According to the TRIZ, situations that satisfy y1 but not y2 characterize under these conditions a so-called technical contradiction noted TC1 in Fig. 1 (b). In the same way, situations that satisfy y2 but not y1 have under these conditions a second technical contradiction noted TC2 in Fig. 1 (b). The situation e9, on the other hand, does not bring a contradiction because none of the objectives is achieved; there is no conflict of objectives in this "solution".

To obtain a physical contradiction in the sense of the TRIZ, it is necessary to be able to assign to the contradictions TC1 and TC2 an action variable (AP) which allows one to move from one technical contradiction to the other by modifying its value as shown in the example in Fig. 1 (c). In this example, x1 = 1 characterizes contradiction TC1 and x1 = 0 characterizes contradiction TC2. In the TRIZ the physical contradiction of the example is stated: the variable x1 must take both the values 1 and 0 to reach the objectives. The system of contradictions described by OTSM-TRIZ is the coherent set of the two technical contradictions TC1 and TC2 and the physical contradiction that "explains" or "causes" TC1 and TC2.

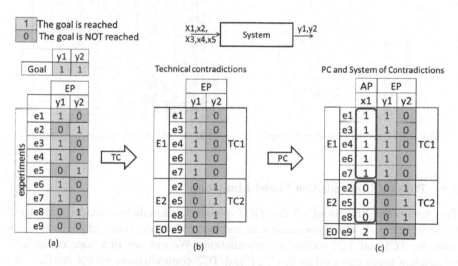

**Fig. 1.** TRIZ system of contradiction out of experimental data

## 2.2 Limitation on Technical Contradiction of the TRIZ Models

The example in Fig. 2, which deals with a problem where six objectives are to be satisfied, illustrates a limitation of the classical TRIZ model of technical contradiction. Indeed, it can be seen from this example that two of the six objectives can always be met at the same time, but that the six objectives can never be met at the same time. In other words, in the sense of the classical TRIZ, there is no contradiction but the problem of conflict between objectives exists. It was therefore necessary to find another way of expressing the technical contradiction. Several proposals called generalized technical contradictions (GTC) have been made to this effect in the literature. They consider at least two or even all objectives simultaneously [18]. We do not elaborate further on this point, which is not the subject of this paper. We will retain for our purpose that as for the system of contradictions of the classical TRIZ, a system of generalized contradictions is composed of two generalized technical contradictions and one generalized physical contradiction. The two generalized technical contradictions GTC1 and GTC2 of a system of contradictions define a partition of the experiments into three sets E1, E2, E0 where E1 represents the experiments for which we have the contradiction GTC1, E2 represents the set of experiments for which we have the contradiction GTC2, and where E0 is constituted by the complementary experiments of the partition. The reader interested in the definitions and the methods of identification of the GTC from the data can refer to the references [12, 13].

| GOAL | 1 | 1 | 1 | 1 | 1 | 1 |
|---|---|---|---|---|---|---|
| | **EP** | | | | | |
| | y1 | y2 | y3 | y4 | y5 | y6 |
| e1 | 1 | 0 | 1 | 1 | 1 | 1 |
| e2 | 0 | 1 | 0 | 0 | 1 | 1 |
| e3 | 1 | 0 | 1 | 0 | 0 | 0 |
| e4 | 1 | 1 | 1 | 1 | 0 | 0 |
| e5 | 1 | 0 | 1 | 0 | 1 | 1 |
| e6 | 0 | 1 | 0 | 1 | 1 | 1 |
| e7 | 1 | 0 | 1 | 0 | 0 | 0 |
| e8 | 1 | 0 | 0 | 1 | 1 | 1 |
| e9 | 0 | 1 | 0 | 1 | 1 | 1 |

(experiments)

**Fig. 2.** TC model limitation example

| | | GOAL→ | | | | | 1 | 1 | |
|---|---|---|---|---|---|---|---|---|---|
| | | **AP** | | | | | **EP** | | |
| | | x1 | x2 | x3 | x4 | x5 | y1 | y2 | |
| E1 | e1 | 1 | 1 | 0 | 0 | 1 | 1 | 0 | |
| | e3 | 1 | 0 | 1 | 0 | 0 | 1 | 0 | |
| | e4 | 1 | 1 | 0 | 0 | 0 | 1 | 0 | TC1 |
| | e5 | 1 | 0 | 1 | 0 | 1 | 1 | 0 | |
| | e7 | 1 | 0 | 1 | 1 | 0 | 1 | 0 | |
| E2 | e2 | 0 | 1 | 1 | 1 | 1 | 0 | 1 | |
| | e6 | 0 | 1 | 0 | 1 | 2 | 0 | 1 | TC2 |
| | e9 | 0 | 1 | 0 | 0 | 2 | 0 | 1 | |
| E0 | e8 | 1 | 0 | 0 | 0 | 1 | 0 | 0 | |

**Fig. 3.** PC model limitation example

## 2.3   Physical Contradiction Model Limitation

To explain the limitations of the TRIZ physical contradiction model consider the example in Fig. 3, when processing data and look for physical contradictions associated with the TC1 and TC2 technical contradictions. We can see that none of the action parameters alone can explain the TC1 and TC2 contradictions with a conflict on its values. Indeed, for x1, when x1 = 0 we have the situations of the set E2 which characterize TC2 but when x1 = 1, we have the situations of E1 which are characteristic of TC1 and situation of E0 namely e8 where none of the objectives is reached. To get around this difficulty two alternative but coherent ways to express the contradiction with the action parameters have been proposed. These contradictions are called by their authors generalized physical contradictions and contextual physical contradictions [19].

## 2.4   The Generalized Physical Contradiction

A first approach consists in determining a logical expression of the action parameters C1 which discriminates the situations of E1 from those of E2 and E0 on the one hand, and in determining a logical expression C2 which discriminates the situations E2 from those of E1 and E0 on the other hand. The two expressions thus obtained are then the equivalent of the conflict between parameters of the physical contradiction of the TRIZ. In the case of the example of Fig. 3, the expressions C1 and C2 below allow to express a generalized physical contradiction (GPC):

C1: $(x1 = 1).(x2 = 1).(x3 = 0).(x4 = 0)$
C2: $(x1 = 0).(x2 = 1).(x3 = 0).(x4 = 0)$

The generalized physical contradiction can then be expressed with the concepts C1 and C2: "to achieve objectives y1 and y2, both C1 and C2 must be satisfied, which is not possible". The association of a generalized physical contradiction with two generalized technical contradictions is called a system of generalized contradictions (SGC).

## 2.5   Contextual Physical Contradiction

The second approach to express the generalized physical contradiction is to add the notion of context [19]. To illustrate this notion, let's take the previous example and observe the expressions C1 and C2. We see that C1 and C2 are distinguished by the value of $x1$ and share the same values for $x2$, $x3$ and $x4$. Let us then note C the logical expression such as is true if $(x2 = 1).(x3 = 0).(x4 = 0)$. We can then reformulate the previous contradiction by introducing the expression C. In situations where the expression C is true, the action parameter $x1$ must take both the value 1 and the value 0 to meet the objectives. Expression C is called the context of the generalized physical contradiction and the system of contradictions.

In the case of our example, we find in the context C a physical contradiction of the classical TRIZ. The generalized contradiction within a given context specifies the domain of validity of the contradiction of the classical TRIZ. This information, which is not easy to find in general, is not evoked in the classical TRIZ. However, it can be important for understanding the problem and interesting for solving a problem.

This paper concerns the improvement of numerical techniques allowing the fast and reliable identification of the concepts C1 and C2 and the context C of generalized physical contradictions.

## 2.6   Seeking for the Causes and Context of the TC

The work of identifying generalized physical contradictions through numerical data analysis techniques is based on the observation that TC1 and TC2 can be considered as discriminant functions between the E1 and E2 sets of experiments. In [20] an exhaustive search algorithm for all generalized physical contradictions associated with two generalized technical contradictions is proposed by modeling this problem as an integer optimization problem. This problem is recognized as NP-hard, which limits the application of this algorithm to problems the number of action variables of which is lower than 13 when those action parameters have only 2 levels. To bypass this problem, the same author proposes to first identify the variables involved in the searched contradictions using SVM learning techniques [21] and the associated discriminant analysis [13]. The same technique was used to identify the parameter-value pairs of the action parameters involved in the physical contradictions [13]. Taking advantage of this last possibility, Bach proposes an approach for interpreting the weights of the SVM discriminant analysis with respect to selected technical contradictions in the Pareto set of the binary matrix of EPs. This last approach avoids the use of the exhaustive algorithm.

The methods mentioned above have been used successfully in real cases. The exhaustive search method may give many contradictions, but only a few of them are relevant. The practical question of the choice of the contradiction then arises. The direct identification method based on learning does not have this drawback [22]. It provides the parameters and values involved in the pair of technical contradictions but it lets the user conclude on the expression of C1 and C2 and does not provide the context C. Moreover, their application requires knowledge and experience in data analysis to correctly interpret the results of the SVM learning algorithm. In some cases, the interpretation of SVM results remains difficult even for an expert in data analysis.

## 3   Problematic and Expected Contribution(S) of the Paper

The objective of our current research is to construct a heuristic that quickly provides a user who is not an expert in data analysis with only the relevant generalized physical contradictions and their context when the number of action parameters and values is large. As discussed in Sect. 2, one disadvantage of SVM based method is the ambiguity that may arise in the interpretation of the weights of the discrimination function provided by the SVM method.

### 3.1   Practical Limitations of SVM Use

To explain these drawbacks, we recall with the example of Fig. 4 the principle of use and interpretation of SVM outputs. In this example, we consider three evaluation parameters y1, y2, and y3 and an action parameter that can take 10 values x1 to x10. We want to know which values xi explain the achievement or non-achievement of the objective yj. To do this, the SVM discrimination function provides weights (see Fig. 4 (a)) which can be interpreted as follows: if the value of the weight is "enough" positive, then xi explains the achievement of the objective for yj and if it is "enough" negative, then xi explains the unsatisfactory achievement of the objective for yj.

The first practical problem concerns the interpretation of "enough". Indeed, the values defining the limit between a positive or negative action and no discriminatory action are not fixed by the method. Moreover, they may vary according to the evaluation parameter yi. To illustrate this point, it is provided in Fig. 4 (b) and (c), two different interpretations of the weights in Fig. 4 (a). Knowledge about the system can help in the interpretation, but we would like to be able to decide on the basis of the data.

The second practical question concerns the sample size of data needed to ensure that the order of values is stable because with different sample size we see different order of variables and we don't understand which one is more accurate and trustable, we would like to know the necessary sample size to be able to interpret the data.

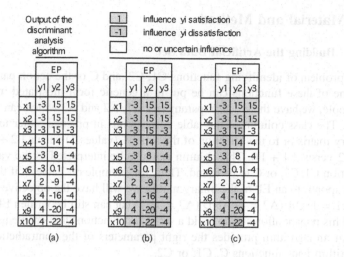

**Fig. 4.** Limitation of SVM weights interpretation

## 3.2 Problematic of the Paper

The main question in this paper is to define which action parameters are involved in generalized physical contradiction (i.e. we do not seek for the contradiction itself). In the SVM-based approaches presented in previous works, the idea is to exploit a learning method and its recognition function. We can imagine using other learning algorithms to recognize the variables involved in the contradictions. Each method can produce different results. The question then arises to compare their performance and to know which one is more accurate or robust.

As soon as we know how to measure the quality of a solution provided by a method we can compare the methods. In this paper, we present an alternative method to the SVM approach named XGBOOST [23] (eXtreme Gradient Boosting), which will be compared to SVM [24].

The main problem that we deal with is imbalanced data that exists in some problems, it's means that number of data for each class or group of data is not balanced and that the number of data that exist in one group is very few. Moreover, when the method can deal with imbalanced data, the usual metric like accuracy can't show overfitting or under-fitting for this kind of dataset. That is the reason why we need measures that allow us to deal with these questions. Some of them are proposed in the literature of machine learning like AUC, and PRC curve. We will test them also in the method we propose bellow because this situation often happens in innovation. Our objective is finding accurate and robust models that can show the importance of features involved in the contradiction. Also, we looking for an algorithm that can (1) easily deal with multi-class problems and have a way to delete ineffective variables, (2) in a next research step, might provide the concepts C1 and C2 of the GPC). The latest point is among main reasons why we explored the use of XGBOOST.

# 4  Material and Method

## 4.1  Building the Artificial Data Set

The problem of identifying functions C1, C2, and C or the action parameters involved in one of these functions can be put in a generic form illustrated in Table 1. In this example, we have three action parameters A1, A2 and A3 which can take two values 1 or 0. The class column of the table corresponds in practice either to a column of the binary matrix or to the selection of the sets E1 (values 1) versus E2 +E0 (zeros values) or E2 versus E1 + E0. This column can also be interpreted as the value of the logical function C1, C2, or C to be found. Thus, for example on Table 1. if the column "class" corresponds to an EP of the binary matrix we will have the objective reached (EP = 1) if (A1 = 1) OR (A2 = 1) AND (A3 = 1). What can still be written EP = A1 + A2.A3.

This remark allows us to build a set of test functions that enable us to check to what extent an algorithm provides the right parameters of the contradiction and later if an algorithm finds functions C, C1, or C2.

At the preprocessing stage of our research methodology, we build different datasets with different numbers of action parameters (10, 15, 20) and also with different sizes of data samples (100, 300, 500, 1000).

**Table 1.** Data sample

| A1 | A2 | A3 | Class |
|----|----|----|-------|
| 1  | 0  | 0  | 1     |
| 0  | 0  | 0  | 0     |
| 0  | 0  | 1  | 0     |
| 0  | 1  | 0  | 0     |
| 0  | 1  | 1  | 1     |
| 0  | 0  | 0  | 0     |
| 0  | 1  | 0  | 0     |

The functions used for the test part are given below, '.' means AND between two variables, and '+' means OR between two variables.

$$\text{Function } 1 = A1.A2 \tag{1}$$

$$\text{Function } 2 = A1.A2 + A1.A3 \tag{2}$$

$$\text{Function } 3 = A1.A2 + A3.A7 + A5 \tag{3}$$

$$\text{Function4} = A1.A2.A3\ldots A10 \tag{4}$$

$$\text{Function } 5 = A1 + A2.A3 + A2.A4 + A3.A5.A6 + A4.A5.A7.A8 \tag{5}$$

They were chosen for their degree of difficulty in treatment. In the following, you can see imbalance ratio (IR) and table of imbalance ratio of these functions.

$$IR = \frac{\text{number of data in Majority Class}}{\text{number of data in Minority Class}} \tag{6}$$

In this formula, for example if we have 2 outputs for the defined function and if the number of zero outputs in our dataset is equal to 1000 and the number of one output in our dataset is equal to 8, then class 1 or data with output 1 is minority class because it has lower number of data inside the dataset and class 0 is majority then IR will be 1000 divide by 8 is 125. It shows that this dataset is highly imbalanced and we need a plan to pass this problem.

It can be seen in the Table 2 that Function 4 has the highest imbalance ratio. Among the other functions, F1 and F2 are most challenging ones because the number of data in majority class is much more than number of data in minority class and this makes learning harder because in learning stage, model focus on majority class and neglect the minority class.

**Table 2.** Imbalance ratio of different function with different sampling

| #Sample | F1 | F2 | F3 | F4 | F5 |
|---------|------|------|------|-------|------|
| 100 | 4.26 | 1.77 | 0.51 | 99.0 | 0.49 |
| 200 | 4.40 | 1.81 | 0.43 | 99.0 | 0.42 |
| 300 | 3.54 | 1.67 | 0.48 | 149.0 | 0.38 |
| 400 | 3.25 | 1.54 | 0.45 | 199.0 | 0.37 |
| 500 | 3.62 | 1.68 | 0.48 | 124.0 | 0.39 |
| 1000 | 3.08 | 1.61 | 0.42 | 249.0 | 0.37 |

Once the test functions are defined, we preprocess the data, it means we binarize the input and output and split the data to training, validation, and test data sets by using 5-fold stratified data sampling. Indeed, as we are dealing with some imbalanced data sets these actions allow having enough data of each value (0 and 1). A stratified sampling ensures that subgroups (strata) of a given class are each adequately represented within the whole sample of classes. In this way, we can see different aspects of the data, and later we can evaluate and check the confidence and robustness of our model in different conditions.

## 4.2 Global Process to Find the Important Variables Involved in Contradiction

In this paper, we want to evaluate the performance of the "extreme gradient boosting" algorithm to extract the important features involved in physical contradiction and compare it performances to SVM approach. The methodology to identify the features is provided below. The two first stages 1) and 2) consist in getting data and preprocessing them as described in the previous section.

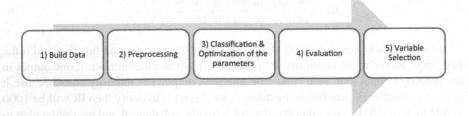

**Fig. 5.** Our proposed methodology to detect the important inputs involved in contradiction

In the next step 3) we classify the data, with a gradient boost tree algorithm (XGBOOST). During the training of step 3), we check the model via a Log loss metric on validation data in order to prevent as much as possible overfitting and underfitting phenomenon.

After training the model, we evaluate it in step 4), to see how much it might be successful in classifying the test data. For evaluating the result, as we deal with imbalanced data, we used metrics that are good when dealing with imbalanced datasets like AUC curve, PRC curve. We consider that in very high-level imbalance dataset PRC curve is a better metric than AUC curve [25, 26]. The measures used so far in step 4) allow the user of the classification method to "decide" whether the classification model obtained in step 3) has identified the Action Parameters without knowing them beforehand as in a real situation.

In step (5), the user of this algorithm should then decide from the measures which variables retains as important features. We can even propose an algorithm that retains itself the relevant features.

As we have just seen, the process in Fig. 5 can be implemented by different learning algorithms coupled to an automatic or human decision process. To compare the performance of these different processes, we propose in our experiments to add a performance measure of different implementations of the parameter identification process. This measure is relevant in our experimentation as in our evaluation examples we already know the important features. Thus, it is possible to check afterward how far the whole process allows to retain the "right" features or not. We called this measure correctness:

$$\text{Correctness} = \frac{f(\text{choice first N}(\text{Sort M}))}{\text{number of actual important features}} \tag{7}$$

In the formula of correctness, M is equal to the value of the importance of each variable extracted from the model, it could be weight in SVM or gain of each feature extracted from the decision tree. "Sort M" means, we sort these M from highest value to lowest value, because feature with highest value means that it has more contribution than others to classify the output of dataset. N is equal to the number of important features in the function, for example, if we are looking to evaluate function 1, then only 2 variables are important in the function, and N value is 2 for this function. Function f in the formula is comparing these selected variables with actual variables that existed in actual function and return number of matching between these two lists, for example, if we have 10 APs and actual function that builds the output is like A1 + A2A4 with 3 important variables. Let us imagine that after training and extraction of the feature importance of model, the provided ranking of feature importance is A1, A3, and A4. Then correctness for this situation is equal to two divides by three, because we can predict 2 of 3 important variables of the actual function and correctness will be 66%. This formula can be used in our experimentation because we already know the actual function and we use this information for evaluating the whole process.

In the next section, we provide the results obtained with this method. The details of the measure and their interpretation for the user are provided.

# 5 Illustration and Evaluation of the Approach

For understanding the problem and to understand which variables play a more important role in contradiction we need to find them inside of the inputs (Action parameters). Thus, after the classifying stage we can check the variable importance from the simulated model. In SVM we can see it via the weights of the kernel. In XGBOOST we can see it via different parameters like gain, cover, weight [27], total gain, total cover, and total gain. In XGBOOST weight is the number of times a feature is used to split the data across all trees, gain is the average gain across all splits the feature is used in, cover is the average coverage across all splits the feature is used in, total gain is the total gain across all splits the feature is used in, and total cover is the total coverage across all splits the feature is used in. In this paper, we first explored which one(s) of the XGBOOST measures better explains the important features and later compare XGBOOST measures with SVM measures to see which one is more robust in imbalanced situations and which one can give the more accurately the important features with the lowest sample size.

To compare the different feature importance provided by XGBOOST we used AUC, PRC curve to check how much results are usable.

In the following we compare the result for different functions, all the functions have 20 inputs with the name of A1 to A20 and one output. But all the input variables are not necessary to describe the function; each of them can be described with one of the 5 functions provided above (Eqs. (1) to (5))

## 5.1 Comparing Different Feature Importance of XGBOOST

Because we build our dataset, we know which variables are important and which are useless we can check if our algorithm can find these important variables or not. But we have a problem, XGBOOST give multiple feature importance and we need to figure out which one(s) among weight, Cover, Gain, Total gain, Total cover is more suitable to detect the important features. However, the notion of importance is always linked to the problem being solved. For us, the important variables are those that allow us to identify our function. For example Function 5 = A1 + A2.A3 + A2.A4 + A3.A5.A6 + A4. A5.A7.A8 we have 20 variables in our dataset, but only 8 of them are useful in this function.

Since we know the types of functions we are trying to identify, we were able to define a rule of importance of variables for this type of function. Moreover, this order relation must also allow us to distinguish from which point in this order the variables are no longer important to describe the function. For example Function 5 = A1 + A2. A3 + A2.A4 + A3.A5.A6 + A4.A5.A7.A8 we have 20 variables in our dataset, but only 8 of them are useful in this function for the GPC. Thus, the algorithm must order in our example first the variables A1 to A8 and then the other variables. In addition, one must be able to distinguish the importance between the variables A1 to A8 and the others. We study below if the measures resulting from our classification algorithm with XGBOOST allow this distinction by a user when reading the measures or automatically. For that reason, we plot different bar chart of 5 feature importance measures of XGBOOST (weight, Cover, Gain, Total gain, Total cover) with different sample size to see which one can show us the uptrend in value when we increase the sample size from 100 to 2000 and also show the downtrend.

As can be seen in Fig. 6, total gain can give A1 to A8 values greater than A9 to A20 values, and when the sample size increases. The value of total gain also increases for the important variables but not necessarily for the others; it means that when we give more data to the model, the model confidence in important features also increases. And we can also see the downtrend from A1 to A8 which shows that the model is ranking A1 as most important feature and A8 as lowest important feature inside of our function. We also expect these characteristics to become more pronounced as sample sizes increase.

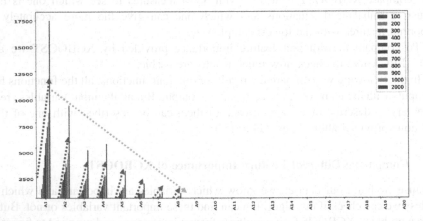

**Fig. 6.** Total gain of each variable of XGBOOST with different sample size of function 5

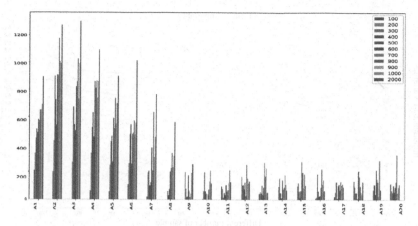

**Fig. 7.** Weight of each variable from XGBOOST with different sample size of function 5

One can see an example of inconsistency of our method when we used weight as importance function in Fig. 7, because there is no sign of uptrend when we increase the sample size and also there is no sign of downtrend from A1 to A8, and value of A1 to A8 are not systematically higher than the values of A9 to A20 in most of case when the sample size increases.

Finally, among the five tested importance features the total gain and total cover could be used for our problem when using bar charts. In order to choose between these two measures, we made more a detailed comparison of them by using line charts to plot them (see Fig. 8 and Fig. 9).

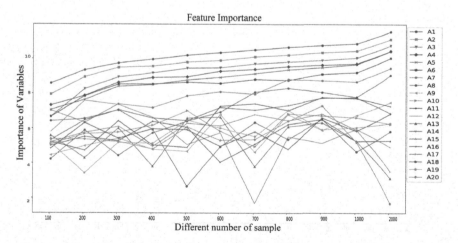

**Fig. 8.** Total Cover of each variable of XGBOOST with different sample size of function 5

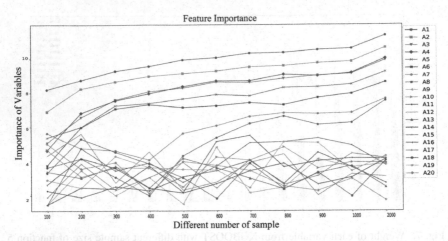

**Fig. 9.** Total gain of each variable of XGBOOST with different sample size of function 5

When we compare these two graphs, we see that the total coverage requires larger sample sizes than the total gain to exhibit the important parameters of the example, namely A1 to A8. We also see that there does not seem to be any trend in the rank of the other variables when the sample size is increased. So, we used the total gain as measure to compare the use of XGBOOST and SVM on our problem (Figs. 10 and 11).

To compare XGBOOST and SVM, we use box plot to see the median, standard deviation, maximum and minimum of feature importance of each algorithm with different sample sizes. We performed this process on the 5 functions mentioned above, but here we just show the result for function 5:

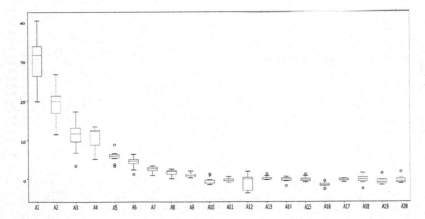

**Fig. 10.** SVM weights range with different sample size from 100 to 2000 of function 5

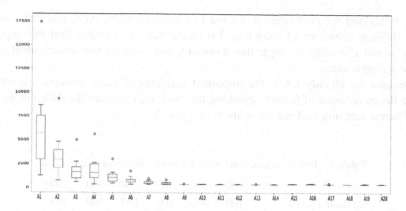

**Fig. 11.** XGBOOST total gain with different sample size from 100 to 2000 of function 5

As you can see in these two figures variable of A1 to A8 have a higher value in comparison to the A9 to A20, but for example A8 in XGBOOST doesn't to much overlap to non-important values, but in contrary A8 in SVM has overlap with different non-important variables like A9, A12, A18. This leaves us to speculate that XGBOOST might better distinguish between important and non-important features of our problem (the same king of result is obtained for our 5 examples and you can find more results on our github[1]). Moreover, XGBOOST was more robust to the non-important features for the 5 examples. Indeed, in box plot with different sample size, standard deviation of non-important features was systematically in a smaller range with XGBOOST compared to SVM; in both case they were around the zero, but in SVM ranges of non-important feature was not consistent as they change below and above the zero with different sample size.

By using Box plot or line chart, we can also detect the non-important features., In box plot we can detect them by removing the narrow boxes around the zero and in line chart with different sample size, non-important feature changes a lot but important features are more robust to these changes and they hold their ranking with different sample size.

Now we make the hypothesis that XGBOOST is more robust on non-important features, then problem that we deal with is that we don't know, which model with how many number of sample we can trust more because we deal with different sample size of the real system or simulated model, and we need a metric for this problem to evaluate the result of classification and also result of features selected from the model [28]. And because of we deal with different kind of data and different ratio of imbalanced dataset, we cannot say exactly how many data we need to have a good performance in the modeling and feature selection before training the model. Our solution for this problem is, at first, we build the model based on different sample size and then, with different measures, we check which one of these models can better modelized the function inside of the data.

---

[1] https://github.com/nasergh/TRIZ-contradiction.

For checking the performance, we use two measurements, AUC and PRC, and we show different scenarios of sampling that model can successfully find the important variables and also some example that it doesn't, and compare the measurement to find the best sample size.

Because we already know the important variables of each function, we can calculate the correctness of feature selection, that why we calculate the different measure for different function and we show them in Table 3.

**Table 3.** Result of functions with different sample size (in percent)

|            |             | 100   | 200   | 300   | 400   | 500   | 1000  |
|------------|-------------|-------|-------|-------|-------|-------|-------|
| Function 1 | AUC         | 100   | 100   | 100   | 100   | 100   | 100   |
|            | PRC         | 100   | 100   | 100   | 100   | 100   | 100   |
|            | Correctness | 100   | 100   | 100   | 100   | 100   | 100   |
| Function 2 | AUC         | 100   | 100   | 100   | 100   | 100   | 100   |
|            | PRC         | 100   | 100   | 100   | 100   | 100   | 100   |
|            | Correctness | 100   | 100   | 100   | 100   | 100   | 100   |
| Function 3 | AUC         | 97.86 | 99.97 | 100   | 100   | 100   | 100   |
|            | PRC         | 98.93 | 99.99 | 100   | 100   | 100   | 100   |
|            | Correctness | 80    | 100   | 100   | 100   | 100   | 100   |
| Function 4 | AUC         | N.A   | 73.48 | 87.91 | 90.45 | 96.47 | 99.24 |
|            | PRC         | N.A   | 4.12  | 18.09 | 6.21  | 63.92 | 61.30 |
|            | Correctness | 40    | 50    | 60    | 40    | 70    | 100   |
| Function 5 | AUC         | 83.70 | 99.50 | 99.80 | 100   | 99.80 | 99.90 |
|            | PRC         | 93.50 | 99.80 | 99.90 | 100   | 99.90 | 100   |
|            | Correctness | 62.50 | 87.50 | 87.50 | 87.50 | 87.50 | 100   |

With these results we can see that, when we increase the sample sizes, if PRC or AUC becomes stable and changing very smoothly then our sample size is large enough to have a good correctness (more than 70%) or in other word we can more trust to the result of feature importance values of the model and in other hand we have an accurate model of the data and model understand the relation between the variables much better. One can see that when we have higher AUC or PRC value, then value of feature important and ranking of them is also improved. For example, for the function 4, PRC decrease 11.88% when we changed the number of samples from 300 to 400 sample. Also, one can see is the correctness of feature selection decrease 20%, it lets us conjecture that there is a relationship between the model accuracy and features extracted from it.

It can also be seen that when there is a big jump in PRC and AUC values, and PRC value comes to more than 60% then it seems that we are very near to a sufficient number of sample size to find the feature important.

# 6  Discussion

In this paper our goal was finding the features important that are involved in contradiction and for that purpose we built artificial dataset with binary functions. At first, we compare different output of feature importance that can be extract from the XGBOOST model and we find out, total gain shows the feature important of each function with better ranking and also with small amount of data, total gain can show the feature important better than others. After that we compare the feature importance of SVM with XGBOOST to see which one is more robust in different functions and data's, then we see that XGBOOST result for non-important features is more stable and robust to the noise and they are very close to zero in compare to the SVM. Also, we see that in some functions XGBOOST with a smaller number of samples in compare to the SVM can give the right order of feature important. With this methodology we build an automatic system that extract the most important variable from the data.

In our experiment we see that if we deal with highly imbalanced dataset then it's hard to find the important features inside of the dataset, and also, it's hard to make the decision about how many numbers of samples is enough for model to give us more trustable feature importance. That is why we evaluate the model with different measurement and we see that there is a relation between the feature importance extracted from the model and the accuracy of the model. Despite this relation was not very clear, it can be used as a guide for the user to continue improving the model and correctness of extracted important features. With the defined metrics we know when a model can understand the relation between the variables, but we don't know with how many samples we will be required to have a high correctness in feature importance. In the future, we will look more closely to this problem.

Another problem that we dealt with it, was imbalanced dataset. We need at least 4 samples that show the minority class, otherwise we cannot have a good feature selection and also accurate model that describe the relation and variable importance inside the dataset.

This methodology can help to find the important features or in other word the action parameters that are involved in identifying the physical contradiction behind the technical contradictions.

# 7  Conclusion

In this paper, first we find out which feature importance of XGBOOST describes the important variables of physical contradiction. Then we compared the performance of SVM and XGBOOST algorithms for getting the important variables involved in generalized physical contradictions. In order to make this comparison and to use XGBOOST, it was necessary to seek for measures providing the important variables for XGBOOST algorithm. The results suggest that, first, XGBOOST is more powerful and robust in noisy dataset and can better detect the non-important features than SVM, second, XGBOOST can show the importance action parameters with a smaller number of data. In the next part, we show that PRC and AUC can give a clue to the user that how much model can understand the actual function and indirectly show how much model can successfully extract the important action parameters.

**Acknowledgement.** This research is carried out within the framework of the Offensive Sciences project number 13.11 "Virtual Innovative Real Time Factory" (VIRTFac) which benefits from the financial support of the Offensive Sciences programme of the Upper Rhine Trinational Metropolitan Region, the INTERREG V Upper Rhine programme and the European Regional Development Fund (ERDF) of the European Union.

# References

1. Altshuller, G.S.: Creativity as an exact science: the theory of the solution of inventive problems. Gordon and Breach (1984)
2. Bach, S., De Guio, R., Nathalie, G.: Combining discrete event simulation, data analysis, and TRIZ for fleet optimization. J. Eur. TRIZ Assoc. Innov. **04**(02), 47–61 (2017)
3. Ben Moussa, F., Benmoussa, R., de Guio, R., Dubois, S., Rasovska, I.: An algorithm for inventive problem solving coupled with optimization for solving inventive problems encountered in supply chains (2016). http://icube-publis.unistra.fr/4-BBdD16
4. Ben Moussa, F.Z., Rasovska, I., Dubois, S., Guio, R.D., Benmoussa, R.: Reviewing the use of the theory of inventive problem solving (TRIZ) in green supply chain problems, J. Clean. Prod. **142**, 2677–2692 (2017). https://doi.org/10.1016/j.jclepro.2016.11.008
5. BenMoussa, F.Z., Dubois, S., De Guio, R., Rasovska, I., Benmoussa, R.: Integrating the theory of inventive problem solving with discrete event simulation in supply chain management. In: Cavallucci, D., De Guio, R., Koziołek, S. (eds.) TFC 2018. IAICT, vol. 541, pp. 330–347. Springer, Cham (2018). https://doi.org/10.1007/978-3-030-02456-7_27
6. Burgard, L., Dubois, S., de Guio, R., Rasovska, I.: Sequential experimentation to perform the Analysis of Initial Situation (2011). http://icube-publis.unistra.fr/4-BDDR11
7. Chibane, H., Dubois, S., De Guio, R.: Automatic extraction and ranking of systems of contradictions out of a design of experiments. In: Cavallucci, D., De Guio, R., Koziołek, S. (eds.) TFC 2018. IAICT, vol. 541, pp. 276–289. Springer, Cham (2018). https://doi.org/10. 1007/978-3-030-02456-7_23
8. Dubois, S., de Guio, R., Rasovska, I.: From simulation to invention, beyond the pareto-frontier (2015). http://icube-publis.unistra.fr/4-DDR15
9. Dubois, S., Eltzer, T., De Guio, R.: A dialectical based model coherent with inventive problems and optimization problems. Comput. Ind. **60**(8), 575–583 (2009)
10. Dubois, S., De Guio, R., Brouillon, A., Angelo, L.: A feedback on an industrial application of the FORMAT methodology. In: Cavallucci, D., De Guio, R., Koziołek, S. (eds.) TFC 2018. IAICT, vol. 541, pp. 290–301. Springer, Cham (2018). https://doi.org/10.1007/978-3-030-02456-7_24
11. Rasovska, I., de Guio, R., Dubois, S.: Using dominance relation to identify relevant generalized technical contradictions in innovative design, October 2017. http://icube-publis. unistra.fr/4-RdD17
12. Lin, L., Dubois, S., De Guio, R., Rasovska, I.: An exact algorithm to extract the generalized physical contradiction. Int. J. Interact. Des. Manuf. (IJIDeM) **9**(3), 185–191 (2014). https:// doi.org/10.1007/s12008-014-0250-3
13. Lin, L., Rasovska, I., De Guio, R., Dubois, S.: Optimization methods for inventive design. TRIZ – The Theory of Inventive Problem Solving, pp. 151–185. Springer, Cham (2017). https://doi.org/10.1007/978-3-319-56593-4_7

14. Parrend, P., Guigou, F., Navarro, J., Deruyver, A., Collet, P.: Artificial immune ecosystems: the role of expert-based learning in artificial cognition. In: ICAROB 2018| The International Conference on Artificial Life and Robotics, p. 5, February 2018. http://icube-publis.unistra.fr/4-PGND18a

15. Dubois, S., Lin, L., De Guio, R., Rasovska, I., Christian Weber, S.H.: From Simulation to Invention, beyond the Pareto-Frontier, Milan, Italy (2015)

16. Dubois, S., Eltzer, T., De Guio, R.: A dialectical based model coherent with inventive and optimization problems. Comput. Ind. **60**(8), 575–583 (2009). https://doi.org/10.1016/j.compind.2009.05.020

17. Dubois, S., Rasovska, I., De Guio, R.: Interpretation of a general model for inventive problems, the generalized system of contradictions (2009)

18. Lin, L., Rasovska, I., De Guio, R., Dubois, S.: Algorithm for identifying generalized technical contradictions in experiments. J. Eur. Systèmes Autom. JESA **47**(4–8), 563–588 (2013)

19. L. Lin, Optimization methods for inventive design, PhD thesis (2016)

20. Madara, D.S.: Theory of inventive problem solving (TRIZ): his-story, IJISET - Int. J. Innov. Sci. Eng. Technol. **2**(7), 86–95 (2015)

21. Hsu, C.-W., Chang, C.-C., Lin, C.-J. et al., A practical guide to support vector classification. Taipei (2003)

22. Bach, S., De Guio, R., Gartiser, N.: Combining discrete event simulation, data analysis, and TRIZ for fleet optimization. J. Eur. TRIZ Assoc. Innov. **4**(2), 47–61 (2017)

23. Chen, T., Guestrin, C.: Xgboost: a scalable tree boosting system. In: Proceedings of the 22nd ACM SIGKDD International Conference on Knowledge Discovery and Data Mining, pp. 785–794 (2016)

24. Malik, U., Barange, M., Ghannad, N., Saunier, J., Pauchet, A.: A generic machine learning based approach for addressee detection in multiparty interaction. In: Proceedings of the 19th ACM International Conference on Intelligent Virtual Agents, pp. 119–126 (2019)

25. Folleco, A., Khoshgoftaar, T.M., Napolitano, A.: Comparison of four performance metrics for evaluating sampling techniques for low quality class-imbalanced data. In: Seventh International Conference on Machine Learning and Applications, pp. 153–158 (2008)

26. Saito, T., Rehmsmeier, M.: The precision-recall plot is more informative than the ROC plot when evaluating binary classifiers on imbalanced datasets. PLoS ONE, **10**(3) (2015)

27. Hastie, T., Tibshirani, R., Friedman, J.: The Elements of Statistical Learning. SSS. Springer, New York (2009). https://doi.org/10.1007/978-0-387-84858-7

28. Cristianini, N., Shawe-Taylor, J., et al.: An Introduction to Support Vector Machines and Other Kernel-Based Learning Methods. Cambridge University Press, Cambridge (2000)

# Flow Structure Information Model for Multi-flow Problem Analysis of Complex Systems

Xuerui Wang[1,2](✉), Jianhui Zhang[1,2](✉), Ruikai Zhao[1,2],
Wenxu Zhang[3], and Congying Wang[3]

[1] School of Mechanical Engineering, Hebei University of Technology,
Tianjin 300130, China
798295382@qq.com, zhjh@hebut.edu.cn
[2] National Engineering Research Center for Technological Innovation Method
and Tool, Hebei University of Technology, Tianjin 300130, China
[3] China Ship Development and Design Center, Wuhan 430061, China

**Abstract.** In the process of the mutual transfer and transformation of material flow, energy flow and information flow in complex system, the property and type change of flow will have a negative effect on other miscarriages, resulting in a variety of flow problems in the system. This paper classifies the system flow based on the property of flow, puts forward 5 kinds of defective problem flow and corresponding 5 kinds of Multi-flow problems, establishes the symbol system of Multi-flow problems in complex system and the flow structure information model for Multi-flow problems analysis, and describes the system Multi-flow and Multi-flow problems by the basic element model in extension theory. In this paper, the flow structure information model of material flow, energy flow and information flow of the system is established. This model, combined with the elementary model, can reveal the mechanism of the Multi-flow problem in essence. A general process model for the analysis of the Multi-flow problem of complex system is proposed, and the feasibility of this model is verified by an example of a full-automatic small particle packaging machine.

**Keywords:** Complex system · Multi-flow problem · Flow structure information model · Primitive model · Particle packaging machine

## 1 Introduction

### 1.1 A Subsection Sample

"Flow" is a new concept developed in modern TRIZ [1], and has formed a systematic method to analyze and solve problems. The three foundations that constitute the objective world are matter, energy and information. Any system is constantly exchanging matter, energy and information between its internal links and between it and the external environment, thus forming material flow, energy flow and information flow in time and space [2].

In this paper, a large number of material flow, energy flow and information flow in a complex system are studied and defined as a system. Multiple flow problems caused by multiple flows in the process of transfer and transformation are called Multi-flow problem.

At present, there are many studies on flow analysis of material flow, energy flow and information flow in complex systems by domestic and foreign scholars. For example, TRIZ masters Simon Litvin [3] and Alex Lyubomirskiy of GEN3 company proposed flow analysis [3] theory. Sun Yongwei [4] stressed that flow analysis should deeply analyze the material flow, energy flow or information flow in the product system, and then identify some possible shortcomings in these flows, such as flow bottleneck, excessive conversion of flow and harmful effects of flow. Yang Jizhong [5] proposed that flow analysis is an analytical tool to identify the defects of material flow, energy flow and information flow in the system, and analyzes the defects not revealed mainly through the recognition function. Li [6] proposed that when using flow analysis to solve problems, engineering technical problems should first be established, and then flow analysis should be used to transform technical problems into defect flow model. Then flow analysis should be carried out with problem analysis tools to analyze the results of defect flow, and finally the final solution should be determined in flow evolution law.

However, with the increasing importance of innovative methods in product innovative design, the research on innovative design methods, especially the innovative design mechanism of complex systems, has become a hotspot in recent years. At present, however, the research results of innovative methods on Multi-flow problems in complex systems are rare, which cannot effectively guide the R & D personnel of enterprises to analyze complex problems. Therefore, it is necessary to carry out the analysis and research on the Multi-flow problems of complex systems, and to determine the scientific problems, so as to propose the solutions in the future.

## 2 Multi-flow Problem Analysis Method

Multi - flow problem of complex systems is a result of the existence of transmission in the process of energy dissipation devices, the conversion efficiency and design a system for complex systems respectively, flow properties and types of changes will produce negative effect to other streams, show the functional defects in the operation of the system caused by in singular, weakened, or function failure conditions, and many other problems. Therefore, the research on Multi-flow properties and types of complex systems is the basis for determining the types of Multi-flow problems in complex systems.

### 2.1 Attribute Analysis of Flows

Zhao Min [7] divided the attributes of the flow as follows:

(1) In the basic nature, it has the property of continuity and motility;
(2) In terms of functional types, it has such properties as useful, harmful, insufficient, excessive, wasteful, neutral, single first-class, composite flow, etc.;
(3) In the direction, there are forward, reverse, alternating properties;

(4) In the shape, there are long, short, thick, thin, curved, straight, cross section characteristics and other properties;

(5) On the ontology, there are properties such as mass, color, density, internal energy and flow rate;

(6) In terms of observation, there are measurable, unmeasurable and uncertain properties;

(7) On the channel, there are other properties such as patency, discontinuity, blockage, stagnation, and mutual damage between flow and channel.

## 2.2 Classification of Flow Problems

According to the attribute analysis of the above flow, in the case of excluding the normal flow, 5 different types of defect flows can be obtained in terms of the attributes of different flows, which are respectively: excessive flow, insufficient flow, stagnant flow, harmful flow and deflected flow.

At the same time, the 5 defect flows described correspond to one flow problem respectively, as shown in Table 1:

**Table 1.** Comparison table of problem flow and flow problem

| Problematic flow | → | Flow problem |
|---|---|---|
| Excessive flow | → | Flow excessiveness |
| Lost flow | → | Flow loss |
| Stagnant flow | → | Flow retention |
| Harmful flow | → | Flow deterioration |
| Deflected flow | → | Flow deflection |

## 2.3 Construction of Multi-flow Problem Analysis for Flow Structure Information

The previous part has classified the Multi-flow problem according to the attribute analysis of the Multi-flow in the Multi-flow problem, but the text description is more abstract, which also has a lot of inconvenience. Symbolized expression is intuitive and clear, which can more intuitively express the Multi-flow problem. In order to further study the generation mechanism of Multi-flow problem and explore its internal correlation, a flow structure information model which can describe the concrete manifestation of Multi-flow problem is proposed. This model is a Multi-flow problem generation mechanism model based on the flow structure information (MFP-FSI), that is, the Multi-flow problem analysis model based on the flow structure information. The whole process from generation to formation of the Multi-flow problem can be systematically analyzed by means of symbolic expression.

**The Symbol of the MFP-FSI Model Represents the System.** The MFP-FSI model is used to analyze the Multi-flow problem, so it is necessary to establish an applicable model notation for the analysis of the structure of the functional flow and the negative effects, so as to realize the description of each object. The negative effects include harmful effects, insufficient effects and excessive effects.

The description of functions in the MFP-FSI model includes normal functions and defective functions, which can be represented by the symbols of the existing model. At the same time, a functional element is added to the model, which may be both the object of negative effects and the source of negative effects. In addition, the representation of convection is further refined, including the classification of Multi-flow problems. At the same time, the representation symbols of negative effects are given in the model to facilitate the analysis of the sources and objects of negative effects. The specific MFP-FSI model symbol system is shown in Table 2.

**Table 2.** MFP-FSI model notation system

| Symbol | Name | Classify | Action |
|--------|------|----------|--------|
| | Normal function | Node symbol | Represents normal function |
| | Defect feature | Node symbol | Represents a functional defect |
| | Functional element | Node symbol | Represents the bearing structure |
| | Super system | Node symbol | Represents super system |
| \| | connection | Connection symbol | Represents the relationship |
| →→ | The normal flow | Connection symbol | Represents normal flow |
| —○→ | Flow excessiveness | Connection symbol | Represents flow excessiveness |
| ●○→ | Flow loss | Connection symbol | Represents flow loss |
| —○-► | Flow retention | Connection symbol | Represents flow retention |
| —○~ | Flow deterioration | Connection symbol | Represents flow deterioration |
| —○⤴ | Flow deflection | Connection symbol | Represents flow deflection |
| ~~~ | Harmful effects | Attribute symbols | Harmful effects |
| – – → | Lack of effects | Attribute symbols | Lack of effects |
| ——→ | Excess effect | Attribute symbols | Excess effect |

**Representation of Multi-flow Problem Under MFP-FSI Model.** The MFP-FSI model is used to formalize the Multi-flow problem. The Multi-flow problem can be divided into many cases according to its different forms. Therefore, the MFP-FSI model is applied to study the root cause of negative effects with flow structure as the key point.

The negative effect between the system flows is exerted on the functional flow or the functional realization carrier, which affects the realization of the system functions. The final expression of the Multi-flow problem is generally expressed in the form of design functional defects, and the final output is the problem flow.

Taking harmful effects as an example, there are 5 manifestations of multiple flow problems caused by them, as shown in Fig. 1:

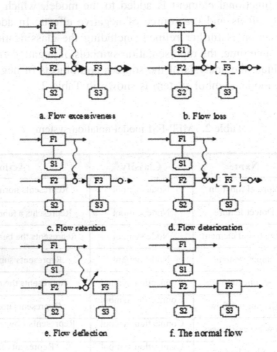

a. Flow excessiveness    b. Flow loss

c. Flow retention    d. Flow deterioration

e. Flow deflection    f. The normal flow

**Fig. 1.** Multi-flow problem analysis model based on flow structure information between multiple flows.

Figure 1.a shows that between functions, the flow has a harmful effect on other flows, resulting in excessive output flow.

Figure 1.b shows that between functions, the harmful effect of flow causes other flow losses, resulting in the final output flow loss.

Figure 1.c shows that between functions, the flow has a harmful effect on other flow retention, resulting in the final output flow retention.

Figure 1.d shows that between functions, the flow has a harmful effect on other flows, resulting in deterioration of the final output flow.

Figure 1.e shows that between functions, the flow has a detrimental effect on other flow deflections, resulting in the final output flow deflections.

In addition to the above 5 forms of Multi-flow problems, Fig. 1.f shows the structural information model of normal flow.

The function defects of Multi-flow problem are different with different objects. In addition to the negative effects on other flows, the Multi-flow problem will generally take the supersystem or the functional implementation carrier as the action object to cause damage to them and produce some undesirable effects. Also take the harmful effect as an example, there are three forms in total: Fig. 2.g shows that the flow will have a harmful effect on the action object in the supersystem; Fig. 2.h shows that the flow acting on the functional realization carrier will have a harmful effect on the corresponding functional realization process. Figure 2.i shows that the harmful effect of the flow in the process of function action causes the function input stream not to be transformed into the desired function output stream as required by function action.

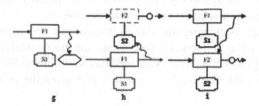

**Fig. 2.** Multi-flow problem analysis model based on flow structure information between the supersystem and the functional implementation carrier.

## 2.4   Standardized Description of Complex System Multi-flow Problems

**Significance of the Canonical Description of the Multi-flow Problem of the Primitive Model.** Before this paper has introduced the flow more symbols as well as information flow structure model of problem, but according to the description of the problem more flow also has many defects, such as the object is not specific, property is not accurate, quantity is not enough precise, etc., which makes the designer in the design process can't be sure what are impact between flow, unable to deeper analysis problem is caused by flow problem what attributes and the severity of the problem. Therefore, the standardized description of the material flow, energy flow, information flow and the Multi-flow problems caused by these flows in complex system is conducive to the analysis and solution of the problems.

Extenics [8] is the extension and innovation of the law of things and the method, its theoretical basis primitive model will be things of the characteristics of the object O, things c and its corresponding value v comprehensive consideration, using the combination of qualitative and quantitative method to comprehensively describe the process of objective things and their changes with ordered three yuan group as the basic unit of describing things, remember to R = (O, c, v). Use the element to describe the relationship between objects, and use the more formal relationship element to describe the interaction between objects, things, people, information and other objects.

$$R = \begin{bmatrix} O & c_1 \, v_1 \, c_2 \, v_2 & \vdots & c_n \, v_n \end{bmatrix} \tag{1}$$

**Analysis and Description of Multi-flow Problem Based on Primitive Model.** In the primitive model of Multi-flow problem, the object of the primitive model is not only the object of Multi-flow problem study, but also the object of taking measures to modify. The feature is the property that the object has, and it is the specific location that causes the effect of functional defect. An object has one or more properties that jointly cause the problem. The parameter is the specific value of the property in the research object, which is the most basic level of the solution. The innovative solution of the problem can be achieved by modifying the value of the quantity. The description of the parameter can be either a specific value or an adjective.

Taking the particle packaging machine as an example, according to the component analysis diagram of the constructed equipment, the paper analyzes it by means of resource analysis, flow analysis and other methods, and obtains the problems that need to be improved. A primitive model is used to normalize the problem, as shown in Table 3:

**Table 3.** Normalized description of Multi-flow problem of particle packaging machine

| Problem flow | Flow defect problem description |
|---|---|
| M1 | Material accumulation |
| E2 | Energy reduction |
| S3 | Signal disappears |

| Problem flow | Standardized description based on primitive model | Symbols for Multi-flow problems |
|---|---|---|
| M1 | R1= (O1, C1, V1) | —O— |
| E2 | E2= (O2, C2, V2) | —O→ |
| S3 | S3= (O3, C3, V3) | —O—▸ |

# 3   Multi-flow Problem Analysis Process Model

## 3.1   System Analysis

**Establish Component Analysis Diagram.** When facing a system, first of all, it is necessary to analyze the system and establish the reverse fishbone diagram of the system. After splitting each level of components through the reverse fishbone diagram of the system, the component analysis diagram is established according to the position of each component in the system and the actual relationship between each component, as shown in Fig. 3. S1–S6 represent the system components.

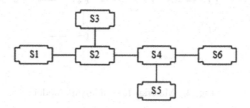

**Fig. 3.**   Component analysis diagram.

The component analysis diagram is different from the functional model of the system in that the components are simply connected with each other and there is no interaction between them. The component analysis diagram is also different from the functional structure of the system in that each block diagram represents not a single functional element.

**Resource Analysis.** Resources for complex systems analysis, first of all, determine the complex systems of material resources, energy resources, information resources, and dug up the function realization of the redundancy in the process of resources, finally according to the complex system of material resources, energy resources, information resources and redundant resources exist in the system of material flow, energy flow, information flow and redundant flow, as shown in Table 4.

**Table 4.**   System resource list and system Multi-flow list

| System resource list | | System Multi-flow list | |
|---|---|---|---|
| Material resources | …… | Material flow | …… |
| Energy resources | …… | Energy flow | …… |
| Information resources | …… | Information flow | …… |

### 3.2    MFP-FSI Model Construction of Material Flow, Energy Flow and Information Flow

After the resource analysis of the system, the specific material flow, energy flow and information flow in the system are determined. Here, the material flow is only taken as an example to establish the material flow analysis model, as shown in Fig. 4.

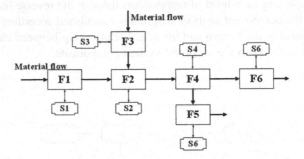

**Fig. 4.** Material flow analysis model

F1–F6 in the Fig. 4 represent the indivisible function elements in the system, and S1–S6 corresponding to them represent the carrier element of each function element. The material flow in the figure is the object of function, which connects the functional elements. The specific form of flow is that it takes the Multi-flow of continuous motion as the function carrier to make action on the object, change or maintain the attribute parameters or attributes of the object.

Next, the problems of material flow in the input stage, process stage and output stage are listed and briefly described. Further, the flow defect problem is standardized by the primitive model, and the type of flow problem is determined to be represented by the above symbol system, as shown in Table 5.

In view of the target system, the 5 flow problems in the system are identified and determined, and the MFP-FSI model of the system about the material flow is established by combining the above Multi-flow problem analysis model based on the flow structure information of a single flow, as shown in Fig. 5.

### 3.3    MFP-FSI General Model Construction Based on Component Analysis Diagram

Previously, corresponding MFP-FSI models have been established for material flow, energy flow and information flow respectively. Here, the mapping of the three MFP-FSI models to the component analysis diagram is made at the same time, and finally, the general mapping diagram of the total Multi-flow structure information is formed. The specific method is shown in Fig. 6.

In the MFP-FSI general model diagram, the structural information among the material flow, energy flow and information flow at the intersection location is identified, and the influence relationship between different types of flows is determined.

**Table 5.** Material flow defect information description

| Problem flow | Flow defect problem description |
|:---:|:---:|
| M1 | ...... |
| M2 | ...... |
| M3 | ...... |
| ...... | ...... |

| Problem flow | Standardized description based on primitive model | Symbols for Multi-flow problems |
|:---:|:---:|:---:|
| M1 | R1= (O1, C1, V1) | —◦➤ |
| M2 | R2= (O2, C2, V2) | —◦➤ |
| M3 | R3= (O3, C3, V3) | —◦➤ |
| ...... | ...... | ...... |

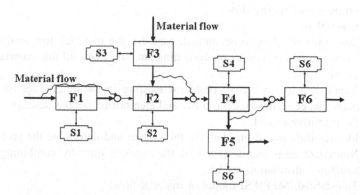

**Fig. 5.** MFP-FSI model of material flow

Then, the mechanism of Multi-flow problem is explored through the mutual restriction of the properties, characteristics and magnitude values between flows.

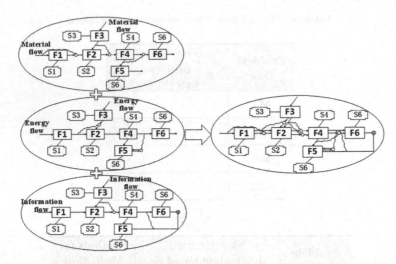

**Fig. 6.** MFP-FSI total model mapping method diagram

## 3.4    Multi-flow Problem Analysis Process Model

Based on the above, the Multi-flow problem analysis process model is established, as shown in Fig. 7, which is divided into 3 stages and 5 steps:

(1) Decompose the functional components of the system, draw the reverse fishbone diagram, and establish the component analysis diagram.

(2) Conduct resource analysis on the system to determine material resources, energy resources and information resources, and then determine material flow, information flow and energy flow.

(3) For material flow:

    A. Determine the flow to be studied, establish the material flow analysis model based on the component analysis diagram, and mark all the material flows in the diagram.

    B. Establish a list to list the problems existing in the input stage, process and output stage of the material flow, and then normalize the description through the primitive model.

    C. Identify the flow of problems in the system and determine the problem type.

    D. Normalize each manifestation of the material flow by combining the flow structure information model.

    E. To establish MFP-FSI model of material flow.

(4) The analysis of information flow and energy flow is the same as above, the last three flow MFP-FSI models map to the component analysis diagram at the same time to form the overall Multi-flow structure information mapping model diagram.

(5) Identify the flow structure information model of material, energy and information at the intersection location, analyze and reveal the mechanism of Multi-flow problem.

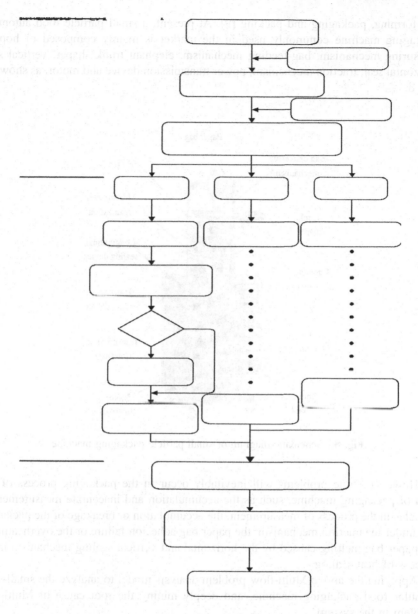

**Fig. 7.** Multi-flow problem analysis process model

# 4  Project Examples

With the rapid development of food processing industry, food packaging machinery rises rapidly. Particle quantification automatic packaging machine is a packaging machine used for granular materials. It has a complex structure and close relationship, and can realize the automation of packaging processes such as bag feeding, bag-making and forming, packaging and packing [9]. At present, a small particle food automatic packaging machine commonly used in the market is mainly composed of hopper, measuring mechanism, bag-feeding mechanism, elephant trunk shaper, vertical seal, horizontal seal, traction mechanism, power transmission device and motor, as shown in Fig. 8.

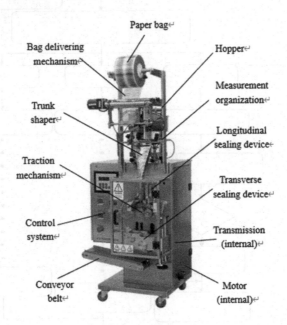

Paper bag

Bag delivering mechanism

Hopper

Trunk shaper

Measurement organization

Traction mechanism

Longitudinal sealing device

Control system

Transverse sealing device

Conveyor belt

Transmission (internal)

Motor (internal)

**Fig. 8.** Schematic diagram of small particle packaging machine

However, some problems will inevitably occur in the packaging process of this kind of packaging machine, such as the accumulation and inaccurate measurement of particles in the process of measurement, the accumulation or breakage of the packaging bag under the traction mechanism, the paper bag adhesion failure or the overheating of the paper bag melting caused by the horizontal and vertical sealing mechanism in the process of heat sealing.

Applying the above Multi-flow problem analysis model to analyze the small-scale granular food packaging machine, and deeply mining the root cause of Multi-flow problem in the system.

## 4.1   System Analysis

The system analysis of the small-scale granular food automatic packaging machine is carried out, and the reverse fishbone diagram separation system is established to obtain the system components, as shown in Fig. 9.

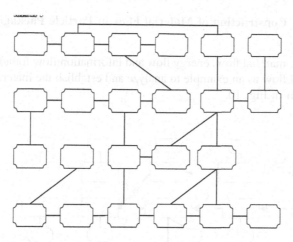

**Fig. 9.** Analysis diagram of packaging machine components

Analyze the resources of the small particle packaging machine, distinguish the material resources, energy resources and information resources in the system, and further determine the material flow, energy flow and information flow in the system, as shown in Table 6:

**Table 6.** System resource list and system Multi-flow list

| Resource type | Resources existing in the system |
|---|---|
| Material resources | Ground, paper bag, particle, packaging finished product, hopper, locking ring, bag conveying fixed rod, paper bag guide rod, measuring cup, scraper, opening and closing valve, quantitative bucket, elephant nose shaper, hot melt block, sensor, longitudinal sealing plate, transverse sealing plate, stepping motor, belt pulley, cutter, conveyor line, main motor, reducer, main shaft and cam, quantitative shaft |
| Energy resources | Electric energy, thermal energy, mechanical energy, gravitational potential energy, Joule heat |
| Information resources | Signal |

| Multi stream type | Multi-flow in the system |
|---|---|
| Material flow | Paper bag, particle and finished package |
| Energy flow | Electric energy, thermal energy, mechanical energy, gravitational potential energy, Joule heat |
| Information flow | Signal flow |

## 4.2    MFP-FSI Construction of Material Flow in Particle Packaging Machine

According to the material flow, energy flow and information flow found above, here we take the material flow as an example to analyze and establish the material flow analysis model, as shown in Fig. 10.

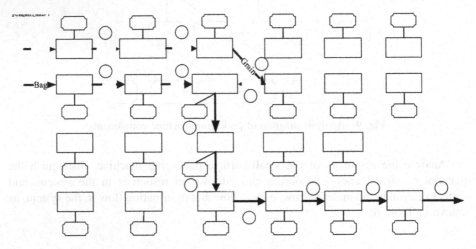

**Fig. 10.** Material flow analysis model

The flow process of "particle" and "paper bag" in the figure represents the flow process of material flow.

Next, based on the actual problems in the work of the particle packaging machine, a list is established. Then, for each problem with defects, the primitive model is used to normalize the description and determine the type of flow problem. The Multi-flow problem symbol system given in the paper is used to represent it, as shown in Table 7:

Establish MFP-FSI model of material flow in particle packaging machine, as shown in Fig. 11:

## 4.3    MFP-FSI General Model Construction of Particle Packaging Machine

After the MFP-FSI models of material flow, energy flow and information flow are established respectively, the flow structure information models of the three flows are mapped to the initial component analysis diagram, and finally the MFP-FSI model general diagram of particle packaging machine is formed, as shown in Fig. 12, which reflects the generation mechanism of Multi-flow problem of particle packaging machine, and Table 8 is a further explanation of Multi-flow problem in Fig. 12.

**Table 7.** Description of material flow defects

| Problem flow | Flow defect problem description |
|---|---|
| M2 | The particles in the quantitative bucket accumulate before the scraper |
| M2 | The scraper flattening material makes the measurement inaccurate |
| M3 | The scraper scratches particles |
| M5 | The paper bag is held in place by a locking ring |
| M6 | The paper bag was pulled and broken |
| M8 | The paper bag is poorly heat-sealed and unglued |
| M10 | Packaging overheating, paper bag melting |

| Problem flow | Standardized description based on primitive model | Symbols for Multi-flow problems |
|---|---|---|
| M2 | R2= (Particles, bulk density, large) | |
| M2 | R2= (Particles, metering accuracy, low) | |
| M3 | R3= (Particles, damage rate, high) | |
| M5 | R5= (Paper bag, conveying efficiency, low) | |
| M6 | R6= (Paper bag, damage rate, high) | |
| M8 | R7= (Paper bag, heat sealing effect, low) | |
| M10 | R8= (Paper bag, heat sealing effect, high) | |

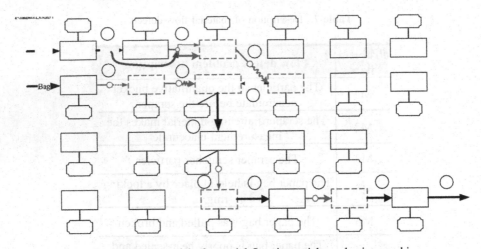

**Fig. 11.** MFP-FSI model of material flow in particle packaging machine

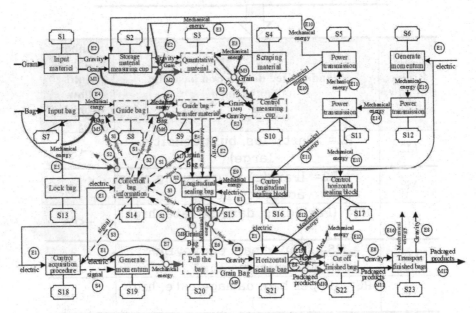

**Fig. 12.** General diagram of MFP-FSI model of particle packaging machine

**Table 8.** Summary of Multi-flow problems of particle packaging machine

| Problem flow | Problem symbol | Mechanism description of Multi-flow problem | Problem flow | Problem symbol | Mechanism description of Multi-flow problem |
|---|---|---|---|---|---|
| M2 | | The particles in the hopper fall too much and accumulate | M2' | | The excessive or too light scraping of the scraper materials resulting in inaccurate measurement |
| M3 | | The scraper has a strong force to scratch particles | M5 | | The paper bag is locked by mechanical force to produce retention |
| M6 | | The paper bag was broken by excessive strain | M8 | | The lack of heat caused the paper bag not to stick |
| M10 | | Excessive heat causes the paper bag to melt | E6 | | The low voltage causes the heating bar to be underheated and produce excess joule heat |
| E7 | | Electrical energy makes the mechanical energy of the stepper motor too large | E13 | | The high voltage causes the heating rod to overheat and produce excess joule heat |
| S2 | | The rupture of the paper bag caused the feedback signal flow to deflect | | | |

## 5   Conclusion

(1) In this paper, a set of flow structure information model for Multi-flow problem analysis in complex product system is proposed. The model can directly show the Multi-flow problems in complex system in the form of chart, and reveal the generation mechanism of Multi-flow problems.

(2) The flow structure information model is applied to the particle packaging machine to reveal the internal problems of the system, which is conducive to the solution of the convection defect problem.

**Acknowledgment.** The research is supported in part by the National Innovation Method Fund, China (No. 2018IM040300).

# References

1. Altshuller, G.: And Suddenly the Inventor Appeared. Technical Innovation Center, Inc., Worcester (1996)
2. Long, Y.: A large system research based on the coordination of material flow, energy flow and information flow. Huazhong University of Science and Technology, Wuhan (2009)
3. Simon, L.: Flow Analysis. GEN3 Partners, Inc., Boston (2015)
4. Sun, Y., Sergei, I.V.: TRIZ: The Golden key to Innovation I. Science Press, Beijing (2015)
5. Yang, J., Yan, H., Wei, Y., et al.: Research on low-frequency vibration reduction track structure based on TRIZ theory. J. Railway Eng. **32**(4), 60–64 (2015)
6. Jun, L., Mike, M.Z.: Deep understanding and applying flow analysis, simplified detective flow classification models. In: Proceedings of MATRIZ TRIZfest 2016 International Conference, pp. 122–130 (2016)
7. Zhao, M., Zhang, W., Wang, G.: TRIZ Advanced and Practical: The Invention Method of Da Dao Jian. China Machine Press, Beijing (2015)
8. Yang, C., Cai, W.: Extension Engineering. Science Press, Beijing (2007)
9. Zhang, H.: Accelerating the development of particle packaging machine in packaging industry. Plast. Manufact. **10**, 42–43 (2015)

# Multi-conflict Problem Resolution Process Model of Complex Technical System

Ruikai Zhao[1,2(✉)], Jianhui Zhang[1,2(✉)], Xinyu Zhang[2], Xuerui Wang[1,2], Congying Wang[3], and Wenxu Zhang[3]

[1] School of Mechanical Engineering, Hebei University of Technology, Tianjin 300130, China
m13672152230@163.com, zhjh@hebut.edu.cn
[2] National Technological Innovation Method and Tool Engineering Research Center, Tianjin 300130, China
[3] China Ship Development and Design Center, Wuhan 430061, China

**Abstract.** In view of the limitations of classical TRIZ theory in dealing with multi-conflict problems in complex technical systems, it is difficult to resolve multi-conflict problems quickly and effectively. The quantitative construction algorithm of multi-conflict problem network based on extension theory is introduced, so as to establish the hierarchical analysis structure of multi-conflict problems, to dig the essential relation between multi-conflict problems, and to quantitatively calculate the correlation degree of multi-conflict problems. On this basis, cluster analysis is carried out to classify conflict groups, in which conflicts belonging to different groups are solved in parallel way. Based on AHP, the serial resolution priority of multi-conflict problem in the same group is determined. Thus, the optimization solution path planning of multi-conflict problem network with unified series and parallel is completed, and the solution is completed by combining with relevant tools of TRIZ theory. In the end, the multi-conflict problem resolution process model of complex technical system is established, which provides necessary theoretical guidance and technical support for relevant research and engineering practice. The validity of the model is verified by the research on the no-avoidance stereo garage.

**Keywords:** Complex system · TRIZ · Multi-conflict problem · Multi-conflict network construction algorithm · Optimization solution path planning · Stereo garage

## 1 Introduction

The product innovation design Theory represented by TRIZ (Theory of inventive problem solving) holds that the elimination of conflicts in the system is the driving force for its development and evolution [1]. However, in the face of multi-conflict problems in complex technical systems, the classical TRIZ theory is difficult to solve directly due to its difficulty in resolution, wide coverage of fields, and complex relations among conflict elements [2].

For this reason, many scholars have carried out researches from their own perspectives. Khomenko [3] proposed OTSM theory (General theory of powerful thinking), which can effectively manage complex system problems. The complex problem is decomposed and iterated layer by layer by applying the problem flow technique, and the problem flow network is constructed to complete the solution. However, there are some problems in the analysis process, which are influenced by subjective factors and inefficient in solving, and there is no clear systematic conflict resolution method. On this basis, Han [4] established a pyramidal initial problem analysis process model in combination with graph theory. Through the analysis and description of the complex problems and the relations among the sub-problems, the difficulty of the subsequent solution is reduced. However, there is still a lack of effective multi-conflict solution. Czinki [5] used Cynefin framework to analyze the problems of complex systems, to divide different problem domains, and to recommend appropriate TRIZ tools for solving different problem types. However, this analysis method is macroscopical and has weak operability in practical engineering application. Zhang [6] analyzed the frequency of application of the invention principle from the perspective of statistics, and on this basis proposed a fast method for solving multiple conflicts, but it lacked consideration of the interaction between multiple conflicts. Zhou [7] integrated TRIZ and extension theory and established a transformation model between them, which can effectively solve two types of conflict problems in system design. But it fails to consider the influence of non-core conflict factors on the solution result, as well as the parameter coupling between multiple conflicts. Zhang [1] formally described complex system problems based on extension theory. The problem flow network is constructed, the key problems are selected, then the conflict network and parameter network are established, and the key conflicts are determined. A systematic multi-conflict network construction and resolution process is formed, but the efficient multi-conflict network solution method is still lacking.

In general, there are still relatively few researches on multi-conflict problem solving of complex technical systems. The analysis process usually relies on the subjective experience of the operator and lacks the consideration of the coupling effect between multi-conflict problems. Moreover, there is no systematic method to guide the determination of optimal solution path of multi-conflict network in engineering practice. For this reason, this paper identifies and analyzes the conflicts in complex technical systems according to the methods in literature [8]. Then, the ENV (Element-name-value) model was used to standardize the expression of the multi-conflict problems, and the essential relationship between them was mined with the help of Extension Theory, so as to propose a quantitative construction algorithm for the network of multi-conflict problems network.

After the construction of the multi-conflict network, the cluster analysis is carried out according to the correlation degree of multi-conflict to classify the conflict groups. The conflicts belonging to different groups were solved in parallel, and the resolution priority of conflicts belonging to the same group was determined by the judgment matrix method in AHP (Analytic Hierarchy Process). Thus, the optimization solution path planning of the multi-conflict problem network with unified series and parallel is completed, and the resolution is completed by combining with TRIZ tool. Finally, the multi-conflict resolution process model of complex technical system is established.

## 2   Multi-conflict Network Construction

### 2.1   ENV Normalization of Conflicts

According to the conflict representation method of ENV model [9], any conflict problem can be composed of one control parameter and multiple evaluation parameters:

$$TC_i = (CP_1^{(i)}, EP_1^{(i)}, EP_2^{(i)}, \cdots, EP_k^{(i)}) \ (k \geq 2) \tag{1}$$

Where $TC_i$ represents the conflict $i$, $CP_1^{(i)}$ represents the control parameter of conflict $i$, and $EP_k^{(i)}$ represents the k-th (k $\geq$ 2) evaluation parameter of conflict $i$.

Figure 1 shows an example of conflicts expressed by the ENV model, where $E_1, E_2$ and $E_3$ are design objects associated with control parameter $CP_1$, evaluation parameter $EP_1$ and evaluation parameter $EP_2$, respectively. While $V_a$ is the positive parameter value and $\overline{V_a}$ is the negative parameter value.

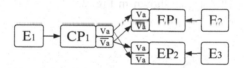

**Fig. 1.** Examples of conflicts expressed by the ENV model

### 2.2   Extension Analysis of Conflict

In order to explore the intrinsic relationship between multiple conflict problems, the extension analysis method in Extension Theory [10] is introduced to study the possibility and formal representation of conflict extension. Extension Theory, a new cross-cutting discipline spanning philosophy, mathematics and engineering, is used to explore ways and possibilities of expanding things. On the basis of the extension primitive model, the characteristics and corresponding values of conflict $i$ are described. Through correlation analysis, the subject matter-element of conflict parameter related to conflict elements is expanded, as shown in Eq. (2).

Among them, $M_1, M_2, \cdots, M_n$ respectively represent the design object's object elements of conflict parameters related to conflict object element $M$. With the help of decomposable analysis, the multiple primitives of each conflict parameter body are decomposed. Then based on the divergence analysis principle, the key feature elements are excavated and the organizational structure is expanded. Based on the formal description of the primitive model, the hierarchical analysis structure of the conflict is obtained, which provides the prerequisite for the quantitative construction of the multi-conflict network.

Suppose the conflict $TC_t$ contains $m$ conflict characteristic parameters, i.e. $TC_t = (X_1^{(t)}, \cdots, X_m^{(t)})$ (Note: $X_m^{(t)}$ represents $CP$ and $EP$ in the previous Sect. 2.1). Each conflict parameter corresponds to a design object, and the conflict parameter $X_i^{(t)}$ corresponds to the design object $S_i^{(t)}$, which contains $n$ functional elements, i.e. $S_i^{(t)} = (T_1^{(t,i)}, \cdots, T_j^{(t,i)}, \cdots, T_n^{(t,i)})$ (Notes: ① $S_i^{(t)}$ represents $E$ in the previous Sect. 2.1; ② Although each conflict parameter corresponds to a design object, the relationship between them is not a one-to-one mapping. Because different conflict parameters may correspond to the same design object). Let the functional element $T_j^{(t,i)}$ have $s$ technical characteristic parameters, expressed as: $T_j^{(t,i)} = \begin{bmatrix} O_j^{(t,i)} & C_j^{(t,i)} & V_j^{(t,i)} \end{bmatrix}$. $O_j^{(t,i)}$ generally refers to the object being described. The characteristic is represented as $C_j^{(t,i)} = \begin{bmatrix} c_1^{(t,i,j)} & \cdots & c_s^{(t,i,j)} \end{bmatrix}^T$, and its corresponding value is represented as $V_j^{(t,i)} = \begin{bmatrix} v_1^{(t,i,j)} & \cdots & v_s^{(t,i,j)} \end{bmatrix}^T$, as shown in Fig. 2.

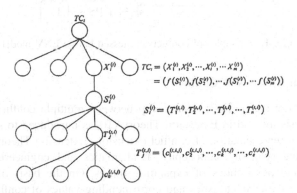

$$TC_t = (X_1^{(t)}, X_2^{(t)}, \cdots, X_i^{(t)}, \cdots X_m^{(t)})$$
$$= (f(S_1^{(t)}), f(S_2^{(t)}), \cdots f(S_i^{(t)}), \cdots f(S_m^{(t)}))$$

$$S_i^{(t)} = (T_1^{(t,i)}, T_2^{(t,i)}, \cdots, T_j^{(t,i)}, \cdots, T_n^{(t,i)})$$

$$T_j^{(t,i)} = (c_1^{(t,i,j)}, c_2^{(t,i,j)}, \cdots, c_k^{(t,i,j)}, \cdots, c_s^{(t,i,j)})$$

**Fig. 2.** The schematic diagram to extend the hierarchical structure of conflict

$$M = (O_m, C_m, V_m) = \begin{bmatrix} conflit\,i & CP & v_1 \\ & \text{Design object} & v_2 \\ & \text{of CP} & \\ & EP_1 & v_3 \\ & \text{Design object} & v_4 \\ & \text{of } EP_1 & \\ & \vdots & \vdots \\ & EP_n & v_{n'} \\ & \text{Design object} & v_{n'+1} \\ & \text{of } EP_1 & \end{bmatrix}$$

$$\sim \begin{cases} M_1 = (O_{m1}, C_{m1}, V_{m1}) \\ \quad = \begin{bmatrix} O_{m1} & \text{The conflit corresponding} & v_1^{(m1)} \\ & \text{to the design object of } CP^1 & \\ & \vdots & \vdots \\ & \text{The conflit corresponding} & v_k^{(m1)} \\ & \text{to the design object of } CP^k & \\ & \text{The conflit corresponding} & v_{k+1}^{(m1)} \\ & \text{to the design object of } EP^1 & \\ & \vdots & \vdots \\ & \text{The conflit corresponding} & v_{k+t}^{(m1)} \\ & \text{to the design object of } EP^t & \end{bmatrix} \\ \qquad\qquad \vdots \\ M_n = (O_{mn}, C_{mn}, V_{mn}) \\ \quad = \begin{bmatrix} O_{mn} & \text{The conflit corresponding} & v_1^{(mn)} \\ & \text{to the design object of } CP^1 & \\ & \vdots & \vdots \\ & \text{The conflit corresponding} & v_{k'}^{(mn)} \\ & \text{to the design object of } CP^{k'} & \\ & \text{The conflit corresponding} & v_{k'+1}^{(mn)} \\ & \text{to the design object of } EP^1 & \\ & \vdots & \vdots \\ & \text{The conflit corresponding} & v_{k'+t'}^{(mn)} \\ & \text{to the design object of } EP^{t'} & \end{bmatrix} \end{cases} \qquad (2)$$

## 2.3 Quantitative Construction Algorithm of Multi-conflict Network

There are two main forms of conflict network, namely one-way connection and two-way connection (undirected line). The advantage of one-way connection is that it is easy to form causal chain. By identifying the key breakthrough of conflict with the nature of "root cause", the multi-conflict network can be solved readily. However, in the complex technical system, it is often difficult to directly judge the relationship between the active and passive impact of conflicts, and sometimes even shows the coupling relationship. Therefore, it is more universal to use undirected line to connect each conflict.

(1) The first step is to make a qualitative analysis on the multi-conflict problem of the standardized expression of ENV, and determine the design object subject corresponding to the conflict parameter through extension correlation analysis.

(2) The second step is to mine the main functional elements and key technical characteristic parameters contained in the design object based on the extension analysis, and form the multi-conflict hierarchical analysis structure.

(3) The third step is to determine the characteristic quantity domain and node characteristic value of each hierarchy. Suppose the conflict parameter body of conflict $TC_t(t = 1, 2, \cdots, l)$ is $S_i^{(t)}(i = 1, 2, \cdots, m)$, including $n$ elements. Taking the j-th component $T_j^{(t,i)}$ $(j = 1, 2, \cdots, n)$ as an example, the extension primitive model is established:

$$
T_j^{(t,i)} = \begin{bmatrix} O_j^{(t,i)} & c_1^{(t,i,j)} & v_1^{(t,i,j)} \\ & \vdots & \vdots \\ & c_k^{(t,i,j)} & v_k^{(t,i,j)} \\ & \vdots & \vdots \\ & c_s^{(t,i,j)} & v_s^{(t,i,j)} \end{bmatrix}
\tag{3}
$$

Corresponding characteristic quantity domain $V_j^{\prime(t,i)}$ and optimal quantity domain $V_j^{\prime\prime(t,i)}$ are expressed as:

$$
V_j^{\prime(t,i)} = \begin{bmatrix} V_1^{\prime(t,i,j)} \\ \vdots \\ V_k^{\prime(t,i,j)} \\ \vdots \\ V_s^{\prime(t,i,j)} \end{bmatrix}, V_j^{\prime\prime(t,i)} = \begin{bmatrix} V_1^{\prime\prime\prime(t,i,j)} \\ \vdots \\ V_k^{\prime\prime(t,i,j)} \\ \vdots \\ V_s^{\prime\prime(t,i,j)} \end{bmatrix}
\tag{4}
$$

Among them, $V_k^{\prime(t,i,j)} = \left\langle c_k^{(t,i,j)}, d_k^{(t,i,j)} \right\rangle (k = 1, 2, \cdots, s)$ represents the quantity domain of the k-th technical characteristic parameter of $T_j^{(t,i)}$, while $V_k^{\prime\prime(t,i,j)} = \left\langle a_k^{(t,i,j)}, b_k^{(t,i,j)} \right\rangle$ is the optimal quantity domain of the k-th feature of $T_j^{(t,i)}$.

(4) The fourth step is to calculate the comprehensive correlation function value of each conflict, as shown below:

$$
K(TC_t) = \sum_i \alpha_i^{(t)} \left[ \sum_j \beta_j^{(t,i)} \left( \sum_k \omega_k^{(t,i,j)} k\left( v_k^{(t,i,j)} \right) \right) \right]
\tag{5}
$$

Where, $\alpha_i^{(t)}$ represents the weight of design objects corresponding to conflict parameters, $\beta_j^{(t,i)}$ represents the weight of functional components, and $\omega_k^{(t,i,j)}$ represents the weight of technical characteristic parameters, satisfying $\sum_i \alpha_i^{(t)} = 1$, $\sum_j \beta_j^{(t,i)} = 1$ and $\sum_k \omega_k^{(t,i,j)} = 1$ respectively. Specific parameters can be assigned according to engineering experience, field expert evaluation, comparative matrix method [11] and other methods. And the correlation function $k\left(v_k^{(t,i,j)}\right)$:

$$
k\left(v_k^{(t,i,j)}\right) = \begin{cases} \dfrac{\rho\left(v_k^{(t,i,j)},v_k''^{(t,i,j)}\right)}{\rho\left(v_k^{(t,i,j)},v_k'^{(t,i,j)}\right)-\rho\left(v_k^{(t,i,j)},v_k''^{(t,i,j)}\right)}, & v_k^{(t,i,j)} \notin V_k''^{(t,i,j)} \\[4mm] \dfrac{-2\rho\left(v_k^{(t,i,j)},v_k'^{(t,i,j)}\right)}{\left|b_k^{(t,i,j)}-a_k^{(t,i,j)}\right|}, & v_k^{(t,i,j)} \in V_k''^{(t,i,j)} \end{cases}
\tag{6}
$$

(5) The fifth step is to obtain the comprehensive correlation function of each conflict by combining Eqs. (3)–(6), and to calculate the Relevance between any two:

$$
R(TC_t, TC_u) = 1 - \lambda(|K(TC_t) - K(TC_u)|)^p
$$
$$
(t, u = 1, 2, \cdots, l)
\tag{7}
$$

Where, $\lambda$ and $p$ are adjustment parameters to normalize the value range to $[0, 1]$, and $l$ is the number of conflicts.

(6) Finally, the conflicts are connected according to their Relevance. The node represents the multi-conflict problem expressed by ENV standardization, and the undirected line represents the connection between conflicts. The number marked on the line represents the corresponding correlation degree, and the value range is $[0, 1]$. The larger the value, the closer the relationship between the two, as shown in Fig. 3.

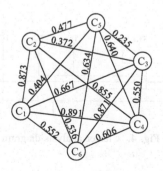

**Fig. 3.** Examples of multi-conflict problem networks

## 3   Determination of Optimal Solution Path for Multi-conflict Network

### 3.1   Cluster Analysis of Multi-conflict Problems

In order to realize the efficient solution of multi-conflict problem networks, this paper proposes an optimal solution path planning method for multi-conflict problem network based on cluster analysis and AHP. Through cluster analysis [12], a large number of multi-conflict problems in the complex technical system are divided into several different conflict groups in an appropriate way.

Firstly, the fuzzy similarity relation between conflicting elements in the multi-conflict problem set is established. Let the domain $X = \{TC_1, \cdots, TC_n\}$ represent the set of multi-conflict problems to be classified, n is the total number of conflicts, and the multi-conflict fuzzy similarity matrix is:

$$(r_{ij})_{n \times n} = R(TC_i, TC_j) \, i, j = 1, 2, \cdots, n \tag{8}$$

The transitive closure is obtained and then fuzzy clustering is carried out, which meets the following requirements:

$$t(R) \circ t(R) \subseteq t(R) \wedge R \subseteq t(R)$$
$$\wedge \, \forall S \supseteq R, \, S^2 \subseteq S \Rightarrow S \supseteq t(R) \tag{9}$$

The clustering stop threshold $\lambda$ can be determined by the average correlation, that is:

$$\lambda = R' = \frac{\sum\limits_{i=1}^{n} \sum\limits_{j=1}^{n} r'_{ij}}{n^2} \tag{10}$$

Thus, the conflict set $X$ is divided into several groups. The conflict in the same group needs to be further determined because of its high correlation degree, while the conflict in different groups can be solved in parallel. The clustering analysis of conflict networks described in Fig. 3 is shown in Fig. 4.

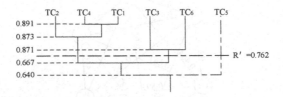

**Fig. 4.** Cluster analysis diagram

## 3.2    Determination of Multi-conflict Resolution Path in the Same Group

In order to determine the solution path of multi-conflict problems under the same group, the judgment matrix method in AHP [13] (Analytic Hierarchy Process) was introduced, and its weight was assigned according to its importance, horizontal influence range and vertical universality. The pairwise comparison matrices of the control parameters and their corresponding evaluation parameters are established respectively. The weight vectors of all control parameters and their evaluation parameters were determined, and the evaluation information at all levels was integrated to obtain the resolution priority sequence of multi-conflict problems in the same group.

Let $A = (a_{ij})_{s \times s}$ be the judgment matrix of the control parameters corresponding to a multi-conflict problem group $TC = \{TC_1, \cdots, TC_s\}$ to be evaluated, and $B_t = (b_{uv})_{k \times k}$ be the judgment matrix of the evaluation parameters corresponding to the control parameters of conflict $TC_t$ $(t \in 1, 2, \cdots, s)$. The scale method of 1–9 was used to compare the different parameters in pairs, as shown in Table 1.

**Table 1.** The scale meaning of the judgment matrix

| Scale | Meaning |
|---|---|
| 1 | The two elements are of equal importance; |
| 3 | The former is slightly more important than the latter |
| 5 | The former is more important than the latter |
| 7 | Compared with the latter, the former is very important |
| 9 | Compared with the latter, the former is extremely important |
| 2, 4, 6, 8 | Represents the intermediate value of the above adjacent judgment |
| Reciprocal | Represents factor $j$ ratio $i$, such as: $a_{ji} = 1/a_{ij}$ |

The weight coefficient $\omega_i^{(CP)}$ of the control parameters in this group is:

$$\omega_i^{(CP)} = \frac{\left( \prod_{j=1}^{s} a_{ij} \right)^{1/s}}{\sum_{i=1}^{s} \left( \prod_{j=1}^{s} a_{ij} \right)^{1/s}} \quad i = 1, 2, \cdots, s \tag{11}$$

The evaluation parameter weight coefficient $\omega_u^{(CP,EP)}$ is calculated similarly (Just replace $a_{ij}$ in Eq. (11) with $b_{ij}$). Then check the consistency of the judgment matrix and calculate the consistency index (CI):

$$CI = \frac{\lambda_{max} - s}{s - 1} \tag{12}$$

And consistency ratio (CR):

$$CR = \frac{CI}{RI} \tag{13}$$

Where, $RI$ is the average random consistency index. Matrix consistency is acceptable when CR is less than 0.10, otherwise it should be appropriately corrected. $IF_u^{(CP,EP)}$ indicates the influence degree of the control parameters on the evaluation parameters, and the value range is $\{1, 2, \cdots, 5\}$. The larger the value is, the stronger the influence degree is.

From this, the comprehensive value $Z(TC_t)$ of each conflict can be obtained.

$$Z(TC_t) = \sum_u \omega_i^{(CP)} \cdot \omega_u^{(CP_i,EP)} \cdot IF_u^{(CP_i,EP)} \tag{14}$$

Thus, the resolution priority sequence of the multi-conflict problem in this group is obtained by descending order of the comprehensive value. By analogy with other groups, the optimal solution path of multi-conflict network with unified series and parallel can be determined and solved by combining with TRIZ tool. If a class group contains only a single conflict, it can be solved directly.

# 4    Multi-conflict Resolution Process Model of Complex Technical System

To sum up, the multi-conflict resolution process model of complex technical system is formed, which is divided into three stages, including 14 main steps, as shown in Fig. 5 and Table 2.

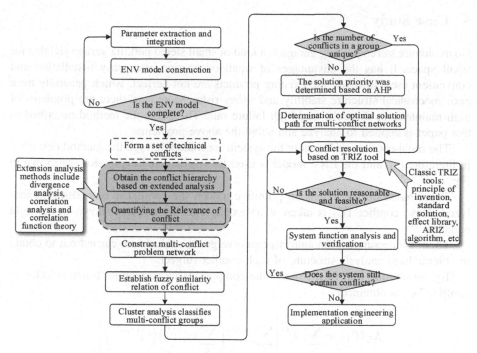

**Fig. 5.** Multi-conflict resolution process model of complex technical system

**Table 2.** Complex technical system multi-conflict problem elimination process model construction process

| Stage | Steps | Operating content |
|---|---|---|
| The first | 1 | Extract the conflict control parameters and their evaluation parameters; |
| | 2 | ENV standardized expression; |
| | 3 | Based on the extended analysis, the structure of conflict hierarchy analysis is obtained |
| | 4 | Quantitative analysis and calculation of conflict Relevance; |
| | 5 | Construct multi-conflict problem network; |
| The second | 6 | To establish the fuzzy similarity between the conflicts; |
| | 7 | The transitive closure is calculated and the clustering analysis is carried out |
| | 8 | Classification of multi-conflict problem groups; |
| | 9 | The priority of conflict resolution was determined based on AHP; |
| | 10 | The optimal solution path of multi-conflict network is determined; |
| The last | 11 | Using TRIZ tool to solve the conflict; |
| | 12 | To test the feasibility of the solution; |
| | 13 | System function analysis and verification; |
| | 14 | Complete innovative solution and implement engineering application |

## 5    Case Study

No avoidance stereo parking garage is a kind of small stereo parking garage suitable for small space. It has the advantages of small occupation area, easy installation and convenient use. However, the existing products are not perfect, which generally have poor mechanical structure stability and safety risks. Moreover, there are problems of high maintenance difficulty and high failure rate. Therefore, the method described in this paper is applied to analyze and solve the above problems.

The multi-conflict problems in the system are mined through the method described in literature [8], and the ENV model is used for standardized expression, as shown in Fig. 6.

Then, based on the extension primitive model, the conflict is extended and analyzed. Now, conflict $TC_1$ is taken as an example to illustrate, as shown in the right equation:

Then, the decomposition analysis and divergence analysis are carried out to obtain the hierarchical analysis structure of each conflict subject.

By substituting into Eqs. (5)–(6), the comprehensive correlation function value of conflict $TC_1$ is obtained:

$$K(TC_1) = \sum_i \alpha_i^{(1)} \left[ \sum_j \beta_j^{(1,i)} \left( \sum_k \omega_k^{(1,i,j)} k\left(v_k^{(1,i,j)}\right) \right) \right]$$

$$= 0.637$$

The calculation method of $K(TC_t)$ for other conflicts is similar, and the results are shown in Table 3. Substitute in formula (7), calculate the Relevance between the conflicts ($\lambda = 5.2, p = 1$), and then establish a multi-conflict problem network, as shown in Fig. 7.

$$M_{TC_1} = (O_{TC_1}, C_{TC_1}, V_{TC_1}) = \begin{bmatrix} TC_1 & CP & \text{Support way} \\ & S_1 & \text{Support frame construction} \\ & EP_1 & \text{Operability} \\ & S_2 & \text{Docking arrangement device} \\ & EP_2 & \text{Safety performance} \\ & S_3 & \text{Carrying car device} \\ & EP_3 & \text{Intensity} \\ & S_4 & \text{Support frame construction} \\ & EP_4 & \text{Structural stability} \\ & S_5 & \text{The device that drives movement} \\ & EP_5 & \text{Structural complexity} \\ & S_6 & \text{The device that drives rotation} \end{bmatrix}$$

$$\sim \left\{ \begin{array}{l} M_{S_1}^{(TC_1)} = \left( O_{S_1}^{(TC_1)}, C_{S_1}^{(TC_1)}, V_{S_1}^{(TC_1)} \right) \\[4pt] = \begin{bmatrix} \text{Support frame construction} & \begin{array}{l}\text{The conflit corresponding} \\ \text{to the design object of } CP^1\end{array} & TC_1 \\ & \begin{array}{l}\text{The conflit corresponding} \\ \text{to the design object of } EP^1\end{array} & TC_1 \\ & \cdots EP^2 & TC_5 \\ & \cdots EP^3 & TC_{10} \end{bmatrix} \\[4pt] M_{S_2}^{(TC_1)} = \left( O_{S_2}^{(TC_1)}, C_{S_2}^{(TC_1)}, V_{S_2}^{(TC_1)} \right) \\[4pt] = \begin{bmatrix} \text{Docking arrangement device} & \begin{array}{l}\text{The conflit corresponding} \\ \text{to the design object of } EP^1\end{array} & TC_1 \\ & \cdots EP^2 & TC_3 \\ & \cdots EP^3 & TC_6 \\ & \cdots EP^4 & TC_8 \\ & \cdots EP^5 & TC_9 \end{bmatrix} \\[4pt] M_{S_3}^{(TC_1)} = \left( O_{S_3}^{(TC_1)}, C_{S_3}^{(TC_1)}, V_{S_3}^{(TC_1)} \right) \\[4pt] = \begin{bmatrix} \text{Carrying car device} & \begin{array}{l}\text{The conflit corresponding} \\ \text{to the design object of } EP^1\end{array} & TC_1 \\ & \cdots EP^2 & TC_2 \\ & \cdots EP^3 & TC_4 \end{bmatrix} \\[4pt] M_{S_4}^{(TC_1)} = \left( O_{S_4}^{(TC_1)}, C_{S_4}^{(TC_1)}, V_{S_4}^{(TC_1)} \right) \\[4pt] = \begin{bmatrix} \begin{array}{l}\text{The device that} \\ \text{drives movement}\end{array} & \begin{array}{l}\text{The conflit corresponding} \\ \text{to the design object of } CP^1\end{array} & TC_6 \\ & \begin{array}{l}\text{The conflit corresponding} \\ \text{to the design object of } EP^1\end{array} & TC_1 \\ & \cdots EP^2 & TC_3 \\ & \cdots EP^3 & TC_5 \\ & \cdots EP^4 & TC_7 \\ & \cdots EP^5 & TC_8 \\ & \cdots EP^6 & TC_9 \end{bmatrix} \\[4pt] M_{S_5}^{(TC_1)} = \left( O_{S_5}^{(TC_1)}, C_{S_5}^{(TC_1)}, V_{S_5}^{(TC_1)} \right) \\[4pt] = \begin{bmatrix} \begin{array}{l}\text{The device that} \\ \text{drives rotation}\end{array} & \begin{array}{l}\text{The conflit corresponding} \\ \text{to the design object of } CP^1\end{array} & TC_3 \\ & \begin{array}{l}\text{The conflit corresponding} \\ \text{to the design object of } EP^1\end{array} & TC_1 \\ & \cdots EP^2 & TC_5 \\ & \cdots EP^3 & TC_{10} \end{bmatrix} \end{array} \right.$$

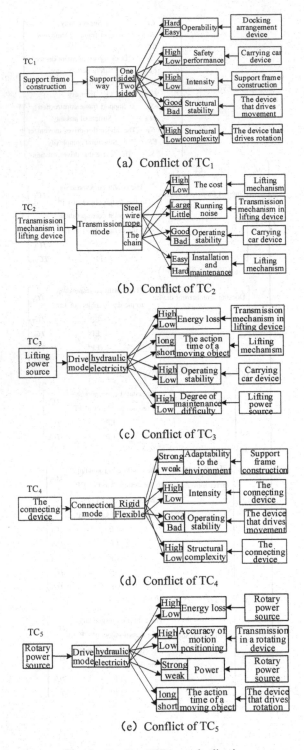

（a）Conflict of TC$_1$

（b）Conflict of TC$_2$

（c）Conflict of TC$_3$

（d）Conflict of TC$_4$

（e）Conflict of TC$_5$

**Fig. 6.** Conflict ENV standardization

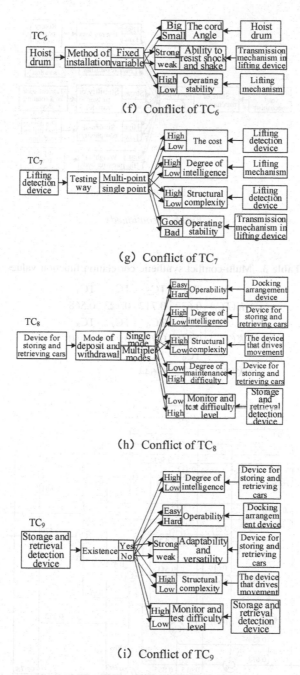

(f)  Conflict of TC$_6$

(g)  Conflict of TC$_7$

(h)  Conflict of TC$_8$

(i)  Conflict of TC$_9$

**Fig. 6.**  (*continued*)

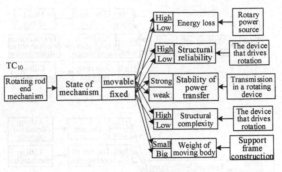

(j)  Conflict of $TC_{10}$

**Fig. 6.**  (*continued*)

**Table 3.**  Multi-conflict synthetic correlation function values

|           | $TC_1$ | $TC_2$ | $TC_3$ | $TC_4$ |
|-----------|--------|--------|--------|--------|
| $K(TC_i)$ | 0.637  | 0.712  | 0.723  | 0.568  |
|           | $TC_5$ | $TC_6$ | $TC_7$ | $TC_8$ |
| $K(TC_i)$ | 0.616  | 0.706  | 0.700  | 0.640  |
|           | $TC_9$ | $TC_{10}$ |     |        |
| $K(TC_i)$ | 0.642  | 0.644  |        |        |

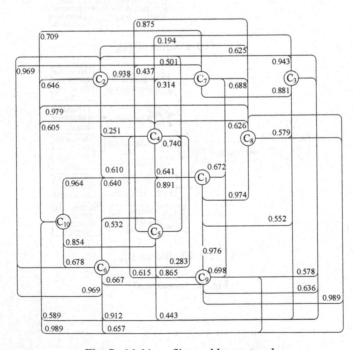

**Fig. 7.**  Multi-conflict problem network

According to Eq. (8), the 10th order fuzzy similarity matrix $R = (r_{ij})_{10 \times 10}$ is obtained, as shown in Table 4.

**Table 4.** Fuzzy similarity matrix for multi-conflict problems

$$R = \begin{bmatrix} 1 & 0.610 & 0.552 & 0.641 & 0.891 & 0.640 & 0.672 & 0.974 & 0.976 & 0.974 \\ 0.610 & 1 & 0.943 & 0.251 & 0.501 & 0.969 & 0.938 & 0.625 & 0.636 & 0.646 \\ 0.552 & 0.943 & 1 & 0.194 & 0.443 & 0.912 & 0.881 & 0.579 & 0.578 & 0.589 \\ 0.641 & 0.251 & 0.194 & 1 & 0.740 & 0.283 & 0.314 & 0.626 & 0.615 & 0.605 \\ 0.891 & 0.501 & 0.443 & 0.740 & 1 & 0.532 & 0.437 & 0.875 & 0.865 & 0.854 \\ 0.640 & 0.969 & 0.912 & 0.283 & 0.532 & 1 & 0.969 & 0.657 & 0.667 & 0.678 \\ 0.672 & 0.938 & 0.881 & 0.314 & 0.437 & 0.969 & 1 & 0.688 & 0.698 & 0.709 \\ 0.974 & 0.625 & 0.579 & 0.626 & 0.875 & 0.657 & 0.688 & 1 & 0.989 & 0.979 \\ 0.976 & 0.636 & 0.578 & 0.615 & 0.865 & 0.667 & 0.698 & 0.989 & 1 & 0.989 \\ 0.974 & 0.646 & 0.589 & 0.605 & 0.854 & 0.678 & 0.709 & 0.979 & 0.989 & 1 \end{bmatrix}$$

The transitive closure is calculated from Eqs. (9)–(10) to complete the clustering, and the result divides the multi-conflict problem set into three categories, i.e. $\{TC_2, TC_3, TC_6, TC_7\}, \{TC_1, TC_5, TC_8, TC_9, TC_{10}\}, \{TC_4\}$ as shown in Fig. 8.

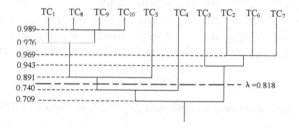

**Fig. 8.** Cluster analysis of multi-conflict problem

For multi-conflicts within the same group, the judgment matrix method in AHP was used to determine the solution priority relation due to its high degree of association. Let's take group $\{TC_1, TC_5, TC_8, TC_9, TC_{10}\}$ as an example.

Firstly, the weight coefficient $\omega_i^{(CP)}$ of each conflict control parameter in the same group and the weight coefficient $\omega_u^{(CP,EP)}$ of the evaluation parameter corresponding to each control parameter were determined. Where: $\omega_1^{(CP)}, \omega_2^{(CP)}, \cdots, \omega_5^{(CP)}$ respectively represent the control parameter weights of conflict $TC_1, TC_5, TC_8, TC_9, TC_{10}$. The judgment matrix of control parameters is established, as shown in Table 5.

**Table 5.** Judgment matrix of control parameters

|        | $CP_1$  | $CP_2$ | $CP_3$  | $CP_4$ | $CP_5$ |
|--------|---------|--------|---------|--------|--------|
| $CP_1$ | 1       | 4      | 0.5     | 3      | 6      |
| $CP_2$ | 0.25    | 1      | 0.1667  | 0.5    | 2      |
| $CP_3$ | 2       | 6      | 1       | 4      | 7      |
| $CP_4$ | 0.3333  | 2      | 0.25    | 1      | 2      |
| $CP_5$ | 0.1667  | 0.5    | 0.1429  | 0.5    | 1      |

According to Eqs. (11)–(13), the weight vector of the control parameter is calculated as:

$(0.2945, 0.0777, 0.4593, 0.1161, 0.0524)^T \lambda_{max} = 5.067$ and consistency ratio $CR = 0.015$.

Determine the weight vectors of evaluation parameters corresponding to each control parameter, as shown in Table 6.

**Table 6.** Evaluation parameter weight coefficients corresponding to each control parameter

| Conflict | $\omega_i^{(CP)}$ | $\omega_1^{(CP,EP)}$ | $\omega_2^{(CP,EP)}$ | $\omega_3^{(CP,EP)}$ | $\omega_4^{(CP,EP)}$ | $\omega_5^{(CP,EP)}$ | $\lambda_{max}$ | CR |
|----------|--------|--------|--------|--------|--------|--------|--------|--------|
| $TC_1$   | 0.2945 | 0.1024 | 0.4490 | 0.2379 | 0.1598 | 0.0510 | 5.2037 | 0.0455 |
| $TC_5$   | 0.0777 | 0.2383 | 0.0924 | 0.2610 | 0.4084 | –      | 4.0975 | 0.0365 |
| $TC_8$   | 0.4593 | 0.3416 | 0.2518 | 0.0684 | 0.1178 | 0.2203 | 5.1498 | 0.0334 |
| $TC_9$   | 0.1161 | 0.2427 | 0.1874 | 0.3676 | 0.0679 | 0.1345 | 5.1774 | 0.0396 |
| $TC_{10}$| 0.0524 | 0.4144 | 0.0764 | 0.2859 | 0.0850 | 0.1384 | 5.0745 | 0.0166 |

Then determine the influence coefficient $IF_u^{(CP,EP)}$, as shown in Table 7.

**Table 7.** Evaluation parameter weight coefficients corresponding to each control parameter

| Change measures of control parameters | Corresponding evaluation parameters | $IF_u^{(CP,EP)}$ |
|------|------|------|
| $TC_1$: The supporting frame is supported on both sides | $EP_1$: Operability of docking arrangement device | 4 |
| | $EP_2$: Safety performance of carrying car device | 5 |
| | $EP_3$: Intensity of support frame construction | 4 |
| | $EP_4$: Structural stability of driving mobile devices | 3 |
| | $EP_5$: The complexity of the rotating mechanism | 2 |
| $TC_5$: The rotating mechanism is driven by hydraulic pressure | $EP_1$: Energy consumption of rotating power source | 4 |
| | $EP_2$: Accuracy of motion positioning of rotating transmission mechanism | 3 |
| | $EP_3$: Power performance of rotating power source | 5 |
| | $EP_4$: Motion action time of rotating mechanism | 2 |

*(continued)*

**Table 7.** (*continued*)

| Change measures of control parameters | Corresponding evaluation parameters | $IF_u^{(CP,EP)}$ |
|---|---|---|
| TC$_8$: There are various ways of storage and retrieval | EP$_1$: Operability of docking arrangement device | 5 |
| | EP$_2$: The degree of intelligence of the depositing and taking mechanism | 4 |
| | EP$_3$: Structural complexity of driving mobile devices | 2 |
| | EP$_4$: Maintainability of storage and retrieval mechanism | 3 |
| | EP$_5$: Monitoring difficulty of storage and retrieval detection devices | 4 |
| TC$_9$: Add storage and retrieval detection devices | EP$_1$: The degree of intelligence of the depositing and taking mechanism | 3 |
| | EP$_2$: Operability of docking arrangement device | 4 |
| | EP$_3$: Adaptability of deposit and withdrawal mechanism | 5 |
| | EP$_4$: Structural complexity of driving mobile devices | 2 |
| | EP$_5$: Monitoring difficulty of storage and retrieval detection devices | 2 |
| TC$_{10}$: The mechanism at the end of the rotating rod is movable | EP$_1$: Energy consumption of rotating power source | 2 |
| | EP$_2$: Reliability of rotating mechanism | 4 |
| | EP$_3$: Power transmission stability of rotating transmission mechanism | 3 |
| | EP$_4$: Rotating mechanism complexity | 2 |
| | EP$_6$: the weight of the moving parts in the supporting frame structure | 3 |

Thus, by substituting into Eq. (14), the comprehensive value $Z(TC_t)$ of each conflict can be calculated, and the results are as follows:

$$Z(TC_1) = 1.2332, Z(TC_5) = 0.2605$$
$$Z(TC_8) = 1.8769, Z(TC_9) = 0.24319$$
$$Z(TC_{10}) = 0.1335$$

Thus, the priority of multi-conflict solution of this class group is determined as follows:

$$TC_8 \gg TC_1 \gg TC_9 \gg TC_5 \gg TC_{10}$$

The rest groups are determined similarly. In particular, $\{TC_4\}$ contains only a single conflict that can be solved directly.

The optimal solution path of multi-conflict problem network of no-avoidance stereo garage is shown in Fig. 9.

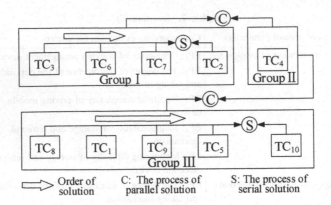

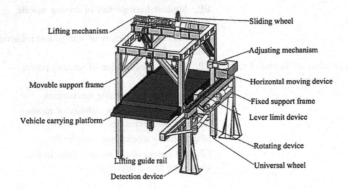

**Fig. 9.** The optimal solution path of multi-conflict problem network

**Fig. 10.** The new concept design scheme of no-avoidance stereo garage

Based on the network optimization solution path of multi-conflict problem, TRIZ tool was used to complete resolution, and an innovative design scheme was obtained [14], as shown in Fig. 10.

# 6 Conclusion

This paper focuses on the resolution of multi-conflicts in complex technical systems. In view of the limitation of the classical TRIZ theory in dealing with the multi-conflict problem of complex technical system directly, a process model for the multi-conflict elimination of complex technical system is proposed to guide the relevant engineering practice. ENV model is used to standardize the expression of multi-conflict problems in complex systems, and the essential relation between multi-conflict problems is mined through extension theory, so as to propose a quantitative algorithm for constructing multi-conflict problem network. Then clustering analysis is carried out according to the degree of multi-conflict correlation to classify conflict groups. Combined with the judgment matrix method in AHP, the path planning for multi-conflict problem network optimization was completed, and TRIZ tool was used to complete the resolution. The effectiveness of the model is verified by the research on the no-avoidance stereo garage, which provides a reference for the relevant engineering design.

**Acknowledgment.** The research is supported in part by the National Innovation Method Fund, China (No. 2018IM040300).

# References

1. Terninko, J., Zusman, A., Zlotin, B.: Systematic Innovation: An Introduction to TRIZ (Theory of Inventive Problem Solving). CRC Press, Boca Raton (1998)
2. Fiorineschi, L., Frillici, F.S., Rissone, P.: A comparison of classical TRIZ and OTSM-TRIZ in dealing with complex problems. Procedia Eng. **131**, 86–94 (2015)
3. Khomenko, N., Ashtiani, M.: Classical TRIZ and OTSM as a Scientific Theoretical Background for Non-Typical Problem Solving Instruments. ETRIA Future, Frankfurt (2007)
4. Han, B., Zhang, J.H., Liu, K.C., et al.: A pyramidal model for initial problem situation analysis process. In: 2014 IEEE International Conference on Management of Innovation and Technology, pp. 436–441. IEEE (2014)
5. Czinki, A., Hentschel, C.: Solving complex problems and TRIZ. Procedia CIRP **39**, 27–32 (2016)
6. Zhang, C., Yang, F., Ren, G.: Research on a rapid multi-contradictions problem solving method and its program design for TRIZ. J. Mach. Des. **31**(10), 8–12 (2014)
7. Zhou, J., Gui, F., Zhao, Y., et al.: Model and application of product conflict problem with integrated TRIZ and Extenics for low-carbon design. Procedia Comput. Sci. **122**, 384–391 (2017)
8. Zhang, J., Liang, R., Han, B., et al.: The problem flow network building and solving process model for complex product. J. Mech. Eng. **54**(23), 160–173 (2018)
9. Khomenko, N., Guio, R.: OTSM network of problems for representing and analysing problem situations with computer support. In: IFIP International Federation for Information Processing, pp. 77–88 (2007)
10. Wen, C.A.I., Chunyan, Y.A.N.G.: The basic theory and method system of extenics. Chin. Sci. Bull. **58**(13), 1190–1199 (2013)
11. Dweiri, F., Kumar, S., Khan, S.A., et al.: Designing an integrated AHP based decision support system for supplier selection in automotive industry. Expert Syst. Appl. **62**, 273–283 (2016)
12. Zadeh, L.A.: Fuzzy sets. Inf. Control **8**(3), 338–353 (1965)
13. Franek, J., Kresta, A.: Judgment scales and consistency measure in AHP. Procedia Econ. Financ. **12**, 164–173 (2014)
14. Zhang, J., Zhao, R., et al.: A new type of no-avoidance stereo garage, China, CN108487723A, 04 September 2018

# Cross-Fertilization of TRIZ for Innovation Management

# A Study on the Effect of Improved Collective Intelligence Combined with TRIZ Methodology for Solving Complex Technology Systems

Sehoon Cho[✉]

Hanwha Precision Machinery, Korea Polytechnic University, Seongnam-Si, Gyeong-Do, South Korea
sh68.cho@gmail.com

**Abstract.** In defining problems from complex situations, overcoming various steps in the solution process, and reaching the final problem-solving situation, the limitations of competencies possessed by some of the most prominent experts have emerged. In many cases, the principles, and concepts for problem-solving are appropriately suggested by TRIZ experts, but in the process of solving a real problem situation, various constraints exist, and large and small subsequent problems occur and are not finally solved.

This paper is organized on the basis of attempted and good results in solving technical problems that have not been solved for a long time in various divisions of large Korean companies (S group). These problem-solving processes are based on TRIZ methodology and additionally, based on distributed cognitive theory, collective intelligence and its solutions have been found and good results have been made. These results show that attempting simultaneous problem solving by multiple specialists is effective in producing a faster and more viable solution, rather than relying on a few problem-solving specialists, in a complex and expanding technology system.

Specifically, TRIZ-Facilitator basically analyzes the initial problem situation to form Cross-Functional Team and get management decisions. The Facilitator analyzes the problem, pre-reviews the problem-solving complexity and constraints at the execution stage, assigns the role of the team's experts at each stage, and follows the TRIZ procedure.

**Keywords:** Collective intelligence · TRIZ · Cross functional team · Ideation · Complexity · Technology system · Distributed cognition theory · Facilitator · Conceptual design

## 1 4th Industrial Revolution and New Issues

### 1.1 Changes in the General Situation

These days, referred to as the 4th Industrial Revolution, Industry 4.0, and so on, many of the technical problems faced by companies continue to increase in complexity and various difficulties arise in attempting to solve the problems. In many cases, the

© IFIP International Federation for Information Processing 2020
Published by Springer Nature Switzerland AG 2020
D. Cavallucci et al. (Eds.): TFC 2020, IFIP AICT 597, pp. 383–398, 2020.
https://doi.org/10.1007/978-3-030-61295-5_29

principles, concepts, and solutions for problem solving have been systematically created and proposed by TRIZ experts. However, in the process of resolving the actual problem situation, various limitations exist, and various subsequent problems that are not expected occur, resulting in cases where the final problem is not solved. As technology advances, it can be thought of as being simplified on the surface in a single technology system, but the level of interaction between actual components is increasing.

## 1.2 Changes in Problem Situation and Complexity

The main feature of the Fourth Industrial Revolution is the combination and convergence of all industries, and the result is accelerating the increase in the complexity of technological systems. In TRIZ's theory, it can be seen that in the trend of artificial technology evolution, the technology system increases its control level and increases the complexity of configuration [1]. From a human point of view, technology systems are being optimized for IFR. In the process, the technology system itself has a complicated system (structure) to obtain functions or performance, and the complexity of the interaction relationship increases (Table 1).

**Table 1.** Law of development of engineered systems and reinterpretation

| 1. Law of completeness of parts of a system | Increasing the level of system integrity |
| --- | --- |
| 2. Law of energy conductivity in a system | Increasing energy efficiency |
| 3. Law of harmonization of rhythms | Increase of rhythm harmony level |
| 4. Law of increasing ideality | – |
| 5. Law of uneven development of parts | Increasing the number of uneven development components |
| 6. Law of transition to a supersystem | Increase of transfer to higher systems |
| 7. Law of transition from macro to micro level | Increasing the degree of micronization |
| 8. Law of increasing substance-field involvement | – |
| 9. Law of increasing dynamics | – |

As this complexity increases, new attempts to solve various problems are emerging. However, creating new methods has the potential to create another complexity. By classifying the characteristics of the problem complexity into four types, research on methodologies suitable for each type is also being conducted [2, 3]. This complexity presents us with a strong challenge, but when it is solved, it becomes a new opportunity and an opportunity for all of us [3].

## 1.3 Problem Complexity and General Reasons for Difficulty

What does it mean to be complicated? It can be largely divided into complexity in terms of result and complexity in process. In the output, it may mean that the interaction relationship between various different components is not simple. Complexity in the process means a situation in which decision-making is difficult or delayed because various organizations or participants involved in the process or decision-making process exist and mutual interests exist. Processes tend to be divided and complicated by work or process expertise. Complexity is also related to the precision of the control of the system or the increase in the level of control, but it is also closely related to the smaller components. Since systems composed of micro-level or smaller parts are linked to other systems of the higher level, the micronized parts increase the complexity of the system, leading to an increase in the configuration for another control. In addition, the complexity of the problem increases proportionally as the number of organizations or people affected by the decision-making process and various effects of it increases. As more departments or people participate, the complexity generally increases and eventually makes decisions difficult or delayed. Another is the increase in complexity as the level of professional skills or knowledge gradually included in one technology system increases or increases in quantity. In order to have a variety of different functions, the interactivity increases, and accordingly, a change in one shape affects other characteristics. Lastly, when a company plans a new service or product or wants to improve an existing product or service, the competitor's patent problem exists. Worldwide, the number of intellectual property information has already exceeded 430 million. Increasingly competitive patents increase the difficulty of designing products in new ways and structures that do not conflict with them.

## 2 Various Attempts to Solve Problems and New Tasks

### 2.1 Collective Intelligence and Its Application Methods

Collective intelligence was said by Levy in 1997 to be "intelligence distributed everywhere, constantly valued, adjusted in real time, and mobilized with real competence" [26]. This means that collective intelligence is meaningful when it becomes a fluid relationship made by members in a space of knowledge that is continuously re-evaluated and adjusted in real time. Team is a group of people who must work together to achieve a given task or goal, and interact and collaborate [4]. The concept of facilitation is known to have started after 1950. The preliminary meaning of facilitation means 'make things easier' and 'promote actions or processes'. It means acting as a leader in such a role to participate in a group activity process from a neutral point of view to guide organizational members to accomplish tasks and cooperate with each other [6]. In other words, to increase the effectiveness of an organized team, it means neutralizing the tasks or topics covered by the team, and diagnosing and intervening to help team members improve problem recognition, problem solving, and decision-making methods [6, 7]. Cross Functional Team (Hereinafter referred to as CFT) is a method that is attempted as a form of problem solving through collective intelligence. CFT is generally a team between functions', which can be an important way for organizations to solve complex problems, reduce costs, reduce resources and increase their competitive advantage [8]. In the work of new product development, there was also a study that the balanced composition and physical proximity of the CFT in the composition and operation of the CFT are important variables that determine the performance of the CFT [9].

The following are empirical examples. Founded in 2001 in the United States, "Innocentive" is also an attempt to solve problems by collective intelligence. Another example is Kaggle, a big data analytics consulting firm founded by Anthony Goldbloom of the United States in 2010. In Korea, a technology problem solving platform called "K-TechNavi" has recently emerged. The operation method is similar to that of the United States. When registering the problem to be solved, the target level, deadline, and compensation conditions are determined, and the technical experts in each field registered on the platform form a team to try to solve the problem. In the field of patents dealing with the results of problem solving, there is a research result that, even when evaluating the quality or value of patents, patents with multiple inventors are qualitatively superior and have higher value [10]. In addition, the number of patents through joint cooperation is increasing worldwide [11, 12]. In addition, there is a tendency to increase the value of patents designed by multiple inventors rather than patents made by a single inventor.

These cases and studies have shown that it is important for many people to try to solve complex problems and problems in various situations, and it produces better results. Nevertheless, little is known about these various attempts, and how the participating experts used the methods and tools used to solve the problem.

## 2.2   Problems that Do not Solve, Features of Complex Problems

The reason why it is difficult to solve the problem situation by the principle or direction of problem solving alone is because there are unique constraints for each problem. In addition, depending on the environment or the situation, depending on the time when the constraints appear or recognize, new and unexpected problems occur and the problem cannot be solved, and eventually, the attempt to solve the problem through the application of the problem solving direction or principle is stopped. When analyzing the process of creating a result rather than the process of analyzing the results, there are various types of steps, and each major step has a decision-making process. In each decision-making step, the criteria, conditions, environment, etc. may change or unpredictable questions may arise. Unexpected conditions or criteria in decision-making often re-analyze and solve problems. In this case, we can say, "Design change by VOC or VOB, specification change" with a very soft expression.

In a situation of increasing complexity, one or two experts can roughly analyze a third party's problem, but rarely know the entire process of problem solving. There are cases in which attempts are made to solve problems by only requesting a problem in a narrower area than the actual problem situation. In this case, the probability of the problem being properly analyzed or resolved by one or two problem solving experts is low. The situations described above can be very complex and difficult in themselves.

On the other hand, however, it lacks information in the process of recognizing and solving problems. Sometimes, in the process of resolving the problem, laws and regulations created by country are involved.

## 2.3  Practical Limitations of TRIZ Experts in Complex Issues

Most TRIZ experts are basically those who majored in engineering at school. In addition, while working in a specific technology field for many years, additional knowledge, skills, and experiences in the field are accumulated. In some special cases, it is often possible to have knowledge and experience in a variety of skills in more diverse fields. However, the problems we need to meet and solve now and in the future must deal with a system in which multiple engineering technologies are converged. We meet with systems that combine mechanical, electrical, electronic, physical, chemical, nano, and magnetic engineering. We are already meeting a lot. We face practical limitations when meeting increasingly complex systems and various engineering needs and customer problems requiring unfamiliar industry expertise. Finally, we meet various difficulties that lead to the resolution of the problem. Sometimes the severity of the problem arises at the border of more than one technology or department.

# 3  Applying Distributed Cognitive Theory in Problem Solving

## 3.1  General Process for the Solution

The process of recognizing and solving human problems has a very general pattern. It is explained by searching and recognizing the problem space composed of various problem states, and goes through the initial, middle, and target state (solution determination) stages [14]. In other words, it consists of the steps of problem recognition, information collection, and problem solving, and can be expressed briefly as shown in Fig. 1. This corresponds to the human problem-solving process from the perspective of human cognitive psychology.

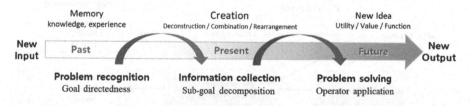

**Fig. 1.** General process for the solution

The various attempts to solve problems related to collective intelligence mentioned above can be understood as distributed cognition in Cognitive psychology or Neuroscience [13].

### 3.2   The Role of CFT and Facilitation

For complex problem situations, a group of experts such as CFT is preferred as a way to raise the level of cognition, especially at each stage. Distributed cognitive theory is a theory that claims that the resources that enable and embody human collective activity are distributed across people, artifacts, and situations [13]. In other words, an individual's cognition is not only present in the person's head, but is seen as being expressed in the whole situation using other people working with the person and tools designed to suit the context of the activity. It occurs when people collaborate and need coordination to achieve a common goal. The common purpose, cooperation and coordination required here can be played by the facilitator in facilitation. The core of its role is to enable rational collective thinking through sharing of information and fair criticism. The Facilitator guides team members through the process of recognizing problems and through which tools and methods they can come up with their own ideas. The role of the facilitator is gradually expanding, and various existing experts, not the facilitator's own domain, complement the facilitation capabilities [15, 16].

## 4   Improved Methods and Procedures

In the process of problem solving, the TRIZ expert's role of facilitation has already been tried and utilized [19, 20, 22]. In this paper, in the basic role of TRIZ Facilitation [22], in the process of resolving a complex problem in parallel with the basic role of the TRIZ expert and the role of the Facilitator, from the recognition of the problem to the conclusion of the final problem situation, And covers supplementary procedures and important checklists.

### 4.1   Problem Recognition and Types and Procedures

Depending on the size and type of the problem, the procedures and methods and tools for solving the problem, organizational structure, duration, and budget vary [17].

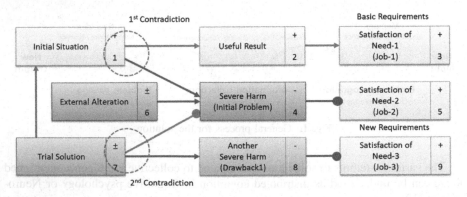

**Fig. 2.** Flow chart of initial problem [23]

Also, in TRIZ, the follow-up procedure may be set slightly differently depending on the type of problem. The problem-solving process differs according to the type of problem [18]. Therefore, first, the problem type should be reviewed by interviewing the problem situation from the department or person in charge. People at the site of the problem are not problem-solving experts. Most do not know what TRIZ is. Therefore, it makes the problem situation visually easy for field engineers and decision makers to understand [Fig. 2 and 23]. The information obtained examines the size of the people and departments involved in the type of problem, and the type and depth of the expertise involved. These reviews should determine what my role should be in the subject matter [Table 2, 18]. Afterwards, as an in-house problem-solving expert, a CFT that includes the technical areas to be roughly analyzed and necessary technical experts is prepared through a certain procedure. Patent experts may be included in cases where continuous analysis of patents is necessary in the creation of solutions [24].

**Table 2.** 3-Tracks: problem type and process [18]

| Tracks | Problem Type | Method | Remark |
|---|---|---|---|
| Workshop + Facilitation (Facilitator) | Unresolved problems, cost innovation, quality problems / defects, New concept design (performance / function), multiple departments Long-term outstanding problems [Complex problem situation] | Operates for a short period of at least 5-10 days depending on the type TRIZ Expert: Facilitation, FOS PL + R & D: Tech. analysis, ideation, verification, execution Necessary Period: 1~2 weeks | (+) Short-term solution (±) Concentration of competency (+) Division of TRIZ experts / capabilities ↑ (-) Point of selection |
| TRIZ Training (Trainer) + Training and support | Technical issues of individual (1 ~ 3) tasks within the development task, single department [Single/Simple Tech. Domain] | Expert course training (Lvl course certification + 5 days) Interworking progress during task period + Individual facilitation of TRIZ experts TRIZ Expert : Training, Facilitation, FOS PL+R&D : Tech. analysis, ideation, verification, execution Necessary Period: 1~4 weeks + 1~6 Months | (+) Separate organization, solve business problems without spending time (+) Securing experts by business (-) Expert training required (-) Long term |
| TRIZ Solving (Solver) | Difficulty difficulties, urgency problems, long-term outstanding problems [Within Tech. Domains] | TRIZ expert-led problem solving by business per year (parallel technology learning) TRIZ Expert : Tech. analysis, FOS, ideation PL+R&D : Technical support (1 ~ 2 weeks), verification, implementation Outcome : Solving Concept, Direction/Principle for Solution Necessary Period: 1~6 Months | (+) Triz expert solves high-quality problems through analysis capabilities (+) Researcher participation ratio is low (-) Solution Product application applied Max 30% or less (-) Long term |

## 4.2 Decision Making and Various Conditions

Every problem situation goes through the steps of recognizing the problem and the area, the process of judging the need for problem solving, and the process of problem solving. And each of these stages involves a decision-making process. Therefore, it is very important that the company recognizes this situation as a problem, judges that it needs to be solved, and pays money and time before the company starts to solve the problem.

**Table 3.** Basic (1st) criteria for evaluation

| List | Contents | Decision maker | Verification Step |
|---|---|---|---|
| Purpose (quality) | Ex) High quality assembly line fits existing facility<br>*Purpose expressed in terms of VOC and VOB* | | |
| Goal (quantitative) | Ex) Size of line is smaller than size of facility<br>*The practical meaning of achieving the objectives, measurable forms such as numerical values, processing speed, capacity, volume, weight, function & parameters* | | |
| Achievement criteria (quantitative) | Ex) Additional cost <5%, weight / volume increase less than 3%, development period 3 months, cost increase less than 1%<br>*Matters related to the scope of investment (decision making) to solve problems* | | |
| Precautions | Ex) Defective pumps produced, Design, weight,<br>*Mandatory requirements for problem solving* | | |

In addition, it is necessary to grasp the core criteria at each decision-making stage. Sometimes the external design cannot be changed, and the manufacturing cost and weight cannot be increased [Table 3]. In addition, it is desirable to set additional target achievement criteria step by step.

If the problem type, level, and organization have been determined through the process so far, if the resolution process is done through facilitation and the CFT member does not have TRIZ knowledge, introduce the tools used by team members as a 1–3-day training course Conduct training.

## 4.3    Creating Ideas to Solve Problems and Acting Step by Step

**Definition of Initial Problems and Investigation of Prior Patents:** Before proceeding with the subsequent work for solving the problem, the prior patent is searched with keywords and function definitions that can be obtained from the problem definition. This must be done essentially. Patent issues can be partially obtained in advance when writing 'Basic Criteria for Evaluation'. However, it is desirable to perform it again in this step for verification.

**Prepare for Resource Analysis and Idea Making:** With CFT, resource analysis is conducted with the initial problems in Fig. 2. As a TRIZ expert, resource analysis has a variety of tables and examines things that have a direct or indirect relationship with, or influence, a problem from various perspectives through questions. In the process of solving problems through team members unfamiliar with TRIZ using Fig. 2, if 'Situational contradiction' is clear, immediately define 'Task' for idea development. This is the same as the procedure proposed by 'Guided Brainstorming LLC' [19]. Here, it is most important that the contradictory situation is expressed in a picture that the team members can easily understand and clearly understand what the task is.

**Generating Multiple Ideas in Silence:** Based on the problem definition shared in the previous step, the resources found, and the personal work area and knowledge and experience of the team members, the invention principle (including the separation principle) is applied sequentially to write or draw each idea on a given idea sheet. Team members think of an idea for a task created together to solve a common problem using only the principles of the invention given within a given time. Here, the principles of invention and separation were used in GB-TRIZ [19, 21]. 40 traditional invention principles can be used, but this is used here as an example. Each task comes up with 30 ideas per person. If there are 5 team members, 150 ideas are created. These ideas have basic feasibility as ideas for solving tasks in their respective fields of expertise. However, it needs to be soundly criticized by other specialties or experts. The team member who presented the idea explains it to the team members on a technical basis.

**Initial Solution Made of Multiple Ideas:** TRIZ experts who participate as facilitators can participate in making ideas with team members. The operator (TRIZ Facilitator, hereinafter called operator) collects and summarizes similar ideas. The operator assembles and shares the initial solution from similar ideas collected. In this process, the ideas of the team members have already been positively collected, so explanations and complementary ideas supporting the initial solution made are added. And the operator conducts a basic evaluation of the initial solutions, a group of ideas gathered [Table 4].

**Table 4.** Evaluation of the initial solutions

| # | Initial Solutions | 문제해결 (Efficiency) | 검증여부 (Feasibility) | 제품구현 (Impl.) | Sum |
|---|---|---|---|---|---|
| 1 | | | | | |
| 2 | | | | | |
| 3 | [Selection of candidates for 1ˢᵗ Solution] * Cost (required cost, mass production standard) review in Next step 1) Potential to remove harmful effects 2) Feasibility-Whether the solution is actually effective 3) Implement ability / implementation | | | | |
| 4 | | | | | |
| 5 | | | | | |
| 6 | | | | | |

| Criterion | 1 | 10 |
|---|---|---|
| 1. Efficiency | Does not counteract Initial Problem | Eliminates Initial Problem completely |
| 2. Feasibility | There is no way to realize this solution or its portion | Realization of solution is obvious and clear |
| 3. Implementability | Never will be implemented | Could be easily implemented tomorrow |

The selected candidates identify the shortcomings or needs of each initial solution and potential problems and severity from team members. Here, the operator should perform the role of providing the TRIZ Tool in a timely manner as an enhanced role rather than the general facilitator. In addition, it provides logical advice on the created ideas, interaction with the results of FOS for the shared task, association, and usage examples.

In this process, the role of the operator is the most important thing, and it is to efficiently connect knowledge, experiences, and skills of distributed team members to share new relationships and results of integrated and overlapping thoughts. When you create a new connection by collecting decentralized things, something different (creative) is created.

**Resetting Problems and Defining New Tasks:** For example, if an initial solution made from 150 ideas is appropriate, proceed to the next step. If you don't get good scores and support in evaluating the initial solutions, analyze the reasons and supplement your team members or use the results of the FOS. When a new problem with the initial solution exists, a new task is determined from the redefined problem as shown in Fig. 3. Then, as in the previous idea creation method, ideas for new tasks are created, assembled, and evaluated. In the second process of creating an idea, attempts are made to generate three ideas for the set tasks: (a) Improve, (b) Counteract, and (c) Resolve the Contradiction. The operator models the contradiction with a new task, presents it to the team members, and explains how to generate ideas to resolve the contradictions.

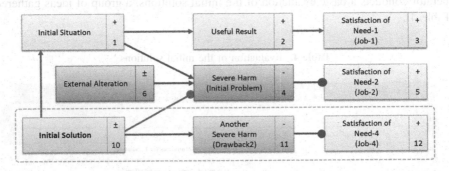

**Fig. 3.** Flow chart of redefining the problem

**Creating Ideas to Resolve Contradictions:** Asking team members who are unfamiliar with TRIZ procedures or tools to resolve contradictions does not help solve the problem. Therefore, the relationship between the beneficial and harmful effects caused by each condition is explained in general terms, and the knowledge and experience of each team member and the shared resources can be transformed temporally and spatially by structure and conditions. And guide each to think of an idea.

**Evaluation and Selection of the Final Solute:** Rather than choosing an initial solution, use more strict criteria. Regarding the task, (a) is it approached as a solution, (b) is the scale of the cost required to solve the problem within the limits, (c) does not produce new harmful results or actions, (d) is the required function and performance verified?, (e) Assemble the evaluation based on the team's unique expertise from 5 perspectives, such as whether there is no problem creating it immediately (Table 5).

**Table 5.** Evaluation of final solutions

| Criterion | 1 | 10 |
|---|---|---|
| 1.Goal / Objective | Does not bring closer to the Goal | Achieves Goal completely |
| 2.Cost | Intolerably huge cost that will never be repaid | Implementation and use of solution do not incur any new cost and even reduces the current costs |
| 3.Intolerable problems | Causes a lot of intolerable problems | No problem |
| 4.Feasibility | There is no way to realize this solution or its portion | Realization of solution is obvious and clear |
| 5.Implementability | Never will be implemented | Could be easily implemented tomorrow |

The candidates for the final solution created through this process have the characteristic of resolving the contradiction in various technical resources and resources given for one task. Attempts to solve other problems that each candidate could potentially have are circulating through the process described above, and the size and impact of the problems gradually develop.

## 5  Case Study

### 5.1  Problem Situation

The surveillance camera installed on the outside of the building is equipped with a transparent cover to protect the system, including the lens, to prevent the ingress of dust and rainwater into the system. The cover can also hide the direction of surveillance from the outside. However, a new problem occurred due to this transparent cover. As shown in Fig. 4, ghost shape caused by several sunlight occurred in the image of the area to be monitored. In particular, it occurred at about 60–90 min, when the sun rises and the sunset time, where the sunlight is about 20° to the optical axis of the lens.

**Fig. 4.** Problem situation and surveillance system photos

### 5.2  Problem Analysis and Problem Definition

As a result of analyzing the cause of the problem phenomenon, as strong sun-light passes through the transparent cover and the lens, partial reflection on the surface of the lens partially occurs and the reflected light is reflected inside the transparent cover to create a ghost image. This was considered a natural physical optical phenomenon (Fig. 5).

**Fig. 5.** Causes of ghost imaging

## 5.3  Solution Approach According to the Type of Problem

As a result of the interview, the research and development department tried various attempts for more than a year. As a result, experiments were conducted to impart new properties to the lens or cover as a physical phenomenon. There was also support from an external TRIZ expert. However, all attempts have resulted in reducing the problem a bit and have not yet made a solution that satisfies the manufacturing quality, reliability, and cost level. In the actual system operation, several engineering knowledges was required, including the processing of image information, the design of optical instruments, and control of the motor. Therefore, it was decided that it was appropriate to construct and approach the CFT with facilitation.

## 5.4  Criteria for Solving Evaluation and Organization of CFT

As for the requirements of the solution, mass production quality and cost level were important. There should be no quality problem of the means to solve the problem, and the cost required to solve the problem should be less than 10 $.

## 5.5  Simple TRIZ Training and Facilitation

The CFT, including the TRIZ facilitator, was organized into nine people. Only one of the technical experts received TRIZ training. For the remaining 6 people, 8 h of training was conducted per day on the introduction of the problem-solving process and the tools and how to use them. The schedule for solving the problem was planned for a total of 5 days. The primary outcome is conceptual design for resolution.

## 5.6  Resource Analysis and FOS

Based on the results of the first interview and the problem situation obtained through CFT, the problem situation is illustrated as in Fig. 6, and the task for solving the problem is decided and shared. For the FOS procedure for the task, the system configuration, material properties, and related scientific principles were analyzed, and similar cases were searched.

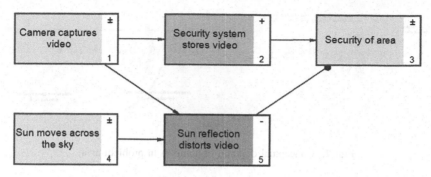

**Fig. 6.** Flow chart of initial problem

## 5.7 Ideation for Initial Solution

As a result of individual ideation of 30 principles of invention, 52 ideas were obtained. And it was classified into 12 idea groups. From the point of view of individual field of expertise of CFT members, we have obtained possible solutions. Each group was selected as an initial solution for four groups through conceptual explanation of ideas, mutual verification and evaluation. Among the candidates for the initial solution evaluated as the fastest solution, a second task was set and silence ideation was performed. This time, a total of 57 ideas were obtained, and a combination of these was suggested as a solution to VOC.

## 5.8 Follow-Up Procedures for Technical Problem Solving (VOB)

Among the initial resolution candidates not selected in the previous step, a new task was set for the highest evaluation score and FOS and resource analysis were performed. The solution is to use an intermediate medium to block the ingress (path) of ghost light. Searched for phenomena and application products that occur when light travels and penetrates or collides with objects.

The solution is to apply the principles found through FOS to parts that can be easily changed, except for configurations that cause new problems when modified in the system. It is a method of arranging the medium between the transparent cover and the lens to partially change the material and shape of the existing parts. That is, the opaque plate installed was changed to prevent image distortion due to the boundary between the straight portion and the curved portion of the transparent cover [Figs. 7 and 8]. The film with polarization function has already been verified for quality, and it has been solved without adding or damaging the configuration of the system by cutting and placing it in the size of the blocking plate. The cost is less than one dollar.

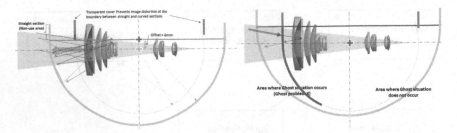

**Fig. 7.** Conceptual diagram of solution in problem area

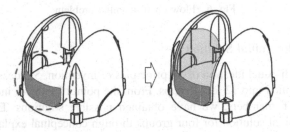

**Fig. 8.** Application of conceptual design in products

## 5.9    Solution Verification and Follow-Up

The verification of the solution was carried out by the quality department, and the results shown in Fig. 9 were obtained.

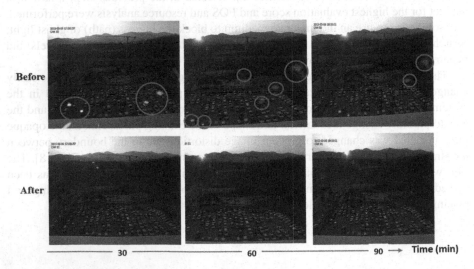

**Fig. 9.** Comparison of effectiveness of solution application

Lastly, the solution is filed with a patent in the exporting country of major products. Currently, the solution has been registered in the United States and China [25].

# 6 Conclusion

The problems introduced were so-called unresolved and complex problems in which various specialized technologies such as optics, motor control, software, material mechanics, and mechanical design interact in a complex way.

It is important to organize a group of experts suitable for the problem situation through the organization of CFT and to use their experience and knowledge. The actual role of the TRIZ expert is to analyze the initial problem situation and act as a facilitator, guide the problem solving and use the TRIZ tool at the appropriate time. And through the CFT, a group of experts organized for problem solving, it is a role to draw their knowledge, experience, and skills for problem solving in the form of ideas and connect their dispersed ideas and ideas.

The limitations of this paper did not prepare for the difference between the amount and quality of information, such as technology, management, and decision-making, about the problem situation between the internal TRIZ expert and the external TRIZ expert. We have confirmed that such information affects the practical solution.

**Acknowledgments.** The author thanks Len Kaplan for reading and helping me with new challenges despite the company's various changes and difficulties right next to me for two years.

# References

1. Zlotin B., Zusman, A.: Patterns of evolution: recent findings on structure and origin. In: Altshuller's TRIZ Institute Conference, TRIZCON 2006, Milwaukee, 29 April–2 May 2006
2. Czinki, A.: Solving complex problems and TRIZ, TFC 2015. Procedia CIRP **39**, 27–32 (2016)
3. Snowden, D.J., Boone, M.E.: A leader's framework for decision making. Harv. Bus. Rev. **85**(11), 69–76 (2007)
4. Reddy, W.B.: Team Building: Blueprints for Productivity and Satisfaction Hardcover, 1 June 1988
5. Osborn, A.F.: Applied Imagination (1953)
6. Weaver, R.G., Farrell, J.D.: Managers as Facilitators, a Practical Guide to Getting Work Done in a Changing Workplace. Berrett-Koehler Publishers, San Francisco (1997)
7. Roger, R.M.: The Skilled Facilitator: A Comprehensive Resource for Consultants, Facilitators, Managers, Trainers, and Coaches. Wiley, San Francisco (2002)
8. Miller, M.A.: Developing High-Performance Cross-Functional Teams: Understanding Motivations, Functional Loyalties and Teaming Fundamentals, LA-13120-T. Los Alamos National Laboratory, 1 August 1996
9. Kim, J., Kim, B.: CFT (cross functional team) as an enabler of fidelity between R&D and manufacturing. In: 9th KASBA (2007)
10. Ko, K.: European Patent Inventor, Invention Process. ReSEAT Analysis Report (2007)
11. Kim, J.: Maximize the Value of National Science and Technology by Strengthen Sharing/Collaboration of National R&D Information

12. Ko, K.: Patent application and technology joint research of invention activity. ReSEAT Analysis Report (2008)
13. Lee, K.-H.: A model of community-based learning system as a socially distributed cognitive system. Korean J. Educ. Method. Stud. **15** (2003)
14. Anderson, J.R.: Cognitive Psychology and Its Implication, 4th edn. WH Freeman and Company, New York (1995)
15. Lee Y.: Facilitator' role and competency, HRD, August 2009
16. Schwarz, R.M.: The Skilled Facilitator. Wiley, San Francisco (2002)
17. Yale University Problem Management Process Guide (2012)
18. Kaplan, L., Cho, S.: Samsung Techwin's in-house TRIZ training and guidance (2014)
19. Guided Brainstorming™ TRIZ Facilitator
20. Harrington, H.J.: Lean TRIZ: How to Dramatically Reduce Product-Development Costs with This Innovative Problem-Solving Tool. CRC Press, Boca Raton (2017)
21. Kaplan, L., Malkin, S.: Inventive Principles. In: Reference Book, OutCompete (2014)
22. Kaplan, L., Malkin, S.; GB TRIZ Facilitation. Basics of GB TRIZ, vol. 1 (2015)
23. Kaplan, L., Cho, S., Prévost, E.: Universal unsolvable problem and process of resolving it. In: Global TRIZ Conference (2015)
24. Cho, S.: Strategic Patent Development Cases using TRIZ and Patent Information in Industry. TFC (2018)
25. Cho, S.: Camera system and photographing method. US 10,084,977, CN ZL20161022 8213.9
26. Levy, P.: Collective Intelligence: Mankind's Emerging World in Cyberspace. Perseus Books, Cambridge (1997)

# Men and Their Technical Systems

Hans-Gert Gräbe[✉]

Leipzig University, 04009 Leipzig, Germany
graebe@informatik.uni-leipzig.de

**Abstract.** With the concept of a technical system the whole TRIZ theory corpus revolves around a term that is not very precisely defined in the TRIZ literature, but left to a "common sense". In this paper an attempt is made to determine how far a notion of technical system takes in this theoretical context and how it can be related to approaches from neighboring theory corpuses. It turns out that focusing on an artifact dimension of technology, as defined by the term technical system, blocks the view on essential relational phenomena that are inherent to a world of technical systems and a notion of technical principle is more suited for the analysis of such relational phenomena.

**Keywords:** TRIZ · Technical system · Technical principle

## 1 Introduction

The whole is more than the sum of its parts. In [4] I show that it is even much more than this sum, because in the system's *relations* the states of the parts multiply and do not just add up. In that direction the TRIZ Body of Knowledge [8] develops the conceptual foundation of the own theory only half-heartedly. Especially for the question, what is a *technical system*, the "common sense" is referenced. The diversity of this "common sense" was visible in a Facebook discussion [3] in August 2019. This is of course no foundation for a scientific approach.

In this paper we develop an approximation to the notion *technical system* and ask whether such a term carries on at all in order to analyze the *world of technical systems* more closely. The rarely surprising answer is no, because the whole, this world, is more than the sum of its parts. Relational conditions in this world become rather visible in the concept of *technical principle* than in the concept *technical system*. To that extent, the approach in [14] is much better suited to analyze evolution in the world of technical systems as the approach in the official MATRIZ document [9]. The term *principle* is not to be misunderstood here as TRIZ principle, because the unfortunate English and German translation of the Russian origin "приём" is better replaced by "method" or "approach pattern".

For a long version of my arguments with a more detailed explanation (in German) I refer to [5].

© IFIP International Federation for Information Processing 2020
Published by Springer Nature Switzerland AG 2020
D. Cavallucci et al. (Eds.): TFC 2020, IFIP AICT 597, pp. 399–410, 2020.
https://doi.org/10.1007/978-3-030-61295-5_30

## 2   Laws of Evolution of Technical Systems

Laws of evolution of technical systems exist in different versions and are one of the pillars of the "TRIZ Body of Knowledge" [8]. They regularly contain a *law of displacement of humans from technical systems*. In this paper I refer to [9] as main reference of the "state of the art", where influential TRIZ theorists with the authority of MATRIZ compiled a systematization of the current state of debates on such "Trends of Engineering Systems Evolution" (TESE).

The opposite view was formulated in the cybernetics discourse of the 1960s to 1980s [2]: "What is the position of man in the highly complex information-technological system? Our answer to that question was always: Man is the only creative productive force, it must be and remain the *subject* of development. Therefore, the concept of full automation, according to which the human is to be gradually eliminated from the process, misses the point!"

The problems of such a "concept of full automation", a world of "automatically moving machines" meanwhile triggered an ecological crisis of planetary dimension. The displacement thesis itself is perceived as a direct threat, that can be formulated as thesis itself:

**Thesis 1:** *An (apparent) displacement of humans from technical systems points to an under-complex, existentially dangerous misperception of the technical systems under consideration.*

However, this is no longer a technical problem only. Harrisburg, Chernobyl, Fukushima or the climate change request a further examination of such contradictory positions. The "trends (or laws) of development of technical systems" refer to a *specific* conceptual level of abstraction of descriptions of a world that develops in contradictory forms itself. In particular the "trends" are in contradiction to lines of development extracted on other levels of abstraction. In short, the ambivalent relationship to a "displacement of humans from technical systems" expanded above in thesis and counter thesis is in no way special just for this trend, but applies in a similar way to the other nine trends. TRIZ offers a good methodology to analyze such contradictions if one does not stop at memorizing these trends only.

## 3   Technology and World Changing Practices

Today operation and use of technical systems is certainly a central element of world-changing human practices. For this purpose planned and coordinated actions based on division of labour is required, because using the benefits of a system requires to operate it. Conversely, it makes little sense to operate a system that is not being used. In computer science this connection is well known as the connection between definition and call of a function – calling a function that has not yet been defined causes a run time error; the definition of a function that is never called points to a design error.

Closely linked to this distinction between definition and call of a function is the distinction between design time and run time. Such a distinction is even more important in the real world of technical systems – during design time the cooperative interactions are *planned in principle*, at run time *the plan is executed*. Hence for technical systems one has to distinguish interpersonally communicated *justified expectations* as *forms of description* and *experienced results* as *forms of performance*.

This is not a simple task as the following example of a concert performance shows. The form of performance, which pleases the listeners, is preceded by the description form, the agreement on the exact interpretation of the work to be performed. This agreement on a *joint plan* is itself a precondition-rich practical process. The requirements result from previous practices – such as the *private procedural skills* of the individual musicians in the mastery of their instruments and the existence of the score as an established form of description of the concert piece to be performed. Since on October 14, 2018 at Leipzig Gewandhaus Alexander Shelley went without this score of Mozart's Piano Concerto KV 491 to the director's podium, we can imagine that this form of description provided at most the raw material basis for director and orchestra in the preceding rehearsals to agree upon a situation-specific special form of description of the performance form. Even more, the opulent gestures of the director towards the orchestra show that during these rehearsals also *language* was generated to transform the results of longer processes of reconciliation into a compact form that meets the time-critical requirements of the tempi of performance. The mere "engineering" dimension was transcended by Gabriela Montero, the soloist of that evening, with her encore: the audience is asked to sing a melody, out of which the virtuoso develops an improvisation as a form of performance to which there is no interpersonal communicable description form, beside the sound recordings of that Gewandhaus evening and the reports from the enthusiastic listeners. That also here technical mastery was only a necessary requirement, is beyond question.

The relationship between men and their technical systems is therefore complex and can be grasped only in a dialectical perspective of further development of already existing technical systems, if not to inescapably end up in unfruitful hen-egg debates.

## 4  Systems and Components

In addition to the dimensions of description and performance, for technical systems the *aspect of reuse* also plays a major role. This applies, at least on the artifact level, but *not* to larger technical systems – these are *unique specimens*, even though assembled using standardized components. Also the majority of computer scientist is concerned with the creation of such unique specimens, because the IT systems that control such systems are also unique.

The special features of a technical system result therefore mainly from the *interplay of components*. For example, the production control systems of various BMW plants differ significantly [7]. The plants were built at different times taking into account the respective state of the art and the likewise changing business model of the company. Once such large technical systems are released they can only be modified to a limited extent and are therefore, after the corresponding amortization periods, also consistently decommissioned. Nevertheless, the aspect of reuse also plays a role in such very different technical systems, but is shifted from the immediate level of technical artifacts to higher levels of abstraction.

Hence the *concept of a technical system* rooted in a planning and real-world context has four dimensions

1. as a real-world unique specimen (e.g. as a product or a service),
2. as a description of this real-world unique specimen (e.g. in the form of a special product configuration)
   and for components produced in larger quantities also
3. as description of the design of the system template (product design) and
4. as description and operation of the delivery and operating structures of the real-world unique specimens of this system produced according to this template (as production, quality assurance, delivery, operational and maintenance plans).

Point 4 in particular hardly plays a role in the TRIZ context, although neither in the private nor in the business environment technical products are sustainably demanded for which foreseeable inadequate service is offered.

As a basis for such a delimiting system concept, the submersive concept of open systems from the theory of dynamical systems [1] is used, which postulates

1. an outer boundary and functionally determined embedding in a (functioning) environment,
2. an inner demarcation against existing systems (components) that are exploited and
3. a (functioning) external throughput that leads to dynamic internal structure formation as source of the performance of the system.

*Technical systems* in such a setting are systems whose design is influenced by cooperatively acting people based on division of labour, where *existing* technical systems are normatively characterized at description level by a *specification* of their interfaces and at performance level (at least normatively) by the *guaranteed specification-compliant operation*.

We are clearly within the range of standard TRIZ terminology of a *system of systems* – a technical system consists of components, which in turn are technical systems, whose *functioning* (both in functional and operational sense) is assume for the currently considered system.

The concept of a technical system thus has a clearly epistemic function of (functional) "reduction to the essential". To Einstein the recommendation is attributed "to make it as simple as possible but not simpler". The *law of completeness of a system* expresses exactly this thought, however, not as a *law*, but as an engineering *modeling directive*. The apparent "natural law" of the observed dynamics therefore essentially addresses *reasonable human action*.

In an approach of "reduction to the essential" and "guaranteed specification-compliant operation" human practices are inherently built in, since only in such a context the terms "essential", "guarantee" and "operation" can be filled with sense in a meaningful way. These essential terms from the socially determined practical relationship of people are deeply rooted in the concept generation processes of descriptions of special technical systems and find their "natural" continuation in the special social settings of a legally constituted societal system.

# 5  The World of Technical Systems. Basics

In the TRIZ literature such conceptual foundations hardly play a role. Relevant textbooks such as [6] consider the term "technical system" as intuitively given from "industrial practices" [6], while other terms such as "process", "product", "service", "resources" and "effects" [6] are carefully introduced. Even the detailed description of the "evolution of technical systems" in 5 laws and 11 trends [6] is based solely on the succinct statement "The existence of technical evolution is a central insight of the TRIZ".

How the concept of a *technical system* can be further sharpened? In [4] we identified "the system concept as descriptional focusing to make real-world phenomena accessible for a description by *reduction to the essentials*". Such a reduction focuses on the following three dimensions [4]:

(1) Outer demarcation of the system against an environment, reduction of these relationships to input/output relationships and guaranteed throughput.
(2) Inner demarcation of the system by combining subareas to components, whose functioning is reduced to "behavioural control" via input/output relations.
(3) Reduction of the relations in the system itself to "causally essential" relationships.

Further, it is stated that – similar to the concert example – such a reductive description (explicitly or implicitly) exploits output from prior life:

(1) An at least vague idea about the (working) input/output services of the environment.
(2) A clear idea of the inner workings of the components (beyond the pure specification).
(3) An at least vague idea about causalities in the system itself, that precedes the detailed modelling.

The description of planning, design and improvement of technical systems in such an approach is based on the performance of already existing technical systems, which are present both in (2) as components and – from the point of view of a system in the supersystem – in (3) as neighbouring systems. Thus engineering practices are embedded into a *world of technical systems*. From the special descriptive perspective of a system the components or neighbouring systems are given with their *specification* only. Such a *reduction to the essential* appears practically as a shortened way of reasoning about social normality, what I call *fiction* for short. This fiction can and does work in daily language use as long as the social circumstances are in operation, that guarantee the maintenance of the social normality, i.e., as long as the *operation of the corresponding infrastructure* is guaranteed. Hence technical systems are – at least in their performance dimension – *always* socio-technical systems.

## 6  Engineering Systems and Socio-economic Evolution

Evolution of engineering systems, as V. Souchkov states in the preface of [9], should be considered as "innovative development since – in contrast to nature – craftsmen and engineers make decisions based on logic, previous experience, and knowledge of basic principles rather than chance." The concentration on "craftsmen and engineers" points to narrow practices, from which the systematization in [9] is drawn.

To identify lines of development, in [9] the term *technical system*[1] is embedded between "technology push" and "market pull" as "simple means for understanding the advancement of man-made systems" [9]. The reference to the even more vague term "man-made systems" is explained afterwards in more detail. Innovation as an "improvement of already-existing systems" is supported by the advance of scientific knowledge. This advancement is the source for new systems, products and services to be created. It is driven by a "market pull, the second trigger for innovation" as a shaping selection process, "that stimulates the development of a system by meeting the needs of that system's users". The exact form of this approach, driven not from engineering requirements, but from innovation-entrepreneurial practices, becomes clear in [9]. The foundations of these implicit conceptualizations are located in the framework of the economic system of a capitalist society as supersystem (I add: of western type, since the transferability to more autocratic economic systems as in China or Russia, for example, require additional considerations). In reality, the conceptualization is even more tightly drawn. The analysis of the examples shows that a distinction between industrial plant construction, mechanical engineering and consumer goods production, as common in economic analysis, is not carried out. It prevails the perspective of a larger market oriented company that estimates the product compatibility of technical systems. The unique specimen character of the vast majority of large technical systems and thus the practices of industrial plant construction are not taken into account.

This renders the subject area of technical systems sufficiently clear, whose "evolution" is examined. But what is the aggregation principle for identifying "trends" in such an evolution? Now that we have identified a supersystem, we can use the TRIZ methodology itself to reconstruct the modeling in [9] and analyze its conceptual foundation.

The starting point is the socio-economic (super) system of an industrial mode of production. "The wealth of these societies", Marx begins his analysis of such a socio-economic system in [10], "appears as a 'vast collection of goods', and individual goods are their elementary form. Our investigation therefore begins with the analysis of the goods." We also start with this term as a high level abstraction. As well known Marx' labour value theory abstracted in the concept of *good* from all qualitative characteristics other than the one, to be a product of human labour. Only on such a level of abstraction, special goods become globally exchangeable and constitute a global market as a *relation* – field in TRIZ terminology – between these special commodities, the *exchange value*.

---

[1] We do not distinguish between the newly introduced term "engineering system" and this old term being in use together with its abbreviation TS in the TRIZ literature for many years.

However, that is not what [9] is about, it is about functional qualities of specific product groups such as washing machines or fountain pens. The general competitive relationship between abstract goods is broken down into more specific competitive conditions of individual product groups on individual markets, and in [9] the "market pull" is the main function of the tool "market", which transforms the objects "engineering systems" into "useful products" – I use the TRIZ terminology of [16] on this unusual target. With the marketability of products we identified a first structural unit in the supersystem – special markets at which *special* goods with *specific* functional characteristics – *use value* in Marx's terminology – are competing with each other.

The use value of a good is characterized by a bundle of specific "useful" functionalities, i.e. by the property of a good to be a specific technical component in the sense developed so far. This ensemble of useful features determines the possibilities and limits of the interchangeability of goods in the overall societal technological process. Such borders lead to a stratification of "the market" into special *technology markets* for specific product groups with different MPV (main parameter of value) – according to [9] a central characteristic of such markets.

Such a technology market is less likely determined by the goods traded on it, as by the companies producing these goods. But this shifts the focus from an MPV as an independent characteristic of goods to the *business ability to produce* technical artifacts with this MPV in a reasonable price-performance ratio. Hence, on these technology markets meet producers updating their *prior experience* on the contradictions between justified expectations and experienced results in the exchange of their work products. This drives the dynamics of such a technology market.

Hence technical evolution should consider these technological production conditions, too. This is also recognized in [9], because the options for action described in the book refer to the organization of corresponding innovation processes within companies. Hence a *second* supersystem *innovation management* (IM) pops up in our TRIZ analysis – the management structures of companies that are responsible for the innovation process. Again we have to take into account the duality of system template – common social practices of the organization of innovation processes as discussed in [12] – and special real-world systems of innovation in the individual companies. The *main function* of those structures is the organization of innovation processes in close connection with the general business strategy. This process is contradictory by itself, since it has to take into account the *contradictory requirements* of different parts of the company (R&D, sales, finance, controlling, SCM, CRM). The recommendations compiled in [9] are *one* aspect in this complex balancing process. But, compared to the analysis in [12], a methodology between "technology push" and "market pull" remains rather on the level of the 1960s compared to contemporary approaches in management theory. In [12] with "state of the art in science and technology" (ST) next to the "needs of society and marketplace" a *third* supersystem pops up. This third supersystem ST is relevant also for patent grants and the concepts *the state of the art* and *level of invention*. Thus we already identified *three* socio-technical supersystems (economy, IM, ST), each with its own terms, structures, components, forms of description and implementation, which, in one way or another, are related to the evolution of technical systems.

The existence of *multiple* supersystems clearly indicates that the term *supersystem* should not be confused with the term *environment*. Supersystems are specific systems with their own language and logic. The relationship supersystem-system is similar to the relationship system-component: they constitute two different perspectives of perception on the "totality of the world" with two different understandings of the *essential* and thus from two different reduction perspectives. From the perspective of the system any supersystem also acts functionally. The description of the system's interface specifies an input and throughput from the supersystem in terms of quantity, quality and structure, required by the system to function at run time. The supersystem guarantees to fulfill these requirements in the performance dimension. Hence from the system's perspective *a supersystem is nothing more than a special kind of component, a neighbouring component.*

# 7   Normalization and Standardization

One of the main roads of technical development is concerned with normalization and standardization as a prerequisite for modularization. Modularization is an important – if not the most important at all – engineering approach that drives the evolution of technical systems. Modular systems are widely used and make it possible to create unique technical real-world specimen in the same way as explained in the concert example. While the private procedural skills of the musicians were an essential prerequisite in that example, now the *logic of the business application* appears as "core concern" of the components and the *logic of networking* of the infrastructure as "cross cutting concerns". Both logics are orthogonal to each other, which devaluates the trends 4.2 "of increasing system completeness" and 4.4 of "transition to the supersystem" in [9] in their separate consideration. This suggests the following second thesis:

**Thesis 2:** *A better descriptive understanding of the infrastructure requirements of interacting components (transition to the supersystem) leads to an* attenuation *of the requirements for completeness of the individual components.*

In particular, the arguments in [9] for trend 4.2 to justify the hierarchization into "operating agent" (as core function), "transmission" (support for the working tool), "energy source" (use of forces of nature) and "control system" (use of – nowadays mainly digital – control elements) are affected by these developments, as a visit to a DIY store immediately shows. The machine systems of reputable manufacturers concentrate on provision of energy. Via appropriate APIs (such as velcro, screw or click fasteners on the mechanical level) suitable tools can be joined with the energy machine[2]. Relational effects as normalization and standardization in this *world of*

---

[2] Progress in material sciences, in particular with hook and loop fasteners, led to a massive return to *mechanical* coupling principles in contrast to the TRIZ principle 28 of *replacement of mechanical schemes.*

*technical systems* play a much greater role than the further development of the technical artifacts only.

Standardization also opens up economies of scale for standard components, i.e. for concepts near to the "ideal final results". Economies of scale lead to *decreasing* cost per individual item and thus move the guiding principle of competition from the *better technical solution* to the *cheaper economic production*. So the S-curve does not necessarily end – and probably rarely does – with the decommissioning in stage 4 [9], but turns at the height of mature *technical* quality (including normalization and standardization) into the direction of *ubiquity*, in which the *ever-less* economic expenditures for the availability of this "state of the art" take on a leading role in further development.

The trend 4.1 "of increasing (technical) value" thus turns to a trend "of decreasing economic value", or – in economic terms – the market previously driven by demand is turning to a supply-driven market. The same (mature) use value has ever lower exchange value. The value of "ideality" [6] indeed goes beyond any limits, but as a consequence of an *economic* law. This corresponds to TRIZ principle 17 of *transition to other dimensions* and can be fixed as a third thesis:

**Thesis 3:** *The (technical) trend 4.1 "of increasing (technical) value" turns in Stage 3 of the S-curve development into an (economic) "trend of decreasing (economic) value".*

This means that in stage 3 the leading function (MPV) of the further development of the production of common tools and standard components turns from the technical driving forces to the economic ones. This process of "commodification" is sufficiently described in [11], hence there is no need to delve into the subject here.

The TRIZ principle 17 of *transition to other dimensions* appears in the above argumentation not as *abstract design pattern*, but as *abstract evolution pattern*, since here it does not operate as a means of active influence of a problem-solving process, but as a description pattern of passively observed real-world developments. In this sense, however, every other of the TRIZ principles as well as the TRIZ standards can be formulated as an abstract evolution pattern. Conversely, the trends of evolution can be interpreted as further abstract design patterns that can be used in addition to the "principles" and the "standards". Although this is not new to experienced TRIZ practitioners, see [15], I formulate this observation as another thesis:

**Thesis 4:** *Each of the TRIZ principles and each of TRIZ standards can convincingly be formulated as a "trend of evolution of technical systems" and vice versa.*

The hierarchy of evolution patterns thus gives cause to develop a "hierarchy of TRIZ principles" [17], as proposed by Dietmar Zobel more than 10 years ago, see also [18]. The approach of M. Rubin in [13] to systematize the connections between such hierarchizations remains to be investigated further.

Normalization and standardization heavily influences the evolution in the world of technical systems in an advanced state. We demonstrate these effects in the *world of bolted joints* with machine screws and wood screws.

For the production of machine screws, high precision and coherence of diameter and angle of attack of the threads is required to ensure that they fit with the counterparts. This precision can be reached not only in an industrial production mode, but – for special applications – also with appropriate private tools – e.g., a thread tap. With slotted, crosshead, hexagonal, countersunk head, socket head etc. screws there is a wide range of ready for use solutions for different application scenarios (TRIZ principle 3 of *local quality*), and corresponding tools: ordinary wrenches, socket wrenches, screwdrivers, Allen keys and so on (once again TRIZ principle 3), both as individual tools and inserts for the cordless screwdriver as an energy machine (TRIZ principle 1 of *decomposition*, TRIZ standard 3.1 of *transition to a bi-system*). Flexible connections[3] (together with the cordless screwdriver TRIZ standard 3.1 *transition to a poly system*) can be used to apply screw connections even in places that are difficult to access and so on. These tools are also used by industrial robots (TRIZ standard 3 *transition to a supersystem* applied twice, because the industrial robots are components in the super-super-system).

The world of wood screws avoids the two-component system (once again TRIZ standard 3.1: bolt and nut), in that the hold in the material itself is sought (trend 4.6 of increasing degree of trimming – why this central TRIZ method is neither part of the "principles" nor the "standards"?), either by predrilling (TRIZ principle 10 of *previous action*) or by a self-tapping screw (TRIZ principle 25 of the *self-service* or again trend 4.6 of *trimming*). Unfortunately some materials do not offer this grip, thus *anchors* were invented (TRIZ non-trend of *anti-trimming*[4]), a world of technical solutions that are at the heart of every TRIZ practitioner. We didn't touch yet special applications of screw connections as in surgery, where essential parameters of material and reliability are determined by the conditions of the supersystem and lead to very special system solutions.

I have described this world in so much detail to clarify three aspects:

1) It is a world of technical systems in which principles of problem solving based on TRIZ play an important role.
2) The structuring moment in that world are not the technical systems, but the *technical principles*.
3) The 10 "trends" in a decontextualized fashion are not very helpful to determine your way through highly volatile requirement situations, if you seek for *special* solutions in *special* contextualizations.

In such a world the "evolution of individual technical systems" is of minor interest compared to a global *evolution of technology*, i.e. the "evolution of the world of technical systems" as a whole.

---

[3] Amazon offers such a 31-piece set of the company Lotex GmbH for 20.99 Euro.

[4] This is a subtle point, since this trend is called "закон развертывания – свертывания" in Russian [8], but from this bidirectional mode only one direction survived in the English (and German) translation.

# 8 Summary

With the concept of a *technical system* the whole TRIZ theoretical body revolves around a term that is not precisely defined in the TRIZ literature, but left to a "common sense". The 40 TRIZ principles, the 76 TRIZ standards and the (in [9]) 10 TRIZ trends of evolution constitute a universe of theoretical reflections of practical inventory experience with a tendency to universalism. Nevertheless overarching generalizations of practical experience and the resulting decontextualization in the TRIZ theoretical body are hardly perceived as a problem in the TRIZ community.

In this paper an attempt was made to determine how far a notion of *technical system* takes in this theoretical context and to relate this with approaches from neighbouring theory corpusses. It turns out that focusing on an artifact dimension of technology, as inherent to the term *technical system*, blocks the view on essential *relational* phenomena in the *world of technical systems*. A notion of *technical principle* as used in [14] is better suited for the analysis of relational phenomena in that world. Hence again: the whole is more than the sum of its parts.

# References

1. Von Bertalanffy, L.: An outline of general system theory. Br. J. Philos. Sci. 1(2), 134–165 (1950)
2. Fuchs-Kittowski, K.: Knowledge co-production. Processing, distribution and creation of information in creative learning organizations. In: Fuchs-Kittowski, K., et al. (eds.) Organisationsinformatik und Digitale Bibliothek in der Wissenschaft. Jahrbuch Wissenschaftsforschung 2000. Gesellschaft für Wissenschaftsforschung, Berlin (2000). ISBN 3-934682-34-0. (in German)
3. Gräbe, H.-G.: A discussion about TRIZ and system thinking reported in my Open Discovery Blog (2019). https://wumm-project.github.io/2019-08-07
4. Gräbe, H.-G.: Reader for the 16th Interdisciplinary Discussion *The concept of resilience as an emergent characteristic in open systems*, Leipzig, 7 February 2020 (2020). http://mint-leipzig.de/2020-02-07/Reader.pdf. (in German)
5. Gräbe, H.-G.: Men and their technical systems. LIFIS Online, 19 May 2020 (2020). https://doi.org/10.14625/graebe_20200519. (in German)
6. Koltze, K., Souchkov, V.: Systematic Innovation, 2nd edn. Hanser, Munich (2017). ISBN 978-3-446-45127-8. (in German)
7. Kropik, M.: Production Control Systems in the Automobile Manufacturing. Springer, Heidelberg (2009). https://doi.org/10.1007/978-3-540-88991-5. ISBN 978-3-540-88991-5. (in German)
8. Litvin, S., Petrov, V., Rubin, M.: TRIZ Body of Knowledge (2007). https://triz-summit.ru/en/203941
9. Lyubomirskiy, A., Litvin, S., et al.: Trends of Engineering System Evolution, Sulzbach-Rosenberg (2018). ISBN 978-3-00-059846-3
10. Marx, K.: Das Kapital, vol. 1. MEW 23. Dietz Verlag, Berlin (1971)
11. Naetar, F.: Commodification, law of values and immaterial labour. Grundrisse **14**, 6–19 (2005). (in German)
12. Preez, N.D.D., Louw, L., Essmann, H.: An innovation process model for improving innovation capability. J. High Technol. Manag. Res. **17**, 1–24 (2006)

13. Rubin, M.S.: On the connection between laws of development of general systems and laws of development of technical systems. Manuscript, November (2019). (in Russian)
14. Shpakovsky, N.: Tree of Technology Evolution. Forum, Moscow (2010). ISBN 978-1-5398-9218-2
15. Shub, L.: Caution! The contradiction table (2006). http://metodolog.ru/conference.html. (in Russian)
16. Target Invention: TRIZ Trainer (2020). https://triztrainer.ru
17. Zobel, D., Hartmann, R.: Pattern of Invention, 2nd edn. Expert Verlag, Renningen (2016). ISBN 978-3-8169-3244-4. (in German)
18. Zobel, D.: Contributions to the further development of TRIZ. LIFIS Online, 19 May 2020 (2020). https://doi.org/10.14625/zobel_20200119. (in German)

# Using Bibliometric Indicators from Patent Portfolio Valuation as Value Factor for Generating Smart Beta Products

Andreas Zagos[1(✉)] and Stelian Brad[2(✉)]

[1] Intracom GmbH, 53127 Bonn, Germany
zagos@intracomgroup.de
[2] Technical University Cluj-Napoca, Cluj-Napoca, Romania
stelian.brad@staff.utcluj.ro

**Abstract.** This paper goal is to present the results of the use of patent valuation indicators as alternative data which can generate a value factor which is suitable to design financial products. Based on different patent value indicators which address the areas "assignee", "technology" and "market" an "IP portfolio index" was designed and back tested with real market data. The outperformance of the IP portfolio index is shown in the current paper.

**Keywords:** Patent valuation · Bibliometric data · Stock picking · IP portfolio index · Smart beta · Factor-investing · Alternative data

## 1 Introduction

Alternative data (proprietary datasets) in different areas like geo-location, credit card, social/sentiment or web traffic became very popular over the last years at financial institutions promising additional insights beside business data.

The financial asset management institutions like discretionary, quantitative or hedgefunds develop own indexes which should outperform in terms of absolute return on investment with low maximum drawdown (A maximum drawdown (MDD) is the maximum observed loss from a peak to a trough of a portfolio, before a new peak is attained. Maximum drawdown is an indicator of downside risk over a specified time period, Investopedia) compared to an underlying (similar) index. These so called 'smart beta products' (Smart beta defines a set of investment strategies that emphasize the use of alternative index construction rules to traditional market capitalization-based indices. Smart beta emphasizes capturing investment factors or market inefficiencies in a rules-based and transparent way, Investopedia) use alternative index construction which is rule-based and including different factors.

Patent data became very popular over the past years because of the currently high quality of the data delivered by the most national patent offices and the possibility to use patent metrics as an indicator to measure the innovation developed by companies [1–8].

In literature have been created as well some "patent indexes" based on different patent metrics. Some of them are described in the study of Michele Grimaldi and Livio Cricelli [9]. In this study an own "patent value index" is described based on different metrics.

© IFIP International Federation for Information Processing 2020
Published by Springer Nature Switzerland AG 2020
D. Cavallucci et al. (Eds.): TFC 2020, IFIP AICT 597, pp. 411–429, 2020.
https://doi.org/10.1007/978-3-030-61295-5_31

The main weakness of the current existing patent indexes is beside of the lack of high-quality data that the meaningfulness of the outcome and the commercial exploitation is doubtful.

## 2  Aim of the Study

The aim of the study is to scientifically prove that patent indicators derived from different metrics have a real market impact especially for the financial sector.

This paper shows that patent value indicators build out of bibliometric data are suitable to determine equities which will outperform on a long-term base and can be used as reliable factor to develop smart beta products based on patent related indicators.

The main theory for using patent indicators is, that the development of the patent portfolio of a company is an early trend indicator and contemporary representing the present status of a company's research- and development output.

The amount and quality of granted and applied patents are an early stage and trend indicator, because first there is a serious time lag between application and grant of a patent which depends on the patent office, the patent quality itself and the technological sector and is stated to 1–10 years [10]. Secondly patents can be found after several years of their filing in products of the applicant.

The patenting activity of a company represents as well the current status of a company in terms of revenues and profits, because filing and counter fighting needs available resources in terms of money and human power. Further the development of patents needs a high-class research and development department, which generates innovations, otherwise no patents will be granted. Last but not least, a company which is filing patents with a high quality believes in its own technology and future growth, and is not only optimizing the corporate structure for cost-savings.

These points make patent analysis for fundamental company rating so interesting. Studies have shown that there is a correlation between stock value and patent development [11–13].

The current paper endorses the basic theory, that measurement of patent quality is a suitable factor for selecting equities and generating indexes for investment purposes.

## 3  Data Sources

For this study different data sources have been used which are described as follows:

### 3.1  Business Data

The business data have been delivered from Moodys product "Orbis" which is Bureau van Dijk's flagship company database [14]. It contains information on companies across the world and focuses on private company information. It has information on around 300 million companies from all countries. The main information which was exported from the database have been:

- Company identifier (ISIN)
- Total assets
- Amount on employees
- Corporate tree with subsidiaries >51% share
- Stock quotes of the equities (closing prices)
- List of constituents for backtested index

## 3.2   Patent Data

The used database for patent data was "Patstat" [15] which is a global database containing bibliographical data relating to more than 100 million patent documents from industrialised and developing countries. It also includes the legal event data from more than 40 patent authorities contained in the EPO worldwide legal event data.

## 3.3   Economic Data

The economic data used for this study is the GDP from each country. This was downloaded from the Worldbank Open Data [16].

# 4   Proposed System for the Main Indicators

Based on different possible indicators, the proposed main indicators determining patent portfolio quality are:

1. Assignee impact [Ai] = ratio alive patent families/employees and total assets of the assignee
2. Technology Impact [Ti] = Number of citing patents
3. Market impact [Mi] = amount of family members and GDP of the countries where the patent family members are alive (=patent country distribution)

The indicators are determined like follows:

## 4.1   Assignee Impact [Ai]

The assignee itself seems to have an impact for the value of a patent because he needs high resources to get the patents in force, to block competitors and to sew infringements. One metric to determine the commercial strength of an assignee is the amount on "total assets". Further the more granted patents a research and development department is producing, the higher the quality of the patents due to standardised processes and intellectual knowledge in patenting.

The total assets are normalized to the maximum of 369.8 B€ on total assets for Toyota Motor Corporation [14], having as industrial, non-governmental owned, the worldwide highest total assets declared in the balance sheet.

The Assignee impact is defined to:

$$[Ai] = \frac{Amount\ on\ alive\ patents}{Amount\ on\ employees} * \frac{Total\ assets}{Maximum\ total\ assets} \tag{1}$$

Both sub-indicators are equalweighted.

## 4.2 Technology Impact [Ti]

There are 2 different types of citation: forward and backward citations. Future citations received by a patent (forward citations) are more important than the backward citations, because in the case of forward citation the main indication is, that an innovation has contributed to the development of subsequent inventions. For this reason, citations have been used in several studies as a measure of the value of an invention [5, 17, 18]. The main thesis is, that the more often a patent is quoted as prior art during examinations of subsequent patent examinations, the more fundamental its technological contribution to the field, the higher the quality [19, 20].

Backward citations are used to determine the inventory step of the innovation and because this is connected with the patent applying process of the attorney it can't be used as good indicator: some attorneys are using a huge amount of backward citations with the aim to show the examiner that the applied patent is very innovative, other attorneys do not use this very intensively. Also, the application process in different countries leads to different amounts of backward citations.

The examiners in the Patent offices have a certain number of patents they always use for citations (because of time reduction for the examination process) – this behaviour from the practical point of view can have influences. This topic was examined by Criscuolo and Verspagen [20] and Juan Alcácer and Michelle Gittelman [21].

Further the cited documents can be also used as an indicator. Usually there are other patents or utility models cited but also NPL (Non-Patent-Literature) [22]. The main conclusion is, that the closer a patent application is to "fundamental research", as reflected by the non-patent references, the higher its technological quality. NPL is also used like backward citation to show the examiner that the state of the art has been approved before applying.

The forward citation is also a main indicator for the litigation process. In the work of Jean O. Lanjouw and Mark Schankerman [23] it is shown that there is a direct impact between citation and litigation.

The current Technology impact is defined as follows: the amount on foreign citations were divided through the amount on alive patents. The normalization was performed under the backward citation index, average per economy (country) [24].

Self-citations (even intra-corporate from subsidiaries) and references to non-patent literature have been excluded from the count. Approximately 11 percent of all citations in the sample from Jaffe and Tratenberg, 2003 are self-citations. To determine this indicator properly the corporate tree from the company must be available [25].

The technology impact [Ti] is defined to:

$$[Ti] = \frac{\text{amount on foreign citations (normalized)}}{\text{amount on alive patents}} \qquad (2)$$

## 4.3 Market Impact [Mi]

A number of authors have argued out that information on family size may be particularly well suited as an indicator of the value of patent rights. The studies by Putnam and Lanjouw et al. [26] have shown that the size of a patent family, measured as the number of jurisdictions in which a patent grant has been sought are highly correlated. To measure the potential power of a "family size", it is recommended to obtained the number of nations in which protection for a particular invention was sought from Derwent's World Patent Index (WPI) database.

The study from Adam B. Jaffe, Gáetan de Rassenfosse [27] shows, that there exists as well a bias for the priority application,

The size of a patent family is an indicator for the market impact that the technology described in the patent may have. The assumption is, that the higher the applicants willingness to pay for a large territory protection, the higher the patents value.

There exist some studies [28] showing that triadic patents (patent family applied and/or granted in Europe, Asia and USA) having a higher value then only filed in single countries, but due own experience of the author in several valuation projects the value of a patent depends much more on the certain economy where the patent is filed.

The market impact is therefore defined to the share of the IPC class (distinct 4-digit IPC subclasses) in the certain country where the patent family is filed, expressing the importance of the technology area in the certain country. The shares for each sub-class are exemplarily shown in a study from InTraCoM [29].

The market impact is further directly correlated with the economic size of the country (expressed in GDP), the importance of the certain technology in that country (expressed in share of the IPC class in the country) and the legal status of the patent family (application, grant or utility model).

The Market impact [Mi] is defined to:

$$[Mi] = \sum_1^n \frac{\text{amount patents in the IPC class in the country}}{\text{total amount on patnets in the IPC class}} * \frac{\text{GPR of the country}}{\text{Global GDP}} * Co$$

$$(3)$$

Co = factor for legal status of the patent family member defined to
Granted patent = 100%
Applied patent = 20%
Utility model = 10%

**4.4    Composite Index**

The calculation of the total patent quality [TPQ] in %, is based on the equal weighted indicators Ai, Ti, Mi, to:

$$TPQ = Ai * Ti * Mi$$

# 5  Data Samples

The IP portfolio index was generated and backtested based on the available indices in the market. Because the constituents (listed and delisted equities) of the index change every year, the backtest is performed static and dynamic. The static tests were designed in that way, that the current constituents have been selected and remained for the past 10 years in the patent value index, and not replaced with the new ones. This is a small failure in the direct benchmarking of the IP portfolio index with the current indices, but there is no other possibility on how to handle this issue for benchmarking on a long time period (>10 years). A second, dynamic backtest was performed too, but for a shorter period, for 4 years. The dynamic tests take into account the change of constituents and there is as well some turnover in the designed IP portfolio index.

The composition of the indexes and other related data like closing prices have been received from Orbis IP database [14].

Some data samples are given in the following tables in order to give an impression about the patent indicators, the sectors and equities used. Table 1 shows data samples are for the STOXX600 index (Table 2):

**Table 1.**  Data samples of patent metrics for a sample set of companies from STOXX600

| No. | Company name | 1 | 2 | 3 | 4 | 5 | 6 | 7 |
|-----|--------------|---|---|---|---|---|---|---|
| 1. | BP PLC | GB | 10.264 | 25.144 | 81 | 90 | 100 | 51 |
| 2. | SIEMENS AG | DE | 208.112 | 297.635 | 95 | 87 | 100 | 99 |
| 3. | HENNES & MAURITZ AB | SE | 7 | 2 | 31 | 36 | 0 | 56 |
| 4. | ASTRAZENECA | GB | 42.525 | 34.160 | 81 | 95 | 100 | 48 |
| 5. | SODEXO | FR | 23 | 19 | 39 | 60 | 0 | 58 |
| 6. | TELEFONAKTIEBOLAGET | SE | 134.219 | 81.995 | 91 | 88 | 100 | 85 |
| 7. | CREDIT AGRICOLE S.A. | FR | 78 | 84 | 51 | 100 | 54 | 0 |
| 8. | HENKEL AG & CO. KGAA | DE | 32.265 | 28.764 | 83 | 94 | 100 | 55 |
| 9. | WM MORRISON SUPERMARKETS | GB | 5 | 4 | 44 | 63 | 13 | 55 |
| 10. | ALLIANZ SE | DE | 86 | 80 | 79 | 91 | 100 | 48 |

1 Country code
2 Number of live publications
3 Number of granted publications
4 Total patent quality in %
5 Technical impact
6 Market impact
7 Assignee impact

**Table 2.** Data samples of financial metrics for a sample set of companies from STOXX600

| No. | Company name | 1 | 2 | 3 | 4 | 5 | 6 | 7 |
|-----|--------------|---|---|---|---|---|---|---|
| 1. | BP PLC | GB | GB0007980591 | 7 | 5 | 5 | 70 | 262 |
| 2. | DAIMLER AG | DE | DE0007100000 | 76 | 45 | 46 | 298 | 302 |
| 3. | TOTAL S.A. | FR | FR0000120271 | 57 | 43 | 46 | 107 | 243 |
| 4. | FIAT CHRYSLER AUTOMOBILES N.V. | NL | NL0010877643 | 22 | 12 | 13 | 191 | 98 |
| 5. | BAYERISCHE MOTOREN WERKE AKTIENGESELLSCHAFT | DE | DE0005190003 | 98 | 69 | 71 | 133 | 228 |
| 6. | NESTLE S.A. | CH | CH0038863350 | 77 | 65 | 71 | 291 | 117 |
| 7. | SIEMENS AG | DE | DE0007236101 | 126 | 100 | 110 | 385 | 150 |
| 8. | DEUTSCHE TELEKOM AG | DE | DE0005557508 | 16 | 13 | 15 | 210 | 170 |
| 9. | ENEL SPA | IT | IT0003128367 | 5 | 4 | 5 | 69 | 165 |
| 10. | TESCO PLC | GB | GB0008847096 | 3 | 2 | 3 | 464 | 57 |

1 Country code
2 ISIN number
3 Market price - high, EUR, year 2018
4 Market price - low, EUR, year 2018
5 Market price - year end, EUR, year 2018
6 Number of employees in 1,000
7 Total assets, b€

The Stoxx600 Index contains in general 20 sectors. The sectors considered for the IP portfolio index are:

1. Automobiles & Parts
2. Basic Resources Services (Basic resources)
3. Chemicals
4. Construction Materials
5. Food & Beverages
6. Industrial Goods
7. Media
8. Medical Engineering (Healthcare)
9. Oil Services, Green Energy (Oil&Gas)
10. Personal & Household Goods
11. Retail
12. Technology
13. Travel & Leisure

The sectors not considered (due low IP activity and importance) are:

1. Banks
2. Basic Resources (producers)
3. Financial Services
4. Healthcare (producers)
5. Insurance

6. Oil & Gas (producers)
7. Real Estate
8. Real Estate Cap
9. Telecommunications
10. Utilities

In the Stoxx600 232 companies were identified having a reasonable amount on patents (Fig. 1):

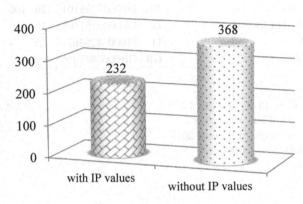

**Fig. 1.** Amount on equities with high quality patents in Stoxx 600 index

In these sectors the equities with highest IP relevance were selected (Fig. 2):

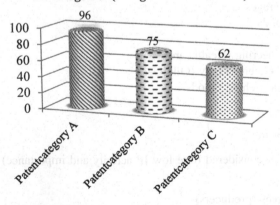

**Fig. 2.** Categories within the IP value index

The selected equities in the Patentcategory A in the IP portfolio listed in Table 3.

**Table 3.** Top equities with highest patent portfolio quality in Stoxx600 index

| | | |
|---|---|---|
| 1. ABB Ltd. | 41. Hexagon AB | 81. STMicroelectronics NV |
| 2. Actelion Ltd. | 42. Infineon | |
| 3. Air Liquide SA | 43. International Consolidated Airlines | 82. SUEZ SA |
| 4. Akzo Nobel N.V. | | 83. Swatch Group Ltd. Bearer |
| 5. Alcatel-Lucent SA | 44. Investor AB | |
| 6. Alstom SA | 45. Johnson Matthey | 84. Syngenta AG |
| 7. Arkema SA | 46. Kone Oyj | 85. Tate & Lyle PLC |
| 8. ARM Holdings plc | 47. LANXESS AG | 86. Technip SA |
| 9. ASML Holding NV | 48. Legrand SA | 87. Telecom Italia |
| 10. ASSA ABLOY AB | 49. LM Ericsson Telefon AB | 88. Telia Company AB |
| 11. Associated British Foods plc | 50. Lonza Group AG | 89. UCB S.A. |
| | 51. L'Oreal SA | 90. Umicore |
| 12. Atlas Copco AB | 52. Metso Oyj | 91. Unilever NV Cert. of shs |
| 13. BASF SE | 53. Nestle S.A. | |
| 14. Bayer AG | 54. Nokia Oyj | 92. Unilever PLC |
| 15. Beiersdorf AG | 55. Novo Nordisk A/S | 93. Veolia Environnement SA |
| 16. BT Group plc | 56. Novozymes A/S | |
| 17. Carlsberg A/S | 57. Orange SA | 94. Vestas Wind Systems A/S |
| 18. CGG | 58. Outotec Oyj | |
| 19. Clariant AG | 59. Petroleum Geo-Services ASA | 95. Vivendi SA |
| 20. Compagnie de Saint-Gobain SA | 60. Porsche Automobil Holding SE Pref | 96. Wartsila Oyj Abp |
| 21. Michelin SCA | 61. Prysmian S.p.A. | |
| 22. Continental AG | 62. Reckitt Benckiser Group plc | |
| 23. Daimler AG | 63. Rolls-Royce Holdings plc | |
| 24. Danone SA | 64. Royal DSM NV | |
| 25. Deutsche Lufthansa | 65. Royal KPN NV | |
| 26. Diageo plc | 66. Royal Philips NV | |
| 27. Electrolux AB | 67. Safran SA | |
| 28. Elekta AB | 68. Salzgitter AG | |
| 29. Essilor International | 69. Sandvik AB | |
| 30. FLSmidth & Co. | 70. SAP SE | |
| 31. Fortum Oyj | 71. SBM Offshore NV | |
| 32. Fresenius Medical | 72. Schneider Electric | |
| 33. Fresenius SE & Co. | 73. SES SA FDR | |
| 34. GEA Group | 74. Siemens AG | |
| 35. Gemalto N.V. | 75. SKF AB | |
| 36. Getinge AB | 76. Sky plc | |
| 37. Givaudan SA | 77. Smith & Nephew | |
| 38. GKN plc | 78. Smiths Group Plc | |
| 39. Grifols, S.A. | 79. Solvay SA | |
| 40. Henkel AG & Co. | 80. Sonova Holding AG | |

# 6 Results

## 6.1 Backtests on STOXX600

The performance of the IP portfolio Index containing the selected 232 equities with high IP quality shows a significant outperformance in opposition to the equal-weighted Stoxx 600 Index, and to the index of No IP Stoxx 600 (Fig. 3):

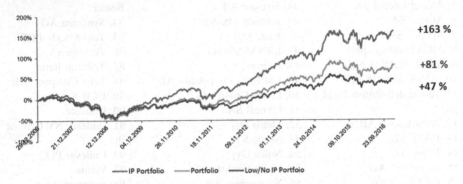

**Fig. 3.** Performance of the static IP portfolio Index for Stoxx600

**Portfolio Construction.** The Stoxx Europe 600 Index is separated in IP and Low/No IP stocks per 30.06.2016. Static, equal weighted portfolios of 232 IP stocks ("IP Stoxx Europe 600") vs 368 Low/No IP stocks ("Low/No IP Stoxx Europe 600") with yearly adjustment per 31.07; Benchmark is equal weighted Stoxx Europe 600 Portfolio ("Stoxx Europe 600"; 600 stocks); degree of investment = 100%; no risk management; no fees; ex dividend; all stock prices are calculated in EUR.

Some performance indicators for the IP portfolio index is shown at following table (Table 4):

**Table 4.** Key performance indicators of static IP portfolio Index Stoxx600

|  | Sharpe ratio | Sortino ratio | Avg 1 Y return | Avg 1 Y volatility | MAX DD |
|---|---|---|---|---|---|
| Patent portfolio index Stoxx600 | 0.54 | 0.87 | 10.2% | 14.4% | −43.3% |
| Stoxx 600 | 0.42 | 0.39 | 6.1% | 14.2% | −44.9% |
| No IP Stoxx 600 | 0.32 | 0.18 | 4.0% | 14.6% | −42.3% |

The Sharpe Ratio is used to help investors understand the return of an investment compared to its risk. Generally, the greater the value of the Sharpe ratio, the more attractive the risk-adjusted return. The sharpe ratio is calculated to:

$$\text{Sharpe Ratio} \; = \; \frac{Rp - Rf}{\sigma p} \qquad (4)$$

Where:

Rp = return of the portfolio
Rf = risk-free rate
σp = standard deviation of the portfolio's excess return

The Sortino ratio is a variation of the Sharpe ratio that differentiates harmful volatility from total overall volatility by using the asset's standard deviation of negative portfolio returns, called downside deviation, instead of the total standard deviation of portfolio returns (Investopedia). The Sortino ratio is a useful way for investors to evaluate an investment's return for a given level of bad risk and is defined to:

$$\text{Sortino Ratio} \; = \; \frac{Rp - Rf}{\sigma d} \qquad (5)$$

Where:

Rp = actual or expected return of the portfolio
rf = risk-free rate
σd = standard deviation of the portfolio's downside

All key performance indicators show a better quality of the IP portfolio index. Especially the correlation of significantly increasing the return with a very slight change of maximum drawdown (Max DD) and volatility makes the IP portfolio index very attractive. The downside risk (Sortino ratio) is as well much better than the index.

This backtest was performed with a static portfolio of selected equities. This means, that the constituents of the IP portfolio index did not change, which does not meet the reality. Therefore, a dynamic index was backtested too, where every year the new composed Stoxx 600 was analysed. The performance is shown in the Fig. 4.

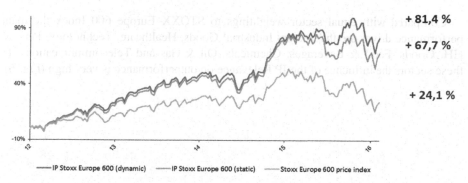

**Fig. 4.** Performance of the dynamic IP portfolio Index for Stoxx600

**Portfolio Construction.** Stoxx Europe 600 Index Portfolio is separated in IP and Low/No IP stocks per 30.06.2016. Static, equal weighted portfolios of 232 IP stocks ("IP Portfolio") vs. 368 Low/No IP stocks ("Low/No IP Portfolio") with yearly adjustment per 31.07; Benchmark is equal weighted Stoxx Europe 600 Portfolio ("Portfolio"; 600 stocks); degree of investment = 100%; no risk management; no fees; ex dividend; all stock prices are calculated in EUR.

**Sector Performance.** The selected sectors for designing the IP Stoxx index intended to show the market neutrality of the composed index. This means that the index should provide positive returns completely independent of the market conditions. Compared to the STOXX Europe 600 Index the main performance driver are the Sectors Industrial Goods, Healthcare, Food & Beverages, Chemicals, Pers. & HH Goods and Technology (Fig. 5).

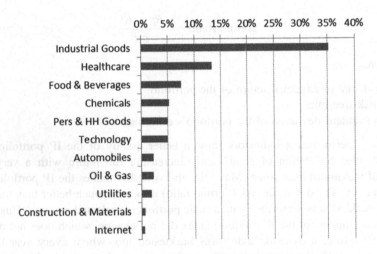

**Fig. 5.** Sector performance of the Stoxx600 Index

Compared with equal sector weightings to STOXX Europe 600 Index the main performance driver are the Sectors Industrial Goods, Healthcare, Technology, Pers. & HH. Goods, Food & Beverages, Chemicals, Oil & Gas and Telecommunications. In these sectors the influence of the IP Relevance on outperformance is very high (Fig. 6).

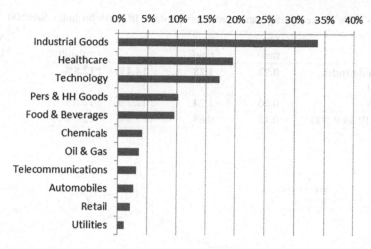

**Fig. 6.** Sector performance of the IP portfolio STOXX600 vs. Stoxx600 Index

Different other indices were backtested, under same conditions like the Stoxx600 which is showed more detailed in this paper. The results for the other indices are the following:

### 6.2 Backtests on S&P500

Backtests on S&P500 show similar results to the STOXX600 index (Fig. 7).

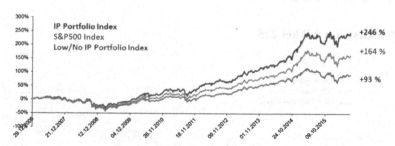

**Fig. 7.** Performance of the static IP portfolio Index for S&P 500

Static, equal weighted portfolios of 238 IP stocks ("IP Portfolio") vs. 248 Low/No IP stocks ("Low/No IP Portfolio") with yearly adjustment per 31.07. All stock prices are calculated in local currency (Table 5) (Fig. 8).

**Table 5.** key performance indicators of static IP portfolio Index S&P500

|  | Sharpe ratio | Sortino ratio | Return | Avg 1 Y volatility | MAX DD |
|---|---|---|---|---|---|
| **IP Portfolio Index S&P 500** | **0.77** | **1.28** | **14.4%** | **12.8%** | **−30.7%** |
| S&P 500 | 0.66 | 1.24 | 11.2% | 12.6% | −33.8% |
| Low/No IP S&P 500 | 0.48 | 0.68 | 7.5% | 12.7% | −41.9% |

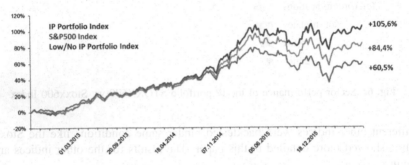

**Fig. 8.** Performance of the dynamic IP portfolio Index for S&P 500

For the IP portfolio S&P index the main improvement is the return. The other factors like MaxDD, Sortino- or Sharpe ratio remain similar but much better than the equities with no or low IP.

## 6.3    Backtests on Nikkei 225

**Fig. 9.** Performance of the static IP portfolio Index for Nickei225

Static, equal weighted portfolios of 132 IP stocks ("IP Portfolio") vs 93 Low/No IP stocks ("Low/No IP Portfolio") with yearly adjustment per 31.07. All stock prices are calculated in local currency (Table 6) (Figs. 9 and 10).

**Table 6.** Key performance indicators of static IP portfolio Index Nikkei225

| | Avg. return (9Y) | Avg volatility (9Y) | Sharpe ratio | Sortino ratio |
|---|---|---|---|---|
| IP Nikkei 225 Index | 5.3% | 14.9% | 0.46 | 0.17 |
| Nikkei 225 Index | 4.0% | 14.9% | 0.42 | 0.10 |
| Low/No IP Nikkei 225 Index | 2.2% | 15.3% | 0.30 | 0.01 |

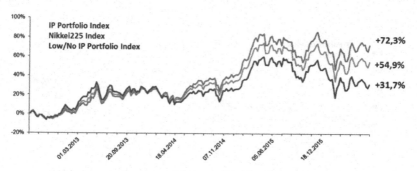

**Fig. 10.** Performance of the dynamic IP portfolio Index for Nickei225

## 6.4    Backtests on CSI300

**Fig. 11.** Performance of the static IP portfolio Index for CSI300

Static, equal weighted portfolio of 40 IP stocks with half-yearly adjustment ("IP CSI 300 Portfolio") vs. 260 Low/No IP stocks in CSI 300 Index per 30/06/2016. All stock prices are calculated in local currency (Fig. 11).

For the Nikkei index the findings are the same like for the S&P index (Table 7) (Fig. 12).

**Table 7.** Key performance indicators of static IP portfolio Index CSI 300

|  | Sharpe ratio | Sortino ratio | Avg. return (6Y) | Avg. 1 Y volatility (6Y) | MAX DD |
|---|---|---|---|---|---|
| IP Portfolio Index | 0.75 | 7.0 | 14.7% | 18.6% | −47.9% |
| CSI 300 Index | 0.16 | 0.85 | 1.6% | 24.8% | −44.8% |

**Fig. 12.** Performance of the dynamic IP portfolio Index for CSI300

For the IP portfolio CSI index the main improvement is the massive increase of return and much better Sortino ratio. The max DD increased slightly.

Summary of the most important key performance indicators (Table 8):

**Table 8.** Summary of most important key performance indicators of the IP portfolio index

| Index | 1 | 2 | 3 | 4 | 5 | 6 | 7 |
|---|---|---|---|---|---|---|---|
| Stoxx600 | 232 | 368 | 39% | 11 | 7 | 4.5 | 157% |
| CSI300 | 40 | 260 | 13% | 14.7 | 1.6 | – | 919% |
| Nickei225 | 132 | 93 | 59% | 5.3 | 4 | 2.2 | 133% |
| S&P500 | 238 | 248 | 49% | 14.4 | 11.2 | 7.5 | 129% |

1 Amount on patent equities in index
2 Amount on No or Low patent equities in index
3 Share of IP equities
4 Average return of the IP portfolio
5 Average return of the equal weighted index
6 Average return of the no IP portfolio
7 Outperformance IP portfolio

## 6.5   Correlations and Sector Bias

A main question which occurs when a new factor is designed and applied to indices is if the factor has a certain attribute bias? Attribute bias describes the fact that equities that are chosen using one predictive model or technique tend to have similar fundamental characteristics. For the patent factor it is obvious that there could be a bias in technology equities, because those are having the most patents. The current analysis showed that different other sectors like "household" or "food and beverages", which are not classified as "hightech" are outperforming as well.

A look-ahead-bias does not exist because the data were produced at point of time.

The next important question is if the factor correlates with any other existing factor? Backtests on the factors value, momentum and others are not correlated like the Fig. 13 shows.

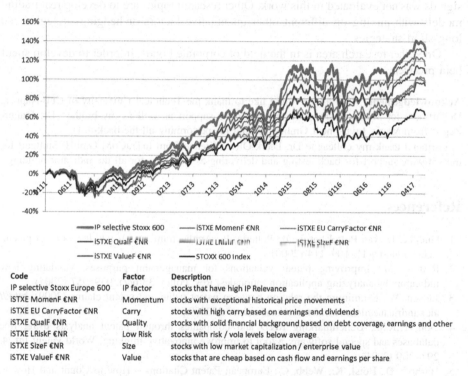

| Code | Factor | Description |
|---|---|---|
| IP selective Stoxx Europe 600 | IP factor | stocks that have high IP Relevance |
| iSTXE MomenF €NR | Momentum | stocks with exceptional historical price movements |
| iSTXE EU CarryFactor €NR | Carry | stocks with high carry based on earnings and dividends |
| iSTXE QualF €NR | Quality | stocks with solid financial background based on debt coverage, earnings and other |
| iSTXE LRiskF €NR | Low Risk | stocks with risk / vola levels below average |
| iSTXE SizeF €NR | Size | stocks with low market capitalization / enterprise value |
| iSTXE ValueF €NR | Value | stocks that are cheap based on cash flow and earnings per share |

**Fig. 13.** Comparison of factors Stoxx 600 versus IP portfolio Index

One could also guess that the amount on patents or research-and development expenditure is correlated. This was analysed in older studies and can be denied [30, 31].

## 7  Conclusions

The current work shows that using patent metrics for defining and applying indicators for stock picking is an appropriate method to develop a new factor which can generate alpha in a designed index. The main requirement to use the IP portfolio Index factor for improving financial products is, that in the selection must be a reasonable amount on equities which operate in a technology field. The backtests do not show correlations for an optimum of the share of IP equities in an index neither focus on a certain world-region or a technology sector.

The basic theory that equities with a high qualitative patent portfolio perform better than those without is proved in the current study because the main global indices like Stoxx600, S&P, Nikkei and CSI showed an outperformance in a backtest period of 10 years.

Further research in this area will be done in the area of o higher granulation of the patent quality in defining more than 3 indicators. The basic selection for the equities was to identify equities with good patent portfolio, the possibility of identifying exit signals was not evaluated in this work. Other research topics are to develop real trading models with mixing up different other quantitative factors or hedging strategies like long-short strategies.

One other research area is in the field of corporate bonds, in order to develop smart beta products.

**Acknowledgement.** The author would like to thank the Technical University of Cluj-Napoca, Department for Management of Research for the support as well as my brother, Dr. Ioannis Zagos from Matrix Investment GmbH, helping me performing all the back-tests.

Further I thank my colleague Dr. Dierk-Oliver Kiehne from InTraCoM GmbH, Stuttgart for the software support for back-testing and delivering as well data for all the indicator building.

# References

1. Guellec, D., van Pottelsberghe de Potterie, B.: Applications, grants and the value of patent. Econ. Lett. **69**(1), 109–114 (2000)
2. Reitzig, M.: Improving patent valuations for management purposes: validating new indicators by analyzing application rationales. Res. Policy **33**(6/7), 939–957 (2004)
3. Jansen, W.: Examining the relation between patent value and patent claims (2009). http://alexandria.tue.nl/extra1/afstversl/tm/Jansen%202009.pdf
4. Dou, H.R.M.: Benchmarking R&D and companies through patent analysis using free databases and special software: a tool to improve innovative thinking. World Patent Inf. **4**, 297–309 (2004)
5. Harhoff, D., Hoisl, K., Webb, C.: European Patent Citations – How to Count and How to Interpret Them, University of Munich (2006)
6. Deng, Y.: Private value of European patents. Eur. Econ. Rev. **51**(7), 1785–1812 (2007)
7. van Zeebroeck, N.: The puzzle of patent value indicators (CEB Working Paper N° 07/023). Université Libre de Bruxelles. Solvay Brussels School of Economics and Management, Brussels, Belgium (2007)
8. PatVal-EU. JHomepage. http://ec.europa.eu/invest-in-research/pdf/download_en/patval_mai nreportandannexes.pdf. Accessed 25 May 2020
9. Grimaldi, M., Cricelli, L.: Valuating and analyzing the patent portfolio: the patent portfolio value index. Eur. J. Innov. Manag. **21**(2), 174–205 (2018). https://doi.org/10.1108/ejim-02-2017-0009
10. WIPO Statistics Database, October 2015

11. Narin, F., Breitzman, A., Thomas, P.: Using patent citation indicators to manage a stock portfolio. In: Moed, H.F., Glänzel, W., Schmoch, U. (eds.) Handbook of Quantitative Science and Technology Research, pp. 553–568. Springer, Dordrecht (2004). https://doi.org/10.1007/1-4020-2755-9_26
12. Hall, B.H., Thoma, G., Torrisi, S.: The market value of patents and R&D: evidence from European firms. Acad. Manag. Proc. **2007**(1) (2007)
13. Hall, B.H., Jaffe, A., Trajtenberg, M.: Market Value and Patent Citations: A First Look, No E00-277, Economics Working Papers, University of California at Berkeley (2000)
14. Business Data Provided from Orbis, Bureau van Dijk (2019)
15. EPO Homepage. https://www.epo.org/searching-for-patents/business/patstat.html. Accessed 25 May 2020
16. World Bank Open Data. https://data.worldbank.org/. Accessed 25 May 2020
17. Abrams, D., Akcigit, U., Popadak, J.: Patent value and citations: Creative destruction or strategic disruption? National Bureau of Economic Research Working Paper No. 19647 (2013)
18. Trajtenberg, M.: Economic Analysis of Product Innovation: The Case of CT Scanners. Harvard Economic Studies, vol. 160. Harvard University Press, Cambridge (1990)
19. Ernst, Leptien, Witt: Technologie-und Innovations management (2000)
20. Criscuolo, P., Verspagen, B.: Does it matter where patent citations come from? Inventor vs. examiner citations in European patents, vol. 37 (2008)
21. Alcácer, J., Gittelman, M.: Patent citations as a measure of knowledge flows: the influence of examiner citations. Rev. Econ. Stat. **88**(4), 774–779 (2006)
22. OECD: Patents citing non-patent literature (NPL), selected technologies, 2007–13: Share of citations to NPL in backward citations, average, EPO patents, in Connecting to knowledge, OECD Publishing, Paris (2015)
23. Lanjouw, J.O., Schankerman, M.: Characteristics of patent litigation: a window on competition. RAND J. Econ. **32**(1), 129–151 (2001)
24. OECD: Calculations Based on PATSTAT (EPO, April 2012), October 2012
25. Hall, B.H., Jaffe, A., Trajtenberg, M.: Market value and patent citations. RAND J. Econ. **36**(1), 16–38 (2005)
26. Lanjouw/Pakes/Putnam, S. 418 ff. How to count patents and value intellectual property: Uses of patent renewal and application data. NBER Working Paper Series, vol. 5741. National Bureau of Economic Research, Cambridge (1996)
27. Jaffe, A.B., de Rassenfosse, G.: Patent citation data in social science research: overview and best practices. J. Assoc. Inf. Sci. Technol. (2017). https://doi.org/10.1002/asi
28. Criscuolo, P.: The 'home advantage' effect and patent families. A comparison of OECD triadic patents, the USPTO and the EPO. Scientometrics **66**(1), 23–41 (2006). https://doi.org/10.1007/s11192-006-0003-6
29. Kiehne, D.-O.: InTraCoM GmbH, What specific technology represents a certain country, August 2016
30. Kiehne, D.-O.: The Correlation Between the Number of Patents and the Patent Portfolio Value of Companies, July 2019 (2019). http://media.intracomgroup.de/InTraCoMCorrelation Patval_and_Patcount_July2019_DOK.pdf
31. Zagos, A.: Correlation Between R&D Expenses and Patent Value, April 2019. http://media.intracomgroup.de/RD_Expenses_Study_ANZ.pdf

# Innovative Method of Patent Design Around Guided by Technological Evolution

Lulu Zhang[1,2]([✉]) [iD], Runhua Tan[1,2]([✉]) [iD], Hao-Yu Li[1,2] [iD],
Fanfan Wang[1,2] [iD], Jianguang Sun[1,2], and Kang Wang[1,2] [iD]

[1] Hebei University of Technology, Tianjin 300401, China
zhanglulu199429@163.com, rhtan@hebutedu.cn
[2] National Engineering Research Center for Technological Innovation Method
and Tool, Tianjin 300401, China

**Abstract.** Patent design around can avoid infringement disputes, but it is hard for enterprises to use this method in the development of innovative products. This paper proposes an innovative method for the patent design around guided by laws of the technological system evolution. Functions of the product is firstly determined using a constructed function-need matrix of patents related to the target product. The potential state of technologies is then predicted according to laws of technological system evolution through analyzing the target function model. The patent design around is then conducted to search patents for relative functions. The solution is finally formed to circumvent any potential infringement. Feasibility of the proposed method is verified in the design of a mosquito catcher.

**Keywords:** Patent design around · Laws of technological system evolution · TRIZ · Mosquito catcher

## 1 Introduction

With the international market competition, enterprises frequently face to the patent barriers in the product innovation [1]. In order to get a place in the market, it is of paramount importance to enhance competitiveness using the core technology with the independent patent. In view of that, the patent design around plays a very important role in the competition for the enterprises.

Schechter [2] explained that patent design around is a circuitous design process in order to avoid the obstruction or attack from other enterprises. At present, different methods have been proposed to implement the patent design around from various perspectives. For example, Liu et al. [3] recommended formulating functional requirements from the patented product using design around the patent by replacing, deleting, adding or combining function elements. Jiang et al. [4] used a function trimming method to construct the function model and built the trimming variation of the new product according to the principle of the component avoidance. Li et al. [5] proposed an evading method for timing, which decomposes technical characteristics in patent claims [6]. Xu et al. [7] proposed a method that combines patent information and axiomatic design. Jiang et al. [8] integrated patent's IPC cluster analysis and technical

D. Cavallucci et al. (Eds.): TFC 2020, IFIP AICT 597, pp. 430–443, 2020.
https://doi.org/10.1007/978-3-030-61295-5_32

maturity to determine the patent clusters and goal. Li et al. [9] constructed the function trimming paths of patent design around for mechanical products.

In this paper, laws of the technological system evolution are applied to guide the direction of patent design around. Patents related to the target product are analyzed by a function-need matrix for mining new requirements of customers and target functions. The future state of the existing technology with the target function could then be predicted by laws of the technological system evolution. In order to avoid the infringement, the patent design around is implemented for patents involved in the target function. TRIZ tools are used to solve derivative technical problems in the improvement design process [10]. The infringement determination is eventually made for the design scheme.

This approach provides new insight for patent design around, aiming at promising innovation for local enterprises. The remainder of this paper is organized as follows. Section 2 describes the method to obtain the target function. Section 3 specifies determination of the potential state as the goal of patent design around. Section 4 shows a procedure flow of the proposed method. Section 5 introduces a case study for design of a mosquito catcher to verify the method. Section 6 concludes the research by highlighting the findings.

## 2 Acquisition of Target Function Based on Patent Analysis

In the requirements analysis phase, main functions of a target product are first obtained by retrieving the relevant patents in the Patsnap patent database (http://www.zhihuiya.com), which are decomposed into sub-functions. The function flow model of each sub-function is then constructed. Functional keywords are added to the existing patent retrieval formula to study the technical background and claims in each patent. Corresponding technical solutions to sub-functions should be deduced. Based on the analysis of the existing invention patents, the relationship between the function category and patent quantity is obtained, as shown in Fig. 1, we can initially identify the function of the target product as the main demand for users. In a chronological order, the number of patents is counted corresponding to each function, and the function-need matrix is constructed to express changes of the demand visually as shown in Fig. 2.

The relationship between the function category and patent quantity can help designers to obtain the importance of various functions to the product, which can be used as a preliminary understanding of the target function in the target product. Similarly, the function-need matrix is established to study the development of various functions. It is a mathematical matrix based on the year of patent application and the function realized by patent. This matrix can visually summarize the change of patent number of each function in the target product with time, so as to study the change of research investment in the target product function in the market, determine the valuable target function in the target product.

By analyzing the relationship between product function category and patent quantity and function-need matrix, it can be found that some functions with the large total number of patents (hot spots) are gradually decreased with time, while others are increased. The decreasing trend indicates a shrinking market share of this function or a

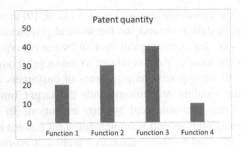

Fig. 1. Function category and patent quantity from patent analysis stage

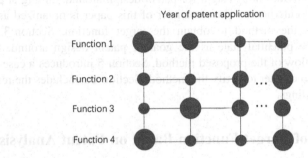

Fig. 2. Function-need matrix

technical bottleneck. On the other hand, an increase implies that the function's demand expands. It has a great research and development value for the fierce competition. Additionally, some potential functions, where the total number of patents is small (sparse), indicating that this function is gradually discovered by the market. It has the research value for low-end market innovation.

According to the information implied in the two figures above, designers can determine functions with the development value from the target product and avoid the investment of functions without the research value. This helps the designers to provide objective data support when determining the target function and avoid mistakes of direction incurred by subjective judgment. In this paper, the function with the large market demand and increasing state is selected as the research object.

# 3 Derivation of Direction for Evading Design Based on Laws of Technological System Evolution

After determining the target function, the relevant patents are analyzed, and the laws of technological system evolution are selected according to the evolutionary state of the patent, the potential direction can be predicted. The target function is then improved along the evolution route, enhancing the innovation level using the patent design around. This can not only develop the future product concepts, but also implement the product development following the evolution route.

## 3.1 Functional Analysis of Target Function

The functional analysis analyzes the system, subsystem and components from the perspective of the function, rather than the technology. This operation is mainly to construct a function component model and a function flow model. The function flow model represents function elements and input/output flows that connect them. In contrast, the function flow model can get the working principle of the target function and provide a reliable basis for the following technological system evolution. In addition, in the process of patent design around, designers can creatively conceive the realization form of the target function at a high level of abstraction. Therefore, the function flow model is selected as the analysis tool in this paper.

Firstly, the target function (input/output relationship) of a product is abstracted. The input/output is composed of energy flow, material flow and signal flow. The general target function is usually not easy to achieve; thus, it should be decomposed into sub-functions until the end of the function element can be directly realized. The function element is concatenated with each flow, forming the function chain as shown in Fig. 3.

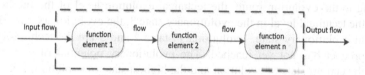

**Fig. 3.** Function chain

## 3.2 Laws of Technological System Evolution

Laws of the technological system evolution [11] are a series of principles established by Altshuller for finding the existence operation and change of a system. He suggested that the same problem usually recurs in the different technology and corresponding solution as well. Laws of the technological system evolution are tools that improve technology from the current state [12, 13]. Fry and Rivin summarized laws of the technological system evolution into nine as follows [14].

(1)  Increasing degree of ideality;
(2)  Non-uniform evolution of sub-systems;
(3)  Increasing dynamism (flexibility);
(4)  Transition to a higher-level system;
(5)  Transition to micro-level;
(6)  Completeness;
(7)  Shortening of energy flow path;
(8)  Increasing substance–field interactions;
(9)  Harmonization of rhythms.

These laws of the technological system evolution indicate the general direction in which evolution routes qualitatively analyze the specific technology. The essence of the technology evolution is to transfer a core technology from the low level to high level. Laws and routes of the technological system evolution play a strong guiding role in the creation of innovative and competitive design concepts.

### 3.3    Evolutionary Potential of the Technology System

The technological evolution routes qualitatively identify specific stages of the technological system in each direction from a microscopic level. The possible structural states reveal the product realization to predict the evolutionary potential of products [15].

After understanding the realization of target function of product through the function analysis, the claims related to target function in the patents are then analyzed to determine the development trend. And match with the law of technological system evolution, select the corresponding evolution route, determine the current technical state of the product, and predict the potential evolution state, and get the innovation direction.

As shown in Fig. 4, there is an evolution route. The evolution route has 5 evolutionary states, with the initial state being state 1 and the highest state being state 5. According to the evolution route, the technical evolution level of the product is analyzed. If the technical level in the evolutionary state 3, the evolutionary state 3 is called the current evolutionary state. Evolutionary states 4 and 5 are the technological level that the product has not yet reached. The evolutionary potential of technology lies between the current state of evolution and the highest state of evolution. Each potential state implies the potential technology with a strategic decision, which can be analyzed to generate innovative ideas about the new generation of products to formulate the development strategy of products.

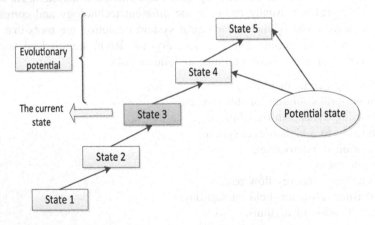

**Fig. 4.** Evolutionary potential of technology system

## 4   Implementation of the Patent Design Around Method Guided by Laws of the Technological System Evolution

The patent design around guided by laws of the technological system evolution is divided into four stages:

(1) Retrieve and analyze relevant patents of the target product; derive the target function with the research value according to changes of patents with different functions.

(2) Obtain the direction of patent design around based on laws of the technological system evolution by predicting the potential state of the existing technical structure of the target function and getting the innovative design direction of the product.

(3) According to the direction and route of evolution, the patent design around related to target function is then implemented. There may be some derivative technical problems in the design, TRIZ tools are used to solve the problems one by one to obtain effective solutions.

(4) Patent infringement determination [16, 17] according to the legal judgment process. A detailed operation process is shown in Fig. 5.

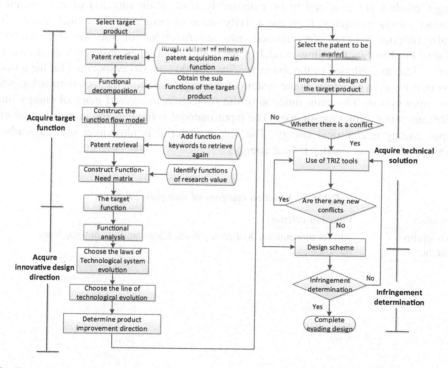

**Fig. 5.** Implementation process of patent design around method guided by laws of technological system evolution

# 5  Case Study

Mosquito catcher is a simple device that attract mosquitoes and catches them. After analyzing the related patents of the product, it is found that the market demand for cleaning the mosquito catcher is increasing gradually. The following will introduce the innovative design process of a mosquito catcher based on the patent design around guided by laws of the technological system evolution.

## 5.1  Acquire Target Function of Product

To start with, the relevant patents are retrieved, and main functions of the product are extracted for the target product of mosquito catchers. The main functions are then decomposed into sub-functions, and the function flow model of each sub-function is abstracted. The Keywords of sub-functions are added to the existing patent retrieval formula to obtain more relevant patents. After browsing the text in each patent, the relationship between the function category and patent quantity is obtained. In a chronological order, the number of patents corresponding to each function is counted, constructing the function-need matrix to express changes of the demand visually.

(1)  Function decomposition and construction of the function flow model

In the Patsnap patent database (http://www.zhihuiya.com), relevant patents for the target product are searched to be extensively read. Main function of the mosquito catcher moves mosquitos from the activity space of people to a confined space. The main function is then decomposed into sub-functions of the mosquito catcher (Table 1). The function flow model of each sub function is abstracted as shown in Fig. 6. Due to limitation of the space, the function flow model is specified for the attract mosquitoes as an example. In the system of the target function, the mosquito belongs to the super system. The main function of the subjects is to convert material energy into substances that attract mosquitoes. The input material is organic and inorganic, and the input energy is electrical energy. The output material is ultraviolet ray and carbon dioxide, the output energy is heat energy.

**Table 1.**  Function category of mosquito catcher

| Product | Function category |
|---------|-------------------|
| Mosquito catcher | Attract mosquitoes, Kill mosquitoes, Clean up mosquitoes, Store mosquitoes |

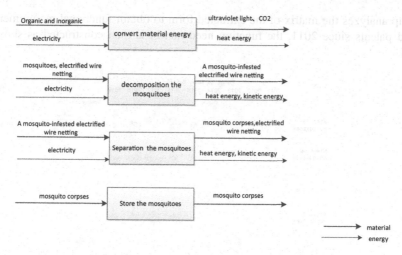

**Fig. 6.** Function flow model for each sub-function

(2) Obtain the relationship between the function category and patent quantity

In the Patsnap patent database, functional keywords are added to the existing patent retrieval formula to retrieve the patent again with the time period from 2011 to 2019 and the patent type as an auxiliary filter. After the weight reduction and noise reduction, 108 patents are selected. The technical background and claims in each patent are studied to obtain corresponding technical solutions of sub-functions. The relationship between function category and patent quantity is then obtained as shown in Fig. 7. 25 patents, 31 patents, 49 patents and 3 patents are respectively involved to attract mosquitoes, kill mosquitoes, clean up mosquitoes and store mosquitoes.

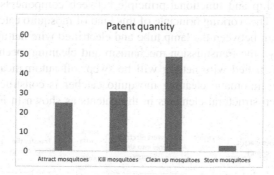

**Fig. 7.** Function category and patent quantity of mosquito catcher from patent analysis

(3) Construction of function-need matrix

The selected patents are extracted according to the application year and functions to derive the extract form of relevant patents. Using the patent analysis function of

Patsnap analyzes the matrix of the extracted form to obtain functional requirements of related patents since 2011, the function-need matrix is then constructed as shown in Fig. 8.

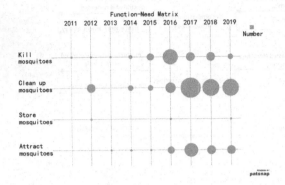

**Fig. 8.** Function-need matrix of the mosquito catcher

Through the comprehensive analysis of the two figures, the market demand for cleaning mosquito is identified as the patent hot spot. The quantity of patents for the function has been steadily increasing since 2014. Therefore, the mosquito cleaning function of the mosquito catcher is the target function to be studied.

## 5.2 Acquisition of Innovative Design Direction

### (1) Target functional analysis

The function, cleaning mosquito, is mainly achieving by the electric device, as the research object. The model about target function is constructed to further clarify the structural relationship and functional principle between components of the mosquito cleaning function. The working principle of this kind of mosquito catchers is to set up a cleaning mechanism between the lamp tube and electrified wire netting, and the power is provided to drive the transmission mechanism and cleaning mechanism. Mosquito corpses on the electrified wire netting will be swept off automatically. The function flow model of the automatic cleaning mosquito catcher is constructed based on the connection between structural elements in the patents as shown in Fig. 9.

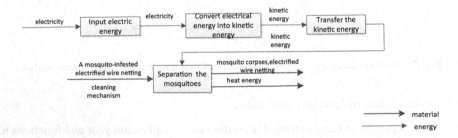

**Fig. 9.** Function flow model for automatic cleaning mosquito catcher

The target function is decomposed to obtain function elements required to realize the function, which is the basis of product improvement. According to the target function of the product, it is divided into three parts: power mechanism, transmission mechanism and cleaning mechanism. Because the cleaning part driven by the power mechanism, the transmission mechanism and move the brush to sweep off the mosquito corpse on the electrified wire netting, the power mechanism, transmission mechanism and cleaning mechanism are parallel. But the rotating rod and brush are components of the cleaning mechanism, and the decomposition is shown in the Fig. 10.

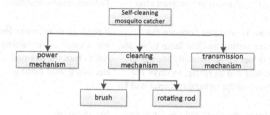

**Fig. 10.** Functional decomposition of mosquito catcher

(2)  Acquisition of new innovative design direction

After understanding the realization of target function of product through the function analysis, the claims related to target function in the patents are then analyzed to determine the development trend. According to the laws of technological system evolution, shortcomings of existing products are uncovered, which are the innovative direction. The specific process of the product innovation direction acquisition is specified as follows.

Step 1: Select the target product and determine the target function. In Subsect. 5.1 we have obtained the target function for the mosquito cleaning function of the mosquito catcher.

Step 2: Read the patent related to the target function, summarize and analyze the realization of the target function. After reading the patent literature related to mosquito cleaning, we have found that the mechanism to clean mosquito corpses as shown in Table 2. After comprehensive analysis, it is found that the existing cleaning methods have shortcomings of the low cleaning efficiency and cleanliness as shown in Table 2.

Step 3: According to the analysis of the evolution trend of target function, we choose two laws as follows.

① Based on the direction of evolution of the cleaning function, the law of increasing dynamism (flexibility) is selected.

② For better control the cleaning, the law of completeness is selected.

Step 4: Choose the routes of the evolution.

① Line 3-3 is selected for the cleaning mechanism which is evolved into fluid and field.

② Line 6-1 is selected for reducing human involvement.

Step 5: Determine product improvement directions. By analyzing the realization mechanism of the target function, shortcomings of the target function are obtained. In order to solve the problem and deficiency, improvement directions of the product are obtained according to two technological evolution routes in Step 4 to design a self-cleaning mosquito catcher.

**Table 2.** Current cleaning methods and inadequacies

| Number | Cleanup methods | Inadequate |
|--------|-----------------|------------|
| 1 | Manual cleaning of mosquito corpses after power failure | Tedious, time-consuming and laborious |
| 2 | A rolling brush is arranged between the electrified wire netting and the lamp tube, and the clockwork device is manually started to drive the rotating rod to rotate, to drive the brush to move, and the mosquito corpse will be swept off | It needs to store power for the spring manually, and it can't work continuously, and the brush can't clean the external surface of the electrified wire netting |
| 3 | The motor drives the shaft and the fan rotates, creating negative pressure to attract mosquitoes | Not clean up |
| 4 | The motor drives brush moves up and down to brush off the mosquito corpse | Brushes doesn't clean the outside of the electrified wire netting very well |
| 5 | The cam mechanism indirectly drives the electrified wire netting up and down, shaking off the mosquito corpse | Not clean up |
| 6 | The mosquito catcher consists of a separable warp and weft mechanism, which is regularly removed to clean the dirt | Tedious, cleaning up is not timely |

## 5.3 Patent Design Around of Mosquito Catcher

(1) Determination of evading the target patent

Following the product innovation design direction, on the premise of realizing the target function, the patent scheme that can be further improved is identified from retrieved product patents. Based on the existing patent technology of the product, the corresponding improvement design is carried out. In this paper, the improvement is based on the patent CN107751149A.

(2) Derivation of the technical solution

After summarizing cleaning methods of the mosquito catcher, we find the evolution process of the cleaning device of a brush-wind field. According to the line 3-3 of transition to fluids and fields, liquid photocatalysts can be used to help decompose corpses on the electrified wire netting. Because photocatalyst can stimulate the oxygen and water molecules attached to the surface of the substance to generate Oh - and O2 free ion groups, these free radicals with strong oxidizing can decompose almost all the organic substances and some inorganic substances harmful to human body or the environment, and finally decompose organic substances and bacteria into carbon dioxide and water. The photocatalyst provides the function of deodorization and self-cleaning.

The functional decomposition results of the cleaning function of the mosquito catcher are then analyzed according route 6-1, i.e. line of completion (dislodging of human involvement). The control mechanism is added for the liquid photocatalyst spraying to regularly clean the electrified wire netting.

Combining the above two directions, we get the following scheme. The motor drives the central guide rail by gear. It again drives the central guide rail to move in a circle by moving up and down as a guide rail. The base has a circular groove for a light that attracts mosquitoes. There is a groove in the central guide for placing the hose for spraying liquid photocatalyst, and the spray head is installed on the bracket. The electrified wire netting is composed of positive and negative roots with a circular and spiral structure, which is easier to clean than the parallel wire netting. When cleaning mosquitoes, a scraper is used to clean the large ones, and a liquid photocatalyst is sprayed at the same time. Under the sunlight, the organic pollutants on the surface of the electrified wire netting can be decomposed into carbon dioxide, which can attract mosquitoes at the same time. The control device can record the discharge times of the electrified wire netting and clean up after reaching a specified number of times. The final design results are shown in Fig. 11, 12, and 13.

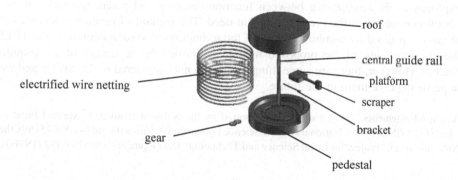

**Fig. 11.** Explosion diagram of the mosquito catcher

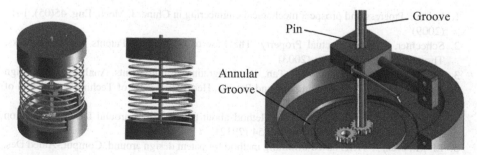

**Fig. 12.** Top view of the mosquito catcher    **Fig. 13.** Zoomed-in view of the mosquito catcher

### 5.4   Infringement Determination

The new scheme is then compared with the existing technology in patents. The original patented core technology cleaning device is redesigned, adding the control device. According to the standard of patent infringement determination, it has successfully evaded the scope of protection of the original patent and formed innovative achievements that can be applied for new patents.

## 6   Conclusions

The current method of patent design around guided by laws of the technological system evolution has comprehended all types of analysis methods and tools of TRIZ to yield the very high success rate of circumvention. The potential development direction of the existing products is predicted by laws of the technological system evolution. The product development direction obtained is used to guide the improvement of the target product. Comparing with the traditional method of patent design around by simply looking for the patent literature language or technology application blank, this method amends defects of the previous patent circumvention design, which uses "accidental discovery of patent loopholes", to render the design method of patent design around more perfect, efficient and accurate. In this paper, the hidden patent knowledge is explored in the relationship between function category and patent quantity and the coordinate matrix of the product function-need. The method of product patent design around is realized by combining laws of the technological system evolution and TRIZ theory. Feasibility of the proposed method is verified in the design of a mosquito catcher. However, there are some things that were not considered in this article and we hope to improve them in the future.

**Acknowledgements.** This research is supported by the National Innovation Method Fund of China (2017IM040100), National Natural Science Foundation of China (Grant No. 51675159), the National Special Project for Local Science and Technology Development (Grant No. 18241837G).

## References

1. Lei, Y.: Progress and prospect mechanical engineering in China. J. Mech. Eng. **45**(05), 1–11 (2009)
2. Schechter, R.E.: Intellectual Property: The Law of Copyrights, Patents and Trademarks. Thomson West, Minnesota (2003)
3. Liu, Y., Jiang, P., Wang, W., Tan, R.: Integrating Requirements Analysis and Design Around Strategy for Designing Around Patents, Hebei University of Technology, School of Mechanical Engineering (2011)
4. Jiang, P., Luo, P., Tan, R., et al.: Method about patent design around based on function trimming. J. Mech. Eng. **48**(11), 46–54 (2012)
5. Li, M., et al.: A TRIZ-based trimming method for patent design around. Comput.-Aided Des. **62**, 20–30 (2015)

6. Cascini, G., Russo, D.: Computer-aided analysis of patent and search for TRIZ contradictions. Int. J. Prod. Dev. **4**(1/2), 52–67 (2007)
7. Xu, Y., Xu, B., Hong, Y.: Development of a design methodology based on patent and axiomatic design. J. Qual. **16**(3), 153–163 (2009)
8. Jiang, P., Wang, C., Sun, J., et al.: Method and application of patented design around by combination of IPC cluster analysis and TRIZ. J. Mech. Eng. **51**(07), 144–154 (2017)
9. Li, H., Liu, L., Zhao, S., et al.: Study on function cutting paths of patent design around for mechanical products. China Mech. Eng. **26**(19), 2581–2589 (2015)
10. Tan, R.: TRIZ and Applications: The Process and Method of Technological Innovation. Higher Education Press, Beijing (2010)
11. Altshuller, G.S.: The Innovation Algorithm. Technical Innovation Center, Worcester (2000)
12. Tan, R., Zhang, Q.: The law and lines of system evolution in TRIZ and the application. Ind. Eng. Manag. **8**(1), 34–36 (2003)
13. Cavallucci, D., Lerch, C., Schenk, E.: Product lines innovation: on the use of technical laws of evolution. In: Thierry, B.H. (ed.) The Economics of Creativity: Ideas, Firms and Markets, pp. 41–57. Lineledge, London (2013)
14. Fey, V.R., Rivin, E.I.: Guided technology evolution (TRIZ technology forecasting) [M/OL]. TRIZ J. (1999). http://www.triz-journal.com
15. Zhang, J., Tan, R., Yang, B., et al.: Study on technique of product technology evolutionary. J. Eng. Des. **3**, 157–163 (2008)
16. Yang, M., Zheng, Z.: Indirect patent infringement and patent infringement determination principle. Intellect. Property Rights **79**(4), 55–58 (2011)
17. Chen, S.: Patent infringement determination is analysed. Household Electr. Appl. **286**(8), 10–12 (2012)

# Dynamization and Real Options – Discussing the Economic Success of Design Inventions

Leonid Chechurin[1] and Mikael Collan[2(✉)]

[1] School of Engineering Science, LUT University, Yliopistonkatu 34,
53851 Lappeenranta, Finland
leonid.chechurin@lut.fi
[2] School of Business and Management, LUT University, Yliopistonkatu 34,
53851 Lappeenranta, Finland
mikael.collan@lut.fi

**Abstract.** This paper discusses the issue of real-world relevance in design invention and specifically discusses the topic from the point of view of dynamization. The dynamization-based idea that more customization, adaptation, and flexibility increase the ideality of a design may not in reality increase the chances for the real-world economic success of the design. The concept of real options is used in the economic evaluation of investments, specifically in the evaluation of the value of flexibility and the ability to adapt to new situations of investments. We introduce and shortly explore the relationship between dynamization and real options and illustrate with two real-world examples, how the context into which design innovations are made and the existence of standards may greatly affect the success of theoretically more ideal designs in real-world contexts. This paper is among the first to tie TRIZ with the concept of real options.

**Keywords:** Dynamization · Real options · Design success

## 1 Introduction

The aim of this paper is to discuss the real-world relevance of design invention and in doing so to contribute to the wider issue of practical relevance of using invention-supporting techniques and specifically the Theory of Inventive Problem Solving (TRIZ). TRIZ was introduced by Shapiro and Altshuller in 1956 [1] and is often referred to as a theory, if not always a scientific one, at least this ambition is directly reflected in the name of the method. What we are interested in is how TRIZ and TRIZ related techniques can perhaps be made more relevant from the point of view of being successful in invention generation from the point of view of being able to generate economically viable inventions.

TRIZ contains several modeling techniques that include modeling by contradictions and Substance-field triples (SuFileds) and modern TRIZ development has included added Function Modelling and Cause Effect Chains (CEC) to the toolkit. There are contradiction elimination rules known as the Altshuller Matrix or Inventive Standards to apply for SuFields. Function model can be changed by Trimming, or just provide the

D. Cavallucci et al. (Eds.): TFC 2020, IFIP AICT 597, pp. 444–451, 2020.
https://doi.org/10.1007/978-3-030-61295-5_33

researcher the new perspective of seeing the problem, together with CEC analysis. The techniques and the framework provide the ontology within which a TRIZ practitioner typically operates. This ontology can also be called "the box of thinking". There is no other way to get out of the box than by introducing something new to the ontology. Ideation in this box is a formal process and new combinations (ideas) appear as the result of the application of formal rules.

*Example.* Famous MATChEM tool gives a pattern of meditation if the required function is of mechanical, acoustic, thermal, chemical, or electro-magnetic nature. G. Altshuller declared that the ideality of a solution would increase, when we move from left to right (in the matrix) or from mechanical solutions toward applications based on electromagnetic fields. There is, however, no statistically based evidence that supports this hypothesis. MATChEM is still used to diversify the ideation for quick brainstorming sessions and the success is measured by the number of ideas, not by their chances to make it to technologically feasible cases or, even more importantly, to sustainable solutions [2]. At least, MATChEM tool grounds the morphological design in basic physical domains.

Other TRIZ techniques like most of contradiction elimination principles or Substance-Filed analysis support the generation of ideas at even more strategic (and therefore less responsible) level, when the physical principle of realization is not even taken into account. At the end of the day it is practical implementation that "crowns" the ideation effort, however, the decision to physically realize an idea is typically driven by an evaluation of economic sustainability. In other words, ideas that are not profitable (even in the long term) will typically never see a physical realization.

Unfortunately, the evaluation of viability of TRIZ-generated ideas, consistent data gathering and analysis of idea evaluation, information about economic assessment of TRIZ generated ideas and, overall, open academic discussion on the two TRIZ basic hypothesis like "Ideality Increase Trend" or the "Dynamization Increase Trend" has never received a lot of attention in the TRIZ community since Altshuller's time. TRIZ literature is full of storytelling and mostly appeals to the common sense instead of assessments, data or fact-based proof, and expertise of professionals.

We present here several examples of how trends of system evolution are treated in TRIZ literature. The basics description of trends of evolution can be found in Petrov [3]. The text, repeating Altshuller, declares that "Replacement of a field type with a field that has a higher degree of control can be done in the following order: gravitational, thermal, mechanical, electromagnetic, chemical, biologic." And later "This sequence is featured by the transition from solid monolithic system to entirely flexible (elastic) object; to an object consisting of powder, to gel, to liquid, to aerosol, to gas, and finally, to a field. In particular, it can be plasma.". Russo et al. [4] formulate the call of dynamization trend as "If an object or system is rigid or inflexible, make it movable or adaptable." Next go several examples of application of this axiom. Park et al. [5] use evolution trends to evaluate the perspective patents. They also apply this approach to applying it to floating wind turbine technology. Cascini et al. [6] use adapted evolution patterns to demonstrate the industry possible conceptual solution for equipment upgrade. TRIZ trends help to demonstrate opportunities in e-commerce in [7] and in food industry [8]. It is important to point out that both cases report that TRIZ trends helped to deliver technical ideas that companies have not thought before, but no economical feasibility study is given. Obviously, it does not help to conclude if these new concepts are actually better in business sense.

There is rather wide invention-selection and innovation-commercialization focused literature, but only few papers specifically connect to TRIZ, for examples see [9, 10]. The discussion of these and other systemic problems in TRIZ can be found in [11]. In this paper we discuss in vein with the above observations, the specific topic of dynamization from the point of view of value creation and tie it with a concept of real options used in understanding and analyzing the value of adaptivity (also called "flexibility" in the real option literature) in financial investment oriented literature. We illustrate our ideas with two real-world examples.

## 2  Dynamization and Functionality Increase

Dynamization is understood as the design trend in which we believe that the more customization, flexibility, and adaptivity is added to a design the more ideal it becomes and the higher the chances it will have to be successful (a successful product) become, see Fig. 1.

Rigid body        Many        Liquid              Field
                  joints
         One             Flexible      Gaseous
         joint

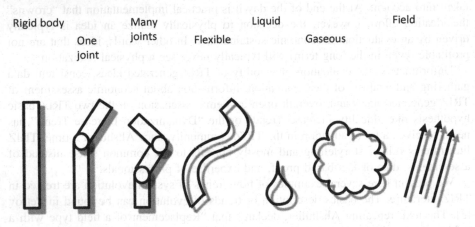

**Fig. 1.** The classical TRIZ view on evolution of the system architecture as it becomes "more and more ideal"

It is often noticed that dynamization can also be seen as the result of contradiction elimination. More specifically, each stage of dynamization eliminates the conflicting requirements for the design. The variable structure helps optimize the response of the system to each requirement, instead of looking for a compromise that can also be a legitimate design strategy. We have to notice that the dynamization perspective provides just another morphology set for modelling, the same way the MATChEM template does. There are a number of classical examples, which are used in TRIZ literature as the qualitative proof or illustration of how the trend works retrospectively.

It is often shown as an example how the airplane wing evolves from eventually one-piece element to the structure with flaps and aileron, how they become more and more movable observing various conditions of take-off and the cruising stages of the flight [12]. And how it ends up in the full variable geometry wing, that turns out to be the basic feature for a class of airplanes, although small and restricted by military use. Importantly, one can observe that variable geometry wing planes have not become the dominant plane-type in aircraft fleets, but exist only as a niche, an alternative that dominates only a very specific segment of the market (military airplanes). Also, otherwise airplane fleets tend to cluster around segments of machines with fixed geometry of the wing, specific for the task for which the specific airplane have been designed for.

Functionality increase trend is given different formulations by Altshuller. It can be read in the Ideality increase, where ideality is functionality over cost (so, more functionality would mean better ideality assuming cost stays the same). Another message is sent by the Trend of Transformation into Supersystem. More precisely, in its subtrend with a difficult name "Mono-Bi-Poli". The idea is the following. The system is designed to perform its single function, so it is called mono system. The next step of evolution should be a system with two functions, or Bi-system. Then the system acquires many functions becoming "Poli-System". The spectrum of functions delivered by the system becomes more and more diverse, the amount of delivered functions is supposed to migrate from discrete to a continuous range. It is assumed that adding more functions ideally does not increase the cost, so those functions convolve. The example of functionality increase is often the wrench evolution, see the Fig. 2.

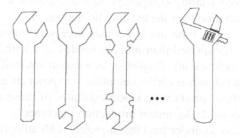

**Fig. 2.** The classical TRIZ view on the evolution of the wrench.

A single wrench quickly evolves to what is known a standard wrench now, that is a bi-system, as it performs two functions (for two different bolting sizes). The next to the right wrenches illustrates acquiring more and more functions (specific sizes) by the wrench. Finally, adjustable wrench (in the right) seems to be the illustration of the poli-system with the infinite amount of functions (any bolting size can be served). It is interesting, how the adjustable wrench kills the second bird: it also can be interpreted as dynamization trend illustration. Indeed, fixed structure of the clamp is made movable (dynamic) now. Here we need to ask: "why has the adjustable wrench not become fully dominant in the wrench market?", but exists as one possibility among the "wrench-space" and is specifically and typically used in the first aid toolkits for home application? Somehow this is contradictory in the TRIZ sense, where the more ideal design does not conquer the markets. To discuss the reasons for this further we turn to the concept of real options.

## 3 Real Options

Having considered dynamization or multi functionality strategy in design as essentially creating more options, we are looking for a bridge to the theory of real options in decision-making science. An option that exists in the realm of the physical world is typically called a real option [13]. Options are possibilities that the holder of the option, typically the owner of the project or the physical machine that contains the option, can exercise if she so desires, but such that she does not have the obligation to use. Real options that exist in the real-world and may be connected to physical investments have an analogy to financial options that give their holder the right, but not the obligation to buy or sell an underlying financial instrument (stock) for a previously agreed upon price (a financial option is a contract). The option is exercised only if it creates benefit to the holder.

There are many types of real options that are connected to real-world projects and investments and they depend on the type of action that they trigger [14]. *Higher-level real options* include the option to wait (to invest) and the option to abandon (an investment). This means that one does not have to rush into things, but may have the flexibility to wait and learn before acting – on the other hand if things do not go the way they were supposed to one may have the flexibility to walk away. This is the main flexibility that a limited liability companies offer to their owners. There may be the option to grow the operation over the existing limitations, due to having acquired such an option by, e.g., acquiring (one size larger than necessary) infrastructure that permits larger volumes to be transported than initially needed at a higher cost (but that, e.g., enable expansion of production). *Project or investment internal real options* include different options to switch inputs and/or outputs into a (production) process and options to change the quantity of production. Good examples of these real options are, e.g., flex-fuel cars and non-batch dependent production machinery.

It is most often easy to understand that a project with an option to change it if the world changes is more valuable than the same project without the option. In TRIZ terminology it simply means that the variable, or adaptive, or self-adaptive design is expected to be more valuable, as it has the ability to adapt itself to changing operational conditions, or to the type of the target. This means that the project with the option is able to adapt to changes and to protect itself against the negative and attempt to reap more benefits from positive changes, while a stationary project with no (or very little) real options is stuck with the modus operandi it has. This discussion also reveals one very important thing about option value, namely that *real options are not valuable when there is no change possible or only little change foreseeable.*

From a design point of view understanding real options and the value of options within the context into which one is creating new designs is important, because designs with real options, or flexible or multi-function design typically have an extra cost attached to them over designs with no real options. This means that options typically come at a cost, which makes designs with options more expensive than designs with no options. The end user, who is the potential buyer of the design, will look at the context and consider the alternative designs typically from a cost-benefit perspective and consider the extra cost of the option against the value from the option (for her in the context into which she is buying the design). If the perceived value from the option is lower than the extra cost that she has to pay for the option she will be likely not choose the design with the option. This means that the objectively technically superior design may be the one that is most often not chosen by the potential buyers, because the contexts in which the added value it brings can be realized are not the majority of use cases. In other words, to be able to design a "most selling" design the added cost of options in the design must be kept very low, or the context to which the option-carrying designs are designed for must be such that they will benefit from the options (and create value).

A context where option value is high is typically one that faces a lot of changes – in statistical terms there is high variance. Interestingly, high variance in one thing in one place does not mean that the same variance exists everywhere. Also, variance must often not only be accompanied with the option to adapt to it, but also with external constructs that support the use of the option. This also means that the same real option may be valuable to one organization, but worthless to another [15]. To illustrate the above, in the next section we give two short examples of how real-world real options add/do not add value to the everyday life of their holders.

## 4  Short Examples of Real-World Value of Options in Design

We consider two hypothetical design case studies, first from a classical TRIZ point of view and then from a real option perspective.

*Example 1. Automotive Engine Design.* Let us be involved in the brainstorming session of motor design, where we are given a chance to come up with adventurous, out of box ideas. TRIZ adept would refer to dynamization trend and conclude that as far as type of the fuel is considered we wish to see automotive engines that run on a larger and larger diversity of fuels. This is already in place: we have more and more hybrid cars, where there are options to switch from petrol to liquid substitutes or electricity. If the ideality increase trend is allowed to speak up, we would imagine a car that can adapt itself to any type of fuel the owner decided to use today. And this type of ideal power generator should be the final stage of evolution according to Altshuller.

Let us now turn to a real world situation: Flex-fuel cars are prevalent in Brazil. It is well-known that such combustion engines can be constructed that are able to operate with 100% ethanol or 100% petroleum or any mixture of the above. These owners of these cars effectively hold the option to switch inputs into their "transportation process". The price of flex-fuel cars is higher than the same models with (only) a conventional petrol engine would be. In Brazil there is an extensive network of fuel stations that services both these fuels and makes this real-option worth something. To realize the value of the option the flex-fuel car holders must know, when refilling, which fuel to choose. Having the choice of selecting the cheaper fuel may mean an average saving of, e.g., three (3) euro per fill-up – if the car is filled twice per week this means the total annual saving of over 300 euro per year. Lifetime saving for a car with ten years of economic life is then over 3000 euro. If the cost of the flex-fuel car is less than 3000 higher than the price of the "only petrol" car, ceteris paribus, then the flex-fuel car (acquiring the real option) is a wealth adding investment. The case for the design with the option is clear in the Brazilian context – the real option adds value (by reducing costs). However, if the same vehicles were taken to Europe, they could operate as they are able to use 100% petrol, but the ability to benefit from the variance (the non-uniform behavior of market prices of petrol and ethanol) of fuel prices would not exist due to the European context not having the infrastructure of ethanol fuel stations in place. In essence the real option with potentially considerable value in the multi-fuel environment would be essentially worthless in the petrol dominated market. *Designing options for one context does not mean that the same strategy is successful for all contexts.*

***Example 2. Wrench Design.*** The TRIZ-driven ideation session on wrenches was already discussed above and it supposed the preferred design to be that of multi-function, adaptation and, ideally, that of the self-adaptive model. Now, consider a fixated engineer that loves the bolt size 12. Everything he constructs is made exclusively by using size 12 only. The machines constructed are as good as their counterparts. The bolts in the machine must be tightened every 3 months in connection with the recurring maintenance. Now, a wrench salesman comes to the machine owner to sell the new adjustable wrench telling her that the product has an unlimited number of options with regards to the bolt sizes it can be used on within the min-max interval and the added cost to the single wrench is moderate. Surprised the salesman leaves without a sale. The option the adjustable wrench carried was worthless in the context of the standardized bolt-size machine. The machine design had circumvented the need for options in maintenance equipment, in essence the complexity reduction brought by standardization worked counter to the option design in the wrench. *When designing options, one must understand the existing standards very well, standards are typically in place to reduce the need for options.*

## 5   Conclusions

We have discussed the issue of real-world relevance of the tools used in support of ideation and specifically how the tools often are detached from the real-world in the sense that they do not guarantee economic feasibility or commercial success of new inventions that may be according to the same tools more ideal than previously existing inventions for the same purpose. This means that a higher level of ideality may be a poor guide in understanding whether a design is economically viable. For this reason, other ways of determining economic viability are needed.

We have focused on the concept of dynamization and explored how it and the investment analysis related concept of real optionality are connected and discussed how real option thinking can contribute to the context of evaluating the success. We suggest that real option analysis has a lot to offer for the feasibility evaluation of new designs.

We have used two real-world examples and discussed what drives the value of the designs (real options) – the examples show that more optionality/more dynamic a project is does not guarantee that the design has more value than a "static" design. Key finding is that understanding the context into which designs are designed carries very high importance from the point of view of commercial success.

We conclude that the claim "the more dynamic the design the more successful it is" has no sense without economical projection.

# References

1. Altschuller, G.S., Shapiro, R.B.: Psychology of inventive activity. Voprosy psikhologii **6**, 37–49 (1956)
2. Belski, Y., Livotov, P., Mayer, O.: Eight fields of MATCEMIB help students to generate more ideas. Proc. CIRP **39**, 85–90 (2016)
3. Petrov, V.: The laws of system evolution. TRIZ future 2001. In: 1st ETRIA Conference 2001. https://triz-journal.com/laws-system-evolution. Accessed 15 July 2020
4. Russo, D., Regazzoni, D., Montecchi, T.: Eco-design with TRIZ laws of evolution. Proc. Eng. **9**, 311–322 (2011)
5. Park, H., Ree, J.J., Kim, K.S.: Identification of promising patents for technology transfers using TRIZ evolution trends. Expert Syst. Appl. **40**(2), 736–743 (2013)
6. Cascini, G., Rotini, F., Russo, D.: Networks of trends: systematic definition of evolutionary scenarios. In: TRIZ Future Conference 2008 Procedia, vol. 9, pp. 355–367 (2011)
7. Barragan-Ferrer, J.-M., Negny, S., Damasius, J., Barragan-Ferrer, D., Cizeikiene, D.: TRIZ evolution trends as an approach for predicting the future development of the technological systems in the food industry. In: Cortés-Robles, G., García-Alcaraz, J.L., Alor-Hernández, G. (eds.) Managing Innovation in Highly Restrictive Environments. MIE, pp. 247–277. Springer, Cham (2019). https://doi.org/10.1007/978-3-319-93716-8_12
8. Chiang, T., Yi, C., Chang, C.: An empirical study of applying Kano model and TRIZ business evolution trends to improve E-commerce service quality. In: Proceedings of 2013 IEEE International Conference on Service Operations and Logistics, and Informatics, Dongguan, pp. 340–344 (2013)
9. Collan, M., Luukka, P.: Using innovation scorecards and lossless fuzzy weighted averaging in multiple-criteria multi-expert innovation evaluation. In: Chechurin, L., Collan, M. (eds.) Advances in Systematic Creativity. MIE, pp. 323–339. Springer, Cham (2019). https://doi.org/10.1007/978-3-319-78075-7_18
10. Pynnönen, M., Hallikas, J., Immonen, M.: Innovation commercialisation: processes, tools and implications. In: Chechurin, L., Collan, M. (eds.) Advances in Systematic Creativity. MIE, pp. 341–366. Springer, Cham (2019). https://doi.org/10.1007/978-3-319-78075-7_19
11. Abramov, O., Sobolev, S.: Current stage of TRIZ evolution and its popularity. In: Chechurin, L., Collan, M. (eds.) Advances in Systematic Creativity. MIE, pp. 3–15. Springer, Cham (2019). https://doi.org/10.1007/978-3-319-78075-7_1
12. Petrov, V.: TRIZ. Theory of Inventive Problem Solving. Springer, Cham (2019). https://doi.org/10.1007/978-3-030-04254-7
13. Trigeorgis, L.: Real Options in Capital Investments. Praeger Publishers, Westport (1995)
14. Amram, M., Kulatilaka, N.: Real Options: Managing Strategic Investment in and Uncertain World. Harvard Business School Press, Boston (1999)
15. Collan, M., Kyläheiko, K.: Forward-looking valuation of strategic patent portfolios under structural uncertainty. J. Intellect. Property Rights **18**, 230–241 (2013)

# TRIZ-Based Approach for Improving the Adoption of Open Innovation 2.0

Eugen Otavă[✉] and Stelian Brad

Research Centre for Engineering and Management of Innovation, Technical University of Cluj-Napoca, Memorandumului 28, 400114 Cluj-Napoca, Romania
eugen.otava@muri.utcluj.ro,
stelian.brad@staff.utcluj.ro

**Abstract.** Openness has increasingly become a global trend. Open Innovation 2.0 (OI2) widens the scope of traditional Open Innovation (OI) and difficulties the organizations with a vision of even more open collaboration that will require business models innovations. In this new paradigm of OI2, innovation happens in ecosystems or networks that go far beyond traditional organizational boundaries. OI has received extensive attention in the scientific research in the past decade, but OI2 is still a new paradigm that opened advanced research opportunities due to the new dimensions of digital collaboration and co-creation at each level of society. OI2 aims to contribute to driving significant societal changes and benefits, due to its inclusive, multidisciplinary and open approach to solving general problems. In this paper, we focus on deriving the enabling factors and barriers to OI2 adoption thru existing literature review, and to propose inventive solutions to identified problems, through a TRIZ based approach. These solutions are analyzed against a set of ranked success influencing factors by means of a quantification method, in order to propose a minimal set of context-free prioritized interventions to facilitate the adoption of OI2.

**Keywords:** Open Innovation (OI) · Open Innovation 2.0 (OI2) · Paradigm shift · TRIZ

## 1 Introduction

While TRIZ (Theory of Inventive Problem Solving) nowadays is primarily used in technological areas and engineering, latest applications in business and management provided encouraging results. In order to facilitate the Open Innovation 2.0 (OI2) adoption in general, a complex and non-linear process, which require business models innovation, due to the paradigm shift, the aim of this paper is to find using TRIZ innovative solutions for the formulated questions/problems, and to propose a minimal set of context-free prioritized interventions.

The challenges we face nowadays are too enormous to consider tackling them in separation, thus we need a new approach, based on the principle of sustainable development [1]. In 2003, Henry Chesbrough conceptualized the idea of open

© IFIP International Federation for Information Processing 2020
Published by Springer Nature Switzerland AG 2020
D. Cavallucci et al. (Eds.): TFC 2020, IFIP AICT 597, pp. 452–464, 2020.
https://doi.org/10.1007/978-3-030-61295-5_34

innovation. This new paradigm was largely discussed in the last decade. And just ten years later after open innovation was introduced, the paradigm was shifting again to OI2, basically has moved from OI to networked and participative innovation, which is an integral characteristic of OI2 [7]. Based on [2], this is consistent with Kurzweil's (1999) law of accelerating returns, which predicts that paradigm shifts will occur more rapidly, especially in technology domains. Also, Munteanu explains in chapter two of [4], that the lifespan of a paradigm is shortened exponentially nowadays, and the germs of a new paradigm appears diffuse and unexpected in the whole volume of concepts and preconceptions that form the "common sense" in which the individual and society evolve at a time. OI evolved rapidly thru an ecosystem-based model, where innovation happens in networks that go far beyond traditional organizational boundaries. As [5] describes, OI2 emerged in the last years, incorporating technological, social, political, environmental dimensions, based on principles of integrated collaboration and co-created shared value, cultivating innovation ecosystems and unleashing the power of exponential technologies [1].

In terms of innovation evolution, we have three phases, as identified by European Union Open Innovation Strategy and Policy Group in 2013. First phase belongs to the closed innovation, the second one to the open innovation and the third one to inno-vation networks and ecosystems, which few years later was associated to the new OI2 evolving paradigm (see Fig. 1).

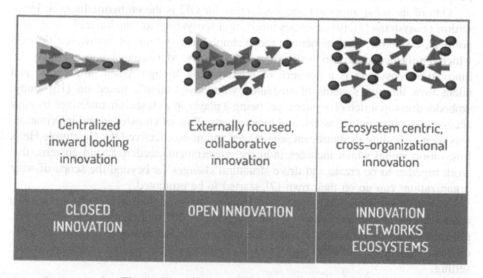

**Fig. 1.** The Evolution of Innovation. Source [2]

As [3] concludes, the original principles of the European open innovation model, differs from the international models through its specific focus on democracy, equality and well-being. According to [6] bibliometric study for 2003–2017 period of time, USA is the leading country and Europe is the leading region in open innovation research in general. This could be justified by a number of driving forces, among which a milestone could be traced in 2010 when the European Union (EU) launched the Innovation Union as one of seven flagship initiatives of the Europe 2020 Strategy [6].

(Sivam, Dieguez, Ferreira, & Silva, 2019) in [6] argues that nowadays a specific innovation can no longer be considered as the result of a predefined and isolated contributions but rather as the outcome of a co-creation process with knowledge flows in and out the entire economic and social environment. As a result, based on [6], there is an increasing need of organizations to open up the innovation process to all active players. OI2 is not something that completely replaces OI but rather it widens the scope and takes it further [8], so OI2 difficulties organizations with a vision of even more open collaboration compared to OI.

## 1.1 Enabling Factors and Barriers to OI2 Adoption

David Teece, professor of global business at the University of California, Berkeley, Haas School of Business, said that innovation is changing so rapidly that no study can aim to comprehensively describe it. In the spirit of his remarks, we propose a list of enabling factors and barriers to OI2, extracted thru literature review, list that we do not claim to be fixed or exhaustive, due to the mentioned dynamics. As a thought leader, Martin Curley wrote: "Today, the concept [of open innovation] is evolving fast. Driven by plummeting communication costs and the ever-increasing numbers of connected people and devices, it has never been so easy to exchange information and ideas" [7].

One of the most important success factors for OI2 is the **embeddedness in innovation ecosystems** [2]. [9] describes innovation ecosystems as "the interorganizational, political, economic, environmental, and technological systems of innovation through which a milieu conducive to business growth is catalyzed, sustained and supported. An innovation ecosystem is a network of relationships through which information and talent flow through systems of sustained value co-creation". Based on [10] study, embeddedness in a rich ecosystem, i.e. being a player in a cluster characterized by easy access to complementary assets, and by an intense flow of knowledge and information, was seen as leading to significant advantages and more effective OIs. Quadruple Helix Innovation model which includes industry, government, academia, and citizens, that work together to co-create and drive structural changes far beyond the scope of what organizations can do on their own [2], started to be promoted.

The **orchestration** at the ecosystem level is important and involves processes that cannot be automated, including the identification of different ecosystems, actor roles, relevant collaboration methods and value capture [3]. According to [5], the ability to orchestrate a rich ecosystem represents an enabling factor for the transition to OI2 setting.

Leveraging organizational culture by spreading openness, sharing and trust, becomes a crucial aspect for OI2 setting. The **common values and vision** drive common purpose-driven actions. According to [9] the "value is co-created for the innovation ecosystem through events, impacts and coalitions/networks that emerge from a shared vision of the desired transformations". [12] study also concludes between other that in order to encourage the active participation of ecosystem actors in the value co-creation process, efforts must be made to ensure a **clear vision and a shared value base** on which the ecosystem activities can be built.

Another important success factor is **trust**. As [13] specifies, any activities for open innovation depend on trust building among stakeholders.

Bror Salmelin highlights in [14] the importance of **new professions** in the dynamic processes necessary at ecosystem level, and he considers that universities, management institutes and institutes of applied science have an important role in developing new innovation-enabling curricula, not just focusing on digital user and on digital professional skills for creating ICT systems [14].

The concept of a user becomes more complex and multi-sided, resulting in various **engagement models** and contractual terms for different user and developer groups [3]. According to [2], an **engagement platform** is the place where people and their environment join so that co-creation can begin. Engagement platforms represents therefore an enabling factor for co-creation and OI2.

Jean-Claude Burgelman was one of the first policymakers to identify the trend of **user-led** and **user centered innovation**, outlining the shift from the user as a research object to the user as a research contributor, and ultimately to the user as a full research participant. The involvement of users is a pivotal component of OI2 [10]. [2] argues that instead of focusing on a product or services features, developers who focus on the user experience are likely to be most successful.

According to [8] **diversity** is an OI2 enabling factor, as diversity results in breakthrough innovations more likely than just collaborating within a single disciplinary. Diversity can refer to multiple dimensions, as for example to different organizational culture, industry, ethnicity, skills set etc. Diversity can be achieved by collaborating with people outside of an organization, like consultants for example, but in OI2 diversity is an attribute of the network or innovation ecosystem. [12] study finds that the more diversity there is among the ecosystem actors, the greater the support for innovativeness within the value co-creation process will be.

Increasingly complex and integrated solutions offer opportunities for **new business models,** and just by evolving and adapting quickly, one organization can resist and be successful. However, this requires a broad understanding of the industry on a system level, which has been the focus in open innovation projects from the beginning [3]. OI is related to the open business model, since the link between technology and new business models is strengthened by the intensive use of OI, as [10] argues. With the rise of Web 2.0, a new generation of business models has emerged, and converged in the new paradigm of OI2 [2].

Innovation activities in OI2 take place in a self-organizing **network**. Power and influence are not derived from rank or exclusive access to specific resources, but from convincing others from the network to accept a particular direction [15]. According to [13] SMEs skills in maintaining few relevant networks are essential for OI activities. Networked product creation has become an industry norm, and a culture of openness and sharing has been established [3]. Together the network members can create value in a way no organization could do by itself [8].

As [10] explains, the control secured thanks to **Intellectual Property** (IP) makes companies more prone to build alliances and collaborate when they can protect their own technologies and knowledge.

Based on [10] study, establishing the **right innovation mix**, the right balance between internal R&D and external sourcing of knowledge and technology remains a serious barrier to implementing OIs. In OI2 the innovation happens in ecosystems or networks, so many stakeholders are involved in the innovation process, with a lack of institutional support. They come from different organizational cultures and have different backgrounds.

**Lack of institutional support** and/or the presence of rules and regulations that prevent innovation constitute a considerable barrier for OI2. Companies in the study conducted by [10] lament the rigidities of policymakers and of the public sector.

[11] in [5] identified the following **internal managerial key factors**: carefully balancing internal and external resources, leveraging organizational culture, developing a sound business model, managing human resources.

Table 1 shows a summary of the factors we have identified to enable the adoption of OI2 and the corresponding barriers.

**Table 1.** Enabling factors versus barriers

| Enabling factors | Corresponding barriers |
|---|---|
| Embeddedness in Innovation Ecosystems e.g. around Digital Innovation Hubs | Institutional barriers Establishing the right innovation mix Mindset not changed from OI to OI2 |
| Ability to orchestrate the rich ecosystem | Institutional barriers |
| Leveraging organizational culture by having a shared value and vision | Organizational culture – lack of openness |
| Trust among stakeholders | Organizational culture – lack of trust |
| Managing human resources: new professions and skills are needed | Institutional barriers Lack of specialization curricula, training |
| Innovation co-creation thru engagement platforms | Mindset not changed from OI to OI2 Organizational culture – lack of openness |
| Adopt a user centric mindset (user centricity) | Mindset not changed from OI to OI2 Organizational culture – lack of openness |
| Continuously innovate business models | Distraction of resources |
| Take advantage of networking effects | Organizational culture – lack of openness |
| Cultivation of diversity | Organizational culture – lack of openness Establishing the right innovation mix |
| Ensure IP protection | Institutional barriers |

Based on the conducted literature review, focused on extracting enabling factors and barriers to the OI2 adoption, we summarized the below list of questions/issues, concerning the business model transformations:

- How can the organizations that are resistant to change due to being afraid of losing control over decisions and identity, be helped to evolve from closed innovation or OI collaborations models and adopt the OI2 principles?
- How do we ensure the active participation of all OI2 actors in the value co-creation process?

- How do we choose the right OI2 actors to collaborate with in order to ensure the required diversity?
- How do we create and maintain a shared vision and trust among all OI2 actors?
- What is the right balance between openness and internalization for each OI2 actor?
- How do we determine the contribution of each OI2 actor and calculate its benefits accordingly?
- How the openness and diversity of the OI2 ecosystem can be ensured e.g. facilitate the involvement of relevant real users, contributors etc.?

## 2   Methodology

The current understanding about the structures and practices supporting value co-creation in innovation ecosystems is still very limited [12]. Studies on enabling factors and barriers to OI2, based on a large number of actors, are practically non-existent. On this work, we aim to identify the key enabling factors and challenges to the OI2 adoption. We extracted the enabling factors and the barriers/challenges to OI2 adoption, through existing literature review, and we formulated a list of questions. Next step was to propose inventive solutions to these questions/problems using TRIZ. These inventive solutions are practically innovating the business models.

The competence of fast and optimized decision making in business and management can be achieved and enhanced by using a TRIZ-based approach for non-technical problems [16]. Based on TRIZ philosophy, humans solve problems by modifying systems and processes, and at abstract level, patterns of such modifications are universal. As a first step, the non-technical problems are formulated in terms of conflicts or contradictions, and based on the TRIZ Contradictions Matrix [17] inventive principles are suggested as generalized solutions to the problems.

The proposed inventive solutions were analyzed against a set of ranked success influencing factors by means of a quantification method (Analytic Hierarchy Process [18]) in order to propose a set of prioritized interventions that we consider useful for facilitating the adoption of OI2 in general, in a context-free approach.

## 3   OI2 as Generic System Analyzed with TRIZ

Using the TRIZ Contradictions Matrix (CM) for Business & Management [17], multiple Inventive Principles (in TRIZ) are suggested as generalized solutions to each contradiction. Table 2. presents the formulated problems, their form corresponding to TRIZ CM, the inventive principles suggested as generic solutions and the outcome, the proposed solutions to overcome the identified challenges.

**Table 2.** Identified challenges for OI2 adoption under TRIZ analysis

| Identified challenge | Challenge expressed in TRIZ CM | Inventive principles (Innovation vectors) | Solutions proposed |
|---|---|---|---|
| How can the organizations that are resistant to change due to being afraid of losing control over decisions and identity, be helped to evolve from closed innovation or OI collaborations models and adopt the OI2 principles? | Increase the importance of the dynamic element (collaboration organizational culture) (1) without reducing the influence (involved engagement) in the task (decision, process) (10) | External support (8) Prior action (10) Exploit resonance (sensibility) (18) Expansion (37) | S1. External support for companies (training, consultancy, trials), in order to understand the benefits of OI2 |
| How can the organizations that are resistant to change due to being afraid of losing control over decisions and identity, be helped to evolve from closed innovation or OI collaborations models and adopt the OI2 principles? | Improve area covered by the dynamic element (communication network) (5) without reducing influence (force, involved engagement) in the task (process) (10) | Extract, retrieve or remove some elements from the system (2) Periodic action (19) Elastic construction (30) Transformation of system properties (35) | S2. Advice organizations to start with partial involvement in OI2 ecosystems (extract just a minimum set of resources, knowledge to contribute in the beginning) |
| How can the organizations that are resistant to change due to being afraid of losing control over decisions and identity, be helped to evolve from closed innovation or OI collaborations models and adopt the OI2 principles? | Increase adaptability of the system (35) without increasing tension (pressure, criticality) (11) | Partial or excessive action (16) Transformation of system properties (35) | S3. Invite organizations as observers into OI2 projects |
| How can the organizations that are resistant to change due to being afraid of losing control over decisions and | Increase effort to involve dynamic elements (person, process, technology, mobile assets etc.) (19) without reducing | Extract, retrieve or remove some elements from the system (2) | S4. Establish in advance different actor roles in the OI2 project e.g. architectural lead, |

*(continued)*

**Table 2.** (*continued*)

| Identified challenge | Challenge expressed in TRIZ CM | Inventive principles (Innovation vectors) | Solutions proposed |
|---|---|---|---|
| identity, be helped to evolve from closed innovation or OI collaborations models and adopt the OI2 principles? | influence (force, involved engagement) in the tsk (decision, process) (10) | Partial or excessive action (16) Rushing through (21) Copying (26) | implementation lead, delivery lead etc. |
| How do we ensure the active participation of all OI2 actors in the value co-creation process? | Increase effort to involve (motivate, activate) dynamic elements (person, innovation ecosystem participants) (19) without affecting the stability of the system (13) | Inversion or reversion (13) Translation into a new dimension (17) Periodic action (19) Mediator (24) | S5. Introduce an OI2 mediator role for all OI2 collaborations levels e.g. organization, OI2 ecosystem, OI2 projects |
| How do we choose the right OI2 actors to collaborate with in order to ensure the required diversity? | Reduce harmful factors acting on the system (30) without affecting the adaptability of the system (openness) (35) | Moderation in advance (11) Convert harm intro benefit (22) Use of permeable units (31) Transformation of system properties (35) | S6. In advance selection of OI2 actors thru democratic decision-making process e.g. voting of all applicants. Rejected actors/potential contributors to be redirected to a different OI2 initiative |
| How do we create and maintain a shared vision and trust among all OI2 actors? | Increase clarity of the flow in the process (18) without creating side harmful effects (31) | Periodic action (19) Changing the transparency (32) Transformation of system properties (35) Inert environment (39) | S7. Create a new-shared virtual identity for every OI2 project (virtual organization) Conduct periodic satisfaction surveys between all participants in the virtual organization |
| What is the right balance between openness and | Increase length of the dynamic element (communication network, knowledge | Reconfigurable construction (29) | S8. Create separate departments open to OI2 collaborations (with skilled |

(*continued*)

**Table 2.** (*continued*)

| Identified challenge | Challenge expressed in TRIZ CM | Inventive principles (Innovation vectors) | Solutions proposed |
|---|---|---|---|
| internalization for each OI2 actor? | sharing) (3) without damaging quantity of substance (money, internal know how, general organization's performance and output) (26) | Transformation of system properties (35) | personnel, pre-defined management processes, clear goals etc.) |
| How do we determine the contribution of each OI2 actor and calculate its benefits accordingly? | Increase importance of the dynamic element (1) without damaging stability of the system (13) | Act for segmenting the system (1) Periodic action (19) Transformation of system properties (35) Inert environment (39) | S9. Introduce a new measure of value added thru the OI2 project lifecycle, which should quantify the tangible contribution (resources spent, hours etc.) & intangible contribution (knowhow, new ideas etc.) of all members |
| How the openness and diversity of the OI2 ecosystem can be ensured e.g. facilitate the involvement of relevant real users, contributors etc.? | Increase convenience in use (33) without increasing the number of harmful factors acting on the system (30) | Extract, retrieve or remove some elements from the system (2) Self-service (25) Replacement of a traditional system (28) Inert environment (39) | S10. Real users should be randomly selected to participate in OI2 innovative projects |

We consider an OI2 setting successful if in this new context, the OI2 ecosystem is able to create and capture value that is successfully implemented and delivered to the targeted group. With this definition in mind, we have identified 6 factors that influence the successful OI2 adoption, and these are: obtained profit (expected to be high by every organization in the ecosystem), value delivered to customer and society as outcome of OI2 collaborations (expected to be high), public reputation (expected to increase for all participants in OI2 setting), employees' satisfaction (expected to increase for all participant organizations), operational costs (expected to reduce in a network-based setup) and risk (expected to be lower). Using Analytic Hierarchy Process (AHP) [19] we have classified these factors as presented in below Fig. 2. The scale of relative importance is as following: 1 - Equal importance, 3 - Moderate importance, 5 - Strong importance, 7 - Very strong importance, 9 - Extreme importance.

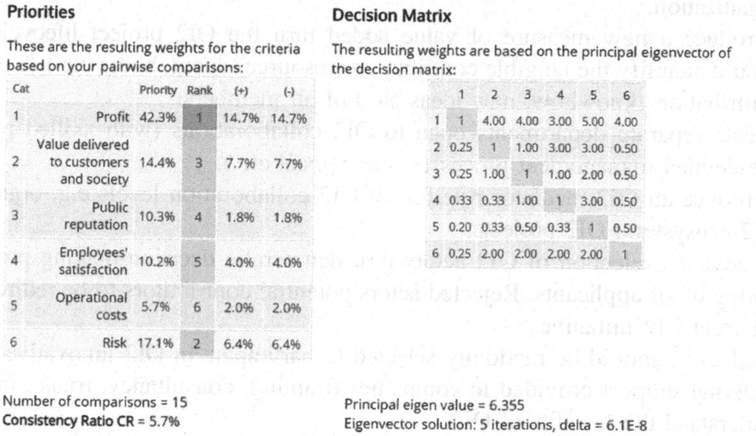

**Priorities**

These are the resulting weights for the criteria based on your pairwise comparisons:

| Cat | | Priority | Rank | (+) | (-) |
|---|---|---|---|---|---|
| 1 | Profit | 42.3% | 1 | 14.7% | 14.7% |
| 2 | Value delivered to customers and society | 14.4% | 3 | 7.7% | 7.7% |
| 3 | Public reputation | 10.3% | 4 | 1.8% | 1.8% |
| 4 | Employees' satisfaction | 10.2% | 5 | 4.0% | 4.0% |
| 5 | Operational costs | 5.7% | 6 | 2.0% | 2.0% |
| 6 | Risk | 17.1% | 2 | 6.4% | 6.4% |

Number of comparisons = 15
**Consistency Ratio CR = 5.7%**

**Decision Matrix**

The resulting weights are based on the principal eigenvector of the decision matrix:

| | 1 | 2 | 3 | 4 | 5 | 6 |
|---|---|---|---|---|---|---|
| 1 | 1 | 4.00 | 4.00 | 3.00 | 5.00 | 4.00 |
| 2 | 0.25 | 1 | 1.00 | 3.00 | 3.00 | 0.50 |
| 3 | 0.25 | 1.00 | 1 | 1.00 | 2.00 | 0.50 |
| 4 | 0.33 | 0.33 | 1.00 | 1 | 3.00 | 0.50 |
| 5 | 0.20 | 0.33 | 0.50 | 0.33 | 1 | 0.50 |
| 6 | 0.25 | 2.00 | 2.00 | 2.00 | 2.00 | 1 |

Principal eigen value = 6.355
Eigenvector solution: 5 iterations, delta = 6.1E-8

**Fig. 2.** Decision Matrix and Classification of identified factors influencing the OI2 adoption using AHP method; Source [20]

Having the priority of each factor identified to influence the successfulness of OI2 adoption, we have moved forward and we analyzed the TRIZ generated solutions to overcome the identified challenges, against this set of ranked factors. Table 3 shows the corresponding data, in a decision matrix format.

**Table 3.** OI2 adoption – inventive solutions decision matrix

| Factors | Profit | Value delivered to customers and society | Public reputation | Employees' satisfaction | Operational costs | Risk | Score |
|---|---|---|---|---|---|---|---|
| Weights | 6 | 4 | 3 | 2 | 1 | 5 | |
| S1 | 2 | 2 | 1 | 4 | 4 | 4 | 55 |
| S2 | 1 | 2 | 2 | 3 | 2 | 5 | 53 |
| S3 | 1 | 1 | 2 | 4 | 2 | 5 | 51 |
| S4 | 1 | 2 | 2 | 4 | 2 | 5 | 55 |
| S5 | 2 | 3 | 1 | 5 | 2 | 5 | 64 |
| S6 | 1 | 4 | 4 | 4 | 1 | 4 | 63 |
| S7 | 2 | 4 | 3 | 5 | 2 | 5 | 74 |
| S8 | 2 | 3 | 3 | 4 | 4 | 5 | 70 |
| S9 | 4 | 4 | 1 | 3 | 3 | 4 | 72 |
| S10 | 1 | 5 | 1 | 3 | 2 | 5 | 62 |

Based on the obtained scores, we generated the prioritized set of TRIZ-based inventive measures that we propose for business models transformation, on the way to OI2 adoption, in general.

1. Create a new-shared virtual identity for every OI2 project (virtual organization) and conduct periodic satisfaction surveys between all participants in the virtual organization.
2. Introduce a new measure of value added thru the OI2 project lifecycle, which should quantify the tangible contribution (resources spent, hours etc.) & intangible contribution (knowhow, new ideas etc.) of all members.
3. Create separate departments open to OI2 collaborations (with skilled personnel, pre-defined management processes, clear goals etc.).
4. Introduce an OI2 mediator role for all OI2 collaboration levels e.g. organization, OI2 ecosystem, OI2 projects.
5. In advance selection of OI2 actors thru democratic decision-making process e.g. voting of all applicants. Rejected actors/potential contributors to be redirected to a different OI2 initiative.
6. Real users should be randomly selected to participate in OI2 innovative projects.
7. External support provided to companies (training, consultancy, trials), in order to understand the benefits of OI2.
8. Establish in advance different actor roles in the OI2 project e.g. architectural lead, implementation lead, delivery lead etc.
9. Advice organizations to start with partial involvement in OI2 ecosystems (extract just a minimum set of resources & knowledge to contribute in the beginning).
10. Invite organizations as observers into OI2 projects.

## 4   Conclusions

OI2 is still a new paradigm in our changing world, on which the problems to be solved become bigger and with an increasing complexity at a tremendous speed. Is believed that the new OI2 will achieve greater outcomes due to promoting extensive networking and co-creative collaboration between all actors in society, beyond all previous collaboration schemes. In OI2 innovation happens in ecosystems or networks that go far beyond traditional organizational boundaries, and it aims to bring many benefits to our society, due to its inclusive, multidisciplinary and open approach on solving the societal problems thru co-creativity and co-creation, that many may benefit from, as for example the environment, business, citizens and also the service providers (e.g. public sector). There are still many challenges for OI2 widespread adoption. On this article, we analyzed OI2 in a general way, as we have not analyzed each economical sector separately, or a specific country/region. Our proposed prioritized list of interventions, inventive solutions generated using a TRIZ-based systematic methodology, aims to facilitate the OI2 adoption, and is general and context-free. Our work leverages the usage of TRIZ methodology for more general use, to support idea generation for a paradigm shift that requires business models transformation, which we think, will bring multiple benefits to our society, and represents an important step in the transition process to a knowledge-based society. From our proposed set of inventive TRIZ-based generated interventions, and prioritized using a decision matrix having a list of ranked success influencing factors using the analytic hierarchy process, the most three weighed ones revealed to be the creation of a shared virtual identity, virtual organization, for each OI2 project, the introduction of a new measure of value added thru the OI2 project lifecycle which should quantify the tangible & intangible members' contribution, and the solution to create separate departments open for OI2 collaborations, within organizations, with OI2 skilled personnel, pre-defined management processes and clear goals. Also, the solution of a mediator for every OI2 collaboration level (organization, project, ecosystem, etc.), revealed to be the fourth measure to be considered based on our inventive methodology. The set of proposed measures opens up further research possibilities, especially for their impact at the organization level and at the OI2 ecosystem level, and for prospecting possible implementation plans, for different contexts.

# References

1. Curley, M., Salmelin, B.: Open Innovation 2.0: The New Mode of Digital Innovation for Prosperity and Sustainability. Springer, Cham (2018). https://doi.org/10.1007/978-3-319-62878-3
2. Curley, M., Salmelin, B.: Open Innovation 2.0: A New Paradigm. OISPG White Paper (2013)
3. Turkama, P.: The future focus for open innovation. In: Open Innovation 2.0 Yearbook 2017–2018. European Commission, Luxembourg, Publications Office of the European Union (2018), pp. 93–98 (2018)
4. Broché, S., Marinescu, P. (coord.): Deschideri spre lumea complexității. Editura Universității din București, București (2008)
5. Pacheco, V., Araújo, N., Rocha, L.: Open innovation: from OI to OI2. In: EconWorld2020@Porto Proceedings, Porto (2020)
6. Le, H.T.T., Dao, Q.T.M., Pham, V.C., Tran, D.T.: Global trend of open innovation research: a bibliometric analysis. Cogent Bus. Manag. 6, 1–21 (2019)
7. Curley, M.: Twelve principles for open innovation 2.0. Nature 533, 314–316 (2016)
8. Morikawa, M.: What Is Open Innovation 2.0 and Why Does It Matter? https://www.viima.com/blog/what-is-open-innovation-2.0-and-why-does-it-matter. Accessed 07 May 2020
9. Russell, M.G., Still, K., Huhytamäki, J., Yu, C., Rubens, N.: Transforming innovation ecosystems through shared vision and network orchestration. In: Triple Helix IX International Conference, p. 21 (2011)
10. Di Minin, A., et al..: Case Studies on Open Innovation in ICT. JRC Science for Policy Report, pp. 1–12 (2016)
11. Di Minin, A., Casprini, E., De Marco, C.E., Ferrigno, G., Marullo, C.: Open innovation: the transition from OI to OI2. In: Open Innovation 2.0 Yearbook 2017–2018. European Commission, Luxembourg, Publications Office of the European Union, pp. 89–92 (2018)
12. Ketonen-Oksi, S., Valkokari, K.: Innovation ecosystems as structures for value cocreation. Technol. Innov. Manag. Rev. 9, 25–35 (2019)
13. Hossain, M.: A review of literature on open innovation in small and medium-sized enterprises. J. Global Entrepr. Res. 5(1), 1–12 (2015). https://doi.org/10.1186/s40497-015-0022-y

14. Salmelin, B.: New skills and attitudes at the heart of modern innovation policy. In: Open Innovation 2.0 Yearbook 2017–2018. European Commission, Luxembourg, Publications Office of the European Union, pp. 9–11 (2018)
15. Cuartielles, D., Nepelski, D., Van Roy, V.: Arduino—A global network for digital innovation. In: Open Innovation 2.0 Yearbook 2017–2018. European Commission, Luxembourg, Publications Office of the European Union (2018), pp. 15–24 (2018)
16. Ruchti, B., Livotov, P.: TRIZ-based innovation principles and a process for problem solving in business and management. TRIZ J. 1, 1–9 (2001)
17. Brad, S.: TRIZ to support creation of innovative shared value business initiatives. In: Koziołek, S., Chechurin, L., Collan, M. (eds.) Advances and Impacts of the Theory of Inventive Problem Solving, pp. 101–112. Springer, Cham (2018). https://doi.org/10.1007/978-3-319-96532-1_10
18. Teknomo, K.: Analytic Hierarchy Process (AHP) Tutorial. https://people.revoledu.com/kardi/tutorial/AHP/. Accessed 01 June 2020
19. Brunelli, M.: Introduction to the Analytic Hierarchy Process. Learning from Failures, p. 83. Springer, Cham (2015). https://doi.org/10.1007/978-3-319-12502-2
20. AHP Online Calculator. https://bpmsg.com/ahp/. Accessed 01 June 2020

# Author Index